Standard & Poor's Educational Version of Market Insight, available at www.mhhe.com/edumarketinsight

Use the same real data professionals use!

McGraw-Hill/Irwin is proud to partner with Standard & Poor's to offer access to the Educational Version of Market Insight FREE with the purchase of a new text. A passcode card is bound into books, which gives you access to six years of financial data, along with industry trends, stock reports, and much more for over 1000 top companies. Relevant chapters contain end-of-chapter problems that use this data to gain a better understanding of practical business situations.

Interactive FinSims

This exciting review tool is at your fingertips!

An exclusive tool developed by McGraw-Hill/Irwin contains multiple simulations of key financial topics. These simulations are ideal for you to use in order to reinforce your knowledge and gain additional practice in sharpening your skills to master the principles of corporate finance.

help you succeed in your finance course!

Corporate Finance Online

Check out this site for more Corporate Finance activities!

Included on the OLC is a link to Corporate Finance Online, another exclusive web tool from McGraw-Hill/Irwin. This value-added site enables faculty and students to engage in corporate finance activities using the Internet for 27 different key financial topics and allows you to complete challenging exercises and discussion questions that draw on recent articles, company reports, government data, and other web-based resources. Use the Finance Tutor series to quiz yourself on corporate finance topics and receive feedback for continuous learning.

With the purchase of a New Book*

You Can Access the Real Financial Data that the Experts Use!

*If you purchased a used book, see other side for access information.

This card entitles the purchaser of a new textbook to a semester of access to the Educational Version of Standard & Poor's Market Insight®, a rich online resource featuring hundreds of the most often researched companies in the Market Insight database.

For 1,000 companies, this website provides you:

- Access to six years' worth of fundamental financial data from the renowned Standard & Poor's COMPUSTAT® database
- 12 Excel Analytics Reports, including balance sheets, income statements, ratio reports and cash flow statements; adjusted prices reports, and profitability; forecasted values and monthly valuation data reports
- Access to Financial Highlights Reports including key ratios
- S & P Stock Reports that offer fundamental, quantitative and technical analysis
- EDGAR reports updated throughout the day
- Industry Surveys, written by S & P's Equity analysts
- News feeds (updated hourly) for companies and industries.

STANDARD &POOR'S

 McGraw-Hill Irwin

See other side for your unique site ID access code.

Welcome to the Educational Version of Market Insight!

www.mhhe.com/edumarketinsight

Check out your textbook's website for details on how this special offer enhances the value of your purchase!

1. To get started, use your web browser to go to **www.mhhe.com/edumarketinsight**

2. Enter your site ID exactly as it appears below.

3. You may be prompted to enter the site ID for future use—please keep this card.

Your site ID is:

ra153423

ISBN: 978-0-07-329352-3
MHID: 0-07-329352-0

STANDARD
&POOR'S

 McGraw-Hill Irwin

*If you purchased a used book, this site ID may have expired. For new password purchase, please go to www.mhhe.com/edumarketinsight. Password activation is good for a 6 month duration.

Foundations of
Financial Management

TWELFTH EDITION

THE MCGRAW-HILL/IRWIN SERIES IN FINANCE, INSURANCE AND REAL ESTATE

Stephen A. Ross, Consulting Editor
Franco Modigliani Professor of Finance and Economics
Sloan School of Management
Massachusetts Institute of Technology

FINANCIAL MANAGEMENT

Adair
Excel Applications for Corporate Finance
Second Edition

Benninga and Sarig
Corporate Finance: A Valuation Approach

Block and Hirt
Foundations of Financial Management
Twelfth Edition

Brealey, Myers, and Allen
Principles of Corporate Finance
Eighth Edition

Brealey, Myers and Marcus
Fundamentals of Corporate Finance
Fifth Edition

Brooks
FinGame Online 4.0

Bruner
Case Studies in Finance: Managing for
Corporate Value Creation
Fifth Edition

Chew
The New Corporate Finance: Where Theory
Meets Practice
Third Edition

Chew and Gillan
Corporate Governance at the Crossroads:
A Book of Readings
First Edition

DeMello
Cases in Finance
Second Edition

Grinblatt and Titman
Financial Markets and Corporate Strategy
Second Edition

Helfert
Techniques of Financial Analysis: A Guide
to Value Creation
Eleventh Edition

Higgins
Analysis for Financial Management
Eighth Edition

Kester, Ruback, and Tufano
Case Problems in Finance
Twelfth Edition

Ross, Westerfield, and Jaffe
Corporate Finance
Eighth Edition

Ross, Westerfield, Jaffe, and Jordan
Corporate Finance: Core Principles and
Applications
First Edition

Ross, Westerfield, and Jordan
Essentials of Corporate Finance
Fifth Edition

Ross, Westerfield, and Jordan
Fundamentals of Corporate Finance
Eighth Edition

Shefrin
Behavioral Corporate Finance: Decisions
That Create Value
First Edition

Smith
The Modern Theory of Corporate Finance
Second Edition

White
Financial Analysis with an Electronic Calculator
Sixth Edition

INVESTMENTS

Bodie, Kane, and Marcus
Essentials of Investments
Sixth Edition

Bodie, Kane, and Marcus
Investments
Seventh Edition

Cohen, Zinbarg, and Zeikel
Investment Analysis and Portfolio
Management
Fifth Edition

Hirt and Block
Fundamentals of Investment Management
Eighth Edition

Hirschey and Nofsinger
Investments: Analysis and Behavior
First Edition

Jordan and Miller
Fundamentals of Investments: Valuation and
Management
Fourth Edition

FINANCIAL INSTITUTIONS AND MARKETS

Cornett and Saunders
Fundamentals of Financial Institutions
Management

Rose and Hudgins
Bank Management and Financial Services
Seventh Edition

Rose and Marquis
Money and Capital Markets: Financial
Institutions and Instruments in a Global
Marketplace
Ninth Edition

Santomero and Babbel
Financial Markets, Instruments, and
Institutions
Second Edition

Saunders and Cornett
Financial Institutions Management: A Risk
Management Approach
Fifth Edition

Saunders and Cornett
Financial Markets and Institutions: An
Introduction to the Risk Management Approach
Third Edition

INTERNATIONAL FINANCE

Beim and Calomiris
Emerging Financial Markets

Eun and Resnick
International Financial Management
Fourth Edition

Kuemmerle
Case Studies in International
Entrepreneurship: Managing and Financing
Ventures in the Global Economy
First Edition

Levich
International Financial Markets: Prices and
Policies
Second Edition

REAL ESTATE

Brueggeman and Fisher
Real Estate Finance and Investments
Thirteenth Edition

Corgel, Ling, and Smith
Real Estate Perspectives: An Introduction to
Real Estate
Fourth Edition

Ling and Archer
Real Estate Principles: A Value Approach
Second Edition

FINANCIAL PLANNING AND INSURANCE

Allen, Melone, Rosenbloom, and Mahoney
Pension Planning: Pension, Profit-Sharing,
and Other Deferred Compensation Plans
Ninth Edition

Altfest
Personal Financial Planning
First Edition

Crawford
Life and Health Insurance Law
Eighth Edition (LOMA)

Harrington and Niehaus
Risk Management and Insurance
Second Edition

Hirsch
Casualty Claim Practice
Sixth Edition

Kapoor, Dlabay, and Hughes
Focus on Personal Finance: An Active
Approach to Help You Develop Successful
Financial Skills
First Edition

Kapoor, Dlabay, and Hughes
Personal Finance
Eighth Edition

Foundations of Financial Management

TWELFTH EDITION

STANLEY B. BLOCK
Texas Christian University

GEOFFREY A. HIRT
DePaul University

Boston   Burr Ridge, IL   Dubuque, IA   Madison, WI   New York   San Francisco   St. Louis
Bangkok   Bogotá   Caracas   Kuala Lumpur   Lisbon   London   Madrid   Mexico City
Milan   Montreal   New Delhi   Santiago   Seoul   Singapore   Sydney   Taipei   Toronto

McGraw-Hill Irwin

FOUNDATIONS OF FINANCIAL MANAGEMENT

Published by McGraw-Hill/Irwin, a business unit of The McGraw-Hill Companies, Inc., 1221 Avenue of the Americas, New York, NY, 10020. Copyright © 2008 by The McGraw-Hill Companies, Inc. All rights reserved. No part of this publication may be reproduced or distributed in any form or by any means, or stored in a database or retrieval system, without the prior written consent of The McGraw-Hill Companies, Inc., including, but not limited to, in any network or other electronic storage or transmission, or broadcast for distance learning.

Some ancillaries, including electronic and print components, may not be available to customers outside the United States.

This book is printed on acid-free paper.

1 2 3 4 5 6 7 8 9 0 DOW/DOW 0 9 8 7 6

ISBN: 978-0-07-302720-3 (student edition)
MHID: 0-07-302720-0 (student edition)

Editorial director: *Brent Gordon*
Executive editor: *Michele Janicek*
Developmental editor II: *Christina Kouvelis*
Senior marketing manager: *Julie Phifer*
Media producer: *Jennifer Wilson*
Senior project manager: *Susanne Riedell*
Lead production supervisor: *Michael R. McCormick*
Senior designer: *Adam Rooke*

Photo research coordinator: *Kathy Shive*
Supplement producer: *Ira C. Roberts*
Lead media project manager: *Becky Szura*
Cover design: *Dave Seidler*
Typeface: *10.5/13 Times Roman*
Compositor: *Techbooks*
Printer: *R. R. Donnelley*

We would like to thank the following companies for permission to use their logos in this text: Nortel Networks, Southwest Airlines, Nestlé, eBay, Mack Trucks, Deutsche Bank, Sony, Sears, 3M, McGraw-Hill, Microsoft, Renault, Johnson & Johnson, Amazon.com, Eli Lilly, McDonald's, Continental Airlines, Coca-Cola, Calloway's Nursery, Celera, General Electric, Ericsson, Textron, Standard & Poor's, IBM, Wendy's International, Honeywell International, Hitachi, Procter & Gamble, Pfizer, Nokia, Kellogg, SBC, Fujitsu, Dell, Dun & Bradstreet, Target, Earthlink, General Motors, Liebert, Mattel, Del Monte, Tootsie Roll, Archer Daniels Midland Company, Echostar Communications, Hewlett-Packard, Viacom, Kmart, Yahoo! Inc., Duke Energy, Schlumberger, and CEMEX.

eBay is a trademark of eBay Inc.
The Sears Logo within this book is reprinted by arrangement with Sears, Roebuck and Co. and is protected under copyright. No duplication is permitted.
Used with permission from McDonald's Corporation.
Kellogg's® is a Registered trademark of Kellogg Company. All rights reserved. Used with permission.
The Dell logo is a trademark of Dell Computer Corporation.
Nestlé and Nest Design is a registered trademark of Nestlé.
Amazon.com is the registered trademark of Amazon.com, Inc.
The SBC logo is a registered trademark of SBC Properties, L.P.
The IBM logo is reprinted with permission and is a registered trademark of International Business Machines Corporation.
Microsoft is a registered trademark of Microsoft Corporation.
Yahoo: Used with permission by Yahoo! Inc. YAHOO! and the YAHOO! logo are trademarks of Yahoo! Inc.
Duke Energy: © & ® 2000 Duke Energy Corp. All Rights Reserved.

Library of Congress Cataloging-in-Publication Data
Block, Stanley B.
    Foundations of financial management / Stanley B. Block, Geoffrey A. Hirt.—12th ed.,
    Annotated instructor's ed.
        p. cm.—(The McGraw-Hill/Irwin series in finance, insurance, and real estate)
    Includes index.
    ISBN-13: 978-0-07-302720-3 (student ed: alk. paper)
    ISBN-10: 0-07-302720-0 (student ed: alk. paper)
    ISBN-13: 978-0-07-325743-3 (AIE: alk. paper)
    ISBN-10: 0-07-325743-5 (AIE: alk. paper)
        1. Corporations—Finance. I. Hirt Geoffrey A. II. Title.
HG4026.B589   2008
658.15—dc22   2006046620

www.mhhe.com

To our wonderful wives, Cathy and Linda, and children—Michelle, Randy, Amy, and Brian.

Stanley B. Block
Geoffrey A. Hirt

About the Authors

Stanley B. Block Professor Block teaches financial management and investments at Texas Christian University, where he received the Burlington Northern Outstanding Teaching Award and the M. J. Neeley School of Business Distinguished Teaching Award. His research interests include financial markets, mergers, and high-yield bonds. He has served as president of the Southwestern Finance Association and is a Chartered Financial Analyst and a Certified Cash Manager. He enjoys sports and has run the NY Marathon. Professor Block holds a BA from the University of Texas at Austin, an MBA from Cornell University, and a PhD from LSU.

In 2001, his former students established the Dr. Stan Block $1.5 million Endowed Chair in Finance at Texas Christian University. He is the first chairholder of the named chair.

Geoffrey A. Hirt Dr. Hirt is currently Professor of Finance at DePaul University. He received his PhD in Finance from the University of Illinois at Champaign-Urbana, his MBA from Miami University of Ohio and his BA from Ohio-Wesleyan University. Geoff directed the Chartered Financial Analysts Study program for the Investment Analysts Society of Chicago (now the CFA Institute of Chicago) from 1987 to 2001 and was on the Board of Directors of the CFA Institute of Chicago from 2002 through 2005. He was also Director of Equity Research at Mesirow Financial from 1998 to 2001. Dr. Hirt developed the real dollar investment fund at Illinois State University, taught real dollar investment classes at TCU, and is currently teaching the real dollar portfolio management course at DePaul University.

Preface

Thirty years have passed since we began writing the first edition of this text, and many things have changed during that time.

First of all, the field of finance has become much more analytical, with the emphasis on decision-oriented approaches to problems rather than the old, descriptive approach. We have increased the use of analytical approaches to financial problems in virtually every chapter of the book. But we also have stayed with our basic mission of making sure the student is able to follow us in our discussions throughout the text. While the 12th edition is considerably more sophisticated than the initial edition, it is still extremely "reader friendly." As the analytical skills demanded of students have increased, so has the authors' care in presenting the material.

Using computers has become considerably more important over the last quarter century, and this is also reflected in the 12th edition. We now offer Web Exercises at the end of every chapter, URL citations throughout the text, Standard & Poor's computer exercises at the end of selected chapters, self-study software for the student, an Online Learning Center for students and faculty, and computerized testing software and Powerpoint® for the faculty.

Throughout the past 30 years, the Block and Hirt text has been a leader in bringing the real world into the classroom, and this has never been more apparent than in the 12th edition. Each section of the book highlights an influential figure in the business world, each chapter opens with a real-world vignette, and the Finance in Action boxes (found in virtually every chapter) describe real-world activities and decisions made by actual businesses. Not only are hundreds of corporations discussed, but actual corporate logos are shown for the most important corporations covered in the book. The authors are also up-to-date on the latest tax and financial reporting legislation.

The international world of finance has become much more important over the last 30 years, and the text has expanded its international coverage tenfold since the first edition. Where there is an international application for a financial issue, you are very likely to find it in the Block and Hirt text.

More recently, the "new" economy, associated with high technology, has gained importance and in this latest edition there are more references to the eBays, Amazon. coms, and Oracles than ever before.

However, there is one thing that has not changed over the last 30 years—the authors still write the entire book and all of the problems themselves! We believe our devotion of time, energy, and commitment over these years is the reason for our reputation for having produced a high-quality and successful text—edition after edition.

Reinforcing Prerequisite Knowledge

Employers of business graduates report that the most successful analysts, planners, and executives are both effective and confident in their financial skills. We concur. One of the best ways to increase your facility in financial planning is to integrate your knowledge from prerequisite courses. Therefore, the text is designed to build on your basic knowledge from courses in accounting and economics. By applying tools learned in these courses, you can develop a conceptual and analytical understanding of financial management.

We realize, however, that for some students time has passed since you have completed your accounting courses. Therefore, we have included Chapter 2, a thorough review of accounting principles, finance terminology, and financial statements. With a working knowledge of Chapter 2, you will have a more complete understanding of the impact of business decisions on financial statements. Furthermore, as you are about to begin your career you will be much better prepared when called upon to apply financial concepts.

Content Improvements

The 12th edition specifically covers the following new topics:

Financial Goals in an International Market Environment Chapter 1 provides a discussion of how 3M manages corporate strategy in an environment in which 60 percent of its sales are foreign.

The Critical Role of the Board of Directors in Corporate Decisions The fiduciary responsibility of the board of directors is covered in Chapter 1. Failure to meet this responsibility is pointed out in the case of Enron and WorldCom along with the presentation of other ethical considerations.

The Use of Technology to Manage the Investment in Working Capital In Chapter 6 the authors discuss the use of sophisticated computer procedures to monitor the investment in inventory as an illustration of the integration of technology into financial management.

The Different Use of Debt by Actual Companies In the discussion of cost of capital in Chapter 11, the reader is able to view the debt strategy of 13 actual companies.

Global Events of the 21st Century In Chapter 14 the authors cover everything from 9/11 to Hurricane Katrina by illustrating the effect of key events on the financial markets.

Changing Capital Markets The use of electronic trading and the changing role of the major financial exchanges is discussed in Chapter 14.

Foreign Exchange Considerations in the Capital Markets The ups and downs of the euro versus the dollar and the impact on financial management is covered in Chapter 21.

Successful improvements from the previous editions that we have built on in the 12th edition include:

Functional Integration We have taken care to include examples that are not just applicable to finance students, but also to marketing, management, and accounting majors.

Small Business Since over two-thirds of jobs created in the U.S. economy are from small businesses, we have continued to note when specific financial techniques are performed differently by large and small businesses.

Comprehensive International Coverage We have updated and expanded coverage on international companies and events throughout the text.

Contemporary Coverage The 12th edition has continued to provide updated real-world examples, using companies easily recognizable by students to illustrate financial concepts presented in the text.

Internet Presence Helpful Web sites are listed throughout the text as well as featured in many of the Finance in Action boxes. Web exercises are featured in each chapter and Standard & Poor's problems are included in relevant chapters to further showcase real-world material.

New Features

New! Practice Problems and Solutions

Two practice problems are featured at the end of each chapter. They review concepts illustrated within the chapter and enable the student to determine whether the material has been understood prior to completion of the problem sets. Detailed solutions to the practice problems are found immediately following each problem.

Expanded! Finance in Action Boxes

These boxed readings highlight specific topics of interest that now relate to four main areas: managerial decisions, global situations, technology issues, and ethics. The addition of ethics is relevant given the many recent corporate scandals and the resulting governance issues. Web site addresses are included in applicable boxes for easy access to more information on that topic or company.

New! Part Openers

In addition to listing the germane chapters, the Part Openers now feature Related Part Web sites so you are able to easily reference the most current and relevant information on the Web.

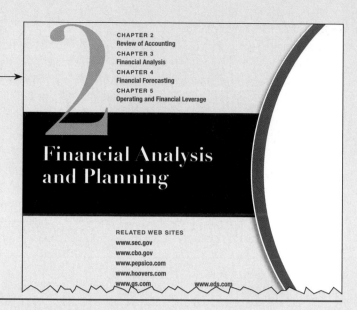

CHAPTER 2
Review of Accounting

CHAPTER 3
Financial Analysis

CHAPTER 4
Financial Forecasting

CHAPTER 5
Operating and Financial Leverage

2

Financial Analysis and Planning

RELATED WEB SITES

www.sec.gov
www.cbo.gov
www.pepsico.com
www.hoovers.com
www.gs.com   www.eds.com

Chapter Features

Updated! News Makers

Each part opens with a News Maker feature that highlights an influential person in finance or business and their contributions to the field. Featured professionals include: Paul Newman, Sallie Krawchek, Indra Nooyi, Steve Jobs, Jim Tyree, and Richard Parsons.

Chapter Concepts

Chapter concepts are listed on the opening page of each chapter as a quick introduction to the material you will learn and as an indication of the key topics you should understand fully before moving to the next chapter.

news makers

Financial management takes place within the context of economic activity as well as within a structure of social and ethical constraints. Unfortunately, in the aftermath of the stock market bubble of the late 1990s, many investors and corporate boards of directors were surprised to find out that the officers of their companies had engaged in misleading and fraudulent financial transactions. Corporate officers of companies such as Tyco, Enron, WorldCom, Adelphia Communications, and many more, were indicted and charged with fraud, tax evasion, embezzlement, and unlawful corporate practices. The stock market took a nosedive; the Securities and Exchange Commission stepped up its investigations into many companies' accounting practices; the U.S. president signed a corporate ethics bill; Congress passed the Sarbanes-Oxley Act, and

Paul Newman's famous recipe for spaghetti sauce marketed under the brand, Newman's Own. Then there came salad dressing, popcorn, salsa, and more. You can check out the "Legend of Newman's Own" on www.newmansown.com.

You may be surprised to find that the profits of his company are donated to more than 1,000 charities. Newman's Own has contributed over $200 million since its inception. One charity that Newman founded is the Hole in the Wall Gang (www.hitwg-camps.org) that in 2006 had five camps servicing 6,700 seriously ill children. Each camp provides recreational and therapeutic experi... for children ... y otherwise ...t on these childhood expe... because of their intensive

Paul Newman espoused some of his corporate philosophy at a forum on corporate philanthropy at the Haas School of Business at the University of California at Berkeley. Newman thinks of

Paul Newman–Newman's Own
Getty Images

charitable giving as an investment in society. "It seems so human

chapter concepts

1 Leverage represents the use of fixed cost items to magnify the firm's results.

2 Operating leverage indicates the extent fixed assets (plant and equipment) are utilized by the firm.

3 Financial leverage shows how much debt the firm employs in its capital structure.

4 By increasing leverage, the firm increases its profit potential, but also its risk of failure.

In the physical sciences as well as in politics, the term leverage has been popularized to mean the use of special force and effects to produce more than normal results from a given course of action. In business the same concept is applied, with the emphasis on the employment of fixed cost items in anticipation of magnifying returns at high levels of operation. The student should recognize that leverage is a two-edged sword—producing highly favorable results when things go well, and quite the opposite under negative conditions.

Just ask the airline industry. Firms such as American Airlines, Continental, Delta, Southwest, and UAL were all flying high at the turn of the century because of favorable economic conditions, high capacity utilization, and relatively low interest rates on debt. Such was not the case in the next decade when high leverage in the form of high-cost fixed assets (airplanes) and high-cost debt was causing severe consequences in a weak economy. Among the affected firms is Atlanta-based Delta Airlines.

Between 2000 and 2005, Delta saw its EPS go from $6.87 to a negative $12.80. That's a pretty scary ride for any company. Delta had to take Chapter 11 bankruptcy on September 14, 2005, although its planes are still flying on a more limited basis under court supervision.

It is widely believed that massive consolidations (mergers) between the weak and the strong within the airline industry will be necessary the next time the warning light on the economy comes on because of the high leverage in the industry.

Revised! Chapter Opening Vignettes

We bring in current events (such as business-to-business online ventures and competition among air carriers) as chapter openers to illustrate the material to be learned in the upcoming chapter.

Updated! Company Logos

In this feature, four-color company logos (such as Microsoft, Nestlé, and Cemex) are included in the margin of the text where a situation involving the company is used as an example. This feature helps to call out our strength in providing many real-world examples. Because logos are so easy to recognize, you will have no trouble identifying them with the financial concepts in the example.

How does the market allocate capital to the thousands of firms that are continually in need of money? Let us assume that you graduate from college as a finance major and are hired to manage money for a wealthy family like the Rockefellers. You are given $250 million to manage and you can choose to invest the money anywhere in the world. For example, you could buy common stock in Microsoft, the American software company, or in Nestlé, the Swiss food company, or in Cemex, the Mexican cement company; you could choose to lend money to the U.S. or Japanese government by purchasing its bonds; or you could lend money to ExxonMobil or British Petroleum. Of course these are only some of the endless choices you would have.

How do you decide to allocate the $250 million so that you will maximize your return and minimize your risk? Some investors will choose a risk level that meets their objective and maximize return for that given level of risk. By seeking this risk-return objective, you will bid up the prices of securities that seem underpriced and have potential for high returns and you will avoid securities of equal risk that, in your judgment, seem overpriced. Since all market participants play the same risk-return game, the financial markets become the playing field, and price movements become the winning or losing score. Let us look at only the corporate sector of the market and 100 companies of equal risk. Those companies with expectations for high return will have higher relative common stock prices than those companies with poor expectations. Since the securities' prices in the market reflect the combined judgment of all the players, price movements provide feedback to corporate managers and let them know whether the market thinks they are winning or losing against the competition.

Those companies that perform well and are rewarded by the market with high-priced securities have an easier time raising new funds in the money and capital markets than their competitors. They are also able to raise funds at a lower cost. Go back to that $250

Functional Use of Four Colors

The 12th edition continues to include the well-received functional use of four colors to enhance your understanding of tables, graphs, and exhibits. For example, the financial analysis chapter (Chapter 3) uses color to make the origin of the ratios easier to follow. For easy identification, the balance sheet appears in blue and the income statement in red. These same two colors continue to be traced through the numerical ratios, with each number appearing in the same color as the financial statement from which it was derived. This linkage helps identify whether the ratio is a balance sheet ratio, an income statement ratio, or a mixed ratio.

In-Book Acetates on Time Value of Money (Chapter 9)

The concept of the "time value of money" is one of the most difficult topics in any financial management course for professors to communicate to students. We think we have created a visual method for teaching future value and present value of money that will help you understand the concept simply and quickly. The 12th edition includes four-color acetates in the text that visually relate future values and present values. We hope you agree that this innovation is an advancement in financial pedagogy.

Summary

Each chapter ends with a summary that ties the material back to the chapter concepts presented at the beginning of the chapter.

Summary

Financial forecasting allows the financial manager to anticipate events before they occur, particularly the need for raising funds externally. An important consideration is that growth may call for additional sources of financing because profit is often inadequate to cover the net buildup in receivables, inventory, and other asset accounts.

A systems approach is necessary to develop pro forma statements. We first construct a pro forma income statement based on sales projections and the production plan, then translate this material into a cash budget, and finally assimilate all previously developed material into a pro forma balance sheet.

An alternative to tracing cash and accounting flows to determine financial needs is to assume that accounts on the balance sheet will maintain a given percentage relationship to sales. We can then indicate a change in the sales level and ascertain our related financing needs. This is known as the percent-of-sales method.

For firms that are in highly seasonal businesses, it is particularly important to identify peaks and slowdowns in the activities of the firm and the associated financial requirements.

Review of Formulas

At the end of every chapter that includes equations, we provide a list of all equations for easy reviewing purposes.

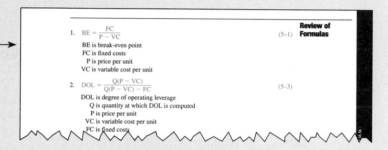

Review of Formulas

1. $BE = \dfrac{FC}{P - VC}$ (5–1)

   BE is break-even point
   FC is fixed costs
   P is price per unit
   VC is variable cost per unit

2. $DOL = \dfrac{Q(P - VC)}{Q(P - VC) - FC}$ (5–3)

   DOL is degree of operating leverage
   Q is quantity at which DOL is computed
   P is price per unit
   VC is variable cost per unit
   FC is fixed costs

List of Key Terms

Similarly, you can use the list of key terms provided at the end of each chapter to test your comprehension and retention. Page numbers are provided for each term and the term is also defined in the glossary at the back of the book.

List of Terms

profitability ratios 55	inflation 65
asset utilization ratios 55	replacement costs 66
liquidity ratios 55	disinflation 66
debt utilization ratios 55	deflation 67
Du Pont system of analysis 57	LIFO 68

Discussion Questions and Problems

The material in the text is supported by over 250 questions and 350 problems in this edition, to reinforce and test your understanding of each chapter. Care has been taken to make the questions and problems consistent with the chapter material, and each problem is labeled with its topic to facilitate that link. Every problem has been revised in this edition, but the level and variety of the complete set is similar to those from previous editions.

Discussion Questions

1. Discuss some financial variables that affect the price-earnings ratio.
2. What is the difference between book value per share of common stock and market value per share? Why does this disparity occur?
3. Explain how depreciation generates actual cash flows for the company.
4. What is the difference between accumulated depreciation and depreciation expense? How are they related?

Problems   All problems are available in Homework Manager. Please see the preface for more information.

Income statement   1. Frantic Fast Foods had earnings after taxes of $390,000 in the year 2006 with 300,000 shares outstanding. On January 1, 2007, the firm issued 25,000 new shares. Because of the proceeds from these new shares and other operating improvements, earnings after taxes increased by 20 percent.

   a. Compute earnings per share for the year 2006.
   b. Compute earnings per share for the year 2007.

Income statement   2. Bettis Bus Company had earnings after taxes of $600,000 in the year 2006 with 300,000 shares of stock outstanding. On January 1, 2007, the firm issued 40,000 new shares. Because of the proceeds from these new shares and other operating improvements, earnings after taxes increased by 25 percent.

   a. Compute earnings per share for the year 2006.
   b. Compute earnings per share for the year 2007.

www.mhhe.com/bhl2e

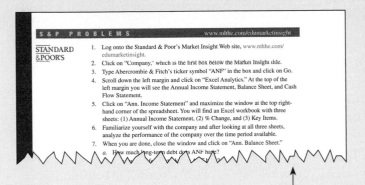

Revised! Standard & Poor's Problems

Relevant chapters contain problems directly incorporating the Educational Version of Market Insight, a service based on Standard & Poor's renowned COMPUSTAT database. Problems are based on market data provided by real companies to gain a better understanding of practical business situations.

Updated! Comprehensive Problems

Several chapters have comprehensive problems, indicated with red sidebars that integrate and require the application of several financial concepts into one problem. Additional comprehensive problems are included in the Instructor's Manual for Chapters 2, 3, and 8.

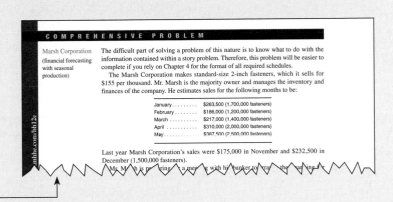

Web Exercises

Each chapter includes at least one Web exercise to help pull more relevant real-world material into the classroom. The exercises ask students to go to a specific Web site of a company and make a complete analysis similar to that demonstrated in the chapter. These exercises provide a strong link between learning chapter concepts and applying them to the actual decision-making process.

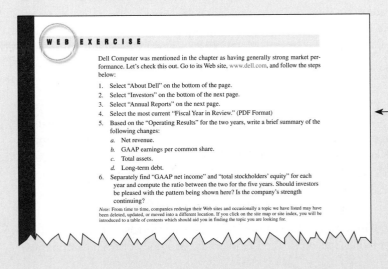

Teaching and Learning Support

For Instructors:

Instructor's Resource CD-ROM (0073257451) Receive all of the supplements in an electronic format! The Instructor's Manual, PowerPoint, Computerized Test Bank, Instructor's Manual to Accompany the Casebook, and Test Bank are all together on one convenient CD. The interface provides instructors with a self-contained program that allows them to arrange the visual resources into their own presentations and add additional files as well.

- *Instructor's Manual with Solutions (0073257478)* Revised to help the instructor integrate the graphs, tables, perspectives, transparencies, and problems into a lecture format. Each chapter opens with a brief overview and a review of key chapter concepts. The chapter is then outlined in an annotated format to be used as an in-class reference guide by the instructor. The manual also includes detailed solutions to all of the problems, set in a larger type font to facilitate their reproduction as transparencies for the classroom. Additional comprehensive problems and solutions are also included.

- *PowerPoint Presentation* Contains lecture outlines and selected exhibits from the book in a four-color, electronic format that you can customize for your own lectures. Selected end-of-chapter solutions (all odd-numbered and some even-numbered questions) are also included.

- *Test Bank* This includes 1,500 multiple-choice and true/false questions, with revisions made by the authors corresponding to the revisions in the 12th edition. Also included are quiz sets and matching quizzes.

- *Computerized Test Bank* Utilizing McGraw-Hill's EZ Test testing software for Windows to quickly create customized exams, this user-friendly program allows instructors to sort questions by format, edit existing questions or add new ones, and scramble questions for multiple versions of the same test.

- *Instructor's Manual to Accompany Cases* This includes a brief synopsis of the purpose of each case, its relation to the text, and its level of complexity. Detailed solutions to the end-of-case questions are also provided. Two new cases are featured in this edition.

DVD (0073261874) These finance videos are 10-minute case studies on topics such as financial markets, careers, TVM (time value of money), capital budgeting, EVA (economic value added), mergers and acquisitions, and international finance.

For Students:

Standard & Poor's Educational Version of Market Insight McGraw-Hill/Irwin is proud to partner with Standard & Poor's to offer access to the Educational Version of Market Insight free with the purchase of a new text. A passcode card is provided, which will give your students access to six years of financial data for over 1,000 top U.S. companies. See www.mhhe.com/edumarketinsight for details on this exclusive partnership!

Study Guide and Workbook (0073257494) This valuable resource, created by Dwight C. Anderson, Louisiana Tech University, provides chapter summaries, outlines with page references, and additional problems and multiple-choice questions with solutions for practice.

Cases (0073257443) These 29 cases, written by the authors, are ideal for in-depth analysis and facilitate an integrated understanding of the topics presented in the book.

Online Learning Center

Visit this full Web resource now available with the 12th edition at www.mhhe.com/bh12e. The Information Center includes information on this new edition and links for special offers. The Instructor's Edition includes all of the teaching resources for the book, and the Student Edition includes free online study materials—such as quizzes and study outlines—developed specifically for this edition. Excel Spreadsheet Templates are also included. A feedback form is available for your questions and comments.

Self-Study Software This tutorial software is available free! It contains a self-study program, with questions written by the authors, to test your understanding of the concepts, as well as provide an infinite number of problems to solve with the random-number generator program. It also includes the glossary of terms, chapter concepts, and summaries.

Virtual Lectures Developed to further enhance the coverage presented in each chapter, a unique set of audio and visual aids details the specifics of the chapter and reviews key concepts to help reinforce their importance.

Corporate Finance Online An exclusive Web tool from McGraw-Hill/Irwin, this value-added site enables faculty and students to engage in financial exercises and activities for 27 different key corporate finance topics. Students can complete challenging exercises and discussion questions that draw on recent articles, company reports, government data, and other Web-based resources. There are also password-protected teaching notes to assist you with classroom integration of the material.

Finance Around the World A link to this global financial resource for researching and exploring corporate finance is also included in the OLC.

Packaging Options

McGraw-Hill's Homework Manager™ Are you looking for a way to spend less time grading and to have more flexibility with the problems you assign as homework and tests? McGraw-Hill's Homework Manager is an exciting new package option developed for this text! Homework Manager is a Web-based tool for instructors and students for delivering, answering, and grading end-of-chapter problems and tests, and providing a limitless supply of self-graded practice for students.

All of the book's end-of-chapter problems are loaded into Homework Manager, and instructors can choose to assign the exact problems as stated in the book, or algorithmic versions of them so each student has a unique set of variables for the problems. You create the assignments and control parameters such as—do you want your students to receive hints, is this a graded assignment or practice, etc. The test bank is also available in Homework Manager, giving you the ability to use the questions for online tests. Both the problems and the tests are automatically graded and the results are stored in a private grade book, which is created when you set up your class. Detailed results let you see at a glance how each student does on an assignment or an individual problem—you can even see how many tries it took them to solve it. If you order this special package, students will receive a Homework Manager User's Guide and an access code packaged with their text. *ISBN: 0073318132*

***McGraw-Hill's Homework Manager Plus*™** There is also an enhanced version of McGraw-Hill's Homework Manager through the Homework Manager Plus package option. If you order the text packaged with Homework Manager Plus, your students will receive Homework Manager as described above, but with an integrated online text included. When students are in Homework Manager and need more help to solve a problem, there will be a link that takes them to the section of the text online that explains the concept they are struggling with. All of McGraw-Hill's media assets, such as videos, narrated lectures, and additional online quizzing, are also integrated at the appropriate places of the online text to provide students with a full learning experience. If you order this special package, students will receive the Homework Manager Plus card packaged with their text, which will give them access to all of these products, as well as an online Homework Manager User's Guide. McGraw-Hill's Homework Manager is powered by Brownstone. *ISBN: 007331840*

The Wall Street Journal Your students can subscribe to *The Wall Street Journal*, both print and online versions, for 15 weeks at a specially priced rate of $20.00 in addition to the price of the text. Students will receive a "How to Use the *WSJ*" handbook and a card explaining how to start the subscription to both versions. Contact your McGraw-Hill sales representative for more information on this package.

BusinessWeek Your students can subscribe to 15 weeks of *BusinessWeek* for a specially priced rate of $8.25 in addition to the price of the text. Students will receive a passcode card shrink-wrapped with their new text. The card directs students to a Web site where they enter the code and then gain access to *BusinessWeek's* registration page to enter address info and set up their print and online subscription. Contact your McGraw-Hill sales representative for more information on this package.

Financial Analysis with an Electronic Calculator, Sixth Edition, by Mark A. White This helpful guide provides your students with information and procedures to master financial calculators and gain a deeper understanding of financial mathematics. Complete instructions are included for solving all major problem types on three popular models of financial calculators: Hewlett-Packard's HP-10B II, Sharp Electronics' EL-733A, and Texas Instruments' BA II Plus. Sixty hands-on problems with detailed solutions will allow you to practice the skills outlined in the book and obtain instant reinforcement. Contact your McGraw-Hill sales representative for more information on this package.

FinGame Online 4.0, by LeRoy Brooks In this comprehensive simulation game, students control a hypothetical company over numerous periods of operation. As students make major financial and operating decisions for their company, they will develop and enhance skills in financial management and financial accounting statement analysis. This valuable asset is $15.00 in addition to the price of the text. Contact your McGraw-Hill sales representative for more information on this package.

Finance and Investments Using The Wall Street Journal, by Peter R. Crabb This text teaches students to evaluate and apply information from *The Wall Street Journal* by presenting three main steps—an overview of the finance/investments topic; a group of exercises based on data or an article that is printed in the workbook or in *The Wall Street Journal*; and step-by-step lessons in analyzing data and articles. Contact your sales representative for a special packaging price.

Acknowledgments

For their valuable reviews and helpful comments, we are grateful to:

Dwight C. Anderson
Eric Anderson
Antonio Apap
Kavous Ardalan
Charles Barngrover
Brian T. Belt
Omar Benkato
Joseph Bentley
William J. Bertin
Debela Birru
Robert Boatler
Alka Bramhandkar
Dallas Brozik
Georgia Buckles
Richard Butler
Ezra Byler
Rosemary Carlson
Alan J. Carper
Cheryl Chamblin
Leo Chan
Rolf Christensen
E. Tylor Claggett
Henry Co
Nanette Cobb
Allan Conway
Tom Copeland
Walter R. Dale
Jeffrey S. Dean

Andrea DeMaskey
James Demello
Bob Diberio
Clifford A. Diebold
Jeff Donaldson
Tom Downs
David Durst
Fred Ebeid
Jeff Eicher
Marumbok Etta
Barry Farber
O. L. Fortier
Mohamed Gaber
Robert Gaertner
Jim Gahlon
James Gentry
Elizabeth Goins
Bernie J. Grablowsky
Bill Greer
Debbie Griest
Kidane Habteselassie
John R. Hall
Thomas R. Hamilton
Walt Hammond
Carole Harris
Charles Higgins
Stanley Jacobs
Bharat Jain

Joel Jankowski
Gerald S. Justin
Fredric S. Kamin
Peter R. Kensicki
Tom Kewley
Jim Keys
Robert Kleiman
Raj Kohli
Charles Kronche
Ronald Kudla
Morris Lamberson
Joe Lavely
Joseph Levitsky
John H. Lewis
Terry Lindenberg
Joe Lipscomb
John P. Listro
Wilson Liu
Doug Lonnstrom
Claude Lusk
Paul Marciano
John D. Markese
Peter Marks
Thomas Maroney
Kooros Maskooki
Joe Massa
Patricia Matthews
Michael Matukonis
K. Gary McClure
Grant McQueen
Wayne E. McWee

Stuart Michelson
Vassil Mihov
Jerry D. Miller
David Minars
Mike Moritz
Heber Moulton
Bryan O'Neil
Dimitrios Pachis
Coleen C. Pantalone
Robert Pavlik
Rosemary C. Peavler
Mario Picconi
Beverly Piper
Harlan Platt
Ralph A. Pope
Roger Potter
Franklin Potts
Dev Prasad
Chris Prestopino
Frances A. Quinn
David Rankin
Dan Raver
Robert Rittenhouse
Mauricio Rodriguez
Frederick Rommel
Marjorie Rubash
Gary Rupp
Philip Russel
Gayle Russell
Robert Saemann
Olgun Fuat Sahin

Ajay Samant	William Smith	Cathyann Tully	Philip L. Wiggle
Atul Saxena	Jan R. Squires	Donald E. Vaughn	Lawrence Wolken
Timothy Scheppa	Sundaram Srinivasan	Mark Vaughan	Annie Wong
Sandra Schickele	Mark Sunderman	Andrew Waisburd	Don Wort
James Scott	Robert Swanson	Ken Washer	Ergun Yener
Abu Selimuddin	Glenn Tanner	William Welch	Lowell Young
Gowri Shankar	Richard Taylor	Gary Wells	Emily Zeitz
Joanne Sheridan	Robert Taylor	Larry White	Terry Zivney
Fred Shipley	Mike Tuberose	Howard R. Whitney	Matt Wirgau

We also wish to thank Brian Hirt for technical computer assistance, Jim Tyree of Mesirow Financial, and Becky Ziberna for researching support. Finally we would like to thank Michele Janicek, executive editor; Christina Kouvelis, developmental editor II; Susanne Riedell, senior project manager; Julie Phifer, senior marketing manager; Adam Rooke, senior designer; Michael McCormick, lead production supervisor; Becky Szura, lead media project manager; Ira Roberts, supplement producer; Jennifer Wilson, media producer; Jen Jelinski, marketing specialist; and the entire team at McGraw-Hill/Irwin for its feedback, support, and enduring commitment to excellence.

Stanley B. Block
Geoffrey A. Hirt

Brief Contents

Contents

List of Selected Real-World Examples and Boxes

Chapter	Subject, Title, Table Number, or Company Name	Page

Chapter	Subject, Title, Table Number, or Company Name	Page

List of Selected International Examples and Boxes

Introduction

news makers

Financial management takes place within the context of economic activity as well as within a structure of social and ethical constraints. Unfortunately, in the aftermath of the stock market bubble of the late 1990s, many investors and corporate boards of directors were surprised to find out that the officers of their companies had engaged in misleading and fraudulent financial transactions. Corporate officers of companies such as Tyco, Enron, WorldCom, Adelphia Communications, and many more, were indicted and charged with fraud, tax evasion, embezzlement, and unlawful corporate practices. The stock market took a nosedive; the Securities and Exchange Commission stepped up its investigations into many companies' accounting practices; the U.S. president signed a corporate ethics bill; Congress passed the Sarbanes-Oxley Act, and investors, lenders, and the general public lost faith in the accuracy of corporate accounting statements.

Then you ask, why in the world are you presenting Paul Newman, famous movie star, as the News Maker for Part 1? Well it is easy, the authors have admired Mr. Newman's business acumen and corporate philanthropy for many years. In the beginning there was Paul Newman's famous recipe for spaghetti sauce marketed under the brand, Newman's Own. Then there came salad dressing, popcorn, salsa, and more. You can check out the "Legend of Newman's Own" on www.newmansown. com.

You may be surprised to find that the profits of his company are donated to more than 1,000 charities. Newman's Own has contributed over $200 million since its inception. One charity that Newman founded is the Hole in the Wall Gang (www.hitwg-camps.org) that in 2006 had five camps servicing 6,700 seriously ill children. Each camp provides recreational and therapeutic experiences for children who may otherwise miss out on these childhood experiences because of their intensive medical care. While Newman's energy and money started the camps, they have outgrown his ability to sustain them, and the camps rely on gifts from other individuals and corporations.

Paul Newman espoused some of his corporate philosophy at a forum on corporate philanthropy at the Haas School of Business at the University of California at Berkeley. Newman thinks of

Paul Newman–Newman's Own
Getty Images

charitable giving as an investment in society. "It seems so human to hold your hand out to other people who are less fortunate," Newman said. "I don't know why that can't be part of the corporate mentality."

The Goals and Functions of Financial Management

1

chapter
concepts

1   The field of finance integrates concepts from economics, accounting, and a number of other areas.

2   The relationship of risk to return is a central focus of finance.

3   The primary goal of financial managers is to maximize the wealth of the shareholders.

4   Financial managers attempt to achieve wealth maximization through daily activities such as credit and inventory

management and through longer-term decisions related to raising funds.

5   Financial managers must carefully consider domestic and international business conditions in carrying out their responsibilities.

6   Daily price changes in the financial markets provide feedback about a company's performance and help investors allocate their capital between firms.

3M is one of those rare companies that is more adept than others at creating products, marketing those products, and being financially astute. 3M is the maker of Post-it® notes, Scotch tape, adhesives, sponges, pharmaceuticals, and thousands of other products. 3M's 2005 annual reports states: "Our new-product pipeline continues to expand significantly. This pipeline is expected to deliver $5.5 billion of total sales over the period 2005 to 2007." In order to accomplish this track record, 3M's research and development for these products has to be financed, the design and production funded, and the products marketed and sold worldwide. This process involves all the functions of business.

Did you ever stop to think about the importance of the finance function for a $20 billion multinational company like 3M where 60 percent of sales are international? Someone has to manage the

3M

international cash flow, bank relationships, payroll, purchases of plant and equipment, and acquisition of capital. Financial decisions must be made concerning the feasibility and profitability of the continuous stream of new products developed through 3M's very creative research and development efforts. The financial manager needs to keep his or her pulse on interest rates, exchange rates, and the tone of the money and capital markets.

Companies don't generally lay out their financial goals in their annual reports because investors might be able to see if they actually accomplished those goals. While goals may change over time with management changes, 3M clearly stated their financial goals in a recent annual report. These goals are very consistent with the financial theory expressed in this book.

We strive to maximize shareholder wealth through solid profitable growth and effective use of capital. Specific financial goals are to achieve (1) at least 30 percent of sales from products introduced during the last four years; (2) growth in earnings per share of more than 10 percent per year on average; (3) growth in economic profit exceeding earnings per share growth, and return on invested capital among the highest of industrial companies.

In order to achieve these goals the financial manager must manage 3M's global affairs and react quickly to changes in financial markets and exchange rate fluctuations. The board of directors and chief executive officer rely on the financial division to provide a precious resource—capital—and to manage it efficiently and profitably. If you would like to do some research on 3M, you can access its home page at www.3M.com. If you would like to understand more about how companies make financial decisions, keep reading.

The Field of Finance

The field of finance is closely related to economics and accounting, and financial managers need to understand the relationships between these fields. Economics provides a structure for decision making in such areas as risk analysis, pricing theory through supply and demand relationships, comparative return analysis, and many other important areas. Economics also provides the broad picture of the economic environment in which corporations must continually make decisions. A financial manager must understand the institutional structure of the Federal Reserve System, the commercial banking system, and the interrelationships between the various sectors of the economy. Economic variables, such as gross domestic product, industrial production, disposable income, unemployment, inflation, interest rates, and taxes (to name a few), must fit into the financial manager's decision model and be applied correctly. These terms will be presented throughout the text and integrated into the financial process.

Accounting is sometimes said to be the language of finance because it provides financial data through income statements, balance sheets, and the statement of cash flows. The financial manager must know how to interpret and use these statements in allocating the firm's financial resources to generate the best return possible in the long run. Finance links economic theory with the numbers of accounting, and all corporate managers—whether in production, sales, research, marketing, management, or long-run strategic planning—must know what it means to assess the financial performance of the firm.

Many students approaching the field of finance for the first time might wonder what career opportunities exist. For those who develop the necessary skills and training, jobs include corporate financial officer, banker, stockbroker, financial analyst, portfolio manager, investment banker, financial consultant, or personal financial planner. As the student progresses through the text, he or she will become increasingly familiar with the important role of the various participants in the financial decision-making process. A financial manager addresses such varied issues as decisions on plant location, the raising of capital, or simply how to get the highest return on x million dollars between 5 o'clock this afternoon and 8 o'clock tomorrow morning.

Evolution of the Field of Finance

Like any discipline, the field of finance has developed and changed over time. At the turn of the century, finance emerged as a field separate from economics when large industrial corporations in oil, steel, chemicals, and railroads were created by early industrialists such as Rockefeller, Carnegie, and Du Pont. In these early days, a student of finance would spend time learning about the financial instruments that were essential to mergers and acquisitions. By the 1930s, the country was in its worst depression ever and financial practice revolved around such topics as the preservation of capital, maintenance of liquidity, reorganization of financially troubled corporations, and the bankruptcy process. By the mid-1950s finance moved away from its descriptive and definitional nature and became more analytical. One of the major advances was the decision-oriented process of allocating **financial capital** (money) for the purchase of **real capital** (long-term plant and equipment). The enthusiasm for more detailed analysis spread to other decision-making areas of the firm—such as cash and inventory management, capital structure theory, and dividend policy. The emphasis also shifted from that of the outsider looking in at the firm, to that of the financial manager making tough day-to-day decisions that would affect the firm's performance.

Recent Issues in Finance

More recently, financial management has focused on risk-return relationships and the maximization of return for a given level of risk. The award of the 1990 Nobel prize in economics to Professors Harry Markowitz and William Sharpe for their contributions to the financial theories of risk-return and portfolio management demonstrates the importance of these concepts. In addition, Professor Merton Miller received the Nobel prize in economics for his work in the area of **capital structure theory** (the study of the relative importance of debt and equity). These three scholars were the first professors of finance to win a Nobel prize in economics, and their work has been very influential in the field of finance over the last 30 years. Since then, others have followed.

Finance continues to become more analytical and mathematical. New financial products with a focus on hedging are being widely used by financial managers to reduce some of the risk caused by changing interest rates and foreign currency exchange rates.

While the increase of prices, or **inflation**, has always been a key variable in financial decisions, it was not very important from the 1930s to about 1965 when it averaged about 1 percent per year. However, after 1965 the annual rate of price increases began to accelerate and became quite significant in the 1970s when inflation reached double-digit levels during several years. Inflation remained relatively high until 1982 when the U.S. economy entered a phase of **disinflation** (a slowing down of price increases). The effects of inflation and disinflation on financial forecasting, the required rates of return for capital budgeting decisions, and the cost of capital are quite significant to financial managers and have become more important in their decision making.

The Impact of the Internet

The Internet craze of the 1990s created what was referred to as the "new economy." With the crash of the stock market from its peak in March 2000, and the accompanying collapse of hundreds of dot.com Internet companies, many writers pronounced the new economy dead. The Internet has been around for a long time and only in the 1990s did it start to be applied to commercial ventures as companies tried to get a return on their previous technology investments. There never was a "new economy," only an economy where companies were constantly moving through a technological transformation that continues to this day.

The rapid development of computer technology, both software and hardware, continued to turn the Internet into a dynamic force in the economy and has affected the way business is conducted. The rapid expansion of the Internet and its acceptance by the U.S. population has allowed the creation of many new business models and companies such as Amazon.com and eBay. It has also enabled the acceleration of e-commerce solutions for "old economy" companies. These e-commerce solutions include different ways to reach customers—the business to consumer model (B2C)—and more efficient ways to interact with suppliers—the business to business model (B2B).

Ralph S. Larsen, former chairman and CEO of Johnson & Johnson said, "The Internet is going to turn the way we do business upside down—and for the better. From the most straightforward administrative functions, to operations, to marketing and sales, to supply chain relationships, to finance, to research and development, to customer relationships—no part of our business will remain untouched by this technological revolution."[1] So far he has been right.

For a financial manager, e-commerce impacts financial management because it affects the pattern and speed with which cash flows through the firm. In the B2C model, products are bought with credit cards and the credit checks are performed by Visa, MasterCard, American Express, or some other credit card company, and the selling firm gets the cash flow faster than it would using its own credit channels. In the B2B model, orders can be placed, inventory managed, and bids to supply product can be accepted, all online. The B2B model can help companies lower the cost of managing inventory, accounts receivable, and cash. Where applicable we have included Internet examples throughout the book to highlight the impact of e-commerce and the Internet on the finance function.

Functions of Financial Management

Having examined the field of finance and some of its more recent developments, let us turn our attention to the functions financial managers must perform. It is the responsibility of financial management to allocate funds to current and fixed assets, to obtain the best mix of financing alternatives, and to develop an appropriate dividend policy within the context of the firm's objectives. These functions are performed on a day-to-day basis as well as through infrequent use of the capital markets to acquire new funds. The daily activities of financial management include credit management, inventory control, and the receipt and disbursement of funds. Less routine functions encompass the sale of stocks and bonds and the establishment of capital budgeting and dividend plans.

As indicated in Figure 1–1, all these functions are carried out while balancing the profitability and risk components of the firm.

The appropriate risk-return trade-off must be determined to maximize the market value of the firm for its shareholders. The risk-return decision will influence not only the operational side of the business (capital versus labor or Product A versus Product B) but also the financing mix (stocks versus bonds versus retained earnings).

---

[1]Johnson & Johnson *1999 Annual Report,* p. 4.

Figure 1–1

Functions of the financial manager

Forms of Organization

The finance function may be carried out within a number of different forms of organizations. Of primary interest are the sole proprietorship, the partnership, and the corporation.

Sole Proprietorship   The **sole proprietorship** form of organization represents single-person ownership and offers the advantages of simplicity of decision making and low organizational and operating costs. Most small businesses with 1 to 10 employees are sole proprietorships. The major drawback of the sole proprietorship is that there is unlimited liability to the owner. In settlement of the firm's debts, the owner can lose not only the capital that has been invested in the business, but also personal assets. This drawback can be serious, and the student should realize that few lenders are willing to advance funds to a small business without a personal liability commitment.

The profits or losses of a sole proprietorship are taxed as though they belong to the individual owner. Thus if a sole proprietorship makes $25,000, the owner will claim the profits on his or her tax return. (In the corporate form of organization, the corporation first pays a tax on profits, and then the owners of the corporation pay a tax on any distributed profits.) Approximately 71 percent of the 25 million business firms in this country are organized as sole proprietorships, and these produce approximately 5 percent of the total revenue and 20 percent of the total profits of the U.S. economy.

Partnership   The second form of organization is the **partnership**, which is similar to a sole proprietorship except there are two or more owners. Multiple ownership makes it possible to raise more capital and to share ownership responsibilities. Most partnerships are formed through an agreement between the participants, known as the **articles of partnership**, which specifies the ownership interest, the methods for distributing profits, and the means for withdrawing from the partnership. For taxing purposes, partnership profits or losses are allocated directly to the partners, and there is no double taxation as there is in the corporate form.

Like the sole proprietorship, the partnership arrangement carries unlimited liability for the owners. While the partnership offers the advantage of *sharing* possible losses, it presents the problem of owners with unequal wealth having to absorb losses. If three people form a partnership with a $10,000 contribution each and the business loses $100,000, one wealthy partner may have to bear a disproportionate share of the losses if the other two partners do not have sufficient personal assets.

To circumvent this shared unlimited liability feature, a special form of partnership, called a **limited partnership**, can be utilized. Under this arrangement, one or more partners are designated general partners and have unlimited liability for the debts of the firm; other partners are designated limited partners and are liable only for their initial contribution. The limited partners are normally prohibited from being active in the management of the firm. You may have heard of limited partnerships in real estate syndications in which a number of limited partners are doctors, lawyers, and CPAs and there is one general partner who is a real estate professional. Not all financial institutions will extend funds to a limited partnership.

Corporation   In terms of revenue and profits produced, the corporation is by far the most important type of economic unit. While only 20 percent of U.S. business firms are corporations, over 85 percent of sales and over 60 percent of profits can be attributed to the corporate form of organization. The **corporation** is unique—it is a legal entity unto itself. Thus the corporation may sue or be sued, engage in contracts, and acquire property. A corporation is formed through **articles of incorporation**, which specify the rights and limitations of the entity.

A corporation is owned by shareholders who enjoy the privilege of limited liability, meaning their liability exposure is generally no greater than their initial investment.[2] A corporation also has a continual life and is not dependent on any one shareholder for maintaining its legal existence.

A key feature of the corporation is the easy divisibility of the ownership interest by issuing shares of stock. While it would be nearly impossible to have more than 10,000 or 20,000 partners in most businesses, a corporation may have several hundred thousand shareholders. For example, General Electric has 10.6 billion shares of common stock outstanding and 660,000 shareholders, and Microsoft with 10.7 billion shares outstanding has 142,000 shareholders. Both corporations have close to 60 percent of their shares held by institutional investors, but GE has many more small investors than Microsoft, which accounts for the large difference in number of shareholders.

The shareholders' interests are ultimately managed by the corporation's board of directors. The directors may include key management personnel of the firm as well as directors from outside the firm. Directors serve in a fiduciary capacity for the shareholders and may be liable for the mismanagement of the firm. After the collapse of corporations such as Enron and WorldCom due to fraud, the role of outside directors became much more important and corporations were motivated to comply with more stringent corporate governance laws mandated by Congress. Outside directors may make from $5,000 per year for serving on the board of small companies to $75,000 to $150,000 per year for serving on the board of large companies such as General Electric. GE pays additional fees for outside directors who chair or are on the audit, the management development, and compensation committees.

Because the corporation is a separate legal entity, it reports and pays taxes on its *own* income. As previously mentioned, any remaining income that is paid to the shareholders

---

[2]An exception to this rule is made if shareholders buy their stock at less than par value. Then they would be liable for up to the par value.

in the form of dividends will require the payment of a second tax by the shareholders. One of the key disadvantages to the corporate form of organization is this potential double taxation of earnings. In 2003, Congress diminished part of this impact by lowering the maximum tax rate on dividends from 38.6 percent to 15 percent.

There is, however, one way to completely circumvent the double taxation of a normal corporation and that is through formation of a Subchapter S corporation. With a **Subchapter S corporation**, the income is taxed as direct income to the stockholders and thus is taxed only once as normal income, similar to a partnership. Nevertheless, the shareholders receive all the organizational benefits of a corporation, including limited liability. The Subchapter S designation can apply to corporations with up to 75 stockholders.[3]

While the proprietorship, traditional partnership, and various forms of limited partnerships are all important, the corporation is given primary emphasis in this text. Because of the all-pervasive impact of the corporation on our economy, and because most growing businesses eventually become corporations, the effects of most decisions in this text are often considered from the corporate viewpoint.

Corporate Governance

As we learned in the previous section, the corporation is governed by the board of directors, led by the chairman of the board. In most companies the chairman of the board is also the CEO or Chief Executive Officer of the company. During the three-year stock market collapse of 2000–2002, many companies went bankrupt due to mismanagement or in some cases, financial statements that did not accurately reflect the financial condition of the firm because of deception and outright fraud. Companies such as WorldCom reported over $9 billion of incorrect or fraudulent financial entries on their income statements. Many of the errors were found after the company filed for bankruptcy and new management came in to try and save the company.

Enron also declared bankruptcy after it became known that their accountants kept many financing transactions "off the books." The company had more debt than most of their investors and lenders knew. Many of these accounting manipulations were too sophisticated for the average analyst, banker, or board member to understand. In the Enron case, the U.S. government indicted its auditor, Arthur Andersen, and because of the indictment, Andersen was dissolved. Other bankruptcies involving WorldCom, Global Crossing, and Adelphia also exhibited fraudulent financial statements. Because of these accounting scandals, there was a public outcry for corporate accountability, ethics reform, and a demand to know why the corporate governance system had failed. Why didn't the boards of directors know what was going on and stop it? Why didn't they fire management and clean house? These questions will be hot topics for discussion for many years.

The issues of corporate governance are really agency problems. **Agency theory** examines the relationship between the owners and the managers of the firm. In privately owned firms, management and owners are usually the same people. Management operates the firm to satisfy its own goals, needs, financial requirements, and the like.

---

[3]If there are more than 75 investors, a master limited partnership can be formed in which there is limited liability and single taxation of owners.

However, as a company moves from private to public ownership, management now represents all the owners. This places management in the agency position of making decisions that will be in the best interests of all shareholders. Because of diversified ownership interests, conflicts between managers and shareholders can arise that impact the financial decisions of the firm. When the chairman of the board is also the chief executive of the firm, stockholders recognize that the executive may act in his or her own best interests rather than those of the stockholders of the firm. In the prior bankruptcy examples, that is exactly what happened. Management filled their own pockets and left the stockholders with little or no value in the company's stock. In the WorldCom case, a share of common stock fell from the $60 range to $.15 per share and eventually ended up being worthless. Because of these potential conflicts of interest, many hold the view that the chairman of the board of directors should be from outside a company rather than an executive of the firm.

Because **institutional investors** such as pension funds and mutual funds own a large percentage of stock in major U.S. companies, these investors are having more to say about the way publicly owned corporations are managed. As a group they have the ability to vote large blocks of shares for the election of a board of directors. The threat of their being able to replace poorly performing boards of directors makes institutional investors quite influential. Since pension funds and mutual funds represent individual workers and investors, they have a responsibility to see that firms are managed in an efficient and ethical way.

Sarbanes-Oxley Act

Because corporate fraud had taken place at some very large and high profile companies, Congress decided that it needed to do something to control corrupt corporate behavior. There were problems that needed correcting. The major accounting firms had failed to detect fraud in their accounting audits, and outside directors were often not provided with the kind of information that would allow them to detect fraud and mismanagement. Because many outside directors were friends of management and had been nominated by management, there was a question about their willingness to act independently in carrying out their fiduciary responsibility to shareholders. Congress has often overreacted and created laws that have unintended consequences and so the jury is still out on the effectiveness of the Sarbanes-Oxley Act that Congress passed in 2002.

The act set up a five member Public Company Accounting Oversight Board with the responsibility for auditing standards within companies, controlling the quality of audits, and setting rules and standards for the independence of the auditors. It also puts great responsibility on the internal audit committee of each publicly traded company to enforce compliance with the act. The major focus of the act is to make sure that publicly traded corporations accurately present their assets, liabilities, and equity and income on their financial statements.

Let us look at several alternative goals for the financial manager as well as the other managers of the firm. One may suggest that the most important goal for financial management is to "earn the highest possible profit for the firm." Under this criterion, each decision would be evaluated on the basis of its overall contribution to the firm's earnings.

Goals of Financial Management

While this seems to be a desirable approach, there are some serious drawbacks to profit maximization as the primary goal of the firm.

First, a change in profit may also represent a change in risk. A conservative firm that earned $1.25 per share may be a less desirable investment if its earnings per share increase to $1.50, but the risk inherent in the operation increases even more.

A second possible drawback to the goal of maximizing profit is that it fails to consider the timing of the benefits. For example, if we could choose between the following two alternatives, we might be indifferent if our emphasis were solely on maximizing earnings.

	Earnings per Share		
	Period One	Period Two	Total
Alternative A	$1.50	$2.00	$3.50
Alternative B	2.00	1.50	3.50

Both investments would provide $3.50 in total earnings, but Alternative B is clearly superior because the larger benefits occur earlier. We could reinvest the difference in earnings for Alternative B one period sooner.

Finally, the goal of maximizing profit suffers from the almost impossible task of accurately measuring the key variable in this case, namely, "profit." As you will observe throughout the text, there are many different economic and accounting definitions of profit, each open to its own set of interpretations. Furthermore, problems related to inflation and international currency transactions complicate the issue. Constantly improving methods of financial reporting offer some hope in this regard, but many problems remain.

A Valuation Approach

While there is no question that profits are important, the key issue is how to use them in setting a goal for the firm. The ultimate measure of performance is not what the firm earns, but how the earnings are *valued* by the investor. In analyzing the firm, the investor will also consider the risk inherent in the firm's operation, the time pattern over which the firm's earnings increase or decrease, the quality and reliability of reported earnings, and many other factors. The financial manager, in turn, must be sensitive to all of these considerations. He or she must question the impact of each decision on the firm's overall valuation. If a decision maintains or increases the firm's overall value, it is acceptable from a financial viewpoint; otherwise, it should be rejected. This principle is demonstrated throughout the text.

Maximizing Shareholder Wealth

The broad goal of the firm can be brought into focus if we say the financial manager should attempt to *maximize the wealth of the firm's shareholders* through achieving the highest possible value for the firm. **Shareholder wealth maximization** is not a simple task, since the financial manager cannot directly control the firm's stock price, but can only act in a way that is consistent with the desires of the shareholders. Since stock prices are affected by expectations of the future as well as by the economic environment, much of what affects stock prices is beyond management's direct control. Even firms with good earnings and favorable financial trends do not always perform well in a declining stock market over the short term.

The concern is not so much with daily fluctuations in stock value as with long-term wealth maximization. This can be difficult in light of changing investor expectations. In the 1950s and 1960s, the investor emphasis was on maintaining rapid rates of earnings growth. In the 1970s and 1980s, investors became more conservative, putting a premium on lower risk and, at times, high current dividend payments.

In the early and mid-1990s, investors emphasized lean, efficient, well-capitalized companies able to compete effectively in the global environment. But by the late 1990s, there were hundreds of high-tech Internet companies raising capital through initial public offerings of their common stock. Many of these companies had dreams, but very little revenue and no earnings, yet their stock sold at extremely high prices. Some in the financial community said that the old valuation models were dead, didn't work, and were out of date; earnings and cash flow didn't matter anymore. Alan Greenspan, chairman of the Federal Reserve Board, made the now famous remark that the high-priced stock market was suffering from "irrational exuberance." By late 2000, many of these companies turned out to be short-term wonders. A few years later, hundreds were out of business.

Management and Stockholder Wealth

Does modern corporate management always follow the goal of maximizing shareholder wealth? Under certain circumstances, management may be more interested in maintaining its own tenure and protecting "private spheres of influence" than in maximizing stockholder wealth. For example, suppose the management of a corporation receives a tender offer to merge the corporation into a second firm; while this offer might be attractive to shareholders, it might be quite unpleasant to present management. Historically, management may have been willing to maintain the status quo rather than to maximize stockholder wealth.

As mentioned earlier, this is now changing. First, in most cases "enlightened management" is aware that the only way to maintain its position over the long run is to be sensitive to shareholder concerns. Poor stock price performance relative to other companies often leads to undesirable takeovers and proxy fights for control. Second, management often has sufficient stock option incentives that motivate it to achieve market value maximization for its own benefit. Third, powerful institutional investors are making management more responsive to shareholders.

Social Responsibility and Ethical Behavior

Is our goal of shareholder wealth maximization consistent with a concern for social responsibility for the firm? In most instances the answer is yes. By adopting policies that maximize values in the market, the firm can attract capital, provide employment, and offer benefits to its community. This is the basic strength of the private enterprise system.

Nevertheless, certain socially desirable actions such as pollution control, equitable hiring practices, and fair pricing standards may at times be inconsistent with earning the highest possible profit or achieving maximum valuation in the market. For example, pollution control projects frequently offer a negative return. Does this mean firms

McDonald's Corporation—Good Corporate Citizen

Given that stock market investors emphasize financial results and the maximization of shareholder value, one can wonder if it makes sense for a company to be socially responsible. Can companies be socially responsible and oriented toward shareholder wealth at the same time? The authors think so, and McDonald's also thinks the two can go together. For a company with thousands of restaurants throughout the world, being a good neighbor is important.

At a recent annual meeting, McDonald's stated, "Community involvement sets McDonald's apart, builds brand loyalty, and promotes local pride and respect. It is the heart of our commitment to exceptional customer satisfaction. The people we serve at the front counter and the people we serve in the communities—are one and the same. People do business with people they feel good about. Many customers visit McDonald's because we are a responsible corporate citizen."

McDonald's supports one of the world's premier philanthropic organizations, Ronald McDonald House Charities (RMHC). RMHC provides comfort and care to children and their families by awarding grants to organizations through chapters in 31 countries and supporting more than 200 Ronald McDonald Houses in 19 countries. Recently, RMHC awarded nearly $4 million in grants to Interplast and Operation Smile to fund 40 medical missions in 28 countries throughout Latin America and Asia. In addition, it awarded $5 million to the United Nations Children's Fund (UNICEF) to fund the immunization of one million African children and their mothers against neonatal tetanus, a disease that kills hundreds of infants a day in developing countries.

Beyond supporting RMHC, McDonald's provides assistance, including free food, water, and other help to disaster victims and volunteers. McDonald's has helped during earthquakes, hurricanes, floods, and other traumatic events. During the tragedy of September 11, 2001, McDonald's provided nearly 750,000 free meals to rescue workers and contributed more than $4 million to a relief fund with the help of RMHC and collections. The restaurant giant is an active promoter of diversity. Today over 30 percent of McDonald's franchise owners are women and minorities, and it purchases over $3 billion worth of goods and services from women and minority suppliers. Furthermore, McDonald's is an active pursuer of employment diversity and a supporter of educational scholarships, providing millions of dollars in educational assistance.

McDonald's emphasizes environmental programs and works with the Environmental Defense Fund to develop effective programs for reducing and recycling waste. It established McRecycle USA with the goal of using recycled materials for construction and remodeling of its restaurants.

Since the 1990s, McDonald's has purchased more than $4 billion worth of products made from recycled materials and it has eliminated approximately 200,000 tons of packaging by redesigning items including straws, napkins, cups, fry cartons, and other packaging items.

McDonald's actions speak louder than words. Other companies may say they are socially responsible, but McDonald's offers proof.

should not exercise social responsibility in regard to pollution control? The answer is no—but certain cost-increasing activities may have to be mandatory rather than voluntary, at least initially, to ensure that the burden falls equally over all business firms.

Unethical and illegal financial practices on Wall Street by corporate financial "deal-makers" have made news headlines from the late 1980s until the present. Insider trading has been one of the most widely publicized issues in recent years. **Insider trading** occurs when someone has information that is not available to the public and then uses this information to profit from trading in a company's publicly traded securities. This practice is illegal and protected against by the Securities and Exchange Commission (SEC). Sometimes the insider is a company manager; other times it is the company's lawyer, investment banker, or even the printer of the company's financial statements.

Anyone who has knowledge before public dissemination of that information stands to benefit from either good news or bad news.

There has been a long history of Wall Street executives like Ivan Boesky, Dennis Levine, and Michael Milken who were sent to jail for insider trading activities. Such activities as insider trading serve no beneficial economic or financial purpose, and it could be argued that they have a negative impact on shareholder interests. Illegal security trading destroys confidence in U.S. securities markets and makes it more difficult for managers to achieve shareholder wealth maximization.

Ethics and social responsibility can take many different forms. Ethical behavior for a person or company should be important to everyone because it creates an invaluable reputation. However, once that reputation is lost because of unethical behavior, it is very difficult to get back. Some companies are more visible than others in their pursuit of these ethical goals and most companies that do a good job in this area are profitable, save money, and are good citizens in the communities where they operate.

The Role of the Financial Markets

You may wonder how a financial manager knows whether he or she is maximizing shareholder value and how ethical (or unethical) behavior may affect the value of the company. This information is provided daily to financial managers through price changes determined in the financial markets. But what are the financial markets? **Financial markets** are the meeting place for people, corporations, and institutions that either need money or have money to lend or invest. In a broad context, the financial markets exist as a vast global network of individuals and financial institutions that may be lenders, borrowers, or owners of public companies worldwide. Participants in the financial markets also include national, state, and local governments that are primarily borrowers of funds for highways, education, welfare, and other public activities; their markets are referred to as **public financial markets**. Corporations such as Coca-Cola, Nike, and General Motors, on the other hand, raise funds in the **corporate financial markets**.

Structure and Functions of the Financial Markets

Financial markets can be broken into many distinct parts. Some divisions such as domestic and international markets, or corporate and government markets, are self-explanatory. Others such as money and capital markets need some explanation. **Money markets** refer to those markets dealing with short-term securities that have a life of one year or less. Securities in these markets can include commercial paper sold by corporations to finance their daily operations, or certificates of deposit with maturities of less than one year sold by banks. Examples of money market securities are presented more fully in Chapter 7.

The **capital markets** are generally defined as those markets where securities have a life of more than one year. While capital markets are long-term markets, as opposed to short-term money markets, it is often common to break down the capital markets into intermediate markets (1 to 10 years) and long-term markets (greater than 10 years). The capital markets include securities such as common stock, preferred stock, and corporate and government bonds. Capital markets are fully presented in Chapter 14.

Now that you have a very basic understanding of the makeup of the financial markets, you need to understand how these markets affect corporate managers.

Allocation of Capital

A corporation relies on the financial markets to provide funds for short-term operations and for new plant and equipment. A firm may go to the markets and raise financial capital either by borrowing money through a debt offering of corporate bonds or shortterm notes, or by selling ownership in the company through an issue of common stock. When a corporation uses the financial markets to raise new funds, the sale of securities is said to be made in the **primary market** by way of a new issue. After the securities are sold to the public (institutions and individuals), they are traded in the **secondary market** between investors. It is in the secondary market that prices are continually changing as investors buy and sell securities based on their expectations of a corporation's prospects. It is also in the secondary market that financial managers are given feedback about their firms' performance.

How does the market allocate capital to the thousands of firms that are continually in need of money? Let us assume that you graduate from college as a finance major and are hired to manage money for a wealthy family like the Rockefellers. You are given $250 million to manage and you can choose to invest the money anywhere in the world. For example, you could buy common stock in Microsoft, the American software company, or in Nestlé, the Swiss food company, or in Cemex, the Mexican cement company; you could choose to lend money to the U.S. or Japanese government by purchasing its bonds; or you could lend money to ExxonMobil or British Petroleum. Of course these are only some of the endless choices you would have.

How do you decide to allocate the $250 million so that you will maximize your return and minimize your risk? Some investors will choose a risk level that meets their objective and maximize return for that given level of risk. By seeking this risk-return objective, you will bid up the prices of securities that seem underpriced and have potential for high returns and you will avoid securities of equal risk that, in your judgment, seem overpriced. Since all market participants play the same risk-return game, the financial markets become the playing field, and price movements become the winning or losing score. Let us look at only the corporate sector of the market and 100 companies of equal risk. Those companies with expectations for high return will have higher relative common stock prices than those companies with poor expectations. Since the securities' prices in the market reflect the combined judgment of all the players, price movements provide feedback to corporate managers and let them know whether the market thinks they are winning or losing against the competition.

Those companies that perform well and are rewarded by the market with high-priced securities have an easier time raising new funds in the money and capital markets than their competitors. They are also able to raise funds at a lower cost. Go back to that $250 million you are managing. If ExxonMobil wants to borrow money from you at 9 percent and Chevron is willing to pay 8 percent but also is riskier, to which company will you lend money? If you chose ExxonMobil you are on your way to understanding finance. The competition between the two firms for your funds will eventually cause Chevron to offer higher returns than ExxonMobil, or they will have to go without funds. In this way the money and capital markets allocate funds to the highest quality companies at the lowest cost and to the lowest quality companies at the highest cost. In other words, firms pay a penalty for failing to perform competitively.

Institutional Pressure on Public Companies to Restructure

Sometimes an additional penalty for poor performance is a forced restructuring by institutional investors seeking to maximize a firm's shareholder value. As mentioned earlier, institutional investors have begun to flex their combined power, and their influence with corporate boards of directors has become very visible. Nowhere has this power been more evident than in the area of corporate restructuring. **Restructuring** can result in changes in the capital structure (liabilities and equity on the balance sheet). It can also result in the selling of low-profit-margin divisions with the proceeds of the sale reinvested in better investment opportunities. Sometimes restructuring results in the removal of the current management team or large reductions in the workforce. Restructuring also has included mergers and acquisitions of gigantic proportions unheard of in earlier decades. Rather than seeking risk reduction through diversification, firms are now acquiring greater market shares, brand name products (i.e., British Petroleum acquiring Amoco), hidden assets values, or technology—or they are simply looking for size to help them compete in an international arena.

The restructuring and management changes at General Motors, IBM, American Express, Sears, and Eastman Kodak during the last decade were a direct result of institutional investors affecting change by influencing the boards of directors to exercise control over all facets of the companies' activities. Quite a few boards of directors were viewed as rubber stamps for management before this time. Large institutional investors have changed this perception. Without their attempt to maximize the value of their investments, many of the above mentioned restructuring deals would not have taken place. And without the financial markets placing a value on publicly held companies, the restructuring would have been much more difficult to achieve.

Internationalization of the Financial Markets

International trade is a growing trend that is likely to continue. Global companies are becoming more common and international brand names like Sony, Coca-Cola, Nestlé, and Mercedes Benz are known the world over. McDonald's hamburgers are eaten throughout the world, and McDonald's raises funds on most major international money and capital markets. The growth of the global company has led to the growth of global fund raising as companies search for low-priced sources of funds.

In a recent annual report, Coca-Cola stated that it conducted business in 59 different currencies and borrowed money in yen, euros and other international currencies.

This discussion demonstrates that the allocation of capital and the search for low-cost sources of financing is now an international game for the multinational companies. As an exclamation point consider all the non-U.S. companies who want to raise money in the United States. More and more foreign companies such as DaimlerChrysler have listed their shares on the New York Stock Exchange, and there are over several hundred foreign companies whose stock is traded in the United States through American Depository Receipts (ADRs).

We live in a world where international events impact economies of all industrial countries and where capital moves from country to country faster than was ever thought possible. Computers interact in a vast international financial network and markets are more vulnerable to the emotions of investors than they have been in the past. The corporate financial manager has an increasing number of external impacts to consider. Future financial managers will need to have the sophistication to understand international capital flows, computerized electronic funds transfer systems, foreign currency hedging strategies, and many other functions.

The Internet and Changes in the Capital Markets

Technology has had a significant impact on the capital markets. The biggest impact has been in the area of cost reduction for trading securities. Those firms and exchanges that are at the front of the technology curve are creating tremendous competitive cost pressures on those firms and exchanges that cannot compete on a cost basis. This has caused consolidations among major stock markets and the merger of brokerage firms with domestic as well as international partners. Advances in computer technology have created electronic communications networks (electronic markets) such as Archipelago and Instinet that have taken market share away from the organized exchanges (such as the New York Stock Exchange and NASDAQ). These electronic markets have speed and cost advantages over the traditional markets and as a result, the New York Stock Exchange is merging with Archipelago, and NASDAQ has bought Instinet from Reuters. The cost pressures and the need for capital have also caused many of the markets to become for-profit publicly traded companies. The most successful has been the Chicago Mercantile Exchange that went public at $35 per share a few years ago and in May of 2006 was trading at $455 per share. Also, the NASDAQ and the New York Stock Exchange are now publicly traded.

Another area where the Internet has played its role is in the area of retail stock trading. Firms like Charles Schwab, E*TRADE, Ameritrade, and other discount brokerage firms allow customers to trade using the Internet and have created a competitive problem for full-service brokers such as Merrill Lynch and Salomon Smith Barney. These discount firms have forced the full-service retail brokers to offer Internet trading to their customers, even though Internet trading is not as profitable for them as trading through their brokers.

Another change that has squeezed profits for market makers is the change to price quotes in decimals rather than the traditional 1/16, 1/8, 1/4, and 1/2 price quotes. The trend is to a lower cost environment for the customers and a profit squeeze on markets and brokers. These issues and others will be developed more fully in the capital market section of the text.

Format of the Text

The material in this text is covered under six major headings. The student progresses from the development of basic analytical skills in accounting and finance to the utilization of decision-making techniques in working capital management, capital budgeting, long-term financing, and other related areas. A total length of 21 chapters should make the text appropriate for one-semester coverage.

The student is given a thorough grounding in financial theory in a highly palatable and comprehensive fashion—with careful attention to definitions, symbols, and formulas. The intent is that the student will develop a thorough understanding of the basic concepts in finance.

Parts

1. Introduction   This section examines the goals and objectives of financial management. The emphasis on decision making and risk management is stressed, with an update of significant events influencing the study of finance.

2. Financial Analysis and Planning   The student first has the opportunity to review the basic principles of accounting as they relate to finance (financial statements and funds flow are emphasized). This review material in Chapter 2 is optional—and the student may judge whether he or she needs this review before progressing through the section.

Additional material in this part includes a thorough study of ratio analysis, budget construction techniques, and development of comprehensive pro forma statements. The effect of heavy fixed commitments, in the form of either debt or plant and equipment, is examined in a discussion of leverage.

3. Working Capital Management   The techniques for managing the short-term assets of the firm and the associated liabilities are examined. The material is introduced in the context of risk-return analysis. The financial manager must constantly choose between liquid, low-return assets (perhaps marketable securities) and more profitable, less liquid assets (such as inventory). Sources of short-term financing are also considered.

4. The Capital Budgeting Process   The decision on capital outlays is among the most significant a firm will have to make. In terms of study procedure, we attempt to carefully lock down "time value of money" calculations, then proceed to the valuation of bonds and stocks, emphasizing present value techniques. The valuation chapter develops the traditional dividend valuation model and examines bond price sensitivity in response to discount rates and inflation. An appendix presents the supernormal dividend growth model, or what is sometimes called the "two-stage" dividend model. After careful grounding in valuation practice and theory, we examine the cost of capital and capital structure. The text then moves to the actual capital budgeting decision, making generous use of previously learned material and employing the concept of marginal analysis. The concluding chapter in this part covers risk-return analysis in capital budgeting, with a brief exposure to portfolio theory and a consideration of market value maximization.

5. Long-Term Financing   The student is introduced to U.S. financial markets as they relate to corporate financial management. The student considers the sources and uses of funds in the capital markets—with warrants and convertibles covered, as well as the more conventional methods of financing. The guiding role of the investment banker in the distribution of securities is also analyzed. Furthermore, the student is encouraged to think of leasing as a form of debt.

6. Expanding the Perspective of Corporate Finance   A chapter on corporate mergers considers external growth strategy and serves as an integrative tool to bring together such topics as profit management, capital budgeting, portfolio considerations, and valuation concepts. A second chapter on international financial management describes the growth of the international financial markets, the rise of multinational business, and the related effects on corporate financial management. The issues discussed in these two chapters highlight corporate diversification and risk-reduction attempts prevalent in the new century.

List of Terms

Discussion Questions

1. What advantages does a sole proprietorship offer? What is a major drawback of this type of organization?

2. What form of partnership allows some of the investors to limit their liability? Explain briefly.

3. In a corporation, what group has the ultimate responsibility for protecting and managing the stockholders' interests?

4. What document is necessary to form a corporation?

5. What issue does agency theory examine? Why is it important in a public corporation rather than in a private corporation?

6. Why are institutional investors important in today's business world?

7. Why is profit maximization, by itself, an inappropriate goal? What is meant by the goal of maximization of shareholder wealth?

8. When does insider trading occur? What government agency is responsible for protecting against the unethical practice of insider trading?

9. In terms of the life of the securities offered, what is the difference between money and capital markets?

10. What is the difference between a primary and a secondary market?

11. Assume you are looking at many companies with equal risk; which ones will have the highest stock prices?

12. What changes can take place under restructuring? In recent times, what group of investors has often forced restructuring to take place?

WEB EXERCISE

Ralph Larsen, former Chairman and CEO of Johnson & Johnson, was quoted in this chapter concerning the use of the Internet. Johnson & Johnson has been one of America's premier companies for decades and has exhibited a high level of social responsibility around the world. Go to the Johnson & Johnson Web site at www.jnj.com.

1. Under Our Credo, click on "View Our Credo."

2. In the "Select by Biography" box, scroll down and click on the United States and then click on Go.

3. You should see the Credo in English. If English is not your native language or you want to practice your second language, click on another region in the world that speaks your language. After you have read the Credo, explain in one paragraph why the Credo is helpful to the company's employees and customers.

4. Return to the prior page and go to the "Investor Relations" option. Then click on "Annual Reports and Proxy." Next click on the first listed annual report.

5. Select "Financials," click on "Consolidated Financial Statements." Scroll down, record the values of the following for the two years shown, and compute the percentage change between the two years. The numbers are in millions of dollars.

    a. Total assets.

    b. Total stockholders' equity.

    c. Sales to customers (last two years).

    d. Net earnings (last two years).

6. Generally speaking, is Johnson & Johnson growing by more or less than 10 percent per year?

Note: From time to time, companies redesign their Web sites and occasionally a topic we have listed may have been deleted, updated, or moved into a different location. If you click on the site map or site index, you will be introduced to a table of contents that should aid you in finding the topic you are looking for.

2

Financial Analysis and Planning

RELATED WEB SITES

www.sec.gov
www.cbo.gov
www.pepsico.com
www.hoovers.com
www.gs.com
www.ml.com
www.smithbarney.com
www.ratefinancials.com
www.dell.com
www.radioshack.com

www.eds.com
www.sony.com
www.honda.com
www.hitachi.com
www.mitsubishi.com
finance.yahoo.com

In this section we address the topic of financial analysis based on an understanding of accounting statements. Problems arise if the financial statements are not accurate, are manipulated, or do not meet generally accepted accounting principles (GAAP). Indra Nooyi is president and chief executive officer of PepsiCo which had sales of $32 billion in 2005. PepsiCo is a well-known international beverage and food company known for its soft drinks and snacks.

Ms. Nooyi currently serves on the board of directors of PepsiCo and was promoted from chief financial officer to chief executive officer in August, 2006. As CFO, she was responsible for all of PepsiCo's corporate functions, including finance, strategy, business process optimization, corporate platforms, innovations, procurement, investor relations, and information technology. In her new role, Ms. Nooyi will take on more responsibilities. She is known to be very competitive and a tough but fair boss. She has been with PepsiCo since 1994 when she moved from Motorola where she was a corporate strategist. After coming to PepsiCo, she negotiated the $13.8 billion purchase of Quaker Oats in 2001 in her role as CFO.

She earned a degree in chemistry, physics, and math at Madras Christian College in India. She also has a master's degree in finance and marketing from the Indian Institute of Management in Calcutta, and holds a master's degree in Public and Private Management from the Yale School of Management. As you can see, there are a lot of educational ways to get to the top. Her scientific background got her jobs at the engineering company, Asea Brown Boveri, and also at Motorola. With this background she moved to a consumer products company.

Ms. Nooyi is on the board of directors of Motorola, the International Rescue Committee, and the Lincoln Center for the Performing Arts. She obviously has a fond spot in her heart for Yale University and serves as a Successor Fellow at Yale Corporation and on the advisory board of Yale University President's Council of International Activities.

Ms. Nooyi is a popular figure at PepsiCo. She is known as

Indra Nooyi—PepsiCo
© *Zack Seckler/Corbis*

someone who likes to sing and has performed at a PepsiCo corporate talent show. Her love of music and singing comes from being a lead singer in an all female rock band when she was in college.

Review of Accounting

2

1 The income statement measures profitability.

2 The price-earnings ratio indicates the relative valuation of earnings.

3 The balance sheet shows assets and the financing of those assets with debt and equity.

4 The statement of cash flows indicates the change in the cash position of the firm.

5 Depreciation provides a tax reduction benefit which increases cash flow.

Have you had a Coke or Pepsi lately? If so, give yourself two extra points on your homework grade because we are about to briefly discuss both companies and their products. Coca-Cola is using strong markets in China, Russia, and South America to help offset weakness in growth in the United States. Nevertheless, the company's growth in EPS between 1997 and 2005 has only been 28 percent for a compound annual increase of 2.8 percent.

PepsiCo, on the other hand, is doing better as indicated on the "News Makers" discussion on the prior page. Not only does the firm sell beverages but also food products such as Doritos, Tostitos, and Cheetos. Throw in a little Gatorade and you have a strong product mix. Its EPS between 1997 and 2005 has grown by 136 percent for a compound annual increase of 11.3 percent.

Without accounting data tracking these important numbers, financial managers, investors, and bankers would be flying blind. The same can be said for the data of IBM, General Motors, Microsoft, or any other major U.S. corporation.

The language of finance flows logically from accounting. To ensure that the student is adequately prepared to study significant financial concepts, we must lock in the preparatory material from the accounting area. Much of the early frustration suffered by students who have difficulty with finance can be overcome if such concepts as retained earnings, shareholders' equity, depreciation, and historical/replacement cost accounting are brought into focus.

In this chapter, we examine the three basic types of financial statements—the income statement, the balance sheet, and the statement of cash flows—with particular attention paid to the interrelationships among these three measurement devices. As special preparation for the finance student, we briefly examine income tax considerations affecting financial decisions.

The **income statement** is the major device for measuring the profitability of a firm over a period of time. An example of the income statement for the Kramer Corporation is presented in Table 2–1.

Table 2–1

KRAMER CORPORATION	
Income Statement	
For the Year Ended December 31, 2007	
1. Sales..	$2,000,000
2. Cost of goods sold	1,500,000
3. Gross profits..	500,000
4. Selling and administrative expense.......................	270,000
5. Depreciation expense.....................................	50,000
6. Operating profit (EBIT)*................................	180,000
7. Interest expense...	20,000
8. Earnings before taxes (EBT).............................	160,000
9. Taxes..	49,500
10. Earnings after taxes (EAT)..............................	110,500
11. Preferred stock dividends...............................	10,500
12. Earnings available to common stockholders...............	$ 100,000
13. Shares outstanding......................................	100,000
14. Earnings per share......................................	$1.00
*Earnings before interest and taxes.	

First, note that the income statement covers a defined period of time, whether it is one month, three months, or a year. The statement is presented in a stair-step or progressive fashion so we can examine the profit or loss after each type of expense item is deducted.

We start with sales and deduct cost of goods sold to arrive at gross profit. The $500,000 thus represents the difference between the cost of purchased or manufactured goods and the sales price. We then subtract selling and administrative expense and depreciation from gross profit to determine our profit (or loss) purely from operations of $180,000. It is possible for a company to enjoy a high gross profit margin (25–50 percent) but a relatively low operating profit because of heavy expenses incurred in marketing the product and managing the company.[1]

Having obtained operating profit (essentially a measure of how efficient management is in generating revenues and controlling expenses), we now adjust for revenues and expenses not related to operational matters. In this case we pay $20,000 in interest and arrive at earnings before taxes of $160,000. The tax payments are $49,500, leaving aftertax income of $110,500.

---

[1]Depreciation was not treated as part of goods sold in this instance, but rather as a separate expense. All or part of depreciation may be treated as part of cost of goods sold, depending on the circumstances.

Return to Capital

Before proceeding further, we should note that there are three primary sources of capital—the bondholders, who received $20,000 in interest (item 7); the preferred stockholders, who receive $10,500 in dividends (item 11); and the common stockholders. After the $10,500 dividend has been paid to the preferred stockholders, there will be $100,000 in earnings available to the common stockholders (item 12). In computing **earnings per share**, we must interpret this in terms of the number of shares outstanding. As indicated in item 13, there are 100,000 shares outstanding, so the $100,000 of earnings available to the common stockholders may be translated into earnings per share of $1. Common stockholders are sensitive to the number of shares outstanding— the more shares, the lower the earnings per share. Before any new shares are issued, the financial manager must be sure the cash received from the sale will eventually generate sufficient earnings to avoid reducing earnings per share.

The $100,000 of profit ($1 earnings per share) may be paid out to the common stockholders in the form of dividends or retained in the company for subsequent reinvestment. The reinvested funds theoretically belong to the common stockholders, who hope they will provide future earnings and dividends. In the case of the Kramer Corporation, we assume $50,000 in dividends will be paid out to the common stockholders, with the balance retained in the corporation for their benefit. A short supplement to the income statement, a statement of retained earnings (Table 2–2), usually indicates the disposition of earnings.[2]

Table 2–2

STATEMENT OF RETAINED EARNINGS	
For the Year Ended December 31, 2007	
Retained earnings, balance, January 1, 2007	$250,000
Add: Earnings available to common stockholders, 2007.	100,000
Deduct: Cash dividends declared in 2007.	50,000
Retained earnings, balance, December 31, 2007	300,000

We see that a net value of $50,000 has been added to previously accumulated earnings of $250,000 to arrive at $300,000.

Price-Earnings Ratio Applied to Earnings per Share

A concept utilized throughout the text is the **price-earnings ratio**. This refers to the multiplier applied to earnings per share to determine current value of the common stock. In the case of the Kramer Corporation, earnings per share were $1. If the firm had a price-earnings ratio of 20, the market value of each share would be $20 ($1 × 20). The price-earnings ratio (or P/E ratio, as it is commonly called) is influenced by the earnings and the sales growth of the firm, the risk (or volatility in performance), the debt-equity structure of the firm, the dividend payment policy, the quality of management, and

---

[2]The statement may also indicate any adjustments to previously reported income as well as any restrictions on cash dividends.

a number of other factors. Since companies have various levels of earnings per share, price-earnings ratios allow us to compare the relative market value of many companies based on $1 of earnings per share.

The P/E ratio indicates expectations about the future of a company. Firms expected to provide returns greater than those for the market in general with equal or less risk often have P/E ratios higher than the market P/E ratio. Expectations of returns and P/E ratios do change over time, as Table 2–3 illustrates.

Corporation	Industry	Jan. 2 1990	Jan. 2 1994	Jan. 2 1998	Jan. 2 2001	Jan. 2 2006
Bank of America	Banking	10	8	19	10	12
Cisco	Networking	25	24	37	91	23
General Motors	Automobiles	7	8	13	6	40
Intel	Integrated circuits	12	11	24	20	21
Johnson & Johnson	Pharmaceuticals	17	15	28	32	22
McDonald's	Restaurants	14	17	24	23	14
Southwest Air	Airlines	15	23	16	31	31
Textron	Diversified	7	11	27	29	19
Wal-Mart	Retail	24	21	31	38	18
Standard & Poor's (500 Stock Index)		15	20	23	26	24

Table 2–3
Price-earnings ratios for selected U.S. companies

Price-earnings ratios can be confusing. When a firm's earnings are dropping rapidly or perhaps even approaching zero, its stock price, though declining too, may not match the magnitude of the falloff in earnings. This process can give the appearance of an increasing P/E ratio under adversity. This happens from time to time in the steel, oil, and other cyclical industries. For example, in 2001 Cisco Systems (as shown in Table 2–3) was trading at a P/E ratio of 91 because of cyclically low earnings.

Limitations of the Income Statement

The economist defines income as the change in real worth that occurs between the beginning and the end of a specified time period. To the economist an increase in the value of a firm's land as a result of a new airport being built on adjacent property is an increase in the real worth of the firm and therefore represents income. Similarly, the elimination of a competitor might also increase the firm's real worth and therefore result in income in an economic sense. The accountant does not ordinarily employ such broad definitions. Accounting values are established primarily by actual transactions, and income that is gained or lost during a given period is a function of verifiable transactions. While the potential sales price of a firm's property may go from $100,000 to $200,000 as a result of new developments in the area, stockholders may perceive only a much smaller gain or loss from actual day-to-day operations.

Also, as will be pointed out in Chapter 3, "Financial Analysis," there is some flexibility in the reporting of transactions, so similar events may result in differing measurements of income at the end of a time period. The intent of this section is not to criticize the accounting profession, for it is certainly among the best-organized, trained, and paid professions, but to alert students to imperfections already well recognized within the profession.

Balance Sheet

The **balance sheet** indicates what the firm owns and how these assets are financed in the form of liabilities or ownership interest. While the income statement purports to show the profitability of the firm, the balance sheet delineates the firm's holdings and obligations. Together, these statements are intended to answer two questions: How much did the firm make or lose, and what is a measure of its worth? A balance sheet for the Kramer Corporation is presented in Table 2–4 on page 29.

Note that the balance sheet is a picture of the firm at a point in time—in this case December 31, 2007. It does not purport to represent the result of transactions for a specific month, quarter, or year, but rather is a cumulative chronicle of all transactions that have affected the corporation since its inception. In contrast, the income statement measures results only over a short, quantifiable period. Generally, balance sheet items are stated on an original cost basis rather than at current market value.

Interpretation of Balance Sheet Items

Asset accounts are listed in order of **liquidity** (convertibility to cash). The first category of *current assets* covers items that may be converted to cash within one year (or within the normal operating cycle of the firm). A few items are worthy of mention. *Marketable securities* are temporary investments of excess cash. The value shown in the account is the lower of cost or current market value. *Accounts receivable* include an allowance for bad debts (based on historical evidence) to determine their anticipated collection value. *Inventory* may be in the form of raw material, goods in process, or finished goods, while *prepaid expenses* represent future expense items that have already been paid, such as insurance premiums or rent.

Investments, unlike marketable securities, represent a longer-term commitment of funds (at least one year). They may include stocks, bonds, or investments in other corporations. Frequently, the account will contain stock in companies that the firm is acquiring.

Plant and equipment is carried at original cost minus accumulated depreciation. Accumulated depreciation is not to be confused with the depreciation expense item indicated in the income statement in Table 2–1. Accumulated depreciation is the sum of all past and present depreciation charges on currently owned assets, while depreciation expense is the current year's charge. If we subtract accumulated depreciation from the original value, the balance ($500,000) tells us how much of the original cost has not been expensed in the form of depreciation.

Total assets are financed through either liabilities or stockholders' equity. Liabilities represent financial obligations of the firm and move from current liabilities (due within one year) to longer-term obligations, such as bonds payable in 2015.

Among the short-term obligations, *accounts payable* represent amounts owed on open account to suppliers, while *notes payable* are generally short-term signed obligations to the banker or other creditors. An *accrued expense* is generated when a service has been provided or an obligation incurred and payment has not yet taken place. The

Table 2–4

KRAMER CORPORATION
Statement of Financial Position (Balance Sheet)
December 31, 2007

Assets

Current assets:

Cash.		$ 40,000
Marketable securities		10,000
Accounts receivable	$ 220,000	
Less: Allowance for bad debts	20,000	200,000
Inventory		180,000
Prepaid expenses		20,000
Total current assets		450,000

Other assets:

Investments		50,000

Fixed assets:

Plant and equipment, original cost	1,100,000	
Less: Accumulated depreciation	600,000	
Net plant and equipment		500,000
Total assets		$1,000,000

Liabilities and Stockholders' Equity

Current liabilities:

Accounts payable		$ 80,000
Notes payable		100,000
Accrued expenses		30,000
Total current liabilities		210,000

Long-term liabilities:

Bonds payable, 2015		90,000
Total liabilities		300,000

Stockholders' equity:

Preferred stock, $100 par value, 500 shares		50,000
Common stock, $1 par value, 100,000 shares		100,000
Capital paid in excess of par (common stock)		250,000
Retained earnings		300,000
Total stockholders' equity		700,000
Total liabilities and stockholders' equity		$1,000,000

firm may owe workers additional wages for services provided or the government taxes on earned income.

In the balance sheet we see the $1,000,000 in total assets of the Kramer Corporation was financed by $300,000 in debt and $700,000 in the form of stockholders' equity. Stockholders' equity represents the total contribution and ownership interest of preferred and common stockholders.

The *preferred stock* investment position is $50,000, based on 500 shares at $100 par. In the case of *common stock,* 100,000 shares have been issued at a total par value of $100,000, plus an extra $250,000 in *capital paid in excess of par* for a sum of $350,000. We can assume that the 100,000 shares were originally sold at $3.50 each as shown below.

100,000 shares	$1.00	Par value	$100,000
	2.50	Capital paid in excess of par	250,000
	$3.50	Price per share	$350,000

Finally, there is $300,000 in *retained earnings* in Table 2–4. This value, previously determined in the statement of retained earnings (Table 2–2), represents the firm's cumulative earnings since inception minus dividends and any other adjustments.

Concept of Net Worth

Stockholders' equity minus the preferred stock component represents the **net worth**, or **book value**, of the firm. There is some logic to the approach. If you take everything that the firm owns and subtract the debt and preferred stock obligation,[3] the remainder belongs to the common stockholder and represents net worth. In the case of the Kramer Corporation, using data from Table 2–4, we show:

Total assets	$1,000,000
Total liabilities	300,000
Stockholders' equity	700,000
Preferred stock obligation	50,000
Net worth assigned to common	$ 650,000
Common shares outstanding	100,000
Net worth, or book value, per share	$6.50

The original cost per share was $3.50; the net worth, or book value, per share is $6.50; and the market value (based on an assumed P/E ratio of 15 and earnings per share of $1) is $15. This last value is of primary concern to the financial manager, security analyst, and stockholders.

Limitations of the Balance Sheet

Lest we attribute too much significance to the balance sheet, we need to examine some of the underlying concepts supporting its construction. Most of the values on the balance sheet are stated on a historical or original cost basis. This may be particularly troublesome in the case of plant and equipment and inventory, which may now be worth two or three times the original cost or—from a negative viewpoint—may require many times the original cost for replacement.

The accounting profession has been grappling with this problem for decades, and the discussion becomes particularly intense each time inflation rears its ugly head. In

---

[3]An additional discussion of preferred stock is presented in Chapter 17, "Common and Preferred Stock Financing." Preferred stock represents neither a debt claim nor an ownership interest in the firm. It is a hybrid, or intermediate, type of security.

October 1979 the Financial Accounting Standards Board (FASB) issued a ruling that required large companies to disclose inflation-adjusted accounting data in their annual reports. This information was to be disclosed in addition to the traditional historical cost data and could show up in footnotes or in a separate full-fledged financial section with detailed explanations. However, with the decline in the inflation rate to historically low levels, the standard is no longer in force, and the inclusion of inflation-adjusted data is no longer required in any form. If a company wishes to adjust its balance sheet or income statement data for inflation, it is purely a voluntary act.

Table 2–5 looks at large disparities between market value per share and historical book value per share for a number of publicly traded companies in January 2006. Besides asset valuation, a number of other factors may explain the wide differences between per share values, such as industry outlook, growth prospects, quality of management, and risk-return expectations.

Table 2–5

Comparison of market value to book value per share in January 2006

Corporation	Market Value per Share	Book Value per Share	Ratio of Market Value to Book Value
Genentech	$80.25	$7.70	10.42
Dell Computer	38.15	4.85	7.86
PepsiCo	55.24	8.90	6.21
Pitney Bowes	45.16	7.65	5.90
UPS	73.60	17.90	4.11
Ford Motor Co.	9.85	11.20	.88
DaimlerChrysler	40.25	50.75	.79
CNA Financial	28.90	38.85	.74
Chesapeake Corp.	22.11	36.35	.61
Hudson Bay Co.	13.44	32.95	.41

Statement of Cash Flows

The accounting profession designates the statement of cash flows as the third required financial statement, along with the balance sheet and income statement. Referred to as *Statement of Financial Accounting Standards (SFAS) No. 95,* it replaces the old statement of changes in financial position.

The purpose of the **statement of cash flows** is to emphasize the critical nature of cash flow to the operations of the firm. According to accountants, cash flow represents cash or cash equivalent items that can easily be converted into cash within 90 days (such as a money market fund).

The income statement and balance sheet that we have studied thus far are normally based on the accrual method of accounting, in which revenues and expenses are recognized as they occur, rather than when cash actually changes hands. For example, a $100,000 credit sale may be made in December 2006 and shown as revenue for that year—despite the fact the cash payment will not be received until March 2007. When the actual payment is finally received under accrual accounting, no revenue is recognized (it has already been accounted for previously). The primary advantage of accrual accounting is that it allows us to match revenues and expenses in the period in which they occur in order to appropriately measure profit; but a disadvantage is that adequate attention is not directed to the actual cash flow position of the firm.

Say a firm made a $1 million profit on a transaction but will not receive the actual cash payment for two years. Or perhaps the $1 million profit is in cash, but the firm increased its asset purchases by $3 million (a new building). If you merely read the income statement, you might assume the firm is in a strong $1 million cash position; but if you go beyond the income statement to cash flow considerations, you would observe the firm is $2 million short of funds for the period.

As a last example, a firm might show a $100,000 loss on the income statement, but if there were a depreciation expense write-off of $150,000, the firm would actually have $50,000 in cash. Since depreciation is a noncash deduction, the $150,000 deduction in the income statement for depreciation can be added back to net income to determine cash flow.

The statement of cash flows addresses these issues by translating income statement and balance sheet data into cash flow information. A corporation that has $1 million in accrual-based accounting profits can determine whether it can afford to pay a cash dividend to stockholders, buy new equipment, or undertake new projects. In the dot.com era of the last decade, cash flow analysis has taken on a very special meaning.

Developing an Actual Statement

We shall use the information previously provided for the Kramer Corporation in this chapter to illustrate how the statement of cash flows is developed.

But first, let's identify the three primary sections of the statement of cash flows:

1. Cash flows from operating activities.
2. Cash flows from investing activities.
3. Cash flows from financing activities.

After each of these sections is completed, the results are added together to compute the net increase or decrease in cash flow for the corporation. An example of the process is shown in Figure 2–1 on page 33. Let's begin with cash flows from operating activities.

Determining Cash Flows from Operating Activities

Basically, we are going to translate *income from operations* from an accrual to a cash basis. According to *SFAS No. 95,* there are two ways to accomplish this objective. First, the firm may use a *direct method,* in which every item on the income statement is adjusted from accrual accounting to cash accounting. This is a tedious process, in which all sales must be adjusted to cash sales, all purchases must be adjusted to cash purchases, and so on. A more popular method is the *indirect method,* in which net income represents the starting point and then adjustments are made to convert net income to cash flows from operations.[4] This is the method we will use. Regardless of whether the direct or indirect method is used, the same final answer will be derived.

We follow these procedures in computing **cash flows from operating activities** using the indirect method.[5] These steps are illustrated in Figure 2–2 and are described on the top of page 34.

---

[4]The indirect method is similar to procedures used to construct the old sources and uses of funds statement.
[5]In addition to the items mentioned, we may need to recognize the gains or losses on the sale of operating and nonoperating assets. We exclude these for ease of analysis.

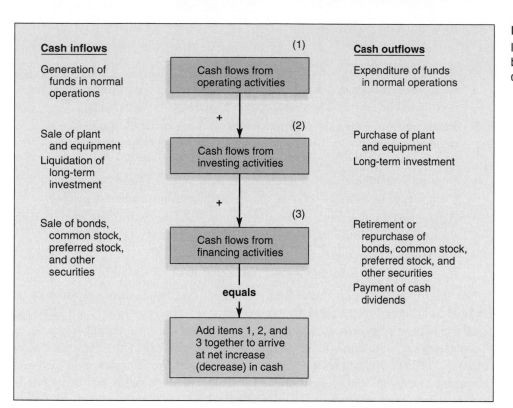

Figure 2–1

Illustration of concepts behind the statement of cash flows

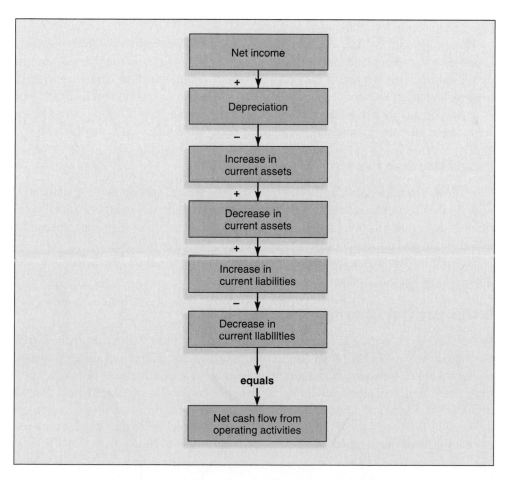

Figure 2–2

Steps in computing net cash flows from operating activities using the indirect method

- Start with net income.
- Recognize that depreciation is a noncash deduction in computing net income and should be added back to net income to increase the cash balance.
- Recognize that increases in current assets are a use of funds and *reduce* the cash balance (indirectly)—as an example, the firm spends more funds on inventory.
- Recognize that decreases in current assets are a source of funds and *increase* the cash balance (indirectly)—that is, the firm reduces funds tied up in inventory.
- Recognize that increases in current liabilities are a source of funds and increase the cash balance (indirectly)—the firm gets more funds from creditors.
- Recognize that decreases in current liabilities are a use of funds and *decrease* the cash balance (indirectly)—that is, the firm pays off creditors.

We will follow these procedures for the Kramer Corporation, drawing primarily on material from Table 2–1 (the previously presented income statement) and from Table 2–6 at the top of page 35 (which shows balance sheet data for the most recent two years).

The analysis is presented in Table 2–7. We begin with net income (earnings after taxes) of $110,500 and add back depreciation of $50,000. We then show that increases in current assets (accounts receivable and inventory) reduce funds and decreases in current assets (prepaid expenses) increase funds. Also, we show increases in current liabilities (accounts payable) as an addition to funds and decreases in current liabilities (accrued expenses) as a reduction of funds.

We see in Table 2–7 that the firm generated $150,500 in cash flows from operating activities. Of some significance is that this figure is $40,000 larger than the net income figure shown on the first line of the table ($110,500). A firm with little depreciation and a massive buildup of inventory might show lower cash flow than reported net income. Once cash flows from operating activities are determined, management has a better feel for what can be allocated to investing or financing needs (such as paying cash dividends).

Determining Cash Flows from Investing Activities

Cash flows from investing activities represent the second section in the statement of cash flows. The section relates to long-term investment activities in other issuers' securities or, more importantly, in plant and equipment. Increasing investments represent a *use* of funds, and decreasing investments represent a *source* of funds.

Examining Table 2–6 for the Kramer Corporation, we show the information in Table 2–8 at the top of page 36.

Determining Cash Flows from Financing Activities

In the third section of the statement of cash flows, **cash flows from financing activities**, we show the effects of financing activities on the corporation in Table 2–9 toward the top of page 36. Financing activities apply to the sale or retirement of bonds, common stock, preferred stock, and other corporate securities. Also, the payment of cash dividends is considered a financing activity. The sale of the firm's securities represents a *source* of funds, and the retirement or repurchase of such securities represents a *use* of funds. The payment of dividends also represents a *use* of funds.

Table 2–6

KRAMER CORPORATION
Comparative Balance Sheets

	Year-End 2006	Year-End 2007
Assets		
Current assets:		
Cash	$ 30,000	$ 40,000
Marketable securities	10,000	10,000
Accounts receivable (net)	170,000	200,000
Inventory	160,000	180,000
Prepaid expenses	30,000	20,000
Total current assets	400,000	450,000
Investments (long-term)	20,000	50,000
Plant and equipment	$1,000,000	1,100,000
Less: Accumulated depreciation	550,000	600,000
Net plant and equipment	450,000	500,000
Total assets	$ 870,000	$1,000,000
Liabilities and Stockholders' Equity		
Current liabilities:		
Accounts payable	$ 45,000	$ 80,000
Notes payable	100,000	100,000
Accrued expenses	35,000	30,000
Total current liabilities	180,000	210,000
Long-term liabilities:		
Bonds payable, 2015	40,000	90,000
Total liabilities	220,000	300,000
Stockholders' equity:		
Preferred stock, $100 par value	50,000	50,000
Common stock, $1 par value	100,000	100,000
Capital paid in excess of par	250,000	250,000
Retained earnings	250,000	300,000
Total stockholders' equity	650,000	700,000
Total liabilities and stockholders' equity	$ 870,000	$1,000,000

Table 2–7

Cash flows from operating activities

Net income (earnings after taxes) (Table 2–1)		$110,500
Adjustments to determine cash flow from operating activities:		
Add back depreciation (Table 2–1)	50,000	
Increase in accounts receivable (Table 2–6)	(30,000)	
Increase in inventory (Table 2–6)	(20,000)	
Decrease in prepaid expenses (Table 2–6)	10,000	
Increase in accounts payable (Table 2–6)	35,000	
Decrease in accrued expenses (Table 2–6)	(5,000)	
Total adjustments		40,000
Net cash flows from operating activities		$150,500

Table 2–8

Cash flows from
investing activities

Increase in investments (long-term securities) (Table 2–6)	($ 30,000)
Increase in plant and equipment (Table 2–6)	(100,000)
Net cash flows from investing activities	($130,000)

In Table 2–9, the financing activities of the Kramer Corporation are shown using data from Tables 2–1, 2–2, and 2–6.

Table 2–9

Cash flows from
financing activities

Increase in bonds payable (Table 2–6)	$50,000
Preferred stock dividends paid (Table 2–1)	(10,500)
Common stock dividends paid (Table 2–2)	(50,000)
Net cash flows from financing activities	($10,500)

Combining the Three Sections of the Statement

We now combine the three sections of the statement of cash flows to arrive at the one overall statement that the corporation provides to security analysts and stockholders. The information is shown in Table 2–10.

Table 2–10

KRAMER CORPORATION
Statement of Cash Flows
For the Year Ended December 31, 2007

Cash flows from operating activities:		
Net income (earnings after taxes)		$110,500
Adjustments to determine cash flow from operating activities:		
Add back depreciation	$ 50,000	
Increase in accounts receivable	(30,000)	
Increase in inventory	(20,000)	
Decrease in prepaid expenses	10,000	
Increase in accounts payable	35,000	
Decrease in accrued expenses	(5,000)	
Total adjustments		40,000
Net cash flows from operating activities		$150,500
Cash flows from investing activities:		
Increase in investments (long-term securities)	(30,000)	
Increase in plant and equipment	(100,000)	
Net cash flows from investing activities		($130,000)
Cash flows from financing activities:		
Increase in bonds payable	50,000	
Preferred stock dividends paid	(10,500)	
Common stock dividends paid	(50,000)	
Net cash flows from financing activities		(10,500)
Net increase (decrease) in cash flows		$ 10,000

We see in Table 2–10 that the firm created excess funds from operating activities that were utilized heavily in investing activities and somewhat in financing activities. As a result, there is a $10,000 increase in the cash balance, and this can also be reconciled with the increase in the cash balance of $10,000 from $30,000 to $40,000, as previously indicated in Table 2–6.

One might also do further analysis on how the buildups in various accounts were financed. For example, if there is a substantial increase in inventory or accounts receivable, is there an associated buildup in accounts payable and short-term bank loans? If not, the firm may have to use long-term financing to carry part of the short-term needs. An even more important question might be: How are increases in long-term assets being financed? Most desirably, there should be adequate long-term financing and profits to carry these needs. If not, then short-term funds (trade credit and bank loans) may be utilized to carry long-term needs. This is a potentially high-risk situation, in that short-term sources of funds may dry up while long-term needs continue to demand funding. In problems at the back of the chapter, you will have an opportunity to further consider these points.

Depreciation and Funds Flow

One of the most confusing items to finance students is whether depreciation is a source of funds to the corporation. In Table 2–7, we listed depreciation as a source of funds (cash flow). This item deserves further clarification. The reason we added back depreciation was not that depreciation was a new source of funds, but rather that we had subtracted this noncash expense in arriving at net income and now have to add it back to determine the amount of actual funds on hand.

Depreciation represents an attempt to allocate the initial cost of an asset over its useful life. In essence, we attempt to match the annual expense of plant and equipment ownership against the revenues being produced. Nevertheless the charging of depreciation is purely an accounting entry and does not directly involve the movement of funds. To go from accounting flows to cash flows in Table 2–7, we restored the noncash deduction of $50,000 for depreciation that was subtracted in Table 2–1, the income statement.

Let us examine a simple case involving depreciation in Table 2–11. Assume we purchase a machine for $500 with a five-year life and we pay for it in cash. Our depreciation schedule calls for equal annual depreciation charges of $100 per year for five years. Assume further that our firm has $1,000 in earnings before depreciation and taxes, and the tax obligation is $300. Note the difference between accounting flows and cash flows for the first two years in Table 2–11.

Since we took $500 out of cash flow originally in year 1 to purchase equipment (in column B), we do not wish to take it out again. Thus we add back $100 in depreciation (in column B) each year to "wash out" the subtraction in the income statement.

Free Cash Flow

A term that has received increasingly greater attention lately is **free cash flow** (FCF). This is actually a by-product of the previously discussed statement of cash flows. Free cash flow is equal to the values shown directly under Table 2–11 in red.

Table 2–11
Comparison of accounting and cash flows

| | Year 1 | |
	(A) Accounting Flows	(B) Cash Flows
Earnings before depreciation and taxes (EBDT)	$1,000	$1,000
Depreciation	100	100
Earnings before taxes (EBT)	900	900
Taxes	300	300
Earnings after taxes (EAT).	$ 600	600
Purchase of equipment		−500
Depreciation charged without cash outlay.		+100
Cash flow.		$ 200

| | Year 2 | |
	(A) Accounting Flows	(B) Cash Flows
Earnings before depreciation and taxes (EBDT)	$1,000	$1,000
Depreciation	100	100
Earnings before taxes	900	900
Taxes	300	300
Earnings after taxes (EAT).	$ 600	600
Depreciation charged without cash outlay.		+100
Cash flow.		$ 700

Free cash flow equals cash flow from operating activities

Minus: Capital expenditures (required to maintain the productive capacity of the firm)

Minus: Dividends (needed to maintain the necessary payout on common stock and to cover any preferred stock obligation).

The concept of free cash flow forces the stock analyst or banker not only to consider how much cash is generated from operating activities, but also to subtract out the necessary capital expenditures on plant and equipment to maintain normal activities. Similarly, dividend payments to shareholders must be subtracted out as these dividends must generally be paid to keep shareholders satisfied.

The balance, free cash flow, is then available for *special financing activities.* In the last decade special financing activities have often been synonymous with leveraged buyouts, in which a firm borrows money to buy its stock and take itself private, with the hope of restructuring its balance sheet and perhaps going public again in a few years at a higher price than it paid. Leveraged buyouts are discussed more fully in Chapter 15. The analyst or banker normally looks at *free cash flow* to determine whether there are sufficient excess funds to pay back the loan associated with the leveraged buyout.

Income Tax Considerations

Virtually every financial decision is influenced by federal income tax considerations. Primary examples are the lease versus purchase decision, the issuance of common stock versus debt decision, and the decision to replace an asset. While the intent

The Auditors Are Being Audited

We take all the numbers presented in this chapter as accurate, but as we learned in the last decade, that is not necessarily the case.

In Table 2–1 of the chapter, sales are shown as $2,000,000 and earnings available to common stockholders are $100,000, but are they really? The event that triggered all this discussion was the collapse of Enron Corporation in the early 2000s. The energy company had falsified its books in regard to profitability, debt, illegal compensation to executives, and a number of other items. Its auditor, Arthur Andersen and Company, went along with these activities and never hesitated in approving the financial statements. When the Securities and Exchange Commission began investigating the possibility of malfeasance, Arthur Andersen not only failed to cooperate, but it shredded important documents. Eventually, Enron collapsed, and Arthur Andersen and Company, a long-time crown jewel of the accounting profession, did too.

Why would Arthur Andersen have taken such a risk in auditing and approving the financial statements of Enron? The answer can be tied to events over the past decade. Arthur Andersen's most profitable activity was not auditing but information technology (IT) consulting. Who was it doing the consulting for? The answer is simple: its auditing clients. A $10 million IT contract was much more important to Arthur Andersen than a $1 million auditing contract. In many cases, in order to get the consulting contract, it had to "go along" with the client in its auditing activities. You scratch my financial statements (back), and I'll scratch your consulting revenues (back).

Arthur Andersen was not alone in engaging in such activities, it was simply much more blatant. Even before the Enron scandal, other members of the "big five" accounting oligopoly were being pressured to separate their consulting activities from their auditing activities. Thus, PricewaterhouseCoopers, KPMG, Ernst and Young, and Deloitte Touche and Tohmatsu were in the process of spinning off their consulting entities. However, for many it was too little too late, and tough legislation came down in the form of the Sarbanes-Oxley Act of 2002. The legislation did the following:

- Authorized the creation of an independent private-sector board to oversee the accounting profession (a work still in process).

- Created new penalties, including long prison terms, for corporate fraud and document destruction.

- Restricted accounting firms from providing most consulting services to audit clients. Also, if and when such services are actually provided, they must be fully divulged. (Most accounting firms are too afraid of this provision to test it by accepting consulting revenue.)

- Held corporate executives legally accountable for the accuracy of their financial statements. The chief executive officer (CEO) and chief financial officer (CFO) of the firm must actually sign a special document attesting to the accuracy of the statements. (Talk about a tough honor code!)

- Created a new federal account to collect civil fines from corporate wrongdoers and use the proceeds to help reimburse defrauded investors.

- Provided new protections for corporate whistle-blowers.

The intent of the act was not only to ensure truth in reporting by accounting firms, but to let investors know they could rely on the financial statements they were analyzing for investment purposes. This was particularly relevant for investors of some of the following firms which had come under attack: Adelphia, Computer Associates, Global Crossing, Kmart, Lucent Technologies, Tyco International, and WorldCom.

**finance in
action**

www.sec.gov

of this section is not to review the rules, regulations, and nuances of the Federal Income Tax Code, we will examine how tax matters influence corporate financial decisions. The primary orientation will be toward the principles governing corporate tax decisions, though many of the same principles apply to a sole proprietorship or a partnership.

Corporate Tax Rates

Corporate federal tax rates have changed four times since 1980. Basically the rate is progressive, meaning lower levels of income (such as $50,000 or $100,000) are taxed at lower rates. Higher levels of income are taxed at higher rates, normally in the mid-30 percent rate. In the illustrations in the text, we will use various rates to illustrate the impact on decision making. The current top rate is 35 percent. However, keep in mind that corporations may also pay some state and foreign taxes, so the effective rate can get to 40 percent or higher in some instances. For corporations with low taxable income, the effective rate may only be 15 to 20 percent.

Cost of a Tax-Deductible Expense

The businessperson often states that a tax-deductible item, such as interest on business loans, travel expenditures, or salaries, costs substantially less than the amount expended, on an aftertax basis. We shall investigate how this process works. Let us examine the tax statements of two corporations—the first pays $100,000 in interest, and the second has no interest expense. An average tax rate of 40 percent is used for ease of computation.

	Corporation A	Corporation B
Earnings before interest and taxes	$400,000	$400,000
Interest	100,000	0
Earnings before taxes (taxable income)	300,000	400,000
Taxes (40%)	120,000	160,000
Earnings after taxes	$180,000	$240,000
Difference in earnings after taxes	$60,000	

Although Corporation A paid out $100,000 more in interest than Corporation B, its earnings after taxes are only $60,000 less than those of Corporation B. Thus we say the $100,000 in interest costs the firm only $60,000 in aftertax earnings. The aftertax cost of a tax-deductible expense can be computed as the actual expense times one minus the tax rate. In this case, we show $100,000 (1 − Tax rate), or $100,000 × 0.60 = $60,000. The reasoning in this instance is that the $100,000 is deducted from earnings before determining taxable income, thus saving $40,000 in taxes and costing only $60,000 on a net basis.

Because a dividend on common stock is not tax-deductible, we say it cost 100 percent of the amount paid. From a purely corporate cash flow viewpoint, the firm would be indifferent between paying $100,000 in interest and $60,000 in dividends.

Depreciation as a Tax Shield

Although depreciation is not a new source of funds, it provides the important function of shielding part of our income from taxes. Let us examine Corporations A and B again, this time with an eye toward depreciation rather than interest. Corporation A charges off $100,000 in depreciation, while Corporation B charges off none. The analysis is shown in the bottom half of page 41.

Now That the Government Is Demanding Honest "Corporate" Accounting—Who Will Be the Next Target?

In August of 2002, Congress passed and the president signed legislation that requires CEOs to sign documents attesting to the truthfulness of their accounting statements (see earlier box). In the event the statements are false, the CEO can be charged with a felony, and large fines and even prison time can follow.

Who will be the next target for honest reporting demands by the government? The quickest place to find the culprit would be in the mirror. Actually, the chastised activities of aggressive revenue accounting and underexpensing by U.S. corporations are "small potatoes" compared to the activities of the federal government.

In 2001, President Bush projected an enormous $5.6 trillion budget surplus over the next 10 years to justify his $1.3 trillion tax cuts for the same period. The budgetary surplus was based on the assumption that there would be no recession over the upcoming decade. Previously, President Clinton had used similar assumptions to indicate there would be adequate revenue to justify spending on social programs. If these ill-conceived projections had taken place in the private sector, there would be enormous stockholder lawsuits with potential liabilities running into billions of dollars. In truth, the government is now running large deficits, not the projected surpluses.

Not only does the government use faulty revenue projections, but it hides expenses through the use of federal agencies that bear expenses on their separate books, thus relieving the federal government of the charges. (This would be any corporate chief financial officer's dream if he or she could get away with it.)

The Congressional Budget Office (CBO) and the Office of Management and Budget (OMB) also project that discretionary spending on such activities as the military, education, homeland security, and so on, will fall by 20 percent relative to the size of the economy over the next 10 years. No one actually believes this will happen, but it makes the problems related to government budgetary control look better.

To complicate the problem, the government counts the current surplus in Social Security and Medicare payments to the government as part of its revenue stream in spite of the fact there will be huge deficits in these programs when the "baby boomers" start retiring over the next decade. However, no reserve accounts are being set up.

Perhaps, it is time the government subpoenas itself for malfeasance in financial reporting. Republicans and Democrats alike would begin to take on the appearance of executives of WorldCom, Enron, and other firms that have been charged with improper financial reporting.

finance in
action

www.cbo.gov

	Corporation A	Corporation B
Earnings before depreciation and taxes.	$400,000	$400,000
Depreciation.	100,000	0
Earnings before taxes	300,000	400,000
Taxes (40%).	120,000	160,000
Earnings after taxes.	180,000	240,000
+ Depreciation charged without cash outlay	100,000	0
Cash flow	$280,000	$240,000
Difference.	$40,000	

We compute earnings after taxes and then add back depreciation to get cash flow. The difference between $280,000 and $240,000 indicates that Corporation A enjoys $40,000 more in cash flow. The reason is that depreciation shielded $100,000 from taxation in Corporation A and saved $40,000 in taxes, which eventually showed up in cash flow. Though depreciation is not a new source of funds, it does provide tax shield benefits that can be measured as depreciation times the tax rate, or in this case $100,000 \times 0.40 = \$40,000$. A more comprehensive discussion of depreciation's effect on cash flow is presented in Chapter 12, as part of the long-term capital budgeting decision.

Summary

The financial manager must be thoroughly familiar with the language of accounting to administer the financial affairs of the firm. The income statement provides a measure of the firm's profitability over a specified period. Earnings per share represents residual income to the common stockholder that may be paid out in the form of dividends or reinvested to generate future profits and dividends. A limitation of the income statement is that it reports income and expense primarily on a transaction basis and thus may not recognize certain major economic events as they occur.

A concept utilized throughout the text is the price-earnings ratio. This refers to the multiplier applied to earnings per share to determine current value of the common stock. The P/E ratio indicates expectations about the future of a company. Firms expected to provide returns greater than those for the market in general with equal or less risk often have P/E ratios higher than the market P/E ratio. Of course, the opposite effect would also be true.

The balance sheet is like a snapshot of the financial position of the firm at a point in time, with the stockholders' equity section purporting to represent ownership interest. Because the balance sheet is presented on a historical cost basis, it may not always reflect the true value of the firm.

The statement of cash flows, the third major statement the corporation presents to stockholders and security analysts, emphasizes the importance of cash flow data to the operations of the firm. It translates the information on the income statement and balance sheet that was prepared on an accrual accounting basis to a cash basis. From these data, the firm can better assess its ability to pay cash dividends, invest in new equipment, and so on.

Depreciation represents an attempt to allocate the initial cost of an asset over its useful life. In essence, we attempt to match the annual expenses of plant and equipment ownership against the revenues being produced. Nevertheless, the charging of depreciation is purely an accounting entry and does not directly involve the movement of funds. To go from accounting flows to cash flows, we restore the noncash deduction for depreciation that was subtracted in the income statement.

List of Terms

cash flows from investing **activities** 34	**depreciation** 37
cash flows from financing **activities** 34	**free cash flow** 37

Discussion Questions

1. Discuss some financial variables that affect the price-earnings ratio.
2. What is the difference between book value per share of common stock and market value per share? Why does this disparity occur?
3. Explain how depreciation generates actual cash flows for the company.
4. What is the difference between accumulated depreciation and depreciation expense? How are they related?
5. How is the income statement related to the balance sheet?
6. Comment on why inflation may restrict the usefulness of the balance sheet as normally presented.
7. Explain why the statement of cash flows provides useful information that goes beyond income statement and balance sheet data.
8. What are the three primary sections of the statement of cash flows? In what section would the payment of a cash dividend be shown?
9. What is free cash flow? Why is it important to leveraged buyouts?
10. Why is interest expense said to cost the firm substantially less than the actual expense, while dividends cost it 100 percent of the outlay?

Practice Problems and Solutions

1. LeBron Furniture Company has the following financial data. Prepare an income statement and compute earnings per share. See Table 2–1 as an example.

Determination of profitability

Sales	$1,300,000
Depreciation expense	70,000
Cost of goods sold.	800,000
Interest expense	30,000
Selling and administrative expense	140,000
Shares outstanding	60,000
Taxes	75,000
Preferred stock dividends	5,000

2. Northern Energy Company has assets of $7,000,000, liabilities of $4,000,000, and $500,000 in preferred stock outstanding. Four hundred thousand common stock shares have been issued.

    a. Compute book value per share.

    b. If the firm has earnings per share of $1.10 and a P/E ratio of 15, what is the stock price per share?

    c. What is the ratio of market value per share to book value per share?

Determination of profitability

Solutions

1.

Sales	$1,300,000
Cost of goods sold	800,000
Gross profit	500,000
Selling and administrative expense	140,000
Depreciation expense	70,000
Operating profit	290,000
Interest expense	30,000
Earnings before taxes	260,000
Taxes	75,000
Earnings after taxes	185,000
Preferred stock dividends	5,000
Earnings available to common stockholders	$ 180,000
Shares outstanding	60,000
Earnings per share	$ 3.00

2. *a.* Use the example material on page 30 to compute book value per share.

Total assets	$7,000,000
Total liabilities	4,000,000
Stockholders equity	3,000,000
Preferred stock obligation	500,000
Net worth assigned to common	2,500,000
Common shares outstanding	400,000
Book value per share	$ 6.25

b. EPS × P/E ratio = Stock price per share

$1.10 × 15 = $16.50

c. $\dfrac{\text{Market value}}{\text{Book value}} = \dfrac{\$16.50}{6.25} = 2.64\times$

Problems

All problems are available in Homework Manager. Please see the preface for more information.

Income statement

1. Frantic Fast Foods had earnings after taxes of $390,000 in the year 2006 with 300,000 shares outstanding. On January 1, 2007, the firm issued 25,000 new shares. Because of the proceeds from these new shares and other operating improvements, earnings after taxes increased by 20 percent.

   a. Compute earnings per share for the year 2006.

   b. Compute earnings per share for the year 2007.

Income statement

2. Bettis Bus Company had earnings after taxes of $600,000 in the year 2006 with 300,000 shares of stock outstanding. On January 1, 2007, the firm issued 40,000 new shares. Because of the proceeds from these new shares and other operating improvements, earnings after taxes increased by 25 percent.

   a. Compute earnings per share for the year 2006.

   b. Compute earnings per share for the year 2007.

3. Arrange the following income statement items so they are in the proper order of an income statement:

Income statement

Taxes	Earnings per share
Shares outstanding	Earnings before taxes
Gross profit shares outstanding	Cost of goods sold
Interest expense	Earnings after taxes
Depreciation expense	Earnings available to common
Preferred stock dividends	stockholders
Operating profit	Selling and administrative expense
Sales	
Gross profit	

4. Given the following information prepare in good form an income statement for the Dental Drilling Company.

Income statement

Selling and administrative expense	$ 60,000
Depreciation expense	70,000
Sales	470,000
Interest expense	40,000
Cost of goods sold	140,000
Taxes	45,000

✕ 5. Prepare in good form an income statement for ATM Cards, Inc. Take your calculations all the way to computing earnings per share.

Determination of profitability

Sales	$800,000
Shares outstanding	100,000
Cost of goods sold	300,000
Interest expense	20,000
Selling and administrative expense	40,000
Depreciation expense	30,000
Preferred stock dividends	80,000
Taxes	110,000

✕ 6. Prepare in good form an income statement for Virginia Slim Wear. Take your calculations all the way to computing earnings per share.

Determination of profitability

Sales	$600,000
Shares outstanding	100,000
Cost of goods sold	200,000
Interest expense	30,000
Selling and administrative expense	40,000
Depreciation expense	20,000
Preferred stock dividends	80,000
Taxes	100,000

7. Censored Books, Inc., sold 1,400 finance textbooks for $160 each to High Tuition University in 2007. These books cost $125 to produce. Censored Books spent $8,000 (selling expense) to convince the university to buy its books.

Determination of earnings and earnings per share

Depreciation expense for the year was $12,000. In addition, Censored Books borrowed $90,000 on January 1, 2007, on which the company paid 10 percent interest. Both the interest and principal of the loan were paid on December 31, 2007. The publishing firm's tax rate is 30 percent.

Did Censored Books make a profit in 2007? Please verify with an income statement presented in good form.

Determination of profitability

8. Lemon Auto Wholesalers had sales of $700,000 in 2007 and cost of goods sold represented 70 percent of sales. Selling and administrative expenses were 12 percent of sales. Depreciation expense was $10,000 and interest expense for the year was $8,000. The firm's tax rate is 30 percent.

    a. Compute earnings after taxes.

    b. Assume the firm hires Ms. Carr, an efficiency expert, as a consultant. She suggests that by increasing selling and administrative expenses to 14 percent of sales, sales can be increased to $750,000. The extra sales effort will also reduce cost of goods sold to 66 percent of sales (there will be a larger markup in prices as a result of more aggressive selling). Depreciation expense will remain at $10,000. However, more automobiles will have to be carried in inventory to satisfy customers, and interest expense will go up to $15,000. The firm's tax rate will remain at 30 percent. Compute revised earnings after taxes based on Ms. Carr's suggestions for Lemon Auto Wholesalers. Will her ideas increase or decrease profitability?

Gross profit

9. *a.* Hillary Swank Clothiers had sales of $360,000 and cost of goods sold of $244,800. What is the gross profit margin (ratio of gross profit to sales)?

    b. If the average firm in the clothing industry had a gross profit of 35 percent, how is the firm doing?

Balance sheet

10. Classify the following balance sheet items as current or noncurrent:

Retained earnings	Bonds payable
Accounts payable	Accrued wages payable
Prepaid expenses	Accounts receivable
Plant and equipment	Capital in excess of par
Inventory	Preferred stock
Common stock	Marketable securities

Cash flow

11. Identify whether each of the following items increases or decreases cash flow:

Increase in accounts receivable	Decrease in prepaid expenses
Increase in notes payable	Increase in inventory
Depreciation expense	Dividend payment
Increase in investments	Increase in accrued expenses
Decrease in accounts payable	

Price/earning ratio

12. Botox Facial Care had earnings after taxes of $280,000 in 2006 with 200,000 shares of stock outstanding. The stock price was $30.80. In 2007, earnings after

taxes increased to $320,000 with the same 200,000 shares outstanding. The stock price was $40.00.

a. Compute earnings per share and the P/E ratio for 2006.
    The P/E ratio equals the stock price divided by earnings per share.

b. Compute earnings per share and the P/E ratio for 2007.

c. Give a general explanation of why the P/E ratio changed.

13. Assume for Botox Facial Care discussed in Problem 12 that in 2008, earnings after taxes declined to $140,000 with the same 200,000 shares outstanding. The stock price declined to $24.50.

    Price/earning ratio

a. Compute earnings per share and the P/E ratio for 2008.

b. Give a general explanation of why the P/E changed. You might want to consult the textbook to explain this surprising result.

14. Okra Snack Delights, Inc., has an operating profit of $210,000. Interest expense for the year was $30,000; preferred dividends paid were $24,700; and common dividends paid were $36,000. The tax was $59,300. The firm has 16,000 shares of common stock outstanding.

    Earnings per share and retained earnings

a. Calculate the earnings per share and the common dividends per share.

b. What was the increase in retained earnings for the year?

15. Quantum Technology had $640,000 of retained earnings on December 31, 2007. The company paid common dividends of $30,000 in 2007 and had retained earnings of $500,000 on December 31, 2006. How much did Quantum Technology earn during 2007, and what would earnings per share be if 40,000 shares of common stock were outstanding?

    Determination of earnings and earnings per share

16. Coastal Pipeline, Inc., anticipated cash flow from operating activities of $8 million in 2008. It will need to spend $1.5 million on capital investments in order to remain competitive within the industry. Common stock dividends are projected at $.6 million and preferred stock dividends at $.25 million.

    Free cash flow

a. What is the firm's projected free cash flow for the year 2008?

b. What does the concept of free cash flow represent?

17. Fill in the blank spaces with categories 1 through 7 below:

    Balance sheet and income statement classification

1. Balance sheet (BS)   5. Current liabilities (CL)

2. Income statement (IS)   6. Long-term liabilities (LL)

3. Current assets (CA)   7. Stockholders' equity (SE)

4. Fixed assets (FA)

Indicate Whether Item Is on Balance Sheet (BS) or Income Statement (IS)	If on Balance Sheet, Designate Which Category	Item
_____	_____	Retained earnings
_____	_____	Income tax expense
_____	_____	Accounts receivable
_____	_____	Common stock
_____	_____	Capital in excess of par value

continued

Indicate Whether Item Is on Balance Sheet (BS) or Income Statement (IS)	If on Balance Sheet, Designate Which Category	Item
_____	_____	Bonds payable, maturity 2012
_____	_____	Notes payable (six months)
_____	_____	Net income
_____	_____	Selling and administrative expenses
_____	_____	Inventories
_____	_____	Accrued expenses
_____	_____	Cash
_____	_____	Plant and equipment
_____	_____	Sales
_____	_____	Operating expenses
_____	_____	Marketable securities
_____	_____	Accounts payable
_____	_____	Interest expense
_____	_____	Income tax payable

Cash flow   ✗   18. The Jupiter Corporation has a gross profit of $700,000 and $240,000 in depreciation expense. The Saturn Corporation also has $700,000 in gross profit, with $40,000 in depreciation expense. Selling and administrative expense is $160,000 for each company.

Given that the tax rate is 40 percent, compute the cash flow for both companies. Explain the difference in cash flow between the two firms.

Development of ✗ 19. Arrange the following items in proper balance sheet presentation;
balance sheet

Accumulated depreciation	$300,000
Retained earnings	96,000
Cash	10,000
Bonds payable	136,000
Accounts receivable	48,000
Plant and equipment—original cost	680,000
Accounts payable	35,000
Allowance for bad debts	6,000
Common stock, $1 par, 100,000 shares outstanding	100,000
Inventory	66,000
Preferred stock, $50 par, 1,000 shares outstanding	50,000
Marketable securities	20,000
Investments	20,000
Notes payable	33,000
Capital paid in excess of par (common stock)	88,000

Book value   20. Landers Nursery and Garden Stores has current assets of $220,000 and fixed assets of $170,000. Current liabilities are $80,000 and long-term liabilities are $140,000. There is $40,000 in preferred stock outstanding and the firm has issued 25,000 shares of common stock. Compute book value (net worth) per share.

21. Amigo Software, Inc., has total assets of $800,000, current liabilities of $150,000, and long-term liabilities of $120,000. There is $65,000 in preferred stock outstanding. Thirty thousand shares of common stock have been issued.

    a. Compute book value (net worth) per share.

    b. If there is $48,000 in earnings available to common stockholders and the firm's stock has a P/E of 20 times earnings per share, what is the current price of the stock?

    c. What is the ratio of market value per share to book value per share? (Round to two places to the right of the decimal point.)

Book value and P/E ratio

22. In Problem 21, if the firm sells at 2.5 times book value per share, what will the P/E ratio be? (Round to the nearest whole number.)

Book value and P/E ratio

23. For December 31, 2006, the balance sheet of Baxter Corporation is as follows:

Construction of income statement and balance sheet

Current Assets		Liabilities	
Cash	$ 10,000	Accounts payable	$ 12,000
Accounts receivable	15,000	Notes payable	20,000
Inventory	25,000	Bonds payable	50,000
Prepaid expenses	12,000		
Fixed Assets		**Stockholders' Equity**	
Plant and equipment (gross)	$250,000	Preferred stock	$ 20,000
Less: Accumulated		Common stock	55,000
depreciation	50,000	Paid-in capital	25,000
Net plant and equipment	200,000	Retained earnings	80,000
		Total liabilities and	
Total assets	$262,000	stockholders' equity	$262,000

Sales for 2007 were $220,000, and the cost of goods sold was 60 percent of sales. Selling and administrative expense was $22,000. Depreciation expense was 8 percent of plant and equipment (gross) at the beginning of the year. Interest expense on the bonds payable was 12 percent. This interest expense is based on December 31, 2006, balances. The tax rate averaged 20 percent.

Two thousand dollars in preferred stock dividends was paid to common stockholders. There were 10,000 shares of common stock outstanding.

During 2007, the cash balance and prepaid expenses balances were unchanged. Accounts receivable and inventory increased by 10 percent. A new machine was purchased on December 31, 2007, at a cost of $35,000.

Accounts payable increased by 25 percent. Notes payable increased by $6,000 and bonds payable decreased by $10,000, both at the end of the year. The common stock and paid-in capital in excess of par accounts did not change.

a. Prepare an income statement for 2007.

b. Prepare a statement of retained earnings for 2007.

c. Prepare a balance sheet as of December 31, 2007.

Statement of cash flows

24. Prepare a statement of cash flows for the Jeter Corporation. Follow the general procedures indicated in Table 2–10 on page 36 of the chapter.

JETER CORPORATION
Income Statement
For the Year Ended December 31, 2007

Sales	$3,300,000
Cost of goods sold	1,950,000
Gross profits	1,350,000
Selling and administrative expense	650,000
Depreciation expense	230,000
Operating income	470,000
Interest expense	80,000
Earnings before taxes	390,000
Taxes	140,000
Earnings after taxes	250,000
Preferred stock dividends	10,000
Earnings available to common stockholders	$ 240,000
Shares outstanding	150,000
Earnings per share	$ 1.60

Statement of Retained Earnings
For the Year Ended December 31, 2007

Retained earnings, balance, January 1, 2007	$800,000
Add: Earnings available to common stockholders, 2007	240,000
Deduct: Cash dividends declared and paid in 2007	140,000
Retained earnings, balance, December 31, 2007	$900,000

Comparative Balance Sheets
For 2006 and 2007

	Year-End 2006	Year-End 2007
Assets		
Current assets:		
Cash	$ 100,000	$ 120,000
Accounts receivable (net)	500,000	510,000
Inventory	610,000	640,000
Prepaid expenses	60,000	30,000
Total current assets	1,270,000	1,300,000
Investments (long-term securities)	90,000	80,000
Plant and equipment	2,000,000	2,600,000
Less: Accumulated depreciation	1,000,000	1,230,000
Net plant and equipment	1,000,000	1,370,000
Total assets	$2,360,000	$2,750,000

Liabilities and Stockholders' Equity	Year-End 2006	Year-End 2007
Current liabilities:		
Accounts payable.	$ 300,000	$ 550,000
Notes payable	500,000	500,000
Accrued expenses	70,000	50,000
Total current liabilities	870,000	1,100,000
Long-term liabilities:		
Bonds payable, 2004	100,000	160,000
Total liabilities	970,000	1,126,000
Stockholders' equity:		
Preferred stock, $100 par value.	90,000	90,000
Common stock, $1 par value	150,000	150,000
Capital paid in excess of par	350,000	350,000
Retained earnings	800,000	900,000
Total stockholders' equity	1,390,000	1,490,000
Total liabilities and stockholders' equity	$2,360,000	$2,750,000

(The following questions apply to the Jeter Corporation, as presented in Problem 24.)

25. Describe the general relationship between net income and net cash flows from operating activities for the firm.

    Net income and cash flows

26. Has the buildup in plant and equipment been financed in a satisfactory manner? Briefly discuss.

    Financing of assets

27. Compute the book value per common share for both 2006 and 2007 for the Jeter Corporation.

    Book value

28. If the market value of a share of common stock is 3.1 times book value for 2007, what is the firm's P/E ratio for 2007? (Round to the nearest whole number.)

    P/E ratio

W E B   E X E R C I S E

PepsiCo was mentioned in the chapter as a company that provides comprehensive financial statements. Go to its Web site, www.pepsico.com and follow the steps below:

1. Under "Investors," click on "Annual Reports." Then click on the most current annual report on the next page.

2. Under the "Pull Down" option scroll way down and indicate the change for the most recent year (in percentages) for the following:

   a. Net revenue   *c.* Cash dividends

   b. Net income   *d.* Total assets

www.mhhe.com/bh12e

3. Under the "Pull Down" option at the top, click on "PepsiCo at a Glance." What percent of "Net Revenue" and "Division Operating Profit" is provided by FritoLay North America?

4. Finally under the "Pull Down" option, select "Management's Responsibility for Financial Reporting." Write a two-sentence summary of the first two paragraphs.

Note: From time to time, companies redesign their Web sites and occasionally a topic we have listed may have been deleted, updated, or moved into a different location. If you click on the site map or site index, you will be introduced to a table of contents which should aid you in finding the topic you are looking for.

S & P   P R O B L E M S   www.mhhe.com/edumarketinsight

STANDARD &POOR'S

1. Log onto the S&P Market Insight Web site, www.mhhe.com/edumarketinsight.
2. Click on "Company," which is the first box below the Market Insight title.
3. Type Abercrombie & Fitch's ticker symbol "ANF" in the box and click on Go.
4. Scroll down the left margin and click on "Excel Analytics." At the top of the left margin you will see the Annual Income Statement, Balance Sheet, and Cash Flow Statement.
5. Click on "Ann. Income Statement" and maximize the window at the top right-hand corner of the spreadsheet. You will find an Excel workbook with three sheets: (1) Annual Income Statement, (2) % Change, and (3) Key Items.
6. Familiarize yourself with the company and after looking at all three sheets, analyze the performance of the company over the time period available.
7. When you are done, close the window and click on "Ann. Balance Sheet."
   a. How much long-term debt does ANF have?
   b. How much preferred stock does ANF have?
   c. What is the difference between their current assets and current liabilities? Are their current liabilities adequately protected by their current assets?
8. When you have finished, close the window and click on "Ann. Cash Flow" for the latest available period.
   a. List the net cash flow from operating activities and identify the major item contributing to an increase and decrease in the operating cash flow.
   b. List the net cash flow from investing activities and identify the major item contributing to an increase and decrease in the cash flow from investment activities.
   c. List the net cash flow from financing activities and identify the major item contributing to an increase and decrease in the cash flow from financing activities.
   d. Finally, what is the increase or decrease in cash and cash equivalents?

3

Financial Analysis

1. Ratio analysis provides a meaningful comparison of a company to its industry.

2. Ratios can be used to measure profitability, asset utilization, liquidity, and debt utilization.

3. The Du Pont system of analysis identifies the true sources of return on assets and return to stockholders.

4. Trend analysis shows company performance over time.

5. Reported income must be further evaluated to identify sources of distortion.

P hiladelphia Eagles quarterback Donovan McNabb's mother knows what she is talking about when she recommends Campbell's soup to his teammates before the big game. But for Campbell's, the product line doesn't just stop with soup. Campbell's offers Pepperidge Farm cookies, Franco-American canned pasta, V8 juice, Prego pasta sauces, and Godiva Chocolates (want to take a quick snack break?).

In 2006 the firm did over seven billion dollars in sales, one-third of which came from foreign markets. The company is over 130 years old, and officers, directors, and heirs own 44 percent of the shares outstanding (that's a high percentage relative to other Fortune 500 companies).

One item of particular interest is the fact that at mid-decade, return on assets stood at approximately 10 percent (a normal figure for most corporations), while return on stockholders' equity was off the charts in the 50–60 percent range. The reason for the divergence is that Campbell's had an exceptionally

high debt ratio of 80 percent. This type of information is important and can be found and understood through the financial ratios discussed in this chapter.

In Chapter 2, we examined the basic assumptions of accounting and the various components that make up the financial statements of the firm. We now use this fundamental material as a springboard into financial analysis—to evaluate the financial performance of the firm.

The format for the chapter is twofold. In the first part we will use financial ratios to evaluate the relative success of the firm. Various measures such as net income to sales and current assets to current liabilities will be computed for a hypothetical company and examined in light of industry norms and past trends.

In the second part of the chapter we will explore the impact of inflation and disinflation on financial operations over the last decade. The student begins to appreciate the impact of rising prices (or at times, declining prices) on the various financial ratios. The chapter concludes with a discussion of how other factors—in addition to price changes—may distort the financial statements of the firm. Terms such as *net income to sales, return on investment,* and *inventory turnover* take on much greater meaning when they are evaluated through the eyes of a financial manager who does more than merely pick out the top or bottom line of an income statement. The examples in the chapter are designed from the viewpoint of a financial manager (with only minor attention to accounting theory).

Ratio Analysis

Ratios are used in much of our daily life. We buy cars based on miles per gallon; we evaluate baseball players by earned run and batting averages, basketball players by field goal and foul-shooting percentages, and so on. These are all ratios constructed to judge comparative performance. Financial ratios serve a similar purpose, but you must know what is being measured to construct a ratio and to understand the significance of the resultant number.

Financial ratios are used to weigh and evaluate the operating performance of the firm. While an absolute value such as earnings of $50,000 or accounts receivable of $100,000 may appear satisfactory, its acceptability can be measured only in relation to other values. For this reason, financial managers emphasize ratio analysis.

For example, are earnings of $50,000 actually good? If we earned $50,000 on $500,000 of sales (10 percent "profit margin" ratio), that might be quite satisfactory—whereas earnings of $50,000 on $5,000,000 could be disappointing (a meager 1 percent return). After we have computed the appropriate ratio, we must compare our results to those achieved by similar firms in our industry, as well as to our own performance record. Even then, this "number-crunching" process is not fully adequate, and we are forced to supplement our financial findings with an evaluation of company management, physical facilities, and numerous other factors.

Dun & Bradstreet

For comparative purposes, a number of organizations provide industry data. For example, Dun & Bradstreet compiles data on 800 different lines of business, while Robert Morris Associates provides ratios on over 150 industry classifications. Often the most valuable industry figures come from the various trade organizations to which firms belong (for example, the National Retail Furniture Association or the National Hardware Association).

Many libraries and universities subscribe to financial services such as Standard & Poor's Industry Surveys and Corporate Reports, the Value Line Investment Survey, and Moody's Corporation. Standard & Poor's also leases a computer database called Compustat to banks, corporations, investment organizations, and universities. Compustat contains financial statement data on over 16,000 companies for a 20-year period. Ratios can also be found on such Internet Web sites as finance.yahoo.com. These data can be used for countless ratios to measure corporate performance. The ratios used in this text are a sample of the major ratio categories used in business, but other classification systems can also be constructed.

Classification System

We will separate 13 significant ratios into four primary categories.

A. Profitability ratios.
1. Profit margin.
2. Return on assets (investment).
3. Return on equity.

B. Asset utilization ratios.
4. Receivable turnover.
5. Average collection period.
6. Inventory turnover.
7. Fixed asset turnover.
8. Total asset turnover.

C. Liquidity ratios.
9. Current ratio.
10. Quick ratio.

D. Debt utilization ratios.
11. Debt to total assets.
12. Times interest earned.
13. Fixed charge coverage.

The first grouping, the **profitability ratios**, allows us to measure the ability of the firm to earn an adequate return on sales, total assets, and invested capital. Many of the problems related to profitability can be explained, in whole or in part, by the firm's ability to effectively employ its resources. Thus the next category is **asset utilization ratios**. Under this heading, we measure the speed at which the firm is turning over accounts receivable, inventory, and longer-term assets. In other words, asset utilization ratios measure how many times per year a company sells its inventory or collects all of its accounts receivable. For long-term assets, the utilization ratio tells us how productive the fixed assets are in terms of generating sales.

In category C, the **liquidity ratios**, the primary emphasis moves to the firm's ability to pay off short-term obligations as they come due. In category D, **debt utilization ratios**, the overall debt position of the firm is evaluated in light of its asset base and earning power.

The users of financial statements will attach different degrees of importance to the four categories of ratios. To the potential investor or security analyst, the critical consideration is profitability, with secondary consideration given to such matters as liquidity and debt utilization. For the banker or trade creditor, the emphasis shifts to the firm's current ability to meet debt obligations. The bondholder, in turn, may be primarily influenced by debt to total assets—while also eyeing the profitability of the firm in terms of its ability to cover debt obligations. Of course, the experienced analyst looks at all the ratios, but with different degrees of attention.

Ratios are also important to people in the various functional areas of a business. The marketing manager, the head of production, the human resource manager, and so on, must all be familiar with ratio analysis. For example, the marketing manager must keep a close eye on inventory turnover; the production manager must evaluate the return on assets; and the human resource manager must look at the effect of "fringe benefits" expenditures on the return on sales.

The Analysis

Definitions alone carry little meaning in analyzing or dissecting the financial performance of a company. For this reason, we shall apply our four categories of ratios to a hypothetical firm, the Saxton Company, as presented in Table 3–1. The use of ratio analysis is rather like solving a mystery in which each clue leads to a new area of inquiry.

Table 3–1

Financial statement for ratio analysis

SAXTON COMPANY Income Statement For the Year Ended December 31, 2007	
Sales (all on credit)	$4,000,000
Cost of goods sold	3,000,000
Gross profit	1,000,000
Selling and administrative expense*	450,000
Operating profit	550,000
Interest expense	50,000
Extraordinary loss	200,000
Net income before taxes	300,000
Taxes (33%)	100,000
Net income	$ 200,000

*Includes $50,000 in lease payments.

Balance Sheet As of December 31, 2007	
Assets	
Cash	$ 30,000
Marketable securities	50,000
Accounts receivable	350,000
Inventory	370,000
Total current assets	800,000
Net plant and equipment	800,000
Net assets	$1,600,000
Liabilities and Stockholders' Equity	
Accounts payable	$ 50,000
Notes payable	250,000
Total current liabilities	300,000
Long-term liabilities	300,000
Total liabilities	600,000
Common stock	400,000
Retained earnings	600,000
Total liabilities and stockholders' equity	$1,600,000

A. Profitability Ratios We first look at profitability ratios. The appropriate ratio is computed for the Saxton Company and is then compared to representative industry data.

Profitability Ratios—

	Saxton Company	Industry Average
1. Profit margin $= \dfrac{\text{Net income}}{\text{Sales}}$	$\dfrac{\$200,000}{\$4,000,000} = 5\%$	6.7%
2. Return on assets (investment) —		
a. $\dfrac{\text{Net income}}{\text{Total assets}}$	$\dfrac{\$200,000}{\$1,600,000} = 12.5\%$	10%
b. $\dfrac{\text{Net income}}{\text{Sales}} \times \dfrac{\text{Sales}}{\text{Total assets}}$	$5\% \times 2.5 = 12.5\%$	$6.7\% \times 1.5 = 10\%$
3. Return on equity $=$		
a. $\dfrac{\text{Net income}}{\text{Stockholders' equity}}$	$\dfrac{\$200,000}{\$1,000,000} = 20\%$	15%
b. $\dfrac{\text{Return on assets (investment)}}{(1 - \text{Debt/Assets})}$	$\dfrac{0.125}{1 - 0.375} = 20\%$	$\dfrac{0.10}{1 - 0.33} = 15\%$

In analyzing the profitability ratios, we see the Saxton Company shows a lower return on the sales dollar (5 percent) than the industry average of 6.7 percent. However, its return on assets (investment) of 12.5 percent exceeds the industry norm of 10 percent. There is only one possible explanation for this occurrence—a more rapid turnover of assets than that generally found within the industry. This is verified in ratio 2b, in which sales to total assets is 2.5 for the Saxton Company and only 1.5 for the industry. Thus Saxton earns less on each sales dollar, but it compensates by turning over its assets more rapidly (generating more sales per dollar of assets).

Return on total assets as described through the two components of profit margin and asset turnover is part of the **Du Pont system of analysis**.

$$\text{Return on assets (investment)} = \text{Profit margin} \times \text{Asset turnover}$$

The Du Pont company was a forerunner in stressing that satisfactory return on assets may be achieved through high profit margins or rapid turnover of assets, or a combination of both. We shall also soon observe that under the Du Pont system of analysis, the use of debt may be important. The Du Pont system causes the analyst to examine the sources of a company's profitability. Since the profit margin is an income statement ratio, a high profit margin indicates good cost control, whereas a high asset turnover ratio demonstrates efficient use of the assets on the balance sheet. Different industries have different operating and financial structures. For example, in the heavy capital goods industry the emphasis is on a high profit margin with a low asset turnover—whereas in food processing, the profit margin is low and the key to satisfactory returns on total assets is a rapid turnover of assets.

Equally important to a firm is its return on equity or ownership capital. For the Saxton Company, return on equity is 20 percent, versus an industry norm of 15 percent. Thus the owners of Saxton Company are more amply rewarded than are other shareholders in the industry. This may be the result of one or two factors: a high return on total assets or a generous utilization of debt or a combination thereof. This can be seen through Equation 3b, which represents a modified or second version of the Du Pont formula.

$$\text{Return on equity} = \frac{\text{Return on assets (investment)}}{(1 - \text{Debt/Assets})}$$

Note the numerator, return on assets, is taken from Formula 2, which represents the initial version of the Du Pont formula (Return on assets = Net income/Sales × Sales/Total assets). Return on assets is then divided by [1 − (Debt/Assets)] to account for the amount of debt in the capital structure. In the case of the Saxton Company, the modified version of the Du Pont formula shows:

$$\text{Return on equity} = \frac{\text{Return on assets (investment)}}{(1 - \text{Debt/Assets})}$$

$$= \frac{12.5\%}{1 - 0.375} = 20\%$$

Actually the return on assets of 12.5 percent in the numerator is higher than the industry average of 10 percent, and the ratio of debt to assets in the denominator of 37.5 percent is higher than the industry norm of 33 percent. Please see ratio 3*b* on page 57 to confirm these facts. Both the numerator and denominator contribute to a higher return on equity than the industry average (20 percent versus 15 percent). Note that if the firm had a 50 percent debt-to-assets ratio, return on equity would go up to 25 percent.[1]

$$\text{Return on equity} = \frac{\text{Return on assets (investment)}}{(1 - \text{Debt/Assets})}$$

$$= \frac{12.5\%}{1 - 0.50} = 25\%$$

This does not necessarily mean debt is a positive influence, only that it can be used to boost return on equity. The ultimate goal for the firm is to achieve maximum valuation for its securities in the marketplace, and this goal may or may not be advanced by using debt to increase return on equity. Because debt represents increased risk, a lower valuation of higher earnings is possible.[2] Every situation must be evaluated individually.

You may wish to review Figure 3–1, which illustrates the key points in the Du Pont system of analysis.

Figure 3–1
Du Pont analysis

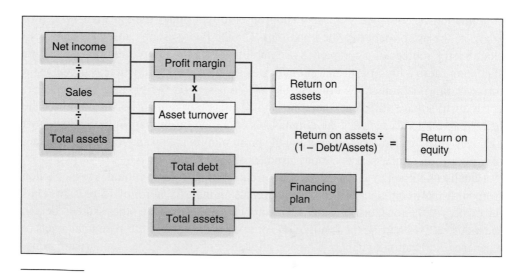

---

[1]The return could be slightly different than 25 percent because of changing financial costs with higher debt.
[2]Further discussion of this point is presented in Chapter 5, "Operating and Financial Leverage," and Chapter 10, "Valuation and Rates of Return."

As an example of the Du Pont analysis, Table 3–2 compares two well-known department store chains, Wal-Mart and Neiman Marcus. In 2005, upscale Neiman Marcus was more profitable in terms of profit margins (6.3 percent versus 3.6 percent). However, Wal-Mart had a 20.8 percent return on equity versus 15.1 percent for Neiman Marcus. Why the reversal in performance? It comes back to the Du Pont system of analysis. Wal-Mart turned over its assets 2.7 times a year versus a considerably slower 1.4 times for Neiman Marcus. Wal-Mart was following the philosophy of its late founder, Sam Walton: Give the customer a bargain in terms of low prices (and low profit margins), but move the merchandise quickly. Wal-Mart was able to turn a low return on sales (profit margin) into a good return on assets. Furthermore, its higher debt ratio (53.4 percent for Wal-Mart versus 41.7 percent for Neiman Marcus) allowed Wal-Mart to turn its higher return on assets into an even higher relative return on equity (20.8 percent versus 15.1 percent). For some firms, a higher debt ratio might indicate additional risk, but for stable Wal-Mart, this is not the case.

	Profit Margin	×	Asset Turnover	=	Return on Assets	÷	(1 – Debt/ Assets)	=	Return on Equity
Wal-Mart	3.6%	×	2.7	=	9.7%	÷	(1 – .534)	=	20.8%
Neiman Marcus	6.3	×	1.4	=	8.8	÷	(1 – .417)	=	15.1

Table 3–2
Return of Wal-Mart versus Neiman Marcus using the Du Pont method of analysis, 2005

Finally as a general statement in computing all the profitability ratios, the analyst must be sensitive to the age of the assets. Plant and equipment purchased 15 years ago may be carried on the books far below its replacement value in an inflationary economy. A 20 percent return on assets purchased in the early 1990s may be inferior to a 15 percent return on newly purchased assets.

B. Asset Utilization Ratios The second category of ratios relates to asset utilization, and the ratios in this category may explain why one firm can turn over its assets more rapidly than another. Notice that all of these ratios relate the balance sheet (assets) to the income statement (sales). The Saxton Company's rapid turnover of assets is primarily explained in ratios 4, 5, and 6.

Asset Utilization Ratios—

	Saxton Company	Industry Average
4. Receivables turnover = $\dfrac{\text{Sales (credit)}}{\text{Receivables}}$	$\dfrac{\$4,000,000}{\$350,000} = 11.4$	10 times
5. Average collection period = $\dfrac{\text{Accounts receivable}}{\text{Average daily credit sales}}$	$\dfrac{\$350,000}{\$11,111} = 32$	36 days
6. Inventory turnover = $\dfrac{\text{Sales}}{\text{Inventory}}$	$\dfrac{\$4,000,000}{\$370,000} = 10.8$	7 times

	Saxton Company	Industry Average
7. Fixed asset turnover =		
$\dfrac{\text{Sales}}{\text{Fixed assets}}$	$\dfrac{\$4,000,000}{\$800,000} = 5$	5.4 times
8. Total asset turnover =		
$\dfrac{\text{Sales}}{\text{Total assets}}$	$\dfrac{\$4,000,000}{\$1,600,000} = 2.5$	1.5 times

Saxton collects its receivables faster than does the industry. This is shown by the receivables turnover of 11.4 times versus 10 times for the industry, and in daily terms by the average collection period of 32 days, which is 4 days faster than the industry norm. Please see these numbers in ratios 4 and 5 on page 59. The average collection period suggests how long, on average, customers' accounts stay on the books. The Saxton Company has $350,000 in accounts receivable and $4,000,000 in credit sales, which when divided by 360 days yields average daily credit sales of $11,111. We divide accounts receivable of $350,000 by average daily credit sales of $11,111 to determine how many days credit sales are on the books (32 days).

In addition the firm turns over its inventory 10.8 times per year as contrasted with an industry average of 7 times.[3] This tells us that Saxton generates more sales per dollar of inventory than the average company in the industry, and we can assume the firm uses very efficient inventory-ordering and cost-control methods.

The firm maintains a slightly lower ratio of sales to fixed assets (plant and equipment) than does the industry (5 versus 5.4) as shown above. This is a relatively minor consideration in view of the rapid movement of inventory and accounts receivable. Finally, the rapid turnover of total assets is again indicated (2.5 versus 1.5).

C. Liquidity Ratios   After considering profitability and asset utilization, the analyst needs to examine the liquidity of the firm. The Saxton Company's liquidity ratios fare well in comparison with the industry. Further analysis might call for a cash budget to determine if the firm can meet each maturing obligation as it comes due.

Liquidity Ratios—

	Saxton Company	Industry Average
9. Current ratio =		
$\dfrac{\text{Current assets}}{\text{Current liabilities}}$	$\dfrac{\$800,000}{\$300,000} = 2.67$	2.1
10. Quick ratio =		
$\dfrac{\text{Current assets} - \text{Inventory}}{\text{Current liabilities}}$	$\dfrac{\$430,000}{\$300,000} = 1.43$	1.0

D. Debt Utilization Ratios   The last grouping of ratios, debt utilization, allows the analyst to measure the prudence of the debt management policies of the firm.

Debt to total assets of 37.5 percent as shown in Equation 11 is slightly above the industry average of 33 percent, but well within the prudent range of 50 percent or less.

---

[3]This ratio may also be computed by using "cost of goods sold" in the numerator. While this offers some theoretical advantages in terms of using cost figures in both the numerator and denominator, Dun & Bradstreet and other credit reporting agencies generally show turnover using sales in the numerator.

Debt Utilization Ratios—

	Saxton Company	Industry Average
11. Debt to total assets =		
$\dfrac{\text{Total debt}}{\text{Total assets}}$	$\dfrac{\$600{,}000}{\$1{,}600{,}000} = 37.5\%$	33%
12. Times interest earned =		
$\dfrac{\text{Income before interest and taxes}}{\text{Interest}}$	$\dfrac{\$550{,}000}{\$50{,}000} = 11$	7 times
13. Fixed charge coverage =		
$\dfrac{\text{Income before fixed charges and taxes}}{\text{Fixed charges}}$	$\dfrac{\$600{,}000}{\$100{,}000} = 6$	5.5 times

Ratios for times interest earned and fixed charge coverage show that the Saxton Company debt is being well managed compared to the debt management of other firms in the industry. Times interest earned indicates the number of times that income before interest and taxes covers the interest obligation (11 times). The higher the ratio, the stronger is the interest-paying ability of the firm. The figure for income before interest and taxes ($550,000) in the ratio is the equivalent of the operating profit figure presented in the upper part of Table 3–1, back on page 56.

Fixed charge coverage measures the firm's ability to meet all fixed obligations rather than interest payments alone, on the assumption that failure to meet any financial obligation will endanger the position of the firm. In the present case the Saxton Company has lease obligations of $50,000 as well as the $50,000 in interest expenses. Thus the total fixed charge financial obligation is $100,000. We also need to know the income before all fixed charge obligations. In this case we take income before interest and taxes (operating profit) and add back the $50,000 in lease payments.

Income before interest and taxes.............	$550,000
Lease payments	50,000
Income before fixed charges and taxes........	$600,000

The fixed charges are safely covered 6 times, exceeding the industry norm of 5.5 times. The various ratios are summarized in Table 3–3 on page 62. The conclusions reached in comparing the Saxton Company to industry averages are generally valid, though exceptions may exist. For example, a high inventory turnover is considered "good" unless it is achieved by maintaining unusually low inventory levels, which may hurt future sales and profitability.

In summary, the Saxton Company more than compensates for a lower return on the sales dollar by a rapid turnover of assets, principally inventory and receivables, and a wise use of debt. The student should be able to use these 13 measures to evaluate the financial performance of any firm.

Trend Analysis

Over the course of the business cycle, sales and profitability may expand and contract, and ratio analysis for any one year may not present an accurate picture of the firm. Therefore we look at the **trend analysis** of performance over a number of years. However, without industry comparisons even trend analysis may not present a complete picture.

Table 3–3
Ratio analysis

	Saxon Company	Industry Average	Conclusion
A. Profitability			
1. Profit margin	5.0%	6.7%	Below average
2. Return on assets.	12.5%	10.0%	Above average due to high turnover
3. Return on equity	20.0%	15.0%	Good, due to ratios 2 and 11
B. Asset Utilization			
4. Receivables turnover	11.4	10.0	Good
5. Average collection period	32.0	36.0	Good
6. Inventory turnover.	10.8	7.0	Good
7. Fixed asset turnover	5.0	5.4	Below average
8. Total asset turnover.	2.5	1.5	Good
C. Liquidity			
9. Current ratio	2.67	2.1	Good
10. Quick ratio.	1.43	1.0	Good
D. Debt Utilization			
11. Debt to total assets.	37.5%	33.0%	Slightly more debt
12. Times interest earned.	11.0	7.0	Good
13. Fixed charge coverage	6.0	5.5	Good

Figure 3–2
Trend analysis

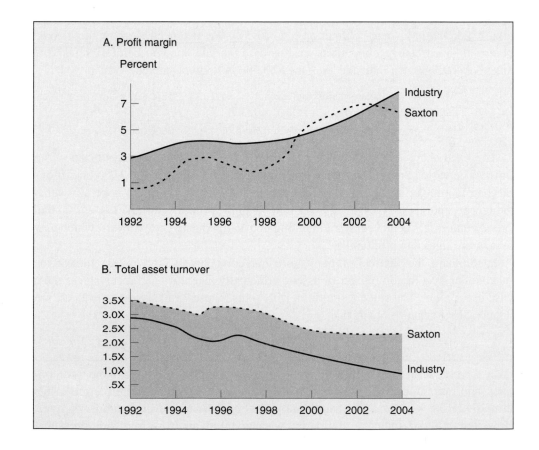

For example, in Figure 3–2 on the bottom of page 62, we see that the profit margin for the Saxton Company has improved, while asset turnover has declined. This by itself may look good for the profit margin and bad for asset turnover. However, when compared to industry trends, we see the firm's profit margin is still below the industry average. With asset turnover, Saxton has improved in relation to the industry even though it is in a downward trend. Similar data could be generated for the other ratios.

By comparing companies in the same industry, the analyst can analyze trends over time. In looking at the computer industry data in Table 3–4, it is apparent that profit margins and returns on equity have declined over time for IBM and Apple. This is primarily due to intensified competition within the industry. IBM began to feel the squeeze on profits first, beginning in 1991, and actually lost money in 1993. By 1994, Lou Gerstner took over as chairman and chief executive officer at IBM and began turning matters around; by 1997, IBM was back to its old levels of profitability and hitting all-time highs for return on stockholders' equity. This continued until the recession of 2001–2002. At the end of 2002, Lou Gerstner announced he was stepping down as head of the firm. Since then, the company has maintained its profit margins.

Dell Computer did not come into the picture until 1992 and, with the exception of 1993, has shown very strong levels of profitability. Founder Michael Dell, now a multibillionaire, has been credited with providing strong leadership to the firm.

Table 3–4

Trend analysis in the computer industry

	IBM		Dell		Apple	
	Profit Margin	**Return on Equity**	**Profit Margin**	**Return on Equity**	**Profit Margin**	**Return on Equity**
1983	13.7%	23.6%	—	—	7.8%	20.3%
1984	14.3	24.8	—	—	3.9	12.7
1985	13.1	20.5	—	—	3.2	11.1
1986	9.3	13.9	—	—	8.1	22.2
1987	9.7	13.7	—	—	8.2	26.0
1988	9.8	14.7	—	—	9.8	39.9
1989	8.4	13.6	—	—	7.7	27.3
1990	8.7	14.1	—	—	8.5	32.8
1991	3.2	5.7	—	—	7.1	25.4
1992	2.2	5.2	5.0	27.5	7.5	24.2
1993	Deficit		Deficit		3.6	14.1
1994	4.6	12.7	4.3	22.9	2.5	9.7
1995	8.8	25.5	5.1	28.0	3.7	12.1
1996	7.7	27.1	6.8	48.9	Deficit	
1997	7.8	30.7	7.7	73.0	Deficit	
1998	7.7	32.6	8.0	62.9	4.8	17.2
1999	8.0	33.9	7.4	35.0	6.8	13.5
2000	8.1	30.0	7.2	41.1	7.0	13.0
2001	9.0	20.5	5.7	37.9	Deficit	
2002	8.4	18.0	6.0	40.0	2.0	3.0
2003	8.5	27.3	6.4	42.1	1.2	1.8
2004	9.0	29.1	6.8	51.0	3.3	5.4
2005	8.6	27.5	7.2	49.0	6.5	13.3

Are Financial Analysts Friends or Foes to Investors? Reader Beware!

Financial analysis is not only done by managers of the firm but by outside analysts as well. These outside analysts normally supply data to stock market investors.

One of the problems that was detected after the great bull market of the 1990s was that analysts were not always as objective as they should be. This unfortunate discovery helped intensify the bear market of the early 2000s.

The reason that many analysts lack objectivity is that they work for investment banking–brokerage firms that are not only involved in providing financial analysis for investors, but also underwriting the securities of the firms they are covering. Underwriting activity involves the distribution of new securities in the public markets and is highly profitable to the investment banker. For example, Goldman Sachs, a major Wall Street investment banking firm, may not only be doing research and financial analysis on General Motors or Eastman Kodak, but also profiting from investment banking business with these firms.

Since the fees from investment banking activities contribute heavily to the overall operations of the investment banker, many analysts for investment banking firms "pulled the punch" in doing financial analysis on their clients in the 1990s.

As an example, Goldman Sachs, Merrill Lynch, or Smith Barney often failed to divulge potential weaknesses in the firms they were investigating for fear of losing the clients' investment banking business. Corporations that were being reported upon were equally guilty. Many a corporate chief officer told an investment banker that "if you come out with a negative report, you will never see another dollar's worth of our investment banking business." Morgan Stanley, a major investment banker, actually had a written internal policy for analysts never to make negative comments about firms providing investment banking fees. Pity the poor investor who naively followed the advice of Morgan Stanley during the mid-1990s.

After the market crash of the early 2000s, the SEC and federal legislators began requiring investment bankers to either fully separate their financial analysis and underwriting business or, at a minimum, fully divulge any such relationships. For example, Merrill Lynch now states in its research reports, "Investors should assume that Merrill Lynch is seeking or will seek investing banking or other business relationships with the companies in this report."

The government is also requiring investment bankers to provide independent reports to accompany their own in-house reports. These independent reports are done by fee-based research firms that do not engage in underwriting activities. Examples of independent firms include Standard & Poor's, Value Line, Morningstar, and other smaller firms. They tend to be totally objective and hard-hitting when necessary.

Some independent research firms know more about a company than it knows about itself. Take the example of Sanford C. Bernstein & Co. and Cisco Systems in late 2000. Bernstein analyst Paul Sagawa downgraded Cisco for investment purposes even though Cisco Chief Executive Officer John T. Chambers respectfully disagreed. The astute independent analyst anticipated the end of the telecom boom and knew the disastrous effect it would have on Cisco because the company would lose key telecom customers. When the disaster finally occurred, CEO Chambers told investors that "No one could have predicted it. It was like a 100-year flood." Apparently he forgot about the Sagawa report he had read and dismissed only a few months before.

The firm that suffered the most steady decline was Apple Computer, with actual losses in 1996 and 1997, and a threat of bankruptcy at that time. However, by 1998 Apple had miraculously turned itself around with a lucrative new line of Macintosh desktop computers and its profit margins and returns on equity were well into the black again. However, Apple too suffered during the recession of 2001–2002 before returning to profitability with its improving personal computer sales and its popular iPod digital music players.

What will be the trends for all three companies for the rest of the decade? Technology is changing so quickly that no one can say. All three are likely to remain lean in terms of operating expenses, but highly innovative in terms of new product development.

Before, coincident with, or following the computation of financial ratios, we should explore the impact of **inflation** and other sources of distortion on the financial reporting of the firm. As illustrated in this section, inflation causes phantom sources of profit that may mislead even the most alert analyst. Disinflation also causes certain problems and we shall consider these as well.

Impact of Inflation on Financial Analysis

The major problem during inflationary times is that revenue is almost always stated in current dollars, whereas plant and equipment or inventory may have been purchased at lower price levels. Thus, profit may be more a function of increasing prices than of satisfactory performance. Although inflation has been moderate throughout most of the 1990s and the current decade, it tends to reappear in almost every decade so you should be aware of its consequences.

An Illustration

The Stein Corporation shows the accompanying income statement for 2007. At year-end the firm also has 100 units still in inventory at $1 per unit.

Table 3–5

STEIN CORPORATION		
Net Income for 2007		
Sales.	$200	(100 units at $2)
Cost of goods sold	100	(100 units at $1)
Gross profit.	100	
Selling and administrative expense	20	(10% of sales)
Depreciation	10	
Operating profit.	70	
Taxes (40%)	28	
Aftertax income	$ 42	

Assume that in the year 2008 the number of units sold remains constant at 100. However, inflation causes a 10 percent increase in price, from $2 to $2.20. Total sales will go up to $220 as shown in Table 3–6, but with no actual increase in physical volume. Further, assume the firm uses FIFO inventory pricing, so that inventory first purchased will be written off against current sales. In this case 2007 inventory will be written off against year 2008 sales revenue.

Table 3–6

STEIN CORPORATION		
Net Income for 2008		
Sales.	$220	(100 units at 2000 price of $2.20)
Cost of goods sold	100	(100 units at $1.00)
Gross profit.	120	
Selling and administrative expense	22	(10% of sales)
Depreciation	10	
Operating profit.	88	
Taxes (40%)	35	
Aftertax income	$ 53	

In Table 3–6, the company appears to have increased profit by $11 compared to that shown in Table 3–5 (from $42 to $53) simply as a result of inflation. But not reflected is the increased cost of replacing inventory and plant and equipment. Presumably, their **replacement costs** have increased in an inflationary environment.

As mentioned in Chapter 2, inflation-related information was formerly required by the FASB for large companies, but this is no longer the case. It is now purely voluntary. What are the implications of this type of inflation-adjusted data? From a study of 10 chemical firms and eight drug companies, using current cost (replacement cost) data found in the financial 10K statements which these companies filed with the Securities and Exchange Commission, it was found that the changes shown in Table 3–7 occurred in their assets, income, and selected ratios.[4]

Table 3–7

Comparison of replacement cost accounting and historical cost accounting

	10 Chemical Companies		8 Drug Companies	
	Replacement Cost	Historical Cost	Replacement Cost	Historical Cost
Increase in assets	28.4%	—	15.4%	—
Decrease in net income before taxes	45.8%	—	19.3%	—
Return on assets	2.8%	6.2%	8.3%	11.4%
Return on equity	4.9%	13.5%	12.8%	19.6%
Debt-to-assets ratio	34.3%	43.8%	30.3%	35.2%
Interest coverage ratio (times interest earned) . . .	7.1×	8.4×	15.4×	16.7×

The comparison of replacement cost and historical cost accounting methods in the table shows that replacement cost reduces income but at the same time increases assets. This increase in assets lowers the debt-to-assets ratio since debt is a monetary asset that is not revalued because it is paid back in current dollars. The decreased debt-to-assets ratio would indicate the financial leverage of the firm is decreased, but a look at the interest coverage ratio tells a different story. Because the interest coverage ratio measures the operating income available to cover interest expense, the declining income penalizes this ratio and the firm has decreased its ability to cover its interest cost.

Disinflation Effect

As long as prices continue to rise in an inflationary environment, profits appear to feed on themselves. The main objection is that when price increases moderate (**disinflation**), there will be a rude awakening for management and unsuspecting stockholders as expensive inventory is charged against softening retail prices. A 15 or 20 percent growth rate in earnings may be little more than an "inflationary illusion." Industries most sensitive to inflation-induced profits are those with cyclical products,

---

[4]Jeff Garnett and Geoffrey A. Hirt, "Replacement Cost Data: A Study of the Chemical and Drug Industry for Years 1976 through 1978." Replacement cost is but one form of current cost. Nevertheless, it is often used as a measure of current cost.

such as lumber, copper, rubber, and food products, and also those in which inventory is a significant percentage of sales and profits.

A leveling off of prices is not necessarily bad. Even though inflation-induced corporate profits may be going down, investors may be more willing to place their funds in financial assets such as stocks and bonds. The reason for the shift may be a belief that declining inflationary pressures will no longer seriously impair the purchasing power of the dollar. Lessening inflation means the required return that investors demand on financial assets will be going down, and with this lower demanded return, future earnings or interest should receive a higher current valuation.

None of the above happens with a high degree of certainty. To the extent that investors question the permanence of disinflation (leveling off of price increases), they may not act according to the script. That is, lower rates of inflation will not necessarily produce high stock and bond prices unless reduced inflation is sustainable over a reasonable period.

Whereas financial assets such as stocks and bonds have the potential (whether realized or not) to do well during disinflation, such is not the case for tangible (real) assets. Precious metals, such as gold and silver, gems, and collectibles, that boomed in the highly inflationary environment of the late 1970s fell off sharply a decade later, as softening prices caused less perceived need to hold real assets as a hedge against inflation. The shifting back and forth by investors between financial and real assets may occur many times over a business cycle.

Deflation   There is also the danger of **deflation**, actual declining prices (which happened in Russia, Asia, and other foreign countries in 1998), in which everyone gets hurt from bankruptcies and declining profits.

Other Elements of Distortion in Reported Income

The effect of changing prices is but one of a number of problems the analyst must cope with in evaluating a company. Other issues, such as the reporting of revenue, the treatment of nonrecurring items, and the tax write-off policy, cause dilemmas for the financial manager or analyst. The point may be illustrated by considering the income statements for two hypothetical companies in the same industry as shown in Table 3–8. Both firms had identical operating performances for 2007—but Company A is very conservative in reporting its results, while Company B has attempted to maximize its reported income.

If both companies had reported income of $280,000 in the prior year of 2006, Company B would be thought to be showing substantial growth in 2007 with net income of $700,000, while Company A is reporting a "flat" or no-growth year in 2007. However, we have already established that the companies have equal operating performances.

Explanation of Discrepancies

Let us examine how the inconsistencies in Table 3–8 could occur. Emphasis is given to a number of key elements on the income statement. The items being discussed here are not illegal but reflect flexibility in financial reporting.

Table 3–8

INCOME STATEMENTS For the Year 2007		
	Conservative Firm A	High Reported Income Firm B
Sales.	$4,000,000	$4,200,000
Cost of goods sold	3,000,000	2,700,000
Gross profit.	1,000,000	1,500,000
Selling and administrative expense	450,000	450,000
Operating profit.	550,000	1,050,000
Interest expense.	50,000	50,000
Extraordinary loss.	100,000	—
Net income before taxes.	400,000	1,000,000
Taxes (30%)	120,000	300,000
Net income	280,000	700,000
Extraordinary loss (net of tax)	—	70,000
Net income transferred to retained earnings	$ 280,000	$ 630,000

Sales   Company B reported $200,000 more in sales, although actual volume was the same. This may be the result of different concepts of revenue recognition.

For example, certain assets may be sold on an installment basis over a long period. A conservative firm may defer recognition of the sales or revenue until each payment is received, while other firms may attempt to recognize a fully effected sale at the earliest possible date. Similarly, firms that lease assets may attempt to consider a long-term lease as the equivalent of a sale, while more conservative firms only recognize as revenue each lease payment as it comes due. Although the accounting profession attempts to establish appropriate methods of financial reporting through generally accepted accounting principles, there is variation of reporting among firms.

Cost of Goods Sold   The conservative firm (Company A) may well be using **LIFO** accounting in an inflationary environment, thus charging the last-purchased, more expensive items against sales, while Company B uses **FIFO** accounting—charging off less expensive inventory against sales. The $300,000 difference in cost of goods sold may also be explained by varying treatment of research and development costs and other items.

Extraordinary Gains/Losses   Nonrecurring gains or losses may occur from the sale of corporate fixed assets, lawsuits, or similar nonrecurring events. Some analysts argue that such extraordinary events should be included in computing the current income of the firm, while others would leave them off in assessing operating performance. Unfortunately, there is inconsistency in the way nonrecurring losses are treated despite attempts by the accounting profession to ensure uniformity. The conservative Firm A has written off its $100,000 extraordinary loss against normally reported income, while Firm B carries a subtraction against net income only after the $700,000 amount has been reported. Both had similar losses of $100,000, but Firm B's loss is shown net of tax implications at $70,000.

RateFinancials Gives Grades to Corporations and Not Everyone Gets an A

What grade did you get on your last accounting or finance exam? A 95 would be great and a 65 disappointing. Corporate chief financial officers may suffer the same fate at the hands of RateFinancials (www.ratefinancials.com). The New York City firm assigns grades to the quality of financial reporting and earnings reported by Fortune 500 companies.

The firm is headed up by Victor Germack, a Harvard MBA, who has a significant background in investment banking and corporate management. Along with senior management, there are 10 well-trained financial analysts on the staff.

Just as your semester grade may be based on quiz grades, homework, and a final exam, RateFinancials gives out grades based on a number of key parameters:

1. Clarity of financial reporting. Is the company telling it like it is or attempting to cover up its tracks? For example, RateFinancials recently cited Krispy Kreme Doughnuts for "baking" its profits through questionable accounting for repurchased franchises and failing to book adequate reserves for doubtful accounts.*

2. Stipulating financial concerns and potential financial exposure. An area of concern might be adequacy of contributions to corporate pension plans.

3. Adequacy of corporate governance. Is the company being run for the benefit of stockholders or top management? Are excessive stock options being granted? Are there truly independent members of the Board of Directors to monitor the activities of top management?

While the SEC concerns itself with many of these same topics, less than 20 percent of corporate annual reports (10Ks) are thoroughly reviewed by the government regulatory agency. Limited funds for federal agencies can only be stretched so far. Of course, there are private sector financial analysts working for Morgan Stanley, Goldman Sachs, Merrill Lynch, and other investment banking houses, but they are often biased in favor of the firm they are recommending to investors.

One of the areas in which RateFinancials grades companies is quality of earnings. This is done by comparing true earnings (earnings adjusted downward for overly generous or aggressive accounting) to reported earnings. The former is taken as a percentage of the latter. Note some of the grades received in 2004–2005 below. As is true for you in your coursework, the higher the grade the better.

Southwest Airlines	49%
Union Pacific	65
Dell Computer Corporation	68
General Motors	73
Honeywell International	77
Harman International	97
Ryder System	99
Standard Pacific	100
Lennar	100
Hershey Foods	100

While the firm charges for its services, coverage of its philosophy and operations can be seen at www.ratefinancials.com.

*Kurt Badenhausen, Jack Gage, Cecily Hall, and Michael K. Ozanian, "How Pretty Are Those Earnings?" *Forbes,* February 14, 2005, p. 64.

Extraordinary gains and losses happen among large companies more often than you might think. General Motors has had "nonrecurring" losses four times in the last decade. In the current age of mergers, tender offers, and buyouts, understanding the finer points of financial statements becomes even more important.

Net Income

Firm A has reported net income of $280,000, while Firm B claims $700,000 before subtraction of extraordinary losses. The $420,000 difference is attributed to different methods of financial reporting, and it should be recognized as such by the analyst. No superior performance has actually taken place. The analyst must remain ever alert in examining each item in the financial statements, rather than accepting bottom-line figures.

Summary

Ratio analysis allows the analyst to compare a company's performance to that of others in its industry. Ratios that initially appear good or bad may not retain that characteristic when measured against industry peers.

There are four main groupings of ratios. Profitability ratios measure the firm's ability to earn an adequate return on sales, assets, and stockholders' equity. The asset utilization ratios tell the analyst how quickly the firm is turning over its accounts receivable, inventory, and longer-term assets. Liquidity ratios measure the firm's ability to pay off short-term obligations as they come due, and debt utilization ratios indicate the overall debt position of the firm in light of its asset base and earning power.

The Du Pont system of analysis first breaks down return on assets between the profit margin and asset turnover. The second step then shows how this return on assets is translated into return on equity through the amount of debt the firm has. Throughout the analysis, the analyst can better understand how return on assets and return on equity are derived.

Over the course of the business cycle, sales and profitability may expand and contract, and ratio analysis for any one year may not present an accurate picture of the firm. Therefore we look at the trend analysis of performance over a period of years.

A number of factors may distort the numbers the accountants actually report. These include the effect of inflation or disinflation, the timing of the recognition of sales as revenue, the treatment of inventory write-offs, the presence of extraordinary gains and losses, and so on. The well-trained financial analyst must be alert to all of these factors.

List of Terms

profitability ratios 55	inflation 65
asset utilization ratios 55	replacement costs 66
liquidity ratios 55	disinflation 66
debt utilization ratios 55	deflation 67
Du Pont system of analysis 57	LIFO 68
trend analysis 61	FIFO 68

Discussion Questions

1. If we divide users of ratios into short-term lenders, long-term lenders, and stockholders, which ratios would each group be *most* interested in, and for what reasons?

2. Explain how the Du Pont system of analysis breaks down return on assets. Also explain how it breaks down return on stockholders' equity.

3. If the accounts receivable turnover ratio is decreasing, what will be happening to the average collection period?

4. What advantage does the fixed charge coverage ratio offer over simply using times interest earned?

5. Is there any validity in rule-of-thumb ratios for all corporations, for example, a current ratio of 2 to 1 or debt to assets of 50 percent?

6. Why is trend analysis helpful in analyzing ratios?

7. Inflation can have significant effects on income statements and balance sheets, and therefore on the calculation of ratios. Discuss the possible impact of inflation on the following ratios, and explain the direction of the impact based on your assumptions.

   a. Return on investment

   b. Inventory turnover

   c. Fixed asset turnover

   d. Debt-to-assets ratio

8. What effect will disinflation following a highly inflationary period have on the reported income of the firm?

9. Why might disinflation prove to be favorable to financial assets?

10. Comparisons of income can be very difficult for two companies even though they sell the same products in equal volume. Why?

---

1. Barnes Appliances has sales of $10,000,000, net income of $450,000, total assets of $4,000,000, and stockholders' equity of $2,000,000.

   a. What is the profit margin?

   b. What is the return on assets?

   c. What is the return on equity?

   d. The debt to assets ratio is currently 50 percent. If it were 60 percent, what would the return on equity be? To answer this question, use formula 3*b* in the text.

2. The Gilliam Corp. has the following balance sheet and income statement. Compute the profitability, asset utilization, liquidity, and debt utilization ratios.

Practice Problems and Solutions

Profitability ratios

All 13 ratios

GILLIAM CORPORATION
Balance Sheet
December 31, 200x

Assets

Current assets:

Cash	$ 70,000
Marketable securities	40,000
Accounts receivable (net)	250,000
Inventory	200,000
Total current assets	$ 560,000
Investments.	100,000
Net plant and equipment	440,000
Total assets.	$1,100,000

Liabilities and Stockholders' Equity

Current liabilities:

Accounts payable	130,000	
Notes payable	120,000	
Accrued taxes	30,000	
Total current liabilities	$ 280,000	

Long-term liabilities:

Bonds payable	200,000	
Total liabilities	$ 480,000	

Stockholders' equity

Preferred stock, $100 par value	150,000
Common stock, $5 par value	50,000
Capital paid in excess of par	200,000
Retained earnings	220,000
Total stockholders' equity	620,000
Total liabilities and stockholders' equity	$1,100,000

GILLIAM CORPORATION
Income Statement
For the Year Ending December 31, 200X

Sales (on credit)	$2,400,000
Less: Cost of goods sold	1,600,000
Gross profit	800,000
Less: Selling and administrative expenses	560,000*
Operating profit (EBIT)	240,000
Less: Interest expense	30,000
Earnings before taxes (EBT)	210,000
Less: Taxes	75,000
Earnings after taxes (EAT)	$ 135,000

*Includes $40,000 in lease payments.

Solutions

1. *a.* $\text{Profit margin} = \dfrac{\text{Net income}}{\text{Sales}} = \dfrac{\$450,000}{\$10,000,000} = 4.5\%$

   b. $\text{Return on assets} = \dfrac{\text{Net income}}{\text{Total assets}} = \dfrac{\$450,000}{\$4,000,000} = 11.25\%$

   c. $\text{Return on equity} = \dfrac{\text{Net income}}{\text{Stockholders' equity}} = \dfrac{\$450,000}{\$2,000,000} = 22.5\%$

   d. $\text{Return on equity} = \dfrac{\text{Return on assets (investment)}}{(1 - \text{Debt/Assets})} = \dfrac{11.25\%}{(1 - .6)}$

   $= \dfrac{11.25\%}{.4} = 28.13\%$

2. **Profitability ratios**

   1. $\text{Profit margin} = \dfrac{\text{Net income}}{\text{Sales}} = \dfrac{\$135,000}{2,400,000} = 5.63\%$

2. Return on assets $= \dfrac{\text{Net income}}{\text{Total assets}} = \dfrac{\$135,000}{1,100,000} = 12.27\%$

3. Return on equity $= \dfrac{\text{Net income}}{\text{Stockholders' equity}} = \dfrac{\$135,000}{620,000} = 21.77\%$

Asset utilization

4. Receivables turnover $= \dfrac{\text{Sales (credits)}}{\text{Accounts receivable}} = \dfrac{\$2,400,000}{250,000} = 9.6x$

5. Average collection period $= \dfrac{\text{Accounts receivable}}{\text{Avg. daily credit sales}} = \dfrac{\$250,000}{6,667} = 37.5 \text{ days}$

6. Inventory turnover $= \dfrac{\text{Sales}}{\text{Inventory}} = \dfrac{\$2,400,000}{200,000} = 12x$

7. Fixed asset turnover $= \dfrac{\text{Sales}}{\text{Fixed assets}} = \dfrac{\$2,400,000}{440,000} = 5.45x$

8. Total asset turnover $= \dfrac{\text{Sales}}{\text{Total assets}} = \dfrac{\$2,400,000}{1,100,000} = 2.18x$

Liquidity ratios

9. Current ratio $= \dfrac{\text{Current assets}}{\text{Current liabilities}} = \dfrac{560,000}{280,000} = 2x$

10. Quick ratio $= \dfrac{\text{Current assets} - \text{inventory}}{\text{Current liabilities}} = \dfrac{\$560,000 - 200,000}{280,000}$

$\qquad = \dfrac{360,000}{280,000} = 1.29x$

Debt utilization ratios

11. Debt to total assets $= \dfrac{\text{Total debt}}{\text{Total assets}} = \dfrac{\$480,000}{1,100,000} = 43.64\%$

12. Times interest earned $= \dfrac{\text{Income before interest and taxes}}{\text{Interest}}$

Note: Income before interest and taxes equals operating profit, $240,000.

Times interest earned $= \dfrac{240,000}{30,000} = 8x$

13. Fixed charge coverage $= \dfrac{\text{Income before fixed charges and taxes}}{\text{Fixed charges}}$

Income before fixed charges and taxes = Operating profit plus Lease payments*

$\$240,000 + \$40,000 = \$280,000$

Fixed charges = Lease payments + Interest

$\$40,000 + \$30,000 = \$70,000$

Fixed charge coverage $= \dfrac{\$280,000}{70,000} = 4x$

*Lease payments are in a footnote on the income statement.

Problems

⊞ ⊡ ™ All problems are available in Homework Manager. Please see the preface for more information.

Profitability ratios

1. Low Carb Diet Supplement, Inc., has two divisions. Division A has a profit of $100,000 on sales of $2,000,000. Division B is only able to make $25,000 on sales of $300,000. Based on the profit margins (returns on sales), which division is superior?

Profitability ratios

2. Database Systems is considering expansion into a new product line. Assets to support expansion will cost $500,000. It is estimated that Database can generate $1,200,000 in annual sales, with a 6 percent profit margin. What would net income and return on assets (investment) be for the year?

Profitability ratios

3. Polly Esther Dress Shops, Inc., can open a new store that will do an annual sales volume of $960,000. It will turn over its assets 2.4 times per year. The profit margin on sales will be 7 percent. What would net income and return on assets (investment) be for the year?

Profitability ratios

4. Billy's Chrystal Stores, Inc., has assets of $5,000,000 and turns over its assets 1.2 times per year. Return on assets is 8 percent. What is the firm's profit margin (return on sales)?

Profitability ratios

5. Dr. Zhivago Diagnostics Corp. income statement for 2007 is as follows:

Sales.	$2,000,000
Cost of goods sold	1,400,000
Gross profit.	600,000
Selling and administrative expense	300,000
Operating profit.	300,000
Interest expense.	50,000
Income before taxes.	250,000
Taxes (30%)	75,000
Income after taxes	$ 175,000

a. Compute the profit margin for 2007.

b. Assume in 2008, sales increase by 10 percent and cost of goods sold increases by 20 percent. The firm is able to keep all other expenses the same. Once again, assume a tax rate of 30 percent on income before taxes. What are income after taxes and the profit margin for 2008?

Profitability ratios

6. Neon Light Company has $1,000,000 in assets and $600,000 of debt. It reports net income of $100,000.

a. What is the return on the assets?

b. What is the return on the stockholders' equity?

c. If the firm has an asset turnover ratio of 3 times, what is the profit margin (return on sales)?

Profitability ratios

7. Network Communications has total assets of $1,400,000 and current assets of $600,000. It turns over its fixed assets 4 times a year. It has $300,000 of debt. Its return on sales is 5 percent. What is its return on stockholders' equity?

Profitability ratios

8. a. Alpha Industries had an asset turnover of 1.4 times per year. If the return on total assets (investment) was 8.4 percent, what was Alpha's profit margin?

b. The following year, on the same level of assets, Alpha's asset turnover declined to 1.2 times and its profit margin was 7 percent.

How did the return on total assets change from that of the previous year?

9. AllState Trucking Co. has the following ratios compared to its industry for 2007.

Du Pont system of analysis

	AllState Trucking	Industry
Return on sales	3%	8%
Return on assets	15%	10%

Explain why the return-on-assets ratio is so much more favorable than the return-on-sales ratio compared to the industry. No numbers are necessary; a one-sentence answer is all that is required.

10. Front Beam Lighting Company has the following ratios compared to its industry for 2008.

Du Pont system of analysis

	Front Beam Lighting	Industry
Return on assets	12%	5%
Return on equity.	16%	20%

Explain why the return-on-equity ratio is so much less favorable than the return-on-assets ratio compared to the industry. No numbers are necessary; a one-sentence answer is all that is required.

11. The King Card Company has a return-on-assets (investment) ratio of 12 percent.

Du Pont system of analysis

a. If the debt-to-total-assets ratio is 40 percent, what is the return on equity?

b. If the firm had no debt, what would the return-on-equity ratio be?

12. Using the Du Pont method, evaluate the effects of the following relationships for the Lollar Corporation.

Du Pont system of analysis

a. Lollar Corporation has a profit margin of 5 percent and its return on assets (investment) is 13.5 percent. What is its assets turnover ratio?

b. If the Lollar Corporation has a debt-to-total-assets ratio of 60 percent, what would the firm's return on equity be?

c. What would happen to return on equity if the debt-to-total-assets ratio decreased to 40 percent?

13. Jerry Rice and Grain Stores has $4,000,000 in yearly sales. The firm earns 3.5 percent on each dollar of sales and turns over its assets 2.5 times per year. It has $100,000 in current liabilities and $300,000 in long-term liabilities.

Du Pont system of analysis

a. What is its return on stockholders' equity?

b. If the asset base remains the same as computed in part a, but total asset turnover goes up to 3, what will be the new return on stockholders' equity? Assume that the profit margin stays the same as do current and long-term liabilities.

Interpreting results from the Du Pont system of analysis

14. Assume the following data for Cable Corporation and Multi-Media, Inc.

	Cable Corporation	Multi-Media, Inc.
Net income	$ 30,000	$ 100,000
Sales.	300,000	2,000,000
Total assets.	400,000	900,000
Total debt	150,000	450,000
Stockholders' equity	250,000	450,000

   a. Compute return on stockholders' equity for both firms using ratio 3*a*. Which firm has the higher return?

   b. Compute the following additional ratios for both firms.

     Net income/Sales

     Net income/Total assets

     Sales/Total assets

     Debt/Total assets

   c. Discuss the factors from part *b* that added or detracted from one firm having a higher return on stockholders' equity than the other firm as computed in part *a*.

Average collection period

15. A firm has sales of $1.2 million, and 10 percent of the sales are for cash. The year-end accounts receivable balance is $180,000. What is the average collection period? (Use a 360-day year.)

Average daily sales

16. The Chamberlain Corporation has an accounts receivable turnover equal to 12 times. If accounts receivable are equal to $90,000, what is the value for average daily credit sales?

Inventory turnover

17. Kamin Corporation has the following financial data for the years 2006 and 2007:

	2006	2007
Sales	$4,000,000	$5,000,000
Cost of goods sold	3,000,000	4,500,000
Inventory.	400,000	500,000

   a. Compute inventory turnover based on ratio number 6, Sales/Inventory, for each year.

   b. Compute inventory turnover based on an alternative calculation that is used by many financial analysts, Cost of goods sold/Inventory, for each year.

   c. What conclusions can you draw from part *a* and part *b*?

Turnover ratios

18. Jim Short's Company makes clothing for schools. Sales in 2007 were $4,000,000. Assets were as follows:

Cash	$ 100,000
Accounts receivable.	800,000
Inventory	400,000
Net plant and equipment	500,000
Total assets.	$1,800,000

    a. Compute the following:
1. Accounts receivable turnover
2. Inventory turnover
3. Fixed asset turnover
4. Total asset turnover

    b. In 2008, sales increased to $5,000,000 and the assets for that year were as follows:

Cash	$ 100,000
Accounts receivable.	900,000
Inventory	975,000
Net plant and equipment	500,000
Total assets	$2,525,000

    Once again, compute the four ratios.

    c. Indicate if there is an improvement or decline in total asset turnover, and based on the other ratios, indicate why this development has taken place.

19. The balance sheet for the Bryan Corporation is shown below. Sales for the year were $3,040,000, with 75 percent of sales sold on credit.   *Overall ratio analysis*

BRYAN CORPORATION
Balance Sheet 200X

Assets		Liabilities and Stockholders' Equity	
Cash	$ 50,000	Accounts payable	$220,000
Accounts receivable	280,000	Accrued taxes	80,000
Inventory	240,000	Bonds payable (long-term)	118,000
Plant and equipment	380,000	Common stock	100,000
		Paid-in capital	150,000
		Retained earnings	282,000
		Total liabilities and	
Total assets	$950,000	stockholders' equity	$950,000

    Compute the following ratios:

    a. Current ratio.

    b. Quick ratio.

    c. Debt-to-total-assets ratio.

    d. Asset turnover.

    e. Average collection period.

20. The Lancaster Corporation's income statement is given on page 78.   *Debt utilization ratios*

    a. What is the times-interest-earned ratio?

    b. What would be the fixed-charge-coverage ratio?

LANCASTER CORPORATION

Sales.	$200,000
Cost of goods sold	116,000
Gross profit.	84,000
Fixed charges (other than interest)	24,000
Income before interest and taxes	60,000
Interest	12,000
Income before taxes	48,000
Taxes (35%)	16,800
Income after taxes	$ 31,200

Debt utilization ✗ and Du Pont system of analysis

21. Using the income statement for J. Lo Wedding Gowns, compute the following ratios:

   a. The interest coverage.

   b. The fixed charge coverage.

   The total assets for this company equal $160,000. Set up the equation for the Du Pont system of ratio analysis, and compute the answer to part *c* below using ratio 2*b* on page 57.

   c. Return on assets (investment).

J. LO WEDDING GOWNS
Income Statement

Sales.	$200,000
Less: Cost of goods sold.	90,000
Gross profit.	110,000
Less: Selling and administrative expense	40,000
Less: Lease expense	10,000
Operating profit*	$ 60,000
Less: Interest expense	5,000
Earnings before taxes.	$ 55,000
Less: Taxes (40%).	22,000
Earnings after taxes	$ 33,000

*Equals income before interest and taxes.

Debt utilization

22. A firm has net income before interest and taxes of $96,000 and interest expense of $24,000.

   a. What is the times-interest-earned ratio?

   b. If the firm's lease payments are $40,000, what is the fixed charge coverage?

Return on assets analysis

23. In January 1998 the Status Quo Company was formed. Total assets were $500,000, of which $300,000 consisted of depreciable fixed assets. Status Quo uses straight-line depreciation of $30,000 per year, and in 1998 it estimated its fixed assets to have useful lives of 10 years. Aftertax income has been $26,000 per year each of the last 10 years. Other assets have not changed since 1998.

    a. Compute return on assets at year-end for 1998, 2000, 2003, 2005, and 2007. (Use $26,000 in the numerator for each year.)

    b. To what do you attribute the phenomenon shown in part *a?*

    c. Now assume income increased by 10 percent each year. What effect would this have on your above answers? (A comment is all that is necessary.)

24. Jodie Foster Care Homes, Inc., shows the following data: Trend analysis

Year	Net Income	Total Assets	Stockholders' Equity	Total Debt
2004	$118,000	$1,900,000	$ 700,000	$1,200,000
2005	131,000	1,950,000	950,000	1,000,000
2006	148,000	2,010,000	1,100,000	910,000
2007	175,700	2,050,000	1,420,000	630,000

    a. Compute the ratio of net income to total assets for each year and comment on the trend.

    b. Compute the ratio of net income to stockholders' equity and comment on the trend. Explain why there may be a difference in the trends between parts *a* and *b.*

25. Quantum Moving Company has the following data. Industry information also is   Trend analysis
shown.

Company Data			Industry Data on Net Income/Total Assets
Year	Net Income	Total Assets	
2005	$350,000	$2,800,000	11.5%
2006	375,000	3,200,000	8.4
2007	375,000	3,750,000	5.5
Year	Debt	Total Assets	Industry Data on Debt/Total Assets
2005	$1,624,000	$2,800,000	54.1%
2006	1,730,000	3,200,000	42.0
2007	1,900,000	3,750,000	33.4

As an industry analyst comparing the firm to the industry, are you likely to praise or criticize the firm in terms of:

    a. Net income/Total assets.

    b. Debt/Total assets.

26. The Global Products Corporation has three subsidiaries.   Analysis by
divisions

	Medical Supplies	Heavy Machinery	Electronics
Sales.	$20,000,000	$5,000,000	$4,000,000
Net income (after taxes)	1,200,000	190,000	320,000
Assets.	8,000,000	8,000,000	3,000,000

    a. Which division has the lowest return on sales?

    b. Which division has the highest return on assets?

    c. Compute the return on assets for the entire corporation.

    d. If the $8,000,000 investment in the heavy machinery division is sold off and redeployed in the medical supplies subsidiary at the same rate of return on assets currently achieved in the medical supplies division, what will be the new return on assets for the entire corporation?

Analysis by affiliates

27. Omni Technology Holding Company has the following three affiliates:

	Software	Personal Computers	Foreign Operations
Sales.	$40,000,000	$60,000,000	$100,000,000
Net income (after taxes)	2,000,000	2,000,000	8,000,000
Assets.	5,000,000	25,000,000	60,000,000
Stockholders' equity	4,000,000	10,000,000	50,000,000

    a. Which affiliate has the highest return on sales?

    b. Which affiliate has the lowest return on assets?

    c. Which affiliate has the highest total asset turnover?

    d. Which affiliate has the highest return on stockholders' equity?

    e. Which affiliate has the highest debt ratio? (Assets minus stockholders' equity equals debt.)

    f. Returning to question *b*, explain why the software affiliate has the highest return on total assets.

    g. Returning to question *d*, explain why the personal computer affiliate has a higher return on stockholders' equity than the foreign operations affiliate even though it has a lower return on total assets.

Inflation and inventory accounting effect

28. The Canton Corporation shows the following income statement. The firm uses FIFO inventory accounting.

CANTON CORPORATION
Income Statement for 2007

Sales.	$100,000	(10,000 units at $10)
Cost of goods sold.	50,000	(10,000 units at $5)
Gross profit	50,000	
Selling and administrative expense	5,000	
Depreciation	10,000	
Operating profit	35,000	
Taxes (30%)	10,500	
Aftertax income.	$ 24,500	

    a. Assume in 2008 the same 10,000-unit volume is maintained, but the sales price increases by 10 percent. Because of FIFO inventory policy, old inventory will still be charged off at $5 per unit. Also assume selling and administrative expense will be 5 percent of sales and depreciation will be unchanged. The tax rate is 30 percent. Compute aftertax income for 2008.

b. In part *a*, by what percent did aftertax income increase as a result of a 10 percent increase in the sales price? Explain why this impact took place.

c. Now assume that in 2009 the volume remains constant at 10,000 units, but the sales price decreases by 15 percent from its year 2008 level. Also, because of FIFO inventory policy, cost of goods sold reflects the inflationary conditions of the prior year and is $5.50 per unit. Further, assume selling and administrative expense will be 5 percent of sales and depreciation will be unchanged. The tax rate is 30 percent. Compute the aftertax income.

29. Construct the current assets section of the balance sheet from the following data. (Use cash as a plug figure after computing the other values.)

Using ratios to construct financial statements

Yearly sales (credit)	$420,000
Inventory turnover	7 times
Current liabilities	$ 80,000
Current ratio	2
Average collection period	36 days

Current assets: $

Cash	_____
Accounts receivable.	_____
Inventory	_____
Total current assets	_____

30. The Shannon Corporation has credit sales of $750,000. Given the following ratios, fill in the balance sheet.

Using ratios to construct financial statements

Total assets turnover	2.5 times
Cash to total assets	2.0 percent
Accounts receivable turnover	10.0 times
Inventory turnover	15.0 times
Current ratio	2.0 times
Debt to total assets	45.0 percent

SHANNON CORPORATION
Balance Sheet 200X

Assets		Liabilities and Stockholders' Equity	
Cash	_____	Current debt.	_____
Accounts receivable	_____	Long-term debt	_____
Inventory	_____	Total debt	_____
Total current assets	_____	Net worth	_____
Fixed assets	_____	Total debt and	
Total assets	_____	stockholder's equity	_____

Using ratios to determine account balances

31. We are given the following information for the Pettit Corporation.

Sales (credit)	$3,000,000
Cash	150,000
Inventory	850,000
Current liabilities	700,000
Asset turnover	1.25 times
Current ratio	2.50 times
Debt-to-assets ratio	40%
Receivables turnover	6 times

Current assets are composed of cash, marketable securities, accounts receivable, and inventory. Calculate the following balance sheet items.

a. Accounts receivable.

b. Marketable securities.

c. Fixed assets.

d. Long-term debt.

Using ratios to construct financial statements

32. The following information is from Harrelson Inc.'s financial statements. Sales (all credit) were $20 million for 2007.

Sales to total assets	2 times
Total debt to total assets	30%
Current ratio	3.0 times
Inventory turnover	5.0 times
Average collection period	18 days
Fixed asset turnover	5.0 times

Fill in the balance sheet:

Cash	_____	Current debt	_____
Accounts receivable	_____	Long-term debt	_____
Inventory	_____	Total debt	_____
Total current assets	_____	Equity	_____
Fixed assets	_____	Total debt and equity	_____
Total assets	_____		

Comparing all the ratios ✗ 33. Using the financial statements for the Snider Corporation, calculate the 13 basic ratios found in the chapter.

SNIDER CORPORATION
Balance Sheet
December 31, 2007

Assets

Current assets:

Cash	$ 50,000
Marketable securities	20,000
Accounts receivable (net)	160,000
Inventory	200,000
Total current assets	$ 430,000
Investments	60,000
Plant and equipment	600,000
Less: Accumulated depreciation	(190,000)
Net plant and equipment	410,000
Total assets	$ 900,000

Liabilities and Stockholders' Equity

Current liabilities:

Accounts payable	$ 90,000
Notes payable	70,000
Accrued taxes	10,000
Total current liabilities	170,000
Long-term liabilities:	
Bonds payable	150,000
Total liabilities	$ 320,000
Stockholders' equity	
Preferred stock, $50 par value	100,000
Common stock, $1 par value	80,000
Capital paid in excess of par	190,000
Retained earnings	210,000
Total stockholders' equity	580,000
Total liabilities and stockholders' equity	$ 900,000

SNIDER CORPORATION
Income Statement
For the Year Ending December 31, 2007

Sales (on credit)	$1,980,000
Less: Cost of goods sold	1,280,000
Gross profit	700,000
Less: Selling and administrative expenses	475,000*
Operating profit (EBIT)	225,000
Less: Interest expense	25,000
Earnings before taxes (EBT)	200,000
Less: Taxes	80,000
Earnings after taxes (EAT)	$ 120,000

*Includes $35,000 in lease payments.

Ratio computation ✕ 34.   Given the financial statements for Jones Corporation and Smith Corporation
and analysis   shown here:

    a. To which one would you, as credit manager for a supplier, approve the
extension of (short-term) trade credit? Why? Compute all ratios before
answering.

    b. In which one would you buy stock? Why?

JONES CORPORATION

Current Assets		**Liabilities**	
Cash	$ 20,000	Accounts payable	$100,000
Accounts receivable	80,000	Bonds payable (long term)........	80,000
Inventory	50,000		
Long-Term Assets		**Stockholders' Equity**	
Fixed assets	$ 500,000	Common stock.................	$150,000
Less: Accumulated depreciation	(150,000)	Paid-in capital	70,000
Net fixed assets*	350,000	Retained earnings	100,000
Total assets	$ 500,000	Total liab. and equity	$500,000

Sales (on credit)	$1,250,000
Cost of goods sold	750,000
Gross profit..........................	500,000
Selling and administrative expense[†]........	257,000
Less: Depreciation expense	50,000
Operating profit.......................	193,000
Interest expense......................	8,000
Earnings before taxes..................	185,000
Tax expense	92,500
Net income	$ 92,500

*Use net fixed assets in computing fixed asset turnover.
[†]Includes $7,000 in lease payments.

SMITH CORPORATION

Current Assets		**Liabilities**	
Cash	$ 35,000	Accounts payable	$ 75,000
Marketable securities	7,500	Bonds payable (long-term)	210,000
Accounts receivable	70,000		
Inventory	75,000		
Long-Term Assets		**Stockholders' Equity**	
Fixed assets	$ 500,000	Common stock.................	$ 75,000
Less: Accum. dep.	(250,000)	Paid-in capital	30,000
Net fixed assets*	250,000	Retained earnings..............	47,500
Total assets	$ 437,500	Total liab. and equity	$437,500

*Use net fixed assets in computing fixed asset turnover.

SMITH CORPORATION (Continued)

Sales (on credit)	$1,000,000
Cost of goods sold	600,000
Gross profit	400,000
Selling and administrative expense[†]	224,000
Less: Depreciation expense	50,000
Operating profit	126,000
Interest expense	21,000
Earnings before taxes	105,000
Tax expense	52,500
Net income	$ 52,500

[†]Includes $7,000 in lease payments.

C O M P R E H E N S I V E   P R O B L E M

Bob Adkins has recently been approached by his first cousin, Ed Lamar, with a proposal to buy a 15 percent interest in Lamar Swimwear. The firm manufactures stylish bathing suits and sunscreen products.

Mr. Lamar is quick to point out the increase in sales that has taken place over the last three years as indicated in the income statement, Exhibit 1. The annual growth rate is 25 percent. A balance sheet for a similar time period is shown in Exhibit 2, and selected industry ratios are presented in Exhibit 3. Note the industry growth rate in sales is only 10 to 12 percent per year.

There was a steady real growth of 3 to 4 percent in gross domestic product during the period under study.

Lamar Swimwear
(trend analysis and industry comparisons)

Exhibit 1

LAMAR SWIMWEAR
Income Sheet

	200X	200Y	200Z
Sales (all on credit)	$1,200,000	$1,500,000	$1,875,000
Cost of goods sold	800,000	1,040,000	1,310,000
Gross profit	$ 400,000	$ 460,000	$ 565,000
Selling and administrative expense*	239,900	274,000	304,700
Operating profit (EBIT)	$ 160,100	$ 186,000	$ 260,300
Interest expense	35,000	45,000	85,000
Net income before taxes	$ 125,100	$ 141,000	$ 175,300
Taxes	36,900	49,200	55,600
Net Income	$ 88,200	$ 91,800	$ 119,700
Shares	30,000	30,000	38,000
Earnings per share	$2.94	$3.06	$3.15

*Includes $15,000 in lease payments for each year.

Exhibit 2

LAMAR SWIMWEAR
Balance Sheet

Assets	200X	200Y	200Z
Cash	$ 30,000	$ 40,000	$ 30,000
Marketable securities.	20,000	25,000	30,000
Accounts receivable.	170,000	259,000	360,000
Inventory	230,000	261,000	290,000
Total current assets	$ 450,000	$ 585,000	$ 710,000
Net plant and equipment	650,000	765,000	1,390,000
Total assets	$1,100,000	$1,350,000	$2,100,000
Liabilities and Stockholders' Equity			
Accounts payable	$ 200,000	$ 310,000	$ 505,000
Accrued expenses	20,400	30,000	35,000
Total current liabilities.	$ 220,400	$ 340,000	$ 540,000
Long-term liabilities	325,000	363,600	703,900
Total liabilities	$ 545,400	$ 703,600	$1,243,900
Common stock ($2 par)	60,000	60,000	76,000
Capital paid in excess of par	190,000	190,000	264,000
Retained earnings	304,600	396,400	516,100
Total stockholders' equity	$ 554,600	$ 646,400	$ 856,100
Total liabilities and stockholders' equity	$1,100,000	$1,350,000	$2,100,000

Exhibit 3

Selected Industry Ratios	200X	200Y	200Z
Growth in sales	—	10.00%	12.00%
Profit margin	7.71%	7.82%	7.96%
Return on assets (investment).	7.94%	8.86%	8.95%
Return on equity	14.31%	15.26%	16.01%
Receivable turnover.	9.02X	8.86X	9.31X
Average collection period	39.9 days	40.6 days	38.7 days
Inventory turnover	4.24X	5.10X	5.11X
Fixed asset turnover	1.60X	1.64X	1.75X
Total asset turnover	1.05X	1.10X	1.12X
Current ratio.	1.96X	2.25X	2.40X
Quick ratio	1.37X	1.41X	1.38X
Debt to total assets	43.47%	43.11%	44.10%
Times interest earned	6.50X	5.99X	6.61X
Fixed charge coverage	4.70X	4.69X	4.73X
Growth in EPS	—	10.10%	13.30%

The stock in the corporation has become available due to the ill health of a current stockholder, who is in need of cash. The issue here is not to determine the exact price for the stock, but rather whether Lamar Swimwear represents an attractive investment situation. Although Mr. Adkins has a primary interest in the profitability ratios, he will take a close look at all the ratios. he has no fast and firm rules about required return on investment, but rather wishes to analyze the overall condition of the firm. The firm does not currently pay a cash dividend, and return to the investor must come from selling the stock in the future. After doing a thorough analysis (including ratios for each year and comparisons to the industry), what comments and recommendations do you offer to Mr. Adkins?

C O M P R E H E N S I V E   P R O B L E M

Sun Microsystems is a leading supplier of computer related products, including servers, workstations, storage devices, and network switches.

Sun Microsystems (trends, ratios, stock performance)

In the letter to stockholders as part of the 2001 annual report, President and CEO Scott G. McNealy offered the following remarks:

> Fiscal 2001 was clearly a mixed bag for Sun, the industry, and the economy as a whole. Still, we finished with revenue growth of 16 percent—and that's significant. We believe it's a good indication that Sun continued to pull away from the pack and gain market share. For that, we owe a debt of gratitude to our employees worldwide, who aggressively brought costs down—even as they continued to *bring exciting new products to market.*

The statement would not appear to be telling you enough. For example, McNealy says the year was a mixed bag with revenue growth of 16 percent. But what about earnings? You can delve further by examining the income statement in Exhibit 1. Also, for additional analysis of other factors, consolidated balance sheet(s) are presented in Exhibit 2 on page 89.

1. Referring to Exhibit 1, compute the annual percentage change in net income per common share-diluted (second numerical line from the bottom) for 1998–1999, 1999–2000, and 2000–2001.

2. Also in Exhibit 1, compute net income/net revenue (sales) for each of the four years. Begin with 1998.

3. What is the major reason for the change in the answer for Question 2 between 2000 and 2001? To answer this question for each of the two years, take the ratio of the major income statement accounts to net revenues (sales).

    Cost of sales

    Research and development

    Selling, general and administrative expense

    Provision for income tax

4. Compute return on stockholders' equity for 2000 and 2001 using data from Exhibits 1 and 2.

Exhibit 1

	2001 Dollars	2000 Dollars	1999 Dollars	1998 Dollars
SUN MICROSYSTEMS, INC.				
Summary Consolidated Statement of Income (in millions)				
Net revenues	$18,250	$15,721	$11,806	$9,862
Costs and expenses:				
Cost of sales	10,041	7,549	5,670	4,713
Research and development	2,016	1,630	1,280	1,029
Selling, general and administrative	4,544	4,072	3,196	2,826
Goodwill amortization	261	65	19	4
In-process research and development	77	12	121	176
Total costs and expenses	16,939	13,328	10,286	8,748
Operating income	1,311	2,393	1,520	1,114
Gain (loss) on strategic investments	(90)	208	—	—
Interest income, net	363	170	85	48
Litigation settlement	—	—	—	—
Income before taxes	1,584	2,771	1,605	1,162
Provision for income taxes	603	917	575	407
Cumulative effect of change in accounting principle, net	(54)	—	—	—
Net income	$ 927	$1,854	$1,030	$ 755
Net income per common share—diluted	$0.27	$ 0.55	$ 0.31	$ 0.24
Shares used in the calculation of net income per common share—diluted	3,417	3,379	3,282	3,180

5. Analyze your results to Question 4 more completely by computing ratios 1, 2*a*, 2*b*, and 3*b* (all from this chapter) for 2000 and 2001. Actually the answer to ratio 1 can be found as part of the answer to question 2, but it is helpful to look at it again.

   What do you think was the main contributing factor to the change in return on stockholders' equity between 2000 and 2001? Think in terms of the Du Pont system of analysis.

6. The average stock prices for each of the four years shown in Exhibit 1 were as follows:

1998	11¼
1999	16¾
2000	28½
2001	9½

   a. Compute the price/earnings (P/E) ratio for each year. That is, take the stock price shown above and divide by net income per common stock-dilution from Exhibit 1.

   b. Why do you think the P/E has changed from its 2000 level to its 2001 level? A brief review of P/E ratios can be found under the topic of *Price-Earnings Ratio Applied to Earnings per Share* in Chapter 2.

Exhibit 2

SUN MICROSYSTEMS, INC.
Consolidated Balance Sheets (in millions)

	2001	2000
Assets		
Current assets:		
Cash and cash equivalents	$ 1,472	$ 1,849
Short-term investments	387	626
Accounts receivable, net of allowances of $410 in 2001 and $534 in 2000	2,955	2,690
Inventories	1,049	557
Deferred tax assets	1,102	673
Prepaids and other current assets	969	482
Total current assets	7,934	6,877
Property, plant and equipment, net	2,697	2,095
Long-term investments	4,677	4,496
Goodwill, net of accumulated amortization of $349 in 2001 and $88 in 2000	2,041	163
Other assets, net	832	521
	$18,181	$14,152
Liabilities and Stockholders' Equity		
Current liabilities:		
Short-term borrowings	$ 3	$ 7
Accounts payable	1,050	924
Accrued payroll-related liabilities	488	751
Accrued liabilities and other	1,374	1,155
Deferred revenues and customer deposits	1,827	1,289
Warranty reserve	314	211
Income taxes payable	90	209
Total current liabilities	5,146	4,546
Deferred income taxes	744	577
Long-term debt and other obligations	1,705	1,720
Total debt	$ 7,595	$ 6,843
Commitments and contingencies		
Stockholders' equity:		
Preferred stock, $0.001 par value, 10 shares authorized (1 share which has been designated as Series A Preferred participating stock); no shares issued and outstanding	—	—
Common stock and additional paid-in-capital, $0.00067 par value, 7,200 shares authorized; issued: 3,536 shares in 2001 and 3,495 shares in 2000	6,238	2,728
Treasury stock, at cost: 288 shares in 2001 and 301 shares in 2000	(2,435)	(1,438)
Deferred equity compensation	(73)	(15)
Retained earnings	6,885	5,959
Accumulated other comprehensive income (loss)	(29)	75
Total stockholders' equity	10,586	7,309
	$18,181	$14,152

7. The book values per share for the same four years discussed in the preceding question were:

    1998 $1.18
    1999 $1.55
    2000 $2.29
    2001 $3.26

    a.   Compute the ratio of price to book value for each year.

    b.   Is there any dramatic shift in the ratios worthy of note?

WEB EXERCISE

Dell Computer was mentioned in the chapter as having generally strong market performance. Let's check this out. Go to its Web site, www.dell.com, and follow the steps below:

1. Select "About Dell" on the bottom of the page.

2. Select "Investors" on the bottom of the next page.

3. Select "Annual Reports" on the next page.

4. Select the most current "Fiscal Year in Review." (PDF Format)

5. Based on the "Operating Results" for the two years, write a brief summary of the following changes:

    a.   Net revenue.

    b.   GAAP earnings per common share.

    c.   Total assets.

    d.   Long-term debt.

6. Separately find "GAAP net income" and "total stockholders' equity" for each year and compute the ratio between the two for the five years. Should investors be pleased with the pattern being shown here? Is the company's strength continuing?

Note: From time to time, companies redesign their Web sites and occasionally a topic we have listed may have been deleted, updated, or moved into a different location. If you click on the site map or site index, you will be introduced to a table of contents which should aid you in finding the topic you are looking for.

S&P PROBLEMS   www.mhhe.com/edumarketinsight

**STANDARD
&POOR'S**

1. Log onto the S&P Market Insight Web site, www.mhhe.com/edumarketinsight.

2. Click on "Company," which is the first box below the Market Insight title.

3. Type Abercrombie & Fitch's ticker symbol "ANF" in the box and click on Go.

4. Scroll down the left margin and click on "Excel Analytics." At the top of the left margin you will see the fourth item listed as Ann. Ratio Report.

5. Find all the ratios presented in Chapter 3, and compare the last two years of data for improvement or deterioration of the ratios. Note that the category titles may not be exactly the same as those in your text, but you can find the items listed separately. If an item is missing or labeled in a slightly different manner, don't get hung up on the titles. For example you might find average assets rather than ending assets in some ratios. As long as the ratios are consistently calculated you can determine whether the company improved or not. Specifically:

    a. Write up an analysis of the profitability ratios.

    b. Write up an analysis of the activity ratios (asset utilization ratios in text).

    c. Write up an analysis of the liquidity ratios.

    d. Write up an analysis of the leverage ratios (debt utilization ratios in text).

6. Close this window and return to the first page. Click on "Industry," which is the second box below the Market Insight title.

7. In the box directly below Industry, scroll to "Apparel Retail" and click Go. You will see "Industry Surveys" as the third major category on the left-hand margin. Click on "Retailing Specialty" to open the industry survey.

8. There is a wealth of information about this industry that you can read. However, go to the last item in the table of contents called: "Comparative Company Analysis." Go to this page and scroll down to the tables with ratios. You will find Abercrombie and Fitch listed first, then Aeropostale, and American Eagle Outfitters. Compare these three companies and rank them from top to bottom in performance. Give your reasons for the rankings.

Financial Forecasting

F orecasting for the future has never been easy, but it has been particularly difficult in the highly volatile economic environment of the post-9/11 era. But that doesn't stop Jim Donald, the new CEO of Starbucks, from looking toward a very bright future. The company continues to percolate with brewed coffee, Italian style espresso beverages, teas, and a variety of food items. You may be surprised to know that in 2005, Starbucks employed 96,700 people in 9,200 stores in the United States and throughout the world.

According to CEO Donald, this is just the launching pad for future growth. He suggests that the future long-term goal is for 25,000 to 30,000 stores. The firm opens approximately 1,500 stores a year. He is also looking for revenue growth of 20 percent annually in the next three to five years and bottom-line growth of 23–25 percent.[1]

Some people say he may be saturating the market with Starbucks, but Donald quickly rejects the notion. He maintains there are 165,000 miles of U.S. roadways that haven't been tapped yet by Starbucks, and the company is quickly moving into foreign markets such as Germany, Switzerland, and other European countries. But watch out China! There are 150 Starbucks now in the world's most populated country, but Donald sees the potential for 2,000 stores as the consumption of upscale goods by young, urban consumers is taking off in China. India may be the firm's next major target.

Of course, not all firms are as fortunate as Starbucks. During the last decade, firms such as GM, Eastman Kodak, EDS, and others have seen hard times because of missed forecasts.

If there is one talent that is essential to the financial manager, it is the ability to plan ahead and to make necessary adjustments before actual events occur. We

---

[1]"Starbucks: The Next Generation," *Fortune,* April 4, 2005, p.30.

likely could construct the same set of external events for two corporations (inflation, recession, severe new competition, and so on), and one firm would survive, while the other would not. The outcome might be a function not only of their risk-taking desires, but also of their ability to hedge against risk with careful planning.

While we may assume that no growth or a decline in volume is the primary cause for a shortage of funds, this is not necessarily the case. A rapidly growing firm may witness a significant increase in accounts receivable, inventory, and plant and equipment that cannot be financed in the normal course of business. Assume sales go from $100,000 to $200,000 in one year for a firm that has a 5 percent profit margin on sales. At the same time, assume assets represent 50 percent of sales and go from $50,000 to $100,000 as sales double. The $10,000 of profit (5 percent × $200,000) will hardly be adequate to finance the $50,000 asset growth. The remaining $40,000 must come from suppliers, the bank, and perhaps stockholders. The student should recognize that profit alone is generally inadequate to finance significant growth and a comprehensive financing plan must be developed. Too often, the small businessperson (and sometimes the big one as well) is mystified by an increase in sales and profits but less cash in the till.

Constructing Pro Forma Statements

The most comprehensive means of financial forecasting is to develop a series of pro forma, or projected, financial statements. We will give particular attention to the **pro forma income statement**, the **cash budget**, and the **pro forma balance sheet**. Based on the projected statements, the firm is able to estimate its future level of receivables, inventory, payables, and other corporate accounts as well as its anticipated profits and borrowing requirements. The financial officer can then carefully track actual events against the plan and make necessary adjustments. Furthermore, the statements are often required by bankers and other lenders as a guide for the future.

A systems approach is necessary to develop pro forma statements. We first construct a pro forma income statement based on sales projections and the production plan, then translate this material into a cash budget, and finally assimilate all previously developed material into a pro forma balance sheet. The process of developing pro forma financial statements is depicted in Figure 4–1. We will use a six-month time frame to facilitate the analysis, though the same procedures could be extended to one year or longer.

Pro Forma Income Statement

Assume the Goldman Corporation has been asked by its bank to provide pro forma financial statements for midyear 2008. The pro forma income statement will provide a projection of how much profit the firm anticipates making over the ensuing time period. In developing the pro forma income statement, we will follow four important steps.

1. Establish a sales projection.
2. Determine a production schedule and the associated use of new material, direct labor, and overhead to arrive at gross profit.
3. Compute other expenses.
4. Determine profit by completing the actual pro forma statement.

Establish a Sales Projection

For purposes of analysis, we shall assume the Goldman Corporation has two primary products: wheels and casters. Our sales projection calls for the sale of 1,000 wheels and 2,000 casters at prices of $30 and $35, respectively. As indicated in Table 4–1, we anticipate total sales of $100,000.

Figure 4–1

Development of pro forma statements

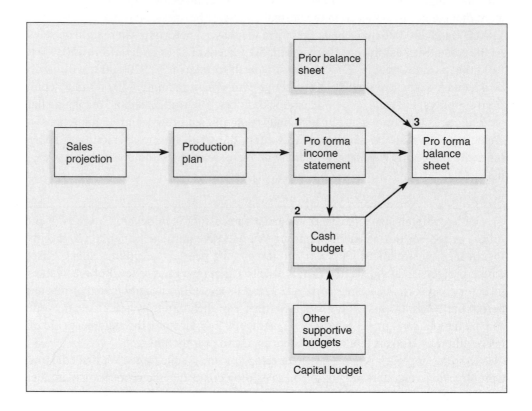

Table 4–1

Projected wheel and caster sales (first six months, 2008)

	Wheels	Casters
Quantity	1,000	2,000
Sales price	$30	$35
Sales revenue	$30,000	$70,000
Total		$100,000

Determine a Production Schedule and the Gross Profit

Based on anticipated sales, we determine the necessary production plan for the six-month period. The number of units produced will depend on the beginning inventory of wheels and casters, our sales projection, and the desired level of ending inventory. Assume that on January 1, 2008, the Goldman Corporation has in stock the items shown in Table 4–2.

	Wheels	Casters	
Quantity............	85	180	
Cost..............	$16	$20	
Total value.........	$1,360	$3,600	
Total......................................			$4,960

Table 4–2
Stock of beginning inventory

We will add the projected quantity of unit sales for the next six months to our desired ending inventory and subtract our stock of beginning inventory (in units) to determine our production requirements. This process is illustrated below.

Units
+ Projected sales
+ Desired ending inventory
− Beginning inventory
= Production requirements

Following this process, in Table 4–3 we see a required production level of 1,015 wheels and 2,020 casters.

	Wheels	Casters
Projected unit sales (Table 4–1)...................	+1,000	+2,000
Desired ending inventory (assumed to represent 10% of unit sales for the time period).............	+100	+200
Beginning inventory (Table 4–2).................	−85	−180
Units to be produced...........................	1,015	2,020

Table 4–3
Production requirements for six months

Sales Forecasting: Where Marketing and Finance Come Together

All the financial analysis in the world can prove useless if a firm does not have a meaningful sales projection. To the extent that the firm has an incorrect sales projection, an inappropriate amount of inventory will be accumulated, projections of accounts receivable and accounts payable will be wrong, and profits and cash flow will be off target. Although a corporate treasurer may understand all the variables influencing income statements, balance sheets, cash budgets, and so on, he or she is out of luck if the sales projection is wrong.

While statistical techniques such as regression and time series analysis may be employed to project sales, it is the marketing staff who are best able to predict future sales. For example, the executives at the Radio Shack Corporation look to the salespeople in their thousands of stores across the country to determine the sales projections for various products. These are the people that are closest to the customer on a daily basis and know which electrical components and products are currently in demand and which are not. Salespeople are also able to judge the economic mood of customers. While an innovative cellular telephone design may bring praise from window shoppers, the question remains, "Is it within the economic boundaries of what customers can afford?" Shoppers vote with their dollars and the salesforce is best able to tabulate the vote count.

Over the last two decades, the marketing profession has developed many sophisticated techniques for analyzing and projecting future sales, and it is important that the financial manager look to the marketing staff to help supply the essential variable for financial forecasting.

finance in
action

www.radioshack.com

We must now determine the cost to produce these units. In previously mentioned Table 4–2 on page 95 we see that the cost of units in stock was $16 for wheels and $20 for casters. However, we shall assume the price of materials, labor, and overhead going into the new products is now $18 for wheels and $22 for casters, as indicated in Table 4–4.

Table 4–4

Unit costs

	Wheels	Casters
Materials...............	$10	$12
Labor.................	5	6
Overhead	3	4
Total................	$18	$22

The *total* cost to produce the required new items for the next six months is shown in Table 4–5.

Table 4–5

Total production costs

	Wheels	Casters	
Units to be produced (Table 4–3)..........	1,015	2,020	
Cost per unit (Table 4–4)	$18	$22	
Total cost	$18,270	$44,440	$62,710

Cost of Goods Sold   The main consideration in constructing a pro forma income statement is the costs specifically associated with units sold during the time period (the **cost of goods sold**). Note that in the case of wheels we anticipate sales of 1,000 units, as indicated in Table 4–1 on page 94, but are producing 1,015, as indicated in Table 4–3, to increase our inventory level by 15 units. For profit measurement purposes, we will *not* charge these extra 15 units against current sales.[2] Furthermore, in determining the cost of the 1,000 units sold during the current time period, we will *not* assume that all of the items sold represent inventory manufactured in this period. We shall assume the Goldman Corporation uses FIFO (first-in, first-out) accounting and it will first allocate the cost of current sales to beginning inventory and then to goods manufactured during the period.

In Table 4–6, we look at the revenue, associated cost of goods sold, and gross profit for both products. For example, 1,000 units of wheels are to be sold at a total revenue of $30,000. Of the 1,000 units, 85 units are from beginning inventory at a $16 cost, and the balance of 915 units is from current production at an $18 cost. The total cost of goods sold for wheels is $17,830, yielding a gross profit of $12,170. The pattern is the same for casters, with sales of $70,000, cost of goods sold of $43,640, and gross profit of $26,360. The combined sales for the two products are $100,000, with cost of goods sold of $61,470 and gross profit of $38,530.

At this point, we also compute the value of ending inventory for later use in constructing financial statements. As indicated in Table 4–7 the value of ending inventory will be $6,200.

---

[2]Later in the analysis we will show the effect these extra units have on the cash budget and the balance sheet.

	Wheels	Casters	Combined
Quantity sold (Table 4–1)	1,000	2,000	3,000
Sales price	$30	$35	
Sales revenue	$30,000	$70,000	$100,000
Cost of goods sold:			
Old inventory (Table 4–2)			
Quantity (units)	85	180	
Cost per unit	$16	$20	
Total	$ 1,360	$ 3,600	
New inventory (the remainder)			
Quantity (units).	915	1,820	
Cost per unit (Table 4–4)	$18	$22	
Total	16,470	40,040	
Total cost of goods sold	17,830	43,640	$ 61,470
Gross profit	$12,170	$26,360	$ 38,530

Table 4–6
Allocation of manufacturing cost and determination of gross profits

+ Beginning inventory (Table 4–2).	$ 4,960
+ Total production costs (Table 4–5)	62,710
Total inventory available for sales	67,670
− Cost of goods sold (Table 4–6)	61,470
Ending inventory	$ 6,200

Table 4–7
Value of ending inventory

Other Expense Items

Having computed total revenue, cost of goods sold, and gross profits, we must now subtract other expense items to arrive at a net profit figure. We deduct general and administrative expenses as well as interest expenses from gross profit to arrive at earnings before taxes, then subtract taxes to determine aftertax income, and finally deduct dividends to ascertain the contribution to retained earnings. For the Goldman Corporation, we shall assume general and administrative expenses are $12,000, interest expense is $1,500, and dividends are $1,500.

Actual Pro Forma Income Statement

Combining the gross profit in Table 4–6 with our assumptions on other expense items, we arrive at the pro forma income statement presented in Table 4–8. As shown toward the bottom of the table, we anticipate earnings after taxes of $20,024, dividends of $1,500, and an increase in retained earnings of $18,524.

Cash Budget

As previously indicated, the generation of sales and profits does not necessarily ensure there will be adequate cash on hand to meet financial obligations as they come due. A profitable sale may generate accounts receivable in the short run but no immediate cash to meet maturing obligations. For this reason, we must translate the pro forma income

Table 4–8

<table>
<tr><td colspan="2" align="center">**Pro Forma Income Statement**
June 30, 2008</td></tr>
<tr><td>Sales revenue. . . . .</td><td>$100,000</td></tr>
<tr><td>Cost of goods sold . . . .</td><td>61,470</td></tr>
<tr><td>Gross profit. . . . .</td><td>38,530</td></tr>
<tr><td>General and administrative expense . . . .</td><td>12,000</td></tr>
<tr><td>Operating profit (EBIT) . . . .</td><td>26,530</td></tr>
<tr><td>Interest expense. . . . .</td><td>1,500</td></tr>
<tr><td>Earnings before taxes (EBT) . . . .</td><td>25,030</td></tr>
<tr><td>Taxes (20%)* . . . .</td><td>5,006</td></tr>
<tr><td>Earnings after taxes (EAT) . . . .</td><td>20,024</td></tr>
<tr><td>Common stock dividends . . . .</td><td>1,500</td></tr>
<tr><td>Increase in retained earnings. . . . .</td><td>$ 18,524</td></tr>
<tr><td colspan="2">*20 percent is applied for simplicity.</td></tr>
</table>

statement into cash flows. In this process we divide the longer-term pro forma income statement into smaller and more precise time frames to anticipate the seasonal and monthly patterns of cash inflows and outflows. Some months may represent particularly high or low sales volume or may require dividends, taxes, or capital expenditures.

Cash Receipts

In the case of the Goldman Corporation, we break down the pro forma income statement for the first half of the year 2008 into a series of monthly cash budgets. In Table 4–1 on page 94, we showed anticipated sales of $100,000 over this time period; we shall now assume these sales can be divided into monthly projections, as indicated in Table 4–9.

Table 4–9

Monthly sales pattern

January	February	March	April	May	June
$15,000	$10,000	$15,000	$25,000	$15,000	$20,000

A careful analysis of past sales and collection records indicates 20 percent of sales is collected in the month of sales and 80 percent in the following month. The cash receipt pattern related to monthly sales is shown in Table 4–10. It is assumed that sales for December 2007 were $12,000.

The cash inflows will vary between $11,000 and $23,000, with the high point in receipts coming in May.

We now examine the monthly outflows.

Cash Payments

The primary considerations for cash payments are monthly costs associated with inventory manufactured during the period (material, labor, and overhead) and disbursements for general and administrative expenses, interest payments, taxes, and dividends. We

Table 4–10   Monthly cash receipts

	December	January	February	March	April	May	June
Sales.................	$12,000	$15,000	$10,000	$15,000	$25,000	$15,000	$20,000
Collections:							
(20% of current sales)...		$ 3,000	$ 2,000	$ 3,000	$ 5,000	$ 3,000	$ 4,000
Collections:							
(80% of previous							
month's sales)		9,600	12,000	8,000	12,000	20,000	12,000
Total cash receipts....		$12,600	$14,000	$11,000	$17,000	$23,000	$16,000

must also consider cash payments for any new plant and equipment, an item that does not show up on our pro forma income statement. Costs associated with units manufactured during the period may be taken from the data provided in Table 4–5 on page 96. In Table 4–11, we simply recast these data in terms of material, labor, and overhead.

Table 4–11   Component costs of manufactured goods

	Wheels			Casters			
	Units Produced	Cost per Unit	Total Cost	Units Produced	Cost per Unit	Total Cost	Combined Cost
Materials.....	1,015	$10	$10,150	2,020	$12	$24,240	$34,390
Labor........	1,015	5	5,075	2,020	6	12,120	17,195
Overhead	1,015	3	3,045	2,020	4	8,080	11,125
							$62,710

We see that the total costs for components in the two products in Table 4–11 are materials, $34,390; labor, $17,195; and overhead, $11,125. We shall assume all these costs are incurred on an equal monthly basis over the six-month period. Even though the sales volume varies from month to month, we assume we are employing level monthly production to ensure maximum efficiency in the use of various productive resources. Average monthly costs for materials, labor, and overhead are as shown in Table 4–12.

	Total Costs	Time Frame	Average Monthly Cost
Materials	$34,390	6 months	$5,732
Labor...............	17,195	6 months	2,866
Overhead	11,125	6 months	1,854

Table 4–12
Average monthly manufacturing costs

We shall pay for materials one month after the purchase has been made. Labor and overhead represent direct monthly cash outlays, as is true of interest, taxes, dividends, and the purchases of $8,000 in new equipment in February and $10,000 in June. We summarize all of our cash payments in Table 4–13. Past records indicate that $4,500 in materials was purchased in December.

Table 4–13   Summary of all monthly cash payments

	December	January	February	March	April	May	June
From Table 4–12:							
Monthly material purchase	$4,500	$ 5,732	$ 5,732	$ 5,732	$ 5,732	$ 5,732	$ 5,732
Payment for material (prior month's purchase)		$ 4,500	$ 5,732	$ 5,732	$ 5,732	$ 5,732	$ 5,732
Monthly labor cost		2,866	2,866	2,866	2,866	2,866	2,866
Monthly overhead		1,854	1,854	1,854	1,854	1,854	1,854
From Table 4–8:							
General and administrative expense ($12,000 over 6 months)		2,000	2,000	2,000	2,000	2,000	2,000
Interest expense							1,500
Taxes (two equal payments)				2,503			2,503
Cash dividend							1,500
Also:							
New equipment purchases			8,000				10,000
Total payments		$11,220	$20,452	$14,955	$12,452	$12,452	$27,953

Actual Budget

We are now in a position to bring together our monthly cash receipts and payments into a cash flow statement, illustrated in Table 4–14. The difference between monthly receipts and payments is net cash flow for the month.

Table 4–14   Monthly cash flow

	January	February	March	April	May	June
Total receipts (Table 4–10)	$12,600	$14,000	$11,000	$17,000	$23,000	$16,000
Total payments (Table 4–13)	11,220	20,452	14,955	12,452	12,452	27,953
Net cash flow	$ 1,380	($ 6,452)	($ 3,955)	$ 4,548	$10,548	($11,953)

The primary purpose of the cash budget is to allow the firm to anticipate the need for outside funding at the end of each month. In the present case, we shall assume the Goldman Corporation wishes to have a minimum cash balance of $5,000 at all times. If it goes below this amount, the firm will borrow funds from the bank. If it goes above $5,000 and the firm has a loan outstanding, it will use the excess funds to reduce the loan. This pattern of financing is demonstrated in Table 4–15—a fully developed cash budget with borrowing and repayment provisions.

Table 4–15 Cash budget with borrowing and repayment provisions

	January	February	March	April	May	June
1. Net cash flow	$1,380	($6,452)	($3,955)	$4,548	$10,548	($11,953)
2. Beginning cash balance	5,000*	6,380	5,000	5,000	5,000	11,069
3. Cumulative cash balance	6,380	(72)	1,045	9,548	15,548	(884)
4. Monthly loan (or repayment)	—	5,072	3,955	(4,548)	(4,479)	5,884
5. Cumulative loan balance	—	5,072	9,027	4,479	—	5,884
6. Ending cash balance	6,380	5,000	5,000	5,000	11,069	5,000

*We assume the Goldman Corporation has a beginning cash balance of $5,000 on January 1, 2008, and it desires a minimum monthly ending cash balance of $5,000.

The first line in Table 4–15 shows net cash flow (from Table 4–14), which is added to the beginning cash balance to arrive at the cumulative cash balance. The fourth entry is the additional monthly loan or loan repayment, if any, required to maintain a minimum cash balance of $5,000. To keep track of our loan balance, the fifth entry represents cumulative loans outstanding for all months. Finally, we show the cash balance at the end of the month, which becomes the beginning cash balance for the next month.

At the end of January the firm has $6,380 in cash, but by the end of February the cumulative cash position of the firm is negative, necessitating a loan of $5,072 to maintain a $5,000 cash balance. The firm has a loan on the books until May, at which time there is an ending cash balance of $11,069. During the months of April and May the cumulative cash balance is greater than the required minimum cash balance of $5,000, so loan repayments of $4,548 and $4,479 are made to retire the loans completely in May. In June the firm is once again required to borrow $5,884 to maintain a $5,000 cash balance.

Pro Forma Balance Sheet

Now that we have developed a pro forma income statement and a cash budget, it is relatively simple to integrate all of these items into a pro forma balance sheet. Because the balance sheet represents cumulative changes in the corporation over time, we first examine the *prior* period's balance sheet and then translate these items through time to represent June 30, 2008. The last balance sheet, dated December 31, 2007, is shown in Table 4–16.

In constructing our pro forma balance sheet for June 30, 2008, some of the accounts from the old balance sheet will remain unchanged, while others will take on new values, as indicated by the pro forma income statement and cash budget. The process is depicted in Figure 4–2.

We present the new pro forma balance sheet as of June 30, 2008, in Table 4–17 on page 103.

Explanation of Pro Forma Balance Sheet

Each item in Table 4–17 can be explained on the basis of a prior calculation or assumption. The explanations begin on the bottom of page 102.

Table 4–16

Balance Sheet December 31, 2007	
Assets	
Current assets:	
Cash	$ 5,000
Marketable securities	3,200
Accounts receivable	9,600
Inventory	4,960
Total current assets	22,760
Plant and equipment	27,740
Total assets	$50,500
Liabilities and Stockholders' Equity	
Accounts payable	$ 4,500
Notes payable	0
Long-term debt	15,000
Common stock	10,500
Retained earnings	20,500
Total liabilities and stockholders' equity	$50,500

Figure 4–2

Development of a pro forma balance sheet

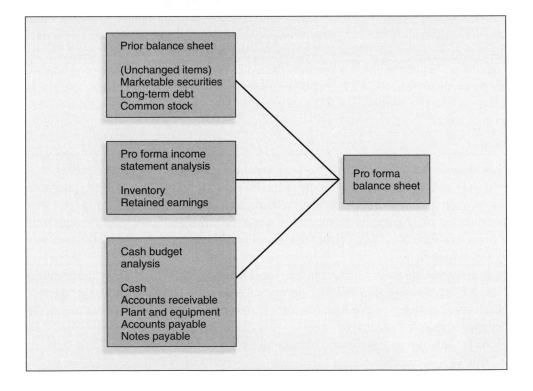

1. Cash ($5,000)—minimum cash balance as shown in Table 4–15.
2. Marketable securities ($3,200)—remains unchanged from prior period's value in Table 4–16.

Table 4–17

Pro Forma Balance Sheet
June 30, 2008

Assets

Current assets:

1. Cash.	$ 5,000
2. Marketable securities	3,200
3. Accounts receivable.	16,000
4. Inventory	6,200
Total current assets	30,400
5. Plant and equipment	45,740
Total assets	$76,140

Liabilities and Stockholders' Equity

6. Accounts payable.	$ 5,732
7. Notes payable	5,884
8. Long-term debt.	15,000
9. Common stock	10,500
10. Retained earnings	39,024
Total liabilities and stockholders' equity	$76,140

3. Accounts receivable ($16,000)—based on June sales of $20,000 in Table 4–10. Twenty percent will be collected that month, while 80 percent will become accounts receivable at the end of the month.

$20,000	Sales
× 80%	
$16,000	Receivables

4. Inventory ($6,200)—ending inventory as shown in Table 4–7.

5. Plant and equipment ($45,740).

Initial value (Table 4–16)	$27,740
Purchases* (Table 4–13)	18,000
Plant and equipment	$45,740

*For simplicity, depreciation is not explicitly considered.

6. Accounts payable ($5,732)—based on June purchases in Table 4–13. They will not be paid until July, and thus are accounts payable.

7. Notes payable ($5,884)—the amount that must be borrowed to maintain the cash balance of $5,000, as shown in Table 4–15.

8. Long-term debt ($15,000)—remains unchanged from prior period's value in Table 4–16.

9. Common stock ($10,500)—remains unchanged from prior period's value in Table 4–16.

10. Retained earnings ($39,024)—initial value plus pro forma income.

Initial value (Table 4–16).	$20,500
Transfer of pro forma income to retained earnings (Table 4–8)	18,524
Retained earnings	$39,024

Analysis of Pro Forma Statement

In comparing the pro forma balance sheet (Table 4–17) to the prior balance sheet (Table 4–16), we note that assets are up by $25,640.

Total assets (June 30, 2005)	$76,140
Total assets (Dec. 31, 2004)	50,500
Increase.	$25,640

The growth was financed by accounts payable, notes payable, and profit (as reflected by the increase in retained earnings). Though the company will enjoy a high degree of profitability, it must still look to bank financing of $5,884 (shown as notes payable in Table 4–17) to support the increase in assets. This represents the difference between the $25,640 buildup in assets, and the $1,232 increase in accounts payable as well as the $18,524 buildup in retained earnings.

Percent-of-Sales Method

An alternative to tracing cash and accounting flows to determine financial needs is to assume that accounts on the balance sheet will maintain a given percentage relationship to sales. We then indicate a change in the sales level and ascertain our related financing needs. This is known as the **percent-of-sales method**. For example, for the Howard Corporation, introduced in Table 4–18, we show the following balance sheet accounts in dollars and their percent of sales, based on a sales volume of $200,000.

Table 4–18

HOWARD CORPORATION
Balance Sheet and Percent-of-Sales Table

Assets		Liabilities and Stockholders' Equity	
Cash	$ 5,000	Accounts payable	$ 40,000
Accounts receivables	40,000	Accrued expenses.	10,000
Inventory	25,000	Notes payable	15,000
Total current assets	$ 70,000	Common stock.	10,000
Plant and equipment	50,000	Retained earnings	45,000
		Total liabilities and	
Total assets	$120,000	stockholders' equity	$120,000

$200,000 Sales
Percent of Sales

Cash	2.5%	Accounts payable	20.0%
Accounts receivable.	20.0	Accrued expenses	5.0
Inventory	12.5		25.0%
Total current assets	35.0		
Plant and equipment	25.0		
	60.0%		

Cash of $5,000 represents 2.5 percent of sales of $200,000; receivables of $40,000 are 20 percent of sales; and so on. No percentages are computed for notes payable, common stock, and retained earnings because they are not assumed to maintain a direct relationship with sales volume.

Once we know how much money we need to finance our growth, we will then decide whether to finance the sales growth with notes payable, sale of common stock, or use long-term debt. There are two possible scenarios for our calculations. First, if the company is operating at full capacity, it will need to buy new plant and equipment to produce more goods to sell. If the company is operating at less than full capacity, it has the ability to increase sales with its current plant and equipment and so it will only need to add more current assets to increase its sales.

In the case of full capacity, any dollar increase in sales will necessitate a 35 percent increase in current assets, as well as a 25 percent increase in plant and equipment. These percentages are found computed in Table 4–18. Of this 60 percent, 25 percent will be spontaneously or automatically financed through accounts payable and accrued expenses, leaving 35 percent to be financed by profit or additional outside sources of financing. We will assume the Howard Corporation has an aftertax return of 6 percent on the sales dollar and 50 percent of profits are paid out as dividends.[3]

If sales increase from $200,000 to $300,000, the $100,000 increase in sales will necessitate $35,000 (35 percent) in additional financing. Since we will earn 6 percent on total sales of $300,000, we will show a profit of $18,000. With a 50 percent dividend payout, $9,000 will remain for internal financing. This means $26,000 out of the $35,000 must be financed from outside sources. Our formula to determine the need for new funds is:

Required new funds—

$$(\text{RNF}) = \frac{A}{S}(\Delta S) - \frac{L}{S}(\Delta S) - PS_2(1 - D) \qquad (4-1)$$

where

$\dfrac{A}{S}$ = Percentage relationship of variable assets to sales [60%]

ΔS = Change in sales [$100,000]

$\dfrac{L}{S}$ = Percentage relationship of variable liabilities to sales [25%]

P = Profit margin [6%]

S_2 = New sales level [$300,000]

D = Dividend payout ratio [0.50]

Plugging in the values, we show:

RNF = 60% ($100,000) − 25% ($100,000) − 6% ($300,000) (1 − .50)

    = $60,000 − $25,000 − $18,000 (.50)

    = $35,000 − $9,000

    = $26,000 required sources of new funds

Presumably the $26,000 can be financed at the bank or through some other appropriate source.

---

[3]Some may wish to add back depreciation under the percent-of-sales method. Most, however, choose the assumption that funds generated through depreciation (in the sources and uses of funds sense) must be used to replace the fixed assets to which depreciation is applied.

What if the company is operating at less than full capacity and doesn't need to buy new plant and equipment. This often happens when the economy is coming out of a recession. In this case we will only need to increase our assets by the 35 percent of spontaneous current assets. Repeating the equation:

$$
\begin{aligned}
\text{RNF} &= 35\% \ (\$100,000) - 25\% \ (\$100,000) - 6\% \ (\$300,000) \ (1 - .50) \\
&= \$35,000 - \$25,000 - \$18,000 \ (.50) \\
&= \$35,000 - \$25,000 - \$9,000 \\
&= \$1,000 \ \text{required sources of new funds.}
\end{aligned}
$$

Notice that when we don't need to buy new equipment, the required new funds amount drops significantly. In this case we only need an extra $1,000 of financing.

Using the percent-of-sales method is much easier than tracing through the various cash flows to arrive at the pro forma statements. Nevertheless, the output is much less meaningful and we do not get a month-to-month breakdown of the data. The percent-of-sales method is a broad-brush approach, while the development of pro forma statements is more exacting. Of course, whatever method we use, the results are only as meaningful or reliable as the assumptions about sales and production that went into the numbers.

Summary

Financial forecasting allows the financial manager to anticipate events before they occur, particularly the need for raising funds externally. An important consideration is that growth may call for additional sources of financing because profit is often inadequate to cover the net buildup in receivables, inventory, and other asset accounts.

A systems approach is necessary to develop pro forma statements. We first construct a pro forma income statement based on sales projections and the production plan, then translate this material into a cash budget, and finally assimilate all previously developed material into a pro forma balance sheet.

An alternative to tracing cash and accounting flows to determine financial needs is to assume that accounts on the balance sheet will maintain a given percentage relationship to sales. We can then indicate a change in the sales level and ascertain our related financing needs. This is known as the percent-of-sales method.

Regardless of what method is used to forecast the future financial needs of the firm (whether it is pro forma financial statements or the percent-of-sales method), the end product is the determination of the amount of new funds needed to finance the activities of the firm.

For firms that are in highly seasonal businesses, it is particularly important to identify peaks and slowdowns in the activities of the firm and the associated financial requirements.

List of Terms

pro forma income statement 93	cost of goods sold 96
cash budget 93	percent-of-sales method 104
pro forma balance sheet 93	

1. What are the basic benefits and purposes of developing pro forma statements and a cash budget?

2. Explain how the collections and purchases schedules are related to the borrowing needs of the corporation.

3. With inflation, what are the implications of using LIFO and FIFO inventory methods? How do they affect the cost of goods sold?

4. Explain the relationship between inventory turnover and purchasing needs.

5. Rapid corporate growth in sales and profits can cause financing problems. Elaborate on this statement.

6. Discuss the advantage and disadvantage of level production schedules in firms with cyclical sales.

7. What conditions would help make a percent-of-sales forecast almost as accurate as pro forma financial statements and cash budgets?

**Practice
Problems and
Solutions**

Cost of goods
sold—FIFO and
LIFO

Schedule of cash
receipts

1. At the end of January, Medical Products Corp. had 625 units in inventory, which had cost $15 to produce. During February, the firm produced 550 units at a cost of $20 per unit. If the firm sold 800 units in February, what was the cost of goods sold?

   a. Assume FIFO inventory accounting

   b. Assume LIFO inventory accounting.

2. Eaton Stores has forecast credit sales for the fourth quarter of the year as:

September (actual)	$100,000
Fourth Quarter	
October.	$ 70,000
November	50,000
December	80,000

   Experience has shown that 30 percent of sales receipts are collected in the month of sale and 60 percent in the following month, and 10 percent are never collected. Prepare a schedule of cash receipts for Eaton Stores covering the fourth quarter (October through December).

Solutions

1. *a.* FIFO Accounting

   Cost of goods sold on 800 units

Old inventory:		
Quantity (units)	625	
Cost per unit	$15	
Total		$ 9,375
New inventory:		
Quantity (units)	175	
Cost per unit	$20	
Total		3,500
Total cost of goods sold		$12,875

b.   LIFO Accounting

Cost of goods sold on 800 units

New inventory:		
Quantity (units)	550	
Cost per unit	$20	
Total		$11,000
Old inventory:		
Quantity (units)	250	
Cost per unit	$15	
Total		3,750
Total cost of goods sold		$14,750

2.

	September	October	November	December
Sales.	$100,000	$70,000	$50,000	$80,000
Collections:				
(30% of current sales).		21,000	15,000	24,000
Collections:				
(60% of previous month's				
sales)		60,000	42,000	30,000
Total cash receipts		$81,000	$57,000	$54,000

The 10 percent that are never collected does not go into the schedule of cash receipts.

Problems

■Ⅴ™
■ⓥ All problems are available in Homework Manager. Please see the preface for more information.

Growth and financing

1.   Philip Morris is excited because sales for his clothing company are expected to double from $500,000 to $1,000,000 next year. Philip notes that net assets (Assets − Liabilities) will remain at 50 percent of Sales. His clothing firm will enjoy a 9 percent return on total sales. He will start the year with $100,000 in the bank and is already bragging about the two Mercedes he will buy and the European vacation he will take. Does his optimistic outlook for his cash position appear to be correct?

Compute his likely cash balance or deficit for the end of the year. Start with beginning cash and subtract the asset buildup (equal to 50 percent of the sales increase) and add in profit.

Growth and financing

2.   In Problem 1 if there had been no increase in sales and all other facts were the same, what would Philip's ending cash balance be? What lesson do the examples in Problems 1 and 2 illustrate?

Sales projections

3.   The Alliance Corp. expects to sell the following number of units of copper cables at the prices indicated, under three different scenarios in the economy. The probability of each outcome is indicated. What is the expected value of the total sales projection?

Outcome	Probability	Units	Price
A	0.30	200	$15
B	0.50	320	30
C	0.20	410	40

4. Bronco Truck Parts expects to sell the following number of units at the prices indicated under three different scenarios in the economy. The probability of each outcome is indicated. What is the expected value of the total sales projection?

Sales projections

Outcome	Probability	Units	Price
A	0.20	300	$16
B	0.50	500	$25
C	0.30	1,000	$30

5. Cyber Security Systems had sales of 3,000 units at $50 per unit last year. The marketing manager projects a 20 percent increase in unit volume sales this year with a 10 percent price increase. Returned merchandise will represent 6 percent of total sales. What is your net dollar sales projection for this year?

Sales projections

6. Dodge Ball Bearings had sales of 10,000 units at $20 per unit last year. The marketing manager projects a 30 percent increase in unit volume sales this year with a 5 percent price decrease (due to a price reduction by a competitor). Returned merchandise will represent 3 percent of total sales. What is your net dollar sales projection for this year?

Sales projections

7. Sales for Western Boot Stores are expected to be 40,000 units for October. The company likes to maintain 15 percent of unit sales for each month in ending inventory (i.e., the end of October). Beginning inventory for October is 8,500 units. How many units should Western Boot produce for the coming month?

Production requirements

8. Vitale Hair Spray had sales of 8,000 units in March. A 50 percent increase is expected in April. The company will maintain 5 percent of expected unit sales for April in ending inventory. Beginning inventory for April was 400 units. How many units should the company produce in April?

Production requirements

9. Delsing Plumbing Company has beginning inventory of 14,000 units, will sell 50,000 units for the month, and desires to reduce ending inventory to 40 percent of beginning inventory. How many units should Delsing produce?

Production requirements

10. On December 31 of last year, Wolfson Corporation had in inventory 400 units of its product, which cost $21 per unit to produce. During January, the company produced 800 units at a cost of $24 per unit. Assuming that Wolfson Corporation sold 700 units in January, what was the cost of goods sold (assume FIFO inventory accounting)?

Cost of goods sold—FIFO

11. At the end of January, Higgins Data Systems had an inventory of 600 units, which cost $16 per unit to produce. During February the company produced 850 units at a cost of $19 per unit. If the firm sold 1,100 units in February, what was its cost of goods sold (assume LIFO inventory accounting)?

Cost of goods sold—FIFO

12. The Bradley Corporation produces a product with the following costs as of July 1, 2007:

Gross profit and ending inventory

Material.	$ 2 per unit
Labor	4 per unit
Overhead	2 per unit

Beginning inventory at these costs on July 1 was 3,000 units. From July 1 to December 1, 2007, Bradley produced 12,000 units. These units had a material cost of $3, labor of $5, and overhead of $3 per unit. Bradley uses FIFO inventory accounting.

Assuming that Bradley sold 13,000 units during the last six months of the year at $16 each, what is its gross profit? What is the value of ending inventory?

Gross profit and ending inventory

13. Assume in Problem 12 that the Bradley Corporation used LIFO accounting instead of FIFO; what would its gross profit be? What would be the value of ending inventory?

Gross profit and ending inventory

14. Sprint Shoes, Inc., had a beginning inventory of 9,000 units on January 1, 2007. The costs associated with the inventory were:

Material.........	$13.00 per unit
Labor	8.00 per unit
Overhead	6.10 per unit

27.10

During 2007, the firm produced 42,500 units with the following costs:

Material.........	$15.50 per unit
Labor	7.80 per unit
Overhead	8.30 per unit

31.60

Sales for the year were 47,250 units at $39.60 each. Sprint Shoes uses LIFO accounting. What was the gross profit? What was the value of ending inventory?

Schedule of cash receipts

15. Victoria's Apparel has forecast credit sales for the fourth quarter of the year as:

September (actual)........	$50,000
Fourth Quarter	
October................	$40,000
November..............	35,000
December..............	60,000

Experience has shown that 20 percent of sales receipts are collected in the month of sale, 70 percent in the following month, and 10 percent are never collected.

Prepare a schedule of cash receipts for Victoria's Apparel covering the fourth quarter (October through December).

Schedule of cash receipts

16. Simpson Glove Company has made the following sales projections for the next six months. All sales are credit sales.

March	$36,000	June..........	$42,000
April	45,000	July...........	53,000
May..........	27,000	August	57,000

Sales in January and February were $41,000 and $39,000 respectively. Experience has shown that of total sales receipts, 10 percent are uncollectible, 40 percent are collected in the month of sale, 30 percent are collected in the following month, and 20 percent are collected two months after sale.

Prepare a monthly cash receipts schedule for the firm for March through August.

17. Watt's Lighting Stores made the following sales projection for the next six months. All sales are credit sales.

Schedule of cash receipts

March	$30,000	June	$34,000
April	36,000	July	42,000
May.	25,000	August	44,000

Sales in January and February were $33,000 and $32,000, respectively.

Experience has shown that of total sales, 10 percent are uncollectible, 30 percent are collected in the month of sale, 40 percent are collected in the following month, and 20 percent are collected two months after sale.

Prepare a monthly cash receipts schedule for the firm for March through August.

Of the sales expected to be made during the six months from March through August, how much will still be uncollected at the end of August? How much of this is expected to be collected later?

18. Ultravision, Inc., anticipates sales of $240,000 from January through April. Materials will represent 50 percent of sales and because of level production, material purchases will be equal for each month during the four months of January, February, March, and April.

Schedule of cash payments

Materials are paid for one month after the month purchased. Materials purchased in December of last year were $20,000 (half of $40,000 in sales). Labor costs for each of the four months are slightly different due to a provision in the labor contract in which bonuses are paid in February and April. The labor figures are:

January	$10,000
February	13,000
March	10,000
April	15,000

Fixed overhead is $6,000 per month. Prepare a schedule of cash payments for January through April.

19. The Denver Corporation has forecast the following sales for the first seven months of the year:

Schedule of cash payments

January	$10,000	May.	$10,000
February	12,000	June	16,000
March	14,000	July	18,000
April	20,000		

Monthly material purchases are set equal to 30 percent of forecasted sales for the next month. Of the total material costs, 40 percent are paid in the month of purchase and 60 percent in the following month. Labor costs will run $4,000 per month, and fixed overhead is $2,000 per month. Interest payments on the debt will be $3,000 for both March and June. Finally, the Denever salesforce will receive a 1.5 percent commission on total sales for the first six months of the year, to be paid on June 30.

Prepare a monthly summary of cash payments for the six-month period from January through June. (Note: Compute prior December purchases to help get total material payments for January.)

Schedule of cash payments

20. The Boswell Corporation forecasts its sales in units for the next four months as follows:

March	6,000
April	8,000
May	5,500
June	4,000

Boswell maintains an ending inventory for each month in the amount of one and one-half times the expected sales in the following month. The ending inventory for February (March's beginning inventory) reflects this policy. Materials cost $5 per unit and are paid for in the month after production. Labor cost is $10 per unit and is paid for in the month incurred. Fixed overhead is $12,000 per month. Dividends of $20,000 are to be paid in May. Five thousand units were produced in February.

Complete a production schedule and a summary of cash payments for March, April, and May. Remember that production in any one month is equal to sales plus desired ending inventory minus beginning inventory.

Schedule of cash payments

21. The Volt Battery Company has forecast its sales in units as follows:

January	800	May	1,350
February	650	June	1,500
March	600	July	1,200
April	1,100		

Volt Battery always keeps an ending inventory equal to 120 percent of the next month's expected sales. The ending inventory for December (January's beginning inventory) is 960 units, which is consistent with this policy.

Materials cost $12 per unit and are paid for in the month after purchase. Labor cost is $5 per unit and is paid in the month the cost is incurred. Overhead costs are $6,000 per month. Interest of $8,000 is scheduled to be paid in March, and employee bonuses of $13,200 will be paid in June.

Prepare a monthly production schedule and a monthly summary of cash payments for January through June. Volt produced 600 units in December.

Cash budget

22. Lansing Auto Parts, Inc., has projected sales of $25,000 in October, $35,000 in November, and $30,000 in December. Of the company's sales, 20 percent are paid for by cash and 80 percent are sold on credit. The credit sales are collected one month after sale. Determine collections for November and December.

Also assume that the company's cash payments for November and December are $30,400 and $29,800, respectively. The beginning cash balance in November is $6,000, which is the desired minimum balance.

Prepare a cash budget with borrowing needed or repayments for November and December. (You will need to prepare a cash receipts schedule first.)

Complete cash budget

23. Harry's Carryout Stores has eight locations. The firm wishes to expand by two more stores and needs a bank loan to do this. Mr. Wilson, the banker,

will finance construction if the firm can present an acceptable three-month financial plan for January through March. The following are actual and forecasted sales figures:

Actual		Forecast		Additional Information	
November.......	$200,000	January.........	$280,000	April forecast.....	$330,000
December.......	220,000	February........	320,000		
		March..........	340,000		

Of the firm's sales, 40 percent are for cash and the remaining 60 percent are on credit. Of credit sales, 30 percent are paid in the month after sale and 70 percent are paid in the second month after the sale. Materials cost 30 percent of sales and are purchased and received each month in an amount sufficient to cover the following month's expected sales. Materials are paid for in the month after they are received. Labor expense is 40 percent of sales and is paid for in the month of sales. Selling and administrative expense is 5 percent of sales and is also paid in the month of sales. Overhead expense is $28,000 in cash per month.

Depreciation expense is $10,000 per month. Taxes of $8,000 will be paid in January, and dividends of $2,000 will be paid in March. Cash at the beginning of January is $80,000, and the minimum desired cash balance is $75,000.

For January, February, and March, prepare a schedule of monthly cash receipts, monthly cash payments, and a complete monthly cash budget with borrowings and repayments.

24. Archer Electronics Company's actual sales and purchases for April and May are shown here along with forecasted sales and purchases for June through September.

Complete cash budget

	Sales	Purchases
April (actual)...............	$320,000	$130,000
May (actual)...............	300,000	120,000
June (forecast).............	275,000	120,000
July (forecast)	275,000	180,000
August (forecast)	290,000	200,000
September (forecast)	330,000	170,000

The company makes 10 percent of its sales for cash and 90 percent on credit. Of the credit sales, 20 percent are collected in the month after the sale and 80 percent are collected two months later. Archer pays for 40 percent of its purchases in the month after purchase and 60 percent two months after.

Labor expense equals 10 percent of the current month's sales. Overhead expense equals $12,000 per month. Interest payments of $30,000 are due in June and September. A cash dividend of $50,000 is scheduled to be paid in June. Tax payments of $25,000 are due in June and September. There is a scheduled capital outlay of $300,000 in September.

Archer Electronics's ending cash balance in May is $20,000. The minimum desired cash balance is $10,000. Prepare a schedule of monthly cash receipts, monthly cash payments, and a complete monthly cash budget with borrowing and repayments for June through September. The maximum desired cash balance is $50,000. Excess cash (above $50,000) is used to buy marketable securities. Marketable securities are sold before borrowing funds in case of a cash shortfall (less than $10,000).

Percent-of-sales method

25. Owen's Electronics has 9 operating plants in seven southwestern states. Sales for last year were $100 million, and the balance sheet at year-end is similar in percentage of sales to that of previous years (and this will continue in the future). All assets (including fixed assets) and current liabilities will vary directly with sales. The firm is working at full capacity.

Balance Sheet
(in $ millions)

Assets		Liabilities and Stockholders' Equity	
Cash.....................	$ 2	Accounts payable............	$15
Accounts receivable	20	Accrued wages	2
Inventory.................	23	Accrued taxes	8
Current assets..........	$45	Current liabilities...........	$25
Fixed assets	40	Notes payable	10
		Common stock..............	15
		Retained earnings	35
		Total liabilities and	
Total assets..............	$85	stockholders' equity	$85

Owen's has an aftertax profit margin of 7 percent and a dividend payout ratio of 40 percent.

If sales grow by 10 percent next year, determine how many dollars of new funds are needed to finance the growth.

Percent-of-sales method

26. The Manning Company has financial statements as shown below and on page 115, which are representative of the company's historical average.

The firm is expecting a 20 percent increase in sales next year, and management is concerned about the company's need for external funds. The increase in sales is expected to be carried out without any expansion of fixed assets, but rather through more efficient asset utilization in the existing store. Among liabilities, only current liabilities vary directly with sales.

Using the percent-of-sales method, determine whether the company has external financing needs, or a surplus of funds. (Hint: A profit margin and payout ratio must be found from the income statement.)

Income Statement

Sales.............................	$200,000
Expenses	158,000
Earnings before interest and taxes	$ 42,000
Interest	7,000
Earnings before taxes.................	$ 35,000
Taxes	15,000
Earnings after taxes	$ 20,000
Dividends	$ 6,000

Balance Sheet

Assets		Liabilities and Stockholders' Equity	
Cash.	$ 5,000	Accounts payable.	$ 25,000
Accounts receivable	40,000	Accrued wages	1,000
Inventory.	75,000	Accrued taxes	2,000
Current assets.	$120,000	Current liabilities.	$ 28,000
Fixed assets	80,000	Notes payable	7,000
		Long-term debt	15,000
		Common stock.	120,000
		Retained earnings	30,000
		Total liabilities and	
Total assets.	$200,000	stockholders' equity	$200,000

---

27. Conn Man's Shops, Inc., a national clothing chain, had sales of $300 million last year. The business has a steady net profit margin of 8 percent and a dividend payout ratio of 25 percent. The balance sheet for the end of last year is shown below.

Percent-of-sales method

Balance Sheet
End of Year
(in $ millions)

Assets		Liabilities and Stockholders' Equity	
Cash.	$ 20	Accounts payable.	$ 70
Accounts receivable	25	Accrued expenses	20
Inventory.	75	Other payables.	30
Plant and equipment	120	Common stock.	40
		Retained earnings	80
		Total liabilities and	
Total assets	$240	stockholders' equity	$240

The firm's marketing staff has told the president that in the coming year there will be a large increase in the demand for overcoats and wool slacks. A sales increase of 15 percent is forecast for the company.

All balance sheet items are expected to maintain the same percent-of-sales relationships as last year,* except for common stock and retained earnings. No change is scheduled in the number of common stock shares outstanding, and retained earnings will change as dictated by the profits and dividend policy of the firm. (Remember the net profit margin is 8 percent.)

a. Will external financing be required for the company during the coming year?

b. What would be the need for external financing if the net profit margin went up to 9.5 percent and the dividend payout ratio was increased to 50 percent? Explain.

---

*This included fixed assets as the firm is at full capacity.

COMPREHENSIVE PROBLEM

Mansfield Corporation

(external funds requirement)

Mansfield Corporation had 2007 sales of $100 million. The balance sheet items that vary directly with sales and the profit margin are as follows:

	Percent
Cash	5%
Accounts receivable	15
Inventory	20
Net fixed assets	40
Accounts payable	15
Accruals	10
Profit margin after taxes	10%

The dividend payout rate is 50 percent of earnings, and the balance in retained earnings at the end of 2007 was $33 million. Notes payable are currently $7 million. Long-term bonds and common stock are constant at $5 million and $10 million, respectively.

a. How much additional external capital will be required for next year if sales increase 15 percent? (Assume that the company is already operating at full capacity.)

b. What will happen to external fund requirements if Mansfield Corporation reduces the payout ratio, grows at a slower rate, or suffers a decline in its profit margin? Discuss each of these separately.

c. Prepare a pro forma balance sheet for 2008 assuming that any external funds being acquired will be in the form of notes payable. Disregard the information in part *b* in answering this question (that is, use the original information and part *a* in constructing your pro forma balance sheet).

COMPREHENSIVE PROBLEM

Marsh Corporation

(financial forecasting with seasonal production)

The difficult part of solving a problem of this nature is to know what to do with the information contained within a story problem. Therefore, this problem will be easier to complete if you rely on Chapter 4 for the format of all required schedules.

The Marsh Corporation makes standard-size 2-inch fasteners, which it sells for $155 per thousand. Mr. Marsh is the majority owner and manages the inventory and finances of the company. He estimates sales for the following months to be:

January	$263,500 (1,700,000 fasteners)
February	$186,000 (1,200,000 fasteners)
March	$217,000 (1,400,000 fasteners)
April	$310,000 (2,000,000 fasteners)
May	$387,500 (2,500,000 fasteners)

Last year Marsh Corporation's sales were $175,000 in November and $232,500 in December (1,500,000 fasteners).

Mr. Marsh is preparing for a meeting with his banker to arrange the financing for the first quarter. Based on his sales forecast and the following information he has provided, your job as his new financial analyst is to prepare a monthly cash budget, monthly and quarterly pro forma income statements, a pro forma quarterly balance sheet, and all necessary supporting schedules for the first quarter.

Past history shows that Marsh Corporation collects 50 percent of its accounts receivable in the normal 30-day credit period (the month after the sale) and the other 50 percent in 60 days (two months after the sale). It pays for its materials 30 days after receipt. In general, Mr. Marsh likes to keep a two-month supply of inventory in anticipation of sales. Inventory at the beginning of December was 2,600,000 units. (This was not equal to his desired two-month supply.)

The major cost of production is the purchase of raw materials in the form of steel rods, which are cut, threaded, and finished. Last year raw material costs were $52 per 1,000 fasteners, but Mr. Marsh has just been notified that material costs have risen, effective January 1, to $60 per 1,000 fasteners. The Marsh Corporation uses FIFO inventory accounting. Labor costs are relatively constant at $20 per thousand fasteners, since workers are paid on a piecework basis. Overhead is allocated at $10 per thousand units, and selling and administrative expense is 20 percent of sales. Labor expense and overhead are direct cash outflows paid in the month incurred, while interest and taxes are paid quarterly.

The corporation usually maintains a minimum cash balance of $25,000, and it puts its excess cash into marketable securities. The average tax rate is 40 percent, and Mr. Marsh usually pays out 50 percent of net income in dividends to stockholders. Marketable securities are sold before funds are borrowed when a cash shortage is faced. Ignore the interest on any short-term borrowings. Interest on the long-term debt is paid in March, as are taxes and dividends.

As of year-end, the Marsh Corporation balance sheet was as follows:

MARSH CORPORATION
Balance Sheet
December 31, 200X

Assets

Current assets:

Cash	$ 30,000	
Accounts receivable	320,000	
Inventory	237,800	
Total current assets		$ 587,800

Fixed assets:

Plant and equipment	1,000,000	
Less: Accumulated depreciation	200,000	800,000
Total assets		$1,387,800

Liabilities and Stockholders' Equity

Accounts payable	$ 93,600	
Notes payable	0	
Long-term debt, 8 percent	400,000	
Common stock	504,200	
Retained earnings	390,000	
Total liabilities and stockholders' equity	$1,387,800	

WEB EXERCISE

EDS was referred to at the beginning of the chapter as a company who missed out on its financial forecast. Let's learn more about the company. Go to its Web site, www.eds.com, and follow the steps below:

1. Click on "About EDS."

2. Then click on "Company Profile."

3. In one paragraph discuss the profile.

4. Click on EDS company profile under "Next Steps" option. Scroll down to "Did you know? EDS," and list three facts you did not previously know about EDS.

5. Return to the home page. Click on "Investor." Then click on "Earnings Reports."

6. Now click on the two most recent quarterly earnings reports, one at a time. Does the company appear to be doing better now in achieving its goals? Write a two-paragraph summary.

Note: From time to time, companies redesign their Web sites and occasionally a topic we have listed may have been deleted, updated, or moved into a different location. If you click on the site map or site index, you will be introduced to a table of contents which should aid you in finding the topic you are looking for.

5

Operating and Financial Leverage

In the physical sciences as well as in politics, the term **leverage** has been popularized to mean the use of special force and effects to produce more than normal results from a given course of action. In business the same concept is applied, with the emphasis on the employment of fixed cost items in anticipation of magnifying returns at high levels of operation. The student should recognize that leverage is a two-edged sword—producing highly favorable results when things go well, and quite the opposite under negative conditions.

Just ask the airline industry. Firms such as American Airlines, Continental, Delta, Southwest, and UAL were all flying high at the turn of the century because of favorable economic conditions, high capacity utilization, and relatively low interest rates on debt. Such was not the case in the next decade when high leverage in the form of high-cost fixed assets (airplanes) and high-cost debt was causing severe consequences in a weak economy. Among the affected firms is Atlanta-based Delta Airlines.

Between 2000 and 2005, Delta saw its EPS go from $6.87 to a negative $12.80. That's a pretty scary ride for any company. Delta had to take Chapter 11 bankruptcy on September 14, 2005, although its planes are still flying on a more limited basis under court supervision.

It is widely believed that massive consolidations (mergers) between the weak and the strong within the airline industry will be necessary the next time the warning light on the economy comes on because of the high leverage in the industry.

119

Leverage in a Business

Assume you are approached with an opportunity to start your own business. You are to manufacture and market industrial parts, such as ball bearings, wheels, and casters. You are faced with two primary decisions.

First, you must determine the amount of fixed cost plant and equipment you wish to use in the production process. By installing modern, sophisticated equipment, you can virtually eliminate labor in the production of inventory. At high volume, you will do quite well, as most of your costs are fixed. At low volume, however, you could face difficulty in making your fixed payments for plant and equipment. If you decide to use expensive labor rather than machinery, you will lessen your opportunity for profit, but at the same time you will lower your exposure to risk (you can lay off part of the workforce).

Second, you must determine how you will finance the business. If you rely on debt financing and the business is successful, you will generate substantial profits as an owner, paying only the fixed costs of debt. Of course, if the business starts off poorly, the contractual obligations related to debt could mean bankruptcy. As an alternative, you might decide to sell equity rather than borrow, a step that will lower your own profit potential (you must share with others) but minimize your risk exposure.

In both decisions, you are making very explicit decisions about the use of leverage. To the extent that you go with a heavy commitment to fixed costs in the operation of the firm, you are employing operating leverage. To the extent that you utilize debt in the financing of the firm, you are engaging in financial leverage. We shall carefully examine each type of leverage and then show the combined effect of both.

Operating Leverage

Operating leverage reflects the extent to which fixed assets and associated fixed costs are utilized in the business. As indicated in Table 5–1, a firm's operational costs may be classified as fixed, variable, or semivariable.

Table 5–1
Classification of costs

Fixed	Variable	Semivariable
Lease	Raw material	Utilities
Depreciation	Factory labor	Repairs and maintenance
Executive salaries	Sales commissions	
Property taxes		

For purposes of analysis, variable and semivariable costs will be combined. In order to evaluate the implications of heavy fixed asset use, we employ the technique of break-even analysis.

Break-Even Analysis

How much will changes in volume affect cost and profit? At what point does the firm break even? What is the most efficient level of fixed assets to employ in the firm? A break-even chart is presented in Figure 5–1 to answer some of these questions. The number of units produced and sold is shown along the horizontal axis, and revenue and costs are shown along the vertical axis.

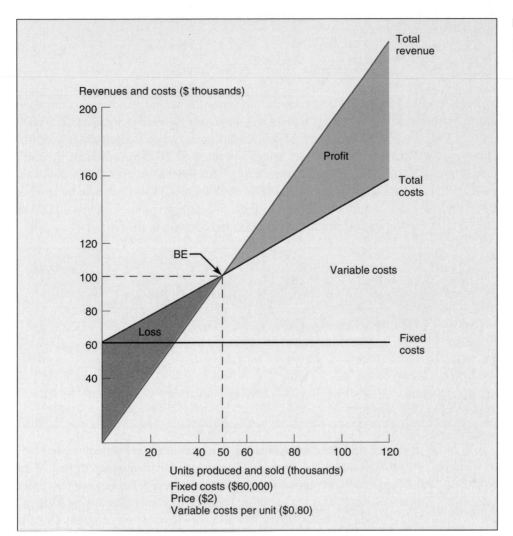

Figure 5–1
Break-even chart:
Leveraged firm

Note, first of all, that our fixed costs are $60,000, regardless of volume, and that our variable costs (at $0.80 per unit) are added to fixed costs to determine total costs at any point. The total revenue line is determined by multiplying price ($2) times volume.

Of particular interest is the break-even (BE) point at 50,000 units, where the total costs and total revenue lines intersect. The numbers are as follows:

Units = 50,000				
Total Variable Costs (TVC)	**Fixed Costs (FC)**	**Total Costs (TC)**	**Total Revenue (TR)**	**Operating Income (loss)**
(50,000 × $0.80)			(50,000 × $2)	
$40,000	$60,000	$100,000	$100,000	0

The break-even point for the company may also be determined by use of a simple formula—in which we divide fixed costs by the contribution margin on each unit sold, with the **contribution margin** defined as price minus variable cost per unit. The formula is shown at the top of the next page.

$$BE = \frac{\text{Fixed costs}}{\text{Contribution margin}} = \frac{\text{Fixed costs}}{\text{Price} - \text{Variable cost per unit}} = \frac{FC}{P - VC} \quad (5\text{–}1)$$

$$\frac{\$60,000}{\$2.00 - \$0.80} = \frac{\$60,000}{\$1.20} = 50,000 \text{ units}$$

Since we are getting a $1.20 contribution toward covering fixed costs from each unit sold, minimum sales of 50,000 units will allow us to cover our fixed costs (50,000 units × $1.20 = $60,000 fixed costs). Beyond this point, we move into a highly profitable range in which each unit of sales brings a profit of $1.20 to the company. As sales increase from 50,000 to 60,000 units, operating profits increase by $12,000 as indicated in Table 5–2; as sales increase from 60,000 to 80,000 units, profits increase by another $24,000; and so on. As further indicated in Table 5–2, at low volumes such as 40,000 or 20,000 units our losses are substantial ($12,000 and $36,000 in the red).

Table 5–2

Volume-cost-profit analysis: Leveraged firm

Units Sold	Total Variable Costs	Fixed Costs	Total Costs	Total Revenue	Operating Income (loss)
0	0	$60,000	$ 60,000	0	$(60,000)
20,000	$16,000	60,000	76,000	$ 40,000	(36,000)
40,000	32,000	60,000	92,000	80,000	(12,000)
50,000	40,000	60,000	100,000	100,000	0
60,000	48,000	60,000	108,000	120,000	12,000
80,000	64,000	60,000	124,000	160,000	36,000
100,000	80,000	60,000	140,000	200,000	60,000

It is assumed that the firm depicted in Figure 5–1, as previously presented on page 121, is operating with a high degree of leverage. The situation is analogous to that of an airline that must carry a certain number of people to break even, but beyond that point is in a very profitable range. This has certainly been the case with Southwest Airlines, which has its home office in Dallas, Texas, but also flies to many other states. The airline systematically offers lower fares than American, Delta, and other airlines to ensure maximum capacity utilization.

A More Conservative Approach

Not all firms would choose to operate at the high degree of operating leverage exhibited in Figure 5–1 on page 121. Fear of not reaching the 50,000-unit break-even level might discourage some companies from heavy utilization of fixed assets. More expensive variable costs might be substituted for automated plant and equipment. Assume fixed costs for a more conservative firm can be reduced to $12,000—but variable costs will go from $0.80 to $1.60. If the same price assumption of $2 per unit is employed, the break-even level is 30,000 units.

$$BE = \frac{\text{Fixed costs}}{\text{Price} - \text{Variable cost per unit}} = \frac{FC}{P - VC} = \frac{\$12,000}{\$2 - \$1.60}$$

$$= \frac{\$12,000}{\$0.40}$$

$$= 30,000 \text{ units}$$

With fixed costs reduced from \$60,000 to \$12,000, the loss potential is small. Furthermore, the break-even level of operations is a comparatively low 30,000 units. Nevertheless, the use of a virtually unleveraged approach has cut into the potential profitability of the more conservative firm, as indicated in Figure 5–2.

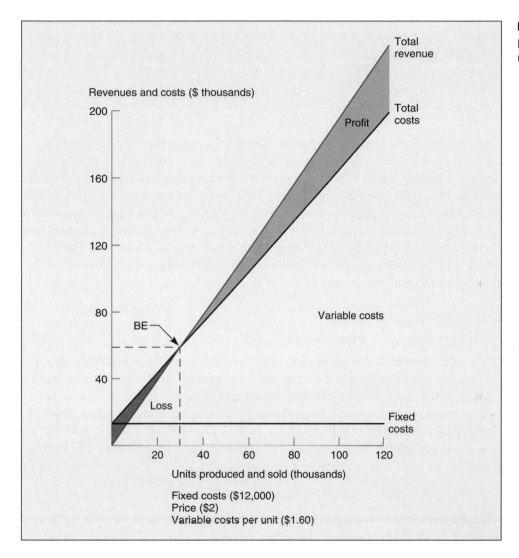

Figure 5–2

Break-even chart: Conservative firm

Even at high levels of operation, the potential profit in Figure 5–2 is rather small. As indicated in Table 5–3 on page 124, at a 100,000-unit volume, operating income is only \$28,000—some \$32,000 less than that for the "leveraged" firm previously analyzed in Table 5–2.

The Risk Factor

Whether management follows the path of the leveraged firm or of the more conservative firm depends on its perceptions about the future. If the vice-president of finance is apprehensive about economic conditions, the conservative plan may be undertaken. For a growing business in times of relative prosperity, management might maintain

Table 5–3

Volume-cost-profit analysis: Conservative firm

Units Sold	Total Variable Costs	Fixed Costs	Total Costs	Total Revenue	Operating Income (loss)
0	0	$ 12,000	$ 12,000	0	$(12,000)
20,000	$ 32,000	12,000	44,000	$ 40,000	(4,000)
30,000	48,000	12,000	60,000	60,000	0
40,000	64,000	12,000	76,000	80,000	4,000
60,000	96,000	12,000	108,000	120,000	12,000
80,000	128,000	12,000	140,000	160,000	20,000
100,000	160,000	12,000	172,000	200,000	28,000

a more aggressive, leveraged position. The firm's competitive position within its industry will also be a factor. Does the firm desire to merely maintain stability or to become a market leader? To a certain extent, management should tailor the use of leverage to meet its own risk-taking desires. Those who are risk averse (prefer less risk to more risk) should anticipate a particularly high return before contracting for heavy fixed costs. Others, less averse to risk, may be willing to leverage under more normal conditions. Simply taking risks is not a virtue—our prisons are full of risk takers. The important idea, which is stressed throughout the text, is to match an acceptable return with the desired level of risk.

Cash Break-Even Analysis

Our discussion to this point has dealt with break-even analysis in terms of accounting flows rather than cash flows. For example, depreciation has been implicitly included in fixed expenses, but it represents a noncash accounting entry rather than an explicit expenditure of funds. To the extent that we were doing break-even analysis on a strictly cash basis, depreciation would be excluded from fixed expenses. In the previous example of the leveraged firm in Formula 5–1 on page 122, if we eliminate $20,000 of "assumed" depreciation from fixed costs, the break-even level is reduced to 33,333 units.

$$\frac{FC}{P - VC} = \frac{(\$60,000 - \$20,000)}{\$2.00 - \$0.80} = \frac{\$40,000}{\$1.20} = 33,333 \text{ units}$$

Other adjustments could also be made for noncash items. For example, sales may initially take the form of accounts receivable rather than cash, and the same can be said for the purchase of materials and accounts payable. An actual weekly or monthly cash budget would be necessary to isolate these items.

While cash break-even analysis is helpful in analyzing the short-term outlook of the firm, particularly when it may be in trouble, break-even analysis is normally conducted on the basis of accounting flows rather than strictly cash flows. Most of the assumptions throughout the chapter are based on concepts broader than pure cash flows.

Degree of Operating Leverage

Degree of operating leverage (DOL) may be defined as the percentage change in operating income that occurs as a result of a percentage change in units sold.

$$\text{DOL} = \frac{\text{Percent change in operating income}}{\text{Percent change in unit volume}} \qquad (5\text{--}2)$$

Highly leveraged firms, such as Ford Motor Company or Dow Chemical, are likely to enjoy a rather substantial increase in income as volume expands, while more conservative firms will participate in an increase to a lesser extent. Degree of operating leverage should be computed only over a profitable range of operations. However, the closer DOL is computed to the company break-even point, the higher the number will be due to a large percentage increase in operating income.[1]

Let us apply the formula to the leveraged and conservative firms previously discussed. Their income or losses at various levels of operation are summarized in Table 5–4.

Units	Leveraged Firm (Table 5–2)	Conservative Firm (Table 5–3)
0	$(60,000)	$(12,000)
20,000	(36,000)	(4,000)
40,000	(12,000)	4,000
60,000	12,000	12,000
80,000	36,000	20,000
100,000	60,000	28,000

Table 5–4
Operating income or loss

We will now consider what happens to operating income as volume moves from 80,000 to 100,000 units for each firm. We will compute the degree of operating leverage (DOL) using Formula 5–2.

Leveraged Firm

$$\text{DOL} = \frac{\text{Percent change in operating income}}{\text{Percent change in unit volume}} = \frac{\dfrac{\$24,000}{\$36,000} \times 100}{\dfrac{20,000}{80,000} \times 100}$$

$$= \frac{67\%}{25\%} = 2.7$$

Conservative Firm

$$\text{DOL} = \frac{\text{Percent change in operating income}}{\text{Percent change in unit volume}} = \frac{\dfrac{\$8,000}{\$20,000} \times 100}{\dfrac{20,000}{80,000} \times 100}$$

$$= \frac{40\%}{25\%} = 1.6$$

---

[1]While the value of DOL varies at each level of output, the beginning level of volume determines the DOL regardless of the location of the end point.

We see on the bottom of page 125 that the DOL is much greater for the leveraged firm, indicating at 80,000 units a 1 percent increase in volume will produce a 2.7 percent change in operating income, versus a 1.6 percent increase for the conservative firm.

The formula for degree of operating leverage may be algebraically manipulated to read:

$$DOL = \frac{Q(P - VC)}{Q(P - VC) - FC} \qquad (5-3)$$

where

Q = Quantity at which DOL is computed.

P = Price per unit.

VC = Variable costs per unit.

FC = Fixed costs.

Using the newly stated formula for the first firm at $Q = 80,000$, with $P = \$2$, $VC = \$0.80$, and $FC = \$60,000$:

$$DOL = \frac{80,000(\$2.00 - \$0.80)}{80,000(\$2.00 - \$0.80) - \$60,000}$$

$$= \frac{80,000(\$1.20)}{80,000(\$1.20) - \$60,000} = \frac{\$96,000}{\$96,000 - \$60,000}$$

$$DOL = 2.7$$

We once again derive an answer of 2.7.[2] The same type of calculation could also be performed for the conservative firm.

Limitations of Analysis

Throughout our analysis of operating leverage, we have assumed that a constant or linear function exists for revenues and costs as volume changes. For example, we have used $2 as the hypothetical sales price at all levels of operation. In the "real world," however, we may face price weakness as we attempt to capture an increasing market for our product, or we may face cost overruns as we move beyond an optimum-size operation. Relationships are not so fixed as we have assumed.

---

[2]The formula for DOL may also be rewritten as:

$$DOL = \frac{Q(P - VC)}{Q(P - VC) - FC} = \frac{QP - QVC}{QP - QVC - FC}$$

We can rewrite the second terms as:

QP = S, or Sales (Quantity × Price)

QVC = TVC, or Total variable costs (Quantity × Variable costs per unit)

FC = Total fixed costs (remains the same term)

We then have:

$$DOL = \frac{S - TVC}{S - TVC - FC}, \text{ or } \frac{\$160,000 - \$64,000}{\$160,000 - \$64,000 - \$60,000} = \frac{\$96,000}{\$36,000} = 2.7$$

Nevertheless, the basic patterns we have studied are reasonably valid for most firms over an extended operating range (in our example that might be between 20,000 and 100,000 units). It is only at the extreme levels that linear assumptions fully break down, as indicated in Figure 5–3.

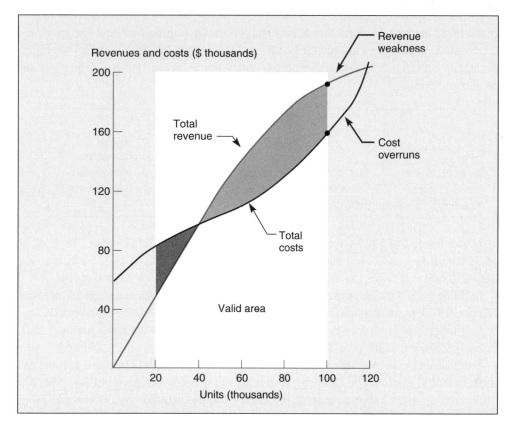

Figure 5–3
Nonlinear break-even analysis

Financial Leverage

Having discussed the effect of fixed costs on the operations of the firm (operating leverage), we now turn to the second form of leverage. **Financial leverage** reflects the amount of debt used in the capital structure of the firm. Because debt carries a fixed obligation of interest payments, we have the opportunity to greatly magnify our results at various levels of operations. You may have heard of the real estate developer who borrows 100 percent of the costs of his project and will enjoy an infinite return on his zero investment if all goes well.

It is helpful to think of *operating leverage* as primarily affecting the left-hand side of the balance sheet and *financial leverage* as affecting the right-hand side.

BALANCE SHEET	
Assets	**Liabilities and Net Worth**
Operating leverage	Financial leverage

Whereas operating leverage influences the mix of plant and equipment, financial leverage determines how the operation is to be financed. It is possible for two firms to have equal operating capabilities and yet show widely different results because of the use of financial leverage.

Impact on Earnings

In studying the impact of financial leverage, we shall examine two financial plans for a firm, each employing a significantly different amount of debt in the capital structure. Financing totaling $200,000 is required to carry the assets of the firm. The facts are presented below.

	Total Assets—$200,000	
	Plan A **(leveraged)**	**Plan B** **(conservative)**
Debt (8% interest)	$150,000 ($12,000 interest)	$ 50,000 ($4,000 interest)
Common stock	50,000 (8,000 shares at $6.25)	150,000 (24,000 shares at $6.25)
Total financing	$200,000	$200,000

Under *leveraged* Plan A we will borrow $150,000 and sell 8,000 shares of stock at $6.25 to raise an additional $50,000, whereas *conservative* Plan B calls for borrowing only $50,000 and acquiring an additional $150,000 in stock with 24,000 shares.

In Table 5–5, we compute earnings per share for the two plans at various levels of "earnings before interest and taxes" (EBIT). These earnings (EBIT) represent the operating income of the firm—before deductions have been made for financial charges or taxes. We assume EBIT levels of 0, $12,000, $16,000, $36,000, and $60,000.

The impact of the two financing plans is dramatic. Although both plans assume the same operating income, or EBIT, for comparative purposes at each level (say $36,000 in calculation 4) the reported income per share is vastly different ($1.50 versus $0.67). It is also evident the conservative plan will produce better results at low income levels—but the leveraged plan will generate much better earnings per share as operating income, or EBIT, goes up. The firm would be indifferent between the two plans at an EBIT level of $16,000 as shown in Table 5–5.

In Figure 5–4 on page 130, we graphically demonstrate the effect of the two financing plans on earnings per share and the indifference point at an EBIT of $16 (thousand).

With an EBIT of $16,000, we are earning 8 *percent* on total assets of $200,000— precisely the percentage cost of borrowed funds to the firm. The use or nonuse of debt does not influence the answer. Beyond $16,000, Plan A, employing heavy financial leverage, really goes to work, allowing the firm to greatly expand earnings per share as a result of a change in EBIT. For example, at the EBIT level of $36,000, an 18 percent return on assets of $200,000 takes place—and financial leverage is clearly working to our benefit as earnings greatly expand.

Degree of Financial Leverage

As was true of operating leverage, degree of financial leverage measures the effect of a change in one variable on another variable. **Degree of financial leverage (DFL)**

Table 5–5

Impact of financing plan on earnings per share

	Plan A (leveraged)	Plan B (conservative)
1. EBIT (0)		
Earnings before interest and taxes (EBIT)	0	0
− Interest (I)	$(12,000)	$ (4,000)
Earnings before taxes (EBT)	(12,000)	(4,000)
− Taxes (T)*.................................	(6,000)	(2,000)
Earnings after taxes (EAT).....................	$ (6,000)	$ (2,000)
Shares......................................	8,000	24,000
Earnings per share (EPS)	$(0.75)	$(0.08)
2. EBIT ($12,000)		
Earnings before interest and taxes (EBIT)	$ 12,000	$12,000
− Interest (I)	12,000	4,000
Earnings before taxes (EBT)	0	8,000
− Taxes (T)	0	4,000
Earnings after taxes (EAT)	$ 0	$ 4,000
Shares......................................	8,000	24,000
Earnings per share (EPS)	0	$0.17
3. EBIT ($16,000)		
Earnings before interest and taxes (EBIT)	$ 16,000	$16,000
− Interest (I)	12,000	4,000
Earnings before taxes (EBT)	4,000	12,000
− Taxes (T)	2,000	6,000
Earnings after taxes (EAT).....................	$ 2,000	$ 6,000
Shares......................................	8,000	24,000
Earnings per share (EPS)	$0.25	$0.25
4. EBIT ($36,000)		
Earnings before interest and taxes (EBIT)	$ 36,000	$36,000
− Interest (I)	12,000	4,000
Earnings before taxes (EBT)	24,000	32,000
− Taxes (T)	12,000	16,000
Earnings after taxes (EAT)	$ 12,000	$16,000
Shares......................................	8,000	24,000
Earnings per share (EPS)	$1.50	$0.67
5. EBIT ($60,000)		
Earnings before interest and taxes (EBIT)	60,000	$60,000
− Interest (I)	12,000	4,000
Earnings before taxes (EBT)	48,000	56,000
− Taxes (T)	24,000	28,000
Earnings after taxes (EAT)	$ 24,000	$28,000
Shares......................................	8,000	24,000
Earnings per share (EPS)	$3.00	$1.17

*The assumption is that large losses can be written off against other income, perhaps in other years, thus providing the firm with a tax savings benefit. The tax rate is 50 percent for ease of computation.

Figure 5–4

Financing plans and earnings per share

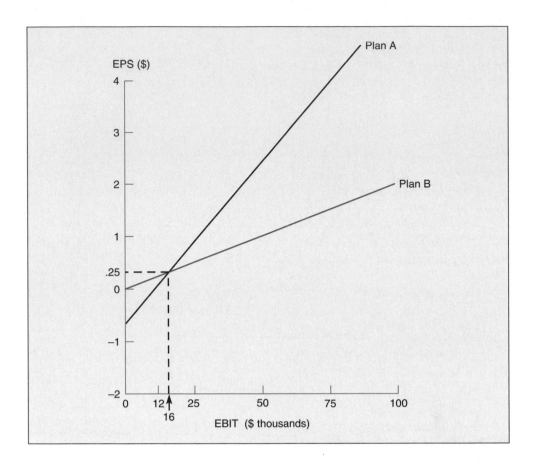

may be defined as the percentage change in earnings (EPS) that occurs as a result of a percentage change in earnings before interest and taxes (EBIT).

$$DFL = \frac{\text{Percent change in EPS}}{\text{Percent change in EBIT}} \tag{5–4}$$

For purposes of computation, the formula for DFL may be conveniently restated as:

$$DFL = \frac{\text{EBIT}}{\text{EBIT} - \text{I}} \tag{5–5}$$

Let's compute the degrees of financial leverage for Plan A and Plan B, previously presented in Table 5–5, at an EBIT level of $36,000. Plan A calls for $12,000 of interest at all levels of financing, and Plan B requires $4,000.

Plan A (Leveraged)

$$DFL = \frac{\text{EBIT}}{\text{EBIT} - \text{I}} = \frac{\$36,000}{\$36,000 - \$12,000} = \frac{\$36,000}{\$24,000} = 1.5$$

Plan B (Conservative)

$$DFL = \frac{\text{EBIT}}{\text{EBIT} - \text{I}} = \frac{\$36,000}{\$36,000 - \$4,000} = \frac{\$36,000}{\$32,000} = 1.1$$

As expected, Plan A has a much higher degree of financial leverage. At an EBIT level of $36,000, a 1 percent increase in earnings will produce a 1.5 percent increase in earnings per share under Plan A, but only a 1.1 percent increase under Plan B. DFL may be computed for any level of operation, and it will change from point to point, but Plan A will always exceed Plan B.

Limitations to Use of Financial Leverage

The alert student may quickly observe that if debt is such a good thing, why sell any stock? (Perhaps one share to yourself.) With exclusive debt financing at an EBIT level of $36,000, we would have a degree of financial leverage factor (DFL) of 1.8.

$$\text{DFL} = \frac{\text{EBIT}}{\text{EBIT} - I} = \frac{\$36,000}{\$36,000 - \$16,000} = \frac{\$36,000}{\$20,000} = 1.8$$

(With no stock, we would borrow the full $200,000.)

$$(8\% \times \$200,000 = \$16,000 \text{ interest})$$

As stressed throughout the text, debt financing and financial leverage offer unique advantages, but only up to a point—beyond that point, debt financing may be detrimental to the firm. For example, as we expand the use of debt in our capital structure, lenders will perceive a greater financial risk for the firm. For that reason, they may raise the average interest rate to be paid and they may demand that certain restrictions be placed on the corporation. Furthermore, concerned common stockholders may drive down the price of the stock—forcing us away from the *objective of maximizing the firm's overall value* in the market. The impact of financial leverage must be carefully weighed by firms with high debt such as UAL (United Airlines).

This is not to say that financial leverage does not work to the benefit of the firm—it does if properly used. Further discussion of appropriate debt-equity mixes is covered in Chapter 11, "Cost of Capital." For now, we accept the virtues of financial leverage, knowing that all good things must be used in moderation. For firms that are in industries that offer some degree of stability, are in a positive stage of growth, and are operating in favorable economic conditions, the use of debt is recommended.

Combining Operating and Financial Leverage

If both operating and financial leverage allow us to magnify our returns, then we will get maximum leverage through their combined use in the form of **combined leverage**. We have said that operating leverage affects primarily the asset structure of the firm, while financial leverage affects the debt-equity mix. From an income statement viewpoint, operating leverage determines return from operations, while financial leverage determines how the "fruits of our labor" will be allocated to debt holders and, more importantly, to stockholders in the form of earnings per share. Table 5–6 shows the combined influence of operating and financial leverage on the income statement. The values in Table 5–6 are drawn from earlier material in the chapter (Tables 5–2 and 5–5). We assumed in both cases a high degree of operating and financial leverage (i.e., the leveraged firm). The sales volume is 80,000 units.

Table 5–6

Income statement

Sales (total revenue) (80,000 units @ $2)	$160,000
− Fixed costs	60,000
− Variable costs ($0.80 per unit)	64,000
Operating income	$ 36,000
Earnings before interest and taxes	$ 36,000
− Interest	12,000
Earnings before taxes	24,000
− Taxes	12,000
Earnings after taxes	$ 12,000
Shares	8,000
Earnings per share	$1.50

Operating leverage brackets the top portion (Sales through Operating income). Financial leverage brackets the lower portion (Earnings before interest and taxes through Earnings per share).

The student will observe, first, that operating leverage influences the top half of the income statement—determining operating income. The last item under operating leverage, operating income, then becomes the initial item for determining financial leverage. "Operating income" and "Earnings before interest and taxes" are one and the same, representing the return to the corporation after production, marketing, and so forth—but before interest and taxes are paid. In the second half of the income statement, we then show the extent to which earnings before interest and taxes are translated into earnings per share. A graphical representation of these points is provided in Figure 5–5.

Figure 5–5

Combining operating and financial leverage

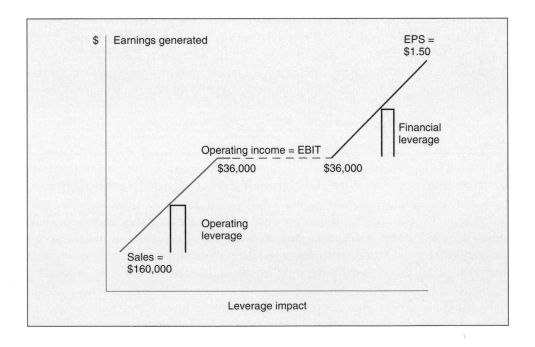

Why Japanese Firms Tend to Be So Competitive

What do firms such as Sony, Honda, Fujitsu, Hitachi, and Mitsubishi have in common? Not only are they all Japanese companies, but they are also highly leveraged, both from operational and financing perspectives.

Japanese companies are world leaders in bringing high technology into their firms to replace slower, more expensive labor. They are known for automated factories, laser technology, robotics, memory chips, digital processing, and other scientific endeavors. Furthermore, the country has government groups such as the Ministry of International Trade and Industry (MITI) and the Science and Technology Agency encouraging further investment and growth through government grants and shared research.

To enjoy the benefits of this technology, Japanese firms have a high fixed cost commitment. Obviously high initial cost technology cannot easily be "laid off" if business slows down. Even the labor necessary to design and operate the technology has somewhat of a fixed cost element associated with it. Unlike in the United States, workers are not normally laid off and many people in Japan consider their jobs to represent a lifetime commitment from their employers.

Not only does the Japanese economy have high operating leverage as described above, but Japanese companies also have high financial leverage. The typical Japanese company has a debt-to-equity ratio two to three times higher than its counterparts in the United States. The reason is that credit tends to be more available in Japan because of the traditional relationship between an industrial firm and its bank. They both may be part of the same cartel or trading company with interlocking directors (directors that serve on both boards). Under such an arrangement, a bank is willing to make a larger loan commitment to an industrial firm and there's a shared humiliation if the credit arrangement goes badly. Contrast this to the United States, where a lending institution such as Citicorp or Bank of America has extensive provisions and covenants in its loan agreements and is prepared to move in immediately at the first sign of a borrower's weakness. None of these comments imply that Japanese firms do not default on their loans. There were, in fact, a number of bad loans sitting on the books of Japanese banks in the mid-2000s.

The key point is that Japanese firms have high operating leverage as well as high financial leverage and that makes them act very competitively. If a firm has a combined leverage of 6 or 8 times, as many Japanese companies do, the loss of unit sales can be disastrous. Leverage not only magnifies returns as volume increases, but magnifies losses as volume decreases. As an example, a Japanese firm that is in danger of losing an order to a U.S. firm for computer chips is likely to drastically cut prices or take whatever action is necessary to maintain its sales volume. A general rule of business is that firms that are exposed to high leverage are likely to act aggressively to cover their large fixed costs and this rule certainly applies to leading Japanese firms. This, of course, may well be a virtue because it ensures that a firm will remain market oriented and progressive.

Degree of combined leverage (DCL) uses the entire income statement and shows the impact of a change in sales or volume on bottom-line earnings per share. Degree of operating leverage and degree of financial leverage are, in effect, being combined. Table 5–7 shows what happens to profitability as the firm's sales go from $160,000 (80,000 units) to $200,000 (100,000 units).

The formula for degree of combined leverage is stated as:

$$\text{Degree of combined leverage (DCL)} = \frac{\text{Percent change in EPS}}{\text{Percent change in sales (or volume)}} \qquad (5\text{–}6)$$

Degree of Combined Leverage

Table 5–7

Operating and financial leverage

	80,000 units	100,000 units
Sales—$2 per unit	$160,000	$200,000
– Fixed costs	60,000	60,000
– Variable costs ($0.80 per unit)	64,000	80,000
Operating income = EBIT	36,000	60,000
– Interest	12,000	12,000
Earnings before taxes	24,000	48,000
– Taxes	12,000	24,000
Earnings after taxes	$ 12,000	$ 24,000
Shares	8,000	8,000
Earnings per share	$1.50	$3.00

Using data from Table 5–7:

$$\frac{\text{Percent change in EPS}}{\text{Percent change in sales}} = \frac{\dfrac{\$1.50}{\$1.50} \times 100}{\dfrac{\$40,000}{\$160,000} \times 100} = \frac{100\%}{25\%} = 4$$

Every percentage point change in sales will be reflected in a 4 percent change in earnings per share at this level of operation (quite an impact).

An algebraic statement of the formula is:

$$\text{DCL} = \frac{Q(P - VC)}{Q(P - VC) - FC - I} \tag{5-7}$$

From Table 5–7: Q (Quantity) = 80,000; P (Price per unit) = $2.00; VC (Variable costs per unit) = $0.80; FC (Fixed costs) = $60,000; and I (Interest) = $12,000.

$$\text{DCL} = \frac{80,000(\$2.00 - \$0.80)}{80,000(\$2.00 - \$0.80) - \$60,000 - \$12,000}$$

$$= \frac{80,000(\$1.20)}{80,000(\$1.20) - \$72,000}$$

$$\text{DCL} = \frac{\$96,000}{\$96,000 - \$72,000} = \frac{\$96,000}{\$24,000} = 4$$

The answer is once again shown to be 4.[3]

---

[3]The formula for DCL may also be rewritten as:

$$\text{DCL} = \frac{Q(P - VC)}{Q(P - VC) - FC - I} = \frac{QP - QVC}{QP - QVC - FC - I}$$

We can rewrite the second terms as:
QP = S, or Sales (Quantity × Price)
QVC = TVC, or Total variable costs (Quantity × Variable costs per unit)
FC = Total fixed costs (remains the same term)
I   = Interest (remains the same term)
We then have:

$$\text{DCL} = \frac{S - TVC}{S - TVC - FC - I}, \text{ or } \frac{\$160,000 - \$64,000}{\$160,000 - \$64,000 - \$60,000 - \$12,000} = \frac{\$96,000}{\$24,000} = 4$$

A Word of Caution

In a sense, we are piling risk on risk as the two different forms of leverage are combined. Perhaps a firm carrying heavy operating leverage may wish to moderate its position financially, and vice versa. One thing is certain—the decision will have a major impact on the operations of the firm.

Summary

Leverage may be defined as the use of fixed cost items to magnify returns at high levels of operation. Operating leverage primarily affects fixed versus variable cost utilization in the operation of the firm. An important concept—degree of operating leverage (DOL)—measures the percentage change in operating income as a result of a percentage change in volume. The heavier the utilization of fixed cost assets, the higher DOL is likely to be.

Financial leverage reflects the extent to which debt is used in the capital structure of the firm. Substantial use of debt will place a great burden on the firm at low levels of profitability, but it will help to magnify earnings per share as volume or operating income increases. We combine operating and financial leverage to assess the impact of all types of fixed costs on the firm. There is a multiplier effect when we use the two different types of leverage.

Because leverage is a two-edged sword, management must be sure the level of risk assumed is in accord with its desires for risk and its perceptions of the future. High operating leverage may be balanced off against lower financial leverage if this is deemed desirable, and vice versa.

Review of Formulas

1. $$BE = \frac{FC}{P - VC} \qquad (5\text{--}1)$$

   BE is break-even point
   FC is fixed costs
     P is price per unit
   VC is variable cost per unit

2. $$DOL = \frac{Q(P - VC)}{Q(P - VC) - FC} \qquad (5\text{--}3)$$

   DOL is degree of operating leverage
     Q is quantity at which DOL is computed
      P is price per unit
    VC is variable cost per unit
    FC is fixed costs

3. $$DOL = \frac{S - TVC}{S - TVC - FC} \qquad (\text{Footnote 2})$$

   DOL is degree of operating leverage
      S is sales (QP) at which DOL is computed
   TVC is total variable costs
     FC is fixed costs

4. $DFL = \dfrac{EBIT}{EBIT - I}$ (5–5)

   DFL is degree of financial leverage
   EBIT is earnings before interest and taxes
        I is interest

5. $DCL = \dfrac{Q(P - VC)}{Q(P - VC) - FC - I}$ (5–7)

   DCL is degree of combined leverage
      Q is quantity at which DCL is computed
      P is price per unit
   VC is variable cost per unit
   FC is fixed costs
      I is interest

6. $DCL = \dfrac{S - TVC}{S - TVC - FC - I}$ (Footnote 3)

   DCL is degree of combined leverage
      S is sales (QP) at which DCL is computed
   TVC is total variable costs
      FC is fixed costs
         I is interest

List of Terms

Discussion Questions

1. Discuss the various uses for break-even analysis.
2. What factors would cause a difference in the use of financial leverage for a utility company and an automobile company?
3. Explain how the break-even point and operating leverage are affected by the choice of manufacturing facilities (labor intensive versus capital intensive).
4. What role does depreciation play in break-even analysis based on accounting flows? Based on cash flows? Which perspective is longer-term in nature?
5. What does risk taking have to do with the use of operating and financial leverage?
6. Discuss the limitations of financial leverage.
7. How does the interest rate on new debt influence the use of financial leverage?
8. Explain how combined leverage brings together operating income and earnings per share.

9. Explain why operating leverage decreases as a company increases sales and shifts away from the break-even point.

10. When you are considering two different financing plans, does being at the level where earnings per share are equal between the two plans always mean you are indifferent as to which plan is selected?

Practice Problems and Solutions

Degree of leverage

1. Meyer Appliance Company makes cooling fans. The firm's income statement is as follows:

Sales (7,000 fans at $20)	$140,000
Less: Variable costs (7,000 fans at $8)	56,000
Fixed costs	44,000
Earnings before interest and taxes (EBIT)	40,000
− Interest (I)	10,000
Earnings before taxes (EBT)	30,000
− Taxes (T)	6,000
Earnings after taxes (EAT)	$ 24,000

Compute:

a. Degree of operating leverage.

b. Degree of financial leverage.

c. Degree of combined leverage.

d. The breakeven point.

2. Hubball Resources has the following capital structure:

Earnings per share and financial leverage

Debt @ 8%	$300,000
Common stock, $10 par (shares 50,000)	500,000
Total	$800,000

a. Compute earnings per share if earnings before interest and taxes is $64,000. (Assume a 20 percent tax rate.)

b. Assume debt goes up by $200,000, common stock goes down by $200,000, and the interest rate on the new debt is 10 percent. The tax rate remains at 20 percent. The par value on the common stock is still $10. Compute earnings per share if earnings before interest and taxes is $80,000.

Solutions

1. *a.*
$$\text{DOL} = \frac{Q(P - VC)}{Q(P - VC) - F} = \frac{7,000\,(\$20 - \$8)}{7,000\,(\$20 - \$8) - \$44,000}$$

$$= \frac{7,000\,(\$12)}{7,000\,(\$12) - \$44,000} = \frac{84,000}{\$84,000 - \$44,000} = \frac{\$84,000}{40,000} = 2.10x$$

b.
$$\text{DFL} = \frac{\text{EBIT}}{\text{EBIT} - I} = \frac{\$40,000}{\$40,000 - \$10,000} = \frac{\$40,000}{30,000} = 1.33x$$

c. $DCL = \dfrac{Q(P - VC)}{Q(P - VC) - FC - I} = \dfrac{7,000\ (\$20 - \$8)}{7,000\ (\$20 - \$8) - \$44,000 - \$10,000}$

$= \dfrac{7,000\ (\$12)}{7,000\ (\$12) - \$54,000} = \dfrac{\$84,000}{\$84,000 - \$54,000}$

$= \dfrac{\$84,000}{\$30,000} = 2.80x$

d. $BE = \dfrac{FC}{P - VC} = \dfrac{\$44,000}{\$20 - \$8} = \dfrac{\$44,000}{\$12} = 3,667 \text{ fans}$

2. a.

Earnings before interest and taxes (EBIT)	$64,000
– Interest (I)	24,000*
Earnings before taxes (EBT)	$40,000
– Taxes (T) 20%	8,000
Earnings after taxes (EAT)	32,000
Shares	50,000
Earnings per share (EPS)	$ .64

*8 percent interest $\times$ $300,000 debt = $24,000

b.

Earnings before interest and taxes (EBIT)	$80,000
– Interest (I)	44,000*
Earnings before taxes (EBT)	$36,000
– Taxes (T) 20%	7,200
Earnings after taxes (EAT)	28,800
Shares	30,000†
Earnings per share (EPS)	$ .96

*Interest on old debt ($24,000) + interest on new debt ($20,000).
10 percent $\times$ $200,000. The total is $44,000.
†50,000 shares reduced by ($200,000/$10 par value) = 50,000 – 20,000
= 30,000

Problems

Break-even
analysis

1. Shock Electronics sells portable heaters for $25 per unit, and the variable cost to produce them is $17. Mr. Amps estimates that the fixed costs are $96,000.

  a. Compute the break-even point in units.

  b. Fill in the table below (in dollars) to illustrate that the break-even point has been achieved.

Sales	_____
– Fixed costs	_____
– Total variable costs	_____
Net profit (loss)	_____

2. The Hartnett Corporation manufactures baseball bats with Pudge Rodriguez's autograph stamped on them. Each bat sells for $13 and has a variable cost of $8. There are $20,000 in fixed costs involved in the production process.

    a. Compute the break-even point in units.

    b. Find the sales (in units) needed to earn a profit of $15,000.

3. Therapeutic Systems sells its products for $8 per unit. It has the following costs:

Rent	$120,000
Factory labor	$1.50 per unit
Executives under contract	$112,000
Raw material	$.70 per unit

    Separate the expenses between fixed and variable costs per unit. Using this information and the sales price per unit of $6, compute the break-even point.

4. Draw two break-even graphs—one for a conservative firm using labor-intensive production and another for a capital-intensive firm. Assuming these companies compete within the same industry and have identical sales, explain the impact of changes in sales volume on both firms' profits.

5. Eaton Tool Company has fixed costs of $200,000, sells its units for $56, and has variable costs of $31 per unit.

    a. Compute the break-even point.

    b. Ms. Eaton comes up with a new plan to cut fixed costs to $150,000. However, more labor will now be required, which will increase variable costs per unit to $34. The sales price will remain at $56. What is the new break-even point?

    c. Under the new plan, what is likely to happen to profitability at very high volume levels (compared to the old plan)?

6. Jay Linoleum Company has fixed costs of $70,000. Its product currently sells for $4 per unit and has variable costs per unit of $2.60. Mr. Thomas, the head of manufacturing, proposes to buy new equipment that will cost $300,000 and drive up fixed costs to $105,000. Although the price will remain at $4 per unit, the increased automation will reduce variable costs per unit to $2.25.

    As a result of Thomas's suggestion, will the break-even point go up or down? Compute the necessary numbers.

7. Calloway Cab Company determines its break-even strictly on the basis of cash expenditures related to fixed costs. Its total fixed costs are $400,000, but 20 percent of this value is represented by depreciation. Its contribution margin (price minus variable cost) for each unit is $3.60. How many units does the firm need to sell to reach the cash break-even point?

8. Air Purifier, Inc., computes its break-even point strictly on the basis of cash expenditures related to fixed costs. Its total fixed costs are $2,400,000, but 15 percent of this value is represented by depreciation. Its contribution margin (price minus variable cost) for each unit is $30. How many units does the firm need to sell to reach the cash break-even point?

Break-even analysis

Break-even analysis

Break-even analysis

Break-even analysis

Break-even analysis

Cash break-even analysis

Cash break-even analysis

Degree of leverage

9. The Sterling Tire Company's income statement for 2007 is as follows:

STERLING TIRE COMPANY
Income Statement
For the Year Ended December 31, 2007

Sales (20,000 tires at $60 each).	$1,200,000
Less: Variable costs (20,000 tires at $30)	600,000
Fixed costs	400,000
Earnings before interest and taxes (EBIT)	200,000
Interest expense.	50,000
Earnings before taxes (EBT)	150,000
Income tax expense (30%).	45,000
Earnings after taxes (EAT)	$ 105,000

Given this income statement, compute the following:

a. Degree of operating leverage.

b. Degree of financial leverage.

c. Degree of combined leverage.

d. Break-even point in units.

Degree of leverage

✂ 10. The Harding Company manufactures skates. The company's income statement for 2007 is as follows:

HARDING COMPANY
Income Statement
For the Year Ended December 31, 2007

Sales (10,000 skates @ $50 each).	$500,000
Less: Variable costs (10,000 skates at $20)	200,000
Fixed costs	150,000
Earnings before interest and taxes (EBIT)	150,000
Interest expense	60,000
Earnings before taxes (EBT)	90,000
Income tax expense (40%)	36,000
Earnings after taxes (EAT)	$ 54,000

Given this income statement, compute the following:

a. Degree of operating leverage.

b. Degree of financial leverage.

c. Degree of combined leverage.

d. Break-even point in units (number of skates).

Break-even point and degree of leverage

11. Mo & Chris's Delicious Burgers, Inc., sells food to Military Cafeterias for $15 a box. The fixed costs of this operation are $80,000, while the variable cost per box is $10.

a. What is the break-even point in boxes?

b. Calculate the profit or loss on 15,000 boxes and on 30,000 boxes.

    c. What is the degree of operating leverage at 20,000 boxes and at 30,000 boxes? Why does the degree of operating leverage change as the quantity sold increases?

    d. If the firm has an annual interest expense of $10,000, calculate the degree of financial leverage at both 20,000 and 30,000 boxes.

    e. What is the degree of combined leverage at both sales levels?

12. United Snack Company sells 50-pound bags of peanuts to university dormitories for $10 a bag. The fixed costs of this operation are $80,000, while the variable costs of peanuts are $.10 per pound.

    a. What is the break-even point in bags?

    b. Calculate the profit or loss on 12,000 bags and on 25,000 bags.

    c. What is the degree of operating leverage at 20,000 bags and at 25,000 bags? Why does the degree of operating leverage change as the quantity sold increases?

    d. If United Snack Company has an annual interest expense of $10,000, calculate the degree of financial leverage at both 20,000 and 25,000 bags.

    e. What is the degree of combined leverage at both sales levels?

Break-even point and degree of leverage

13. U.S. Steal has the following income statement data:

Use of different formulas for operating leverage

Units Sold	Total Variable Costs	Fixed Costs	Total Costs	Total Revenue	Operating Income (Loss)
40,000	$ 80,000	$50,000	$130,000	$160,000	$30,000
60,000	120,000	50,000	170,000	240,000	70,000

    a. Compute DOL based on the formula below (see page 125 for an example):

$$DOL = \frac{\text{Percent change in operating income}}{\text{Percent change in units sold}}$$

    b. Confirm that your answer to part *a* is correct by recomputing DOL using formula 5–3 on page 126. There may be a slight difference due to rounding.

$$DOL = \frac{Q(P - VC)}{Q(P - VC) - FC}$$

Q represents beginning units sold (all calculations should be done at this level). P can be found by dividing total revenue by units sold. VC can be found by dividing total variable costs by units sold.

14. Cain Auto Supplies and Able Auto Parts are competitors in the aftermarket for auto supplies. The separate capital structures for Cain and Able are presented below.

Earnings per share and financial leverage

Cain		Able	
Debt @ 10%	$ 50,000	Debt @ 10%	$100,000
Common stock, $10 par	100,000	Common stock, $10 par	50,000
Total	$150,000	Total	$150,000
Common shares	10,000	Common shares	5,000

a. Compute earnings per share if earnings before interest and taxes are $10,000, $15,000, and $50,000 (assume a 30 percent tax rate).

b. Explain the relationship between earnings per share and the level of EBIT.

c. If the cost of debt went up to 12 percent and all other factors remained equal, what would be the break-even level for EBIT?

P/E Ratio

15. In Problem 14, compute the stock price for Cain if it sells at 18 times earnings per share and EBIT is $40,000.

Leverage and stockholder wealth

16. Sterling Optical and Royal Optical both make glass frames and each is able to generate earnings before interest and taxes of $120,000.

The separate capital structures for Sterling and Royal are shown below:

Sterling		Royal	
Debt @ 12%	$ 600,000	Debt @ 12%	$ 200,000
Common stock, $5 par	400,000	Common stock, $5 par.	800,000
Total	$1,000,000	Total	$1,000,000
Common shares	80,000	Common shares	160,000

a. Compute earnings per share for both firms. Assume a 25 percent tax rate.

b. In part *a*, you should have gotten the same answer for both companies' earnings per share. Assuming a P/E ratio of 20 for each company, what would its stock price be?

c. Now as part of your analysis, assume the P/E ratio would be 16 for the riskier company in terms of heavy debt utilization in the capital structure and 25 for the less risky company. What would the stock prices for the two firms be under these assumptions? (Note: Although interest rates also would likely be different based on risk, we will hold them constant for ease of analysis.)

d. Based on the evidence in part *c*, should management only be concerned about the impact of financing plans on earnings per share or should stockholders' wealth maximization (stock price) be considered as well?

Japanese firm and combined leverage

17. Firms in Japan often employ both high operating and financial leverage because of the use of modern technology and close borrower-lender relationships. Assume the Mitaka Company has a sales volume of 125,000 units at a price of $25 per unit; variable costs are $5 per unit and fixed costs are $1,800,000. Interest expense is $400,000. What is the degree of combined leverage for this Japanese firm?

Combining operating and financial leverage

18. Sinclair Manufacturing and Boswell Brothers Inc. are both involved in the production of brick for the homebuilding industry. Their financial information is as follows:

Capital Structure	Sinclair	Boswell
Debt @ 12%..............................	$ 600,000	0
Common stock, $10 per share................	400,000	$ 1,000,000
Total.....................................	$ 1,000,000	$ 1,000,000
Common shares..........................	40,000	100,000
Operating Plan		
Sales (50,000 units at $20 each)...............	$ 1,000,000	$ 1,000,000
Less: Variable costs	800,000	500,000
....	($16 per unit)	($10 per unit)
Fixed costs	0	300,000
Earnings before interest and taxes (EBIT)........	$ 200,000	$ 200,000

a. If you combine Sinclair's capital structure with Boswell's operating plan, what is the degree of combined leverage? (Round to two places to the right of the decimal point.)

b. If you combine Boswell's capital structure with Sinclair's operating plan, what is the degree of combined leverage?

c. Explain why you got the results you did in part b.

d. In part *b*, if sales double, by what percentage will EPS increase?

19. The Norman Automatic Mailer Machine Company is planning to expand production because of the increased volume of mailouts. The increased mailout capacity will cost $2,000,000. The expansion can be financed either by bonds at an interest rate of 12 percent or by selling 40,000 shares of common stock at $50 per share. The current income statement (before expansion) is as follows:

Expansion and leverage

NORMAN AUTOMATIC MAILER Income Statement 200X		
Sales.................................		$3,000,000
Less: Variable costs (40%)	$1,200,000	
Fixed costs......................	800,000	
Earnings before interest and taxes........		1,000,000
Less: Interest expense		400,000
Earnings before taxes..................		600,000
Less: Taxes (@ 35%).................		210,000
Earnings after taxes		$ 390,000
Shares		100,000
Earnings per share....................		$ 3.90

Assume that after expansion, sales are expected to increase by $1,500,000. Variable costs will remain at 40 percent of sales, and fixed costs will increase by $550,000. The tax rate is 35 percent.

a.   Calculate the degree of operating leverage, the degree of financial leverage, and the degree of combined leverage before expansion. (For the degree of operating leverage, use the formula developed in footnote 2 of this chapter; for the degree of combined leverage, use the formula developed in footnote 3. These instructions apply throughout this problem.)

b.   Construct the income statement for the two financial plans.

c.   Calculate the degree of operating leverage, the degree of financial leverage, and the degree of combined leverage, after expansion, for the two financing plans.

d.   Explain which financing plan you favor and the risks involved.

Leverage and sensitivity analysis

20.   Dickinson Company has $12 million in assets. Currently half of these assets are financed with long-term debt at 10 percent and half with common stock having a par value of $8. Ms. Smith, vice-president of finance, wishes to analyze two refinancing plans, one with more debt (D) and one with more equity (E). The company earns a return on assets before interest and taxes of 10 percent. The tax rate is 45 percent.

   Under Plan D, a $3 million long-term bond would be sold at an interest rate of 12 percent and 375,000 shares of stock would be purchased in the market at $8 per share and retired.

   Under Plan E, 375,000 shares of stock would be sold at $8 per share and the $3,000,000 in proceeds would be used to reduce long-term debt.

a.   How would each of these plans affect earnings per share? Consider the current plan and the two new plans.

b.   Which plan would be most favorable if return on assets fell to 5 percent? Increased to 15 percent? Consider the current plan and the two new plans.

c.   If the market price for common stock rose to $12 before the restructuring, which plan would then be most attractive? Continue to assume that $3 million in debt will be used to retire stock in Plan D and $3 million of new equity will be sold to retire debt in Plan E. Also assume for calculations in part *c* that return on assets is 10 percent.

Leverage and sensitivity analysis

21.   Edsel Research Labs has $24 million in assets. Currently half of these assets are financed with long-term debt at 8 percent and half with common stock having a par value of $10. Ms. Edsel, the vice-president of finance, wishes to analyze two refinancing plans, one with more debt (D) and one with more equity (E). The company earns a return on assets before interest and taxes of 8 percent. The tax rate is 40 percent.

   Under Plan D, a $6 million long-term bond would be sold at an interest rate of 10 percent and 600,000 shares of stock would be purchased in the market at $10 per share and retired. Under Plan E, 600,000 shares of stock would be sold at $10 per share and the $6,000,000 in proceeds would be used to reduce long-term debt.

a. How would each of these plans affect earnings per share? Consider the current plan and the two new plans. Which plan(s) would produce the highest EPS?

b. Which plan would be most favorable if return on assets increased to 12 percent? Compare the current plan and the two new plans. What has caused the plans to give different EPS numbers?

c. Assuming return on assets is back to the original 8 percent, but the interest rate on new debt in Plan D is 6 percent, which of the three plans will produce the highest EPS? Why?

22. The Lopez-Portillo Company has $10 million in assets, 80 percent financed by debt and 20 percent financed by common stock. The interest rate on the debt is 15 percent and the par value of the stock is $10 per share. President Lopez-Portillo is considering two financing plans for an expansion to $15 million in assets.

    Under Plan A, the debt-to-total-assets ratio will be maintained, but new debt will cost a whopping 18 percent! Under Plan B, only new common stock at $10 per share will be issued. The tax rate is 40 percent.

Leverage and sensitivity analysis

a. If EBIT is 15 percent on total assets, compute earnings per share (EPS) before the expansion and under the two alternatives.

b. What is the degree of financial leverage under each of the three plans?

c. If stock could be sold at $20 per share due to increased expectations for the firm's sales and earnings, what impact would this have on earnings per share for the two expansion alternatives? Compute earnings per share for each.

d. Explain why corporate financial officers are concerned about their stock values.

23. Mr. Gold is in the widget business. He currently sells 1 million widgets a year at $5 each. His variable cost to produce the widgets is $3 per unit, and he has $1,500,000 in fixed costs. His sales-to-assets ratio is five times, and 40 percent of his assets are financed with 8 percent debt, with the balance financed by common stock at $10 par value per share. The tax rate is 40 percent.

Operating leverage and ratios

    His brother-in-law, Mr. Silverman, says he is doing it all wrong. By reducing his price to $4.50 a widget, he could increase his volume of units sold by 40 percent. Fixed costs would remain constant, and variable costs would remain $3 per unit. His sales-to-assets ratio would be 6.3 times. Furthermore, he could increase his debt-to-assets ratio to 50 percent, with the balance in common stock. It is assumed that the interest rate would go up by 1 percent and the price of stock would remain constant.

a. Compute earnings per share under the Gold plan.

b. Compute earnings per share under the Silverman plan.

c. Mr. Gold's wife, the chief financial officer, does not think that fixed costs would remain constant under the Silverman plan but that they would go up by 15 percent. If this is the case, should Mr. Gold shift to the Silverman plan, based on earnings per share?

Expansion, break-
even analysis, and
leverage

24. Delsing Canning Company is considering an expansion of its facilities. Its
current income statement is as follows:

Sales	$5,000,000
Less: Variable expense (50% of sales)	2,500,000
Fixed expense	1,800,000
Earnings before interest and taxes (EBIT)	700,000
Interest (10% cost)	200,000
Earnings before taxes (EBT)	500,000
Tax (30%)	150,000
Earnings after taxes (EAT)	$ 350,000
Shares of common stock—200,000	
Earnings per share	$1.75

The company is currently financed with 50 percent debt and 50 percent
equity (common stock, par value of $10). In order to expand the facilities,
Mr. Delsing estimates a need for $2 million in additional financing. His
investment banker has laid out three plans for him to consider:

1. Sell $2 million of debt at 13 percent.

2. Sell $2 million of common stock at $20 per share.

3. Sell $1 million of debt at 12 percent and $1 million of common stock at
$25 per share.

Variable costs are expected to stay at 50 percent of sales, while fixed
expenses will increase to $2,300,000 per year. Delsing is not sure how
much this expansion will add to sales, but he estimates that sales will rise
by $1 million per year for the next five years.

Delsing is interested in a thorough analysis of his expansion plans and methods of
financing. He would like you to analyze the following:

a. The break-even point for operating expenses before and after expansion (in
sales dollars).

b. The degree of operating leverage before and after expansion. Assume sales
of $5 million before expansion and $6 million after expansion. Use the
formula in footnote 2 of the chapter.

c. The degree of financial leverage before expansion and for all three
methods of financing after expansion. Assume sales of $6 million for this
question.

d. Compute EPS under all three methods of financing the expansion at
$6 million in sales (first year) and $10 million in sales (last year).

e. What can we learn from the answer to part *d* about the advisability of the
three methods of financing the expansion?

COMPREHENSIVE PROBLEM

Ryan Boot
Company

(review of Chapters 2
through 5)

RYAN BOOT COMPANY
Balance Sheet
December 31, 2007

Assets		Liabilities and Stockholders' Equity	
Cash	$ 50,000	Accounts payable	$2,200,000
Marketable securities	80,000	Accrued expenses	150,000
Accounts receivable	3,000,000	Notes payable (current)	400,000
Inventory	1,000,000	Bonds (10%)	2,500,000
Gross plant and equipment	6,000,000	Common stock (1.7 million	
Less:		shares, par value $1)	1,700,000
Accumulated depreciation	2,000,000	Retained earnings	1,180,000
		Total liabilities and	
Total assets	$8,130,000	stockholders' equity	$8,130,000

Income Statement—2007

Sales (credit)	$7,000,000
Fixed costs*	2,100,000
Variable costs (0.60)	4,200,000
Earnings before interest and taxes	700,000
Less: Interest	250,000
Earnings before taxes	450,000
Less: Taxes @ 35%	157,500
Earnings after taxes	$ 292,500
Dividends (40% payout)	117,000
Increased retained earnings	$ 175,500

*Fixed costs include (a) lease expense of $200,000 and (b) depreciation of $500,000.

Note: Ryan Boots also has $65,000 per year in sinking fund obligations associated with its bond issue. The sinking fund represents an annual repayment of the principal amount of the bond. It is not tax-deductible.

Ratios

	Ryan Boot (to be filled in)	Industry
Profit margin	_____	5.75%
Return on assets	_____	6.90%
Return on equity	_____	9.20%
Receivables turnover	_____	4.35×
Inventory turnover	_____	6.50×
Fixed-asset turnover	_____	1.85×
Total-asset turnover	_____	1.20×
Current ratio	_____	1.45×
Quick ratio	_____	1.10×
Debt to total assets	_____	25.05%
Interest coverage	_____	5.35×
Fixed charge coverage	_____	4.62×

a. Analyze Ryan Boot Company, using ratio analysis. Compute the ratios on the prior page for Ryan and compare them to the industry data that is given. Discuss the weak points, strong points, and what you think should be done to improve the company's performance.

b. In your analysis, calculate the overall break-even point in sales dollars and the cash break-even point. Also compute the degree of operating leverage, degree of financial leverage, and degree of combined leverage. (Use footnote 2 for DOL and footnote 3 in the chapter for DCL.)

c. Use the information in parts *a* and *b* to discuss the risk associated with this company. Given the risk, decide whether a bank should loan funds to Ryan Boot.

Ryan Boot Company is trying to plan the funds needed for 2008. The management anticipates an increase in sales of 20 percent, which can be absorbed *without increasing fixed assets.*

d. What would be Ryan's needs for external funds based on the current balance sheet? Compute RNF (required new funds). Notes payable (current) and bonds are not part of the liability calculation.

e. What would be the required new funds if the company brings its ratios into line with the industry average during 2008? Specifically examine receivables turnover, inventory turnover, and the profit margin. Use the new values to recompute the factors in RNF (assume liabilities stay the same).

f. Do not calculate, only comment on these questions. How would required new funds change if the company:

(1) Were at full capacity?

(2) Raised the dividend payout ratio?

(3) Suffered a decreased growth in sales?

(4) Faced an accelerated inflation rate?

WEB EXERCISE

At the start of the chapter, we talked about how risky and volatile airlines' operations were. Let's examine this further. Go to finance.yahoo.com.

1. Enter AMR for American Airlines in the "Get Quotes" box.

2. Go to "Company Profile" along the left-hand margin and write a one-paragraph description of the company.

3. Scroll down and click on the "Income Statement." Describe the pattern of change for "Total Revenue" and "Net Income from Continuing Operations" in one paragraph.

4. Next go to the "Balance Sheet". In one sentence, describe the pattern of change in Stockholders' Equity and indicate whether this does or does not appear to be a matter of concern.

5. Click on "Analyst Estimates." Does AMR's earnings estimates appear to be more or less promising for the future?

6. Finally, click on "Competitors." How does AMR compare to the other airlines and the industry in terms of Operating Margin?

Note: From time to time, companies redesign their Web sites and occasionally a topic we have listed may have been deleted, updated, or moved into a different location. If you click on the site map or site index, you will be introduced to a table of contents which should aid you in finding the topic you are looking for.

S & P   P R O B L E M S   www.mhhe.com/edumarketinsight

STANDARD &POOR'S

1. Log onto the S&P Market Insight Web site, www.mhhe.com/edumarketinsight.

2. Click on "Company," which is the first box below the Market Insight title.

3. Type Chevron's ticker symbol "CVX" in the box and click on Go.

4. Scroll down the left margin to the second major category and click on "S&P Stock Reports" and then click on the first S&P Stock Report at the top of the list. Scroll down to the bottom of the page and you will find an abbreviated income statement.

5. Using the most recent two years of available data, compute Chevron's degree of operating leverage. You will have to use the formula, percentage change in pretax income divided by percentage change in revenues.

6. Using the last two years of available data, compute Chevron's degree of financial leverage. You will have to use the formula, percentage change in net income divided by percentage change in pretax income (EBIT).

7. Multiply the degree of financial leverage times the degree of operating leverage to determine the degree of combined leverage.

8. Repeat steps 5, 6, and 7 for the years 2002 and 2003 and compare the leverage ratios. Did the degrees of leverage stay the same? Explain the differences between the two periods.

part 3

Working Capital Management

RELATED WEB SITES

www.stlouisfed.org

www.calloways.com

www.mcgraw-hill.com

www.abercrombie.com

www.abercrombiekids.com

www.covisint.com

www.freemarkets.com

www.ebreviate.com

www.perfect.com

www.nacha.org

www.swift.com

www.nasa.gov

www.bankofamerica.com

www.punchtaverns.com

www.ge.com

Section 3 presents discussions of working capital decisions involving short term credit and the management of cash, marketable securities, accounts receivable, and inventory. One of the biggest participants in the international arena of finance is Citigroup and its Citibank unit, the largest bank in the United States. Citigroup's chief financial officer is Sally Krawcheck, a South Carolina native who turned 40 years old in 2005. She left her position as chairman and CEO of Sanford Bernstein in 2002 to move to Citigroup to run the bank's Smith Barney research and brokerage functions. In 2005 she moved into the role of CFO.

Ms. Krawcheck started out as an equity analyst following the banking industry. She is known as a real numbers person and has been tagged as "Mrs. Clean" because of her focus on ethics and her direct communication style. *Fortune* magazine once called Sally Krawcheck "The Last Honest Analyst." She is considered one of the most influential women executives in the Wall Street financial community.

Citigroup was charged by the New York state attorney general, Eliot Spitzer, for spinning initial public offerings and making biased stock recommendations in its Smith Barney division. Citigroup settled the charges out of court with the state. Additionally, the Federal Reserve imposed merger restrictions on Citigroup over "ethical lapses." Krawcheck, because of her reputation for high ethical standards, has been the right person in the right place and is considered by many to be a stabilizing force at Citigroup. In 2006 the Federal Reserve removed the merger restrictions.

Besides being responsible for number crunching, she is also in charge of investor relations, strategic planning, and mergers and acquisitions. She says that she spends eight weeks out of each year getting ready for the quarterly earnings reporting season. It is a grueling job but she says she loves it.

Ms. Krawcheck graduated from the University of North Carolina in 1987 and received her MBA. from Columbia University. In 2005 she shared the wisdom of her career with students at MIT. The talk was sponsored by the MIT Leadership Center. She had this advice for students. ". . .learn the art of persuasion . . . know how to read people . . . it's very important for everyone to know what they are good and

Sally Krawcheck—Citigroup
© Mark Peterson/Corbis

bad at . . . execution is all about communication." Last she said, "You'll be working for a long time, make sure you do something you like. At the end of the day all you have is your skills, your reputation, and your ethics."

Working Capital and the Financing Decision

6

chapter concepts

1. Working capital management involves financing and controlling the current assets of the firm.

2. Management must distinguish between those current assets that are easily converted to cash and those that are more permanent.

3. The financing of an asset should be tied to how long the asset is likely to be on the balance sheet.

4. Long-term financing is usually more expensive than short-term financing based on the theory of the term structure of interest rates.

5. Risk, as well as profitability, determines the financing plan for current assets.

The rapid growth of business firms in the last two decades has challenged the ingenuity of financial managers to provide adequate financing. Rapidly expanding sales may cause intense pressure for inventory and receivables buildup—draining the cash resources of the firm. As indicated in Chapter 4, "Financial Forecasting," a large sales increase creates an expansion of current assets, especially accounts receivable and inventory. Some of the increased current assets can be financed through the firm's retained earnings, but in most cases internal funds will not provide enough financing and some external sources of funds must be found. In fact, the faster the growth in sales, the more likely it is that an increasing percentage of financing will be external to the firm. These funds could come from the sale of common stock, preferred stock, long-term bonds, short-term securities, and bank loans, or from a combination of short- and long-term sources of funds.

There is also the problem of seasonal sales that affects many industries such as soft drinks, toys, retail sales, and textbook publishing. Seasonal demand for products makes forecasting cash flows and receivables and inventory management difficult. The Internet is beginning to alleviate some of these problems and help management make better plans.

If you have had a marketing course, you have heard about supply chain management. Well, financial executives are also interested in the supply chain as an area where the Internet can help control working capital through online software. McDonald's Corporation of Big Mac fame formed eMac Digital to explore opportunities in business-to-business (B2B) online ventures. One of the first things on the agenda was to have eMac Digital help McDonald's reduce costs. McDonald's wanted to create an online marketplace where restaurants can buy supplies online from food companies. McDonald's, like Wal-Mart, Harley Davidson, and Ericsson, has

A Great Inventory Tracking System May Be Helping You

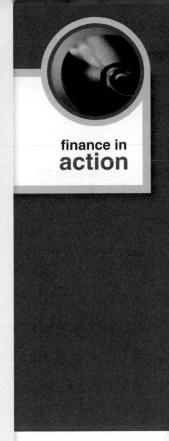

RFID (radio frequency identification technology), a system that has been around since World War II and used by the military to keep track of airplanes, is now the latest rage in inventory/supply chain management. RFID chips have been used in trains, ships, and trucks to track shipment containers. They are also used in automatic toll systems that allow drivers to pass through tolling areas without stopping. The state of Michigan has used these chips to track livestock; marathon officials have used them to track a runner's time, and the Defense Department has used them to track the shelf life of their food rations. Additionally, they are now being used to make sure that shipping containers entering U.S. ports have not been tampered with after inspection.

Hewlett-Packard in a business briefing paper indicates that there may be as much as $45 billion of excess inventory in the retail supply chain that is unaccounted for at any given time. In short, RFID chips can help a company track goods and make sure that the right goods get to the right places on time. Wal-Mart has mandated that its suppliers must have

RFID chips in each pallet of goods shipped to their distribution centers. By October 2005, Wal-Mart had 13 distribution centers and 600 stores and SAM's CLUB locations with live and up-and-running RFID tracking systems. Their top 100 suppliers are already using RFID technology and by January 2006, Wal-Mart plans to have the next top 200 suppliers using the system.

A.T. Kearney, a consulting firm, estimates that the system Wal-Mart and other retailers are putting into place will save billions of dollars. The bad news for Wal-Mart's suppliers is that they are required to pay the entire cost of buying and applying the tags. Kearney estimates that a grocery manufacturer with $5 billion in sales could use more than 220 million tags annually, which could cost $33 million at the current price of 15 cents per tag. You can do the math. If prices of tags fall to 5 cents, the $11 million would still reduce the supplier's profit. The bright side of this is that for expensive and sensitive goods such as pharmaceuticals, the use of RFID chips will also cut down on theft, which might more than cover the cost of the tags.

embraced supply chain management using Web-based procedures. The goal is to squeeze out inefficiencies in the supply chain and thereby lower costs. One of the big benefits is a reduction in inventory through online communications between the buyer and supplier, which speeds up the ordering and delivery process and reduces the amount of inventory needed on hand. These systems may also be able to attract a large number of suppliers to bid on the company's business at more competitive prices.

Another new wrinkle is that retailers like Wal-Mart are requiring suppliers to ship their goods with radio frequency identification chips (RFID) embedded in their shipments. The use of these chips is expected to eliminate processing delays, reduce theft, and result in better inventory management. From the financial manager's viewpoint, anything that can reduce inventory levels without creating out of stock situations will reduce the amount of money needed to finance inventory. If you wish, you can read more about Wal-Mart and RFID chips in the above Finance in Action Box.

Working capital management involves the financing and management of the current assets of the firm. The financial executive probably devotes more time to working capital management than to any other activity. Current assets, by their very nature, are changing daily, if not hourly, and managerial decisions must be made. "How much inventory is to be carried, and how do we get the funds to pay for it?" Unlike long-term decisions, there can be no deferral of action. While long-term decisions involving plant and equipment or market strategy may well determine the eventual success of the firm, short-term decisions on working capital determine whether the firm gets to the long term.

In this chapter we examine the nature of asset growth, the process of matching sales and production, financial aspects of working capital management, and the factors that go into development of an optimum policy.

The Nature of Asset Growth

Any company that produces and sells a product, whether the product is consumer or manufacturer oriented, will have current assets and fixed assets. If a firm grows, those assets are likely to increase over time. The key to current asset planning is the ability of management to forecast sales accurately and then to match the production schedules with the sales forecast. Whenever actual sales are different from forecasted sales, unexpected buildups or reductions in inventory will occur that will eventually affect receivables and cash flow.

In the simplest case, all of the firm's current assets will be **self-liquidating assets** (sold at the end of a specified time period). Assume that at the start of the summer you buy 100 tires to be disposed of by September. It is your intention that all tires will be sold, receivables collected, and bills paid over this time period. In this case your working capital (current asset) needs are truly short term.

Now let us begin to expand the business. In stage two you add radios, seat covers, and batteries to your operation. Some of your inventory will again be completely liquidated, while other items will form the basic stock for your operation. To stay in business, you must maintain floor displays and multiple items for selection. Furthermore, not all items will sell. As you eventually grow to more than one store, this "permanent" aggregate stock of current assets will continue to increase. Problems of inadequate financing arrangements are often the result of the businessperson's failure to realize the firm is carrying not only self-liquidating inventory, but also the anomaly of **"permanent" current assets**.

The movement from stage one to stage two of growth for a typical business is depicted in Figure 6–1. In Panel A the buildup in current assets is **temporary**—while in Panel B, part of the growth in current assets is temporary and part is permanent. (Fixed assets are included in the illustrations, but they are not directly related to the present discussion.)

Controlling Assets— Matching Sales and Production

In most firms, fixed assets grow slowly as productive capacity is increased and old equipment is replaced, but current assets fluctuate in the short run, depending on the level of production versus the level of sales. When the firm produces more than it sells, inventory rises. When sales rise faster than production, inventory declines and receivables rise.

As discussed in the treatment of the cash budgeting process in Chapter 4, some firms employ **level production** methods to smooth production schedules and use manpower and equipment efficiently at a lower cost. One consequence of level production is that current assets go up and down when sales and production are not equal. Other firms may try to match sales and production as closely as possible in the short run. This allows current assets to increase or decrease with the level of sales and eliminates the large seasonal bulges or sharp reductions in current assets that occur under level production.

Publishing companies are good examples of companies with seasonal sales and inventory problems. By the nature of the textbook market, heavy sales are made in the third quarter of each year for fall semester sales. Most sales occur in July, August, September, and again in December for the second semester. The actual printing and

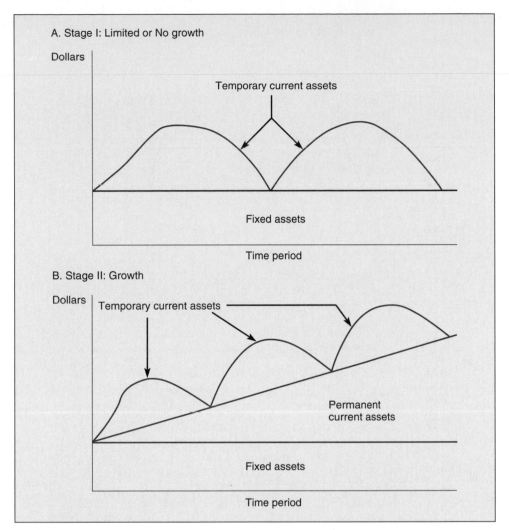

Figure 6–1
The nature of asset
growth

binding of a book have fixed costs that make printing many copies more efficient. Since publishing companies cannot reproduce books on demand, they contract with the printing company to print a fixed number of copies, depending on expected sales over at least one year and sometimes based on sales over several years. If the books sell better than expected, the publishing company will order a second or third printing. Orders may have to be placed as much as nine months before the books will actually be needed, and reorders will be placed as much as three or four months ahead of actual sales. If the book declines in popularity, the publisher could get stuck with a large inventory of obsolete books.

Figure 6–2 depicts quarterly sales and earnings per share for McGraw-Hill Companies, Inc., a diversified publisher of textbooks (*Foundations of Financial Management*), magazines (*BusinessWeek*), databases (*DRI*), and the owner of Standard and Poor's. This major publishing company is a good example of a firm with seasonal sales. McGraw-Hill has a significant share of its sales and earnings in the third and fourth quarters. As mentioned above and you know from experience, most textbooks

Figure 6–2

Quarterly sales and earnings per share for McGraw-Hill

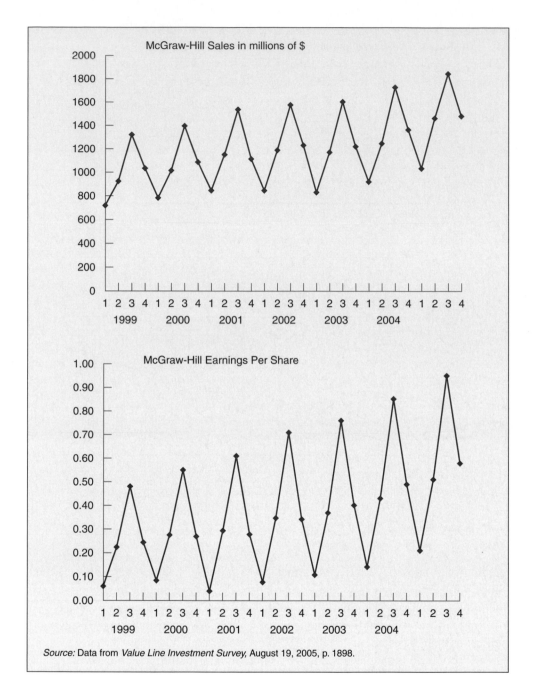

Source: Data from *Value Line Investment Survey,* August 19, 2005, p. 1898.

are sold to bookstores in August, September, and December. The smallest sales are in the first quarter and second quarters of the year and the heavy fixed costs of publishing cause very low earnings per share in these two quarters. You can see from Figure 6–2 that the long-term trend in sales for the firm is up and earnings per share are following the same pattern as sales.

While not all revenues at McGraw-Hill are seasonal, book revenues have a major impact on the company's sales pattern. Because of the seasonal nature of the textbook publishing business, lenders as well as financial managers need to understand the need for inventory financing and inventory management. If management has not planned inventory correctly, lost sales due to stock outs could be a serious problem.

Retail firms, such as Target and Limited Brands, also have seasonal sales patterns. Figure 6–3 shows the quarterly sales and earnings per share of these two companies, with the quarters ending in April, July, October, and January. These retail companies do not stock a year or more of inventory at one time as do publishers. They are selling products that are either manufactured for them by others or manufactured by their subsidiaries. Most retail stores are not involved in deciding on level versus seasonal

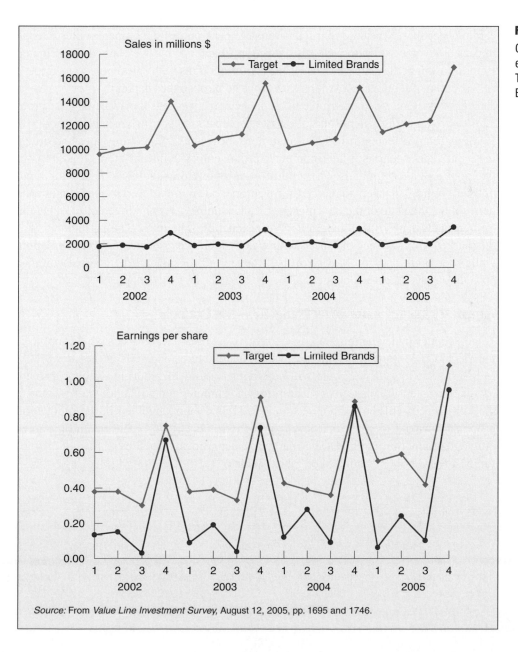

Figure 6–3

Quarterly sales and earnings per share, Target and Limited Brands production but rather in matching sales and inventory. Their suppliers must make the decision to produce on either a level or a seasonal basis. Since the selling seasons are very much affected by the weather and holiday periods, the suppliers and retailers cannot avoid the inventory risk. The fourth quarter for retailers, which begins in November and ends in January, is their biggest quarter and accounts for as much as one-half of their earnings. You can be sure that inventory not sold during the Christmas season will be put on sale during January.

Both Target and Limited Brands show seasonal peaks and troughs in sales that will also be reflected in their cash balances, accounts receivable, and inventory. Notice in Figure 6–3 that Target is growing much faster than Limited Brands which has a rather flat trendline. Even so, Limited Brands' peak earnings per share are almost as high as Target's earnings per share when the fourth quarter sales peak out. Both companies illustrate the impact of leverage on earnings as discussed in Chapter 5, but we can tell that Limited Brands has higher leverage because its EPS rises and falls with sales more than Target's EPS (bottom of Figure 6–3). We shall see as we go through the chapter that seasonal sales can cause asset management problems. A financial manger must be aware of these problems to avoid getting caught short of cash or unprepared to borrow when necessary.

Many retail-oriented firms have been more successful in matching sales and orders in recent years because of new, computerized inventory control systems linked to on-line point-of-sales terminals. These **point-of-sales terminals** allow either digital input or use of optical scanners to record the inventory code numbers and the amount of each item sold. At the end of the day, managers can examine sales and inventory levels item by item and, if need be, adjust orders or production schedules. The predictability of the market will influence the speed with which the manager reacts to this information, while the length and complexity of the production process will dictate just how fast production levels can be changed.

Temporary Assets under Level Production—An Example

To get a better understanding of how current assets fluctuate, let us use the example of the Yawakuzi Motorcycle Company, which manufactures and sells in the snowy U.S. Midwest. Not too many people will be buying motorcycles during October through March, but sales will pick up in early spring and summer and will again trail off during the fall. Because of the fixed assets and the skilled labor involved in the production process, Yawakuzi decides that level production is the least expensive and the most efficient production method. The marketing department provides a 12-month sales forecast for October through September (Table 6–1).

Table 6–1   Yawakuzi sales forecast (in units)

1st Quarter		2nd Quarter		3rd Quarter		4th Quarter	
October	300	January	0	April	1,000	July	2,000
November	150	February	0	May	2,000	August	1,000
December	50	March	600	June	2,000	September	500

Total sales of 9,600 units at $3,000 each = $28,800,000 in sales.

After reviewing the sales forecast, Yawakuzi decides to produce 800 motorcycles per month, or one year's production of 9,600 divided by 12. A look at Table 6–2 shows how level production and seasonal sales combine to create fluctuating inventory. Assume that October's beginning inventory is one month's production of 800 units. The ending inventory level is computed for each month and then multiplied by the production cost per unit of $2,000.

Table 6–2

Yawakuzi's production schedule and inventory

	Beginning Inventory	+	Production (level production)	−	Sales	=	Ending Inventory	Inventory (at cost of $2,000 per unit)
October.......	800		800		300		1,300	$2,600,000
November.....	1,300		800		150		1,950	3,900,000
December.....	1,950		800		50		2,700	5,400,000
January.......	2,700		800		0		3,500	7,000,000
February......	3,500		800		0		4,300	8,600,000
March........	4,300		800		600		4,500	9,000,000
April..........	4,500		800		1,000		4,300	8,600,000
May..........	4,300		800		2,000		3,100	6,200,000
June	3,100		800		2,000		1,900	3,800,000
July..........	1,900		800		2,000		700	1,400,000
August........	700		800		1,000.....		500	1,000,000
September.....	500		800		500.....		800	1,600,000

The inventory level at cost fluctuates from a high of $9 million in March, the last consecutive month in which production is greater than sales, to a low of $1 million in August, the last month in which sales are greater than production. Table 6–3 on page 160 combines a sales forecast, a cash receipts schedule, a cash payments schedule, and a brief cash budget in order to examine the buildup in accounts receivable and cash.

In Table 6–3 the *sales forecast* is based on assumptions in Table 6–1. The unit volume of sales is multiplied by a sales price of $3,000 to get sales dollars in millions. Next, *cash receipts* represent 50 percent collected in cash during the month of sale and 50 percent from the prior month's sales. For example, in October this would represent $0.45 million from the current month plus $0.75 million from the prior month's sales.

Cash payments in Table 6–3 are based on an assumption of level production of 800 units per month at a cost of $2,000 per unit, or $1.6 million, plus payments for overhead, dividends, interest, and taxes.

Finally the *cash budget* in Table 6–3 represents a comparison of the cash receipts and cash payments schedules to determine cash flow. We further assume the firm desires a minimum cash balance of $0.25 million. Thus in October, a negative cash flow of $1.1 million brings the cumulative cash balance to a negative $0.85 million and $1.1 million must be borrowed to provide an ending cash balance of $0.25 million. Similar negative cash flows in subsequent months necessitate expanding the bank loan. For example, in November there is a negative cash flow of $1.325 million. This brings the cumulative cash balance to −$1.075 million, requiring additional borrowings of $1.325 million to ensure a minimum cash balance of $0.25 million. The cumulative

Table 6–3 Sales forecast, cash receipts and payments, and cash budget

	Oct.	Nov.	Dec.	Jan.	Feb.	March	April	May	June	July	Aug.	Sept.
Sales Forecast ($ millions)												
Sales (units)	300	150	50	0	0	600	1,000	2,000	2,000	2,000	1,000	500
Sales (unit price, $3,000)	$0.9	$0.45	$0.15	$0	$0	$1.8	$3.0	$6.0	$6.0	$6.0	$3.0	$1.5
Cash Receipts Schedule ($ millions)												
50% cash	$0.45	$0.225	$0.075	$ 0	$0	$0.9	$1.5	$3.0	$3.0	$3.0	$1.5	$0.75
50% from prior month's sales	0.75*	0.450	0.225	0.075	0	0	0.9	1.5	3.0	3.0	3.0	1.50
Total cash receipts	$1.20	$0.675	$0.300	$0.075	0	$0.9	$2.4	$4.5	$6.0	$6.0	$4.5	$2.25
Cash Payments Schedule ($ millions)												
Constant production of 800 units/ month (cost, $2,000 per unit)	$1.6	$1.6	$1.6	$1.6	$1.6	$1.6	$1.6	$1.6	$1.6	$1.6	$1.6	$1.6
Overhead	0.4	0.4	0.4	0.4	0.4	0.4	0.4	0.4	0.4	0.4	0.4	0.4
Dividends and interest	—	—	—	—	—	—	—	—	—	—	1.0	—
Taxes	0.3	—	—	0.3	—	—	0.3	—	—	0.3	—	—
Total cash payments	$2.3	$2.0	$2.0	$2.3	$2.0	$2.0	$2.3	$2.0	$2.0	$2.3	$3.0	$2.0
Cash Budget ($ millions; required minimum balance is $0.25 million)												
Cash flow	$(1.1)	$(1.325)	$(1.7)	$(2.225)	$(2.0)	$(1.1)	$0.1	$2.5	$4.0	$3.7	$1.5	$0.25
Beginning cash	0.25†	0.25	0.25	0.250	0.25	0.25	0.25	0.25	0.25	0.25	1.1	2.60
Cumulative cash balance	$(0.85)	$(1.075)	$(1.45)	$(1.975)	$(1.75)	$(0.85)	$0.35	$2.75	$4.25	$3.95	$2.6	$2.85
Monthly loan or (repayment)	1.1	1.325	1.7	2.225	2.0	1.1	(0.1)	(2.5)	(4.0)	(2.85)	0	0
Cumulative loan	1.1	2.425	4.125	6.350	8.35	9.45	9.35	6.85	2.85	0	0	0
Ending cash balance	0.25	0.25	0.25	0.25	0.25	0.25	0.25	0.25	0.25	1.1	2.6	2.85

*Assumes September sales of $1.5 million.

†Assumes cash balance of $0.25 million at the beginning of October and that this is the desired minimum cash balance.

loan through November (October and November borrowings) now adds up to $2.425 million. Our cumulative bank loan is highest in the month of March.

We now wish to ascertain our total current asset buildup as a result of level production and fluctuating sales for October through September. The analysis is presented in Table 6–4. The cash figures come directly from the last line of Table 6–3. The accounts receivable balance is based on the assumption that accounts receivable represent 50 percent of sales in a given month, as the other 50 percent is paid for in cash. Thus the accounts receivable figure in Table 6–4 represents 50 percent of the sales figure from the second numerical line in Table 6–3. Finally, the inventory figure in Table 6–4 is taken directly from the last column of Table 6–2 on page 159, which presented the production schedule and inventory data.

	Cash	Accounts Receivable	Inventory	Total Current Assets
October	$0.25	$0.450	$2.6	$ 3.30
November	0.25	0.225	3.9	4.375
December	0.25	0.075	5.4	5.725
January	0.25	0.00	7.0	7.25
February	0.25	0.00	8.6	8.85
March	0.25	0.90	9.0	10.15
April	0.25	1.50	8.6	10.35
May	0.25	3.00	6.2	9.45
June	0.25	3.00	3.8	7.05
July	1.10	3.00	1.4	5.50
August	2.60	1.50	1.0	5.10
September	2.85	0.75	1.6	5.20

Table 6–4
Total current assets, first year ($millions)

Total current assets (last column in Table 6–4) start at $3.3 million in October and rise to $10.35 million in the peak month of April. From April through August, sales are larger than production, and inventory falls to its low of $1 million in August, but accounts receivable peak at $3 million in the highest sales months of May, June, and July. The cash budget in Table 6–3 (on page 160) explains the cash flows and external funds borrowed to finance asset accumulation. From October to March, Yawakuzi borrows more and more money to finance the inventory buildup, but from April forward it eliminates all borrowing as inventory is liquidated and cash balances rise to complete the cycle. In October the cycle starts over again; but now the firm has accumulated cash it can use to finance next year's asset accumulation, pay a larger dividend, replace old equipment, or—if growth in sales is anticipated—invest in new equipment to increase productive capacity. Table 6–5 on page 162 presents the cash budget and total current assets for the second year. Under a simplified no-growth assumption, the monthly cash flow is the same as that of the first year, but beginning cash in October is much higher than the first year's ending cash balance and this lowers the borrowing requirement and increases the ending cash balance and total current assets at year-end. Higher current assets are present despite the fact that accounts receivable and inventory do not change.

Table 6-5 Cash budget and assets for second year with no growth in sales ($millions)

| | End of First Year | | | | | | | Second Year | | | | | |
	Sept.	Oct.	Nov.	Dec.	Jan.	Feb.	March	April	May	June	July	Aug.	Sept.
Cash flow	$0.25	$(1.1)	$(1.325)	$(1.7)	$(2.225)	$(2.0)	$(1.1)	$0.1	$2.5	$4.0	$3.7	$1.5	$0.25
Beginning cash	2.60	2.85	1.750	0.425	0.25	0.25	0.25	0.25	0.25	0.25	0.25	3.7	5.2
Cumulative cash balance . . .		1.75	0.425	(1.275)	(1.975)	(1.75)	(0.85)	0.35	2.75	4.25	3.95	5.2	5.45
Monthly loan (or repayment) . .	—	—	—	1.525	2.225	2.0	1.1	(0.1)	(2.5)	(4.0)	(0.25)	—	—
Cumulative loan	—	—	—	1.525	3.750	5.75	6.85	6.75	4.25	0.25	0	—	—
Ending cash balance	$2.85	$1.75	$0.425	$0.25	$0.25	$0.25	$0.25	$0.25	$0.25	$0.25	$3.70	$5.2	$5.45
Total Current Assets													
Ending cash balance	$2.85	$1.75	$0.425	$0.25	$0.25	$0.25	$0.25	$0.25	$0.25	$0.25	$3.70	$5.2	$5.45
Accounts receivable	0.75	0.45	0.225	0.075	0	0	0.95	1.50	3.0	3.0	3.0	1.5	0.75
Inventory	1.6	2.6	3.9	5.4	7.0	8.6	9.0	8.6	6.2	3.8	1.4	1.0	1.60
Total current assets	$5.2	$4.8	$4.55	$5.725	$7.25	$8.85	$10.20	$10.35	$9.45	$7.05	$8.1	$7.7	$7.80

Figure 6–4 is a graphic presentation of the current asset cycle. It includes the two years covered in Tables 6–4 and 6–5 assuming level production and no sales growth.

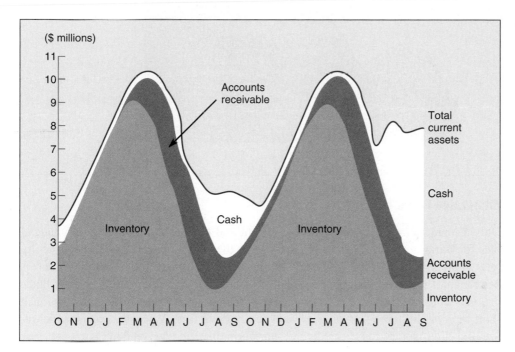

Figure 6–4
The nature of asset growth (Yawakuzi)

The financial manager's selection of external sources of funds to finance assets may be one of the firm's most important decisions. The axiom that all current assets should be financed by current liabilities (accounts payable, bank loans, commercial paper, etc.) is subject to challenge when one sees the permanent buildup that can occur in current assets. In the Yawakuzi example, the buildup in inventory was substantial at $9 million. The example had a logical conclusion in that the motorcycles were sold, cash was generated, and current assets became very liquid. What if a much smaller level of sales had occurred? Yawakuzi would be sitting on a large inventory that needed to be financed and would be generating no cash. Theoretically, the firm could be declared technically insolvent (bankrupt) if short-term sources of funds were used but were unable to be renewed when they came due. How would the interest and principal be paid without cash flow from inventory liquidation? The most appropriate financing pattern would be one in which asset buildup and length of financing terms are perfectly matched, as indicated in Figure 6–5.

In the upper part of Figure 6–5 we see that the temporary buildup in current assets (represented by orange) is financed by short-term funds. More importantly, however, permanent current assets and fixed assets (both represented by blue) are financed with long-term funds from the sale of stock, the issuance of bonds, or retention of earnings.

Patterns of Financing

Figure 6–5

Matching long-term and short-term needs

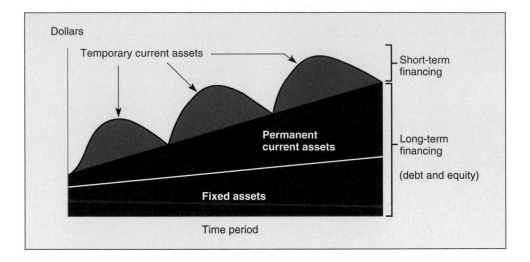

Alternative Plans

Only a financial manager with unusual insight and timing could construct a financial plan for working capital that adhered perfectly to the design in Figure 6–5. The difficulty rests in determining precisely what part of current assets is temporary and what part is permanent. Even if dollar amounts could be ascertained, the exact timing of asset liquidation is a difficult matter. To compound the problem, we are never quite sure how much short-term or long-term financing is available at a given time. While the precise synchronization of temporary current assets and short-term financing depicted in Figure 6–5 may be the most desirable and logical plan, other alternatives must be considered.

Long-Term Financing

To protect against the danger of not being able to provide adequate short-term financing in tight money periods, the financial manager may rely on long-term funds to cover some short-term needs. As indicated in Figure 6–6, long-term capital is now being used to finance fixed assets, permanent current assets, and part of *temporary current assets*.

Figure 6–6

Using long-term financing for part of short-term needs

By using long-term capital to cover part of short-term needs, the firm virtually assures itself of having adequate capital at all times. The firm may prefer to borrow a million dollars for 10 years—rather than attempt to borrow a million dollars at the beginning of each year for 10 years and pay it back at the end of each year.

Short-Term Financing (Opposite Approach)

This is not to say that all financial managers utilize long-term financing on a large scale. To acquire long-term funds, the firm must generally go to the capital markets with a bond or stock offering or must privately place longer-term obligations with insurance companies, wealthy individuals, and so forth. Many small businesses do not have access to such long-term capital and are forced to rely heavily on short-term bank and trade credit.

Furthermore, short-term financing offers some advantages over more extended financial arrangements. As a general rule, the interest rate on short-term funds is lower than that on long-term funds. We might surmise then that a firm could develop a working capital financing plan in which short-term funds are used to finance not only temporary current assets, but also part of the permanent working capital needs of the firm. As depicted in Figure 6–7, bank and trade credit as well as other sources of short-term financing are now supporting part of the permanent capital asset needs of the firm.

Figure 6–7
Using short-term financing for part of long-term needs

Some corporations are more flexible than others because they are not locked into a few available sources of funds. Corporations would like many financing alternatives in order to minimize their cost of funds at any point. Unfortunately, not many firms are in this enviable position through the duration of a business cycle. During an economic boom period, a shortage of low-cost alternatives exists, and firms often minimize their financing costs by raising funds in advance of forecasted asset needs.

Not only does the financial manager encounter a timing problem, but he or she also needs to select the right type of financing. Even for companies having many alternative sources of funds, there may be only one or two decisions that will look good in retrospect. At the time the financing decision is made, the financial manager is never sure it is the right one. Should the financing be long-term or short-term, debt

The Financing Decision

or equity, and so on? Figure 6–8 is a decision-tree diagram that shows many of the financing choices available to a chief financial officer. A decision is made at each point until a final financing method is chosen. In most cases a corporation will use a combination of these financing methods. At all times the financial manager will balance short-term versus long-term considerations against the composition of the

Figure 6–8

Decision tree of the financing decision

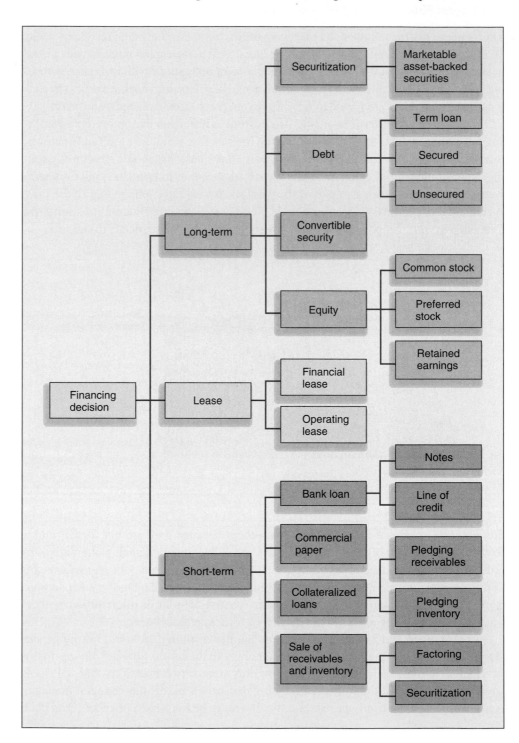

firm's assets and the firm's willingness to accept risk. The ratio of long-term financing to short-term financing at any point in time will be greatly influenced by the *term structure of interest rates*.

Term Structure of Interest Rates

The **term structure of interest rates** is often referred to as a **yield curve**. It shows the relative level of short-term and long-term interest rates at a point in time. Knowledge of changing interest rates and interest rate theory is extremely valuable to corporate executives making decisions about how to time and structure their borrowing between short- and long-term debt. Generally U.S. government securities are used to construct yield curves because they are free of default risk and the large number of maturities creates a fairly continuous curve. Yields on corporate debt securities will move in the same direction as government securities, but will have higher interest rates because of their greater financial risk. Yield curves for both corporations and government securities change daily to reflect current competitive conditions in the money and capital markets, expected inflation, and changes in economic conditions.

Three basic theories describe the shape of the yield curve. The first theory is called the **liquidity premium theory** and states that long-term rates should be higher than short-term rates. This premium of long-term rates over short-term rates exists because short-term securities have greater liquidity and, therefore, higher rates have to be offered to potential long-term bond buyers to entice them to hold these less liquid and more price-sensitive securities. The **market segmentation theory** (the second theory) states that Treasury securities are divided into market segments by the various financial institutions investing in the market. Commercial banks prefer short-term securities of one year or less to match their short-term lending strategies. Savings and loans and other mortgage-oriented financial institutions prefer the intermediate length securities of between 5 and 7 years, while pension funds and life insurance companies prefer long-term 20- to 30-year securities to offset the long-term nature of their commitments to policyholders. The changing needs, desires, and strategies of these investors tend to strongly influence the nature and relationship of short-term and long-term interest rates.

The third theory describing the term structure of interest rates is called the **expectations hypothesis**. This theory explains the yields on long-term securities as a function of short-term rates. The expectations theory says long-term rates reflect the average of short-term expected rates over the time period that the long-term security is outstanding. Using a four-year example and simple averages,[1] we demonstrate this theory in Table 6–6. In the left-hand panel of the table, we show the anticipated one-year rate

Table 6–6   The expectations theory

1 year T-bill at beginning of year 1 = 4%	
1-year T-bill at beginning of year 2 = 5%	2-year security (4% + 5%)/2 = 4.5%
1-year T-bill at beginning of year 3 = 6%	3-year security (4% + 5% + 6%)/3 = 5.0%
1-year T-bill at beginning of year 4 = 7%	4-year security (4% + 5% + 6% + 7%)/4 = 5.5%

[1]Using a geometric mean return rather than a simple average return creates a more exact rate of return. For example for the four-year security a geometric return would provide a return of 5.494% rather than the 5.5% simple average in Table 6–6.

on T-bill (Treasury bill) securities at the beginning of each of four years in the future. Treasury bills are short-term securities issued by the government. In the right-hand panel, we show averages of the one-year anticipated rates.

For example the two-year security rate is the average of the expected yields of two one-year T-bills, while the rate on the four-year security is the average of all four one-year rates. In this example, the progressively higher rates for two-, three- and four-year securities represent a reflection of higher anticipated one-year rates in the future. The expectations hypothesis is especially useful in explaining the shape and movement of the yield curve. The result of the expectations hypothesis is that, when long-term rates are much higher than short-term rates, the market is saying it expects short-term rates to rise. When long-term rates are lower than short-term rates, the market is expecting short-term rates to fall. This theory is useful to financial managers in helping them set expectations for the cost of financing over time and, especially, in making choices about when to use short-term debt or long-term debt.

In fact, all three theories of the term structure just discussed have some impact on interest rates. At times the liquidity premium or segmentation theory dominates the shape of the curve and, at other times, the expectations theory is the most important.

Figure 6–9 shows a Treasury yield curve that is published by the St. Louis Federal Reserve Bank in *Monetary Trends,* a weekly online publication that can be directly accessed on www.stlouisfed.org. The bottom axis shows time periods (months and years) and the vertical axis indicates rates. In this figure on the top curve, yields rise from about 3.5 percent for three-month Treasury bills, to 4.0 percent for five-year Treasury

Figure 6–9

Treasury yield curve

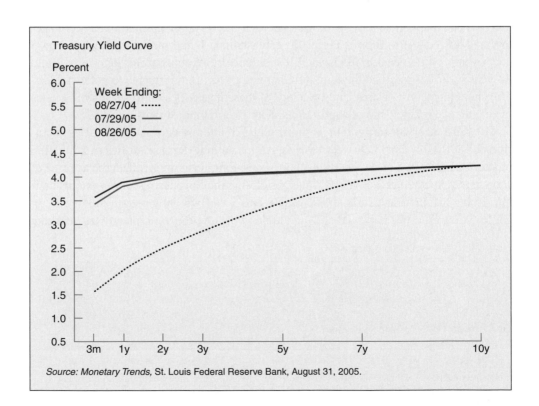

notes, and continue up to 4.2 percent for 10-year Treasury bonds. This upward-sloping yield curve has the normal shape.

The bottom line in the chart represents the yield curve for the same time period one year earlier. Monetary policy has moved yields all along the curve to higher levels. The three-month yields have risen from about 1.50 percent to 3.5 percent or 200 **basis points** (one basis point equals 1/100 of 1 percent).

An *upward-sloping* yield curve is considered normal, but the difference between short-term and long-term rates has often been quite wide, such as in October of 1993 when short-term rates were less than 3 percent and long-term rates were close to 7 percent. Generally, the more upward sloping the yield curve the greater the expectation that interest rates will rise. When faced with a *downward-sloping,* or inverted, yield curve, the expectation would be the opposite. A good example of this occurred in September of 1981 when short-term rates were over 17 percent and long-term rates were close to 15 percent. A little over one year later, in December of 1982, short-term rates were 8 percent and long-term rates were about 10.5 percent. This example also illustrates that interest rates can move dramatically in a relatively short time (in this case 15 months).

In designing working capital policy, the astute financial manager is interested not only in the term structure of interest rates but also the relative volatility and the historical level of short-term and long-term rates. Figure 6–10 covers a 35-year period of time and demonstrates that short-term rates (red) are more volatile than

Figure 6–10   Long- and short-term annual interest rates

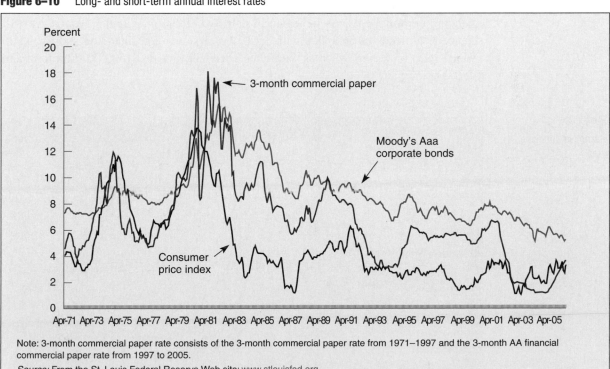

Note: 3-month commercial paper rate consists of the 3-month commercial paper rate from 1971–1997 and the 3-month AA financial commercial paper rate from 1997 to 2005.
Source: From the St. Louis Federal Reserve Web site: www.stlouisfed.org.

long-term rates (blue). This volatility is what makes a short-term financing strategy risky. Figure 6–10 also shows that interest rates follow the general trend of inflation as measured by the consumer price index (black). As inflation goes up or down, so do interest rates. While this relationship seems simple, it explains financial managers' and lenders' preoccupations with forecasting inflation. Unfortunately, most economists will admit to the uncertainty of forecasting. While we can see that short- and long-term interest rates are closely related to each other and to inflation, the record of the professionals for accurate interest rate predictions for periods longer than a few months is spotty at best.

How should the financial manager respond to fluctuating interest rates and changing term structures? When interest rates are high and expected to decline, the financial manager generally tries to borrow short term (if funds are available). As rates decline, the chief financial officer will try to lock in the lower rates with heavy long-term borrowing. Some of these long-term funds will be used to reduce short-term debt and the rest will be available for future expansion of plant and equipment and working capital if necessary.

A Decision Process

Assume we are comparing alternative financing plans for working capital. As indicated in Table 6–7, $500,000 of working capital (current assets) must be financed for the Edwards Corporation. Under Plan A, we will finance all our current asset needs with short-term funds (fourth numerical line), while under Plan B we will finance only a relatively small portion of current assets with short-term money—relying heavily on long-term funds. In either case we will carry $100,000 of fixed assets with long-term financing commitments. As indicated in part 3 of Table 6–7, under Plan A we will finance total needs of $600,000 with $500,000 of short-term financing and $100,000 of long-term financing, whereas with Plan B we will finance $150,000 short term and $450,000 long term.

Table 6–7

Alternative financing plans

EDWARDS CORPORATION	Plan A	Plan B
Part 1. Current assets		
Temporary..	$250,000	$250,000
Permanent	250,000	250,000
Total current assets	500,000	500,000
Short-term financing (6%)............................	500,000	150,000
Long-term financing (10%)	0	350,000
	$500,000	$500,000
Part 2. Fixed assets	$100,000	$100,000
Long-term financing (10%)	$100,000	$100,000
Part 3. Total financing (summary of parts 1 and 2)		
Short term (6%)	$500,000	$150,000
Long term (10%)....................................	100,000	450,000
	$600,000	$600,000

Plan A carries the lower cost of financing, with interest of 6 percent on $500,000 of the $600,000 required. We show the impact of both plans on bottom-line earnings in Table 6–8.[2] Assuming the firm generates $200,000 in earnings before interest and taxes, Plan A will provide aftertax earnings of $80,000, while Plan B will generate only $73,000.

Table 6–8

Impact of financing plans on earnings

EDWARDS CORPORATION
Plan A

Earnings before interest and taxes	$200,000
Interest (short term), 6% × $500,000	− 30,000
Interest (long term), 10% × $100,000	− 10,000
Earnings before taxes	160,000
Taxes (50%)	80,000
Earnings after taxes	$ 80,000

Plan B

Earnings before interest and taxes	$200,000
Interest (short term), 6% × $150,000	− 9,000
Interest (long term), 10% × $450,000	− 45,000
Earnings before taxes	146,000
Taxes (50%)	73,000
Earnings after taxes	$ 73,000

Introducing Varying Conditions

Although Plan A, employing cheaper short-term sources of financing, appears to provide $7,000 more in return, this is not always the case. During **tight money** periods, when capital is scarce, short-term financing may be difficult to find or may carry exorbitant rates. Furthermore, inadequate financing may mean lost sales or financial embarrassment. For these reasons, the firm may wish to evaluate Plans A and B based on differing assumptions about the economy and the money markets.

Expected Value

Past history combined with economic forecasting may indicate an 80 percent probability of normal events and a 20 percent chance of extremely tight money. Using Plan A, under normal conditions the Edwards Corporation will enjoy a $7,000 superior return over Plan B (as previously indicated in Table 6–8). Let us now assume that under disruptive tight money conditions, Plan A would provide a $15,000 lower return than Plan B because of high short-term interest rates. These conditions are summarized in Table 6–9, and an expected value of return is computed. The **expected value** represents the sum of the expected outcomes under the two conditions.

---

[2]Common stock is eliminated from the example to simplify the analysis. If it were included, all of the basic patterns would remain the same.

Table 6–9

Expected returns under different economic conditions

EDWARDS CORPORATION				
1. Normal conditions	Expected higher return under Plan A		Probability of normal conditions	Expected outcome
	$7,000	×	.80	= +$5,600
2. Tight money	Expected lower return under Plan A		Probability of tight money	
	($15,000)	×	.20	= (3,000)
Expected value of return for Plan A versus Plan B				= +$2,600

We see that even when downside risk is considered, Plan A carries a higher expected return of $2,600. For another firm, XYZ, in the same industry that might suffer $50,000 lower returns during tight money conditions, Plan A becomes too dangerous to undertake, as indicated in Table 6–10. Plan A's expected return is now $4,400 less than that of Plan B.

Table 6–10

Expected returns for high-risk firm

XYZ CORPORATION				
1. Normal conditions	Expected higher return under Plan A		Probability of normal conditions	Expected outcome
	$7,000	×	.80	= +$ 5,600
2. Tight money	Expected lower return under Plan A		Probability of tight money	
	($50,000)	×	.20	= (10,000)
Negative expected value of return for Plan A versus Plan B				= ($ 4,400)

Shifts in Asset Structure

For large U.S. nonfinancial corporations as represented by the Standard & Poor's Industrial companies, the percentage of working capital (Current assets – Current liabilities) divided by Sales has declined from about 23 percent in the mid-1960s to its current level of between 7 and 15 percent. The latter values are shown in Figure 6–11. Over the time period 1993 to 2004, this ratio declined from almost 14 percent in 1994 to its low of 7 percent during the recession of 2000–2001 and then recovered to 15 percent by year-end 2004. This demonstrates the cyclical nature of working capital that we discussed earlier in the chapter. During a recession, sales decline or stay even, but cash, receivables, and inventory fall and short-term debt may rise, causing a large decline in the working capital to sales ratio. As the firm's profitability increases during the upswing, cash, receivables, and inventory rise, and short-term debt may fall or be replaced by low-cost long-term debt in the low-interest rate environment of a recession. These two effects cause the ratio to rise.

However the long-term decrease in liquidity since the late 1960s can be traced to more efficient inventory management such as just-in-time inventory programs, point-of-sales terminals, and other methods of more efficient inventory management methods. The long-term decline in working capital can also be traced to electronic cash flow transfer systems, and the ability to sell accounts receivable through the securitization of assets (more fully explained in the next chapter).

Figure 6–11   Percentage of working capital to sales for the Standard & Poor's Industrials

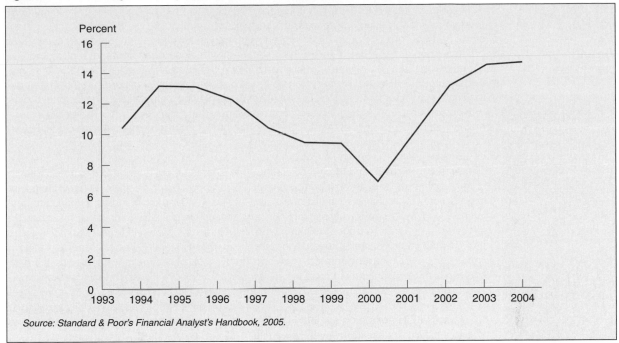

Source: Standard & Poor's Financial Analyst's Handbook, 2005.

As previously indicated, the firm should attempt to relate asset liquidity to financing patterns, and vice versa. In Table 6–11, a number of working capital alternatives are presented. Along the top of the table, we show asset liquidity; along the side, the type of financing arrangement. The combined impact of the two variables is shown in each of the four panels of the table.

Toward an Optimal Policy

Table 6–11

Asset liquidity and financing assets

	Asset Liquidity	
Financing Plan	**Low Liquidity**	**High Liquidity**
Short-term	1 High profit High risk	2 Moderate profit Moderate risk
Long-term	3 Moderate profit Moderate risk	4 Low profit Low risk

In using Table 6–11, each firm must decide how it wishes to combine asset liquidity and financing needs. The aggressive, risk-oriented firm in Panel 1 will borrow short term and maintain relatively low levels of liquidity, hoping to increase profit. It will benefit from low-cost financing and high-return assets, but it will be vulnerable to a credit crunch. The more conservative firm, following the plan in Panel 4, will utilize

Working Capital Problems in a Small Business

Many small businesses that are seasonal in nature have difficult financing problems. This is particularly true of retail nursery (plants) stores, greeting card shops, boating stores, and so on. The problem is that each of these businesses has year-round fixed commitments, but the business is seasonal. For example, Calloway's Nursery, located in the Dallas–Ft. Worth Metroplex, as well as in Houston and San Antonio, does approximately half of its business in the April to June quarter, yet it must make lease payments for its 26 retail outlets every month of the year. The problem is compounded by the fact that during seasonal peaks it must compete with large national retail chains such as Lowe's and Home Depot who can easily convert space allocated to nursery products to other purposes when winter comes. While Calloway's Nursery can sell garden-related arts and crafts in its off-season, the potential volume is small compared to the boom periods of April, May, and June.

Seasonality is not a problem that is exclusive to small businesses. However, its effects can be greater because of the difficulty that small businesses have in attracting large pools of permanent funds through the use of equity capital. The smaller business firm is likely to be more dependent on suppliers, commercial banks, and others to provide financing needs. Suppliers are likely to provide the necessary funds during seasonal peaks, but are not a good source of financ-ing during the off-season. Banks may provide a line of credit (a commitment to provide funds) for the off-season, but the small firm can sometimes find it difficult to acquire bank financing. This has become particularly true with the consolidation of the banking industry through mergers. Twenty years ago, the small businessperson was usually on a first-name, golf-playing basis with the local banker who knew every aspect of his or her business. Now a loan request may have to go to North Carolina, Ohio, California, New York, or else-where, for final approval.

The obvious answer to seasonal working capital problems is sufficient financial planning to insure that profits produced during the peak season are available to cover losses during the off-season. Calloway's Nursery and many other small firms literally predict at the beginning of their fiscal period the movement of cash flow for every week of the year. This includes the expansion and reduction of the workforce during peak and slow periods, and the daily tracking of inventory. However, even such foresight cannot fully prepare a firm for an unexpected freeze, a flood, the entrance of a new competitor into the marketplace, a zoning change that redirects traffic in the wrong direction, and so on.

Thus, the answer lies not just in planning, but in flexible planning. If sales are down by 10 per-cent, then a similar reduction in employees, sal-aries, fringe benefits, inventory, and other areas must take place. Plans for expansion must be changed into plans for contraction.

established long-term financing and maintain a high degree of liquidity. In Panels 2 and 3, we see more moderate positions in which the firm compensates for short-term financing with highly liquid assets (2) or balances off low liquidity with precommitted, long-term financing (3).

Each financial manager must structure his or her working capital position and the associated risk-return trade-off to meet the company's needs. For firms whose cash flow patterns are predictable, typified by the public utilities sector, a low degree of liquidity can be maintained. Immediate access to capital markets, such as that enjoyed by large, prestigious firms, also allows a greater risk-taking capability. In each case, the ultimate concern must be for maximizing the overall valuation of the firm through a judicious consideration of risk-return options.

In the next two chapters, we will examine the various methods for managing the individual components of working capital. In Chapter 7 we consider the techniques for managing cash, marketable securities, receivables, and inventory. In Chapter 8 we look at trade and bank credit and also at other sources of short-term funds.

Summary

Working capital management involves the financing and controlling of the current assets of the firm. These current assets include cash, marketable securities, accounts receivable, and inventory. A firm's ability to properly manage current assets and the associated liability obligations may determine how well it is able to survive in the short run.

Because a firm with continuous operations will always maintain minimum levels of current assets, management must be able to distinguish between those current assets that are permanent and those that are temporary or cyclical. In order to determine the permanent or cyclical nature of current assets, the financial manager must give careful attention to the growth in sales and the relationship of the production process to sales. Level production in a seasonal sales environment increases operating efficiency, but it also calls for more careful financial planning.

In general, we advocate tying the maturity of the financing plan to the maturity of the current assets. That is, finance short-term cyclical current assets with short-term liabilities and permanent current assets with long-term sources of funds. In order to carry out the company's financing plan with minimum cost, the financial manager must keep an eye on the general cost of borrowing, the term structure of interest rates, the relative volatility of short- and long-term rates, and predict, if possible, any change in the direction of interest rate movements.

Because the yield curve is usually upward sloping, long-term financing is generally more expensive than short-term financing. This lower cost in favor of short-term financing must be weighed against the risk that short-term rates are more volatile than long-term rates. Additionally, if long-term rates are expected to rise, the financial manager may want to lock in long-term financing needs before they do.

The firm has a number of risk-return decisions to consider. Though long-term financing provides a safety margin for the availability of funds, its higher cost may reduce the profit potential of the firm. On the asset side, carrying highly liquid current assets assures the bill-paying capability of the firm—but detracts from profit potential. Each firm must tailor the various risk-return trade-offs to meet its own needs. The peculiarities of a firm's industry will have a major impact on the options open to its management.

List of Terms

working capital management   153
self-liquidating assets   154
permanent current assets   154
temporary current assets   154
level production   154
point-of-sales terminals   158
term structure of interest rates
   (yield curve)   167

liquidity premium theory   167
market segmentation theory   167
expectations hypothesis   167
basis points   169
tight money   171
expected value   171

Discussion Questions

1. Explain how rapidly expanding sales can drain the cash resources of a firm.
2. Discuss the relative volatility of short- and long-term interest rates.

3. What is the significance to working capital management of matching sales and production?

4. How is a cash budget used to help manage current assets?

5. "The most appropriate financing pattern would be one in which asset buildup and length of financing terms are perfectly matched." Discuss the difficulty involved in achieving this financing pattern.

6. By using long-term financing to finance part of temporary current assets, a firm may have less risk but lower returns than a firm with a normal financing plan. Explain the significance of this statement.

7. A firm that uses short-term financing methods for a portion of permanent current assets is assuming more risk but expects higher returns than a firm with a normal financing plan. Explain.

8. What does the *term structure of interest rates* indicate?

9. What are three theories for describing the shape of the term structure of interest rates (the yield curve)? Briefly describe each theory.

10. Since the mid-1960s, corporate liquidity has been declining. What reasons can you give for this trend?

Practice Problems and Solutions

Expected value

1. Meyer Electronics expects sales next year to be $3,000,000 if the economy is strong, $1,200,000 if the economy is steady, and $800,000 if the economy is weak. Mr. Meyer believes there is a 30 percent probability the economy will be strong, a 60 percent probability of a steady economy, and a 10 percent probability of a weak economy. What is the expected level of sales for the next year?

Alternative financing plans

2. Otis Resources is trying to develop an asset-financing plan. The firm has $200,000 in temporary current assets and $500,000 in permanent current assets. Otis also has $300,000 in fixed assets.

    a. Construct two alternative financing plans for the firm. One of the plans should be conservative, with 70 percent of assets financed by long-term sources and the rest financed by short-term sources. The other plan should be aggressive, with only 20 percent of assets financed by long-term sources and the remaining assets financed by short-term sources. The current interest rate is 12 percent on long-term funds and 5 percent on short-term financing. Compute the annual interest payments under each plan.

    b. Given that Otis's earnings before interest and taxes are $234,000, calculate earnings after taxes for each of your alternatives. Assume a tax rate of 35 percent.

Solutions

1.

State of Economy	Sales	Probability	Expected Outcome
Strong	$3,000,000	.30	$ 900,000
Steady	1,200,000	.60	720,000
Weak	800,000	.10	80,000
		Expected level of sales =	$1,700,000

2. *a.*

Temporary current assets	$ 200,000
Permanent current assets	500,000
Fixed assets.	300,000
Total assets	$1,000,000

Conservative Plan

Total Assets	Percent of Total	Dollar Amount	Interest Rate	Interest Expense
$1,000,000	Long term (.70)	$700,000	.12	$84,000
1,000,000	Short term (.30)	300,000	.05	15,000
			Total Interest	$99,000

Aggressive Plan

Total Assets	Percent of Total	Dollar Amount	Interest Rate	Interest Expense
$1,000,000	Long term (.20)	$200,000	.12	$24,000
1,000,000	Short term (.80)	800,000	.05	40,000
			Total Interest	$64,000

b.

	Conservative	Aggressive
EBIT	$234,000	$234,000
I.	99,000	64,000
EBT.	135,000	170,000
Tax 35%	47,250	59,500
EAT	$ 87,750	$110,500

Problems

All problems are available in Homework Manager. Please see the preface for more information.

Expected value

1. Austin Electronics expects sales next year to be $900,000 if the economy is
    strong, $650,000 if the economy is steady, and $375,000 if the economy is
    weak. The firm believes there is a 15 percent probability the economy will
    be strong, a 60 percent probability of a steady economy, and a 25 percent
    probability of a weak economy.
         What is the expected level of sales for next year?

Expected value

2. Sharpe Knife Company expects sales next year to be $1,500,000 if the
    economy is strong, $800,000 if the economy is steady, and $500,000 if the
    economy is weak. Mr. Sharpe believes there is a 20 percent probability the
    economy will be strong, a 50 percent probability of a steady economy, and
    a 30 percent probability of a weak economy. What is the expected level of
    sales for the next year?

External financing

3. Cobb Tie Shops, Inc., expects sales next year to be $300,000. Inventory and accounts receivable will increase by $60,000 to accommodate this sales level. The company has a steady profit margin of 10 percent with a 30 percent dividend payout. How much external financing will the firm have to seek? Assume there is no increase in liabilities other than that which will occur with the external financing.

External financing

4. Antivirus, Inc., expects its sales next year to be $2,000,000. Inventory and accounts receivable will increase by $430,000 to accommodate this sales level. The company has a steady profit margin of 12 percent with a 25 percent dividend payout. How much external financing will the firm have to seek? Assume there is no increase in liabilities other than that which will occur with the external financing.

Self-liquidating inventory and finance

5. Antonio Banderos & Scarves sells headwear that is very popular in the fall-winter season. Units sold are anticipated as:

October	1,000
November	2,000
December	4,000
January	3,000
	10,000 units

If seasonal production is used, it is assumed that inventory will directly match sales for each month and there will be no inventory buildup.

Antonio thinks the above assumption is too optimistic and decides to go with level production to avoid being out of merchandise. He will produce the 10,000 items over four months at a level of 2,500 per month.

a. What is the ending inventory at the end of each month? Compare the unit sales to the units produced and keep a running total.

b. If the inventory costs $5 per unit and will be financed at the bank at a cost of 12 percent, what is the monthly financing cost and the total for the four months?

Short-term versus longer-term borrowing

6. Boatler Used Cadillac Co. requires $800,000 in financing over the next two years. The firm can borrow the funds for two years at 9 percent interest per year. Mr. Boatler decides to do economic forecasting and determines that if he utilizes short-term financing instead, he will pay 6.75 percent interest in the first year and 10.55 percent interest in the second year. Determine the total two-year interest cost under each plan. Which plan is less costly?

Short-term versus longer-term borrowing

7. Stern Educational TV, Inc., has decided to buy a new computer system with an expected life of three years at a cost of $200,000. The company can borrow $200,000 for three years at 12 percent annual interest or for one year at 10 percent annual interest.

a. How much would the firm save in interest over the three-year life of the computer system if the one-year loan is utilized, and the loan is rolled over (reborrowed) each year at the same 10 percent rate? Compare this to the 12 percent three-year loan.

b. What if interest rates on the 10 percent loan go up to 15 percent in the second year and 18 percent in the third year? What would be the total interest cost compared to the 12 percent, three-year loan?

8. Assume that Hogan Surgical Instruments Co. has $2,000,000 in assets. If it goes with a low-liquidity plan for the assets, it can earn a return of 18 percent, but with a high-liquidity plan, the return will be 14 percent. If the firm goes with a short-term financing plan, the financing costs on the $2,000,000 will be 10 percent, and with a long-term financing plan, the financing costs on the $2,000,000 will be 12 percent. (Review Table 6–11 for parts *a, b,* and *c* of this problem.)

Optimal policy mix

a. Compute the anticipated return after financing costs with the most aggressive asset-financing mix.

b. Compute the anticipated return after financing costs with the most conservative asset-financing mix.

c. Compute the anticipated return after financing costs with the two moderate approaches to the asset-financing mix.

d. Would you necessarily accept the plan with the highest return after financing costs? Briefly explain.

9. Assume that Atlas Sporting Goods, Inc., has $800,000 in assets. If it goes with a low-liquidity plan for the assets, it can earn a return of 15 percent, but with a high-liquidity plan the return will be 12 percent. If the firm goes with a short-term financing plan, the financing costs on the $800,000 will be 8 percent, and with a long-term financing plan, the financing costs on the $800,000 will be 10 percent. (Review Table 6–11 on page 173 for parts *a, b,* and *c* of this problem.)

Optimal policy mix

a. Compute the anticipated return after financing costs with the most aggressive asset-financing mix.

b. Compute the anticipated return after financing costs with the most conservative asset-financing mix.

c. Compute the anticipated return after financing costs with the two moderate approaches to the asset-financing mix.

d. If the firm used the most aggressive asset-financing mix described in part *a* and had the anticipated return you computed for part *a*, what would earnings per share be if the tax rate on the anticipated return was 30 percent and there were 20,000 shares outstanding?

e. Now assume the most conservative asset-financing mix described in part *b* will be utilized. The tax rate will be 30 percent. Also assume there will only be 5,000 shares outstanding. What will earnings per share be? Would it be higher or lower than the earnings per share computed for the most aggressive plan computed in part *d*?

10. Winfrey Diet Food Corp. has $4,500,000 in assets.

Matching asset mix and financing plans

Temporary current assets	$1,000,000
Permanent current assets	1,500,000
Fixed assets.	2,000,000
Total assets	$4,500,000

Short-term rates are 8 percent. Long-term rates are 13 percent. Earnings before interest and taxes are $960,000. The tax rate is 40 percent.

If long-term financing is perfectly matched (synchronized) with long-term asset needs, and the same is true of short-term financing, what will earnings after taxes be? For an example of perfectly matched plans, see Figure 6–5 on page 164.

Impact of term structure of interest rates on financing plan

11. In Problem 10, assume the term structure of interest rates becomes inverted, with short-term rates going to 12 percent and long-term rates 4 percentage points lower than short-term rates.

If all other factors in the problem remain unchanged, what will earnings after taxes be?

Conservative versus aggressive financing

12. Collins Systems, Inc., is trying to develop an asset-financing plan. The firm has $300,000 in temporary current assets and $200,000 in permanent current assets. Collins also has $400,000 in fixed assets.

a. Construct two alternative financing plans for the firm. One of the plans should be conservative, with 80 percent of assets financed by long-term sources and the rest financed by short-term sources. The other plan should be aggressive, with only 30 percent of assets financed by long-term sources and the remaining assets financed by short-term sources. The current interest rate is 15 percent on long-term funds and 10 percent on short-term financing. Compute the annual interest payments under each plan.

b. Given that Collins's earnings before interest and taxes are $180,000, calculate earnings after taxes for each of your alternatives. Assume a tax rate of 40 percent.

Alternative financing plans

13. Lear, Inc., has $800,000 in current assets, $350,000 of which are considered permanent current assets. In addition, the firm has $600,000 invested in fixed assets.

a. Lear wishes to finance all fixed assets and half of its permanent current assets with long-term financing costing 10 percent. The balance will be financed with short-term financing, which currently costs 5 percent. Lear's earnings before interest and taxes are $200,000. Determine Lear's earnings after taxes under this financing plan. The tax rate is 30 percent.

b. As an alternative, Lear might wish to finance all fixed assets and permanent current assets plus half of its temporary current assets with long-term financing and the balance with short-term financing. The same interest rates apply as in part *a*. Earnings before interest and taxes will be $200,000. What will be Lear's earnings after taxes? The tax rate is 30 percent.

c. What are some of the risks and cost considerations associated with each of these alternative financing strategies?

Expectations hypothesis and interest rates

14. Using the expectations hypothesis theory for the term structure of interest rates, determine the expected return for securities with maturities of two, three, and four years based on the data at the top of page 181. Do an analysis similar to that in the right-hand portion of Table 6–6 on page 167.

1-year T-bill at beginning of year 1	5%
1-year T-bill at beginning of year 2	6%
1-year T-bill at beginning of year 3	8%
1-year T-bill at beginning of year 4	10%

15. Carmen's Beauty Salon has estimated monthly financing requirements for the next six months as follows:

Interest costs under alternative plans

January	$8,000	April	$8,000
February	2,000	May	9,000
March	3,000	June	4,000

Short-term financing will be utilized for the next six months. Projected annual interest rates are:

January	8.0%	April	15.0%
February	9.0	May	12.0
March	12.0	June	12.0

   a. Compute total dollar interest payments for the six months. To convert an annual rate to a monthly rate, divide by 12. Then multiply this value times the monthly balance. To get your answer sum up the monthly interest payments.

   b. If long-term financing at 12 percent had been utilized throughout the six months, would the total-dollar interest payments be larger or smaller? Compute the interest owed over the six months and compare your answer to that in part *a*.

16. In Problem 15, what long-term interest rate would represent a break-even point between using short-term financing as described in part *a* and long-term financing? Hint: Divide the interest payments in 15*a* by the amount of total funds provided for the six months and multiply by 12.

Break-even point in interest rates

17. Garza Electronics expects to sell 500 units in January, 250 units in February, and 1,000 units in March. December's ending inventory is 700 units. Expected sales for the year are 7,200 units. Garza has decided on a level production schedule of 600 units (7,200 units for the year/12 months = 600 units per month). What is the expected unit volume of end-of-month inventory for January, February, and March? Show the beginning inventory, production, and sales for each of the three months that are used to derive the ending inventory.

Sales and inventory buildup

18. Bombs Away Video Games Corporation has forecasted the following monthly sales:

Level production and related financing effects

January	$95,000	July	$ 40,000
February	88,000	August	40,000
March	20,000	September	50,000
April	20,000	October	80,000
May	15,000	November	100,000
June	30,000	December	118,000
	Total sales = $696,000		

Bombs Away Video Games sells the popular Strafe and Capture video game cartridge. It sells for $5 per unit and costs $2 per unit to produce. A level production policy is followed. Each month's production is equal to annual sales (in units) divided by 12.

Of each month's sales, 30 percent are for cash and 70 percent are on account. All accounts receivable are collected in the month after the sale is made.

a. Construct a monthly production and inventory schedule in units. Beginning inventory in January is 20,000 units. (Note: To do part *a*, you should work in terms of units of production and units of sales.)

b. Prepare a monthly schedule of cash receipts. Sales in the December before the planning year are $100,000. Work part *b* using dollars.

c. Determine a cash payments schedule for January through December. The production costs of $2 per unit are paid for in the month in which they occur. Other cash payments, besides those for production costs, are $40,000 per month.

d. Prepare a monthly cash budget for January through December using the cash receipts schedule from part *b* and the cash payments schedule from part *c*. The beginning cash balance is $5,000, which is also the minimum desired.

Level production and related financing effects

19. Esquire Products, Inc., expects the following monthly sales:

January	$24,000	May.........	$ 4,000	September	$25,000
February	15,000	June	2,000	October	30,000
March	8,000	July	18,000	November	38,000
April	10,000	August	22,000	December	20,000

Total sales = $216,000

Cash sales are 40 percent in a given month, with the remainder going into accounts receivable. All receivables are collected in the month following the sale. Esquire sells all of its goods for $2 each and produces them for $1 each. Esquire uses level production, and average monthly production is equal to annual production divided by 12.

a. Generate a monthly production and inventory schedule in units. Beginning inventory in January is 8,000 units. (Note: To do part *a,* you should work in terms of units of production and units of sales.)

b. Determine a cash receipts schedule for January through December. Assume that dollar sales in the prior December were $20,000. Work part *b* using dollars.

c. Determine a cash payments schedule for January through December. The production costs ($1 per unit produced) are paid for in the month in which they occur. Other cash payments (besides those for production costs) are $7,000 per month.

d. Construct a cash budget for January through December using the cash receipts schedule from part *b* and the cash payments schedule from part *c*. The beginning cash balance is $3,000, which is also the minimum desired.

e. Determine total current assets for each month. Include cash, accounts receivable, and inventory. Accounts receivable equal sales minus 40 percent of sales for a given month. Inventory is equal to ending inventory (part *a*) times the cost of $1 per unit.

WEB EXERCISE

McGraw-Hill was mentioned in the chapter as a company that has a high degree of seasonality (and associated working capital issues). Let's use the Internet to examine the seasonality:

1. Go to www.mcgraw-hill.com.
2. Click on "Investors."
3. Click on "Investor Fact Book" on the right-hand margin.
4. Click on "Financial Information" in the Investor Fact Book table of contents.
5. Scroll all the way down until you get to "Quarterly Revenue and Operating Profit by Segment."
6. Under Revenue, record total revenue for the latest year (second column from the right).
7. Next divide each quarter's (Q1, Q2, Q3, Q4) revenue for the latest year into total operating revenue for the latest year. Which quarter represents the highest percent of total revenue? Refer to the discussion of McGraw-Hill in the text to see why this is the case.
8. Under Operating Profit, record total operating profit for the latest year. Next divide each quarter's operating profit for the latest year into total operating profit for the latest year. What quarter represents the highest percent of total operating profit? Is your answer to Question 8 consistent with Question 7?
9. Which of the three segments (McGraw-Hill Education, Financial Services, or Information and Media Services) appears to be the most sensitive in quarterly performance? Compute McGraw-Hill Education's percent of total operating revenue for the first and third quarters. Do the same for the other two segments. What conclusion did you reach about the segment that performs best in the third quarter? Once again, why is this the case?

Note: From time to time, companies redesign their Web sites and occasionally a topic we have listed may have been deleted, updated, or moved into a different location. If you click on the site map or site index, you will be introduced to a table of contents which should aid you in finding the topic you are looking for.

S&P PROBLEMS   www.mhhe.com/edumarketinsight

1. Log onto the S&P Market Insight Web site, www.mhhe.com/edumarketinsight.
2. Click on "Company," which is the first box below the Market Insight title.

STANDARD
&POOR'S

3. In this problem we are going to compare the differences in working capital policy between Nordstrom Inc. (JWN), Target (TGT), and Wal-Mart (WMT). These companies all use different retail models to sell goods to consumers.

4. Type Nordstrom's ticker symbol "JWN" in the box and click on Go.

5. Scroll down the left margin and click on "Excel Analytics" and then go to "Quarterly Income Statements," and click on the first one. Record the sales figure or print the report for the six quarters and determine if there is any seasonal sales pattern.

6. Return to the previous menu and now click on the "Quarterly Ratio Report." Examine the activity ratios (asset utilization ratios in Chapter 3) and analyze Nordstrom for efficiency. Also note the profitability ratios.

7. Repeat steps 5 and 6 using Target (TGT).

8. Repeat steps 5 and 6 using Wal-Mart (WMT).

9. Now compare the three companies and determine which has the most efficient model for working capital management.

10. Given that efficient working capital management should lead to better profitability, write up a short analysis of the three companies' working capital management and how it might affect each company's profitability.

Current Asset Management

1 Current asset management is an extension of concepts discussed in the previous chapter and involves the management of cash, marketable securities, accounts receivable, and inventory.

2 Cash management involves control over the receipt and payment of cash so as to minimize nonearning cash balances.

3 The management of marketable securities involves selecting between various short-term investments.

4 Accounts receivable and inventory management require credit and inventory level decisions to be made with an eye toward profitability.

5 An overriding concept is that the less liquid an asset is, the higher the required return.

Retailing is one of the most challenging industries for managing current assets. Weather, economic conditions, changing customer tastes, and seasonal purchasing influence retail industry sales. The industry reports monthly sales figures and so becomes a barometer of consumers' spending attitudes. Forecasting inventory needs and cash flows are extremely difficult when sales don't go according to plan.

The Christmas selling season is the biggest time of the year for most retailers, and the economy, as well as the weather, has a large impact on how much consumers will spend. In 2002 consumers were still reeling from a recession and spending was disappointing. In 2006, retail stores were concerned about the continuing effects of Hurricane Katrina and Hurricane Rita and the very high prices of gasoline and heating oil. The high prices of necessities such as these would have an impact on the average consumer's disposable income and retail stores were prepared for a rather lackluster Christmas season (which

had been preceded by a rather tepid back-to-school selling season).

Many retailers carry light inventories into these holiday periods with low expectations trying to avoid large after-Christmas discounts. This strategy doesn't always work well because consumers are often not predictable. Sometimes stores such as Abercrombie & Fitch do so well that they run out of popular merchandise, while stores like Sears suffer subpar sales and end up with more merchandise than they need.

These retail companies have their hands full managing their current assets. Those that do it well, such as Wal-Mart, establish a competitive advantage that helps increase their market share and often creates an increase in shareholder value through a rising stock price. This is why the financial manager must carefully allocate resources among the current assets of the firm—cash, marketable securities, accounts receivable, and inventory. In managing cash and marketable securities,

185

the primary concern should be for safety and liquidity—with secondary attention placed on maximizing profitability. As we move to accounts receivable and inventory, a stiffer profitability test must be met. The investment level should not be a matter of happenstance or historical determination, but must meet the same return-on-investment criteria applied to any decision. We may need to choose between a 20 percent increase in inventory and a new plant location or a major research program. We shall examine the decision techniques that are applied to the various forms of current assets.

Cash Management

Managing cash is becoming ever more sophisticated in the global and electronic age of the new century as financial managers try to squeeze the last dollar of profit out of their cash management strategies. Despite whatever lifelong teachings you might have learned about the virtues of cash, the corporate financial manager actively seeks to keep this nonearning asset to a minimum. The less cash you have, generally the better off you are, but still you do not want to get caught without cash when you need it. Minimizing cash balances as well as having accurate knowledge of when cash moves into and out of the company can improve overall corporate profitability. First we discuss the reasons for holding cash and then examine the cash flow cycle for the typical firm.

Reasons for Holding Cash Balances

There are several reasons for holding cash: for transactions balances, for compensating balances for banks, and for precautionary needs. The transactions motive involves the use of cash to pay for planned corporate expenses such as supplies, payrolls, and taxes, but also can include planned acquisitions of long-term fixed assets. The second major reason for holding cash results from the practice of holding balances to compensate a bank for services provided rather than paying directly for those services.

Holding cash for precautionary motives assumes management wants cash for emergency purposes when cash inflows are less than projected. Precautionary cash balances are more likely to be important in seasonal or cyclical industries where cash inflows are more uncertain. Firms with precautionary needs usually rely on untapped lines of bank credit. For most firms the primary motive for holding cash is the transactions motive.

Cash Flow Cycle

Cash balances are largely determined by cash flowing through the company on a daily, weekly, and monthly basis as determined by the **cash flow cycle**. As discussed in Chapter 4, the cash budget is a common tool used to track cash flows and resulting cash balances. Cash flow relies on the payment pattern of customers, the speed at which suppliers and creditors process checks, and the efficiency of the banking system. The primary consideration in managing the cash flow cycle is to ensure that inflows and outflows of cash are properly synchronized for transaction purposes. In Chapter 6 we

Figure 7–1
The cash flow cycle

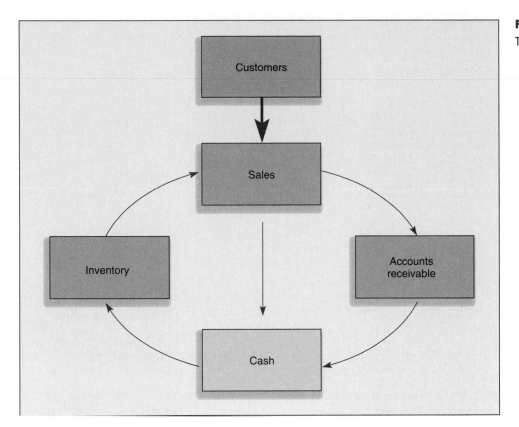

discussed the cyclical nature of asset growth and its impact on cash, receivables, and inventory, and we now expand on that by examining the cash flow process more fully.

Figure 7–1 illustrates the simple cash flow cycle where the sale of finished goods or services produces either a cash sale or account receivable for future collection. Eventually the accounts receivable are collected and become cash, which is used to buy or produce inventory that is then sold. Thus the cash-generating process is continuous even though the cash flow may be unpredictable and uneven.

Sales, receivables, and inventory form the basis for cash flow, but other activities in the firm can also affect cash inflows and outflows. The cash flow cycle presented in Figure 7–2 on page 188 expands the detail and activities that influence cash. Cash inflows are driven by sales and influenced by the type of customers, their geographical location, the product being sold, and the industry.

A sale can be made for cash (McDonald's) or on credit (Nordstrom). Some industries like textbook publishing will grant credit terms of 60 days to bookstores, and others like department stores will grant customers credit for 30 days.

One trend that is having a positive effect on cash flow is the rise of e-commerce sales. Most retailers have shopping Web sites. You can go to a search engine and type in the name of a retail chain and be directed to their Web site where, most likely, you can sign up for the gift registry or create a wish list. Wal-Mart, Kmart, and Target, all discount chains, have shopping Web sites and upscale popular retailers like

Figure 7–2

Expanded cash flow cycle

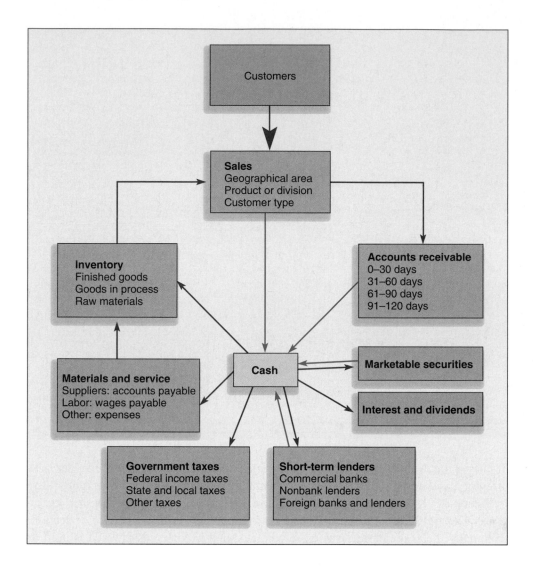

Abercrombie and Fitch also have them. Abercrombie lists both www.abercrombie.com and www.abercrombiekids.com. One of the benefits of selling on the Internet is that customers have to buy with credit or debit cards which generate cash flow much faster than a sale made with the retailer's own credit card that has 30-day payment terms. The credit card companies advance the cash to the retailer within 7–10 days. Because cash flow starts with the sale, financial managers have to pay attention to the percentage of sales that are generated by cash, by outside credit cards, and by the company's own credit cards.

When an account receivable is collected or the credit card company advances payment, cash balances increase and the firm uses cash to pay interest to lenders, dividends to stockholders, taxes to the government, accounts payable to suppliers, wages to workers, and to replace inventory. When the firm has excess cash, it will invest in marketable securities, and when it needs cash for current assets, it will usually either sell marketable securities or borrow funds from short-term lenders.

The Impact of the Internet on Working Capital Management

The Internet is having a significant effect on the way companies manage the purchase of their inventory, the way they sell their goods, how they collect their money, and how they manage their cash. Electronic funds transfer systems, discussed later in the chapter, have been around for over 20 years, although their growth has accelerated in the last several years.

There are two major trends that will affect corporate practices and profitability for decades to come. The first trend is the creation and use of business-to-business (B2B) industry supply exchanges usually initiated by the "old" economy companies. The second trend is the use of auction markets, which have been created by "new" economy companies to allow businesses to buy and sell goods among themselves.

There are several examples of supply exchanges that will have a major impact on the industry. Covisint (www.covisint.com) is one of the highest profile B2B exchanges and was launched in 2000. It is an industry-specific exchange supported by five of the largest automobile manufacturers in the world, including founders Ford, General Motors, DaimlerChrysler, Nissan, and Renault. Covisint stands for cooperation, vision, and integration, and is an online marketplace where original equipment manufacturers (OEMs) and suppliers come together to do business in a single business environment using the same tools and user interface. It was created to reduce costs and increase efficiencies through its purchasing and bidding system. In 2002, over 500 online bidding events were processed through Covisint with a total procurement volume of over 30 billion euros.

By 2005, Covisint, which is a division of Compuware, had over 190,000 users in 96 countries and in addition to its founding members, also included Mitsubishi Motors and Peugeot-Citroen. In August 2005, it also announced plans to create a health care platform with Michigan Blue Cross and Blue Shield.

The second trend in working capital management is the use of online auction companies for business to business markets such as FreeMarkets (www.freemarkets.com), eBreviate (www.ebreviate.com), and Perfect Commerce (www.perfect.com).

FreeMarkets started the online business-to-business auctions for buyers of various industries and was acquired by Ariba in January of 2003. It developed specialties and qualified buyers and suppliers for more than 70 product categories such as coal, injection molded plastic parts, metal fabrications, chemicals, printed circuit boards, and more. Now it is part of Ariba, and the information on the auctions is not very transparent.

eBreviate which is now owned by A.T. Kearney Procurment, the consulting arm of Electronic Data Systems (EDS), is another e-sourcing auction company which helps purchasing organizations use Internet technology to determine what they are buying, from whom, and under what commercial terms. It started up in 2000 and boasts major customers such as Volkswagen, Procter & Gamble, and JP Morgan Chase, as well as the U.S. Navy. eBreviate is not industry specific like Covisint.

Commerce One started out as a B2B auction site but like the others has broadened its scope to include what has developed into the word "spend policy." In other words these companies help other companies spend their money wisely and efficiently through the use of e-commerce technology. Commerce One has a stellar client list that includes Boeing, Deutsche Telekom, Eastman Chemical, Schlumberger, and others. In 2006 Commerce One was acquired by Perfect Commerce.

The advantage of these auction sites is that they eliminate geographical barriers and allow suppliers from all over the world to bid on business that they would never have thought of soliciting before the Internet. The bidding processes have a time limit, which can be several hours or days. Just like any other auction the participants get feedback on the bids made and can compete on price. The suppliers are prequalified so that they meet the manufacturing standards of the purchaser.

finance in action

www.ford.com

www.gm.com

www.daimlerchrysler.com

www.nissanusa.com

Managing the cash inflows and payment outflows is one of the critical functions of the financial manager. New electronic transfer mediums are changing the time period between the mailing of a check and the collection period. While the cash flow cycle is still affected by collection mechanisms such as lockboxes, the U.S. mail system,

Collections and Disbursements

and international sales, to name a few, the use of float became much less significant when the U.S. Congress passed the Check Clearing for the 21st Century Act, which took effect on October 28, 2004. These issues are presented in detail in the following section.

Float

Some people are shocked to realize that cash listed on a balance sheet does not necessarily represent the company's actual cash in the bank. There are actually two cash balances of importance: the corporation's recorded amount and the amount credited to the corporation by the bank. The difference between the two is called **float**. Float arises from time delays in mailing, processing, and clearing checks through the banking system. Once a check is received in the mail and a deposit is made, the deposited funds are not available for use until the check has cleared the banking system and been credited to the corporate bank account. This works for checks written to pay suppliers as well as the checks deposited from customers. This means that float can be managed to some extent through a combination of disbursement and collection strategies.

One of the major bottlenecks in the collection and disbursement process has been the physical presentation of the original check to the issuing bank. This process always took mail time, delivery time, and processing time. The **Check Clearing for the 21st Century Act (Check 21)** mentioned above allows banks and others to electronically process a check. According to the Federal Reserve Board, Check 21

> . . . is designed to foster innovation in the payments system and to enhance its efficiency by reducing some of the legal impediments to check truncation. The law facilitates check truncation by creating a new negotiable instrument called a substitute check, which permits banks to truncate original checks, to process check information electronically, and to deliver substitute checks to banks that want to continue receiving paper checks. A substitute check is the legal equivalent of the original check and includes all the information contained on the original check.[1]

This new law has not yet been fully implemented by all corporations and banks, but its impact will be to reduce the processing and delivery times and reduce float to the number of days it takes to send U.S. mail. In the event that companies wire deposits and make payments electronically through the banking system, float will be reduced all together. The Federal Reserve states that in 2003 more payments were made electronically by businesses and consumers than by check. Even before Check 21 was passed, the Federal Reserve estimates that in 1990, 50 billion checks were used and by 2003, the number had fallen by 25 percent to 37 billion checks. The ease of credit card and debit card payments and online banking for consumers, wire transfers for corporations, and the rise of Internet commerce, continues to move us to the checkless society.

We continue with our example of float, because despite Check 21, float will still exist to some extent because of one- to three-day mail delivery and because not all banks will immediately embrace the use of substitute checks. Float caused by processing time will eventually disappear.

---

[1]From **www.federalreserve.gov/paymentsys.htm**.

We examine the use of float in Tables 7–1 and 7–2. Our firm has deposited $1,000,000 in checks received from customers during the week and has written $900,000 in checks to suppliers. With the new Check 21 act, most of the $1,000,000 deposited will clear the day the checks are received. However, the $900,000 in checks we sent to our suppliers by mail could take up to three days to reach them. The company's books would show that $900,000 has been taken out of its bank account, but the bank would not subtract that amount until the original or substitute checks were presented for payment. That means that even with Check 21, the bank might still have a larger balance in the company's account than the company has listed on its books. If it takes one day for the mail to be delivered, this $500,000 float will only last the one day.

Table 7–1
Day one

	Corporate Books	Bank Books (amounts actually cleared)	
Initial amount	$ 100,000	$ 100,000	
Deposits	+1,000,000	+1,000,000	(Check 21—no float)
Checks sent to suppliers	− 900,000	− 400,000	(Mail float)
Balance	+$ 200,000	+$ 700,000	(Usable funds)
		+$500,000 Float	

Assume that the bank debits the company's account on day two for $300,000 of checks that cleared. This would reduce the float by a corresponding $300,000 to $200,000.

Table 7–2
Day two

	Corporate Books	Bank Books (amounts actually cleared)	
Initial amount	$ 100,000	$ 100,000	
Deposits	+1,000,000	+1,000,000	(Check 21—no float)
Checks sent to suppliers	− 900,000	− 700,000	(Mail float)
Balance	+$ 200,000	+$ 400,000	(Usable funds)
		+$200,000 Float	

Some companies actually operate with a negative cash balance on their corporate books, knowing float will carry them through at the bank. Of course, float will eventually catch up with a company and it will have to deposit more funds into its accounts to cover the checks written. Most companies who play this game have a line of credit at their bank so that if the float disappears faster than they expected, they can borrow against their line of credit. This loan may last for a day, a week, or even longer.

Improving Collections

We may expedite the collection and check-clearing process through a number of strategies.[2] A popular method is to utilize a variety of collection centers throughout the marketing area. An insurance company such as Allstate, with headquarters in Chicago,

---

[2]Larger banks have cash management advisory groups that can offer valuable consultation on these matters.

may have 75 collection offices disbursed throughout the country, each performing billing and collection-deposit functions.

For those who wish to enjoy the benefits of expeditious check clearance at lower costs, a **lockbox system** may replace the network of regional collection offices. Under this plan, customers are requested to forward their checks to a post office box in their geographic region and a local bank picks up the checks. The bank can then process the local checks through the local clearinghouse for rapid collection and have the funds available for use the same day.[3] Whether the corporation uses a collection system or the less expensive lockbox system, excess cash balances at the local banks are remitted to the corporate headquarter bank through a daily wire transfer or automated clearinghouse that makes the funds immediately available for corporate use.

Extending Disbursements

Perhaps you have heard of the multimillion-dollar corporation with its headquarters located in the most exclusive office space in downtown Manhattan, but with its primary check disbursement center in Fargo, North Dakota. Though the firm may engage in aggressive speedup techniques in the processing of incoming checks, a slowdown pattern more aptly describes the payment procedures.

While the preceding example represents an extreme case, the slowing of disbursements is not uncommon in cash management. It has even been given the title "extended disbursement float." Many full-service banks offer services to control disbursements, and also reconcile discrepancies between the Federal Reserve's check processing system and the bank's totals. This allows the company to time their payments so that they hold their cash balances as long as possible. While it is not the intent of this text to encourage or discourage such practices, their fairly widespread use is worthy of note.

Cost-Benefit Analysis

An efficiently maintained cash management program can be an expensive operation. The use of remote collection and disbursement centers involves additional costs, and banks involved in the process will require that the firm maintain adequate deposit balances or pay sufficient fees to justify the services. Though the use of a lockbox system may reduce total corporate overhead, the costs may still be substantial.

These expenses must be compared to the benefits that may accrue through the use of **cost-benefit analysis**. If a firm has an average daily remittance of $2 million and 1.5 days can be saved in the collection process by establishing a sophisticated collection network, the firm has freed $3 million for investment elsewhere. Also, through stretching the disbursement schedule by one day, perhaps another $2 million will become available for alternate uses. An example of this process is shown in Figure 7–3. If the firm is able to earn 10 percent on the $5 million that is freed up, as much as

---

[3]Checks deposited with a bank are cleared through the Federal Reserve System, through a correspondent bank, or through a locally established clearinghouse system. A check is collected when it is remitted to the payer's bank and actually paid by that bank to the payee's bank.

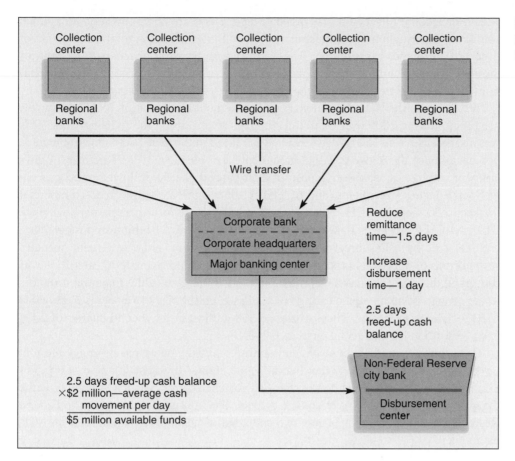

Figure 7–3
Cash management network

$500,000 may be expended on the administrative costs of cash management before the new costs are equal to the generated revenue.

Electronic Funds Transfer

In the current decade, some of the techniques of delaying payment and using float are being reduced through the techniques of **electronic funds transfer**, a system in which funds are moved between computer terminals without the use of a "check." Through the use of terminal communication between the store and the bank, your payment to the supermarket is automatically charged against your account at the bank before you walk out the door.

Most large corporations have computerized cash management systems. For example, a firm may have 55 branch offices and 56 banks, one bank for each branch office and a lead bank in which the major corporate account is kept. At the end of each day the financial manager can check all the company's bank accounts through an online computer terminal. He or she can then electronically transfer all excess cash balances from each branch or regional bank to the corporate lead bank for overnight investment in money market securities.

Automated clearinghouses (ACH) are an important element in electronic funds transfers. An ACH transfers information between one financial institution and another and from account to account via computer tape. There are approximately 30 regional automated clearinghouses throughout the United States, claiming total membership of over 12,000 financial institutions. These institutions transmit or receive ACH entries through central clearing facilities operated by the American Clearing House Association, the Federal Reserve system, the Electronic Payment Network, and VISA.

According to the National Automated Clearinghouse Association (NACHA) www. nacha.org, during 2005 over 5 million companies were using the ACH network. This was an increase from 750,000 in 1997 and 2 million in the year 2000. One of the most popular uses of the network is the direct deposit of checks. Over 99 percent of government employees use direct deposit of their payroll checks, followed by 82 percent of Social Security recipients, and 65 percent of the private workforce. Commercial transactions using the ACH network have grown by close to 17 percent per year since 1989. NACHA estimates that Americans saved more than $1 billion in postage costs and late fees by using direct payments, while companies and government agencies save billions of dollars. This is not surprising given that approximately $30 trillion was processed through automated clearing houses in 2005. One of the major contributors to the growth of automated clearing houses has been the rise of Accounts Receivable (ARC) e-check payments. These exceeded 208 million in the second quarter of 2004 and 383 million by the second quarter of 2005.

The growth in this medium of funds transfer has the same motivating force that has driven Amazon.com and other Internet companies—low cost and ease of use. For example, the unit price charged by the Fed for check processing is 4.5 cents while the unit price for an ACH payment is 1.8 cents. The unit price charged by the Federal Reserve System for a check is now two and a half times higher than that for an ACH payment.

Figure 7–4 diagrams the flow of funds through the ACH network. The originator can be an individual, corporation, or other entity that initiates entries into the automated clearinghouse network. The originator forwards the credit or debit transaction data to an originating depository financial institution (ODFI), which then sorts and transmits the file to an automated clearinghouse operator. The ACH then distributes the file to the

Figure 7–4
ACH network

Source: www.nacha.org.

receiving depository financial institution (RDFI), which then makes the funds available to the individual, corporation, or other entity that has authorized the originator to initiate a credit or debit entry to the receiver's account held at the RDFI.

International electronic funds transfer is mainly carried out through SWIFT (www.swift.com). SWIFT is an acronym for the Society for Worldwide Interbank Financial Telecommunications. During 2005 SWIFT provided around-the-clock international payments between 7,750 financial institutions in 204 countries. SWIFT uses a proprietary secure messaging system (electronic funds transfer system) in which each message represents a transfer of currencies for payments, treasury, securities, and trade. A single message could be instructions to transfer $100 or $1 billion from one institution to another. Figure 7–5 shows the number of annual messages in millions and the annual growth in messages. Total volume of 2.3 trillion messages represents many trillions of dollars.

Figure 7–5   Five-year SWIFTNet FIN message traffic

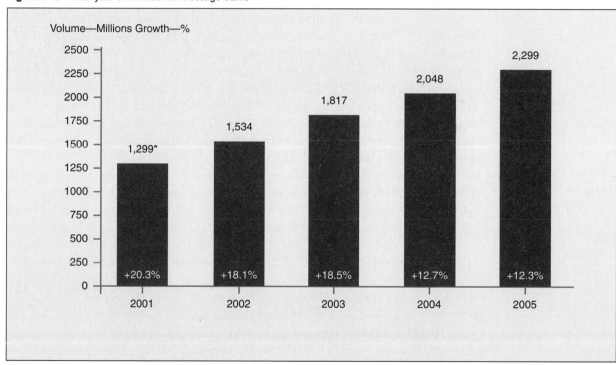

Rigid security standards are enforced, each message is encrypted (secretly coded), and every money transaction is authenticated by another code. These security measures are important to the members as well as to SWIFT, which assumes the financial liability for the accuracy, completeness, and confidentiality of transaction instructions from and to the point of connection to member institution circuits. One area of increasing concern has been electronic fraud, and SWIFT is using advanced smart card technology to improve its security system. Additionally it will automate the process by which financial institutions exchange secret authentication keys with each other.

International Cash Management

Multinational corporations can shift funds around from country to country much as a firm may transfer funds from regional banks to the lead bank. Just as financial institutions in the United States have become more involved in electronic funds transfer, an international payments system has also developed. However, international cash management has many differences from domestic-based cash management systems. Payment methods differ from country to country. For example in Poland, Russia, and other eastern European countries, checks were seldom used in preference to cash, and in other countries, electronic payments are more common than in the United States. International cash management is more complex because liquidity management, involving short-term cash balances and deficits, has to be managed across international boundaries and time zones and is subject to the risks of currency fluctuations and interest rate changes in all countries. There are also differences in banking systems and check clearing processes, account balance management, information reporting systems, and cultural, tax, and accounting differences.

A company may prefer to hold cash balances in one currency rather than another or to take advantage of the high interest rates available in a particular country for short-term investments in marketable securities. In periods in which one country's currency is rising in value relative to other currencies, an astute financial manager will try to keep as much cash as possible in the country with the strong currency. In periods in which the dollar is rising relative to other currencies, many balances are held in U.S. bank accounts or in dollar-denominated bank accounts in foreign banks, more commonly known as Eurodollar deposits. The international money markets have been growing in scope and size, so these markets have become a much more important aspect of efficient cash management.

International and domestic cash managers employ the same techniques and rely on forecasting methods using cash budgets and daily cash reports to predict cash balances. For those companies that are unable to actively manage their cash balances, banks often provide them special accounts to manage their cash flow and earn a return on their excess cash. The **sweep account** is one such account that allows companies to maintain zero balances with all their excess cash swept into an interest-earning account. Most banks have accounts that allow corporate clients to write checks on zero balance accounts with the understanding that when the check is presented for payment, money will be moved from the interest-bearing account to the appropriate account. These examples illustrate the way banks help manage excess cash for their corporate customers. The next section explains how companies manage their own excess cash balances by purchasing marketable securities.

Marketable Securities

The firm may hold excess funds in anticipation of a cash outlay. When funds are being held for other than immediate transaction purposes, they should be converted from cash into interest-earning marketable securities.[4]

---

[4]The one possible exception to this principle is found in the practice of holding compensating balances at commercial banks—a topic for discussion in Chapter 8.

The financial manager has a virtual supermarket of securities from which to choose. Among the factors influencing that choice are yield, maturity, minimum investment required, safety, and marketability. Under normal conditions, the longer the maturity period of the security, the higher the yield, as indicated in Figure 7–6.

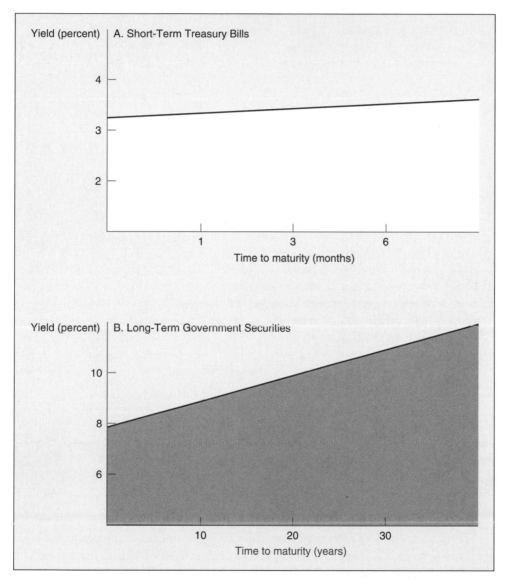

Figure 7–6

An examination of yield and maturity characteristics

The problem in "stretching out" the maturity of your investment is that you may have to take a loss. A $5,000 Treasury note issued initially at 5.5 percent, with three years to run, may only be worth $4,800 if the going interest rate climbs to 7 percent and the investor has to cash in before maturity. This risk is considerably greater as the maturity date is extended. A complete discussion of the "interest rate risk" is presented in Chapter 16, "Long-Term Debt and Lease Financing."

Table 7–3 Types of short-term investments

	Maturity	Minimum Amount	Safety	Marketability	Yield March 22, 1980	Yield July 14, 2000	Yield January 9, 2003	Yield September 12, 2005
Federal government securities:								
Treasury bills*	3 months	$1,000	Excellent	Excellent	14.76	6.06%	1.18%	3.45%
Treasury bills	6 months	1,000	Excellent	Excellent	13.85	6.34	1.24	3.67
Treasury notes	1–10 years	5,000	Excellent	Excellent	13.86	6.29	2.24	4.13
Treasury Inflation Protection Securities (TIPS)†	10 years	1,000	Excellent	Excellent	—	4.03	2.39	1.68
Federal agency securities:								
Federal Home Loan Bank	1 year	5,000	Excellent	Excellent	14.40	6.78	1.40	3.92
Nongovernment securities:								
Certificates of deposit (large)	3 months	100,000	Good	Good	16.97	6.65	1.29	3.75
Certificates of deposit (small)	3 months	500	Good	Poor	15.90	6.00	1.31	2.85
Commercial paper	3 months	25,000	Good	Fair	17.40	6.50	1.28	3.71
Banker's acceptances	3 months	None	Good	Good	17.22	6.51	1.31	3.83
Eurodollar deposits‡	3 months	25,000	Good	Excellent	18.98	6.75	1.32	3.84
Savings accounts	Open	None	Excellent	None	5.25	3.00	1.25	1.00
Money Market funds	Open	500	Good	None	14.50	6.00	0.96	2.87
Money market deposit accounts (financial institutions)	Open	1,000	Excellent	None	—	5.50	1.20	2.26

Several of the above securities can be purchased with maturities longer than those indicated. The above are the most commonly quoted.
*Treasury Bills are quoted on a coupon yield basis rather than on a discount basis. Since 1970 investors could only buy T-bills in $10,000 amounts but beginning August 10, 1998, this amount was lowered to $1,000.
†Treasury Inflation Protection Securities are quoted in real interest rates. An inflation premium is added on to the principal amount making the comparable yields competitive.
‡Though not marketable, these investments are still highly liquid in that funds may be withdrawn without penalty.

Sources: The Wall Street Journal, July 13, 2000 and September 14, 2005, pp. B4, C8, C10, and the St. Louis Federal Reserve Bank.

The various forms of marketable securities and investments, emphasizing the short term, are presented in Table 7–3 above. The key characteristics of each investment will be reviewed along with examples of yields at four different time periods.

As shown in Table 7–3, yields are given for four periods starting with March 22, 1980, when interest rates were extremely high because of double digit inflation and ending with September 2005, when interest rates were rising off their all-time lows reached in 2003. Perhaps, the July 2000 rates represent more normal rates than any of the other three periods. The low rates in 2003 represented an attempt by the Federal Reserve Board to stimulate an economy that had gone into recession during March 2001 and whose recovery was uncertain due to the terrorist attacks of 9/11, 2001. Note that interest rates for various securities had fallen 10 to 16 percent between 1980 and 2003.

Comparing the data for 2000 with data of 2003 and 2005 also demonstrates the ability of interest rates to rise and fall quickly. Table 7–3 may very well show the high and low of interest rates for the post-World War II period.

Let us examine the characteristics of each security in Table 7–3. **Treasury bills** are short-term obligations of the federal government and are a popular place to "park funds" because of a large and active market. Although these securities are originally issued with maturities of 91 days and 182 days, the investor may buy an outstanding T-bill with as little as one day remaining (perhaps two prior investors have held it for 45 days each).

With the government issuing new Treasury bills weekly, a wide range of choices is always available. Treasury bills are unique in that they trade on a discount basis— meaning the yield you receive occurs as a result of the difference between the price you pay and the maturity value.

Treasury notes are government obligations with a maturity of 1 to 10 years, and they may be purchased with short- to intermediate-term funds. In 1997, the U.S. Treasury introduced inflation-indexed Treasury securities referred to as **Treasury Inflation Protection Securities (TIPS)**. This security pays interest semiannually that equals a real rate of return specified by the U.S. Treasury, plus principal at maturity that is adjusted annually to reflect inflation's impact on purchasing power. TIPS are a useful short-term investment if interest rates should rise quickly because of rapid increases in inflation. Even if the investor owns a long-term issue, the principal value will not fluctuate much in response to rising or falling market interest rates. This price stability occurs because the principal amount is adjusted for inflation each year.

Federal agency securities represent the offerings of such governmental organizations as the Federal Home Loan Bank and the Student Loan Marketing Association. Though lacking the direct backing of the U.S. Treasury, they are guaranteed by the issuing agency and provide all the safety that one would normally require. There is an excellent secondary market for agency securities that allows investors to sell an outstanding issue in an active and liquid market before the maturity date. Government agency issues pay slightly higher yields than direct Treasury issues.

Another outlet for investment is a **certificate of deposit (CD)**, offered by commercial banks, savings and loans, and other financial institutions. The investor places his or her funds on deposit at a specified rate over a given time period as evidenced by the certificate received. This is a two-tier market, with small CDs ($500 to $10,000) carrying lower interest rates, while larger CDs ($100,000 and more) have higher interest provisions and a degree of marketability for those who wish to sell their CDs before maturity. The CD market became fully deregulated by the federal government in 1986. CDs are normally insured (guaranteed) by the federal government for up to $100,000.

Comparable in yield and quality to large certificates of deposit, **commercial paper** represents unsecured promissory notes issued to the public by large business corporations. When Ford Motor Credit Corporation needs short-term funds, it may choose to borrow at the bank or expand its credit resources by issuing its commercial paper to the general public in minimum units of $25,000. Commercial paper is usually held to maturity by the investor, with no active secondary market in existence.

Banker's acceptances are short-term securities that generally arise from foreign trade. The acceptance is a draft drawn on a bank for payment when presented to the bank. The difference between a draft and a check is that a company does not have to deposit funds at the bank to cover the draft until the bank has accepted the draft for payment and presented it to the company. In the case of banker's acceptances arising from foreign trade, the draft may be accepted by the bank for *future* payment of the required amount. This means the exporter who now holds the banker's acceptance may have to wait 30, 60, or 90 days to collect the money. Because there is an active market for banker's acceptances, the exporter can sell the acceptance on a discount basis to any buyer and in this way receive the money before the importer receives the goods. This provides a good investment opportunity in banker's acceptances. Banker's acceptances rank close behind Treasury bills and certificates of deposit as vehicles for viable short-term investments.

Another popular international short-term investment arising from foreign trade is the **Eurodollar certificate of deposit.** The rate on this investment is usually higher than the rates on U.S. Treasury bills and bank certificates of deposit at large U.S. banks. Eurodollars are U.S. dollars held on deposit by foreign banks and in turn lent by those banks to anyone seeking dollars. Since the U.S. dollar is the only international currency accepted worldwide, any country can use it to help pay for goods purchased through international trade. Therefore, there is a large market for Eurodollar deposits and loans.

The lowest yielding investment may well be a **passbook savings account** at a bank or a savings and loan. Although rates on savings accounts are no longer prescribed by federal regulation, they are still a relatively unattractive form of investment in terms of yield.

Of particular interest to the smaller investor is the **money market fund**—a product of the tight money periods of the 1970s and early 1980s. For as little as $500 or $1,000, an investor may purchase shares in a money market fund, which in turn reinvests the proceeds in higher-yielding $100,000 bank CDs, $25,000 to $100,000 commercial paper, and other large-denomination, higher-yielding securities. The investor then receives his or her pro rata portion of the interest proceeds daily as a credit to his or her shares.

Money market funds allow the small businessperson or investor to participate directly in higher-yielding securities. All too often in the past, the small investor was forced to place funds in low-yielding savings accounts, while "smart" money was parked at higher yields in large-unit investments. Examples of money market funds are Dreyfus Liquid Assets Inc. and Fidelity Daily Income Trust. The investor can normally write checks on a money market fund.

Beginning in December 1982, money market funds got new competition when commercial banks, savings and loans, and credit unions were permitted by the regulatory agencies and Congress to offer **money market accounts** modeled after the money market funds. Due to deregulation, financial institutions are able to pay competitive market rates on money market deposit accounts. While there is not a federally prescribed minimum balance, the normal minimum is $1,000. Terms do vary from institution to institution. Generally these accounts may have only three deposits and three withdrawals per month and are not meant to be transaction accounts, but a place to keep excess cash balances. They may be used by individuals or corporations, but are more attractive to smaller firms than to larger firms (which have many more alternatives available). These accounts are insured up to $100,000 by federal agencies, which makes them slightly less risky than money market funds.

Although not a short-term investment as such, most financial institutions also offer NOW accounts. NOW accounts are checking accounts that pay interest. (These accounts are not included in Table 7–3 because their primary purpose is for check writing.)

An increasing portion of the investment in corporate assets has been in accounts receivable as expanding sales, fostered at times by inflationary pressures, have placed additional burdens on firms to carry larger balances for their customers. Frequently, recessions have also stretched out the terms of payment as small customers have had to rely on suppliers for credit. Accounts receivable as a percentage of total assets have increased relative to inventory, and this is a matter of concern for some corporations in their management of current assets.[5]

Management of Accounts Receivable

Accounts Receivable as an Investment

As is true of other current assets, accounts receivable should be thought of as an investment. The level of accounts receivable should not be judged too high or too low based on historical standards of industry norms, but rather the test should be whether the level of return we are able to earn from this asset equals or exceeds the potential gain from other investments. For example, if we allow our customers five extra days to clear their accounts, our accounts receivable balance will increase—draining funds from marketable securities and perhaps drawing down the inventory level. We must ask whether we are optimizing our return, in light of appropriate risk and liquidity considerations.

An example of a buildup in accounts receivable is presented in Figure 7–7, with supportive financing provided through reducing lower-yielding assets and increasing lower-cost liabilities.

Credit Policy Administration

In considering the extension of credit, there are three primary policy variables to consider in conjunction with our profit objective.

1. Credit standards
2. Terms of trade
3. Collection policy

Credit Standards   The firm must determine the nature of the credit risk on the basis of prior records of payment, financial stability, current net worth, and other factors. When an account receivable is created, credit has been extended to the customer who is

---

[5]Federal Trade Commission and Securities and Exchange Commission, *Quarterly Report for Manufacturing Corporations,* 4th quarter, 1971, and 2nd quarter, 2005.

Figure 7–7

Financing growth in accounts receivable

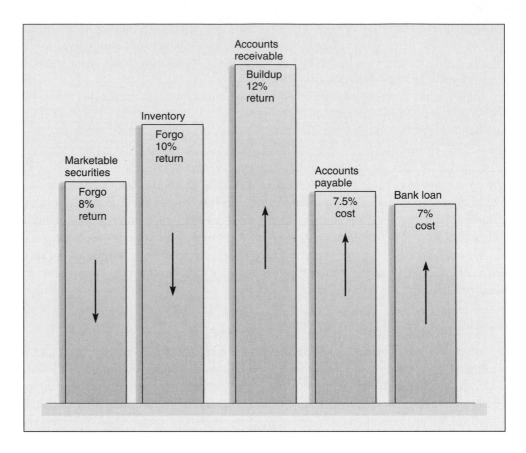

expected to repay according to the terms of trade. Bankers sometimes refer to the **5 Cs of credit** (character, capital, capacity, conditions, and collateral) as an indication of whether a loan will be repaid on time, late, or not at all. *Character* refers to the moral and ethical quality of the individual who is responsible for repaying the loan. A person of principle or a company run by people of high ethical standards is expected to be a good credit risk. A decision on character is a judgment call on the part of the lender and is considered one of the most significant considerations when making a loan. *Capital* is the level of financial resources available to the company seeking the loan and involves an analysis of debt to equity and the firm's capital structure. *Capacity* refers to the availability and sustainability of the firm's cash flow at a level high enough to pay off the loan. *Conditions* refers to the sensitivity of the operating income and cash flows to the economy. Some industries such as automobiles, chemicals, and paper are quite cyclical and exhibit wide fluctuations in cash flows as the economy moves through the economic cycle of contraction and expansion. The more sensitive the cash flow to the economy, the more the credit risk of the firm. When the economy is in a recession, business health in general is weaker, and most firms are riskier. *Collateral* is determined by the assets that can be pledged against the loan. Much as an automobile serves as collateral for a car loan or a house for a mortgage, companies can pledge assets that are available to be sold by the lender if the loan is not repaid. Obviously, the better the quality of the collateral, the lower the risk of the loan.

The assessment of credit risk and the setting of reasonable credit standards that allow marketing and finance to set goals and objectives together are based on the ability to get information and analyze it. An extensive electronic network of credit information has been developed by credit agencies throughout the country. The most prominent source of business information is **Dun & Bradstreet Information Services (DBIS)**, which produces business information analysis tools, publishes reference books, and provides computer access to information contained in its international database of more than 40 million businesses. DBIS has a large staff of analysts constantly updating information from public and private sources. Information is gathered, detailing the line of business, net worth, size of the company, years in business, management, and much more. DBIS produces many different reports, but its Business Information Report (BIR) is its cornerstone information product and a credit decision support tool.

In addition to the BIR, Dun & Bradstreet is known for a variety of credit scoring reports that rank a company's payment habits relative to its peer group. This is very important when, for example, a company is doing business with a new customer and there is no track record of orders and payment. Some of the other reports include a Supplier Evaluation, a Commercial Credit Scoring Report, a Small Business Credit Scoring Report, a Payment Analysis Report, a Financial Stress Report, and an Industry Credit Score Report. Table 7–4 presents the first page of the Trucking Industry Credit Score Report. Understanding the details is not as important as understanding the general concept.

Dun & Bradstreet's Credit Scoring products help facilitate credit decisions on more than 10 million U.S. businesses. Credit Score reports can help predict the likelihood that a company will become severely delinquent (90+ days past term) in paying its bills for a 12-month period. Small business and industry-specific credit score reports are available and the information is continuously updated.

The credit scores are based on D&B's statistical models, which are designed to analyze the risk of a bad debt. Some of the more important variables that go into these models include the age of the company in years, negative public records (suits, liens, judgments, and virtually all business bankruptcy filing, etc.), total number of employees, facility ownership, financial statement data, payment index information, and satisfactory or slow payment experiences. The model is intended to predict payment problems as much as 12 months before they occur.

Given that the world is doing more and more business on a global scale, being able to track companies around the world using a database containing over 40 million listings is a big advantage. The companies in the database can be verified through a D-U-N-S® Number, which is accepted by the United Nations and other international organizations as a global business identification standard. The **Data Universal Number System (D-U-N-S)** is a unique nine-digit code assigned by Dun & Bradstreet Information Services (DBIS) to each business in its information base. The D-U-N-S number can be used to track whole families of companies that are related through ownership. Subsidiaries, divisions, and branches can be linked to their ultimate parent company at the top of the family pyramid. For example, this tracking ability could be useful to identify additional sales opportunities within a corporate family. An example

Table 7–4   Dun & Bradstreet report

Trucking Industry Credit Score Level 2:
Gorman Manufacturing Company

TRUCKING INDUSTRY CREDIT SCORE REPORT
LEVEL TWO

D-U-N-S: 80-473-5132

DATE PRINTED: January 20, 1999
BUSINESS RECORD DATE: October 12, 1998

GORMAN MANUFACTURING COMPANY, INC
(AND BRANCH(ES) OR DIVISION(S))

BUSINESS SUMMARY
CONTROL: 1965

492 KOLLER STREET
EMPLOYS: 105
SAN FRANCISCO, CA 94110
NET WORTH: $2,838,982
    TEL: 650-555-0000

SIC: 27 52

LOB: COMMERCIAL PRINTING

PAYMENTS REPORTED FROM MEMBERS OF THE TRUCKING INDUSTRY
(amounts may be rounded to nearest figure in prescribed ranges)

Antic	- Anticipated	(Payments received prior to date of invoice)
Disc	- Discounted	(Payments received within trade discount period)
Ppt	- Prompt	(Payments received within terms granted)

REPORTED	PAYING RECORD	HIGH CREDIT	NOW OWES	PAST DUE	SELLING TERMS	LAST SALE WITHIN
06/98	Ppt	1,000	500	0	N30	
04/98	(002)	0	0	0		
	Satisfactory					
03/98	Ppt	100,000	20,000	0	N30	1 mo
	Slow 15	90,000	70,000	0	N30	1 mo
	Slow 210	2,500	2,500	2,500		1 mo
	(006)	7,500	7,500	7,500		1 mo
	Placed for collection					
	(007)	2,500	1,000	1,000	N30	1 mo

Accounts are sometimes placed for collection even though the existence or amount of the debt is disputed.

Payment experiences reflect how bills are met in relation to the terms granted. In some instances payment beyond terms can be the result of disputes over merchandise, skipped invoices etc.

Each experience shown represents a separate account reported by a supplier. Updated trade experiences replace those previously reported.

The TRUCKING INDUSTRY CREDIT RISK SCORE predicts the likelihood of a firm paying trucking bills in a delinquent manner (90 Days Past Terms) during the next 12 months, based on the information in Dun & Bradstreet's files. The score was calculated using statistically valid models derived from D&B's extensive information files and includes analysis of the trucking industry payment information.

The PERCENTILE ranks the firm relative to all businesses who use trucking services. For example, a firm in the 80th percentile is a better risk than 79% of all trucking customers.

The INCIDENCE OF DELINQUENT PAYMENT is the proportion of trucking customers with scores in this range that were reported 90 days past due by members of the trucking industry. The incidence of delinquent payment for the entire population of trucking customers was 11.8% over the past year.

TRUCKING INDUSTRY CREDIT RISK SCORE: (1 HIGHEST RISK - 100 LOWEST RISK)	24
PERCENTILE:	1
INCIDENCE OF DELINQUENT PAYMENT FOR TRUCKING CUSTOMERS WITH SCORES 21 - 25:	74.2%

Source: Reprinted with permission of Dun & Bradstreet.

of this hierarchical relationship is shown in Figure 7–8 for Gorman Printing Company, Inc. Clearly the use of information databases will continue to save companies time and money in their credit decisions.

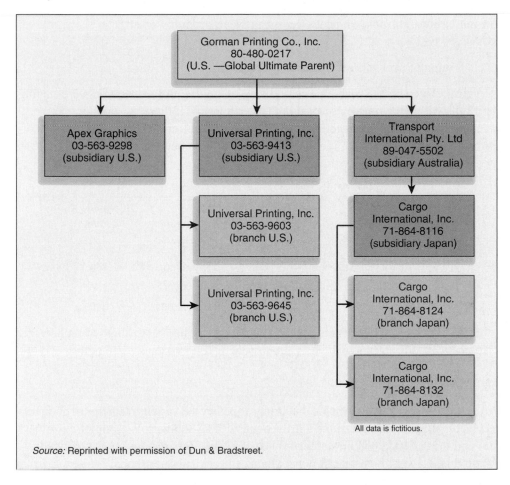

Figure 7–8
Dun's numerical tracking system

Source: Reprinted with permission of Dun & Bradstreet.

Terms of Trade   The stated terms of credit extension will have a strong impact on the eventual size of the accounts receivable balance. If a firm averages $5,000 in daily credit sales and allows 30-day terms, the average accounts receivable balance will be $150,000. If customers are carried for 60 days, we must maintain $300,000 in receivables and much additional financing will be required.

In establishing credit terms the firm should also consider the use of a cash discount. Offering the terms 2/10, net 30, enables the customer to deduct 2 percent from the face amount of the bill when paying within the first 10 days, but if the discount is not taken, the customer must remit the full amount within 30 days. We have been discussing credit standards and terms of trade. Another key area is collection policy.

Collection Policy   In assessing collection policy, a number of quantitative measures may be applied to the credit department of the firm.

a.   Average collection period $= \dfrac{\text{Accounts receivable}}{\text{Average daily credit sales}}$

An increase in the **average collection period** may be the result of a predetermined plan to expand credit terms or the consequence of poor credit administration.

b. Ratio of bad debts to credit sales.

An increasing ratio may indicate too many weak accounts or an aggressive market expansion policy.

c. Aging of accounts receivables.

Aging of accounts receivable is one way of finding out if customers are paying their bills within the time prescribed in the credit terms. If there is a buildup in receivables beyond normal credit terms, cash inflows will suffer and more stringent credit terms and collection procedures may have to be implemented. An aging schedule is presented below to illustrate the concept.

	Age of Receivables, May 31, 200X		
Month of Sales	**Age of Account (days)**	**Amounts**	**Percent of Account Due**
May.	0–30	$ 60,000	60%
April	31–60	25,000	25
March	61–90	5,000	5
February	91–120	10,000	10
Total receivables		$100,000	100%

If the normal credit terms are 30 days, the firm is doing something wrong because 40 percent of accounts are overdue with 10 percent over 90 days outstanding.

An Actual Credit Decision

We now examine a credit decision that brings together the various elements of accounts receivable management. Assume a firm is considering selling to a group of customers that will bring $10,000 in new annual sales, of which 10 percent will be uncollectible. While this is a very high rate of nonpayment, the critical question is, What is the potential contribution to profitability?

Assume the collection cost on these accounts is 5 percent and the cost of producing and selling the product is 77 percent of the sales dollar. We are in a 40 percent tax bracket. The profit on new sales is as follows:

Additional sales	$10,000
Accounts uncollectible (10% of new sales)	1,000
Annual incremental revenue	9,000
Collection costs (5% of new sales)	500
Production and selling costs (77% of new sales)	7,700
Annual income before taxes	800
Taxes (40%)	320
Annual incremental income after taxes	$ 480

Though the return on sales is only 4.8 percent ($480/$10,000), the return on invested dollars may be considerably higher. Let us assume the only new investment in this case is a buildup in accounts receivable. (Present working capital and fixed assets are sufficient to support the higher sales level.) Assume an analysis of our accounts indicates a turnover ratio of 6 to 1 between sales and accounts receivable. Our new accounts receivable balance will average $1,667.

$$\text{Accounts receivable} = \frac{\text{Sales}^6}{\text{Turnover}} = \frac{\$10,000}{6} = \$1,667$$

Thus we are committing an average investment of only $1,667 to provide an aftertax return of $480, so that the yield is a very attractive 28.8 percent. If the firm had a minimum required aftertax return of 10 percent, this would clearly be an acceptable investment. We might ask next if we should consider taking on 12 percent or even 15 percent in uncollectible accounts—remaining loyal to our concept of maximizing return on investment and forsaking any notion about risky accounts being inherently good or bad.

Inventory Management

In a manufacturing company, inventory is usually divided into the three basic categories: raw materials used in the product; work in progress, which reflects partially finished products; and finished goods, which are ready for sale. All these forms of inventory need to be financed, and their efficient management can increase a firm's profitability. The amount of inventory is not always totally controlled by company management because it is affected by sales, production, and economic conditions.

Because of its cyclical sales that are highly sensitive to the U.S. economic business climate, the automobile industry is a good case study in inventory management. The automakers have often suffered from inventory buildups when sales declined because adjusting production levels required time. During the 1980s, again in 2002–03 and in 2005, the big three (General Motors, Ford, and Chrysler) took turns implementing buyer incentive programs such as discount financing at rates well below market rates and cash rebate programs to stimulate sales. These programs cut profit margins per car but generated cash flow and reduced investment expenses associated with holding high inventories.

Because inventory is the least liquid of current assets, it should provide the highest yield to justify the investment. While the financial manager may have direct control over cash management, marketable securities, and accounts receivable, control over inventory policy is generally shared with production management and marketing. Let us examine some key factors influencing inventory management.

Level versus Seasonal Production

A manufacturing firm must determine whether a plan of level or seasonal production should be followed. Level production was discussed in Chapter 6. While level (even) production throughout the year allows for maximum efficiency in the use of manpower and machinery, it may result in unnecessarily high inventory buildups before shipment, particularly in a seasonal business. For example, a bathing suit manufacturer would not want excess suits in stock in November.

---

[6]We could actually argue that our out-of-pocket commitment to sales is 82 percent (77 percent production and sales costs plus 5 percent collection costs) times $10,000, or $8,200. This would indicate an even smaller commitment to receivables.

If we produce on a seasonal basis, the inventory problem is eliminated, but we will then have unused capacity during slack periods. Furthermore, as we shift to maximum operations to meet seasonal needs, we may be forced to pay overtime wages to labor and to sustain other inefficiencies as equipment is overused.

We have a classic problem in financial analysis. Are the cost savings from level production sufficient to justify the extra expenditure in carrying inventory? Let us look at a typical case.

	Production	
	Level	Seasonal
Average inventory	$100,000	$70,000
Operating costs—aftertax	50,000	60,000

Though $30,000 more will have to be invested in average inventory under level production (first line), $10,000 will be saved in operating costs (second line). This represents a 33 percent return on investment. If the required rate of return is 10 percent, this would clearly be an acceptable alternative.

Inventory Policy in Inflation (and Deflation)

The price of copper went from $3.00 to $0.50 a pound and back up again during the last two decades. Similar price instability has occurred in wheat, sugar, lumber, and a number of other commodities. Only the most astute inventory manager can hope to prosper in this type of environment. The problem can be partially controlled by taking moderate inventory positions (do not fully commit at one price).

Another way of protecting an inventory position would be by hedging with a futures contract to sell at a stipulated price some months from now.

Rapid price movements in inventory may also have a major impact on the reported income of the firm, a process described in Chapter 3, "Financial Analysis." A firm using FIFO (first-in, first-out) accounting may experience large inventory profits when old, less expensive inventory is written off against new high prices in the marketplace. The benefits may be transitory, as the process reverses itself when prices decline.

The Inventory Decision Model

Substantial research has been devoted to determining optimum inventory size, order quantity, usage rate, and similar considerations. An entire branch in the field of operations research is dedicated to the subject.

In developing an inventory model, we must evaluate the two basic costs associated with inventory: the carrying costs and the ordering costs. Through a careful analysis of both of these variables, we can determine the optimum order size that minimizes costs.

Carrying Costs   **Carrying costs** include interest on funds tied up in inventory and the costs of warehouse space, insurance premiums, and material handling expenses. There is also an implicit cost associated with the dangers of obsolescence or perishability and rapid price change. The larger the order we place, the greater the average inventory we will have on hand, and the higher the carrying costs.

Ordering Costs   As a second factor, we must consider the **cost of ordering** and processing inventory into stock. If we maintain a relatively low average inventory in stock, we must order many times and total ordering costs will be high. The opposite patterns associated with the two costs are portrayed in Figure 7–9.

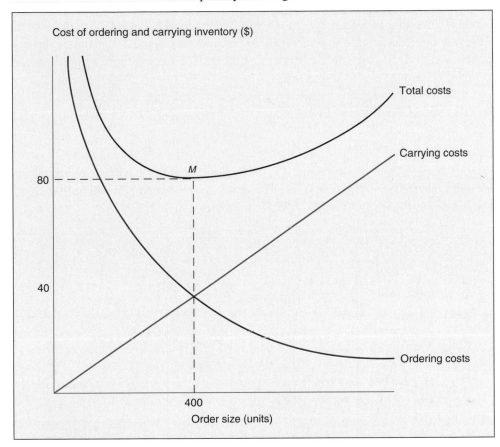

Figure 7–9

Determining the optimum inventory level

As the order size increases, carrying costs go up because we have more inventory on hand. With larger orders, of course, we will order less frequently and overall ordering costs will go down. The trade-off between the two can best be judged by examining the total cost curve. At point *M* on that curve, we have appropriately played the advantages and disadvantages of the respective costs against each other. With larger orders, carrying costs will be excessive, while at a reduced order size, constant ordering will put us at an undesirably high point on the ordering cost curve.

Economic Ordering Quantity

The question becomes, How do we mathematically determine the minimum point (*M*) on the total cost curve? We may use the following formula.

$$\text{EOQ} = \sqrt{\frac{2SO}{C}} \tag{7–1}$$

EOQ is the **economic ordering quantity**, the most advantageous amount for the firm to order each time. We will determine this value, translate it into average inventory size, and determine the minimum total cost amount (*M*). The terms in the EOQ formula are defined as follows:

S = Total sales in units
O = Ordering cost for each order
C = Carrying cost per unit in dollars

Let us assume that we anticipate selling 2,000 units; it will cost us $8 to place each order; the price per unit is $1, and with a 20 percent carrying cost to maintain the average inventory; the carrying charge per unit is $0.20. Plugging these values into our formula, we show:

$$\text{EOQ} = \sqrt{\frac{2SO}{C}} = \sqrt{\frac{2 \times 2,000 \times \$8}{\$0.20}} = \sqrt{\frac{\$32,000}{\$0.20}} = \sqrt{160,000}$$

$$= 400 \text{ units}$$

The optimum order size is 400 units. On the assumption that we will use up inventory at a constant rate throughout the year, our average inventory on hand will be 200 units, as indicated in Figure 7–10 below. Average inventory equals EOQ/2.

Figure 7–10

Inventory usage pattern

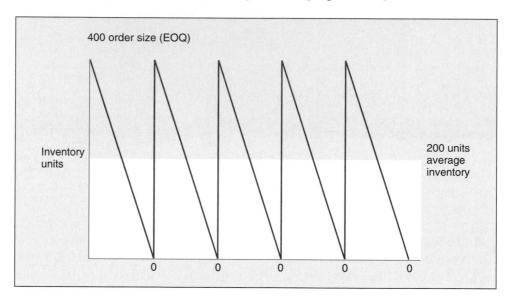

Our total costs with an order size of 400 and an average inventory size of 200 units are computed in Table 7–5 below.

Table 7–5

Total costs for inventory

1. Ordering costs = $\frac{2,000}{400}$ $\frac{\text{Units}}{\text{Order size}}$ = 5 orders

    5 orders at $8 per order = $40

2. Carrying costs = Average inventory in units × Carrying cost per unit

    200 × $0.20 = $40

3. Order cost $40
    Carrying cost   + 40
    Total cost $80

Point *M* in Figure 7–9 on page 209 can be equated to a total cost of $80 at an order size of 400 units. At no other order point can we hope to achieve lower costs. The same basic principles of total cost minimization that we have applied to inventory can be applied to other assets as well. For example, we may assume cash has a carrying cost (opportunity cost of lost interest on marketable securities as a result of being in cash) and an ordering cost (transaction costs of shifting in and out of marketable securities) and then work toward determining the optimum level of cash. In each case we are trying to minimize the overall costs and increase profit.

Safety Stock and Stock Outs

In our analysis thus far we have assumed we would use inventory at a constant rate and would receive new inventory when the old level of inventory reached zero. We have not specifically considered the problem of being out of stock.

A stock out occurs when a firm is out of a specific inventory item and is unable to sell or deliver the product. The risk of losing sales to a competitor may cause a firm to hold a **safety stock** to reduce this risk. Although the company may use the EOQ model to determine the optimum order quantity, management cannot always assume the delivery schedules of suppliers will be constant or that there will be delivery of new inventory when old inventory reaches zero. A safety stock will guard against late deliveries due to weather, production delays, equipment breakdowns, and the many other things that can go wrong between the placement of an order and its delivery.

A minimum safety stock will increase the cost of inventory because the carrying cost will rise. This cost should be offset by eliminating lost profits on sales due to stock outs and also by increased profits from unexpected orders that can now be filled.

In the prior example, if a safety stock of 50 units were maintained, the average inventory figure would be 250 units.

$$\text{Average inventory} = \frac{\text{EOQ}}{2} + \text{Safety stock} \qquad (7\text{–}2)$$

$$\text{Average inventory} = \frac{400}{2} + 50$$

$$= 200 + 50 = 250$$

The inventory carrying cost will now increase to $50.

$$\text{Carrying costs} = \text{Average inventory in units} \times \text{Carrying cost per unit}$$

$$= 250 \times \$0.20 = \$50$$

The amount of safety stock that a firm carries is likely to be influenced by the predictability of inventory usage and the time period necessary to fill inventory orders. The following discussion indicates safety stock may be reduced in the future.

Just-in-Time Inventory Management

Just-in-time inventory management (JIT) was designed for Toyota by the Japanese firm Shigeo Shingo and found its way to the United States. Just-in-time inventory management is part of a total production concept that often interfaces with a total quality control program. A JIT program has several basic requirements: (1) quality production that continually satisfies customer requirements; (2) close ties between suppliers, manufacturers, and customers; and (3) minimization of the level of inventory.

Usually suppliers are located near manufacturers and are able to make orders in small lot sizes because of short delivery times. One side effect has been for manufacturers to reduce their number of suppliers to assure quality as well as to ease the complexity of ordering and delivery. Computerized ordering/inventory tracking systems both on the assembly line and in the supplier's production facility are necessary for JIT to work.

Cost Savings from Lower Inventory   Cost savings from lower levels of inventory and reduced financing costs are supposed to be the major benefits of JIT. On average, it is estimated that over the last decade just-in-time inventory systems have reduced inventory to sales ratios by over 10 percent. Some individual cases are more dramatic.

Harley-Davidson reduced its in-process and in-transit inventory by $20 million at a single plant, and General Electric trimmed inventory by 70 percent in 40 plants. In one sense the manufacturer pushes some of the cost of financing onto the supplier. If the supplier also imposes JIT on its suppliers, these efficiencies work their way down the supplier chain to create a leaner production system for the whole economy.

Other Benefits   There are other, not so obvious cost savings to just-in-time inventory systems. Because of reduced warehouse space for inventory, some plants in the automotive industry have reduced floor space by 70 percent over the more traditional plants that warehoused inventory. This saves construction costs and reduces overhead expenses for utilities and manpower. The JIT systems have been aided in the last few years by the development of the Internet and electronic data interchange systems (EDI) between suppliers and production and manufacturing departments. EDI reduces rekeying errors and duplication of forms for the accounting and finance functions. Xerox implemented a quality process along with JIT and reduced its supplier list to 450, which provided a $15 million saving in quality control programs. Reductions in costs from quality control are often overlooked by financial analysts because JIT prevents defects rather than detecting poor quality; therefore, no cost savings are recognized. One last item is the elimination of waste, which is one of the side benefits of a total quality control system coupled with just-in-time inventory systems.

It is important to realize that the just-in-time inventory system is very compatible with the concept of economic ordering quantity. The focus is to balance reduced carrying costs from maintaining less inventory with increased ordering costs. Fortunately electronic data interchange minimizes the impact of having to place orders more often.

The Downside of JIT   Major U.S. companies such as Wal-Mart, Harley-Davidson, Mattel, Papa John's Pizza, Dell, Cisco, and Gap use just-in-time inventory management. When JIT methods work as planned, firms are able to maintain very little inventory, reduce warehouse storage space, and reduce the cost of financing a large inventory. Some JIT management systems allow inventory levels ranging from 1 hour's worth of parts to a maximum of 16 hours' worth. However, there are costs associated with an integrated JIT system. These costs should not be overlooked.

NASA—The National Aeronautics and Space Administration Inventory Control System

When it comes to inventory management, finance textbooks usually focus on a company's ability to order the right amount of inventory in order to minimize cost. This "right" amount of inventory depends on the production schedule, the number of units sold, the cost of storing the inventory, and the inventory methods used. There are also inventory control issues that are different from the manufacturing and sales cycles. What about inventory on hand that is not for sale?

For example, NASA has an inventory of ground support equipment (GSE) that is constantly being used and needs to be available at a moment's notice. The National Aeronautics and Space Administration operates a 47-square-mile facility at the Kennedy Space Center in Florida. The inventory control system has to be able to locate any of 300,000 inventory items stored in 100 buildings around the complex. The inventory could be anything from torque wrenches to the orbiter support braces used when the space shuttles are refitted. Trying to locate the equipment used to be a real struggle and wasted many man-hours per day.

NASA, with the help of their prime contractor, United Space Alliance (USA), installed a radio frequency data communications system that can pinpoint the location of 98 percent of the equipment in a few seconds. It is estimated that this system saves almost $1 billion annually as a result of reducing the time it takes to locate needed equipment. This makes everyone more efficient by eliminating downtime.

The inventory control system operates much like systems found in grocery stores—only grocery stores are not 47 square miles. Whenever a piece of equipment is moved, the employee scans in the equipment's bar code on a handheld computer. The data stored has the model number and the location of the item. The handheld computer transfers the information collected using a radio signal that goes to a repeater high above the ground. There are several repeaters located throughout the complex and this allows the information to be passed on to any handheld computer on a real-time basis.

Source: Transportation & Distribution, December 1999, Volume 40, p. SCF6.

When JIT works, it saves money, but there can be problems. This is a lesson the electronics market learned very well in 2000. Parts shortages led to lost sales and slowing growth for the electronics industry. Parts that took 4 weeks to get in 1998 and 1999 were taking 40 weeks in July of 2000. Some high-frequency cellular phone transistors needed to be ordered 18 months in advance. Industry experts said that the huge multinationals used to have one month's supplies of inventory but at this time nobody wanted to have any inventory, and the industry got caught short without capacity to produce parts for the hot growth items of cell phones, computers, handheld devices, and more. The failure of JIT was that sales increased much more rapidly than forecast and manufacturers could not keep up with the demand. In this case a 30-day supply of inventory would have helped the cell phone manufacturers but only for a short time.

The opposite happened during the recession and the slow economy of 2001–2002. Sales dropped so fast that even with JIT systems, inventory piled up at suppliers and manufacturers. Eventually, sales forecasts and production schedules were adjusted and inventory levels changed.

General Motors learned a different lesson in 1998, when strikes by the United Automobile Workers closed down production of GM cars very quickly because GM had no finished inventory available for continued manufacturing.

Such failures of JIT management systems will cause a revaluation of their use in high-growth industries with changing technologies.

Summary

This chapter on current asset management extends our discussion of Chapter 6 by focusing on the management of cash, marketable securities, accounts receivable, and inventory. An overriding concept in current asset management is that the less liquid an asset, the higher the required return.

In cash management the primary goal should be to keep the cash balances as low as possible, consistent with the notion of maintaining adequate funds for transactions purposes and compensating balances. Cash moves through the firm in a cycle, as customers make payments and the firm pays its bills. We try to speed the inflow of funds and defer their outflow in managing the company's cash balances. The increased use of electronic funds transfer systems both domestically and internationally is reducing float and making collections and disbursements more timely. The use of electronic payment mechanisms, such as automated clearing houses and the new Check 21 Act, have changed the way management manages their collections and payments. We are moving towards a checkless society.

One principle of cash management is not to let excess cash sit in banks and checking accounts when those cash balances could be earning a rate of return. Excess short-term funds may be placed in marketable securities—with a wide selection of issues, maturities, and yields from which to choose. The choices are summarized in Table 7–3.

The management of accounts receivable calls for the determination of credit standards and the forms of credit to be offered as well as the development of an effective collection policy. There is no such thing as bad credit—only unprofitable credit extension. It should also be understood that the accounts receivable policy is related to the inventory management policy.

Inventory is the least liquid of the current assets, so it should provide the highest yield. We recognize three different inventory types: raw materials, work in progress, and finished goods. We manage inventory levels through models such as the economic ordering quantity (EOQ) model, which helps us determine the optimum average inventory size that minimizes the total cost of ordering and carrying inventory. The just-in-time inventory management model (JIT) focuses on the minimization of holding inventory, through quality production techniques and close ties between manufacturers and suppliers. Both EOQ and JIT models are compatible and can work together in the management of inventory.

It seems like a simple concept, but it needs to be stated that the company that manages its current assets efficiently will minimize (or optimize) its investment in them, thereby freeing up funds for other corporate uses. The result will be higher profitability and return on total assets for the firm.

List of Terms

cash flow cycle   186
float   190
Check Clearing for the 21st Century
   Act (Check 21)   190
lockbox system   192
cost-benefit analysis   192

electronic funds transfer   193
automated clearinghouse (ACH)   193
international electronic funds
   transfer   195
sweep account   196
Treasury bills   199

Discussion Questions

1. In the management of cash and marketable securities, why should the primary concern be for safety and liquidity rather than maximization of profit?

2. Explain the similarities and differences of lockbox systems and regional collection offices.

3. Why would a financial manager want to slow down disbursements?

4. Use *The Wall Street Journal* or some other financial publication to find the going interest rates for the list of marketable securities in Table 7–3. Which security would you choose for a short-term investment? Why?

5. Why are Treasury bills a favorite place for financial managers to invest excess cash?

6. Explain why the bad debt percentage or any other similar credit-control percentage is not the ultimate measure of success in the management of accounts receivable. What is the key consideration?

7. What are three quantitative measures that can be applied to the collection policy of the firm?

8. What are the 5 Cs of credit that are sometimes used by bankers and others to determine whether a potential loan will be repaid?

9. What does the EOQ formula tell us? What assumption is made about the usage rate for inventory?

10. Why might a firm keep a safety stock? What effect is it likely to have on carrying cost of inventory?

11. If a firm uses a just-in-time inventory system, what effect is that likely to have on the number and location of suppliers?

Practice Problems and Solutions

1. Abbott Communications has annual credit sales of $1,800,000 and accounts receivable of $190,000. What is the average collection period?

    Average collection period

2. Archer Chemical is thinking about extending trade credit to new customers. Sales would increase by $80,000 if credit were extended to these customers. Of the

    Credit policy decision

new accounts receivable related to these sales, 8 percent would be uncollectible. Additional collection costs would be 4 percent of sales, and selling and collection costs would be 80 percent of sales. The firm is in a 30 percent tax bracket.

a. Compute the new income after taxes.

b. What will be the percentage return on the new sales?

c. If accounts receivable are turned over four times a year, what will be the new investment in accounts receivable?

d. What will be the return on investment assuming the only new investment will be in accounts receivable?

Solutions

1. Average collection period $= \dfrac{\text{Accounts receivable}}{\text{Average daily credit sales}}$

    Accounts receivable $= \$190,000$

    Average daily credit sales $= \dfrac{\text{Credit sales}}{360} = \dfrac{\$1,800,000}{360} = \$5,000$

    Average collection period $= \dfrac{\$190,000}{5,000} = 38$ days

2. *a.*

Additional sales	$80,000
Accounts uncollectible (8% of new sales)	6,400
Annual incremental revenue	$73,600
Collection costs (4% of new sales)	3,200
Production and selling costs (80% of new sales)	64,000
Annual income before taxes	6,400
Taxes (30%).	1,920
Annual incremental income after taxes	$ 4,480

   b. $\dfrac{\text{Incremental income}}{\text{Sales}} = \dfrac{\$4,480}{80,000} = 5.6\%$

   c. Accounts receivable $= \dfrac{\text{Sales}}{\text{Accounts receivable turnover}}$

   $= \dfrac{\$80,000}{4} = \$20,000$

   d. Return on investment $= \dfrac{\text{Incremental income}}{\text{Accounts receivable}} = \dfrac{\$4,480}{20,000} = 22.40\%$

Problems

All problems are available in Homework Manager. Please see the preface for more information.

Determining float

1. Porky's Sausage Co. shows the following values on its corporate books.

Corporate Books	
Initial amount	$10,000
Deposits	+ 80,000
Checks	− 50,000
Balance	$40,000

The initial amount on the bank's books is also $10,000. However, only $70,000 in deposits have been recorded and only $25,000 in checks have cleared. Fill in the table below and indicate the amount of float.

Bank's Books	
Initial amount	$10,000
Deposits	
Checks	————
Balance	
Float	

2. Beth's Society Clothiers, Inc., has collection centers across the country to speed up collections. The company also makes payments from remote disbursement centers so the firm's checks will take longer to clear the bank. Collection time has been reduced by two and one-half days and disbursement time increased by one and one-half days because of these policies. Excess funds are being invested in short-term instruments yielding 6 percent per annum.

   a. If the firm has $4 million per day in collections and $3 million per day in disbursements, how many dollars has the cash management system freed up?

   b. How much can the firm earn in dollars per year on short-term investments made possible by the freed-up cash?

   Cost-benefit analysis of cash management

3. Neon Light Company of Kansas City ships lamps and lighting appliances throughout the country. Ms. Neon has determined that through the establishment of local collection centers around the country, she can speed up the collection of payments by one and one-half days. Furthermore, the cash management department of her bank has indicated to her that she can defer her payments on her accounts by one-half day without offending suppliers. The bank has a remote disbursement center in Florida.

   a. If Neon Light Company has $2 million per day in collections and $1 million per day in disbursements, how many dollars will the cash management system free up?

   b. If Neon Light Company can earn 9 percent per annum on freed-up funds, how much will the income be?

   c. If the total cost of the new system is $375,000, should it be implemented?

   Cost-benefit analysis of cash management

4. Postal Express has outlets throughout the world. It also keeps funds for transactions purposes in many foreign countries. Assume that in 2007 it held 200,000 reals in Brazil worth 70,000 dollars. It drew 10 percent interest, but the Brazilian real declined 20 percent against the dollar.

   a. What is the value of the holdings, based on U.S. dollars, at year-end? (Hint: multiply $70,000 times 1.10 and then multiply the resulting value by 80 percent.)

   b. What is the value of its holdings, based on U.S. dollars, at year-end if it drew 8 percent interest and the real went up by 12 percent against the dollar?

   International cash management

5. Sanders' Prime Time Company has annual credit sales of $1,800,000 and accounts receivable of $210,000. Compute the value of the average collection period.

   Average collection period

Accounts receivable balance

6. Barney's Antique Shop has annual credit sales of $1,080,000 and an average collection period of 40 days in 2007. Assume a 360-day year. What is the company's average accounts receivable balance? Accounts receivable are equal to the average daily credit sales times the average collection period.

Credit policy

7. In Problem 6, if accounts receivable change in 2007 to $140,000, while credit sales are $1,440,000, should we assume the firm has a more or a less lenient credit policy? Hint: Recompute the average collection period.

Determination of credit sales

8. Mervyn's Fine Fashions has an average collection period of 40 days. The accounts receivable balance is $80,000. What is the value of its credit sales?

Aging of accounts receivable   𝕏

9. Route Canal Shipping Company has the following schedule for aging of accounts receivable:

	Age of Receivables April 30, 2007		
(1)	**(2)**	**(3)**	**(4)**
	Age of		**Percent of**
Month of Sales	**Account**	**Amounts**	**Amount Due**
April	0–30	$105,000	_____
March	31–60	60,000	_____
February	61–90	90,000	_____
January	91–120	45,000	_____
Total receivables		$300,000	100%

  a. Fill in column (4) for each month.
  b. If the firm had $1,440,000 in credit sales over the four-month period, compute the average collection period. Average daily sales should be based on a 120-day period.
  c. If the firm likes to see its bills collected in 30 days, should it be satisfied with the average collection period?
  d. Disregarding your answer to part *c* and considering the aging schedule for accounts receivable, should the company be satisfied?
  e. What additional information does the aging schedule bring to the company that the average collection period may not show?

Economic ordering quantity

10. Midwest Tires has expected sales of 12,000 tires this year, an ordering cost of $6 per order, and carrying costs of $1.60 per tire.
  a. What is the economic ordering quantity?
  b. How many orders will be placed during the year?
  c. What will the average inventory be?

Economic ordering quantity

11. Fisk Corporation is trying to improve its inventory control system and has installed an online computer at its retail stores. Fisk anticipates sales of 75,000 units per year, an ordering cost of $8 per order, and carrying costs of $1.20 per unit.
  a. What is the economic ordering quantity?
  b. How many orders will be placed during the year?
  c. What will the average inventory be?
  d. What is the total cost of ordering and carrying inventory?

12. (See Problem 11 for basic data.) In the second year, Fisk Corporation finds that it can reduce ordering costs to $2 per order but that carrying costs stay the same at $1.20. Also, volume remains at 75,000 units.

    a. Recompute *a*, *b*, *c*, and *d* in Problem 11 for the second year.

    b. Now compare years one and two and explain what happened.

13. Diagnostic Supplies has expected sales of 135,000 units per year, a carrying cost of $3 per unit, and an ordering cost of $4 per order.

    a. What is the economic order quantity?

    b. What is average inventory? What is the total carrying cost?

    c. Assume an additional 80 units of inventory will be required as safety stock. What will the new average inventory be? What will the new total carrying cost be?

14. Wisconsin Snowmobile Corp. is considering a switch to level production. Cost efficiencies would occur under level production, and aftertax costs would decline by $30,000, but inventory costs would increase by $250,000. Wisconsin Snowmobile would have to finance the extra inventory at a cost of 13.5 percent.

    a. Should the company go ahead and switch to level production?

    b. How low would interest rates need to fall before level production would be feasible?

15. Johnson Electronics is considering extending trade credit to some customers previously considered poor risks. Sales would increase by $100,000 if credit is extended to these new customers. Of the new accounts receivable generated, 10 percent will prove to be uncollectible. Additional collection costs will be 3 percent of sales, and production and selling costs will be 79 percent of sales. The firm is in the 40 percent tax bracket.

    a. Compute the incremental income after taxes.

    b. What will Johnson's incremental return on sales be if these new credit customers are accepted?

    c. If the receivable turnover ratio is 6 to 1, and no other asset buildup is needed to serve the new customers, what will Johnson's incremental return on new average investment be?

16. Henderson Office Supply is considering a more liberal credit policy to increase sales, but expects that 8 percent of the new accounts will be uncollectible. Collection costs are 5 percent of new sales; production and selling costs are 78 percent; and accounts receivable turnover is five times. Assume income taxes of 30 percent and an increase in sales of $60,000. No other asset buildup will be required to service the new accounts.

    a. What is the level of accounts receivable to support this sales expansion?

    b. What would be Henderson's incremental aftertax return on investment?

    c. Should Henderson liberalize credit if a 15 percent aftertax return on investment is required?

    Assume that Henderson also needs to increase its level of inventory to support new sales and that inventory turnover is four times.

Economic ordering quantity

Economic ordering quantity with safety stock

Level versus seasonal production

Credit policy decision

Credit policy decision— receivables and inventory

d. What would be the total incremental investment in accounts receivable and inventory to support a $60,000 increase in sales?

e. Given the income determined in part *b* and the investment determined in part *d,* should Henderson extend more liberal credit terms?

Credit policy decision with changing variables

17. Comiskey Fence Co. is evaluating the extension of credit to a new group of customers. Although these customers will provide $180,000 in additional credit sales, 12 percent are likely to be uncollectible. The company will also incur $15,700 in additional collection expense. Production and marketing costs represent 70 percent of sales. The firm is in a 34 percent tax bracket and has a receivables turnover of five times. No other asset buildup will be required to service the new customers. The firm has a 10 percent desired return.

a. Should Comiskey Fence Co. extend credit to these customers?

b. Should credit be extended if 15 percent of the new sales prove uncollectible?

c. Should credit be extended if the receivables turnover drops to 1.5, and 12 percent of the accounts are uncollectible (as in part *a*)?

Continuation of Problem 17

18. Reconsider Problem 17*c.* Assume the average collection period is 120 days. All other factors are the same (including 12 percent uncollectibles). Should credit be extended?

Credit policy and return on investment

19. Global Services is considering a promotional campaign that will increase annual credit sales by $400,000. The company will require investments in accounts receivable, inventory, and plant and equipment. The turnover for each is as follows:

Accounts receivable	4x
Inventory	8x
Plant and equipment	2x

All $400,000 of the sales will be collectible. However, collection costs will be 4 percent of sales, and production and selling costs will be 76 percent of sales. The cost to carry inventory will be 8 percent of inventory. Depreciation expense on plant and equipment will be 5 percent of plant and equipment. The tax rate is 30 percent.

a. Compute the investments in accounts receivable, inventory, and plant and equipment based on the turnover ratios. Add the three together.

b. Compute the accounts receivable collection costs and production and selling costs and add the two figures together.

c. Compute the costs of carrying inventory.

d. Compute the depreciation expense on new plant and equipment.

e. Add together all the costs in parts *b*, *c*, and *d*.

f. Subtract the answer from part *e* from the sales figure of $400,000 to arrive at income before taxes. Subtract taxes at a rate of 30 percent to arrive at income after taxes.

g. Divide the aftertax return figure in part *f* by the total investment figure in part *a*. If the firm has a required return on investment of 12 percent, should it undertake the promotional campaign described throughout this problem.

20. In Problem 19, if inventory turnover had only been 4 times:

    a. What would be the new value for inventory investment?

    b. What would be the return on investment? You need to recompute the total investment and the total costs of the campaign to work toward computing income after taxes. Should the campaign be undertaken?

Continuation of
Problem 19

(Problems 21–24 are a series and should be taken in order.)

21. Dome Metals has credit sales of $144,000 yearly with credit terms of net 30 days, which is also the average collection period. Dome does not offer a discount for early payment, so its customers take the full 30 days to pay. What is the average receivables balance? Receivables turnover?

Credit policy
decision with
changing variables

22. If Dome offered a 2 percent discount for payment in 10 days and every customer took advantage of the new terms, what would the new average receivables balance be? Use the full sales of $144,000 for your calculation of receivables.

23. If Dome reduces its bank loans, which cost 10 percent, by the cash generated from reduced receivables, what will be the net gain or loss to the firm (don't forget the 2 percent discount)? Should it offer the discount?

24. Assume that the new trade terms of 2/10, net 30 will increase sales by 15 percent because the discount makes Dome's price competitive. If Dome earns 20 percent on sales before discounts, should it offer the discount? (Consider the same variables as you did for Problems 21 through 23 as well as increased sales.)

COMPREHENSIVE PROBLEM

Logan Distributing Company of Atlanta sells fans and heaters to retail outlets throughout the Southeast. Joe Logan, the president of the company, is thinking about changing the firm's credit policy to attract customers away from competitors. The present policy calls for a 1/10, net 30 cash discount. The new policy would call for a 3/10, net 50 cash discount. Currently, 30 percent of Logan customers are taking the discount, and it is anticipated that this number would go up to 50 percent with the new discount policy. It is further anticipated that annual sales would increase from a level of $400,000 to $600,000 as a result of the change in the cash discount policy.

Logan Distributing
Company
(receivables and
inventory policy)

The increased sales would also affect the inventory level. The average inventory carried by Logan is based on a determination of an EOQ. Assume sales of fans and heaters increase from 15,000 to 22,500 units. The ordering cost for each order is $200, and the carrying cost per unit is $1.50 (these values will not change with the discount). The average inventory is based on EOQ/2. Each unit in inventory has an average cost of $12.

Cost of goods sold is equal to 65 percent of net sales, general and administrative expenses are 15 percent of net sales, and interest payments of 14 percent will only be necessary for the increase in the accounts receivable and inventory balances. Taxes will be 40 percent of before-tax income.

a. Compute the accounts receivable balance before and after the change in the cash discount policy. Use the net sales (total sales minus cash discounts) to determine the average daily sales.

b. Determine EOQ before and after the change in the cash discount policy. Translate this into average inventory (in units and dollars) before and after the change in the cash discount policy.

c. Complete the following income statement.

	Before Policy Change	After Policy Change
Net sales (Sales − Cash discounts)		
Cost of goods sold		
Gross profit		
General and administrative expense		
Operating profit		
Interest on increase in accounts receivable and inventory (14%)		
Income before taxes		
Taxes		
Income after taxes		

d. Should the new cash discount policy be utilized? Briefly comment.

WEB EXERCISE

One of the items discussed in this chapter was the impact of the Internet on working capital management, and FreeMarkets and Perfect Commerce were two companies that were highlighted as being at the forefront of the B2B trend. Go to the Perfect Commerce Web site at www.perfect.com.

1. Click on "Company" and read the description. In one short paragraph, describe what Perfect Commerce does.

2. Click on "Solutions." Scroll down to "SRM Solutions." In two short paragraphs, explain what solutions they offer to buyers and sellers.

3. Click on "Customers" at the top of the page. List three types of customers.

Note: From time to time, companies redesign their Web sites and occasionally a topic we have listed may have been deleted, updated, or moved into a different location. If you click on the site map or site index, you will be introduced to a table of contents which should aid you in finding the topic you are looking for.

8

Sources of Short-Term Financing

chapter concepts

1. Trade credit from suppliers is normally the most available form of short-term financing.

2. Bank loans are usually short term in nature and should be paid off from funds from the normal operations of the firm.

3. Commercial paper represents a short-term, unsecured promissory note issued by the firm.

4. Through borrowing in foreign markets, a firm may lower its borrowing costs.

5. By using accounts receivable and inventory as collateral for a loan, the firm may be able to borrow larger amounts.

In Chapter 8 we examine the cost and availability of the various sources of short-term funds, with primary attention to trade credit from suppliers, bank loans, corporate promissory notes, foreign borrowing, and loans against receivables and inventory. It is sometimes said the only way to be sure a bank loan will be approved is to convince the banker that you don't really need the money. The learning objective of this chapter is the opposite—namely, to demonstrate how badly needed funds can be made available on a short-term basis from the **VIACOM** various credit suppliers.

For example, Viacom Inc., the parent company of MTV and other media companies, has line of credit agreements with banks that allow it to prepay its loans and reduce its commitments in whole or in part. Information about Viacom's credit agreements is found in its 10K report to the Securities and Exchange Commission. Its 10K statement for 2005 shows that Viacom has a $4.5 billion line of credit with $3.0 billion due in four years and the other $1.5 billion due in 15 months. Lines of credit are sometimes referred to as a revolving credit facility. The interest cost on these loans is based on the LIBOR (the London Interbank Offering Rate) plus a percentage margin based on the company's senior unsecured credit rating.

Viacom also pays commitment fees based on the total $4.5 billion line of credit and even if they don't draw down the line of credit, they still pay the fee. This is like an insurance policy; just in case Viacom needs the money, it is guaranteed for the period stated in the agreement. Because Viacom states that the primary purpose of these credit facilities is to back up its commercial paper borrowings, it is clear that if Viacom were unable to raise money in the commercial paper market, it could tap its line of credit instead. Additionally these lines of credit contain certain covenants (restrictions). The major covenant requires Viacom to maintain a minimum interest coverage ratio.

International companies such as Hewlett-Packard also rely on international borrowings and lines of credit. Hewlett-Packard states in its financial statements that it had a $1.5 billion 365-day credit facility and a $1.5 billion five-year credit facility. It states its interest rates are a function of its external credit rating at the time of borrowing and that it pays 8 basis points (8/100th of one percent) on the unused portion of its line of credit. Companies have many choices for borrowing money. These range from bank borrowing through lines of credit and various types of loans, the use of commercial paper, and even international borrowing opportunities. In all cases, the borrowers are trying to minimize their costs through the use of a mix of financing arrangements. We now look at the various forms of credit.

Trade Credit

The largest provider of short-term credit is usually at the firm's doorstep—the manufacturer or seller of goods and services. Approximately 40 percent of short-term financing is in the form of accounts payable or trade credit. Accounts payable is a **spontaneous source of funds**, growing as the business expands on a seasonal or long-term basis and contracting in a like fashion when business declines.

Payment Period

Trade credit is usually extended for 30 to 60 days. Many firms attempt to "stretch the payment period" to receive additional short-term financing. This is an acceptable form of financing as long as it is not carried to an abusive extent. Going from a 30- to a 35-day average payment period may be tolerated within the trade, while stretching payments to 65 days might alienate suppliers and cause a diminishing credit rating with Dun & Bradstreet and local credit bureaus. A major variable in determining the payment period is the possible existence of a cash discount.

Cash Discount Policy

A **cash discount** allows a reduction in price if payment is made within a specified time period. A 2/10, net 30 cash discount means we can deduct 2 percent if we remit our funds 10 days after billing, but failing this, we must pay the full amount by the 30th day.

On a $100 billing, we could pay $98 up to the 10th day or $100 at the end of 30 days. If we fail to take the cash discount, we will get to use $98 for 20 more days at a $2 fee. The cost is a high 36.72 percent. Note that we first consider the interest cost and then convert this to an annual basis. The standard formula for this example is:

$$\frac{\text{Cost of failing to}}{\text{take a cash discount}} = \frac{\text{Discount percent}}{100 \text{ percent} - \text{Discount percent}} \times \frac{360}{\text{Final due date} - \text{Discount period}} \tag{8–1}$$

$$\frac{2\%}{100\% - 2\%} \times \frac{360}{(30 - 10)} = 2.04\% \times 18 = 36.72\%$$

Cash discount terms may vary. For example, on a 2/10, net 90 basis, it would cost us only 9.18 percent not to take the discount and to pay the full amount after 90 days.

$$\frac{2\%}{100\% - 2\%} \times \frac{360}{(90 - 10)} = 2.04\% \times 4.5 = 9.18\%$$

In each case, we must ask ourselves whether bypassing the discount and using the money for a longer period is the cheapest means of financing. In the first example, with a cost of 36.72 percent, it probably is not. We would be better off borrowing $98 for 20 days at some lesser rate. For example, at 10 percent interest we would pay 54 cents[1] in interest as opposed to $2 under the cash discount policy. With the 2/10, net 90 arrangement, the cost of missing the discount is only 9.18 percent and we may choose to let our suppliers carry us for an extra 80 days.

Net Credit Position

In Chapter 2, "Review of Accounting," we defined accounts receivable as a use of funds and accounts payable as a source of funds. The firm should closely watch the relationship between the two to determine its **net trade credit** position. Net trade credit is positive when accounts receivable are greater than accounts payable and vice versa. If a firm has average daily sales of $5,000 and collects in 30 days, the accounts receivable balance will be $150,000. If this is associated with average daily purchases of $4,000 and a 25-day average payment period, the average accounts payable balance is $100,000—indicating $50,000 more in credit is extended than received. Changing this situation to an average payment period of 40 days increases the accounts payable to $160,000 ($4,000 × 40). Accounts payable now exceed accounts receivable by $10,000, thus leaving these funds for other needs. Larger firms tend to be net providers of trade credit (relatively high receivables), with smaller firms in the user position (relatively high payables).

Bank Credit

Banks may provide funds for the financing of seasonal needs, product line expansion, and long-term growth. The typical banker prefers a **self-liquidating loan** in which the use of funds will ensure a built-in or automatic repayment scheme. Actually, two-thirds of bank loans are short-term in nature. Nevertheless, through the process of renewing old loans, many of these 90- or 180-day agreements take on the characteristics of longer-term financing.

Major changes occurring in banking today are centered on the concept of "full-service banking." The modern banker's function is much broader than merely accepting deposits, making loans, and processing checks. A banking institution may be providing trust and investment services, a credit card operation, real estate lending, data processing services, cash management services both domestically and internationally, pension fund management, and many other services for large and small businesses.

The banking scene today has become more international to accommodate increased world trade and the rise of international corporations. The largest international banks are expanding into the United States through bank acquisitions and branch offices. Every major financial center from New York to San Francisco has experienced an increase in the number of foreign banks.

---

[1] $\frac{20}{360} \times 10\% \times \$98 = 54¢.$

Bank deregulation has created greater competition among financial institutions, such as commercial banks, savings and loans, credit unions, brokerage houses, and new companies offering financial services. During the late 1980s and early 1990s the whole U.S. financial system faced difficult problems brought on by the collapse of real estate values, the increased debt load of highly leveraged companies, risky loans to less-developed countries, and competition with international banks. During this time a record number of commercial banks and savings and loans went bankrupt or merged with healthy institutions. The economic recovery following 1991, and relatively low interest rates, created record bank profits, and by the late 1990s financial institutions showed great improvement in their ability to lend money to businesses and households. Additionally, new banking laws allowed more competition and gave banks the right to expand across state lines to create larger, more competitive banks.

Also, large banks made acquisitions to either expand their geographical reach, such as the merger of Bank of America (www.bankofamerica.com) and NationsBank, or to become more competitive in their own market area, as Chase Manhattan did when it acquired Chemical Bank and later merged with J.P. Morgan. Several years later, J.P. Morgan Chase acquired Bank One of Chicago to become the second largest commercial bank in the United States behind Citigroup's Citibank.

It may be a surprise to some, but General Electric Corporation's finance subsidiary, General Electric Capital Services (GECS) would rank as one of the top 10 largest U.S. banks with assets of $618 billion at the end of 2004. It should also be noted that this subsidiary is not regulated as are commercial banks. GECS, with almost half its revenues from international operations, accounted for close to 45 percent of General Electric's 2005 revenues and 49.8 percent of its profits.

We will look at a number of terms generally associated with banking (and other types of lending activity) and consider the significance of each. Attention is directed to the prime interest rate, LIBOR, compensating balances, the term loan arrangement, and methods of computing interest.

Prime Rate and LIBOR

The **prime rate** is the rate a bank charges its most creditworthy customers, and it usually increases as a customer's credit risk gets higher. At certain slack loan periods in the economy, or because of international competition, banks may actually charge top customers less than the published prime rate; however, such activities are difficult to track. The average customer can expect to pay one or two percentage points above prime, while in tight money periods a builder in a speculative construction project might have to pay five or more percentage points over prime.

Since the U.S. dollar is the world's international currency, and because the United States has run up huge foreign trade deficits over the last 10 years, there are several trillion dollars floating around the world's money markets. London is the center of Eurodollar deposits and a majority of these U.S. dollars can be found there. Because U.S. companies can borrow dollars from London banks quite easily, large borrowers shop for the lowest interest rate in either London, New York, or any other major money market center. This means that the U.S. prime rate competes with the **London Interbank Offered Rate (LIBOR)** for those companies with an international presence or those sophisticated enough to use the London Eurodollar market for loans. For example, in the fall of 2005, LIBOR one-year loans were at 4.40 percent versus a U.S. prime rate of 6.75 percent. A loan at 2.0 percent above LIBOR would still be less than the U.S. prime rate.

Figure 8–1 shows the relationship between LIBOR and the prime rate between January 1990 and September 2005. Notice that during this period the prime rate was always higher than LIBOR.

Figure 8–1   The prime rate versus the London Interbank Offered Rate on U.S. dollar deposits

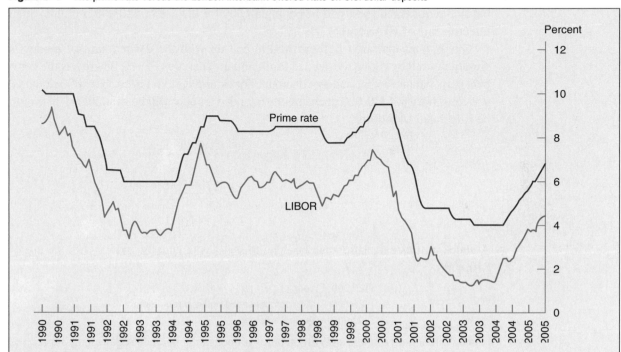

Some of the institutional arrangements mentioned above are likely to be modified with the emergence of the euro currency, but they will still continue to be important. You can read Chapter 21, "International Financial Management," for further discussion of this subject.

Compensating Balances

In providing loans and other services, a bank may require that *business* customers either pay a fee for the service or maintain a minimum average account balance, referred to as a compensating balance. In some cases both fees and compensating balances are required. When interest rates are in the 8.5 percent range, large commercial banks may require compensating balances of over $20,000 to offset $100 in service fees. As interest rates go down this compensating balance rises and so under the 2003 prime rate of 4.25 percent, the compensating balances could be over $40,000 per $100 in service fees. Because the funds do not generate as much revenue at lower interest rates, the compensating balance amount is higher.

When compensating balances are required to obtain a loan, the required amount is usually computed as a percentage of customer loans outstanding, or as a percentage of bank commitments toward future loans to a given account. A common ratio is 20 percent against outstanding loans or 10 percent against total future commitments, though market conditions tend to influence the percentages.

Some view the compensating balance requirement as an unusual arrangement. Where else would you walk into a business establishment, buy a shipment of goods, and then be told you could not take 20 percent of the purchase home with you? If you borrow $100,000, paying 8 percent interest on the full amount with a 20 percent compensating balance requirement, you will be paying $8,000 for the use of $80,000 in funds, or an effective rate of 10 percent.

The amount that must be borrowed to end up with the desired sum of money is simply figured by taking the needed funds and dividing by $(1 - c)$, where c is the compensating balance expressed as a decimal. For example, if you need $100,000 in funds, you must borrow $125,000 to ensure the intended amount will be available. This would be calculated as follows:

$$\text{Amount to be borrowed} = \frac{\text{Amount needed}}{(1 - c)}$$
$$= \frac{\$100,000}{(1 - 0.2)}$$
$$= \$125,000$$

A check on this calculation can be done to see if you actually end up with the use of $100,000.

$125,000	Loan
− 25,000	20% compensating balance requirement
$100,000	Available funds

The intent here is not to suggest that the compensating balance requirement represents an unfair or hidden cost. If it were not for compensating balances, quoted interest rates would be higher or gratuitous services now offered by banks would carry a price tag.

In practice, some corporate clients pay a fee for cash management or similar services while others eliminate the direct fee with compensating balances. Fees and compensating balances vary widely among banks. As the competition heats up among the providers of financial services, corporations can be expected to selectively shop for high-quality, low-cost institutions.

Maturity Provisions

As previously indicated, bank loans have been traditionally short term in nature (though perhaps renewable). In the last decade there has been a movement to the use of the term loan, in which credit is extended for one to seven years. The loan is usually repaid in monthly or quarterly installments over its life rather than in one single payment. Only superior credit applicants, as measured by working capital strength, potential profitability, and competitive position, can qualify for term loan financing. Here the banker and the business firm are said to be "climbing into bed together" because of the length of the loan.

Bankers are hesitant to fix a single interest rate to a term loan. The more common practice is to allow the interest rate to change with market conditions. Thus the interest rate on a term loan may be tied to the prime rate or LIBOR. Often loans will be priced at a premium over one of these two rates reflecting the risk of the borrower. For example a loan may be priced at 1.5 percentage points above LIBOR and the rate will move up and down with changes in the base rate.

Cost of Commercial Bank Financing

The effective interest rate on a loan is based on the loan amount, the dollar interest paid, the length of the loan, and the method of repayment. It is easy enough to observe that $60 interest on a $1,000 loan for one year would carry a 6 percent interest rate, but what if the same loan were for 120 days? We use the formula:

$$\text{Effective rate} = \frac{\text{Interest}}{\text{Principal}} \times \frac{\text{Days in the year (360)}}{\text{Days loan is outstanding}} \qquad (8\text{--}2)$$

$$= \frac{\$60}{\$1,000} \times \frac{360}{120} = 6\% \times 3 = 18\%$$

Since we have use of the funds for only 120 days, the effective rate is 18 percent. To highlight the impact of time, if you borrowed $20 for only 10 days and paid back $21, the effective interest rate would be 180 percent—a violation of almost every usury law.

$$\frac{\$1}{\$20} \times \frac{360}{10} = 5\% \times 36 = 180\%$$

Not only is the time dimension of a loan important, but also the way in which interest is charged. We have assumed that interest would be paid when the loan comes due. If the bank uses a **discounted loan** and deducts the interest in advance, the effective rate of interest increases. For example, a $1,000 one-year loan with $60 of interest deducted in advance represents the payment of interest on only $940, or an effective rate of 6.38 percent.

$$\begin{array}{c}\text{Effective rate on} \\ \text{discounted loan}\end{array} = \frac{\text{Interest}}{\text{Principal} - \text{Interest}} \times \frac{\text{Days in the year (360)}}{\text{Days loan is outstanding}} \qquad (8\text{--}3)$$

$$= \frac{\$60}{\$1,000 - \$60} \times \frac{360}{360} = \frac{\$60}{\$940} = 6.38\%$$

Interest Costs with Compensating Balances

When a loan is made with compensating balances, the effective interest rate is the stated interest rate divided by $(1 - c)$, where c is the compensating balance expressed as a decimal. Assume that 6 percent is the stated annual rate and that a 20 percent compensating balance is required.

$$\begin{array}{c}\text{Effective rate with} \\ \text{compensating balances}\end{array} = \frac{\text{Interest}}{(1 - c)} \qquad (8\text{--}4)$$

$$= \frac{6\%}{(1 - 0.2)}$$

$$= 7.5\%$$

In the prior examples, if dollar amounts are used and the stated rate is unknown, Formula 8–5 can be used. The assumption is that we are paying $60 interest on a $1,000 loan, but are able to use only $800 of the funds. The loan is for a year.

$$\begin{array}{c} \text{Effective rate with} \\ \text{compensating} \\ \text{balances} \end{array} = \frac{\text{Interest}}{\begin{array}{c}\text{Principal} - \text{Compensating} \\ \text{balance in dollars}\end{array}} \times \frac{\begin{array}{c}\text{Days in the} \\ \text{year (360)}\end{array}}{\begin{array}{c}\text{Days loan is} \\ \text{outstanding}\end{array}} \qquad (8–5)$$

$$= \frac{60}{\$1,000 - \$200} \times \frac{360}{360} = \frac{\$60}{\$800} = 7.5\%$$

Only when a firm has idle cash balances that can be used to cover compensating balance requirements would the firm not use the higher effective-cost formulas (Formulas 8–4 and 8–5).

Rate on Installment Loans

The most confusing borrowing arrangement to the average bank customer or a consumer is the installment loan. An **installment loan** calls for a series of equal payments over the life of the loan. Though federal legislation prohibits a misrepresentation of interest rates on loans to customers, a loan officer or an overanxious salesperson may quote a rate on an installment loan that is approximately half the true rate.

Assume that you borrow $1,000 on a 12-month installment basis, with regular monthly payments to apply to interest and principal, and the interest requirement is $60. While it might be suggested that the rate on the loan is 6 percent, this is clearly not the case. Though you are paying a total of $60 in interest, you do not have the use of $1,000 for one year—rather, you are paying back the $1,000 on a monthly basis, with an average outstanding loan balance for the year of approximately $500. The effective rate of interest is 11.08 percent.

$$\begin{array}{c} \text{Effective rate on} \\ \text{installment loan} \end{array} = \frac{2 \times \text{Annual no. of payments} \times \text{Interest}}{(\text{Total no. of payments} + 1) \times \text{Principal}} \qquad (8–6)$$

$$= \frac{2 \times 12 \times \$60}{13 \times \$1,000} = \frac{\$1,440}{\$13,000} = 11.08\%$$

Annual Percentage Rate

Because the way interest is calculated often makes the effective rate different from the stated rate, Congress passed the Truth in Lending Act in 1968. This act required that the actual **annual percentage rate (APR)** be given to the borrower. The APR is really a measure of the effective rate we have presented. Congress was primarily trying to protect the unwary consumer from paying more than the stated rate without his or her knowledge. For example, the stated rate on an installment loan might be 6 percent but the APR might be 11.08 percent. It has always been assumed that businesses should be well versed in business practices and financial matters and, therefore, the Truth in Lending Act was not intended to protect business borrowers but, rather, individuals.

The annual percentage rate requires the use of the actuarial method of compounded interest when calculating the APR. This requires knowledge of the time-value-of-money techniques presented in Chapter 9. For our purposes in this chapter, it is enough to know that the lender must calculate interest for the period on the outstanding loan balance at the beginning of the period. Any payments are first credited against interest due, and any amount left is used to reduce the principal or loan balance. Because there are so many ways to structure loan repayment schedules, no one formula is applicable for computing the APR. For example, loans do not all have 365 days—some have only 10 or 15 days or other portions of a year.

Since most consumer loans are installment types, the APR is usually based on the assumption of amortization. Amortization means an equal dollar amount is paid each period to retire principal and interest. According to the law, a loan amortization schedule is the final authority in the calculation of the APR. The amortization schedule always has an annual percentage rate that diminishes the principal to zero over the loan period. You will learn how to develop an amortization schedule in Chapter 9.

The Credit Crunch Phenomenon

In 1969–70, 1973–74, and 1979–81, the economy went through periods of extreme credit shortages in the banking sector and in other financial markets. We seem to find ourselves in the midst of a tight money situation every few years. The anatomy of a credit crunch is as follows. The Federal Reserve tightens the growth in the money supply in its battle against inflation, causing a decrease in lendable funds and an increase in interest rates. To compound the difficulty, business requirements for funds may be increasing to carry inflation-laden inventory and receivables. A third problem is the massive withdrawal of savings deposits at banking and thrift institutions, all in search of higher returns. There simply are not enough lendable funds.

Recent history has taught us that the way *not* to deal with credit shortages is to impose artificial limits on interest rates in the form of restrictive usury laws or extreme governmental pressure. In 1969–70 the prime rate went to 8.5 percent in a tight money period—a level not high enough to bring the forces of demand and supply together, and little credit was available. In 1974 the prime rose to 12 percent, a rate truly reflecting market conditions, and funds were available. The same was true in 1980 and 1981 as the prime went to 20 percent and higher, but lendable funds were available.

In the early 1990s, the financial system suffered from bad loans made to real estate investors, Third World countries, and high-risk corporations. These bad loans resulted in the partial collapse of the savings and loan industry, and created problems for many banks and insurance companies. In 1998 Russia defaulted on its sovereign debt and the international credit markets reacted by restricting their loans. Credit conditions can change dramatically and suddenly because of unexpected defaults, causing changes in monetary policy, economic recessions, and other shocks to economies around the world. Available funds can simply dry up as lenders become more risk-averse and refuse to lend to high-risk borrowers or even borrowers of moderate risk. Not all credit crunches are caused by high interest rates.

For large and prestigious firms, commercial paper may provide an outlet for raising funds. **Commercial paper** represents a short-term, unsecured promissory note issued to the public in minimum units of $25,000. As Figure 8–2 indicates, the total amount of commercial paper outstanding has increased dramatically, rising from slightly more than

Financing through Commercial Paper

$500 billion in 1991 to $1.58 trillion by late 2005. This large increase in the amount of commercial paper outstanding reflects the willingness of qualified companies to borrow at the lowest rate available. The size of the market has made it easier for corporations to raise short-term funds. Notice that between 2000 and 2003, the commercial paper market declined by almost $400 billion dollars. This decline can be traced to the slower pace of business activity and the resulting recession in 2001. Even after the economy came out of the recession in November 2001, the economy grew very slowly. It was not until 2003 that the economy began to grow at a faster pace and the pickup in short-term borrowing through the commercial paper market is reflected in Figure 8–2.

Figure 8–2   Total commercial paper outstanding

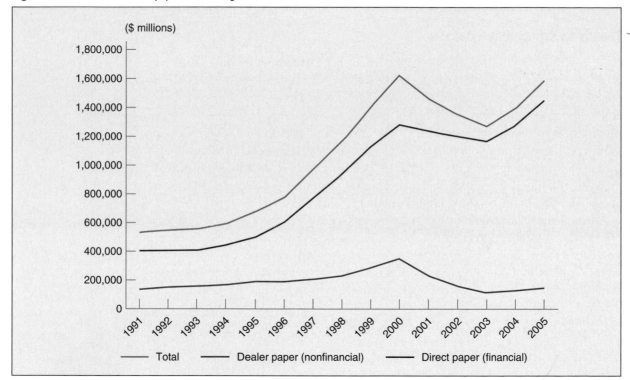

Commercial paper falls into two categories. First, there are finance companies, such as General Motors Acceptance Corporation (GMAC) and General Electric Credit, that issue paper primarily to institutional investors such as pension funds, insurance companies, and money market mutual funds. It is probably the growth of money market mutual funds that has had such a great impact on the ability of companies to sell such an increased amount of commercial paper in the market. Paper sold by financial firms such as GMAC is referred to as **finance paper**, and since it is usually sold directly to the lender by the finance company, it is also referred to as **direct paper**. The second type of commercial paper is sold by industrial companies, utility firms, or financial companies too small to have their own selling network. These firms use an intermediate dealer network to distribute their paper, and so this type of paper is referred to as **dealer paper**.

Traditionally commercial paper is just that. A paper certificate is issued to the lender to signify the lender's claim to be repaid. This certificate could be lost, stolen, misplaced, or damaged and, in rare cases, someone could fail to cash it in at maturity. It is common among companies that sell commercial paper directly to computerize the handling of commercial paper with what is called **book-entry transactions,** in which no actual certificate is created. All transactions simply occur on the books. The use of computer-based electronic issuing methods lowers cost and simplifies administration, as well as linking the lender and the issuing company. General Motors Acceptance Corporation, the largest single issuer of commercial paper, has been a heavy user of the book-entry method and currently has the majority of its commercial paper in this form. As the market becomes more accustomed to this electronic method, large users ($500 million or more) will likely find it profitable to switch from physical paper to the book-entry system, where all transfers of money are done by wiring cash between lenders and commercial paper issuers.

Advantages of Commercial Paper

The growing popularity of commercial paper can be attributed to other factors besides the rapid growth of money market mutual funds and their need to find short-term securities for investment. For example, commercial paper may be issued at below the prime interest rate. As indicated in the last column of Table 8–1, this rate differential is normally 2 to 3 percent.

Table 8–1

Comparison of commercial paper rate to prime rate (annual rate)*

Year	Finance Co. Paper (directly placed) 3 months	Average Bank Prime Rate	Prime Rate Minus Finance Paper
1982	11.23	14.86	3.63
1983	8.70	10.79	2.09
1984	9.73	12.04	2.31
1985	7.77	9.93	2.16
1986	6.38	8.33	1.95
1987	6.54	8.21	1.67
1988	7.38	9.32	1.94
1989	8.72	10.87	2.15
1990	7.87	10.01	2.14
1991	5.71	8.46	2.75
1992	3.65	6.25	2.60
1993	3.16	6.00	2.84
1994	4.53	7.15	2.62
1995	5.78	8.83	3.05
1996	5.29	8.27	2.98
1997	5.48	8.44	2.96
1998	5.37	8.35	2.98
1999	5.22	7.99	2.77
2000	6.33	9.23	2.90
2001	3.64	6.92	3.28
2002	1.70	4.68	2.98
2003	1.13	4.13	3.00
2004	1.52	4.34	2.82
2005	3.10	6.19	3.09

*Averages for the year.

Source: St. Louis Federal Reserve Bank (FRED).

A second advantage of commercial paper is that no compensating balance requirements are associated with its issuance, though the firm is generally required to maintain commercial bank lines of approved credit equal to the amount of the paper outstanding (a procedure somewhat less costly than compensating balances). Finally, a number of firms enjoy the prestige associated with being able to float their commercial paper in what is considered a "snobbish market" for funds.

Limitations on the Issuance of Commercial Paper

The commercial paper market is not without its problems. The bankruptcies of United Airlines, Kmart, Global Crossing, Enron, and WorldCom during the 2001–2002 period caused many lenders in the commercial paper market to become risk-averse. Because only high quality companies with good credit ratings can access this market, many firms that had their credit quality downgraded by credit rating agencies no longer had access to commercial paper. These companies were forced to draw down more expensive lines of credit at their banks to replace the commercial paper they couldn't roll over with new paper. Previously presented Figure 8–2 on page 232 demonstrates a decline of over $400 billion in the amount of commercial paper outstanding during the 2000–2003 period.

Although the funds provided through the issuance of commercial paper are cheaper than bank loans, they are also less predictable. While a firm may pay a higher rate for a bank loan, it is also buying a degree of loyalty and commitment that is unavailable in the commercial paper market.

Foreign Borrowing

An increasing source of funds for U.S. firms has been overseas banks. This trend started several decades ago with the Eurodollar market centered in London. A **Eurodollar loan** is a loan denominated in dollars and made by a foreign bank holding dollar deposits. Such loans are usually short term to intermediate term in maturity. LIBOR is the base interest rate paid on such loans for companies of the highest quality. As Figure 8–1 on page 227 shows, Eurodollar loans at LIBOR (rather than the prime interest rate) can be cheaper than U.S. domestic loans. International companies are always looking in foreign markets for cheaper ways of borrowing.

One approach to borrowing has been to borrow from international banks in foreign currencies either directly or through foreign subsidiaries. In using a subsidiary to borrow, the companies may convert the borrowed currencies to dollars, which are then sent to the United States to be used by the parent company. While international borrowing can often be done at lower interest rates than domestic loans, the borrowing firm may suffer a currency risk. That is, the value of the foreign funds borrowed may rise against the dollar and the loan will take more dollars to repay. Companies generating foreign revenue streams may borrow in those same currencies and thereby reduce or avoid any currency risk. Currency risk will be given greater coverage later in the chapter.

McDonald's, with it widespread international operations, borrows money in many currencies. At the end of 2004 it had borrowed $2.5 billion in the United States, 2.9 billion euros, and 1.15 billion British pounds. It also had borrowed smaller amounts in Swiss francs, Swedish kronor, Korean won, Chinese reniminbi, Australian dollars, Hong Kong dollars, and Singapore dollars. At the end of 2004, McDonald's had foreign debt of $6.6 billion, which accounted for 72 percent of its total debt. This discussion has simply shown that as the world financial markets have become more sophisticated, so must financial managers.

Use of Collateral in Short-Term Financing

Almost any firm would prefer to borrow on an unsecured (no-collateral) basis; but if the borrower's credit rating is too low or its need for funds too great, the lending institution will require that certain assets be pledged. A secured credit arrangement might help the borrower obtain funds that would otherwise be unavailable.

In any loan the lender's primary concern, however, is whether the borrower's capacity to generate cash flow is sufficient to liquidate the loan as it comes due. Few lenders would make a loan strictly on the basis of collateral. Collateral is merely a stopgap device to protect the lender when all else fails. The bank or finance company is in business to collect interest, not to repossess and resell assets.

Though a number of different types of assets may be pledged, our attention will be directed to accounts receivable and inventory. All states have now adopted the Uniform Commercial Code, which standardizes and simplifies the procedures for establishing security on a loan.

Accounts Receivable Financing

Accounts receivable financing may include **pledging accounts receivable as collateral for a loan or an outright *sale* (factoring) of receivables.** Receivables financing is popular because it permits borrowing to be tied directly to the level of asset expansion at any point in time. As the level of accounts receivable goes up, a firm is able to borrow more.

A drawback is that this is a relatively expensive method of acquiring funds, so it must be carefully compared to other forms of credit. Accounts receivable represent one of the firm's most valuable short-term assets, and they should be committed only where the appropriate circumstances exist. An ill-advised accounts receivable financing plan may exclude the firm from a less expensive bank term loan.

Pledging Accounts Receivable

The lending institution will generally stipulate which of the accounts receivable is of sufficient quality to serve as collateral for a loan. On this basis, we may borrow 60 to 90 percent of the value of the acceptable collateral. The loan percentage will depend on the financial strength of the borrowing firm and on the creditworthiness of its accounts. The lender will have full recourse against the borrower if any of the accounts go bad. The interest rate in a receivables borrowing arrangement is generally well in excess of the prime rate.

The interest is computed against the loan balance outstanding, a figure that may change quite frequently, as indicated in Table 8–2 on the next page. In the illustration,

Table 8–2

Receivables loan balance

	Month 1	Month 2	Month 3	Month 4
Total accounts receivable	$11,000	$15,100	$19,400	$16,300
Acceptable accounts receivable (to finance company)	10,000	14,000	18,000	15,000
Loan balance (80%)	8,000	11,200	14,400	12,000
Interest 12% annual–1% per month	80	112	144	120

interest is assumed to be 12 percent annually, or 1 percent per month. In month 1, we are able to borrow $8,000 against $10,000 in acceptable receivables and we must pay $80 in interest. Similar values are developed for succeeding months.

Factoring Receivables

When we factor receivables, they are sold outright to the finance company. Our customers may be instructed to remit the proceeds directly to the purchaser of the account. The factoring firm generally does not have recourse against the seller of the receivables. As a matter of practice, the finance company may do part or all of the credit analysis directly to ensure the quality of the accounts. As a potential sale is being made, the factoring firm may give immediate feedback to the seller on whether the account will be purchased.

When the factoring firm accepts an account, it may forward funds immediately to the seller, in anticipation of receiving payment 30 days later as part of the normal billing process. The factoring firm is not only absorbing risk, but also is actually advancing funds to the seller a month earlier than the seller would normally receive them.

For taking the risk, the factoring firm is generally paid on a fee or commission basis equal to 1 to 3 percent of the invoices accepted. In addition, it is paid a lending rate for advancing the funds early. If $100,000 a *month* is processed at a 1 percent commission and a 12 percent annual borrowing rate, the total effective cost will be 24 percent on an *annual* basis.

1%	Commission
1%	Interest for one month (12% annual/12)
2%	Total fee monthly
2%	Monthly × 12 = 24% annual rate

If one considers that the firm selling the accounts is transferring risk as well as receiving funds early, which may allow it to take cash discounts, the rate may not be considered exorbitant. Also the firm is able to pass on much of the credit-checking cost to the factor.

Asset-Backed Public Offerings

While factoring has long been one way of selling receivables, public offerings of securities backed by receivables as collateral gained respectability when General Motors Acceptance Corporation (GMAC) made a public offering of $500 million of asset-backed securities in December of 1985. In 2002, GMAC-RFC, a wholly owned subsidiary of GMAC, issued $27.3 billion of mortgage-backed securities.

Liquid Assets as Collateral—Punch Taverns Securitizes Liquid Assets

In the United States, asset-backed securities usually take the form of accounts receivable for car loans, credit card loans, or equipment loans. Europe does not have large integrated markets for these types of assets and so asset-backed lending is individualized for specific companies and situations. One of the most interesting asset-backed lending deals was one made by Punch Taverns, a UK pub company. It is not unusual in Britain for companies owning pubs to use the cash flow from those pubs as collateral for loans. The unusual aspect of the Punch Taverns offering was the flexibility that was created in the structure of the loans.

In June of 1999, Punch Taverns issued £305 million of securitized credit that was structured by Bankers Trust and offered to the market through Deutsche Bank and Barclays Capital. There were several maturity dates created with a specific loan amount attached to each maturity. The combination of loan amount and maturity is called a tranche. The Standard and Poor's and Fitch credit rating services gave each tranche a separate credit rating with three of the four tranches rated A. One tranche was rated BBB and was sold primarily to high-yield bond funds and insurance companies. One tranche had a floating rate of 100 basis points over LIBOR and an average maturity of 10.6 years. Three tranches carried fixed rates and had average lives of 6 years, 17.5 years, and 24.2 years, respectively. The fixed-rate loans were priced competitively against securities of equal risk and carried premiums of 235 to 245 basis points over the rate paid on British government securities, called gilts.

Punch Taverns has been growing through its acquisition of large pub companies that own many individual pubs and then selling those pubs that did not fit their portfolio. Punch Taverns needed a flexible lending facility that would allow them to add to their collateral as they bought pubs and to subtract from their collateral as they sold pubs. Punch Taverns arranged asset-backed loans with a maximum loan amount, which allowed them to draw down the loan against their limit as needed while the rest of the proceeds stayed in cash with Bankers Trust. In February of 2000, Punch Taverns used £109 million of its securitization to buy 662 pubs from Swallow. These pubs were located in the north of England and gave Punch Taverns good quality pubs and improved their geographical distribution.

The purchase increased the average beer sale per pub, created economies of scale, and increased the value of Punch Taverns' total holdings. The total pubs owned by the firm sold 368,000 barrels of beer in 1999 and generated £22.4 million in rent. One could say that the liquidity of the loan in financial terms was backed by the liquidity of the underlying assets.

finance in action

www.punchtaverns. com

These **asset-backed securities are nothing more than the sale of receivables**. In former years companies that sold receivables were viewed as short of cash, financially shaky, or in some financial trouble. This negative perception has been diminished by new issues of receivables-backed securities by such companies as Bank of America (credit card receivables), GMAC (car loan receivables), and Mack Trucks (truck loan receivables).

These asset-backed public offerings have continued to be popular, and IBM has added a new wrinkle by selling a public offering of receivables due from state and municipal governments. The interest paid to the owners of these securities is not taxable by the federal government. This allows IBM to raise cash at below-market rates. This strategy may be available only to large companies having significant business with state and local government units. Investment bankers continue to develop new types of asset-backed securities, and they are optimistic that the use of all asset-backed securities will continue to grow because of the predictable cash flows they offer investors.

One of the benefits to the issuer is that they trade future cash flows for immediate cash. The asset-backed security is likely to carry a high credit rating of AA or better, even when the issuing firm may have a low credit rating. This allows the issuing firm to acquire lower cost funds than it could with a bank loan or a bond offering. While this short-term market is still relatively small by money market standards, it can provide an important avenue for corporate liquidity and short-term financing.

However, several problems face the public sale of receivables. One consideration for the buyer of these securities is the probability that the receivables will actually be paid. Even though the loss rate on loans was about one-half of 1 percent in the past, bad debts can be much more than that in times of recession. For example, a serious recession might cause many car owners to default on their car payments to GMAC, and thus leave the owners of the asset-backed security without the promised cash flows. To counteract these fears, many issuers set up a loan-loss reserve fund to partially insure against the possibility of a loss.

Figure 8–3 shows the breakdown of the major asset classes used for the securitization of assets. In an ever-growing market, asset-backed securities (ABS) have been dominated by home equity loan receivables, followed by auto receivables and credit card receivables.

Figure 8–3

Asset-backed securities by categories

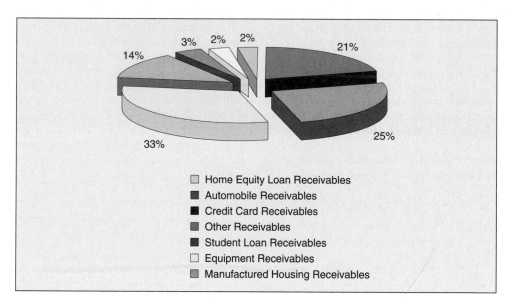

One thing Ford Motor Company found about auto receivables was that when it couldn't use the commercial paper markets because of a debt downgrade to a less than an investment grade credit, the asset-backed securities market was still there for its use. During 2002, Ford sold $16 billion in automobile receivables.

Inventory Financing

We may also borrow against inventory to acquire funds. The extent to which inventory financing may be employed is based on the marketability of the pledged goods, their associated price stability, and the perishability of the product. Another significant factor is the degree of physical control that can be exercised over the product by the lender. We can relate some of these factors to the stages of inventory production and the nature of lender control.

Stages of Production

Raw materials and finished goods are likely to provide the best collateral, while goods in process may qualify for only a small percentage loan. To the extent that a firm is holding such widely traded raw materials as lumber, metals, grain, cotton, and wool, a loan of 70 to 80 percent or higher is possible. The lender may have to place only a few quick phone calls to dispose of the goods at market value if the borrower fails to repay the loan. For standardized finished goods, such as tires, canned goods, and building products, the same principle would apply. Goods in process, representing altered but unfinished raw materials, may qualify for a loan of only one-fourth of their value or less.

Nature of Lender Control

The methods for controlling pledged inventory go from the simple to the complex, providing ever greater assurances to the lender but progressively higher administrative costs. Typical arrangements are as follows:

Blanket Inventory Liens   The simplest method is for the lender to have a general claim against the inventory of the borrower through **blanket inventory liens**. Specific items are not identified or tagged, and there is no physical control.

Trust Receipts   A **trust receipt** is an instrument acknowledging that the borrower holds the inventory and proceeds from sales in trust for the lender. Each item is carefully marked and specified by serial number. When sold, the proceeds are transferred to the lender and the trust receipt is canceled. Also known as *floor planning*, this financing device is very popular among auto and industrial equipment dealers and in the television and home appliance industries. Although it provides tighter control than does the blanket inventory lien, it still does not give the lender direct physical control over inventory—only a better and more legally enforceable system of tracing the goods.

Warehousing   Under this arrangement goods are physically identified, segregated, and stored under the direction of an independent warehousing company. The firm issues a warehouse receipt to the lender, and goods can be moved only with the lender's approval.

The goods may be stored on the premises of the warehousing firm, an arrangement known as **public warehousing**, or on the *borrower's premises*—under a **field warehousing** agreement. When field warehousing is utilized, it is still an independent warehousing company that exercises control over inventory.

Appraisal of Inventory Control Devices

While the more structured methods of inventory financing appear somewhat restrictive, they are well accepted in certain industries. For example, field warehousing is popular in grain storage and food canning. Well-maintained control measures involve substantial administrative expenses, and they raise the overall costs of borrowing. The costs of inventory financing may run 15 percent or higher. However, as is true of accounts receivable financing, the extension of funds is well synchronized with the need.

Hedging to Reduce Borrowing Risk

Those who are in continual need of borrowed funds to operate their firms are exposed to the risk of interest rate changes. One way to partially reduce that risk is through interest rate hedging activities in the financial futures market. **Hedging** means to engage in a transaction that partially or fully reduces a prior risk exposure.

The **financial futures market** is set up to allow for the trading of a financial instrument at a future point in time. For example, in January 2006 one might sell a Treasury bond contract that is to be closed out in June 2006. The sales price of the June 2006 contract is established by the initial January transaction. However, a subsequent purchase of a June 2006 contract at a currently unknown price will be necessary to close out the transaction. In the financial futures market, you do not physically deliver the goods; you merely execute a later transaction that reverses your initial position. Thus, if you initially sell a futures contract, you later buy a contract that covers your initial sale. If you initially buy a futures contract, the opposite is true and you later sell a contract that covers your initial purchase position.

In the case of selling a Treasury bond futures contract, the subsequent pattern of interest rates will determine whether it is profitable or not. If interest rates go up, Treasury bond prices will go down and you will be able to buy a subsequent contract at a lower price than the sales value you initially established. This will result in a profitable transaction. Note the following example.

Sales price, June 2006 Treasury bond contract* (sale occurs in January 2006)	$100,000
Purchase price, June 2006 Treasury bond contract (purchase occurs in June 2006)	95,000
Profit on futures contract	$ 5,000

*Only a small percentage of the actual dollars involved must be invested to initiate the contract. This is known as margin.

The reason Treasury bond prices went down is that interest rates and bond prices move in opposite directions, and interest rates went up. The lesson to be learned from this example is that rising interest rates can mean profits in the financial futures market if you initially sell a contract and later buy it back.

The financial manager who continually needs to borrow money and fears changes in interest rates can partially hedge his or her position by engaging in the type of futures contract described above. If interest rates do rise, the extra cost of borrowing money to actually finance the business can be offset by the profit on a futures contract. If interest rates go down, there will be a loss on the futures contract as bond prices go up, but this will be offset by the more desirable lower borrowing costs of financing the firm.

The financial futures market can be used to partially or fully hedge against almost any financial event. In addition to Treasury bonds, trades may be initiated in Treasury bills, certificates of deposits, GNMA certificates,[2] and many other instruments. The trades may be executed on such exchanges as the Chicago Board of Trade, the Chicago Mercantile Exchange, or the New York Futures Exchange.

---

[2]GNMA stands for Government National Mortgage Association, also known as Ginnie Mae.

Large international firms such as Procter and Gamble or ExxonMobil may also need to hedge against foreign exchange risk. For example, if a company borrows money in Japanese yen and intends to repay the loan using U.S. dollars, it has some concern that the exchange rate between the Japanese yen and the U.S. dollar may change in a way that would make the loan more expensive. If the value of the Japanese yen increases against the U.S. dollar, more dollars would be needed to repay the loan. This movement in the exchange rate would increase the total cost of the loan by making the principal repayment more expensive than the original amount of the loan.

The company could hedge against a rise in the Japanese yen by using the Chicago Mercantile Exchange's International Monetary Market where Japanese yen futures contracts are traded as well as those in euros, Canadian dollars, Mexican pesos, and other currencies. If a ¥100-million Japanese yen loan were due in six months, the company could buy a Japanese yen futures contract that could be closed out six months in the future. The purchase price on the futures contract is established at the time of the initial purchase transaction. The eventual sales price for the contract will be determined at a later point in time. If the value of the Japanese yen increases against the dollar, profit will be made on the futures contract. The money made on the futures contract can offset the higher cost of the company's loan payment. The currency exposure has thus been effectively hedged.[3]

Summary

A firm in search of short-term financing must be aware of all the institutional arrangements that are available. Trade credit from suppliers is normally the most available form of short-term financing and is a natural outgrowth of the buying and reselling of goods. Larger firms tend to be net providers of trade credit, while smaller firms are net users.

Bank loans are usually short term in nature and are self-liquidating, being paid back from funds from the normal operations of the firm. A financially strong customer will be offered the lowest rate with the rates to other customers scaled up to reflect their risk category. Bankers use either the prime rate or LIBOR as their base rate and add to that depending on the creditworthiness of the customer. Banks also use compensating balances as well as fees to increase the effective yield to the bank.

An alternative to bank credit for the large, prestigious firm is the use of commercial paper which represents a short-term unsecured promissory note issued by the firm. Though generally issued at a rate below prime, it is an impersonal means of financing that may "dry up" during difficult financing periods.

Firms are increasingly turning to foreign markets for lower cost sources of funds. They may borrow in the Eurodollar market (foreign dollar loans) or borrow foreign currency directly from banks in an attempt to lower their borrowing costs.

By using accounts receivable and inventory as collateral for a loan, the firm may be able to turn these current assets into cash more quickly than by waiting for the normal cash flow cycle. By using a secured form of financing, the firm ties its borrowing requirements directly to its asset buildup. The firm may also sell its accounts

---

[3]For a more complete discussion of corporate hedging in the futures market, see "Commodities and Financial Futures" in Chapter 16 of Geoffrey Hirt and Stanley Block, *Fundamentals of Investment Management,* 7th ed. (New York: McGraw-Hill, 2003).

receivable to a factor. These secured forms of borrowing may be expensive but may fit the credit needs of the firm, particularly the needs of a small firm that cannot qualify for lower cost bank financing or the commercial paper market.

Finally, the financial manager may wish to consider the use of hedging through the financial futures market. The consequences of rapid interest rate or currency changes can be reduced through participation in the futures market.

List of Terms

spontaneous source of funds 224	direct paper 232
cash discount 224	dealer paper 232
net trade credit 225	book-entry transaction 233
self-liquidating loan 225	Eurodollar loan 234
prime rate 226	pledging accounts receivable 235
London Interbank Offered Rate (LIBOR) 226	factoring 235
	asset-backed securities 237
compensating balance 227	blanket inventory liens 239
term loan 228	trust receipt 239
discounted loan 229	public warehousing 239
installment loan 230	field warehousing 239
annual percentage rate (APR) 230	hedging 240
commercial paper 231	financial futures market 240
finance paper 232	

Discussion Questions

1. Under what circumstances would it be advisable to borrow money to take a cash discount?

2. Discuss the relative use of credit between large and small firms. Which group is generally in the net creditor position, and why?

3. How have new banking laws influenced competition?

4. What is the prime interest rate? How does the average bank customer fare in regard to the prime interest rate?

5. What does LIBOR mean? Is LIBOR normally higher or lower than the U.S. prime interest rate?

6. What advantages do compensating balances have for banks? Are the advantages to banks necessarily disadvantages to corporations?

7. A borrower is often confronted with a stated interest rate and an effective interest rate. What is the difference, and which one should the financial manager recognize as the true cost of borrowing?

8. Commercial paper may show up on corporate balance sheets as either a current asset or a current liability. Explain this statement.

9. What are the advantages of commercial paper in comparison with bank borrowing at the prime rate? What is a disadvantage?

10. What is the difference between pledging accounts receivable and factoring accounts receivable?

11. What is an asset-backed public offering?

12. Briefly discuss three types of lender control used in inventory financing.

13. What is meant by hedging in the financial futures market to offset interest rate risks?

---

1. Automatic Machinery is being offered a 2/10, net 50 cash discount. The firm will have to borrow the funds at 12 percent to take the discount. Should it proceed with the discount?

2. A company plans to borrow $2 million for a year. The stated interest rate is 12 percent. Compute the effective interest rate under each of these assumptions. Each part stands alone.

   a. The interest is discounted.

   b. There is a 20 percent compensating balance requirement.

   c. It is a 12-month installment loan.

   d. Assume the interest is only $45,000 and the loan is for 90 days.

Solutions

1. First compute the cost of not taking the cash discount.

$$\text{Cost of failing to take a cash discount} = \frac{\text{Discount \%}}{100\% - \text{Discount \%}}$$

$$\times \frac{360}{\text{Final due date} - \text{Discount period}}$$

$$= \frac{2\%}{100\% - 2\%} \times \frac{360}{50 - 10}$$

$$= 2.04\% \times 9 = 18.36\%$$

   Since money can be borrowed at 12 percent, the firm should borrow the funds and take the discount.

2. a. $\text{Effective rate on discounted loan} = \dfrac{\text{Interest}}{\text{Principal} - \text{Interest}}$

$$\times \frac{\text{Days in the year (360)}}{\text{Days loan is outstanding}}$$

$$= \frac{\$240,000}{\$2,000,000 - 240,000} \times \frac{360}{360}$$

$$= \frac{\$240,000}{1,760,000} \times 1 = 13.64\%$$

   b. Effective rate with compensating balances

$$= \frac{\text{Interest}}{\text{Principal} - \text{Compensating balance in dollars}} \times \frac{\text{Days in the year (360)}}{\text{Days loan is outstanding}}$$

   Compensating balance = 20% × $2,000,000 = $400,000

$$\text{Effective rate} = \frac{\$240,000}{1,600,000} \times 1 = 15\%$$

c. Effective rate on installment loan

$$= \frac{2 \times \text{Annual number of payments} \times \text{Interest}}{(\text{Total number of payments} + 1) \times \text{Principal}}$$

$$= \frac{2 \times 12 \times \$240{,}000}{(12 + 1) \times \$2{,}000{,}000} \times \frac{\$576{,}000}{2{,}600{,}000} = 22.15\%$$

d. $\text{Effective rate} = \dfrac{\text{Interest}}{\text{Principal}} \times \dfrac{\text{Days in the year (360)}}{\text{Days loan is outstanding}}$

$$= \frac{\$45{,}000}{\$2{,}000{,}000} \times \frac{360}{90} = 2.25\% \times 4 = 9\%$$

Problems

Cash discount

1. Compute the cost of not taking the following cash discounts.
    a. 2/10, net 50.
    b. 2/15, net 40.
    c. 3/10, net 45.
    d. 3/10, net 180.

Cash discount decision

2. Regis Clothiers can borrow from its bank at 11 percent to take a cash discount. The terms of the cash discount are 2/15, net 60. Should the firm borrow the funds?

Cash discount decision

3. Simmons Corp. can borrow from its bank at 12 percent to take a cash discount. The terms of the cash discount are 1.5/10, net 60. Should the firm borrow the funds?

Effective rate of interest

4. Your bank will lend you $2,000 for 45 days at a cost of $25 interest. What is your effective rate of interest?

Effective rate of interest

5. A pawn shop will lend $100 for 10 days at a cost of $5 interest. What is the effective rate of interest?

Effective rate on discounted loan

6. Sol Pine is going to borrow $3,000 for one year at 8 percent interest. What is the effective rate of interest if the loan is discounted?

Effective rate on discounted loan

7. Mary Ott is going to borrow $5,000 for 90 days and pay $140 interest. What is the effective rate of interest if the loan is discounted?

Prime vs. LIBOR

8. Dr. Ruth is going to borrow $5,000 to help write a book. The loan is for one year and the money can either be borrowed at the prime rate or the LIBOR rate. Assume the prime rate is 6 percent and LIBOR 1.5 percent less. Also assume there will be a $40 transaction fee with LIBOR (this amount must be added to the interest cost with LIBOR). Which loan has the lower effective interest cost?

Dollar cost of a loan

9. Talmud Book Company borrows $16,000 for 30 days at 9 percent interest. What is the dollar cost of the loan?

$$\frac{\text{Dollar cost}}{\text{of loan}} = \frac{\text{Amount}}{\text{borrowed}} \times \frac{\text{Interest}}{\text{rate}} \times \frac{\text{Days loan is outstanding}}{\text{Days in the year (360)}}$$

10. McGriff Dog Food Company normally takes 20 days to pay for average daily credit purchases of $9,000. Its average daily sales are $10,000, and it collects accounts in 25 days.

    Net credit position

    a. What is its net credit position? That is, compute its accounts receivable and accounts payable and subtract the latter from the former.

    $$\text{Accounts receivable} = \frac{\text{Average daily credit sales} \times}{\text{Average collection period}}$$

    $$\text{Accounts payable} = \frac{\text{Average daily credit purchases} \times}{\text{Average payment period}}$$

    b. If the firm extends its average payment period from 20 days to 32 days (and all else remains the same), what is the firm's new net credit position? Has it improved its cash flow?

11. Logan Drilling Corp. plans to borrow $200,000 for one year. Northern National Bank will lend the money at 10 percent interest and require a compensating balance of 20 percent. What is the effective rate of interest?

    Compensating balances

12. Computer Graphics Company needs $250,000 in funds for a project.

    Compensating balances

    a. With a compensating balance requirement of 20 percent, how much will the firm need to borrow?

    b. Given your answer to part *a* and a stated interest rate of 10 percent on the *total* amount borrowed, what is the effective rate on the $250,000 actually being used?

13. The Dade Company is borrowing $300,000 for one year and paying $27,000 in interest to Miami National Bank. The bank requires a 20 percent compensating balance. What is the effective rate of interest? What would be the effective rate if the company were required to make 12 monthly payments to retire the loan? The principal, as used in Formula 8–6 on page 230, refers to funds the firm can effectively utilize (Amount borrowed − Compensating balance).

    Compensating balances and installment loans

14. Randall Corporation plans to borrow $200,000 for one year at 12 percent from the Waco State Bank. There is a 20 percent compensating balance requirement. Randall Corporation keeps minimum transaction balances of $10,000 in the normal course of business. This idle cash counts toward meeting the compensating balance requirement. What is the effective rate of interest?

    Compensating balances with idle cash

15. The treasurer for the Macon Blue Sox baseball team is seeking a $20,000 loan for one year from the 4th National Bank of Macon. The stated interest rate is 10 percent, and there is a 15 percent compensating balance requirement. The treasurer always keeps a minimum of $1,500 in the baseball team's checking accounts. These funds count toward meeting any compensating balance requirements. What will be the effective rate of interest on this loan?

    Compensating balances with idle cash

16. Your company plans to borrow $5 million for 12 months, and your banker gives you a stated rate of 14 percent interest. You would like to know the effective rate of interest for the following types of loans. (Each of the following parts stands alone.)

    Effective rate under different terms

    a. Simple 14 percent interest with a 10 percent compensating balance.

    b. Discounted interest.

    c. An installment loan (12 payments).

    d. Discounted interest with a 5 percent compensating balance.

Effective rate under different terms

17. If you borrow $4,000 at $500 interest for one year, what is your effective interest rate for the following payment plans?

    a. Annual payment.

    b. Semiannual payments.

    c. Quarterly payments.

    d. Monthly payments.

Effective rate under different terms

18. Zerox Copying Company plans to borrow $150,000. New Jersey National Bank will lend the money at one-half percentage point over the prime rate at the time of 8 1/2 percent (9 percent total) and requires a compensating balance of 20 percent. The principal in this case will be funds that the firm can effectively use in the business. This loan is for one year. What is the effective rate of interest? What would the effective rate be if Zerox were required to make four quarterly payments to retire the loan?

Installment loan for multiyears

19. Lewis and Clark Camping Supplies Inc. is borrowing $45,000 from Western State Bank. The total interest is $12,000. The loan will be paid by making equal monthly payments for the next three years. What is the effective rate of interest on this installment loan?

Cash discount under special circumstance

20. Mr. Hugh Warner is a very cautious businessman. His supplier offers trade credit terms of 3/10, net 80. Mr. Warner never takes the discount offered, but he pays his suppliers in 70 days rather than the 80 days allowed so he is sure the payments are never late. What is Mr. Warner's cost of not taking the cash discount?

Bank loan to take cash discount

21. The Reynolds Corporation buys from its suppliers on terms of 2/10, net 55. Reynolds has not been utilizing the discounts offered and has been taking 55 days to pay its bills.

    Mr. Duke, Reynolds Corporation vice president, has suggested that the company begin to take the discounts offered. Duke proposes that the company borrow from its bank at a stated rate of 14 percent. The bank requires a 20 percent compensating balance on these loans. Current account balances would not be available to meet any of this compensating balance requirement.

    Do you agree with Duke's proposal?

Bank loan to take cash discount

22. In Problem 21, if the compensating balance requirement were 10 percent instead of 20 percent, would you change your answer? Do the appropriate calculation.

Bank loan to take cash discount

23. Neveready Flashlights, Inc., needs $300,000 to take a cash discount of 2/10, net 70. A banker will loan the money for 60 days at an interest cost of $5,500.

    a. What is the effective rate on the bank loan?

    b. How much would it cost (in percentage terms) if the firm did not take the cash discount, but paid the bill in 70 days instead of 10 days?

    c. Should the firm borrow the money to take the discount?

    d. If the banker requires a 20 percent compensating balance, how much must the firm borrow to end up with the $300,000?

e. What would be the effective interest rate in part *d* if the interest charge for 60 days were $6,850? Should the firm borrow with the 20 percent compensating balance? (The firm has no funds to count against the compensating balance requirement.)

24. Harper Engine Company needs $600,000 to take a cash discount of 1.5/10, net 60. A banker will loan the money for 50 days at an interest cost of $12,100.

    a. What is the effective rate on the bank loan?

    b. How much would it cost (in percentage terms) if Harper did not take the cash discount, but paid the bill in 60 days instead of 10 days?

    c. Should Harper borrow the money to take the discount?

    d. If another banker requires a 10 percent compensating balance, how much must Harper borrow to end up with $600,000?

    e. What would be the effective interest rate in part *d* if the interest charge for 50 days were $8,300? Should Harper borrow with the 10 percent compensating balance? (There are no funds to count against the compensating balance requirement.)

Bank loan to take cash discount

25. Summit Record Company is negotiating with two banks for a $100,000 loan. Fidelity Bank requires a 20 percent compensating balance, discounts the loan, and wants to be paid back in four quarterly payments. Southwest Bank requires a 10 percent compensating balance, does not discount the loan, but wants to be paid back in 12 monthly installments. The stated rate for both banks is 9 percent. Compensating balances will be subtracted from the $100,000 in determining the available funds in part *a*.

    a. Which loan should Summit accept?

    b. Recompute the effective cost of interest, assuming that Summit ordinarily maintains at each bank $20,000 in deposits that will serve as compensating balances.

    c. Does your choice of banks change if the assumption in part *b* is correct?

Competing terms from banks

✗ 26. Charmin Paper Company sells to the 12 accounts listed below.

Accounts receivable financing

Account	Receivable Balance Outstanding	Average Age of the Account over the Last Year
A	$ 60,000	28
B	120,000	43
C	70,000	10
D	20,000	52
E	50,000	42
F	220,000	34
G	30,000	16
H	300,000	65
I	40,000	33
J	90,000	50
K	210,000	14
L	60,000	35

Capital Financial Corporation will lend 90 percent against account balances that have averaged 30 days or less; 80 percent for account balances between 31 and 40 days; and 70 percent for account balances between 41 and 45 days. Customers that take over 45 days to pay their bills are not considered acceptable accounts for a loan.

The current prime rate is 8.5 percent, and Capital charges 3.5 percent over prime to Charmin as its annual loan rate.

a. Determine the maximum loan for which Charmin Paper Company could qualify.

b. Determine how much one month's interest expense would be on the loan balance determined in part *a.*

Hedging to offset risk

27. The treasurer for Pittsburgh Iron Works wishes to use financial futures to hedge her interest rate exposure. She will sell five Treasury futures contracts at $107,000 per contract. It is July and the contracts must be closed out in December of this year. Long-term interest rates are currently 7.3 percent. If they increase to 8.5 percent, assume the value of the contracts will go down by 10 percent. Also if interest rates do increase by 1.2 percent, assume the firm will have additional interest expense on its business loans and other commitments of $63,000. This expense, of course, will be separate from the futures contracts.

a. What will be the profit or loss on the futures contract if interest rates go to 8.5 percent by December when the contract is closed out?

b. Explain why a profit or loss took place on the futures contracts.

c. After considering the hedging in part *a*, what is the net cost to the firm of the increased interest expense of $63,000? What percent of this $63,000 cost did the treasurer effectively hedge away?

d. Indicate whether there would be a profit or loss on the futures contracts if interest rates went down.

WEB EXERCISE

This chapter explores the various sources of financing working capital needs. It also mentions General Electric Capital as a formidable competitor to the banking community. This exercise examines General Electric Capital's various services. Go to General Electric's Web site at www.ge.com.

1. Go to "Financial Services" on the home page. Click on "Business Finance."

2. List three types of services GE Capital provides for Business Lending.

3. List three types of services for "Cash Management & Treasury."

4. Once again click on "Financial Services." Click on "Personal Finances." As shown in the "Directory," list the three services that GE Capital provides in "Personal Finances." Click on "Home Loans," and list three types of mortgages or loans.

5. Based on the information you have seen, does it appear that GE Capital is competitive with more traditional financial institutions?

Note: From time to time, companies redesign their Web sites and occasionally a topic we have listed may have been deleted, updated, or moved into a different location. If you click on the site map or site index, you will be introduced to a table of contents which should aid you in finding the topic you are looking for.

part **4**

The Capital Budgeting Process

RELATED WEB SITES

www.microsoft.com

www.cisco.com

www.oracle.com

www.intel.com

www.corp.aol.com

finance.yahoo.com

www.lilly.com   www.celera.com

www.northropgrumman.com   www.deltagen.com

www.alcoa.com   www.marvell.com

www.lexicon-genetics.com   www.ciena.com

The long-term decisions concerning the appropriate capital structure and the selection of capital projects such as new products and equipment are the decisions that will maximize or diminish shareholder wealth. Someone who knows how to build companies and create significant value is Steve Jobs.

Steve Jobs and two partners created Apple Computer in 1976 and with it, the personal computer age. After many years of running Apple Computer, Jobs was forced out. He formed NeXT Computer and developed a new operating system that streamlined data processing and incorporated many new features into its software. In 1986, Jobs bought Lucasfilm's computer graphics division from George Lucas for $10 million and named it Pixar Animation Studios. Eventually Pixar revolutionized the animated film business that Walt Disney had dominated. Pixar produced blockbuster films like *Toy Story*, *Finding Nemo*, and *The Incredibles* and used Disney as the film distributor and coinvestor. In 2006 the distribution agreement between Pixar and Disney was scheduled to expire and Jobs threatened to take his movies somewhere else. In January of 2006, Disney bought Pixar for $7.4 billion of Disney common stock, and Steve Jobs became Disney's largest shareholder with 7 percent ownership.

While Jobs was building Pixar, Apple Computer was falling on hard times; in 1996 Apple bought NeXT, and Jobs returned to the company he had founded. Jobs continued as chairman and CEO of Pixar and also re-created Apple with a new operating system and developed a new series of desktop and laptop computers. Jobs also cut a deal with Microsoft to create its popular Office Suite for Apple. Eventually in 2006, Apple came out with a computer that ran on Intel chips and could run both the Microsoft Windows applications and Apple's OS applications.

Perhaps Jobs' greatest creation, that may have single-handedly saved Apple, was the iPod. The iPod was perhaps the slickest technology innovation using great design and marketing since Sony had created the Walkman. The iPod became the leader in digital music players and quickly took a majority of the market from other companies' MP3 players. Additionally, Apple created the iTunes store where people could download songs for $.99 each. The buzz around Apple and the iPod spilled over to its computers and as people found the iPod to be user friendly, they started to realize that Apple computers were more user friendly than the PCs, and sales of iMacs

Steve Jobs–Apple Computer
AP/Wide World Photos

and iBooks increased. The stock price of Apple Computer went from a low of $6.20 in 2003 to a high of $86.40 in 2006. (Prices are adjusted for a 2 for 1 stock split in 2005.) After you read these next four chapters you will realize that these capital budgeting initiatives by Apple Computer added extensive value for its shareholders. Steve Jobs is estimated to be worth about $4.4 billion.

The Time Value of Money

1 Money has a time value associated with it and therefore a dollar received today is worth more than a dollar to be received in the future.

2 The future value and present value of a dollar are based on the number of periods involved and the going interest rate.

3 Tables for future value and present value can be applied to any problem to ease the analysis.

4 Not only can future value and present value be computed, but other factors such as yield (rate of return) can be determined as well.

I n 1624 the Native Americans sold Manhattan Island at the ridiculously low figure of $24. But wait, was it really ridiculous? If they had merely taken the $24 and reinvested it at 6 percent annual interest up to 2007, they would have had $115 billion, an amount sufficient to repurchase a good part of New York City. If the Native Americans had invested the $24 at 7.5 percent compounded annually, they would now have over $17 trillion—and tribal chiefs would now rival oil sheiks and Bill Gates as the richest people in the world. Another popular example is that $1 received 2,007 years ago, invested at 6 percent, could now be used to purchase all the wealth in the world.

While not all examples are this dramatic, the time value of money applies to many day-to-day decisions. Understanding the effective rate on a business loan, the mortgage payment in a real estate transaction, or the true return on an investment depends on understanding the time value of money. As long as an investor can garner a positive return on idle dollars, distinctions must be made between money received today and money received in the future. The investor/lender essentially demands that a financial "rent" be paid on his or her funds as current dollars are set aside today in anticipation of higher returns in the future.

Relationship to the Capital Outlay Decision

The decision to purchase new plant and equipment or to introduce a new product in the market requires using capital allocating or capital budgeting techniques. Essentially we must determine whether future benefits are sufficiently large to justify current outlays. It is important that we develop the mathematical tools of the time value of money as the first step toward making capital allocation decisions. Let us now examine the basic terminology of "time value of money."

Future Value— Single Amount

In determining the **future value**, we measure the value of an amount that is allowed to grow at a given interest rate over a period of time. Assume an investor has $1,000 and wishes to know its worth after four years if it grows at 10 percent per year. At the end of the first year, the investor will have $1,000 × 1.10, or $1,100. By the end of year two, the $1,100 will have grown to $1,210 ($1,100 × 1.10). The four-year pattern is indicated below.

1st year	$1,000 × 1.10 = $1,100
2nd year	$1,100 × 1.10 = $1,210
3rd year	$1,210 × 1.10 = $1,331
4th year	$1,331 × 1.10 = $1,464

After the fourth year, the investor has accumulated $1,464. Because compounding problems often cover a long period, a more generalized formula is necessary to describe the compounding procedure. We shall let:

FV = Future value
PV = Present value
i = Interest rate
n = Number of periods

The simple formula is:

$$FV = PV(1 + i)^n$$

In this case, PV = $1,000, i = 10 percent, n = 4, so we have:

$$FV = \$1,000(1.10)^4, \text{ or } \$1,000 \times 1.464 = \$1,464$$

The term $(1.10)^4$ is found to equal 1.464 by multiplying 1.10 four times itself (the fourth power) or by using logarithms. An even quicker process is using an interest rate table, such as Table 9–1 for the future value of a dollar. With n = 4 and i = 10 percent, the value is also found to be 1.464.

Table 9–1

Future value of $1 ($FV_{IF}$)

Periods	1%	2%	3%	4%	6%	8%	10%
1	1.010	1.020	1.030	1.040	1.060	1.080	1.100
2	1.020	1.040	1.061	1.082	1.124	1.166	1.210
3	1.030	1.061	1.093	1.125	1.191	1.260	1.331
4	1.041	1.082	1.126	1.170	1.262	1.360	1.464
5	1.051	1.104	1.159	1.217	1.338	1.469	1.611
10	1.105	1.219	1.344	1.480	1.791	2.159	2.594
20	1.220	1.486	1.806	2.191	3.207	4.661	6.727

The table tells us the amount that $1 would grow to if it were invested for any number of periods at a given interest rate. We multiply this factor times any other amount to determine the future value. An expanded version of Table 9–1 is presented at the back of the text in Appendix A.

In determining the future value, we will change our formula from $FV = PV(1 + i)^n$ to:

$$FV = PV \times FV_{IF} \qquad\qquad (9\text{–}1)$$

where FV_{IF} equals the **interest factor** found in the table.

If $10,000 were invested for 10 years at 8 percent, the future value, based on Table 9–1, would be:

$$FV = PV \times FV_{IF} \ (n = 10, i = 8\%)$$
$$FV = \$10,000 \times 2.159 = \$21,590$$

In recent years the sports pages have been filled with stories of athletes who receive multimillion-dollar contracts for signing with sports organizations. Perhaps you have wondered how the New York Yankees or Los Angeles Lakers can afford to pay such fantastic sums. The answer may lie in the concept of present value—a sum payable in the future is worth less today than the stated amount.

The **present value** is the exact opposite of the future value. For example, earlier we determined that the future value of $1,000 for four periods at 10 percent was $1,464. We could reverse the process to state that $1,464 received four years into the future, with a 10 percent interest or **discount rate**, is worth only $1,000 today—its present value. The relationship is depicted in Figure 9–1.

Present Value— Single Amount

Figure 9–1   Relationship of present value and future value

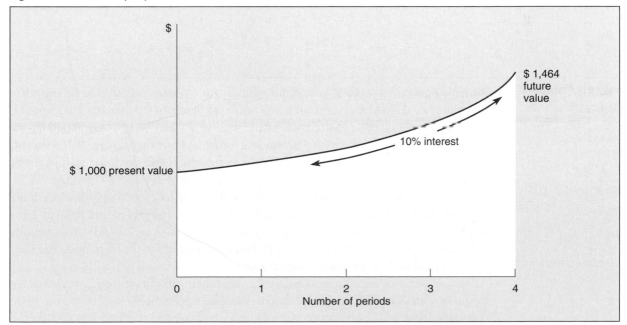

The formula for present value is derived from the original formula for future value.

$$FV = PV(1 + i)^n \quad \text{Future value}$$

$$PV = FV \left[\frac{1}{(1 + i)^n} \right] \quad \text{Present value}$$

The present value can be determined by solving for a mathematical solution to the formula above, or by using Table 9–2, the present value of a dollar. In the latter instance, we restate the formula for present value as:

$$PV = FV \times PV_{IF} \tag{9–2}$$

Once again PV_{IF} represents the interest factor found in Table 9–2.

Table 9–2

Present value of $1
(PV_{IF})

Periods	1%	2%	3%	4%	6%	8%	10%
1	0.990	0.980	0.971	0.962	0.943	0.926	0.909
2	0.980	0.961	0.943	0.925	0.890	0.857	0.826
3	0.971	0.942	0.915	0.889	0.840	0.794	0.751
4	0.961	0.924	0.888	0.855	0.792	0.735	0.683
5	0.951	0.906	0.863	0.822	0.747	0.681	0.621
10	0.905	0.820	0.744	0.676	0.558	0.463	0.386
20	0.820	0.673	0.554	0.456	0.312	0.215	0.149

An expanded table is presented in Appendix B.

Let's demonstrate that the present value of $1,464, based on our assumptions, is $1,000 today.

$$PV = FV \times PV_{IF} \quad (n = 4, i = 10\%) \text{ [Table 9–2]}$$

$$PV = \$1,464 \times 0.683 = \$1,000$$

Future Value—Annuity

Our calculations up to now have dealt with single amounts rather than an **annuity**, which may be defined as a series of consecutive payments or receipts of equal amount. The annuity values are generally assumed to occur at the end of each period. If we invest $1,000 at the end of each year for four years and our funds grow at 10 percent, what is the future value of this annuity? We may find the future value for each payment and then total them to find the **future value of an annuity** (Figure 9–2 on page 257).

The future value for the annuity in Figure 9–2 is $4,641. Although this is a four-period annuity, the first $1,000 comes at the *end* of the first period and has but three periods to run, the second $1,000 at the *end* of the second period, with two periods remaining—and so on down to the last $1,000 at the end of the fourth period. The final payment (period 4) is not compounded at all.

Because the process of compounding the individual values is tedious, special tables are also available for annuity computations. We shall refer to Table 9–3, the future value of an annuity of $1. Let us define A as the annuity value and use Formula 9–3 for the

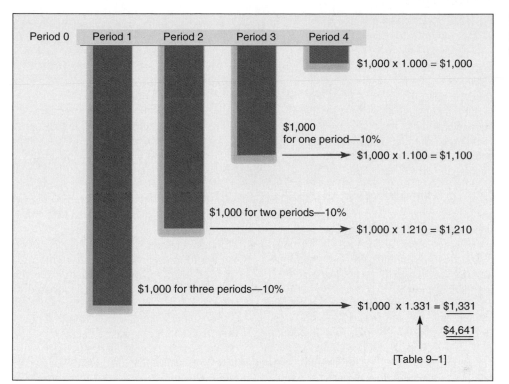

Figure 9–2

Compounding process for annuity

Periods	1%	2%	3%	4%	6%	8%	10%
1	1.000	1.000	1.000	1.000	1.000	1.000	1.000
2	2.010	2.020	2.030	2.040	2.060	2.080	2.100
3	3.030	3.060	3.091	3.122	3.184	3.246	3.310
4	4.060	4.122	4.184	4.246	4.375	4.506	4.641
5	5.101	5.204	5.309	5.416	5.637	5.867	6.105
10	10.462	10.950	11.464	12.006	13.181	14.487	15.937
20	22.019	24.297	26.870	29.778	36.786	45.762	57.275
30	34.785	40.588	47.575	56.085	79.058	113.280	164.490

An expanded table is presented in Appendix C.

Table 9–3

Future value of an annuity of $1 (FV$_{IFA}$)

future value of an annuity.[1] Note that the A part of the subscript on both the left- and right-hand side of the formula below indicates we are dealing with tables for an annuity rather than a single amount. Using Table 9–3 for A = $1,000, n = 4, and i = 10%:

$$FV_A = A \times FV_{IFA} \quad (n = 4, i = 10\%) \tag{9–3}$$
$$FV_A = \$1,000 \times 4.641 = \$4,641$$

---

[1]$FV_A = A(1 + i)^{n-1} + A(1 + i)^{n-2} + \ldots A(1 + i)^1 + A(1 + i)^0$

$\quad = A \left[\dfrac{(1 + i)^n - 1}{i} \right] = A \times FV_{IFA}$

Starting Salaries 50 Years from Now—Will $284,280 Be Enough?

The answer is probably yes if inflation averages 4 percent a year for the next 50 years. Over the last 50 years the inflation rate was in the 3 to 4 percent range, so $284,280 might allow a college graduate to have enough money to pay his or her bills in 50 years if inflation rates stay about the same. The $284,280 is based on a starting salary of $40,000 today and the future value of a dollar for 50 periods at 4 percent. Of course, $40,000 may be too low for some majors, and too high for others.

Inflation in the United States actually was as high as 11.4 percent in 1979 and 13.4 percent in 1980. Conversely, there were declining prices during the depression of the 1930s. If inflation averages 6 percent over the next 50 years, it would require $736,800 to replace a $40,000 salary today. At a 10 percent rate of inflation, the college graduate in 50 years would need to ask an employer for a starting salary of $4,695,600 to be as well-off as his or her predecessor today. Those graduating in the more popular majors would certainly not take a penny under $5 million. While 10 percent inflation seems high for the United States, in countries such as Brazil, Israel, and Mexico, 10 percent inflation would be a welcome occurrence.

Returning to a more realistic 4 percent rate of inflation for the future, the college graduate in 50 years can expect to see his or her domestic airfare for a two-thousand mile round trip go from $400 to approximately $2,843. Tuition at an average private university (over four years) will go from $90,000 to $639,630, and at an Ivy League School from $160,000 to $1,137,120. Save your money for that brilliant grandchild you're planning to have. Tickets for four persons to an NFL football game will increase from $200 to $1,421. But that might be a bargain to watch the descendants of Donovan McNabb and Eli Manning play—quarterbacks who then will be paid $90 million a year. Actually, the salaries of pro football quarterbacks are growing at a rate of 20 percent a year, so a more realistic figure for their annual salary in 50 years might be over $100 billion.

The intent of this discussion is to demonstrate the effects of the time value of money. So far, all of the discussion has been forward-looking. Now, let's look back. How much would one of your grandparents have had to make 50 years ago to equal a $40,000 salary today, assuming a 4 percent rate of inflation? The answer is $5,628.

If a wealthy relative offered to set aside $2,500 a year for you for the next 20 years, how much would you have in your account after 20 years if the funds grew at 8 percent? The answer is as follows:

$$FV_A = A \times FV_{IFA} \quad (n = 20, i = 8\%)$$
$$FV_A = \$2,500 \times 45.762 = \$114,405$$

A rather tidy sum considering that only a total of $50,000 has been invested over the 20 years.

Present Value— Annuity

To find the **present value of an annuity**, the process is reversed. In theory each individual payment is discounted back to the present and then all of the discounted payments are added up, yielding the present value of the annuity.[2] Once

Table 9–4 allows us to eliminate extensive calculations and to find our answer directly. In Formula 9–4 the term PV_A refers to the present value of the annuity.[2] Once

---

[2] $PV_A = A \left[\frac{1}{(1 + i)}\right]^1 + A \left[\frac{1}{(1 + i)}\right]^2 + \ldots A \left[\frac{1}{(1 + i)}\right]^n = A \left[\frac{1 - \frac{1}{(1 + i)^n}}{i}\right]$

$= A \times PV_{IFA}$

again, assume A = $1,000, n = 4, and i = 10 percent—only now we want to know the present value of the annuity. Using Table 9–4:

$$PV_A = A \times PV_{IFA} \quad (n = 4, i = 10\%) \tag{9-4}$$
$$PV_A = \$1,000 \times 3.170 = \$3,170$$

Periods	1%	2%	3%	4%	6%	8%	10%
1	0.990	0.980	0.971	0.962	0.943	0.926	0.909
2	1.970	1.942	1.913	1.886	1.833	1.783	1.736
3	2.941	2.884	2.829	2.775	2.673	2.577	2.487
4	3.902	3.808	3.717	3.630	3.465	3.312	3.170
5	4.853	4.713	4.580	4.452	4.212	3.993	3.791
8	7.652	7.325	7.020	6.773	6.210	5.747	5.335
10	9.471	8.983	8.530	8.111	7.360	6.710	6.145
20	18.046	16.351	14.877	13.590	11.470	9.818	8.514
30	25.808	22.396	19.600	17.292	13.765	11.258	9.427

An expanded table is presented in Appendix D.

Table 9–4

Present value of an annuity of $1 ($PV_{IFA}$)

To reinforce your understanding of the material you have just covered, please proceed to the graphical presentation that follows.

Exhibit 9–1   Future value of $.68 at 10%

Graphical Presentation of Time Value Relationships

This section is designed to supplement the previous discussion of future value, present value, and annuities and to reinforce your understanding of these concepts before you continue into the next sections. This material is nonmathematical and focuses on time value concepts using a visual approach. If you want to skip this graphical presentation, you can go directly to page 266.

The Relationship between Present Value and Future Value

Earlier in this chapter we presented the future value of a single amount as well as the present value of a single amount and applied the concept of annuities to both future value and present value. In the following special section, we use transparencies to help clarify the relationships between future and present value.

In Exhibits 9–1 and 9–2, we show how the future value and present value of a single amount are inversely related to each other. Future value takes a value today, for example $.68, and computes its value in the future assuming that it earns a rate of return each period. In Exhibit 9–1, the $.68 is invested at 10 percent and grows to $1.00 at the end of period 4. Because we want to avoid large mathematical rounding errors, we actually carry the decimal points 3 places. The $.683 that we invest today (period 0), grows to $.751 after one period, $.826 after two periods, $.909 after three periods and $1.00 at the end of the fourth period. In this example, the $.68 is the present value and the $1.00 is the future value.

Exhibit 9–2   Present value of $1.00 at 10%

If you turn the transparency to Exhibit 9–2, you notice that the future value and present value graphs are the flip side of each other. In the present value table, it becomes clear that if I have $1.00 in period 0, it is worth its present value of $1.00. However, if I have to wait one period to receive my dollar, it is worth only $.909 if I can earn a 10 percent return on my money. You can see this by flipping the transparency back to the future value graph. The $.909 at the end of period 3 will grow to $1.00 during period 4. Or by letting $.909 compound at a 10 percent rate for one period, you have $1.00.

Because you can earn a return on your money, $1.00 received in the future is worth less than $1.00 today, and the longer you have to wait to receive the dollar, the less it is worth. For example, if you are to receive $1.00 at the end of four periods, how much is its present value? Flip the transparency to Exhibit 9–2 and you see that the answer is $.68, the same value that we started with in period 0 in the future value graph in Exhibit 9–1. As you change the rate of return that can be earned, the values in Exhibits 9–1 and 9–2 will change, but the relationship will remain the same as presented in this example.

Exhibit 9–3 Present value of $1.00 at 10%

The Relationship between the Present Value of a Single Amount and the Present Value of an Annuity

Exhibit 9–3 shows the relationship between the present value of $1.00 and the present value of a $1.00 annuity. The assumption is that you will receive $1.00 at the end of each period. This is the same concept as a lottery, where you win $2 million over 20 years and receive $100,000 per year for 20 years. In this example we receive only four payments of $1.00 each and we use the transparency format to build up one year at a time.

Looking at Exhibit 9–3 without the transparencies, you see the present value of $1.00 to be received at the end of period 1 is $.909; $1.00 received at the end of period 2 is $.826; $1.00 received at the end of period 3 is $.751; and $1.00 received at the end of period 4 is $.683. These numbers should look very familiar. Exhibit 9–3 has the same values as Exhibit 9–2, except there is no period 0.

Turn the first transparency over Exhibit 9–3. If you are to receive two $1.00 payments, the first at the end of period 1 and the second at the end of period 2, the total present value will simply be the sum of the present value of each $1.00 payment. You can see that the total present value of $1.74 represents the present value of $1.00 to be received at the end of the first period ($.909) and the present value of $1.00 to be received at the end of the second period. The second transparency builds the present value of a three-period annuity equaling $2.49, and the last transparency illustrates the present value of four $1.00 payments equaling $3.17.

This $3.17 is the sum of each present value. The color coding helps illustrate the relationships. The top box is always $.909 and represents the present value of $1.00 received at the end of the first period; the second box from the top is always $.826 and is the present value of the $1.00 received at the end of the second year; the box third from the top is $.751 and is the present value of the $1.00 received at the end of the third year; and finally, the present value of the $1.00 received at the end of the fourth year is $.683. To help solidify this relationship in your memory, look up the present value of $1.00 at 12 percent for periods 1 through 4 in Appendix B. Then create the present value of a $1.00 annuity at 12 percent for two years, three years, and four years. Check your answers in Appendix D. Your answers should match the numbers in Appendix D under the 12 percent column for periods 2 through 4.

Exhibit 9–4 Future value of $1.00 at 10%

Future Value Related to the Future Value of an Annuity

The next relationship is between the future value of a single sum and the future value of an annuity. We start with Exhibit 9–4, which graphically depicts the future value of $1.00 that is growing at a 10 percent rate of return each period. If we start with a present value of $1.00 today (period 0), at the end of period 1 we will have $1.10; at the end of period 2 we will have $1.21; and at the end of period 3 the $1.00 will have grown to $1.33.

One of the confusing features between the future value of $1.00 and the future value of a $1.00 annuity is that they have different assumptions concerning the timing of cash flows. The future value of $1.00 (Appendix A) assumes the $1.00 is invested at the beginning of the period and grows to the end of the period. The future value of an annuity (Appendix C) assumes $1.00 is invested at the end of the period and grows to the end of the next period. This means the last $1.00 invested has no time to increase its value by earning a return. This relationship is shown in the transparencies by adding a period 0 to the future value graph and by creating a transparency overlay that replaces the period 0 in the future value with a period 1 for the future value of an annuity.

The calculation for the future value of a $1.00 annuity simply adds together the future value of a series of equal $1.00 investments. When you turn the first transparency, notice the periods have changed to represent the annuity assumptions. Since the last $1.00 invested does not have a chance to compound, the future value of a two-period annuity equals $2.10. This $2.10 comes from adding the $1.00 invested at the end of period 2 plus the first $1.00 that has grown to $1.10. When you flip the second transparency, notice the future value of a three-period annuity is $3.31. This $3.31 is a combination of the $1.00 invested at the end of period 3, the $1.10 from the second $1.00 invested and $1.21 from the first dollar invested.

Finally, the last transparency demonstrates that the future value of a four-period annuity totals $4.64. The explanation of how each value creates the total is given on the transparency. Since the transparencies are color-coded, you might notice the pattern that exists. The $1.00 amount is always the top box and is the same color. This is the $1.00 that is always invested at the end of the period and has no time to compound. The $1.10 is always the second box from the top and represents the $1.00 that has been invested for only one period, while the $1.21 is always the third box from the top and represents the $1.00 invested for two periods. The $1.33 is the fourth box from the top and represents $1.00 invested for three periods.

Determining the Annuity Value

In our prior discussion of annuities, we assumed the unknown variable was the future value or the present value—with specific information available on the annuity value (A), the interest rate, and the number of periods or years. In certain cases our emphasis may shift to solving for one of these other values (on the assumption that future value or present value is given). For now, we will concentrate on determining an unknown annuity value.

Annuity Equaling a Future Value

Assuming we wish to accumulate $4,641 after four years at a 10 percent interest rate, how much must be set aside at the end of each of the four periods? We take the previously developed statement for the future value of an annuity and solve for A.

$$FV_A = A \times FV_{IFA}$$
$$A = \frac{FV_A}{FV_{IFA}} \tag{9-5}$$

The future value of an annuity (FV_A) is given as $4,641, and FV_{IFA} may be determined from Table 9–3 on page 257 (future value for an annuity). Whenever you are working with an annuity problem relating to future value, you employ Table 9–3 regardless of the variable that is unknown. For n = 4, and i = 10 percent, FV_{IFA} is 4.641. Thus A equals $1,000.

$$A = \frac{FV_A}{FV_{IFA}} = \frac{\$4,641}{4.641} = \$1,000$$

The solution is the exact reverse of that previously presented under the discussion of the future value of an annuity. As a second example, assume the director of the Women's Tennis Association must set aside an equal amount for each of the next 10 years to accumulate $1,000,000 in retirement funds and the return on deposited funds is 6 percent. Solve for the annual contribution, A, using Table 9–3.

$$A = \frac{FV_A}{FV_{IFA}} \quad (n = 10, i = 6\%)$$
$$A = \frac{\$1,000,000}{13.181} = \$75,867$$

Annuity Equaling a Present Value

In this instance, we assume you know the present value and you wish to determine what size annuity can be equated to that amount. Suppose your wealthy uncle presents you with $10,000 now to help you get through the next four years of college. If you are able to earn 6 percent on deposited funds, how many equal payments can you withdraw at the end of each year for four years? We need to know the value of an annuity equal to a given present value. We take the previously developed statement for the present value of an annuity and reverse it to solve for A.

$$PV_A = A \times PV_{IFA}$$
$$A = \frac{PV_A}{PV_{IFA}} \qquad (9\text{–}6)$$

The appropriate table is Table 9–4 on page 259 (present value of an annuity). We determine an answer of $2,886.

$$A = \frac{PV_A}{PV_{IFA}} \quad (n = 4, i = 6\%)$$

$$A = \frac{\$10,000}{3.465} = \$2,886$$

The flow of funds would follow the pattern in Table 9–5. Annual interest is based on the beginning balance for each year.

Year	Beginning Balance	Annual Interest (6%)	Annual Withdrawal	Ending Balance
1	$10,000.00	$600.00	$2,886.00	$7,714.00
2	7,714.00	462.84	2,886.00	5,290.84
3	5,290.84	317.45	2,886.00	2,722.29
4	2,722.29	163.71	2,886.00	0

Table 9–5
Relationship of present value to annuity

The same process can be used to indicate necessary repayments on a loan. Suppose a homeowner signs a $40,000 mortgage to be repaid over 20 years at 8 percent interest. How much must he or she pay annually to eventually liquidate the loan? In other words, what annuity paid over 20 years is the equivalent of a $40,000 present value with an 8 percent interest rate?[3]

$$A = \frac{PV_A}{PV_{IFA}} \qquad (n = 20, i = 8\%)$$

$$A = \frac{\$40,000}{9.818} = \$4,074$$

Part of the payments to the mortgage company will go toward the payment of interest, with the remainder applied to debt reduction, as indicated in Table 9–6.

Period	Beginning Balance	Annual Payment	Annual Interest (8%)	Repayment on Principal	Ending Balance
1	$40,000	$4,074	$3,200	$ 874	$39,126
2	39,126	4,074	3,130	944	38,182
3	38,182	4,074	3,055	1,019	37,163

Table 9–6
Payoff table for loan (amortization table)

---

[3]The actual mortgage could be further refined into monthly payments of approximately $340.

If this same process is followed over 20 years, the balance will be reduced to zero. The student might note that the homeowner will pay over $41,000 of *interest* during the term of the loan, as indicated below.

Total payments ($4,074 for 20 years)	$81,480
Repayment of principal	−40,000
Payments applied to interest	$41,480

Determining the Yield on an Investment

In our discussion thus far, we have considered the following time value of money problems.

		Formula	Table	Appendix
Future value—single amount	(9–1)	$FV = PV \times FV_{IF}$	9–1	A
Present value—single amount	(9–2)	$PV = FV \times PV_{IF}$	9–2	B
Future value—annuity	(9–3)	$FV_A = A \times FV_{IFA}$	9–3	C
Present value—annuity	(9–4)	$PV_A = A \times PV_{IFA}$	9–4	D
Annuity equaling a future value	(9–5)	$A = \dfrac{FV_A}{FV_{IFA}}$	9–3	C
Annuity equaling a present value	(9–6)	$A = \dfrac{PV_A}{PV_{IFA}}$	9–4	D

In each case we knew three out of the four variables and solved for the fourth. We will follow the same procedure again, but now the unknown variable will be i, the interest rate, or yield on the investment.

Yield—Present Value of a Single Amount

An investment producing $1,464 after four years has a present value of $1,000. What is the interest rate, or **yield**, on the investment?

We take the basic formula for the present value of a single amount and rearrange the terms.

$$PV = FV \times PV_{IF}$$
$$PV_{IF} = \frac{PV}{FV} = \frac{\$1,000}{\$1,464} = 0.683 \tag{9–7}$$

The determination of PV_{IF} does not give us the final answer—but it scales down the problem so we may ascertain the answer from Table 9–2, the present value of $1. A portion of Table 9–2 is reproduced below.

Periods	1%	2%	3%	4%	5%	6%	8%	10%
2	0.980	0.961	0.943	0.925	0.907	0.890	0.857	0.826
3	0.971	0.942	0.915	0.889	0.864	0.840	0.794	0.751
4	0.961	0.924	0.888	0.855	0.823	0.792	0.735	0.683

Read down the left-hand column of the table above until you have located the number of periods in question (in this case n = 4), and read across the table for n = 4 until you have located the computed value of PV_{IF} from Formula 9–7. We see that for n = 4 and PV_{IF} equal to 0.683, the interest rate, or yield, is 10 percent. This is the rate that will equate $1,464 received in four years to $1,000 today.

If a PV_{IF} value does not fall under a given interest rate, an approximation is possible. For example, with n = 3 and PV_{IF} = 0.861, using the table on the prior page, 5 percent may be suggested as an approximate answer.

Interpolation may also be used to find a more precise answer. In the above example, we write out the two PV_{IF} values that the designated PVIF (0.861) falls between and take the difference between the two.

PV_{IF} at 5%	0.864
PV_{IF} at 6%	0.840
	0.024

We then find the difference between the PV_{IF} value at the lowest interest rate and the designated PV_{IF} value.

PV_{IF} at 5%.	0.864
PV_{IF} designated	0.861
	0.003

We next express this value (0.003) as a fraction of the preceding value (0.024) and multiply by the difference between the two interest rates (6 percent minus 5 percent). The value is added to the lower interest rate (5 percent) to get a more exact answer of 5.125 percent rather than the estimated 5 percent.

$$5\% + \frac{0.003}{0.024}(1\%) =$$
$$5\% + 0.125\,(1\%) =$$
$$5\% + 0.125\% \quad = 5.125\%$$

Yield—Present Value of an Annuity

We may also find the yield related to any other problem. Let's look at the present value of an annuity. Take the basic formula for the present value of an annuity, and rearrange the terms.

$$PV_A = A \times PV_{IFA}$$
$$PV_{IFA} = \frac{PV_A}{A} \tag{9–8}$$

The appropriate table is Table 9–4 (the present value of an annuity of $1). Assuming a $10,000 investment will produce $1,490 a year for the next 10 years, what is the yield on the investment?

$$PV_{IFA} = \frac{PV_A}{A} = \frac{\$10,000}{\$1,490} = 6.710$$

If the student will flip back to Table 9–4 on page 259 and read across the columns for n = 10 periods, he or she will see that the yield is 8 percent.

The same type of approximated or interpolated yield that applied to a single amount can also be applied to an annuity when necessary.

| **Special Considerations in Time Value Analysis** | We have assumed interest was compounded or discounted on an annual basis. This assumption will now be relaxed. Contractual arrangements, such as an installment purchase agreement or a corporate bond contract, may call for semiannual, quarterly, or monthly compounding periods. The adjustment to the normal formula is quite simple. To determine n, multiply the number of years by the number of compounding periods during the year. The factor for i is then determined by dividing the quoted annual interest rate by the number of compounding periods. |

Case 1—Find the future value of a $1,000 investment after five years at 8 percent annual interest, **compounded semiannually**.

$$n = 5 \times 2 = 10 \quad i = 8 \text{ percent} \div 2 = 4 \text{ percent}$$

Since the problem calls for the future value of a single amount, the formula is $FV = PV \times FV_{IF}$. Using Table 9–1 for n = 10 and i = 4 percent, the answer is $1,480.

$$FV = PV \times FV_{IF}$$
$$FV = \$1,000 \times 1.480 = \$1,480$$

Case 2—Find the present value of 20 quarterly payments of $2,000 each to be received over the next five years. The stated interest rate is 8 percent per annum. The problem calls for the present value of an annuity. We again follow the same procedure as in Case 1 in regard to n and i.

$$PV_A = A \times PV_{IFA} \quad (n = 20, i = 2\%) \text{ [Table 9–4]}$$
$$PV_A = A \times \$2,000 \times 16.351 = \$32,702$$

Patterns of Payment

Time value of money problems may evolve around a number of different payment or receipt patterns. Not every situation will involve a single amount or an annuity. For example a contract may call for the payment of a different amount each year over a three-year period. To determine present value, each payment is discounted (Table 9–2) to the present and then summed.

(Assume 8% discount rate)
1. $1,000 \times 0.926 = \$ \ 926$
2. $2,000 \times 0.857 = \ 1,714$
3. $3,000 \times 0.794 = \ \underline{2,382}$
$\$5,022$

A more involved problem might include a combination of single amounts and an annuity. If the annuity will be paid at some time in the future, it is referred to as a deferred annuity and it requires special treatment. Assume the same problem as above, but with an annuity of $1,000 that will be paid at the end of each year from the fourth through the eighth year. With a discount rate of 8 percent, what is the present value of the cash flows?

1. $1,000 ⎫
2. 2,000 ⎬ Present value = $5,022
3. 3,000 ⎭
4. 1,000 ⎫
5. 1,000 ⎪
6. 1,000 ⎬ Five-year annuity
7. 1,000 ⎪
8. 1,000 ⎭

We know the present value of the first three payments is $5,022, from our calculation near the bottom of page 270, but what about the annuity? Let's diagram the five annuity payments.

The information source is Table 9–4, the present value of an annuity of $1 on page 259. For n = 5, i = 8 percent, the discount factor is 3.993—leaving a "present value" of the annuity of $3,993. However, tabular values only discount to the beginning of the first stated period of an annuity—in this case the beginning of the fourth year, as diagrammed below.

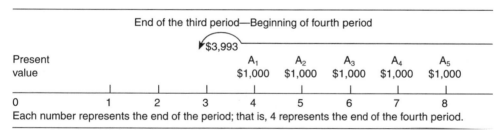

The $3,993 must finally be discounted back to the present. Since this single amount falls at the beginning of the fourth period—in effect, the equivalent of the end of the third period—we discount back for three periods at the stated 8 percent interest rate. Using Table 9–2, we have:

$$PV = FV \times PV_{IF} \qquad (n = 3, i = 8\%)$$
$$PV = \$3,993 \times 0.794 = \$3,170 \text{ (actual present value)}$$

The last step in this discounting process for the annuity is shown below.

A *second method* for finding the present value of a deferred annuity is to:

1. Find the present value factor of an annuity for the total time period. In this case, where n = 8, i = 8%, the PV_{IFA} is 5.747.
2. Find the present value factor of an annuity for the total time period (8) minus the deferred annuity period (5).

$$8 - 5 = 3$$
$$n = 3, i = 8\%$$

The PV_{IFA} value is 2.577.

3. Subtract the value in step 2 from the value in step 1, and multiply by A.

$$\begin{array}{r} 5.747 \\ -\ 2.577 \\ \hline 3.170 \end{array}$$

$3.170 \times \$1,000 = \$3,170$ (present value of the annuity)

$3,170 is the same answer for the present value of the annuity as that reached by the first method. The present value of the five-year annuity may now be added to the present value of the inflows over the first three years to arrive at the total value.

$$\begin{array}{rl} \$5,022 & \text{Present value of first three period flows} \\ +3,170 & \text{Present value of five-year annuity} \\ \hline \$8,192 & \text{Total present value} \end{array}$$

Special Review of the Chapter

In working a time-value-of-money problem, the student should determine first whether the problem deals with future value or present value and second whether a single sum or an annuity is involved. The major calculations in Chapter 9 are summarized below.

1. *Future value of a single amount.*

$$\text{Formula: } FV = PV \times FV_{IF}$$

Table: 9–1 or Appendix A.
When to use: In determining the future value of a single amount.
Sample problem: You invest $1,000 for four years at 10 percent interest. What is the value at the end of the fourth year?

2. *Present value of a single amount.*

$$\text{Formula: } PV = FV \times PV_{IF}$$

Table: 9–2 or Appendix B.
When to use: In determining the present value of an amount to be received in the future.
Sample problem: You will receive $1,000 after four years at a discount rate of 10 percent. How much is this worth today?

3. *Future value of an annuity.*

$$\text{Formula: } FV_A = A \times FV_{IFA}$$

Table: 9–3 or Appendix C.
When to use: In determining the future value of a series of consecutive, equal payments (an annuity).
Sample problem: You will receive $1,000 at the end of each period for four periods. What is the accumulated value (future worth) at the end of the fourth period if money grows at 10 percent?

4. *Present value of an annuity.*

$$\text{Formula: } PV_A = A \times PV_{IFA}$$

Table: 9–4 or Appendix D.
When to use: In determining the present worth of an annuity.
Sample problem: You will receive $1,000 at the end of each period for four years. At a discount rate of 10 percent, what is this cash flow currently worth?

5. *Annuity equaling a future value.*

$$\text{Formula: } A = \frac{FV_A}{FV_{IFA}}$$

Table: 9–3 or Appendix C.
When to use: In determining the size of an annuity that will equal a future value.
Sample problem: You need $1,000 after four periods. With an interest rate of 10 percent, how much must be set aside at the end of each period to accumulate this amount?

6. *Annuity equaling a present value.*

$$\text{Formula: } A = \frac{PV_A}{PV_{IFA}}$$

Table: 9–4 or Appendix D.
When to use: In determining the size of an annuity equal to a given present value.
Sample problems:
  a. What four-year annuity is the equivalent of $1,000 today with an interest rate of 10 percent?
  b. You deposit $1,000 today and wish to withdraw funds equally over four years. How much can you withdraw at the end of each year if funds earn 10 percent?
  c. You borrow $1,000 for four years at 10 percent interest. How much must be repaid at the end of each year?

7. *Determining the yield on an investment.*

Formulas	Tables	
a. $PV_{IF} = \dfrac{PV}{FV}$	9–2, Appendix B	Yield—present value of a single amount
b. $PV_{IFA} = \dfrac{PV_A}{A}$	9–4, Appendix D	Yield—present value of an annuity

When to use: In determining the interest rate (i) that will equate an investment with future benefits.

Sample problem: You invest $1,000 now, and the funds are expected to increase to $1,360 after four periods.

What is the yield on the investment? Use

$$PV_{IF} = \frac{PV}{FV}$$

8. *Less than annual compounding periods.*

Semiannual	Multiply n × 2	Divide i by 2	⎛then use⎞
Quarterly	Multiply n × 4	Divide i by 4	⎜ normal ⎟
Monthly	Multiply n × 12	Divide i by 12	⎝ formula ⎠

When to use: If the compounding period is more (or perhaps less) frequent than once a year.

Sample problem: You invest $1,000 compounded semiannually at 8 percent per annum over four years. Determine the future value.

9. *Patterns of payment—deferred annuity.*

Formulas	Tables	
$PV_A = A \times PV_{IFA}$	9–4, Appendix D	⎫
$PV = FV \times PV_{IF}$	9–2, Appendix B	⎬ Method 1 ⎭

When to use: If an annuity begins in the future.

Sample problem: You will receive $1,000 per period, starting at the end of the fourth period and running through the end of the eighth period. With a discount rate of 8 percent, determine the present value.

The student is encouraged to work the many problems found at the end of the chapter.

List of Terms

future value   254
interest factor   255
present value   255
discount rate   255
annuity   256

future value of an annuity   256
present value of an annuity   258
yield   268
compounded semiannually   270

Discussion Questions

1. How is the future value (Appendix A) related to the present value of a single sum (Appendix B)?

2. How is the present value of a single sum (Appendix B) related to the present value of an annuity (Appendix D)?

3. Why does money have a time value?

4. Does inflation have anything to do with making a dollar today worth more than a dollar tomorrow?

5. Adjust the annual formula for a future value of a single amount at 12 percent for 10 years to a semiannual compounding formula. What are the interest factors (FV_{IF}) before and after? Why are they different?

6. If, as an investor, you had a choice of daily, monthly, or quarterly compounding, which would you choose? Why?

7. What is a deferred annuity?

8. List five different financial applications of the time value of money.

Practice Problems and Solutions

1. *a.* You invest $12,000 today at 9 percent per year. How much will you have after 15 years?

   b. What is the current value of $100,000 after 10 years if the discount rate is 12 percent?

   c. You invest $2,000 a year for 20 years at 11 percent. How much will you have after 20 years?

2. *a.* How much must Katie Wilson set aside each year to accumulate $80,000 after 15 years? The interest rate is 10 percent.

   b. How much must Josh Thompson repay each year for five years to pay off a $20,000 loan that he just took out. The interest rate is 8 percent.

Future value
Present value
Future value

Solving for an annuity

Solving for an annuity

Solutions

1. *a.* This is the future value of a single amount.

$$FV = PV \times FV_{IF} \ (n = 15, i = 9\%) \qquad \text{Appendix A}$$
$$FV = \$12,000 \times 3.642 = \$43,704$$

   b. This is the present value of a single amount.

$$PV = FV \times PV_{IF} \ (n = 10, i = 12\%) \qquad \text{Appendix B}$$
$$PV = \$100,000 \times .322 = \$32,200$$

   c. This is the future value of an annuity.

$$FV_A = A \times FV_{IFA} \ (n = 20, i = 11\%) \qquad \text{Appendix C}$$
$$FV_A = \$2,000 \times 64.203 = \$128,406$$

2. *a.* This calls for solving for an annuity to equal a future value.

$$A = \frac{FV_A}{FV_{IFA}} \qquad (n = 15, i = 10\%) \qquad \text{Appendix C}$$

$$A = \frac{\$80,000}{31.772} = \$2,517.94$$

   b. The $20,000 he is borrowing represents an amount he owes today. He will make future annual payments to pay off this current (present) obligation. This calls for solving for an annuity equal to a present value.

$$A = \frac{PV_A}{PV_{IFA}} \qquad (n = 5, i = 8\%) \qquad \text{Appendix D}$$

$$A = \frac{\$20,000}{3.993} = \$5,008.77$$

Problems

Future value

1. You invest $2,500 a year for three years at 8 percent.

   a. What is the value of your investment after one year? Multiply $2,500 × 1.08.

   b. What is the value of your investment after two years? Multiply your answer to part *a* by 1.08.

   c. What is the value of your investment after three years? Multiply your answer to part *b* by 1.08. This gives your final answer.

   d. Confirm that your final answer is correct by going to Appendix A (future value of $1), and looking up the future value for n = 3, and i = 8 percent. Multiply this tabular value by $2,500 and compare your answer to the answer in part *c*. There may be a slight difference due to rounding.

Present value

2. What is the present value of:

   a. $8,000 in 10 years at 6 percent?

   b. $16,000 in 5 years at 12 percent?

   c. $25,000 in 15 years at 8 percent?

   d. $1,000 in 40 periods at 20 percent?

Present value

3. You will receive $4,000, three years from now. The discount rate is 10 percent.

   a. What is the value of your investment two years from now? Multiply $4,000 × .909 (one year's discount rate at 10 percent).

   b. What is the value of your investment one year from now? Multiply your answer to part *a* by .909 (one year's discount rate at 10 percent).

   c. What is the value of your investment today? Multiply your answer to part *b* by .909 (one year's discount rate at 10 percent).

   d. Confirm that your answer to part *c* is correct by going to Appendix B (present value of $1) for n = 3 and i = 10%. Multiply this tabular value by $4,000 and compare your answer to the answer in part *c*. There may be a slight difference due to rounding.

Future value

4. If you invest $12,000 today, how much will you have:

   a. In 6 years at 7 percent?

   b. In 15 years at 12 percent?

   c. In 25 years at 10 percent?

   d. In 25 years at 10 percent (compounded semiannually)?

Present value

5. Your aunt offers you a choice of $20,000 in 50 years or $45 today. If money is discounted at 13 percent, which should you choose?

Present value

6. How much would you have to invest today to receive:

   a. $12,000 in 6 years at 12 percent?

   b. $15,000 in 15 ycars at 8 percent?

   c. $5,000 each year for 10 years at 8 percent?

   d. $40,000 each year for 40 years at 5 percent?

Future value

7. If you invest $8,000 per period for the following number of periods, how much would you have?

  a. 7 years at 9 percent.

  b. 40 years at 11 percent.

8. You invest a single amount of $12,000 for 5 years at 10 percent. At the end of 5 years you take the proceeds and invest them for 12 years at 15 percent. How much will you have after 17 years?

                      Future value

9. Mrs. Crawford will receive $6,500 a year for the next 14 years from her trust. If an 8 percent interest rate is applied, what is the current value of the future payments?

                      Present value

10. John Longwaite will receive $100,000 in 50 years. His friends are very jealous of him. If the funds are discounted back at a rate of 14 percent, what is the present value of his future "pot of gold"?

                      Present value

11. Carrie Tune will receive $19,500 a year for the next 20 years as a result of the new song she has written. If a 10 percent rate is applied, should she be willing to sell out her future rights now for $160,000?

                      Present value

12. General Mills will receive $27,500 per year for the next 10 years as a payment for a weapon he invented. If a 12 percent rate is applied, should he be willing to sell out his future rights now for $160,000?

                      Present value

13. The Western Sweepstakes has just informed you that you have won $1 million. The amount is to be paid out at the rate of $50,000 a year for the next 20 years. With a discount rate of 12 percent, what is the present value of your winnings?

                      Present value

14. Rita Gonzales won the $60 million lottery. She is to receive $1 million a year for the next 50 years plus an additional lump sum payment of $10 million after 50 years. The discount rate is 10 percent. What is the current value of her winnings?

                      Present value

15. Bruce Sutter invests $2,000 in a mint condition Nolan Ryan baseball card. He expects the card to increase in value by 20 percent a year for the next five years. After that, he anticipates a 15 percent annual increase for the next three years. What is the projected value of the card after eight years?

                      Future value

16. Martha Reed has been depositing $1,500 in her savings account every December since 1998. Her account earns 6 percent compounded annually. How much will she have in December of 2007? (Assume that a deposit is made in 2007. Make sure to count the years carefully.)

                      Future value

17. At a growth (interest) rate of 8 percent annually, how long will it take for a sum to double? To triple? Select the year that is closest to the correct answer.

                      Future value

18. If you owe $30,000 payable at the end of five years, what amount should your creditor accept in payment immediately if she could earn 11 percent on her money?

                      Present value

19. Barney Smith invests in a stock that will pay dividends of $3.00 at the end of the first year, $3.30 at the end of the second year, and $3.60 at the end of the third year. Also, he believes that at the end of the third year he will be able to sell the stock for $50. What is the present value of all future benefits if a discount rate of 11 percent is applied? (Round all values to two places to the right of the decimal point.)

                      Present value

Present value

20. Mr. Flint retired as president of the Color Tile Company but is currently on a consulting contract for $45,000 per year for the next 10 years.

   a. If Mr. Flint's opportunity cost (potential return) is 10 percent, what is the present value of his consulting contract?

   b. Assuming that Mr. Flint will not retire for two more years and will not start to receive his 10 payments until the end of the third year, what would be the value of his deferred annuity?

Quarterly compounding

21. Cousin Bertha invested $100,000 10 years ago at 12 percent, compounded quarterly. How much has she accumulated?

Special compounding

22. Determine the amount of money in a savings account at the end of five years, given an initial deposit of $3,000 and an 8 percent annual interest rate when interest is compounded (a) annually, (b) semiannually, and (c) quarterly.

Annuity due

23. As stated in the chapter, annuity payments are assumed to come at the end of each payment period (termed an ordinary annuity). However, an exception occurs when the annuity payments come at the beginning of each period (termed an annuity due). To find the present value of an annuity due, subtract 1 from n an add 1 to the tabular value. To find the future value of an annuity, add 1 to n and subtract 1 from the tabular value. For example, to find the future value of a $100 payment at the beginning of each period for five periods at 10 percent, go to Appendix C for n = 6 and i = 10 percent. Look up the value of 7.716 and subtract 1 from it for an answer of 6.716 or $671.60 ($100 × 6.716).

   What is the future value of a 10-year annuity of $2,000 per period where payments come at the beginning of each period? The interest rate is 8 percent.

Annuity due

24. Related to the discussion in problem 23, what is the present value of a 10-year annuity of $3,000 per period in which payments come at the beginning of each period? The interest rate is 12 percent.

Present value alternative

25. Your grandfather has offered you a choice of one of the three following alternatives: $5,000 now; $1,000 a year for eight years; or $12,000 at the end of eight years. Assuming you could earn 11 percent annually, which alternative should you choose? If you could earn 12 percent annually, would you still choose the same alternative?

Payments required

26. You need $23,956 at the end of nine years, and your only investment outlet is a 7 percent long-term certificate of deposit (compounded annually). With the certificate of deposit, you make an initial investment at the beginning of the first year.

   a. What single payment could be made at the beginning of the first year to achieve this objective?

   b. What amount could you pay at the end of each year annually for nine years to achieve this same objective?

Quarterly compounding

27. Beverly Hills started a paper route on January 1, 2001. Every three months, she deposits $300 in her bank account, which earns 8 percent annually but is compounded quarterly. On December 31, 2004, she used the entire balance in her bank account to invest in an investment at 12 percent annually. How much will she have on December 31, 2007?

28. Tom Phillips has just invested $8,760 for his son (age one). This money will be used for his son's education 17 years from now. He calculates that he will need $60,000 by the time the boy goes to school. What rate of return will Mr. Phillips need in order to achieve this goal?

Yield

29. On January 1, 2005, Mr. Dow bought 100 shares of stock at $12 per share. On December 31, 2008, he sold the stock for $18 per share. What is his annual rate of return? Interpolate to find the answer.

Yield with interpolation

30. C. D. Rom has just given an insurance company $30,000. In return, he will receive an annuity of $3,200 for 20 years.

Yield with interpolation

At what rate of return must the insurance company invest this $30,000 in order to make the annual payments? Interpolate.

31. Frank Bell has just retired from the telephone company. His total pension funds have an accumulated value of $200,000, and his life expectancy is 16 more years. His pension fund manager assumes he can earn a 12 percent return on his assets.

Solving for an annuity

What will be his yearly annuity for the next 16 years?

32. Dr. Oats, a nutrition professor, invests $80,000 in a piece of land that is expected to increase in value by 14 percent per year for the next five years. She will then take the proceeds and provide herself with a 10-year annuity. Assuming a 14 percent interest rate for the annuity, how much will this annuity be?

Solving for an annuity

33. You wish to retire in 20 years, at which time you want to have accumulated enough money to receive an annual annuity of $12,000 for 25 years after retirement. During the period before retirement you can earn 8 percent annually, while after retirement you can earn 10 percent on your money.

Solving for an annuity

What annual contributions to the retirement fund will allow you to receive the $12,000 annuity?

34. Rusty Steele will receive the following payments at the end of the next three years: $4,000, $7,000, and $9,000. Then from the end of the fourth year through the end of the tenth year, he will receive an annuity of $10,000. At a discount rate of 10 percent, what is the present value of all future benefits?

Deferred annuity

35. Kelly Greene has a contract in which she will receive the following payments for the next five years: $3,000, $4,000, $5,000, $6,000 and $7,000. She will then receive an annuity of $9,000 a year from the end of the sixth through the end of the 15th year. The appropriate discount rate is 13 percent. If she is offered $40,000 to cancel the contract, should she do it?

Present value

36. Kay Mart has purchased an annuity to begin payment at the end of 2009 (the date of the first payment). Assume it is now the beginning of 2007. The annuity is for $12,000 per year and is designed to last eight years.

Deferred annuity

If the discount rate for the calculation is 11 percent, what is the most she should have paid for the annuity?

37. If you borrow $9,725 and are required to pay back the loan in five equal annual installments of $2,500, what is the interest rate associated with the loan?

Yield

Loan repayment 38. Tom Busby owes $20,000 now. A lender will carry the debt for four more years at 8 percent interest. That is, in this particular case, the amount owed will go up 8 percent per year for four years. The lender then will require Busby to pay off the loan over 12 years at 11 percent interest. What will his annual payments be?

Loan repayment 39. If your aunt borrows $50,000 from the bank at 10 percent interest over the eight-year life of the loan, what equal annual payments must be made to discharge the loan, plus pay the bank its required rate of interest (round to the nearest dollar)? How much of her first payment will be applied to interest? To principal? How much of her second payment will be applied to each?

Loan repayment 40. Jim Thomas borrows $70,000 toward the purchase of a home at 12 percent interest. His mortgage is for 30 years.

    a. How much will his annual payments be? (Although home payments are usually on a monthly basis, we shall do our analysis on an annual basis for ease of computation. We will get a reasonably accurate answer.)

    b. How much interest will he pay over the life of the loan?

    c. How much should he be willing to pay to get out of a 12 percent mortgage and into a 10 percent mortgage with 30 years remaining on the mortgage? Suggestion: Find the annual savings and then discount them back to the present at the current interest rate (10 percent).

Annuity with changing interest rates 41. You are chairperson of the investment fund for the Continental Soccer League. You are asked to set up a fund of semiannual payments to be compounded semi-annually to accumulate a sum of $200,000 after 10 years at an 8 percent annual rate (20 payments). The first payment into the fund is to take place six months from today, and the last payment is to take place at the end of the 10th year.

    a. Determine how much the semiannual payment should be. (Round to whole numbers.)

    On the day after the sixth payment is made (the beginning of the fourth year) the interest rate goes up to a 10 percent annual rate, and you can earn a 10 percent annual rate on funds that have been accumulated as well as all future payments into the fund. Interest is to be compounded semiannually on all funds.

    b. Determine how much the revised semiannual payments should be after this rate change (there are 14 payments and compounding dates). The next payment will be in the middle of the fourth year. (Round all values to whole numbers.)

Annuity consideration 42. Your younger sister, Jennifer, will start college in five years. She has just informed your parents that she wants to go to Eastern State U., which will cost $18,000 per year for four years (cost assumed to come at the end of each year). Anticipating Jennifer's ambitions, your parents started investing $3,000 per year five yeas ago and will continue to do so for five more years.

    How much more will your parents have to invest each year for the next five years to have the necessary funds for Jennifer's education? Use 10 percent as the appropriate interest rate throughout this problem (for discounting or compounding). Round all values to whole numbers.

43. Jennifer (from problem 42) is now 18 years old (five years have passed), and she wants to get married instead of going to college. Your parents have accumulated the necessary funds for her education.

    Instead of her schooling, your parents are paying $7,000 for her current wedding and plan to take year-end vacations costing $2,000 per year for the next three years.

    How much money will your parents have at the end of three years to help you with graduate school, which you will start then? You plan to work on a master's and perhaps a PhD. If graduate school costs $18,930 per year, approximately how long will you be able to stay in school based on these funds? Use 10 percent as the appropriate interest rate throughout this problem. (Round all values to whole numbers.)

Special considerations of annuities and time periods

COMPREHENSIVE PROBLEM

Mr. Rambo, President of Assault Weapons, Inc., was pleased to hear that he had three offers from major defense companies for his latest missile firing automatic ejector. He will use a discount rate of 12 percent to evaluate each offer.

Assault Weapons, Inc.

(Comprehensive time value of money)

Offer I $500,000 now plus $120,000 from the end of year 6 through 15. Also, if the product goes over $50 million in cumulative sales by the end of year 15, he will receive an additional $1,500,000. Rambo thought there was a 75 percent probability this would happen

Offer II   Twenty-five percent of the buyer's gross margin for the next four years. The buyer in this case is Air Defense, Inc. (ADI). Its gross margin is 65 percent. Sales for year 1 are projected to be $1 million and then grow by 40 percent per year. This amount is paid today and is not discounted.

Offer III   A trust fund would be set up for the next nine years. At the end of that period, Rambo would receive the proceeds (and discount them back to the present at 12 percent). The trust fund called for semiannual payments for the next nine years of $80,000 (a total of $160,000 per year). The payments would start immediately. Since the payments are coming at the beginning of each period instead of the end, this is an annuity due. To look up the future value of the annuity due in the tables, add 1 to n (18 + 1) and subtract 1 from the value in the table. Assume the annual interest rate on this annuity is 12 percent annually (6 percent semiannually). Determine the present value of the trust fund's final value.

Required: Find the present value of each of the three offers and then indicate which one has the highest present value.

Valuation and Rates of Return

1 The valuation of a financial asset is based on the present value of future cash flows.

2 The required rate of return in valuing an asset is based on the risk involved.

3 Bond valuation is based on the process of determining the present value of interest payments plus the principal payment at maturity.

4 Stock valuation is based on determining the present value of the future benefits of equity ownership.

5 A price-earnings ratio may also be applied to a firm's earnings to determine value.

Valuation appears to be a fickle process to stockholders of some corporations. For example, if you held EchoStar Communications common stock in January 2006, you would be pleased to see that stockholders were valuing your stock at 40 times earnings. Certainly there was some justification for such a high valuation. The firm was one of the leading providers of satellite television products and services, including satellite ECHOSTAR television receiver dishes, receivers, and so on. It boasted of having over 11 million subscribers and had nine satellites in orbit.

But keep in mind the company had 10 straight years of operating deficits until 2003, and that AT&T and other telecommunications giants plan to begin offering fiber-optic infrastructures in the coming years, which will mean new competition.

If stockholders of EchoStar were happy in January 2006 with their strong P/E ratio of 40, those who invested in Dow Chemical were not. The renowned manufacturer of basic chemicals and plastics was only trading at a P/E of 10 despite double-digit growth in EPS over the last few years. Furthermore, the firm paid a dividend of $1.34 per share for a dividend yield (dividend per share/price) of approximately 3 percent.

The question becomes, why are P/E ratios so different and why do they change so much? Informed investors care a lot about their money and vote with their dollars, and they were saying they would pay four times more (40 versus 10) for a dollar of EchoStar's earnings than for Dow's earnings.

The factors that determine valuation are varied, and you will be exposed to many of them in this chapter.

In Chapter 9 we considered the basic principles of the time value of money. In this chapter we will use many of those concepts to determine how financial assets (bonds, preferred stock, and common stock) are valued and how investors establish the rates of return they demand. In the next chapter we will use material from this chapter to determine the overall cost of financing to the firm. We merely turn the coin over. Once we know how much bondholders and stockholders demand in the way of rates of return, we will then observe what the corporation is required to pay them to attract their funds. The cost of corporate financing (capital) is subsequently used in analyzing whether a project is acceptable for investment or not. These relationships are depicted in Figure 10–1.

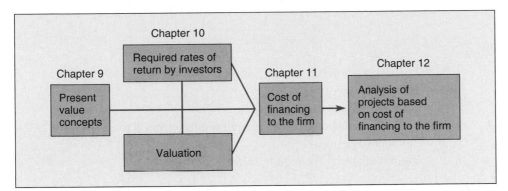

Figure 10–1

The relationship between time value of money, required return, cost of financing, and investment decisions

Valuation Concepts

The valuation of a financial asset is based on determining the present value of future cash flows. Thus we need to know the value of future cash flows and the discount rate to be applied to the future cash flows to determine the current value.

The market-determined **required rate of return**, which is the discount rate, depends on the market's perceived level of risk associated with the individual security. Also important is the idea that required rates of return are competitively determined among the many companies seeking financial capital. For example ExxonMobil, due to its low financial risk, relatively high return, and strong market position, is likely to raise debt capital at a significantly lower cost than can United Airlines, a financially troubled firm. This implies that investors are willing to accept low return for low risk, and vice versa. The market allocates capital to companies based on risk, efficiency, and expected returns—which are based to a large degree on past performance. The reward to the financial manager for efficient use of capital in the past is a lower required return for investors than that of competing companies that did not manage their financial resources as well.

Throughout the balance of this chapter, we apply concepts of valuation to corporate bonds, preferred stock, and common stock. Although we describe the basic characteristics of each form of security as part of the valuation process, extended discussion of each security is deferred until later chapters.

Valuation of Bonds

As previously stated, the value of a financial asset is based on the concept of the present value of future cash flows. Let's apply this approach to bond valuation. A bond provides an annuity stream of interest payments and a $1,000 principal payment at maturity.[1] These cash flows are discounted at Y, the yield to maturity. The value of Y

---

[1]The assumption is that the bond has a $1,000 par value. If the par value is higher or lower, then this value would be discounted to the present from the maturity date.

is determined in the bond market and represents the required rate of return for bonds of a given risk and maturity. More will be said about the concept of yield to maturity in the next section.

The price of a bond is thus equal to the present value of regular interest payments discounted by the yield to maturity added to the present value of the principal (also discounted by the yield to maturity).

This relationship can be expressed mathematically as follows.

$$P_b = \sum_{t=1}^{n} \frac{I_t}{(1+Y)^t} + \frac{P_n}{(1+Y)^n} \qquad (10\text{--}1)$$

where

P_b = Price of the bond
I_t = Interest payments
P_n = Principal payment at maturity
t = Number corresponding to a period; running from 1 to n
n = Number of periods
Y = Yield to maturity (or required rate of return)

The first term in the equation says to take the sum of the present values of the interest payments (I_t); the second term directs you to take the present value of the principal payment at maturity (P_n). The discount rate used throughout the analysis is the yield to maturity (Y). The answer derived is referred to as P_b (the price of the bond). The analysis is carried out for n periods.

Let's assume that I_t (interest payments) equals $100; P_n (principal payment at maturity) equals $1,000; Y (yield to maturity) is 10 percent; and n (total number of periods) equals 20. We could say that P_b (the price of the bond) equals:

$$P_b = \sum_{t=1}^{n} \frac{\$100}{(1+.10)^t} + \frac{\$1,000}{(1+.10)^{20}}$$

Although the price of the bond could be determined with extensive calculations, it is much simpler to use present value tables. We take the present value of the interest payments and then add this value to the present value of the principal payment at maturity.

Present Value of Interest Payments   In this case we determine the present value of a $100 annuity for 20 years.[2] The discount rate is 10 percent. Using Appendix D at the end of the book, the present value of an annuity, we find the following:

$$PV_A = A \times PV_{IFA} \quad (n = 20, i = 10\%)$$
$$PV_A = \$100 \times 8.514 = \$851.40$$

Present Value of Principal Payment (Par Value) at Maturity   This single value of $1,000 will be received after 20 years. Note the term *principal payment at maturity* is used interchangeably with *par value* or *face value* of the bond. We discount $1,000 back to the present at 10 percent. Using end-of-the-book Appendix B, the present value of a single amount, we find the following:

---

[2]For now we are using *annual* interest payments for simplicity. Later in the discussion, we will shift to semiannual payments, and more appropriately determine the value of a bond.

$$PV = FV \times PV_{IF} \quad (n = 20, i = 10\%)$$
$$PV = \$1{,}000 \times .149 = \$149$$

The current price of the bond, based on the present value of interest payments and the present value of the principal payment at maturity, is $1,000.40.

Present value of interest payments	$ 851.40
Present value of principal payment at maturity	149.00
Total present value, or price, of the bond	$1,000.40

The price of the bond in this case is essentially the same as its par, or stated, value to be received at maturity of $1,000.[3] This is because the annual interest rate is 10 percent (the annual interest payment of $100 divided by $1,000) and the yield to maturity, or discount rate, is also 10 percent. When the interest rate on the bond and the yield to maturity are equal, the bond will trade at par value. Later we will examine the mathematical effects of varying the yield to maturity above or below the interest rate on the bond. But first let's examine more fully the concept of yield to maturity.

Concept of Yield to Maturity

In the previous example, the yield to maturity that was used as the discount rate was 10 percent. The **yield to maturity,** or discount rate, is the rate of return required by bondholders. The bondholder, or any investor for that matter, will allow *three* factors to influence his or her required rate of return.

1.   The required **real rate of return**—This is the rate of return the investor demands for giving up the current use of the funds on a noninflation-adjusted basis. It is the financial "rent" the investor charges for using his or her funds for one year, five years, or any given period. Although it varies from time to time, historically the real rate of return demanded by investors has been about 2 to 3 percent.

2.   **Inflation premium**—In addition to the real rate of return discussed above, the investor requires a premium to compensate for the eroding effect of inflation on the value of the dollar. It would hardly satisfy an investor to have a 3 percent total rate of return in a 5 percent inflationary economy. Under such circumstances, the lender (investor) would be paying the borrower 2 percent (in purchasing power) for use of the funds. This would represent an irrational action. No one wishes to *pay* another party to use his or her funds. The inflation premium added to the real rate of return ensures that this will not happen. The size of the inflation premium will be based on the investor's expectations about future inflation. In the last two decades, the inflation premium has been 2 to 4 percent. In the late 1970s, it was in excess of 10 percent.

If one combines the real rate of return (part 1) and the inflation premium (part 2), the **risk-free rate of return** is determined. This is the rate that compensates the investor for the current use of his or her funds and for the loss in purchasing power due to inflation, but not for taking risks. As an example, if the real rate of return were 3 percent and the inflation premium were 4 percent, we would say the risk-free rate of return is 7 percent.[4]

---

[3]The slight difference of $0.40 is due to the rounding procedures in the tables.

[4]Actually a slightly more accurate representation would be: Risk-free rate = (1 + Real rate of return)(1 + Inflation premium) − 1. We would show: (1.03)(1.04) − 1 = 1.0712 − 1 = .0712 = 7.12 percent.

3.   **Risk premium**—We must now add the risk premium to the risk-free rate of return. This is a premium associated with the special risks of a given investment. Of primary interest to us are two types of risk: **business risk** and **financial risk**. Business risk relates to the inability of the firm to hold its competitive position and maintain stability and growth in its earnings. Financial risk relates to the inability of the firm to meet its debt obligations as they come due. In addition to the two forms of risk mentioned above, the risk premium will be greater or less for different types of investments. For example, because bonds possess a contractual obligation for the firm to pay interest to bondholders, they are considered less risky than common stock where no such obligation exists.[5]

The risk premium of an investment may range from as low as zero on a very-short-term U.S. government–backed security to 10 to 15 percent on a gold mining expedition. The typical risk premium is 2 to 6 percent. Just as the required real rate of return and the inflation premium change over time, so does the risk premium. For example, high-risk corporate bonds (sometimes referred to as junk bonds) normally require a risk premium of about 5 percentage points over the risk-free rate. However, in September 1989 the bottom fell out of the junk bond market as Campeau Corp., International Resources, and Resorts International began facing difficulties in making their payments. Risk premiums almost doubled. As is emphasized in many parts of the text, there is a strong correlation between the risk the investor is taking and the return the investor demands. Supposedly, in finance as in other parts of business, "There is no such thing as a free lunch." If you want a higher return, you must take a greater risk.

We shall assume that in the investment we are examining the risk premium is 3 percent. If we add this risk premium to the two components of the risk-free rate of return developed in parts 1 and 2, we arrive at an overall required rate of return of 10 percent.

+ Real rate of return	3%
+ Inflation premium	4
= Risk-free rate	7%
+ Risk premium	3
= Required rate of return	10%

In this instance, we assume we are evaluating the required return on a bond issued by a firm. If the security had been the common stock of the same firm, the risk premium might be 5 to 6 percent and the required rate of return 12 to 13 percent.

Finally, in concluding this section, you should recall that the required rate of return on a bond is effectively the same concept as required yield to maturity.

Changing the Yield to Maturity and the Impact on Bond Valuation

In the earlier bond value calculation, we assumed the interest rate was 10 percent ($100 annual interest on a $1,000 par value bond) and the yield to maturity was also 10 percent. Under those circumstances, the price of the bond was basically equal to par value. Now let's assume conditions in the market cause the yield to maturity to change.

[5]On the other hand, common stock carries the potential for very high returns when the corporation is quite profitable.

Increase in Inflation Premium   For example, assume the inflation premium goes up from 4 to 6 percent. All else remains constant. The required rate of return would now be 12 percent.

+ Real rate of return	3%
+ Inflation premium	6
= Risk-free rate	9%
+ Risk premium	3
= Required rate of return	12%

With the required rate of return, or yield to maturity, now at 12 percent, the price of the bond will change.[6] A bond that pays only 10 percent interest when the required rate of return (yield to maturity) is 12 percent will fall below its current value of approximately $1,000. The new price of the bond, as computed below, is $850.90.

Present Value of Interest Payments—We take the present value of a $100 annuity for 20 years. The discount rate is 12 percent. Using Appendix D:

$$PV_A = A \times PV_{IFA} \quad (n = 20, i = 12\%)$$
$$PV_A = \$100 \times 7.469 = \$746.90$$

Present Value of Principal Payment at Maturity—We take the present value of $1,000 after 20 years. The discount rate is 12 percent. Using Appendix B:

$$PV = FV \times PV_{IF} \quad (n = 20, i = 12\%)$$
$$PV = \$1,000 \times .104 = \$104$$

Total Present Value—

Present value of interest payments	$746.90
Present value of principal payment at maturity	104.00
Total present value, or price, of the bond	$850.90

In this example we assumed increasing inflation caused the required rate of return (yield to maturity) to go up and the bond price to fall by approximately $150. The same effect would occur if the business risk increased or the demanded level for the *real* rate of return became higher.

Decrease in Inflation Premium   The opposite effect would happen if the required rate of return went down because of lower inflation, less risk, or other factors. Let's assume the inflation premium declines and the required rate of return (yield to maturity) goes down to 8 percent.

The 20-year bond with the 10 percent interest rate would now sell for $1,196.80 as shown in the following calculations.

Present Value of Interest Payments—

$$PV_A = A \times PV_{IFA} \quad (n = 20, i = 8\%) \quad (\text{Appendix D})$$
$$PV_A = \$100 \times 9.818 = \$981.80$$

---

[6]Of course the required rate of return on all other financial assets will also go up proportionally.

Present Value of Principal Payment at Maturity—

$$PV = FV \times PV_{IF} \quad (n = 20, i = 8\%) \quad \text{(Appendix B)}$$

$$PV = \$1,000 \times .215 = \$215$$

Total Present Value—

Present value of interest payments.	$ 981.80
Present value of principal payment at maturity.	215.00
Total present value, or price, of the bond	$1,196.80

The bond is now trading at $196.80 over par value. This is certainly the expected result because the bond is paying 10 percent interest when the yield in the market is only 8 percent. The 2 percentage point differential on a $1,000 par value bond represents $20 per year. The investor will receive this differential for the next 20 years. The present value of $20 for the next 20 years at the current market rate of interest of 8 percent is approximately $196.80. This explains why the bond is trading at $196.80 over its stated, or par, value.

The further the yield to maturity on a bond changes from the stated interest rate on the bond, the greater the price change effect will be. This is illustrated in Table 10–1 for the 10 percent interest rate, 20-year bonds discussed in this chapter.

Table 10–1

Bond price table

(10% Interest Payment, 20 Years to Maturity)	
Yield to Maturity	**Bond Price**
2%.	$2,308.10
4	1,815.00
6	1,459.00
7	1,317.40
8	1,196.80
9	1,090.90
10	1,000.00
11	920.30
12	850.90
13	789.50
14	735.30
16	643.90
20	513.00
25%.	$ 407.40

We clearly see the impact that different yields to maturity have on the price of a bond.[7]

---

[7]The reader may observe in Table 10–1 that the impact of a decrease or increase in interest rates is not equal. For example, a 2 percent decrease in interest rates initially at 10 percent will produce a $196.80 gain in the bond price and an increase of 2 percent causes a $149.10 loss. While price movements are not symmetrical around the price of the bond when the time dimension is the maturity date of the bond, they are symmetrical around the duration of the bond. The duration represents the weighted average time period to recapture the interest and principal on the bond. While these concepts go beyond that appropriate for an introductory finance text, the interested reader may wish to consult Geoffrey A. Hirt and Stanley B. Block, *Fundamentals of Investment Management,* 8th ed. (Burr Ridge, IL: Irwin/McGraw-Hill, 2006).

Time to Maturity

The impact of a change in yield to maturity on valuation is also affected by the remaining time to maturity. The effect of a bond paying 2 percentage points more or less than the going rate of interest is quite different for a 20-year bond than it is for a 1-year bond. In the latter case, the investor will only be gaining or giving up $20 for one year. That is certainly not the same as having this $20 differential for an extended period. Let's once again return to the 10 percent interest rate bond and show the impact of a 2 percentage point decrease or increase in yield to maturity for varying *times* to maturity. The values are shown in Table 10–2 below and graphed in Figure 10–2 on page 290. The upper part of Figure 10–2 shows how the amount (premium) above par value is reduced as the number of years to maturity becomes smaller and smaller. Figure 10–2 should be read from left to right. The lower part of the figure shows how the amount (discount) below par value is reduced with progressively fewer years to maturity. Clearly, the longer the maturity, the greater the impact of changes in yield.

Time Period in Years (of 10% bond)	Bond Price with 8% Yield to Maturity	Bond Price with 12% Yield to Maturity
0	$1,000.00	$1,000.00
1	1,018.60	982.30
5	1,080.30	927.50
10	1,134.00	887.00
15	1,170.90	864.11
20	1,196.80	850.90
25	1,213.50	843.30
30	1,224.80	838.50

Table 10–2

Impact of time to maturity on bond prices

Determining Yield to Maturity from the Bond Price

Until now we have used yield to maturity as well as other factors, such as the interest rate on the bond and number of years to maturity, to compute the price of the bond. We shall now assume we know the price of the bond, the interest rate on the bond, and the years to maturity, and we wish to determine the yield to maturity. Once we have computed this value, we have determined the rate of return that investors are demanding in the marketplace to provide for inflation, risk, and other factors.

Let's once again present Formula 10–1:

$$P_b = \sum_{t=1}^{n} \frac{I_t}{(1 + Y)^t} + \frac{P_n}{(1 + Y)^n}$$

We now determine the value of Y, the yield to maturity, that will equate the interest payments (I_t) and the principal payment (P_n) to the price of the bond (P_b).

Assume a 15-year bond pays $110 per year (11 percent) in interest and $1,000 after 15 years in principal repayment. The current price of the bond is $932.21. We wish to compute the yield to maturity, or discount rate, that equates future flows with the current price.

Figure 10–2

Relationship between time to maturity and bond price*

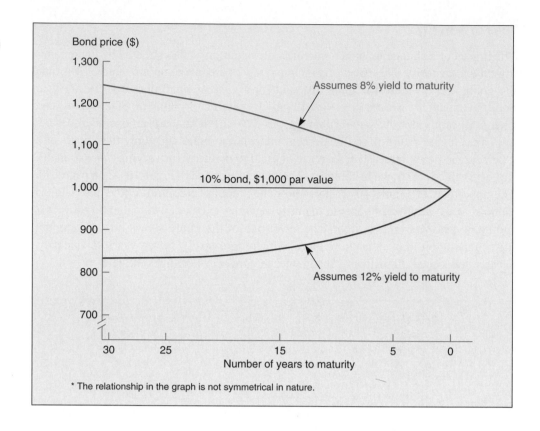

* The relationship in the graph is not symmetrical in nature.

In this trial and error process, the first step is to choose an initial percentage in the tables to try as the discount rate. Since the bond is trading below the par value of $1,000, we can assume the yield to maturity (discount rate) must be above the quoted interest rate of 11 percent. Let's begin the trial and error process.

A 13 Percent Discount Rate   As a first approximation, we might try 13 percent and compute the present value of the bond as follows:

Present Value of Interest Payments—

$$PV_A = A \times PV_{IFA} \quad (n = 15, i = 13\%) \quad \text{(Appendix D)}$$
$$PV_A = \$110 \times 6.462 = \$710.82$$

Present Value of Principal Payment at Maturity—

$$PV = FV \times PV_{IF} \quad (n = 15, i = 13\%) \quad \text{(Appendix B)}$$
$$PV = \$1,000 \times .160 = \$160$$

Total Present Value—

Present value of interest payments	$710.82
Present value of principal payment at maturity	160.00
Total present value, or price, of the bond	$870.82

The answer of $870.82 is below the current bond price of $932.21 as stated toward the bottom of page 289. This indicates we have used too high a discount rate in creating too low a value.

A 12 Percent Discount Rate   As a next step in the trial and error process, we will try 12 percent.

Present Value of Interest Payments—

$$PV_A = A \times PV_{IFA} \quad (n = 15, i = 12\%) \quad \text{(Appendix D)}$$
$$PV_A = \$110 \times 6.811 = \$749.21$$

Present Value of Principal Payment at Maturity—

$$PV = FV \times PV_{IF} \quad (n = 15, i = 12\%) \quad \text{(Appendix B)}$$
$$PV = \$1,000 \times .183 = \$183$$

Total Present Value—

Present value of interest payments	$749.21
Present value of principal payment at maturity	183.00
Total present value, or price, of the bond	$932.21

The answer precisely matches the bond price of $932.21 that we are evaluating. That indicates the correct yield to maturity for the bond is 12 percent. If the computed value were slightly different from the price of the bond, we could use interpolation to arrive at the correct answer. An example of interpolating to derive yield to maturity is presented in Appendix 10A at the end of the chapter.

Formula for Bond Yield   Because it is tedious to determine the bond yield to maturity through trial and error, an approximate answer can also be found by using Formula 10–2.[8]

Approximate yield to maturity (Y′) =

$$\frac{\text{Annual interest payment} + \dfrac{\text{Principal payment} - \text{Price of the bond}}{\text{Number of years to maturity}}}{0.6(\text{Price of the bond}) + 0.4(\text{Principal payment})} \quad (10\text{--}2)$$

Plugging in the values from the just completed analysis of yield to maturity, we show:

$$Y' = \frac{\$110 + \dfrac{\$1,000 - 932.21}{15}}{0.6(\$932.21) + 0.4(\$1,000)}$$
$$= \frac{\$110 + \dfrac{\$67.79}{15}}{\$559.33 + \$400}$$

(continued on page 292)

[8]This formula is developed by Gabriel A. Hawawini and Ashok Vora, "Yield Approximations: A Historical Perspective," *Journal of Finance* 37 (March 1982), pp. 145–56. It tends to provide the best approximation.

(concluded)
$$= \frac{\$110 + \$4.52}{\$959.33}$$

$$= \frac{\$114.52}{\$959.33}$$

$$Y' = 11.94\%$$

The answer of 11.94 percent is a reasonably good approximation of the exact yield to maturity of 12 percent.[9] We use the prime (') symbol after Y to indicate the answer based on Formula 10–2 is only an approximation.

Note that the numerator of Formula 10–2 represents the average annual income over the life of the bond and the denominator represents the average investment. That is, in the numerator, we take the annual interest payment of $110 and add that to the average annual change in the bond value over 15 years, which is computed as $4.52. This provides average annual income of $114.52. In the denominator, we take a *weighted* average of the original price of $932.21 and the final value of $1,000 that we will receive at maturity to get the average investment over the 15-year holding period.[10]

It should be pointed out that in computing yield to maturity on a bond, financially oriented handheld calculators and software programs for personal computers can be extremely helpful. Appendix 10B at the end of the chapter presents material related to calculators.

As we have discussed throughout, the yield to maturity is the required rate of return bondholders demand. More importantly for our purposes here, it also indicates the current cost to the corporation to issue bonds. In the prior example, the corporation had issued bonds at 11 percent, but market conditions changed and the current price of the bond fell to $932.21. At this current price, the ongoing yield to maturity increased to 12 percent (11.94 percent, using the approximation method). If the corporate treasurer were to issue new bonds today, he or she would have to respond to the current market-demanded rate of 12 percent rather than the initial yield of 11 percent. Only by understanding how investors value bonds in the marketplace can the corporate financial officer properly assess the cost of that source of financing to the corporation.

Semiannual Interest and Bond Prices

We have been assuming that interest was paid annually in our bond analysis. In actuality most bonds pay interest semiannually. Thus a 10 percent interest rate bond may actually pay $50 twice a year instead of $100 annually. To make the conversion from an annual to semiannual analysis, we follow three steps.

1. Divide the annual interest rate by two.
2. Multiply the number of years by two.
3. Divide the annual yield to maturity by two.

Assume a 10 percent, $1,000 par value bond has a maturity of 20 years. The annual yield to maturity is 12 percent. In following the three steps above, we would show:

---

[9]The greater the premium or discount and the longer the period to maturity, the less accurate the approximation.
[10]As indicated by the Hawawini and Vora study (cited in footnote 8), this weighting procedure gives a better approximation than the simple arithmetic mean of the two values.

1. 10%/2 = 5% semiannual interest rate; therefore, 5% × $1,000 = $50 semiannual interest.
2. 20 × 2 = 40 periods to maturity.
3. 12%/2 = 6% yield to maturity, expressed on a semiannual basis.

In computing the price of the bond issued, on a semiannual analysis, we show:

Present Value of Interest Payments—We take the present value of a $50 annuity for 40 periods. The semiannual discount rate is 6 percent. Using Appendix D:

$$PV_A = A \times PV_{IFA} \quad (n = 40, i = 6\%)$$
$$PV_A = \$50 \times 15.046 = \$752.30$$

Present Value of Principal Payment at Maturity—We take the present value of $1,000 after 40 periods, using a 6 percent discount rate. Note that once we go to a semiannual analysis with the interest payments, we consistently follow the same approach in discounting back the principal payment; otherwise we would be using semiannual and annual calculations on the same bond. Using Appendix B:

$$PV = FV \times PV_{IF} \quad (n = 40, i = 6\%)$$
$$PV = \$1,000 \times .097 = \$97$$

We now add together the two values to get total present value.

Total Present Value—

Present value of interest payments	$752.30
Present value of principal payment at maturity	97.00
Total present value, or price, of the bond	$849.30

   The answer of $849.30 is slightly below what we found previously for the same bond, assuming an annual interest rate ($850.90). This value was previously shown on page 287. In terms of accuracy, the semiannual analysis is a more acceptable method and is the method used in bond tables. As is true in many finance texts, we present the annual interest rate approach first for ease of presentation, and then the semiannual basis is given. In the problems at the back of the chapter, you will be asked to do problems on both an annual and semiannual interest payment basis.

Preferred stock usually represents a **perpetuity** or, in other words, has no maturity date. It is valued in the market without any principal payment since it has no ending life. If preferred stock had a maturity date, the analysis would be similar to that of the preceding bond example. Preferred stock has a fixed dividend payment carrying a higher order of precedence than common stock dividends, but not the binding contractual obligation of interest on debt. Preferred stock, being a hybrid security, has neither the ownership privilege of common stock nor the legally enforceable provisions of debt. To value a perpetuity such as preferred stock, we first consider the formula:

Valuation and Preferred Stock

$$P_p = \frac{D_p}{(1 + K_p)^1} + \frac{D_p}{(1 + K_p)^2} + \frac{D_p}{(1 + K_p)^3} + \dots + \frac{D_p}{(1 + K_p)^\infty} \qquad (10\text{–}3)$$

where

P_p = the price of preferred stock

D_p = the annual dividend for preferred stock (a constant value)

K_p = the required rate of return, or discount rate, applied to preferred stock dividends

Note the formula calls for taking the present value of an infinite stream of constant dividend payments at a discount rate equal to K_p. Because we are dealing with an infinite stream of payments, Formula 10–3 can be reduced to a much more usable form as indicated in Formula 10–4.

$$P_p = \frac{D_p}{K_p} \qquad\qquad (10\text{–}4)$$

According to Formula 10–4, all we have to do to find the price of preferred stock (P_p) is to divide the constant annual dividend payment (D_p) by the required rate of return that preferred stockholders are demanding (K_p). For example, if the annual dividend were $10 and the stockholder required a 10 percent rate of return, the price of preferred stock would be $100.

$$P_p = \frac{D_p}{K_p} = \frac{\$10}{.10} = \$100$$

As was true in our bond valuation analysis, if the rate of return required by security holders changes, the value of the financial asset (in this case, preferred stock) will change. You may also recall that the longer the life of an investment, the greater the impact of a change in required rate of return. It is one thing to be locked into a low-paying security for one year when the rate goes up; it is quite another to be locked in for 10 or 20 years. With preferred stock, you have a *perpetual* security, so the impact is at a maximum. Assume in the prior example that because of higher inflation or increased business risk, K_p (the required rate of return) increases to 12 percent. The new value for the preferred stock shares is:

$$P_p = \frac{D_p}{K_p} = \frac{\$10}{.12} = \$83.33$$

If the required rate of return were reduced to 8 percent, the opposite effect would occur. The preferred stock price would be computed as:

$$P_p = \frac{D_p}{K_p} = \frac{\$10}{.08} = \$125$$

It is not surprising that preferred stock is now trading well above its original price of $100. It is still offering a $10 dividend (10 percent of the original offering price of $100), and the market is demanding only an 8 percent yield. To match the $10 dividend with the 8 percent rate of return, the market price will advance to $125.

Determining the Required Rate of Return (Yield) from the Market Price

In our analysis of preferred stock, we have used the value of the annual dividend (D_p) and the required rate of return (K_p) to solve for the price of preferred stock (P_p). We could change our analysis to solve for the required rate of return (K_p) as the unknown, given that we know the annual dividend (D_p) and the preferred stock price (P_p). We take Formula 10–4 and rewrite it as Formula 10–5, where the unknown is the required rate of return (K_p).

$$P_p = \frac{D_p}{K_p} \quad \text{(reverse the position of } K_p \text{ and } P_p\text{)} \tag{10–4}$$

$$K_p = \frac{D_p}{P_p} \tag{10–5}$$

Using Formula 10–5, if the annual preferred dividend (D_p) is $10 and the price of preferred stock (P_p) is $100, the required rate of return (yield) would be 10 percent as follows.

$$K_p = \frac{D_p}{P_p} = \frac{\$10}{\$100} = 10\%$$

If the price goes up to $130, the yield will be only 7.69 percent.

$$K_p = \frac{\$10}{\$130} = 7.69\%$$

We see the higher market price provides quite a decline in the yield.

The value of a share of common stock may be interpreted by the shareholder as the *present value* of an expected stream of *future dividends*. Although in the short run stockholders may be influenced by a change in earnings or other variables, the ultimate value of any holding rests with the distribution of earnings in the form of dividend payments. Though the stockholder may benefit from the retention and reinvestment of earnings by the corporation, at some point the earnings must be translated into cash flow for the stockholder. A stock valuation model based on future expected dividends, which is termed a **dividend valuation model,** can be stated as:

Valuation of Common Stock

$$P_0 = \frac{D_1}{(1 + K_e)^1} + \frac{D_2}{(1 + K_e)^2} + \frac{D_3}{(1 + K_e)^3} + \dots + \frac{D_\infty}{(1 + K_e)^\infty} \tag{10–6}$$

where

P_0 = Price of stock today
D = Dividend for each year
K_e = the required rate of return for common stock (discount rate)

This formula, with modification, is generally applied to three different circumstances:

1. No growth in dividends.
2. Constant growth in dividends.
3. Variable growth in dividends.

No Growth in Dividends

Under the no-growth circumstance, common stock is very similar to preferred stock. The common stock pays a constant dividend each year. For that reason, we merely translate the terms in Formula 10–4, which applies to preferred stock, to apply to common stock. This is shown as new Formula 10–7.

$$P_0 = \frac{D_0}{K_e} \qquad (10\text{–}7)$$

P_0 = Price of common stock today
D_0 = Current annual common stock dividend (a constant value)
K_e = Required rate of return for common stock

Assume D_0 = $1.87 and K_e = 12 percent; the price of the stock would be $15.50:

$$P_0 = \frac{\$1.87}{0.12} = \$15.58$$

A no-growth policy for common stock dividends does not hold much appeal for investors and so is seen infrequently in the real world.

Constant Growth in Dividends

A firm that increases dividends at a constant rate is a more likely circumstance. Perhaps a firm decides to increase its dividends by 5 or 7 percent per year. The general valuation approach is shown in Formula 10–8.

$$P_0 = \frac{D_0(1 + g)^1}{(1 + K_e)^1} + \frac{D_0(1 + g)^2}{(1 + K_e)^2} + \frac{D_0(1 + g)^3}{(1 + K_e)^3} + \dots + \frac{D_0(1 + g)^\infty}{(1 + K_e)^\infty} \qquad (10\text{–}8)$$

where

P_0 = Price of common stock today
$D_0(1 + g)^1$ = Dividend in year 1, D_1
$D_0(1 + g)^2$ = Dividend in year 2, D_2, and so on
g = Constant growth rate in dividends
K_e = Required rate of return for common stock (discount rate)

As shown in Formula 10–8, the current price of the stock is the present value of the future stream of dividends growing at a constant rate. If we can anticipate the growth pattern of future dividends and determine the discount rate, we can ascertain the price of the stock.

For example, assume the following information:
D_0 = Last 12-month's dividend (assume $1.87)
D_1 = First year, $2.00 (growth rate, 7%)
D_2 = Second year, $2.14 (growth rate, 7%)
D_3 = Third year, $2.29 (growth rate, 7%) etc.
K_e = Required rate of return (discount rate), 12%

then

$$P_0 = \frac{\$2.00}{(0.12)^1} + \frac{\$2.14}{(0.12)^2} + \frac{\$2.29}{(0.12)^3} + \dots + \frac{\text{Infinite dividend}}{(0.12)^\infty}$$

To find the price of the stock, we take the present value of each year's dividend. This is no small task when the formula calls for us to take the present value of an *infinite* stream of growing dividends. Fortunately Formula 10–8 above can be compressed into a much more usable form if two circumstances are satisfied.

1. The firm must have a constant dividend growth rate (g).
2. The discount rate (K_e) must exceed the growth rate (g).

For most introductory courses in finance, these assumptions are usually made to reduce the complications in the analytical process. This then allows us to reduce or rewrite Formula 10–8 as Formula 10–9. Formula 10–9 is the basic equation for finding the value of common stock and is referred to as the constant growth dividend valuation model.

$$P_0 = \frac{D_1}{K_e - g} \qquad (10\text{–}9)$$

This is an extremely easy formula to use in which:

P_0 = Price of the stock today
D_1 = Dividend at the end of the first year
K_e = Required rate of return (discount rate)
g = Constant growth rate in dividends

Based on the current example:

$D_1 = \$2.00$
$K_e = .12$
$g = .07$

and P_0 is computed as:

$$P_0 = \frac{D_1}{K_e - g} = \frac{\$2.00}{0.12 - 0.07} = \frac{\$2.00}{0.05} = \$40$$

Thus, given that the stock has a $2 dividend at the end of the first year, a discount rate of 12 percent, and a constant growth rate of 7 percent, the current price of the stock is $40.

Let's take a closer look at Formula 10–9 above and the factors that influence valuation. For example, what is the anticipated effect on valuation if K_e (the required rate of return, or discount rate) increases as a result of inflation or increased risk? Intuitively, we would expect the stock price to decline if investors demand a higher return and the dividend and growth rate remain the same. This is precisely what happens.

If D_1 remains at $2.00 and the growth rate (g) is 7 percent, but K_e increases from 12 percent to 14 percent, using Formula 10–9, the price of the common stock will now be $28.57 as shown below. This is considerably lower than its earlier value of $40.

$$P_0 = \frac{D_1}{K_e - g} = \frac{\$2.00}{0.14 - 0.07} = \frac{\$2.00}{0.07} = \$28.57$$

Similarly, if the growth rate (g) increases while D_1 and K_e remain constant, the stock price can be expected to increase. Assume $D_1 = \$2.00$, K_e is set at its earlier level of 12 percent, and g increases from 7 percent to 9 percent. Using Formula 10–9 once again, the new price of the stock would be $66.67.

$$P_0 = \frac{D_1}{K_e - g} = \frac{\$2.00}{0.12 - 0.09} = \frac{\$2.00}{0.03} = \$66.67$$

We should not be surprised to see that an increasing growth rate has enhanced the value of the stock.

Stock Valuation Based on Future Stock Value   The discussion of stock valuation to this point has related to the concept of the present value of future dividends. This is a valid concept, but suppose we wish to approach the issue from a slightly different viewpoint. Assume we are going to buy a stock and hold it for three years and then sell it. We wish to know the present value of our investment. This is somewhat like the bond valuation analysis. We will receive a dividend for three years (D_1, D_2, D_3) and then a price (payment) for the stock at the end of three years (P_3). What is the present value of the benefits? What we do is add the present value of three years of dividends and the present value of the stock price after three years. Assuming a constant growth dividend analysis, the stock price after three years is simply the present value of all future dividends after the third year (from the fourth year on). Thus the current price of the stock in this case is nothing other than the present value of the first three dividends, plus the present value of all future dividends (which is equivalent to the stock price after the third year). Saying the price of the stock is the present value of all future dividends is also the equivalent of saying it is the present value of a dividend stream for a number of years, plus the present value of the price of the stock after that time period. The appropriate formula is still $P_0 = D_1/(K_e - g)$, which we have been using throughout this part of the chapter.

Determining the Required Rate of Return from the Market Price

In our analysis of common stock, we have used the first year's dividend (D_1), the required rate of return (K_e), and the growth rate (g) to solve for the stock price (P_0) based on Formula 10–9.

$$P_0 = \frac{D_1}{K_e - g} \text{ (previously presented in Formula 10–9)}$$

We could change the analysis to solve for the required rate of return (K_e) as the unknown, given that we know the first year's dividend (D_1), the stock price (P_0), and the growth rate (g). We take the formula above and algebraically change it to provide Formula 10–10.

$$P_0 = \frac{D_1}{K_e - g} \tag{10–9}$$

$$K_e = \frac{D_1}{P_0} + g \tag{10–10}$$

Formula 10–10 allows us to compute the required return (K_e) from the investment.

Returning to the basic data from the common stock example:

K_e = Required rate of return (to be solved)
D_1 = Dividend at the end of the first year, $2.00
P_0 = Price of the stock today, $40
g = Constant growth rate .07, or 7%

$$K_e = \frac{\$2.00}{\$40} + 7\% = 5\% + 7\% = 12\%$$

In this instance we would say the stockholder demands a 12 percent return on the common stock investment. Of particular interest are the individual parts of the formula for K_e that we have been discussing. Let's write out Formula 10–10 again.

$$K_e = \frac{\text{First year's dividend}}{\text{Common stock price}} \left(\frac{D_1}{P_0}\right) + \text{Growth (g)}$$

The first term represents the **dividend yield** the stockholder will receive, and the second term represents the anticipated growth in dividends, earnings, and stock price. While we have been describing the growth rate primarily in terms of dividends, it is assumed the earnings and stock price will also grow at that same rate over the long term if all else holds constant. You should also observe that the formula above represents a total-return concept. The stockholder is receiving a current dividend plus anticipated growth in the future. If the dividend yield is low, the growth rate must be high to provide the necessary return. Conversely, if the growth rate is low, a high dividend yield will be expected. The concepts of dividend yield and growth are clearly interrelated.

The Price-Earnings Ratio Concept and Valuation

In Chapter 2 we introduced the concept of the price-earnings ratio. The **price-earnings ratio** represents a multiplier applied to current earnings to determine the value of a share of stock in the market. It is considered a pragmatic, everyday approach to valuation. If a stock has earnings per share of $3 and a price-earnings (P/E) ratio of 15 times, it will carry a market value of $45. Another company with the same earnings but a P/E ratio of 20 times will enjoy a market price of $60.

The price-earnings ratio is influenced by the earnings and sales growth of the firm, the risk (or volatility in performance), the debt-equity structure of the firm, the dividend policy, the quality of management, and a number of other factors. Firms that have bright expectations for the future tend to trade at high P/E ratios while the opposite is true for low P/E firms.

For example the average P/E ratio for all New York Stock Exchange firms was 24 in early 2006, but Amazon.com traded at a P/E of 47 because of its overall strength. Ford traded at a relatively low P/E of 9 because of anemic automobile sales.

P/E ratios can be looked up in *The Wall Street Journal* or the business section of most newspapers. Quotations from *The Wall Street Journal* are presented in Table 10–3 on page 300. The first column (Div) after the company name and symbol (Sym) shows the annual dividend, and the second column (Yld %) shows the dividend yield. This represents the annual dividend divided by the closing stock price. The next column (PE) is of primary interest in that it shows the current price-earnings ratio. For American Power Conversion Corp., which is highlighted in white, it is 27, indicating the closing stock price of $24.83 represents 27 times annual earnings.[11] The remaining columns show the daily volume, closing prices for the day, plus any changes from the previous day.

The dividend valuation approach (based on the present value of dividends) that we have been using throughout the chapter is more theoretically sound than P/E ratios and more likely to be used by sophisticated financial analysts. To some extent, the two

---

[11]The price-earnings ratio is not shown for some companies because they do not have positive earnings on which to base the calculation, or because the preferred stock of the company is shown, in which case, the P/E ratio is not relevant because preferred stock does not have earnings per share.

Table 10–3

Quotations from *The Wall Street Journal*

YTD %CHG	52-WEEK HI	LO	STOCK (SYM)	DIV	YLD %	PE	VOL 100s	CLOSE	NET CHG
19.6	56.10	21	Amerco UHAL	.53p	...	22	1229	55	1.19
-1.1	12.76	10	AmFstApt APRO	1.00	8.4	dd	z6743	11.87	-0.07
13.8	61.01	31.50	AmMov ADS A AMOV	.26e	.4	...	z6644	59.23	-0.98
-25.3	30.41	18.79	AmSvcGp ASGR s	...	...	17	z39045	20	...
↓ 7.6	35.89	26.85	AmCapStrg ACAS	3.00f	8.4	...	3856	35.88	0.16
35.6	26.20	15.17	AmDntlPtnr ADPI	...	...	23	z10148	25.71	0.56
↓ 36.2	31.92	13.75	AmEagleOut AEOS s	.19e	.6	20	22030	32.08	0.95
42.7	18	8.47	AmEcology ECOL	.40e	2.3	14	1061	17.08	-0.52
18.9	42.98	25.04	AmHlthways AMHC	...	...	40	5125	39.27	-0.11
-11.0	17.25	12.04	AmerIndep AMIC	...	...	20	z16619	13	...
-3.2	21.84	14.25	AmMedSysHldg AMMD s	...	...	cc	1923	20.24	0.33
-0.8	25.53	20.70	AmNtlBcsh AMNB	.84f	3.5	17	z4684	24.02	-0.06
12.0	120.14	89.25	AmNatIns ANAT	2.96	2.5	11	z2018	116.69	-0.26
13.0	58.73	21.28	AmPhmPtnrs APPX	...	...	45	4565	42.29	-0.25
0.4	37.99	22.69	AmPhysCap ACAP	...	...	15	1561	36.18	0.07
16.0	27.16	14.55 ♣	AmPwrConv APCC	.40	1.6	27	11339	24.83	0.23
-4.3	23.75	18.57	AmRvrBksh AMRB	.52	2.4	16	10	21.40	-0.08
2.9	49.50	18.15	AmSciEng ASEI	...	...	34	2081	42.40	-0.18
-7.5	6.80	5.01	AmSftwr A AMSWA	.28	5.0	25	z66189	5.58	-0.08
-39.4	15.13	6.91	AmSuprcnd AMSC	...	...	dd	z96059	9.02	-0.02
-1.7	22.59	16.01	AmWBcp AWBC	stk	...	23	z11803	19.90	-0.25
-27.8	48.75	27.29	AmWdmk AMWD s	.12	.4	15	1520	31.54	0.57
-7.8	25.70	19.18 ♣	AmerCarMart CRMT s	...	...	15	z13199	23.37	0.37
1.5	5.99	4.59	AmServFncl ASRV	...	...	dd	114	5.25	-0.12
27.3	29.13	11.94 ♣	AmeristarCno ASCA s	.32	1.1	23	1566	27.43	0.43
↓ 25.7	15.44	9.35	AmeriTrade A AMTD	...	...	26	813621	17.87	3.05
-5.1	65.24	52	Amgen AMGN	...	...	31	52781	60.88	-0.27
-27.2	9.05	2.87	AmkorTch AMKR	...	...	dd	20262	4.86	-0.02
-7.0	29.99	20.04	AmSurg AMSG	...	...	21	1358	27.47	0.56
-16.2	24.95	14.50 ♣	AmylinPharm AMLN	...	...	dd	27006	19.58	0.13
15.0	9.61	4.53	AnadysPharma ANDS	...	...	dd	z19917	8.61	-0.07
4.7	47.81	36.76 ♣	Analogic ALOG	.32	.7	22	1391	46.91	-0.18
-2.5	16.54	9.29	Anaren ANEN	...	...	35	z47612	12.64	0.19
↓ 3.4	29.93	24.52	AncrBcpWI ABCW	.54f	1.8	...	2962	30:13	0.24
36.0	35	16.45 ♣	Andersons ANDE	.34f	1.0	13	z9592	34.67	-0.03
-3.8	21.08	9.30	AndrewCp ANDW	...	...	57	8203	13.11	-0.04
-5.8	28.92	14.75	AndrxGp ADRX	...	...	20	12563	20.57	0.47
1.7	27.30	8.90	AngloDynmcs ANGO	...	...	58	2192	22.52	0.75
-23.9	21.43	12.65	AngiotchPhrm ANPI	...	...	16	2245	14.01	0.06
44.0	17.87	7.89	AnikaThrptcs ANIK	...	...	33	z31228	13.18	-0.14
23.9	22.50	12.08	AnimasCp PUMP	...	...	...	1251	19.37	0.46
18.6	28.69	11.83 ♣	AnsoftCp ANST	...	...	...	z33501	23.96	0.62
-26.2	**6.68**	**3.10**	answerthink ANSR	...	dd	1892		3.44	-0.23
-45.1	11.38	4.51	Antigenics AGEN	...	...	dd	1668	5.56	-0.07
13.5	16.05	9.63	ApogeeEnt APOG	.25	1.6	24	1947	15.22	-0.13
-3.1	94.31	62.55 ♣	ApolloGp A APOL	...	...	77	10768	78.19	-0.01
21.2	18.50	11.36	ApolloInv AINV	.80e	4.4	...	5129	18.30	0.24
19.7	45.44	14.37	AppleCptr AAPL s	...	...	43	148298	38.55	0.69

concepts of P/E ratios and dividend valuation models can be brought together. A stock that has a high required rate of return (K_e) because of its risky nature will generally have a low P/E ratio. Similarly, a stock with a low required rate of return (K_e) because of the predictability of positive future performance will normally have a high P/E ratio. In the first example, both methods provide a low valuation, while in the second case, both methods provide a high valuation.

Variable Growth in Dividends

In the discussion of common stock valuation, we have considered procedures for firms that had no growth in dividends and for firms that had a constant growth. Most of the discussion and literature in finance assumes a constant growth dividend model. However, there is also a third case, and that is one of variable growth in dividends. The most common variable growth model is one in which the firm experiences supernormal (very rapid) growth for a number of years and then levels off to more normal, constant growth. The **supernormal growth** pattern is often experienced by firms in emerging industries, such as in the early days of electronics or microcomputers.

Valuation of High Technology Companies— Throw Away the Book

While the valuation concepts discussed in this chapter apply to 70 to 80 percent of publicly traded companies, a different approach is necessary for high-technology, Internet-related companies. First of all, dividend payments are virtually unheard of. Consider the fact that Cisco Systems, Oracle, and almost every other company in the industry pay no cash dividends and do not intend to pay them in the foreseeable future. Under such circumstances, it is impossible to use the dividend valuation model discussed in the chapter.

What about P/E ratios? For a few select companies, valuation based on P/E ratios may be possible, but the ratios tend to be inordinately high. For most companies in the industry it is not possible to compute a P/E ratio because there are no earnings. This applies to such well-known names as Earthlink, E*TRADE, and most others. You cannot multiply a negative value (earnings) times a positive value (the P/E ratio) to arrive at a stock price.

Newer measures of valuation are replacing traditional measures. When Andy Grove of Intel was asked at an early stage of growth what his ROI (return on investment) was, he responded with the famous quote, "What's my ROI on e-commerce? Are you crazy? This is Columbus in the New World. What was his ROI?"

At the time AOL made its offer for Time Warner (January 10, 2000) for $183 billion (or 71 percent over Time Warner's market capitalization), AOL only had one-fifth of the revenue of Time Warner and 15 percent of the workforce (16,000 employees versus 82,000). It comes down to the new economy versus the old economy.

Just as traditional companies can be compared to others in their industry on the basis of their price/earnings ratios, new age companies can be compared on the basis of their price/sales ratios. These can be computed as total market capitalization over total revenue or as stock price over revenue per share. If a company has a price/sales ratio of 20 when the industry ratio is 10, then analysts view the company much more favorably than they do its competitors.

But once again, be careful. Just as companies with high P/E ratios may be great companies but not always great investments, the same may be true of high price/sales companies. The question becomes, is the high ratio justified by a superior business model or a "first mover advantage," or excess optimism?

Price-to-sales ratios can be supplemented by any number of other ratios to get a better feel for the company and its future. Other measures to take into consideration might include customer acquisition costs, page views per month, customers versus visitors, dollar value per customer, sales growth per customer, and market cap to page views. The list can go on and on. It is most important to understand the goals and objectives of the business model the company is undertaking, and how well the company is achieving its targets. Many companies that had high valuations in the last decade did not fulfill expectations.

In evaluating a firm with an initial pattern of supernormal growth, we first take the present value of dividends during the exceptional growth period. We then determine the price of the stock at the end of the supernormal growth period by taking the present value of the normal, constant dividends that follow the supernormal growth period. We discount this price to the present and add it to the present value of the supernormal dividends. This gives us the current price of the stock.

A numerical example of a supernormal growth rate evaluation model is presented in Appendix 10C at the end of this chapter.

Finally, in the discussion of common stock valuation models, readers may ask about the valuation of companies that currently pay no dividends. Since virtually all our discussion has been based on values associated with dividends, how can this "no dividend" circumstance be handled? One approach is to assume that even for the firm that

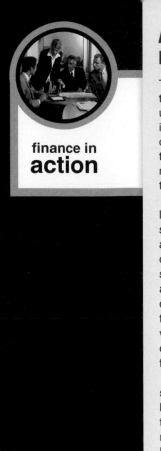
An Important Question—What's a Small Business Really Worth?

The value of a small, privately held business takes on importance when the business is put up for sale, is part of a divorce settlement, or is being valued for estate purposes at the time of the owner's death. The same basic principles that establish valuation for Fortune 500 companies apply to small businesses as well. However, there are important added considerations.

One factor is that private businesses often lack liquidity. Unlike a firm trading in the public securities market, there is no ready market for a local clothing goods store, a bowling alley, or even a doctor's clinic. Therefore, after the standard value has been determined, it is usually reduced for lack of liquidity. Although circumstances vary, the normal reduction is in the 30 percent range. Thus, a business that is valued at $100,000 on the basis of earnings or cash flow may be assigned a value of $70,000 for estate valuation purposes.

There are other factors that are important to small business valuation as well. For example, how important was a key person to the operation of a business? If the founder of the business was critical to its functioning, the firm may have little or no value in his or her absence. For example, a bridal consulting shop or a barber shop may have minimal value upon the death of the owner. On the other hand, a furniture company with established brand names or a small TV station with programming under contract may retain most of its value.

Another consideration that is important in valuing a small business is the nature of the company's earnings. They are often lower than they would be in a publicly traded company. Why? First of all, the owners of many small businesses intermingle personal expenses with business expenses. Thus, family cars, health insurance, travel, and so on, may be charged as business expenses when, in fact, they have a personal element to them. While the IRS tries to restrict such practices, there are fine lines in distinguishing between personal and business uses. As a general rule, small, private businesses try to report earnings as low as possible to minimize taxes. Contrast this with public companies that report earnings quarterly with the intent of showing ever-growing profitability. For this reason, in valuing a small, privately held company, analysts often rework stated earnings in an attempt to demonstrate earning power that is based on income less necessary expenditures. The restated earnings are usually higher.

After these and many other factors are taken into consideration, the average small, private company normally sells at 5 to 10 times average adjusted earnings for the previous three years. It is also important to identify recent sale prices of comparable companies, and business brokers may be able to supply such information. When establishing final value, many people often look to their CPA or a business consultant to determine the true worth of a firm.

pays no current dividends, at some point in the future, stockholders will be rewarded with cash dividends. We then take the present value of their deferred dividends.

A second approach to valuing a firm that pays no cash dividend is to take the present value of earnings per share for a number of periods and add that to the present value of a future anticipated stock price. The discount rate applied to future earnings is generally higher than the discount rate applied to future dividends.

Summary and Review of Formulas

The primary emphasis in this chapter is on valuation of financial assets: bonds, preferred stock, and common stock. Regardless of the security being analyzed, valuation is normally based on the concept of determining the present value of future cash flows. Thus we draw on many of the time-value-of-money techniques developed in Chapter 9. Inherent in the valuation process is a determination of the rate of return that investors demand. When we have computed this value, we have also identified what it will cost the corporation to raise new capital. Let's specifically review the valuation techniques associated with bonds, preferred stock, and common stock.

Bonds

The price, or current value, of a bond is equal to the present value of interest payments (I_t) over the life of the bond plus the present value of the principal payment (P_n) at maturity. The discount rate used in the analytical process is the yield to maturity (Y). The yield to maturity (required rate of return) is determined in the marketplace by such factors as the real rate of return, an inflation premium, and a risk premium.

The equation for bond valuation was presented as Formula 10–1.

$$P_b = \sum_{t=1}^{n} \frac{I_t}{(1+Y)^t} + \frac{P_n}{(1+Y)^n} \qquad (10\text{–}1)$$

The actual terms in the equation are solved by the use of present value tables. We say the present value of interest payments is:

$$PV_A = A \times PV_{IFA} \quad \text{(Appendix D)}$$

The present value of the principal payment at maturity is:

$$PV = FV \times PV_{IF} \quad \text{(Appendix B)}$$

We add these two values together to determine the price of the bond. We use both annual or semiannual analysis.

The value of the bond will be strongly influenced by the relationship of the yield to maturity in the market to the interest rate on the bond and also the length of time to maturity.

If you know the price of the bond, the size of the interest payments, and the maturity of the bond, you can solve for the yield to maturity through a trial and error approach (discussed in the chapter and expanded in Appendix 10A), by an approximation approach as presented in Formula 10–2, or by using financially oriented calculators (in Appendix 10B at the end of the chapter) or appropriate computer software.

Preferred Stock

In determining the value of preferred stock, we are taking the present value of an infinite stream of level dividend payments. This would be a tedious process if the mathematical calculations could not be compressed into a simple formula. The appropriate equation is Formula 10–4.

$$P_p = \frac{D_p}{K_p} \qquad (10\text{–}4)$$

According to Formula 10–4, to find the preferred stock price (P_p) we take the constant annual dividend payment (D_p) and divide this value by the rate of return that preferred stockholders are demanding (K_p).

If, on the other hand, we know the price of the preferred stock and the constant annual dividend payment, we can solve for the required rate of return on preferred stock as:

$$K_p = \frac{D_p}{P_p} \qquad (10\text{–}5)$$

Common Stock

The value of common stock is also based on the concept of the present value of an expected stream of future dividends. Unlike preferred stock, the dividends are not necessarily level. The firm and shareholders may experience:

1. No growth in dividends.
2. Constant growth in dividends.
3. Variable or supernormal growth in dividends.

It is the second circumstance that receives most of the attention in the financial literature. If a firm has constant growth (g) in dividends (D) and the required rate of return (K_e) exceeds the growth rate, Formula 10–9 can be utilized.

$$P_0 = \frac{D_1}{K_e - g} \tag{10–9}$$

In using Formula 10–9, all we need to know is the value of the dividend at the end of the first year, the required rate of return, and the discount rate. Most of our valuation calculations with common stock utilize Formula 10–9.

If we need to know the required rate of return (K_e) for common stock, Formula 10–10 can be employed.

$$K_e = \frac{D_1}{P_0} + g \tag{10–10}$$

The first term represents the dividend yield on the stock and the second term the growth rate. Together they provide the total return demanded by the investor.

List of Terms

required rate of return 283	financial risk 286
yield to maturity 285	perpetuity 293
real rate of return 285	dividend valuation model 295
inflation premium 285	dividend yield 299
risk-free rate of return 285	price-earnings ratio 299
risk premium 286	supernormal growth 300
business risk 286	

Discussion Questions

1. How is valuation of any financial asset related to future cash flows?
2. Why might investors demand a lower rate of return for an investment in ExxonMobil as compared to United Airlines?
3. What are the three factors that influence the required rate of return by investors?
4. If inflationary expectations increase, what is likely to happen to yield to maturity on bonds in the marketplace? What is also likely to happen to the price of bonds?

5. Why is the remaining time to maturity an important factor in evaluating the impact of a change in yield to maturity on bond prices?

6. What are the three adjustments that have to be made in going from annual to semiannual bond analysis?

7. Why is a change in required yield for preferred stock likely to have a greater impact on price than a change in required yield for bonds?

8. What type of dividend pattern for common stock is similar to the dividend payment for preferred stock?

9. What two conditions must be met to go from Formula 10–8 to Formula 10–9 in using the dividend valuation model?

$$P_0 = \frac{D_1}{K_e - g} \qquad (10\text{--}9)$$

10. What two components make up the required rate of return on common stock?

11. What factors might influence a firm's price-earnings ratio?

12. How is the supernormal growth pattern likely to vary from the normal, constant growth pattern?

13. What approaches can be taken in valuing a firm's stock when there is no cash dividend payment?

---

1. The Titan Corp. issued a $1,000 par value bond paying 8 percent interest with 15 years to maturity. Assume the current yield to maturity on such bonds is 10 percent. What is the price of the bond? Do annual analysis.

2. Host Corp. will pay a $2.40 dividend ($D_1$) in the next 12 months. The required rate of return (K_e) is 13 percent and the constant growth rate (g) is 5 percent.

    a. Compute the stock price (P_0).

    b. If K_e goes up to 15 percent, and all else remains the same, what will be the stock price (P_0)?

    c. Now assume in the next year, $D_1 = \$2.70$, $K_e = 12$ percent, and g is equal to 6 percent. What is the price of the stock?

Practice Problems and Solutions

Bond value

Common stock value

Solutions

1. **Present Value of Interest Payments**

    $PV_A = A \times PV_{IFA}$ $(n = 15, i = 10\%)$ Appendix D

    $PV_A = \$80 \times 7.606 = \$608.48$

    Present Value of Principal Payment at Maturity

    $PV = FV \times PV_{IF}$ $(n = 15, i = 10\%)$ Appendix B

    $PV = \$1,000 \times .239 = \$239$

    Total Present Value (Bond Price)

Present value of interest payments	$608.48
Present value of principal payment at maturity	239.00
Bond price	$847.48

2.
$$P_0 = \frac{D_1}{K_e - g} \qquad (10\text{--}9)$$

a. $P_0 = \dfrac{\$2.40}{0.13 - 0.05} = \dfrac{\$2.40}{0.08} = \$30.00$

b. $P_0 = \dfrac{\$2.40}{0.15 - 0.05} = \dfrac{\$2.40}{0.10} = \$24.00$

c. $P_0 = \dfrac{\$2.70}{0.12 - 0.06} = \dfrac{\$2.70}{0.06} = \$45.00$

Problems

:=:=:TM All problems are available in Homework Manager. Please see the preface for more information.

(For the first 18 bond problems, assume interest payments are on an annual basis.)

Bond value
1. The Lone Star Company has $1,000 par value bonds outstanding at 9 percent interest. The bonds will mature in 20 years. Compute the current price of the bonds if the present yield to maturity is:
    a. 6 percent.
    b. 8 percent.
    c. 12 percent.

Bond value
2. Applied Software has $1,000 par value bonds outstanding at 12 percent interest. The bonds will mature in 25 years. Compute the current price of the bonds if the present yield to maturity is:
    a. 11 percent.
    b. 13 percent.
    c. 16 percent.

Bond value
3. Barry's Steroids Company has $1,000 par value bonds outstanding at 12 percent interest. The bonds will mature in 50 years. Compute the current price of the bonds if the percent yield to maturity is:
    a. 4 percent.
    b. 14 percent.

Bond value
4. Referring back to Problem 3, part *b,* what percent of the total bond value does the repayment of principal represent?

Bond value
5. Essex Biochemical Co. has a $1,000 par value bond outstanding that pays 10 percent annual interest. The current yield to maturity on such bonds in the market is 7 percent. Compute the price of the bonds for these maturity dates:
    a. 30 years.
    b. 15 years.
    c. 1 year.

Bond value
6. The Hartford Telephone Company has a $1,000 par value bond outstanding that pays 11 percent annual interest. The current yield to maturity on such bonds in the market is 14 percent. Compute the price of the bonds for these maturity dates:

    a. 30 years.

    b. 15 years.

    c. 1 year.

7. For Problem 6 graph the relationship in a manner similar to the bottom half of Figure 10–2 on page 290. Also explain why the pattern of price change takes place.

    Bond maturity effect

8. Go to Table 10–1 on page 288 which is based on bonds paying 10 percent interest for 20 years. Assume interest rates in the market (yield to maturity) go from 12 percent to 9 percent:

    Interest rate effect

    a. What is the bond price at 12 percent?

    b. What is the bond price at 9 percent?

    c. What would be your percentage return on investment if you bought when rates were 12 percent and sold when rates were 9 percent?

9. Using Table 10–2 on page 289:

    Effect of maturity on bond price

    a. Assume the interest rate in the market (yield to maturity) goes down to 8 percent for the 10 percent bonds. Using column 2, indicate what the bond price will be with a 5-year, a 15-year, and a 30-year time period.

    b. Assume the interest rate in the market (yield to maturity) goes up to 12 percent for the 10 percent bonds. Using column 3, indicate what the bond price will be with a 5-year, a 10-year, and a 30-year period.

    c. Based on the information in part *a,* if you think interest rates in the market are going down, which bond would you choose to own?

    d. Based on information in part *b,* if you think interest rates in the market are going up, which bond would you choose to own?

10. Ron Rhodes calls his broker to inquire about purchasing a bond of Golden Years Recreation Corporation. His broker quotes a price of $1,170. Ron is concerned that the bond might be overpriced based on the facts involved. The $1,000 par value bond pays 13 percent interest, and it has 18 years remaining until maturity. The current yield to maturity on similar bonds is 11 percent.

    Bond value

    Do you think the bond is overpriced? Do the necessary calculations.

11. Tom Cruise Lines, Inc., issued bonds five years ago at $1,000 per bond. These bonds had a 25-year life when issued and the annual interest payment was then 12 percent. This return was in line with the required returns by bondholders at that point as described below:

    Effect of yield to maturity on bond price

Real rate of return	3%
Inflation premium	5
Risk premium	4
Total return	12%

Assume that five years later the inflation premium is only 3 percent and is appropriately reflected in the required return (or yield to maturity) of the bonds. The bonds have 20 years remaining until maturity. Compute the new price of the bond.

Analyzing bond price changes

12. Further analysis of Problem 11.

   a. Find the present value of 2 percent × $1,000 (or $20) for 20 years at 10 percent. The $20 is assumed to be an annual payment.

   b. Add this value to $1,000.

   c. Explain why the answers to problem 12*b* and problem 11 are basically the same. (There is a slight difference due to rounding in the tables.)

Effect of yield to maturity on bond price

13. Media Bias, Inc. issued bonds 10 years ago at $1,000 per bond. These bonds had a 35-year life when issued and the annual interest payment was then 10 percent. This return was in line with the required returns by bondholders at that point in time as described below:

Real rate of return	2%
Inflation premium	4
Risk premium	4
Total return	10%

Assume that 10 years later, due to good publicity, the risk premium is now 2 percent and is appropriately reflected in the required return (or yield to maturity) of the bonds. The bonds have 25 years remaining until maturity. Compute the new price of the bond.

Effect of yield to maturity on bond price

14. Wilson Oil Company issued bonds five years ago at $1,000 per bond. These bonds had a 25-year life when issued and the annual interest payment was then 8 percent. This return was in line with the required returns by bondholders at that point in time as described below:

Real rate of return	2%
Inflation premium	3
Risk premium	3
Total return	8%

Assume that 10 years later, due to bad publicity, the risk premium is now 6 percent and is appropriately reflected in the required return (or yield to maturity) of the bonds. The bonds have 15 years remaining until maturity. Compute the new price of the bond.

Deep discount bonds

15. Lance Whittingham IV specializes in buying deep discount bonds. These represent bonds that are trading at well below part value. He has his eye on a bond issued by the Leisure Time Corporation. The $1,000 par value bond pays 4 percent annual interest and has 16 years remaining to maturity. The current yield to maturity on similar bonds is 10 percent.

   a. What is the current price of the bonds?

   b. By what percent will the price of the bonds increase between now and maturity?

   c. What is the annual compound rate of growth in the value of the bonds? (An approximate answer is acceptable.)

16. Bonds issued by the Coleman Manufacturing Company have a par value of $1,000, which, of course, is also the amount of principal to be paid at maturity. The bonds are currently selling for $850. They have 10 years remaining to maturity. The annual interest payment is 8 percent ($80).

    Compute the approximate yield to maturity, using Formula 10–2.

Approximate yield to maturity

17. Bonds issued by the Tyler Food Corporation have a par value of $1,000, are selling for $1,080, and have 20 years remaining to maturity. The annual interest payment is 12.5 percent ($125).

    Compute the approximate yield to maturity, using Formula 10–2.

Approximate yield to maturity

18. Optional—for Problem 17, use the techniques in Appendix 10A to combine a trial-and-error approach with interpolation to find a more exact answer. You may choose to use a handheld calculator instead.

More exact yield to maturity

(For the next two problems, assume interest payments are on a semiannual basis.)

19. Heather Smith is considering a bond investment in Locklear Airlines. The $1,000 par value bonds have a quoted annual interest rate of 9 percent and interest is paid semiannually. The yield to maturity on the bonds is 12 percent annual interest. There are 15 years to maturity. Compute the price of the bonds based on semiannual analysis.

Bond value—semiannual analysis

20. You are called in as a financial analyst to appraise the bonds of Olsen's Clothing Stores. The $1,000 par value bonds have a quoted annual interest rate of 13 percent, which is paid semiannually. The yield to maturity on the bonds is 10 percent annual interest. There are 25 years to maturity.

    a. Compute the price of the bonds based on semiannual analysis.

    b. With 20 years to maturity, if yield to maturity goes down substantially to 8 percent, what will be the new price of the bonds?

Bond value—semiannual analysis

21. The preferred stock of Denver Savings and Loan pays an annual dividend of $5.60. It has a required rate of return of 8 percent. Compute the price of the preferred stock.

Preferred stock value

22. Bedford Mattress Company issued preferred stock many years ago. It carries a fixed dividend of $8 per share. With the passage of time, yields have gone down from the original 8 percent to 6 percent (yield is the same as required rate of return).

    a. What was the original issue price?

    b. What is the current value of this preferred stock?

Preferred stock value

23. X-Tech Company issued preferred stock many years ago. It carries a fixed dividend of $5.00 per share. With the passage of time, yields have soared from the original 5 percent to 12 percent (yield is the same as required rate of return).

    a. What was the original issue price?

    b. What is the current value of this preferred stock?

    c. If the yield on the Standard & Poor's Preferred Stock Index declines, how will the price of the preferred stock be affected?

Preferred stock value

24. Grant Hillside Homes, Inc., has preferred stock outstanding that pays an annual dividend of $9.80. Its price is $110. What is the required rate of return (yield) on the preferred stock?

Preferred stock rate of return

(All of the following problems pertain to the common stock section of the chapter.)

Common
stock value

X 25. Stagnant Iron and Steel currently pays a $4.20 annual cash dividend (D_0). They plan to maintain the dividend at this level for the foreseeable future as no future growth is anticipated. If the required rate of return by common stockholders (K_e) is 12 percent, what is the price of the common stock?

Common stock
value

26. Laser Optics will pay a common stock dividend of $1.60 at the end of the year (D_1). The required rate of return on common stock (K_e) is 13 percent. The firm has a constant growth rate (g) of 7 percent. Compute the current price of the stock (P_0).

Common
stock value
under different
market conditions

X 27. Ecology Labs, Inc., will pay a dividend of $3 per share in the next 12 months (D_1). The required rate of return (K_e) is 10 percent and the constant growth rate is 5 percent.

a. Compute P_0.

(For parts *b, c, d* in this problem, all variables remain the same except the one specifically changed. Each question is independent of the others.)

b. Assume K_e, the required rate of return, goes up to 12 percent; what will be the new value of P_0?

c. Assume the growth rate (g) goes up to 7 percent; what will be the new value of P_0? K_e goes back to its original value of 10 percent.

d. Assume D_1 is $3.50; what will be the new value of P_0? Assume K_e is at its original value of 10 percent and g goes back to its original value of 5 percent.

Common stock
value

28. Sterling Corp. paid a dividend of $.80 last year. Over the next 12 months, the dividend is expected to grow at a rate of 10 percent, which is the constant growth rate for the firm (g). The new dividend after 12 months will represent D_1. The required rate of return (K_e) is 14 percent. Compute the price of the stock (P_0).

Common stock
value based on
determining
growth rate

29. Justin Cement Company has had the following pattern of earnings per share over the last five years:

Year	Earnings per Share
2003	$4.00
2004	4.20
2005	4.41
2006	4.63
2007	4.86

The earnings per share have grown at a constant rate (on a rounded basis) and will continue to do so in the future. Dividends represent 40 percent of earnings. Project earnings and dividends for the next year (2008).

If the required rate of return (K_e) is 13 percent, what is the anticipated stock price (P_0) at the beginning of 2008?

Common
stock required
rate of return

X 30. A firm pays a $3.80 dividend at the end of year one (D_1), has a stock price of $50, and a constant growth rate (g) of 4 percent. Compute the required rate of return (K_e).

31. A firm pays a $1.50 dividend at the end of year one (D_1), has a stock price of $60 ($P_0$), and a constant growth rate (g) of 8 percent.

    a. Compute the required rate of return (K_e).

    Indicate whether each of the following changes would make the required rate of return (K_e) go up or down. (Each question is separate from the others. That is, assume only one variable changes at a time.) No actual numbers are necessary.

    b. The dividend payment increases.

    c. The expected growth rate increases.

    d. The stock price increases.

Common stock required rate of return

32. Hunter Petroleum Corporation paid a $2 dividend last year. The dividend is expected to grow at a constant rate of 5 percent over the next three years. The required rate of return is 12 percent (this will also serve as the discount rate in this problem). Round all values to three places to the right of the decimal point where appropriate.

    a. Compute the anticipated value of the dividends for the next three years. That is, compute D_1, D_2, and D_3; for example, D_1 is $2.10 ($2.00 × 1.05).

    b. Discount each of these dividends back to the present at a discount rate of 12 percent and then sum them.

    c. Compute the price of the stock at the end of the third year (P_3).

    $$P_3 = \frac{D_4}{K_e - g}$$

    (D_4 is equal to D_3 times 1.05)

    d. After you have computed P_3, discount it back to the present at a discount rate of 12 percent for three years.

    e. Add together the answers in part *b* and part *d* to get P_0, the current value of the stock. This answer represents the present value of the first three periods of dividends, plus the present value of the price of the stock after three periods (which, in turn, represents the value of all future dividends).

    f. Use Formula 10–9 to show that it will provide approximately the same answer as part *e*.

    $$P_0 = \frac{D_1}{K_e - g} \qquad (10\text{–}9)$$

    For Formula 10–9 use D_1 = $2.10, K_e = 12 percent, and g = 5 percent. (The slight difference between the answers to part *e* and part *f* is due to rounding.)

Common stock value based on PV calculations

33. Beasley Ball Bearings paid a $4 dividend last year. The dividend is expected to grow at a constant rate of 6 percent over the next four years. The required rate of return is 13 percent (this will also serve as the discount rate in this problem). Round all values to three places to the right of the decimal point where appropriate.

    a. Compute the anticipated value of the dividends for the next four years. That is, compute D_1, D_2, D_3, and D_4; for example D_1 is $4.24 ($4 × 1.06).

    b. Discount each of these dividends back to present at a discount rate of 13 percent and then sum them.

Common stock value based on PV calculations

www.mhhe.com/bh12e

c. Compute the price of the stock at the end of the fourth year (P_4).

$$P_4 = \frac{D_5}{K_e - g}$$

(D_5 is equal to D_4 times 1.06)

d. After you have computed P_4, discount it back to the present at a discount rate of 13 percent for four years.

e. Add together the answers in part *b* and part *d* to get P_0, the current value of the stock. This answer represents the present value of the four periods of dividends, plus the present value of the price of the stock after four periods, (which, in turn, represents the value of all future dividends).

f. Use Formula 10–9 to show that it will provide approximately the same answer as part *e*.

$$P_0 = \frac{D_1}{K_e - g}$$

For Formula 10–9 use $D_1 = \$4.24$, $K_e = 13$ percent, and $g = 6$ percent. (The slight difference between the answers to part *e* and part *f* is due to rounding.)

g. If current EPS were equal to $5.70 and the P/E ratio is 1.2 times higher than the industry average of 9, what would the stock price be?

h. By what dollar amount is the stock price in part *g* different from the stock price in part *f*?

i. In regard to the stock price in part *f*, indicate which direction it would move if (1) D_1 increases, (2) K_e increases, (3) g increases.

COMPREHENSIVE PROBLEM

Healthy Products (Dividend valuation model, P/E ratio)

Allie Reynolds, the Chief Financial Officer of Healthy Products, Inc., has been asked to do an evaluation of Fiber Cereals, Inc., by the President and Chairman of the Board, Gail Martinez. Healthy Products was planning a joint venture with Fiber Cereals (which was privately traded), and Gail and Allie needed a better feel for Fiber Cereals' common stock value because they thought they might be interested in buying the firm in the future.

Fiber Cereals paid a dividend at the end of year 1 of $1.20; the anticipated growth rate was 10 percent; and the required rate of return was 13 percent.

a. What is the value of the stock based on the dividend valuation model (Formula 10–9 on page 297)?

b. Indicate that the value you computed in part *a* is correct by showing the value of D_1, D_2, and D_3 and discounting each to the present 13 percent. D_1 is $1.20 and it increases by 10 percent (g) each year. Also discount back the anticipated stock price at the end of year 3 to the present and add it to the present value of the three dividend payments.

The value of the stock at the end of year 3 is:

$$P_3 = \frac{D_4}{K_e - g} \qquad D_4 = D_3(1 + g)$$

If you have done all these steps correctly, you should get an answer approximately equal to the answer in part *a*.

c. As an alternative measure, you also examine the value of the firm based on the price-earnings (P/E) ratio times earnings per share.

   Since the company is privately traded (not in the public stock market), you will get your anticipated P/E ratio by taking the average value of five publicly traded food industry companies. These P/E ratios were as follows during the time period under analysis:

	P/E Ratio
Del Monte.	12
General Mills	15
Heinz	14
Kellogg.	22
Kraft	17

   Assume Fiber Cereals has earnings per share of $2.45. What is the stock value based on the P/E ratio approach? Multiply the average P/E ratio you computed times earnings per share. How does this value compare to the dividend valuation model values that you computed in parts *a* and *b*?

d. If in computing the industry average P/E, you decide to weight Kellogg by 40 percent and the other four firms by 15 percent, what would be the new weighted average industry P/E? (Note: You decided to weight Kellogg more heavily because it is similar to Fiber Cereals.) What will the new stock price be? Earnings per share will stay at $2.45.

e. By what percent will the stock price change as a result of using the weighted average industry P/E ratio in part *d* as opposed to that in part *c*?

WEB EXERCISE

Dow Chemical was referred to at the beginning of the chapter as a firm that had a low valuation in the marketplace. Go to **finance.yahoo.com** and type Dow into the "Get Quotes" box.

1. Click on the "Profile" section on the home page and write a one paragraph description of the company's activities.

2. Return to the home page and write down the company's P/E ratio. Is it still relatively low (under 20)?

3. Click on "Competitors" and compare Dow to DuPont (DD) based on the P/E ratio and the PEG ratio (the P/E ratio divided by annual growth). Are Dow's ratios higher or lower than Du Pont's?

4. Go back to the home page. Is the stock up or down from the prior day? (See "change" on the home page).

5. What is its 52-week range?

6. Scroll down and click on "Analysts Opinion." What is the Mean Target, the High Target, and the Low Target? How many brokers follow the firm?

Note: From time to time, companies redesign their Web sites and occasionally a topic we have listed may have been deleted, updated, or moved into a different location. If you click on the site map or site index, you will be introduced to a table of contents which should aid you in finding the topic you are looking for.

APPENDIX | 10A

The Bond Yield to Maturity Using Interpolation

We will use a numerical example to demonstrate this process. Assume a 20-year bond pays $118 per year (11.8 percent) in interest and $1,000 after 20 years in principal repayment. The current price of the bond is $1,085. We wish to determine the yield to maturity or discount rate that equates the future flows with the current price.

Since the bond is trading above par value at $1,085, we can assume the yield to maturity must be below the quoted interest rate of 11.8 percent (the yield to maturity would be the full 11.8 percent at a bond price of $1,000). As a first approximation, we will try 10 percent. Annual analysis is used.

Present Value of Interest Payments—

$$PV_A = A \times PV_{IFA} \quad (n = 20, i = 10\%) \quad \text{(Appendix D)}$$
$$PV_A = \$118 \times 8.514 = \$1,004.65$$

Present Value of Principal Payment at Maturity—

$$PV = FV \times PV_{IF} \quad (n = 20, i = 10\%) \quad \text{(Appendix B)}$$
$$PV = \$1,000 \times .149 = \$149$$

Total Present Value—

Present value of interest payments	$1,004.65
Present value of principal payment at maturity	149.00
Total present value, or price, of the bond	$1,153.65

The discount rate of 10 percent gives us too high a present value in comparison to the current bond price of $1,085. Let's try a higher discount rate to get a lower price. We will use 11 percent.

Present Value of Interest Payments—

$$PV_A = A \times PV_{IFA} \quad (n = 20, i = 11\%) \quad \text{(Appendix D)}$$
$$PV_A = \$118 \times 7.963 = \$939.63$$

Present Value of Principal Payment at Maturity—

$$PV = FV \times PV_{IF} \quad (n = 20, i = 11\%) \quad \text{(Appendix B)}$$
$$PV = \$1,000 \times .124 = \$124$$

Total Present Value—

Present value of interest payments.	$ 939.63
Present value of principal payment at maturity	124.00
Total present value, or price, of the bond.	$1,063.63

The discount rate of 11 percent gives us a value slightly lower than the bond price of $1,085. The rate for the bond must fall between 10 and 11 percent. Using linear interpolation, the answer is 10.76 percent

$1,153.65 PV @ 10%	$1,153.65 PV @ 10%
1,063.63 PV @ 11%	1,085.00 bond price
$ 90.02	$ 68.65

$$10\% + \frac{\$68.65}{\$90.02}(1\%) = 10\% + .76(1\%) = 10.76\%$$

Problem

Yield to maturity and interpolation

10A–1. Bonds issued by the Peabody Corporation have a par value of $1,000, are selling for $890, and have 18 years to maturity. The annual interest payment is 8 percent.

Find yield to maturity by combining the trial-and-error approach with interpolation, as shown in this appendix. (Use an assumption of annual interest payments.)

APPENDIX   I   10B

Using Calculators for Financial Analysis

This appendix is designed to help you use either an algebraic calculator (Texas Instruments BA-35 Student Business Analyst or the Hewlett-Packard 12C financial calculator). We realize that most calculators come with comprehensive instructions, and this appendix is meant only to provide basic instructions for commonly used financial calculations.

There are always two things to do before starting your calculations as indicated in the first table: Clear the calculator and set the decimal point. If you do not want to lose data stored in memory, do not perform steps 2 and 3 in the first box on page 316.

Each step is listed vertically as a number followed by a decimal point. After each step you will find either a number or a calculator function denoted by a box [ ]. Entering the number on your calculator is one step and entering the function is another. Notice that the HP 12C is color coded. When two boxes are found one after another, you may have an [f] or a [g] in the first box. An [f] is orange coded and refers to the orange functions above the keys. After typing the $\boxed{f}$ function, you will automatically look for an orange coded key to punch. For example, after $\boxed{f}$ in the first Hewlett-Packard box (right-hand panel), you will punch in the orange color coded $\boxed{\text{REG}}$. If the $\boxed{f}$ function is not followed by another box, you merely type in $\boxed{f}$ and the value indicated.

	Texas Instruments BA-35	Hewlett-Packard 12C
First clear the calculator	1. $\boxed{\text{ON/C}}$ $\boxed{\text{ON/C}}$ 2. 0 3. $\boxed{\text{STO}}$ Clears memory	1. $\boxed{\text{CLX}}$ Clears screen 2. $\boxed{f}$ 3. $\boxed{\text{REG}}$ Clears memory
Set the decimal point The TI BA-35 has two choices: 2 decimal points or variable decimal points. The screen will indicate Dec 2 or the decimal will be variable. The HP 12C allows you to choose the number of decimal points. If you are uncertain, just provide the indicated input exactly as shown on the right.	1. $\boxed{\text{2nd}}$ 2. $\boxed{\text{STO}}$	1. $\boxed{f}$ 2. 4 (# of decimals)

The $\boxed{g}$ is coded blue and refers to the functions on the bottom of the function keys. After the $\boxed{g}$ function key, you will automatically look for blue coded keys. This first occurs later in the appendix.

Familiarize yourself with the keyboard before you start. In the more complicated calculations, keystrokes will be combined into one step.

In the first four calculations that follow, we simply instruct you how to get the interest factors for Appendixes A, B, C, and D. We have chosen to use examples as our method of instruction.

	Texas Instruments BA-35	Hewlett-Packard 12C
A. Appendix A Future value of $1 i = 9% or .09; n = 5 years $FV_{IF} = (1 + i)^n$ Future value = Present value $\times$ FV_{IF} $FV = PV \times FV_{IF}$ Check the answer against the number in Appendix A. Numbers in the appendix are rounded. Try different rates and years.	To find interest factor 1. 1 2. + 3. 09 (interest rate) 4. $\boxed{=}$ 5. $\boxed{y^x}$ 6. 5 (# of periods) 7. = answer 1.538624	To find interest factor 1. 1 2. $\boxed{\text{enter}}$ 3. .09 (interest rate) 4. + 5. 5 (# of periods) 6. $\boxed{y^x}$ Answer 1.5386

		Texas Instruments BA-35	**Hewlett-Packard 12C**
B.	Appendix B Present value of $1 $i = 9\%$ or .09; $n = 5$ years $PV_{IF} = 1/(1 + i)^n$ Present value = Future value $\times$ PV$_{IF}$ $PV = FV \times PV_{IF}$ Check the answer against the number in Appendix B. Numbers in the appendix are rounded.	To find interest factor Repeat steps 1 through 7 above. Continue with step 8. 8. \[1/x \] Answer .6499314	To find interest factor Repeat steps 1 through 6 above. Continue with step 7. 7. \[1/x \] Answer .6499

		Texas Instruments BA-35	**Hewlett-Packard 12C**
C.	Appendix C Future value of an annuity of $1 $i = 9\%$ or .09; $n = 5$ years $FV_{IFA} = \dfrac{(1 + i)^n - 1}{i}$ Future value = Annuity $\times$ FV$_{IFA}$ $FV_A = A \times FV_{IFA}$ Check your answer with Appendix C. Repeat example using different numbers and check your results with the number in Appendix C. Numbers in appendix are rounded.	To find interest factor Repeat steps 1 through 7 in part *A* of this section. Continue with step 8. 8. \[− \] 9. 1 10. \[= \] 11. \[÷ \] 12. .09 13. \[= \] Answer 5.9847106	To find interest factor Repeat steps 1 through 6 in part *A* of this section. Continue with step 7. 7. 1 8. \[− \] 9. .09 10. \[÷ \] Answer 5.9847

		Texas Instruments BA-35	**Hewlett-Packard 12C**
D.	Appendix D Present value of an annuity of $1 $i = 9\%$ or .09; $n = 5$ years $PV_{IFA} = \dfrac{1 - [1/(1 + i)^n]}{i}$ Present value = Annuity $\times$ PV$_{IFA}$ $PV_A = A \times PV_{IFA}$ Check your answer with Appendix D. Repeat example using different numbers and check your results with the number in Appendix D. Numbers in appendix are rounded.	To find interest factor Repeat steps 1 through 8 in parts *A* & *B*. Continue with step 9. 9. \[− \] 10. 1 11. \[= \] 12. \[+/− \] 13. \[÷ \] 14. .09 15. \[= \] Answer 3.8896513	To find interest factor Repeat steps 1 through 7 in parts *A* & *B*. Continue with step 8. 8. 1 9. \[− \] 10. \[CHS \] 11. .09 12. \[÷ \] Answer 3.8897

On the following pages, you can determine bond valuation, yield to maturity, net present value of an annuity, net present value of an uneven cash flow, internal rate of return for an annuity, and internal rate of return for an uneven cash flow.

Bond Valuation Using Both the TI BA-35 and the HP 12C

Solve for P_b = Price of the bond
Given:

I_t = \$80 annual coupon payments or 8% coupon (\$40 semiannually)
P_n = \$1,000 principal (par value)
n = 10 years to maturity (20 periods semiannually)
Y = 9.0% yield to maturity or required rate of return (4.5% semiannually)

You may choose to refer to Chapter 10 for a complete discussion of bond valuation.

	Texas Instruments BA-35	Hewlett-Packard 12C

BOND VALUATION
 	
All steps begin with number 1.
 	
Numbers following each step are keystrokes followed by a box ☐.
 	
Each box represents a keystroke and indicates which calculator function is performed.
 	
The Texas Instruments calculator requires that data be adjusted for semiannual compounding, otherwise it assumes annual compounding.
 	
The Hewlett-Packard 12C internally assumes that semiannual compounding is used and requires annual data to be entered. The HP 12C is more detailed in that it requires the actual day, month, and year. If you want an answer for a problem that requires a given number of years (e.g., 10 years), simply start on a date of your choice and end on the same date 10 years later, as in the example.
	Set finance mode [2nd] [FIN]
	
	Set decimal to 2 places
	
	    Decimal
	
	[2nd] [STO]
	
	1. 40 (semiannual coupon)
	
	2. [PMT]
	
	3. 4.5 (yield to maturity)
	    semiannual basis
	
	4. [% i]
	
	5. 1000 (principal)
	
	6. [FV]
	
	7. 20 (semiannual periods to maturity)
	
	8. [N]
	
	9. [CPT]
	
	10. [PV] Answer 934.96
	
	Answer is given in dollars, rather than % of par value.
		Clear memory [f] [REG]
		
		Set decimal to 3 places
		
		[f] [3]
		
		1. 9.0 (yield to maturity)
		
		2. [i]
		
		3. 8.0 (coupon in percent)
		
		4. [PMT]
		
		5. 1.092007 (today's date
		        month–day–year)*
		
		6. [enter]
		
		7. 1.092017 (maturity date
		        month–day–year)*
		
		8. [f]
		
		9. [Price] Answer 93.496
		
		Answer is given as % of par value and equals \$934.96.
		
		If Error message occurs, clear memory and start over.
		
		*See instructions in the third paragraph of the first column.

Yield to Maturity on Both the TI BA-35 and HP 12C

Solve for Y = Yield to maturity
Given:

P_b = \$895.50 price of bond
I_t = \$80 annual coupon payments or 8% coupon (\$40 semiannually)
P_n = \$1,000 principal (par value)
n = 10 years to maturity (20 periods semiannually)

You may choose to refer to Chapter 10 for a complete discussion of yield to maturity.

YIELD TO MATURITY	Texas Instruments BA-35	Hewlett-Packard 12C
All steps are numbered. All numbers following each step are keystrokes followed by a box ☐. Each box represents a keystroke and indicates which calculator function is performed.	Set finance mode 2nd FIN Set decimal to 2 places Decimal 2nd STO 1. 20 (semiannual periods) 2. N 3. 1000 (par value) 4. FV 5. 40 (semiannual coupon) 6. PMT 7. 895.50 (bond price) 8. PV 9. CPT 10. % i Answer 4.83% 11. × 12. 2 13. = Answer 9.65% (annual rate)	Clear memory f REG Set decimal f 2 1. 89.55 (bond price as a percent of par) 2. PV 3. 8.0 (annual coupon in %) 4. PMT 5. 1.092007 (today's date month–day–year)* 6. enter 7. 1.092017 (maturity date month–day–year)* 8. f 9. YTM Answer 9.65% In case you receive an Error message, you have probably made a keystroke error. Clear the memory f REG and start over. *See instructions in the third paragraph of the first column

The Texas Instruments BA-35 does not internally compute a semiannual rate, so the data must be adjusted to reflect semiannual payments and periods. The answer received in step 10 is a semiannual rate, which must be multiplied by 2 to reflect an annual yield.

The Hewlett-Packard 12C internally assumes that semiannual payments are made and, therefore, the answer in step 9 is the annual yield to maturity based on semiannual coupons. If you want an answer on the HP for a given number of years (e.g., 10 years), simply start on a date of your choice and end on the same date 10 years later, as in the example.

Net Present Value of an Annuity on Both the TI BA-35 and the HP 12C

Solve for PV = Present value of annuity

    n = 10 years (number of years cash flow will continue)

    PMT = $5,000 per year (amount of the annuity)

    i = 12% (cost of capital K_a)

    Cost = $20,000

You may choose to refer to Chapter 12 for a complete discussion of net present value.

	Texas Instruments BA-35	Hewlett-Packard 12C
NET PRESENT VALUE OF AN ANNUITY All steps are numbered and some steps include several keystrokes. All numbers following each step are keystrokes followed by a box ☐. Each box represents a keystroke and indicates which calculator function is performed on that number. The calculation for the present value of an annuity on the TI BA-35 requires that the project cost be subtracted from the present value of the cash inflows. The HP 12C could solve the problem exactly with the same keystrokes as the TI. However, since the HP uses a similar method to solve uneven cash flows, we elected to use the method that requires more keystrokes but includes a negative cash outflow for the cost of the capital budgeting project. To conserve space, several keystrokes have been put into one step.	Set finance mode ☐2nd ☐FIN Set decimal to 2 places Decimal ☐2nd ☐STO 1. 10 (years of cash flow) 2. ☐N 3. 5000 (annual payments) 4. ☐PMT 5. 12 (cost of capital) 6. ☐%i 7. ☐CPT 8. ☐PV 9. ☐− 10. 20,000 11. ☐= Answer $8,251.12	Set decimal to 2 places ☐f ☐2 ☐f ☐REG clears memory 1. 20000 (cash outflow) 2. ☐CHS changes sign 3. ☐g 4. ☐CFo 5. 5000 (annual payments) 6. ☐g ☐CFj 7. 10 ☐g ☐Nj (years) 8. 12 ☐i (cost of capital) 9. ☐f ☐NPV Answer $8,251.12 If Error message appears, start over by clearing the memory with ☐f ☐REG.

Net Present Value of an Uneven Cash Flow on Both the TI BA-35 and the HP 12C

Solve for NPV = Net present value
        n = 5 years (number of years cash flow will continue)
    PMT = $5,000 (yr. 1); $6,000 (yr. 2); $7,000 (yr. 3); $8,000 (yr. 4);
           $9,000 (yr. 5)
        i = 12% (cost of capital K_a)
    Cost = $25,000

You may choose to refer to Chapter 12 for a complete discussion of net present value concepts.

	Texas Instruments BA-35	Hewlett-Packard 12C
NET PRESENT VALUE OF AN UNEVEN CASH FLOW All steps are numbered and some steps include several keystrokes. All numbers following each step are keystrokes followed by a box ☐ . Each box represents a keystroke and indicates which calculator function is performed on that number. Because we are dealing with uneven cash flows, each number must be entered. The TI BA-35 requires that you make sure of the memory. In step 2, you enter the future cash inflow in year 1 and, in step 3, you determine its present value, which is stored in memory. After the first 1-year calculation, following year present values are calculated in the same way and added to the stored value using the SUM key. Finally, the recall key RCL is used to recall the present value of the total cash inflows. The HP 12C requires each cash flow to be entered in order. The CFo key represents the cash flow in time period 0. The CFj key automatically counts the year of the cash flow in the order entered and so no years need be entered. Finally, the cost of capital of 12% is entered and the f key and NPV key are used to complete the problem.	Clear memory ON/C 0 STO Set decimal to 2 places Decimal 2nd STO Set finance mode 2nd FIN 1. 12 % i 2. 5000 FV 3. 1 N CPT PV SUM 4. 6000 FV 5. 2 N CPT PV SUM 6. 7000 FV 7. 3 N CPT PV SUM 8. 8000 FV 9. 4 N CPT PV SUM 10. 9000 FV 11. 5 N CPT PV SUM 12. RCL (answer 24420.90) 13. − 14. 25000 (cash outflow) 15. = Answer −$579.10 Negative net present value	Set decimal to 2 places f 2 f REG clears memory 1. 25000 (cash outflow) 2. CHS changes sign 3. g CFo 4. 5000 g CFj 5. 6000 g CFj 6. 7000 g CFj 7. 8000 g CFj 8. 9000 g CFj 9. 12 i 10. f NPV Answer −$579.10 Negative net present value If you receive an Error message, you have probably made a keystroke error. Clear memory with f REG and start over with step 1.

Internal Rate of Return for an Annuity on Both the TI BA-35 and the HP 12C

Solve for IRR = Internal rate of return

n = 10 years (number of years cash flow will continue)

PMT = $10,000 per year (amount of the annuity)

Cost = $50,000 (this is the present value of the annuity)

You may choose to refer to Chapter 12 for a complete discussion of internal rate of return.

	Texas Instruments BA-35	Hewlett-Packard 12C
INTERNAL RATE OF RETURN ON AN ANNUITY All steps are numbered and some steps include several keystrokes. All numbers following each step are keystrokes followed by a box ☐. Each box represents a keystroke and indicates which calculator function is performed on that number. The calculation for the internal rate of return on an annuity on the TI BA-35 requires relatively few keystrokes. The HP 12C requires more keystrokes than the TI BA-35, because it needs to use the function keys `f` and `g` to enter data into the internal programs. The HP method requires that the cash outflow be expressed as a negative, while the TI BA-35 uses a positive number for the cash outflow. To conserve space, several keystrokes have been put into one step.	Clear memory `ON/C` 0 `STO` Set finance mode `2nd` `FIN` Set decimal to 2 places Decimal `2nd` `STO` 1. 10 (years of cash flow) 2. `N` 3. 10000 (annual payments) 4. `PMT` 5. 50000 (present value) 6. `PV` 7. `CPT` 8. `% i` Answer is 15.10% At an internal rate of return of 15.10%, the present value of the $50,000 outflow is equal to the present value of $10,000 cash inflows over the next 10 years.	Set decimal to 2 places `f` 2 `f` `REG` clears memory 1. 50000 (cash outflow) 2. `CHS` changes sign 3. `g` 4. `CFo` 5. 10000 (annual payments) 6. `g` `CFj` 7. 10 `g` `Nj` (years) 8. `f` `IRR` Answer is 15.10% If an Error message appears, start over by clearing the memory with `f` `REG`.

Internal Rate of Return with an Uneven Cash Flow on Both the TI BA-35 and the HP 12C

Solve for IRR = Internal rate of return (return which causes present value of outflows to equal present value of the inflows)

  n = 5 years (number of years cash flow will continue)

  PMT = $5,000 (yr. 1); 6,000 (yr. 2); 7,000 (yr. 3); 8,000 (yr. 4); 9,000 (yr. 5)

  Cost = $25,000

You may choose to refer to Chapter 12 for a complete discussion of internal rate of return.

	Texas Instruments BA-35	**Hewlett-Packard 12C**
INTERNAL RATE OF RETURN ON UNEVEN CASH FLOW All steps are numbered and some steps include several keystrokes. All numbers following each step are keystrokes followed by a box ☐ . Each box represents a keystroke and indicates which calculator function is performed on that number. Because we are dealing with uneven cash flows, the mathematics of solving this problem with the TI BA-35 is not possible. A more advanced algebraic calculator would be required. However, for the student willing to use trial and error, the student can use the NPV method and try different discount rates until the NPV equals zero. Check Chapter 12 on methods for approximating the IRR. This will provide a start. The HP 12C requires each cash flow to be entered in order. The ⌷ CFo ⌷ key represents the cash flow in time period 0. The ⌷ CFj ⌷ key automatically counts the year of the cash flow in the order entered and so no years need be entered. To find the internal rate of return, use the ⌷ f ⌷ ⌷ IRR ⌷ keys and complete the problem.	Clear memory ⌷ ON/C ⌷ 0 ⌷ STO ⌷ Set decimal to 2 places Decimal ⌷ 2nd ⌷ ⌷ STO ⌷ Set finance mode ⌷ 2nd ⌷ ⌷ FIN ⌷ 1. 12 ⌷ % i ⌷ (your IRR est.) 2. 5000 ⌷ FV ⌷ 3. 1 ⌷ N ⌷ ⌷ CPT ⌷ ⌷ PV ⌷ ⌷ STO ⌷ 4. 6000 ⌷ FV ⌷ 5. 2 ⌷ N ⌷ ⌷ CPT ⌷ ⌷ PV ⌷ ⌷ SUM ⌷ 6. 7000 ⌷ FV ⌷ 7. 3 ⌷ N ⌷ ⌷ CPT ⌷ ⌷ PV ⌷ ⌷ SUM ⌷ 8. 8000 ⌷ FV ⌷ 9. 4 ⌷ N ⌷ ⌷ CPT ⌷ ⌷ PV ⌷ ⌷ SUM ⌷ 10. 9000 ⌷ FV ⌷ 11. 5 ⌷ N ⌷ ⌷ CPT ⌷ ⌷ PV ⌷ ⌷ SUM ⌷ 12. ⌷ RCL ⌷ (answer 24,420.90) 13. ⌷ − ⌷ 14. 25000 (cash outflow) 15. ⌷ = ⌷ Answer −$579.10 Negative NPV. Start over with a lower discount rate (try 11.15). Answer is 24999.75. With a cash outflow of $25,000, the IRR would be 11.15%.	Set decimal to 2 places ⌷ f ⌷ 2 ⌷ f ⌷ ⌷ REG ⌷ clears memory 1. 25000 (cash outflow) 2. ⌷ CHS ⌷ changes sign 3. ⌷ g ⌷ ⌷ CFo ⌷ 4. 5000 ⌷ g ⌷ ⌷ CFj ⌷ 5. 6000 ⌷ g ⌷ ⌷ CFj ⌷ 6. 7000 ⌷ g ⌷ ⌷ CFj ⌷ 7. 8000 ⌷ g ⌷ ⌷ CFj ⌷ 8. 9000 ⌷ g ⌷ ⌷ CFj ⌷ 9. ⌷ f ⌷ ⌷ IRR ⌷ Answer $11.15% If you receive an Error message, you have probably made a keystroke error. Clear memory with ⌷ f ⌷ ⌷ REG ⌷ and start over with step 1.

APPENDIX | 10C

Valuation of a Supernormal Growth Firm

The equation for the valuation of a supernormal growth firm is:

$$P_0 = \sum_{t=1}^{n} \frac{D_t}{(1 + K_e)^t} + P_n\left(\frac{1}{1 + K_e}\right) \qquad (10C\text{--}1)$$

        (Supernormal   (After supernormal
        growth period)   growth period)

The formula is not difficult to use. The first term calls for determining the present value of the dividends during the supernormal growth period. The second term calls for computing the present value of the future stock price as determined at the end of the supernormal growth period. If we add the two, we arrive at the current stock price. We are adding together the present value of the two benefits the stockholder will receive: a future stream of dividends during the supernormal growth period and the future stock price.

Let's assume the firm paid a dividend over the last 12 months of $1.67; this represents the current dividend rate. Dividends are expected to grow by 20 percent per year over the supernormal growth period (n) of three years. They will then grow at a normal constant growth rate (g) of 5 percent. The required rate of return (discount rate) as represented by K_e is 9 percent. We first find the present value of the dividends during the supernormal growth period.

1. Present Value of Supernormal Dividends—

        $D_0 = \$1.67$. We allow this value to grow at 20 percent per year over the
             three years of supernormal growth.
        $D_1 = D_0(1 + .20) = \$1.67(1.20) = \$2.00$
        $D_2 = D_1(1 + .20) = \$2.00(1.20) = \$2.40$
        $D_3 = D_2(1 + .20) = \$2.40(1.20) = \$2.88$

We then discount these values back at 9 percent to find the present value of dividends during the supernormal growth period.

	Supernormal Dividends	Discount Rate $K_e = 9\%$	Present Value of Dividends during the Supernormal Period
D_1	$2.00	.917	$1.83
D_2	2.40	.842	2.02
D_3	2.88	.772	2.22
			$6.07

The present value of the supernormal dividends is $6.07. We now turn to the future stock price.

2. Present Value of Future Stock Price—

We first find the future stock price at the end of the supernormal growth period. This is found by taking the present value of the dividends that will be growing at a normal, constant rate after the supernormal period. This will begin *after* the third (and last) period of supernormal growth.

Since after the supernormal growth period the firm is growing at a normal, constant rate (g = 5 percent) and K_e (the discount rate) of 9 percent exceeds the new, constant growth rate of 5 percent, we have fulfilled the two conditions for using the constant dividend growth model after three years. That is, we can apply Formula 10–9 (without subscripts for now).

$$P = \frac{D}{K_e - g}$$

In this case, however, D is really the dividend at the end of the fourth period because this phase of the analysis starts at the beginning of the fourth period and D is supposed to fall at the *end* of the first period of analysis in the formula. Also the price we are solving for now is the price at the beginning of the fourth period, which is the same concept as the price at the end of the third period (P_3).

We thus say:

$$P_3 = \frac{D_4}{K_e - g} \tag{10C–2}$$

D_4 is equal to the previously determined value for D_3 of $2.88 compounded for one period at the constant growth rate of 5 percent.

$$D_4 = \$2.88(1.05) = \$3.02$$

Also:

K_e = .09 discount rate (required rate of return)
g = .05 constant growth rate

$$P_3 = \frac{D_4}{K_e - g} = \frac{\$3.02}{.09 - .05} = \frac{\$3.02}{.04} = \$75.50$$

This is the value of the stock at the end of the third period. We discount this value back to the present.

Stock Price after Three Years	Discount Rate* K_e = 9%	Present Value of Future Price
$75.50	.772	$58.29

*Note: n is equal to 3.

The present value of the future stock price (P_3) of $75.50 is $58.29.

By adding together the answers in parts (1) and (2) of this appendix, we arrive at the total present value, or price, of the supernormal growth stock.

(1) Present value of dividends during the normal growth period. . . . . $ 6.07
(2) Present value of the future stock price 58.29
    Total present value, or price $64.36

The process is also illustrated in Figure 10C–1.

Figure 10C–1

Stock valuation under supernormal growth analysis

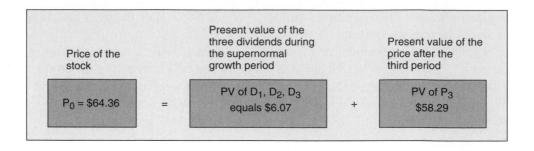

Problem

Valuation of supernormal growth firm

10C–1.   The McMillan Corporation paid a dividend of $2.40 per share of stock over the last 12 months. The dividend is expected to grow at a rate of 25 percent over the next three years (supernormal growth). It will then grow at a normal, constant rate of 6 percent for the foreseeable future. The required rate of return is 14 percent (this will also serve as the discount rate). Round to two places to the right of the decimal point throughout the problem.

a.   Compute the anticipated value of the dividends for the next three years (D_1, D_2, and D_3).

b.   Discount each of these dividends back to the present at a discount rate of 14 percent and then sum them.

c.   Compute the price of the stock at the end of the third year (P_3).

$$P_3 = \frac{D_4}{K_e - g} \quad \text{[Review Appendix 10B for the definition of } D_4\text{]}$$

d.   After you have computed P_3, discount it back to the present at a discount rate of 14 percent for three years.

e.   Add together the answers in part *b* and part *d* to get the current value of the stock. (This answer represents the present value of the first three periods of dividends plus the present value of the price of the stock after three periods.)

11

Cost of Capital

chapter concepts

1 The cost of capital represents the overall cost of financing to the firm.

2 The cost of capital is normally the discount rate to use in analyzing an investment.

3 The cost of capital is based on the valuation techniques from the previous chapter and is applied to bonds, preferred stock, and common stock.

4 A firm attempts to find a minimum cost of capital through varying the mix of its sources of financing.

5 The cost of capital may eventually increase as larger amounts of financing are utilized.

Throughout the previous two chapters, a number of references were made to discounting future cash flows in solving for the present value. How do you determine the appropriate interest rate or discount rate in a real situation? Suppose that a young doctor is rendered incapable of practicing medicine due to an auto accident in the last year of his residency. The court determines that he could have made $100,000 a year for the next 30 years. What is the present value of these inflows? We must know the appropriate discount rate. If 10 percent is used, the value is $942,700; with 5 percent, the answer is $1,537,300—over half a million dollars is at stake.

In the corporate finance setting, the more likely circumstance is that an investment will be made today—promising a set of inflows in the future—and we need to know the appropriate discount rate. This chapter sets down the methods and procedures for making such a determination.

First, the student should observe that if we invest money today to receive benefits in the future, we must be absolutely certain we are earning at least as much as it costs us to acquire the funds for investment—that, in essence, is the minimum acceptable return. If funds cost the firm 10 percent, then all projects must be tested to make sure they earn at least 10 percent. By using this as the discount rate, we can ascertain whether we have earned the financial cost of doing business.

The Overall Concept

How does the firm determine the cost of its funds or, more properly stated, the **cost of capital**? Suppose the plant superintendent wishes to borrow money at 6 percent to purchase a conveyor system, while a division manager suggests stock be sold at an effective cost of 12 percent to develop a new product. Not only would it be foolish for each investment to be judged against the specific means of financing used to implement it, but this would also make investment selection decisions inconsistent. For example, imagine financing a conveyor system having an 8 percent return with 6 percent debt and also evaluating a new product having an 11 percent return but financed with 12 percent common stock. If projects and financing are matched in this way, the project with the lower return would be accepted and the project with the higher return would be rejected. In reality if stock and debt are sold in equal proportions, the average cost of financing would be 9 percent (one-half debt at 6 percent and one-half stock at 12 percent). With a 9 percent average cost of financing, we would now reject the 8 percent conveyor system and accept the 11 percent new product. This would be a rational and consistent decision. Though an investment financed by low-cost debt might appear acceptable at first glance, the use of debt might increase the overall risk of the firm and eventually make all forms of financing more expensive. Each project must be measured against the overall cost of funds to the firm. We now consider cost of capital in a broader context.

The determination of cost of capital can best be understood by examining the capital structure of a hypothetical firm, the Baker Corporation, in Table 11–1. Note that the aftertax costs of the individual sources of financing are shown, then weights are assigned to each, and finally a weighted average cost is determined. (The costs under consideration are those related to new funds that can be used for future financing, rather than historical costs.) In the remainder of the chapter, each of these procedural steps is examined.

Table 11–1

Cost of capital—Baker Corporation

		(1) Cost (aftertax)	(2) Weights	(3) Weighted Cost
Debt	K_d	7.05%	30%	2.12%
Preferred stock	K_p	10.94	10	1.09
Common equity (retained earnings)	K_e	12.00	60	7.20
Weighted average cost of capital	K_a			10.41%

Each element in the capital structure has an explicit, or opportunity, cost associated with it, herein referred to by the symbol K. These costs are directly related to the valuation concepts developed in the previous chapter. If a reader understands how a security is valued, then there is little problem in determining its cost. The mathematics involved in the cost of capital are not difficult. We begin our analysis with a consideration of the cost of debt.

Cost of Debt

The cost of debt is measured by the interest rate, or yield, paid to bondholders. The simplest case would be a $1,000 bond paying $100 annual interest, thus providing a 10 percent yield. The computation may be more difficult if the bond is priced at a discount or premium from par value. Techniques for computing such bond yields were presented in Chapter 10.

Assume the firm is preparing to issue new debt. To determine the likely cost of the new debt in the marketplace, the firm will compute the yield on its currently outstanding debt. This is not the rate at which the old debt was issued, but the rate that investors are demanding today. Assume the debt issue pays $101.50 per year in interest, has a 20-year life, and is currently selling for $940. To find the current yield to maturity on the debt, we could use the trial and error process described in the previous chapter. That is, we would experiment with discount rates until we found the rate that would equate the current bond price of $940 with interest payments of $101.50 for 20 years and a maturity payment of $1,000. A simpler process would be to use Formula 10–2, which gives us the approximate yield to maturity. We reproduce the formula below and relabel it Formula 11–1.

Approximate yield to maturity $(Y') =$

$$\frac{\text{Annual interest payment} + \dfrac{\text{Principal payment} - \text{Price of the bond}}{\text{Number of years to maturity}}}{.6(\text{Price of the bond}) + .4(\text{Principal payment})} \qquad (11\text{--}1)$$

For the bond under discussion, the approximate yield to maturity (Y') would be:

$$Y' = \frac{\$101.50 + \dfrac{\$1,000 - \$940}{20}}{.6(\$940) + .4(\$1,000)}$$

$$= \frac{\$101.50 + \dfrac{60}{20}}{\$564 + \$400}$$

$$Y' = \frac{\$101.50 + 3}{\$964} = \frac{\$104.50}{\$964} = 10.84\%$$

In many cases you will not have to compute the yield to maturity. It will simply be given to you. The practicing corporate financial manager also can normally consult a source such as *Standard & Poor's Bond Guide* to determine the yield to maturity on the firm's outstanding debt. An excerpt from this bond guide is presented in Table 11–2 on page 330. If the firm involved is MediaOne Group, for example, the financial manager could observe that debt maturing in 2032 would have a yield to maturity of 7.41 percent as shown in the last column of the table.

Once the bond yield is determined through the formula or the tables (or is given to you), you must adjust the yield for tax considerations. Yield to maturity indicates how much the corporation has to pay on a *before-tax* basis. But keep in mind the interest payment on debt is a tax-deductible expense. Since interest is tax-deductible, its true cost is less than its stated cost because the government is picking up part of the tab by allowing the firm to pay less taxes. The aftertax cost of debt is actually the yield to maturity times one minus the tax rate.[1] This is presented as Formula 11–2 below Table 11–2.

---

[1] The yield may also be thought of as representing the interest cost to the firm after considering all selling and distribution costs, though no explicit representation is given above to these costs in relationship to debt. These costs are usually quite small, and they are often bypassed entirely in some types of loans. For those who wish to explicitly include this factor in Formula 11–2, we would have:

$$K_d = [\text{Yield}/(1 - \text{Distribution costs})]\,(1 - T)$$

Table 11–2   Excerpt from *Standard & Poor's Bond Guide*

		Corporate Bonds											MED-MER 133

Title-Industry Code & Co. Finances (In Italics)	I n d	Fixed Charge Coverage			Year End	Million $			Balance Sheet Date	L. Term Debt (Mil $)	Capital- ization (Mil $)	Total Debt % Capital	
		2002	2003	2004		Cash & Equiv.	Curr. Assets	Curr. Liab.					

Exchange	Interest Dates	S&P Rating	Date of Last Rating Change	Prior Rating	Eligible Bond Form	Regular Price	Regular (Begins) Thru	Sinking Fund Price	Sinking Fund (Begins) Thru	Refund/Other Restriction Price	Refund/Other Restriction (Begins) Thru	Outst'g (Mil $)	Underwriting Firm / Year	Price Range 2005 High / Low	Mo. End Price Sale(s) or Bid	Curr. Yield	Yield to Mat.

MediaOne Group *(Cont.)*

Issue		Rating															
Nts¹ 6.31s 2005 .... mN		BBB+ 12/01	A–	X	BE	NC	....	....	....	....	....	3.10	M2 '95	101.61 100.71	100.72	6.26	....
Nts¹ 7.30s 2007 .... Jj15		BBB+ 12/01	A–	X	BE	NC	....	....	....	....	....	39.9	M2 '97	106.60 104.26	104 43	6.99	4.92
Deb¹ 7.90s 2027 .... Fa		BBB+ 12/01	A–	X	BE	NC	....	....	....	....	....	2.00	M2 '97	122.37 113.01	120.44	6.56	6.18
Deb¹ 8 15s 2032 .... Fa		BBB+ 6/04	BBB+	X	BE	104 075	(Begins)	....	....	....	....	2.00	M2 '97	113.38 107.82	108.49	7.51	7.41
Deb¹ 6.95s 2037 .... Jj15		BBB+ 12/01	A–	X	BE	NC	....	....	....	....	....	0.12	M2 '97	....	....	6.52	6.46
²Meditrust Corp 57		*1.20 0.08*	*0.83*	*Dc*		*80.30*	*183.0*	*252.0*	*3-31-05*	*790.0*	*2404*						
Nts⁷ 7s 2007 .... fA15		BB– 2/00	BB	Y	BE	NC	....	....	....	....	....	160	M2 '97	106.12 101.00	102.50	6.83	5.64
Nts³ 7. 2s 2026 .... mS10		BB– 2/00	BB	Y	BE	⁴Z100	....	....	....	....	....	175	M2 '96	....	....	....	....
⁵MedPartners Inc. 30a		....	....														
Sr Nts 7⅞s 2006 .... aO		BBB– 3/04	BB+	X	R	NC	....	....	....	....	....	450	S7 '96	105.80 103.43	103.46	7.13	3.78
Mellon Bank N.A. 10		*Now Mellon Fin'l,see*															
Sub Nts 7⅞s 2007 .... Mn15		A+ 5/98	A	X	BE	NC	....	....	....	....	....	300	C5 '97	108.04 105.82	105.95	6.96	4.21
Mellon Fin'l⁸. 25		*4.60 5.22*	*5.01*	*Dc*					*3-31-05*	*5408*	*9726*	*57.4*					
Sub⁷Deb 6.70s 2008 .... Ms		A		X	BE	NC	....	....	....	....	....	250	G1 '96	108.51 106.06	106.57	6.29	4.32
Sub⁷Deb 6⅛s 2010 .... Fa15		A 5/98	A–	X	BE	NC	....	....	....	....	....	350	M5 '98	108.91 105.36	107.55	5.93	4.65
Mellon Funding 25b		*Subsid & gtd by Mellon Fin'l,see*															
Sr Nts⁸ 7½s 2005 .... Jd15		A+		X	BE	NC	....	....	....	....	....	300	C6 2000	101.93 100.13	100.13	7.49	....
Sr Nts⁸ 4⅝s 2007 .... Jd15		A+		X	BE	NC	....	....	....	....	....	400	M5 2002	102.93 101.19	101.58	4.80	4.04
Sub Nts⁸ 6.40s 2011 .... Mn14		A		X	BE	⁹Z100	....	....	....	....	....	300	G1 2001	111.61 107.46	110.54	5.79	4.37
Sub Nts⁸ 5s 2014 .... jD		A		X	BE	⁸Z100	....	....	....	....	....	300	C6 2002	103.82 98.51	102.46	4.88	4.69
Mercantile Bancorp. 10		*Acqd by Firstar Corp,see*															
Sub Nts 7.30s 2007 .... Jd15		A 7/03	A–	X	BE	NC	....	....	....	....	....	200	S1 '97	108.23 105.96	106.24	6.87	3 99
Merck & Co 21a		*25.49 26.21*	*25.24*	*Dc*		*9439*	*15760*	*10902*	*3-31-05*	*5646*	*24920*	*29.2*					
Nts 5⅛s 2006 .... jJ		AA– 11/04	AAA	X	BE	NC	....	....	....	....	....	500	M5 2001	102.37 101.13	101.13	5.19	4.07
Nts 4⅜s 2013 .... Fa15		AA– 11/04	AAA	X	BE	NC	....	....	....	....	....	500	M5 2003	99.13 95.42	98.92	4.42	4.53
Nts 4⅞s 2015 .... Ms		NR		X	BE	⁸Z100	....	....	....	....	....	1000	M6 2005	100.08 95.44	100.08	4.75	4.74
Deb 6.30s 2026 .... Jj		AA– 11/04	AAA	X	BE	NC	....	....	....	....	....	250	M6 '96	112.57 106.27	112.57	5.60	5.30
Deb 6.40s 2028 .... Ms		AA– 11/04	AAA	X	BE	⁹Z100	....	....	....	....	....	500	M7 '98	114.53 107.18	114.53	5.59	5.30
Deb 5.95s 2028 .... jD		AA– 11/04	AAA	X	BE	⁹Z100	....	....	....	....	....	500	M5 '98	109.10 101.90	109.10	5.45	5.28
M-T Nts 'B'¹⁰ 5.76s 2037 ....¹¹mn13		AA– 11/04	AAA	X	BE	¹²NC	....	....	....	....	....	120	M6 '97	113 41 106.02	109.19	5.27	5.16
F/R¹³M-T Nts¹⁴'E' 2042 ....QAug22		AA– 11/04	AAA	X	BE	105	(8-22-32)	....	....	....	....	66.0	S4 2002	97.81 97.43	97.81	....	....
Mercury General 35c		*15.80 81.43*	*97.60*	*Dc*					*3-31-05*	*136.0*	*1620*	*8.4*					
Sr Nts 7¼s 2011 .... fA15		A		X	BE	⁹Z100	....	....	....	....	....	125	2001	112.85 108.49	111.86	6.48	4.91
MeriStar Hospitality 57		*NA 0.38*	*0.39*	*Dc*					*3-31-05*	*1601*	*2272*	*70.5*					
Sr¹⁵Nts¹⁶ 9s 2008 .... Jj15		CCC+ 9/03	B–	Y	BE	NC	....	....	....	....	....	300	Exch 2001	107.00 98.50	102.00	8.82	8.22
MeriStar Hosp Op Ptnr/Fin. 57		*Gtd by MeriStar Hospitality Corp,see*															
Sr¹⁵Nts¹⁶ 10½s 2009 .... Jd15		CCC+ 9/03	B–	Y	BE	105.25	(12-15-05)	....	....	....	....	250	Exch. 2001	109.37 104.25	107.00	9.81	8.37
MeriStar Hospitality 57		*NA 0.38*	*0.39*	*Dc*					*3-31-05*	*1601*	*2272*	*70.5*					
Sr¹⁶Nts¹⁵ 9¼s 2011 .... Jj15		CCC+ 9/03	B–	Y	BE	NC	....	....	....	....	....	0.25	Exch. 2001	....	....	8.74	8.21

Uniform Footnote Explanations–See Page 1. Other: ¹ Was US WEST Cap Fndg. ² Now La Quinta Props. ³ (HRO)On 9-10-03 at 100. ⁴ Plus Make-Whole Amt. ⁵ Now Caremark Rx. ⁶ See Mellon Funding. ⁷ Gtd by Mellon Bank Corp. ⁸ Gtd by Mellon Fin'l. ⁹ Red at greater of 100 or amt based on formula. ¹⁰ (HRO)Ea May 3 to 2036 at 100. ¹¹ Due 5-3-37. ¹² Callable at 100 if less than $25M outstanding. ¹³ Int adj qtrly (3 Mo LIBOR less 0.45%). ¹⁴ (HRO)On ea Aug 22, 2003-13 & ea 3rd Aug 22 att at 98-100. ¹⁵ (HRO)On Chge of Ctrl at 101. ¹⁶ Gtd by MeriStar Hospitality Corp.

Source: Standard & Poor's Bond Guide, June 2006, p. 133.

$$K_d \text{ (Cost of debt)} = Y \text{ (Yield)}(1 - T) \tag{11–2}$$

The term *yield* in the formula is interchangeable with yield to maturity or approximate yield to maturity. In using the approximate yield to maturity formula earlier in this section, we determined that the existing yield on the debt was 10.84 percent. We shall assume new debt can be issued at the same going market rate,[2] and that the firm is paying a 35 percent tax (a nice, easy rate with which to work). Applying the tax adjustment factor, the aftertax cost of debt would be 7.05 percent.

$$\begin{aligned} K_d \text{ (Cost of debt)} &= Y \text{ (Yield)}(1 - T) \\ &= 10.84\% \, (1 - .35) \\ &= 10.84\% \, (.65) \\ &= 7.05\% \end{aligned}$$

Please refer back to Table 11–1 on page 328 and observe in column (1) that the aftertax cost of debt is the 7.05 percent that we have just computed.

---

[2] Actually the rate might be slightly lower to reflect that bonds trading at a discount from par ($940 in this case) generally pay a lower yield to maturity than par value bonds because of potential tax advantages and higher leverage potential. This is not really a major issue in this case.

The cost of preferred stock is similar to the cost of debt in that a constant annual payment is made, but dissimilar in that there is no maturity date on which a principal payment must be made. Determining the yield on preferred stock is simpler than determining the yield on debt. All you have to do is divide the annual dividend by the current price (this process was discussed in Chapter 10). This represents the rate of return to preferred stockholders as well as the annual cost to the corporation for the preferred stock issue.

Cost of Preferred Stock

We need to make one slight alteration to this process by dividing the dividend payment by the net price or proceeds received by the firm. Since a new share of preferred stock has a selling cost (**flotation cost**), the proceeds to the firm are equal to the selling price in the market minus the flotation cost. The cost of preferred stock is presented as Formula 11–3.[3]

$$K_p \text{ (Cost of preferred stock)} = \frac{D_p}{P_p - F} \qquad (11\text{–}3)$$

where

K_p = Cost of preferred stock
D_p = The annual dividend on preferred stock
P_p = The price of preferred stock
F = Flotation, or selling cost

In the case of the Baker Corporation, we shall assume the annual dividend is $10.50, the preferred stock price is $100, and the flotation, or selling cost is $4. The effective cost is:

$$K_p = \frac{D_p}{P_p - F} = \frac{\$10.50}{\$100 - \$4} = \frac{\$10.50}{\$96} = 10.94\%$$

Because a preferred stock dividend is not a tax-deductible expense, there is no downward tax adjustment.

Please refer back to Table 11–1 on page 328 and observe in column (1) that 10.94 percent is the value we used for the cost of preferred stock.

Determining the cost of common stock in the capital structure is a more involved task. The out-of-pocket cost is the cash dividend, but is it prudent to assume the percentage cost of common stock is simply the current year's dividend divided by the market price?

Cost of Common Equity

$$\frac{\text{Current dividend}}{\text{Market price}}$$

If such an approach were followed, the common stock costs for selected U.S. corporations in January 2006 would be Intel (0.9 percent), Disney (1.0 percent), Wal-Mart

---

[3]Note that in Chapter 10, K_p was presented without any adjustment for flotation costs. The instructor may wish to indicate that we have altered the definition slightly. Some may wish to formally add an additional subscript to K_p to indicate we are now talking about the cost of *new* preferred stock. The adjusted symbol would be K_{pn}.

(1.2 percent), and PepsiCo (2.2 percent). Ridiculous, you say! If new common stock costs were assumed to be so low, the firms would have no need to issue other securities and could profitably finance projects that earned only 1 or 2 percent. How then do we find the correct theoretical cost of common stock to the firm?

Valuation Approach

In determining the cost of common stock, the firm must be sensitive to the pricing and performance demands of current and future stockholders. An appropriate approach is to develop a model for valuing common stock and to extract from this model a formula for the required return on common stock.

In Chapter 10 we discussed the constant growth **dividend valuation model** and said the current price of common stock could be stated to equal:

$$P_0 = \frac{D_1}{K_e - g}$$

where

P_0 = Price of the stock today
D_1 = Dividend at the end of the first year (or period)
K_e = Required rate of return
g = Constant growth rate in dividends

We then stated we could arrange the terms in the formula to solve for K_e instead of P_0. This was presented in Formula 10–10. We present the formula once again and relabel it Formula 11–4.

$$K_e = \frac{D_1}{P_0} + g \tag{11–4}$$

The required rate of return (K_e) is equal to the dividend at the end of the first year (D_1), divided by the price of the stock today (P_0), plus a constant growth rate (g). Although the growth rate basically applies to dividends, it is also assumed to apply to earnings and stock price over the long term.

If D_1 = $2, P_0 = $40, and g = 7%, we would say K_e equals 12 percent.

$$K_e = \frac{D_1}{P_0} + g = \frac{\$2}{\$40} + 7\% = 5\% + 7\% = 12\%$$

This means stockholders expect to receive a 5 percent dividend yield on the stock price plus a 7 percent growth in their investment, making a total return of 12 percent.

Required Return on Common Stock Using the Capital Asset Pricing Model

The required return on common stock can also be calculated by an alternate approach called the capital asset pricing model. This topic is covered in Appendix 11A, so only brief mention will be made at this point. Some accept the capital asset pricing model as an important approach to common stock valuation, while others suggest it is not a valid description of how the real world operates.

Under the **capital asset pricing model (CAPM)**, the required return for common stock (or other investments) can be described by the following formula:

$$K_j = R_f + \beta(K_m - R_f) \tag{11-5}$$

where

K_j = Required return on common stock

R_f = Risk-free rate of return; usually the current rate on Treasury bill securities

β = Beta coefficient. The beta measures the historical volatility of an individual stock's return relative to a stock market index. A beta greater than 1 indicates greater volatility (price movements) than the market, while the reverse would be true for a beta less than 1.

K_m = Return in the market as measured by an appropriate index

For the Baker Corporation example, we might assume the following values:

$R_f = 5.5\%$

$K_m = 12\%$

$\beta = 1.0$

K_j, based on Formula 11–5, would then equal:

$$K_j = 5.5\% + 1.0(12\% - 5.5\%) = 5.5\% + 1.0(6.5\%)$$
$$= 5.5\% + 6.5\% = 12\%$$

In this calculation, we have assumed that K_j (the required return under the capital asset pricing model) would equal K_e (the required return under the dividend valuation model). They are both computed to equal 12 percent. Under this equilibrium circumstance, the dividend valuation model and the capital asset pricing model would produce the same answer.

For now we shall use the dividend valuation model exclusively; that is, we shall use $K_e = (D_1/P_0) + g$ in preference to $K_j = R_f + \beta(K_m - R_f)$.

Those who wish to study the capital asset pricing model further are referred to Appendix 11A. This appendix is optional and not required for further reading in the text.

Cost of Retained Earnings

Up to this point, we have discussed the cost (required return) of common stock in a general sense. We have not really specified who is supplying the funds. One obvious supplier of **common stock equity** capital is the purchaser of new shares of common stock. But this is not the only source. For many corporations the most important source of ownership or equity capital is in the form of retained earnings, an internal source of funds.

Accumulated retained earnings represent the past and present earnings of the firm minus previously distributed dividends. Retained earnings, by law, belong to the current stockholders. They can either be paid out to the current stockholders in the form of dividends or reinvested in the firm. As current funds are retained in the firm for reinvestment, they represent a source of equity capital that is being supplied by the current stockholders. However, they should not be considered as free in nature. An opportunity cost is involved. As previously indicated, the funds could be paid out to the current stockholders in the form of dividends, and then redeployed by the stockholders in other stocks, bonds, real estate, and so on. What is the expected rate of return on these alternative investments? That is, what is the opportunity cost? We assume stockholders could at least earn an equivalent return to that provided by their present investment in the firm (on an equal risk basis). This represents $D_1/P_0 + g$. In the security markets, there are thousands of investments from which to choose, so it is not implausible to assume the stockholder could take dividend payments and reinvest them for a comparable yield.

Thus when we compute the cost of retained earnings, this takes us back to the point at which we began our discussion of the cost of common stock. The cost of retained earnings is equivalent to the rate of return on the firm's common stock.[4] This is the opportunity cost. Thus we say the cost of common equity in the form of retained earnings is equal to the required rate of return on the firm's stock as shown as follows.

$$K_e \text{ (Cost of common equity in the form of retained earnings)} = \frac{D_1}{P_0} + g \qquad (11\text{--}6)$$

Thus K_e not only represents the required return on common stock as previously defined, but it also represents the cost of equity in the form of retained earnings. It is a symbol that has double significance.

For ease of reference, the terms in Formula 11–6 are reproduced in the box that follows. They are based on prior values presented in this section on the cost of common equity.

K_e = Cost of common equity in the form of retained earnings
D_1 = Dividend at the end of the first year, $2
P_0 = Price of the stock today, $40
g = Constant growth rate in dividends, 7%
We arrive at the value of 12%.

$$K_e = \frac{D_1}{P_0} + g = \frac{\$2}{\$40} + 7\% = 5\% + 7\% = 12\%$$

The cost of common equity in the form of retained earnings is equal to 12 percent. Please refer back to Table 11–1 on page 328 and observe in column (1) that 12 percent is the value we have used for common equity.

---

[4]One could logically suggest this is not a perfectly equivalent relationship. For example, if stockholders receive a distribution of retained earnings in the form of dividends, they will have to pay taxes on the dividends before they can reinvest them in equivalent yield investments. Also the stockholder may incur brokerage costs in the process. For these reasons, one might suggest the opportunity cost of retained earnings is less than the rate of return on the firm's common stock. The authors have generally supported this position in the past. However, the current predominant view is that the appropriate cost for retained earnings is equal to the rate of return on the firm's common stock. The strongest argument for this equality position is that, in a publicly traded company, a firm always has the option of buying back its stock in the market. Given that this is the case, it is assured a return of K_e. Thus, the firm should not make a physical asset investment that has an expected equity return of less than K_e. Having presented both sides of the argument, the authors have adopted the equality position in recent editions and have used it throughout this chapter. Nevertheless, some instructors may wish to discuss both sides of the issue.

Cost of New Common Stock

Let's now consider the other source of equity capital, new common stock. If we are issuing *new* common stock, we must earn a slightly higher return than K_e, which represents the required rate of return of *present* stockholders. The higher return is needed to cover the distribution costs of the new securities. Assume the required return for present stockholders is 12 percent and shares are quoted to the public at $40. A new distribution of securities must earn slightly more than 12 percent to compensate the corporation for not receiving the full $40 because of sales commissions and other expenses. The formula for K_e is restated as K_n (the cost of new common stock) to reflect this requirement.

$$\text{Common stock} \qquad K_e = \frac{D_1}{P_0} + g$$

$$\text{New common stock} \qquad K_n = \frac{D_1}{P_0 - F} + g \qquad (11\text{--}7)$$

The only new term is F (flotation, or selling costs).

Assume:

$$D_1 = \$2$$
$$P_0 = \$40$$
$$F = \$4$$
$$g = 7\%$$

then

$$K_n = \frac{\$2}{\$40 - \$4} + 7\%$$

$$= \frac{\$2}{\$36} + 7\%$$

$$= 5.6\% + 7\% = 12.6\%$$

The cost of new common stock to the Baker Corporation is 12.6 percent. This value will be used more extensively later in the chapter. New common stock is not assumed to be in the original capital structure for the Baker Corporation presented in Table 11–1.

Overview of Common Stock Costs

For those of you who are suffering from an overexposure to Ks in the computation of cost of common stock, let us boil down the information to the only two common stock formulas that you will be using in the rest of the chapter and in the problems at the back of the chapter.

$$K_e \text{ (Cost of common equity in the form of retained earnings)} = \frac{D_1}{P_0} + g$$

$$K_n \text{ (Cost of new common stock)} = \frac{D_1}{P_0 - F} + g$$

The primary emphasis will be on K_e for now, but later in the chapter we will also use K_n when we discuss the marginal cost of capital.

Optimal Capital Structure— Weighting Costs

Having established the techniques for computing the cost of the various elements in the capital structure, we must now discuss methods of assigning weights to these costs. We will attempt to weight capital components in accordance with our desire to achieve a minimum overall cost of capital. This represents an **optimum capital structure**. For the purpose of this discussion, Table 11–1 (Cost of Capital for the Baker Corporation) is reproduced.

		Cost (aftertax)	Weights	Weighted Cost
Debt.	K_d	7.05%	30%	2.12%
Preferred stock	K_p	10.94	10	1.09
Common equity (retained earnings)	K_e	12.00	60	7.20
Weighted average cost of capital	K_a			10.41%

How does the firm decide on the appropriate weights for debt, preferred stock, and common stock financing? Though debt is the cheapest form of financing, it should be used only within reasonable limits. In the Baker Corporation example, debt carried an aftertax cost of 7.05 percent, while other sources of financing cost at least 10.94 percent. Why not use more debt? The answer is that the use of debt beyond a reasonable point may greatly increase the firm's financial risk and thereby drive up the costs of all sources of financing.

Assume you are going to start your own company and are considering three different capital structures. For ease of presentation, only debt and equity (common stock) are being considered. The costs of the components in the capital structure change each time we vary the debt-assets mix (weights).

	Cost (aftertax)	Weights	Weighted Cost
Financial Plan A:			
Debt	6.5%	20%	1.3%
Equity	12.0	80	9.6
. . . .			10.9%
Financial Plan B:			
Debt	7.0%	40%	2.8%
Equity	12.5	60	7.5
. . . .			10.3%
Financial Plan C:			
Debt	9.0%	60%	5.4%
Equity	15.0	40	6.0
			11.4%

The firm is able to initially reduce the **weighted average cost of capital** with debt financing, but beyond Plan B the continued use of debt becomes unattractive and greatly increases the costs of the sources of financing. Traditional financial theory maintains that there is a U-shaped cost-of-capital curve relative to debt utilization by the firm, as illustrated in Figure 11–1. In this example, the optimum capital structure occurs at a 40 percent debt-to-assets ratio.

Most firms are able to use 30 to 50 percent debt in their capital structure without exceeding norms acceptable to creditors and investors. Distinctions should be made,

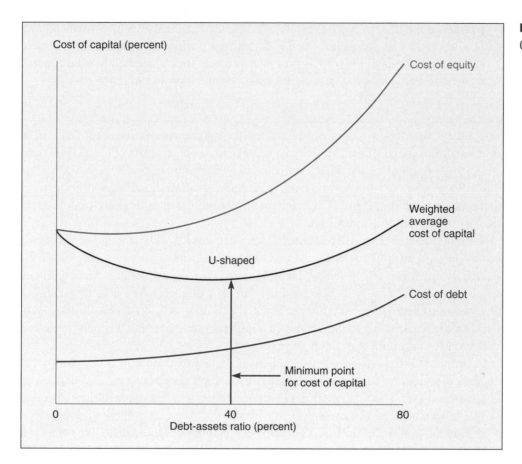

Figure 11–1
Cost of capital curve

however, between firms that carry high or low business risks. As discussed in Chapter 5, "Operating and Financial Leverage," a growth firm in a reasonably stable industry can afford to absorb more debt than its counterparts in cyclical industries. Examples of debt use by companies in various industries are presented in Table 11–3.

Selected Companies with Industry Designations	Percent
Mylan Labs (pharmaceuticals)	18%
Microsoft (software)	19
Intel (semiconductor chips)	20
Liz Claiborne (women's clothing)	39
Diebold (automatic transmissions)	42
Ennis Business Forms (office supplies)	48
Gannett (newspapers and publishing)	50
Motorola (electronics)	56
IBM (computers)	66
Alcan Aluminum (aluminum products)	68
Hilton Hotels (lodging)	70
Dow Chemical (petrochemicals)	73
Delta Airlines (air travel)	98

Table 11–3
Debt as a percentage of total assets (2006)

In determining the appropriate capital mix, the firm generally begins with its present capital structure and ascertains whether its current position is optimal.[5] If not, subsequent financing should carry the firm toward a mix that is deemed more desirable. Only the costs of new or incremental financing should be considered.

Capital Acquisition and Investment Decision Making

So far the various costs of financial capital and the optimum capital structure have been discussed. **Financial capital**, as you may have figured out, consists of bonds, preferred stock, and common equity. These forms of financial capital appear on the corporate balance sheet under liabilities and equity. The money raised by selling these securities and retaining earnings is invested in the real capital of the firm, the long-term productive assets of plant and equipment.

Long-term funds are usually invested in long-term assets, with several asset-financing mixes possible over the business cycle. Obviously a firm wants to provide all of the necessary financing at the lowest possible cost. This means selling common stock when prices are relatively high to minimize the cost of equity. The financial manager also wants to sell debt at low interest rates. Since there is short-term and long-term debt, the manager needs to know how interest rates move over the business cycle and when to use short-term versus long-term debt.

A firm has to find a balance between debt and equity to achieve its minimum cost of capital. Although we discussed minimizing the overall cost of capital (K_a) at a single debt-to-equity ratio, in reality a firm operates within a relevant range of debt to equity before it becomes penalized with a higher overall cost because of increased risk.

Figure 11–2 shows a theoretical cost-of-capital curve at three different points. As we move from time period t to time period t + 2, falling interest rates and rising stock prices cause a downward shift in K_a. This graph illuminates two basic points: (1) The firm wants to keep its debt-to-assets ratio between *x* and *y* along the bottom axis at all times because this is the lowest area on each of the three curves; and (2) The firm would like to finance its long-term needs at time period t + 2 rather than the other two time periods because overall costs are lowest during this time frame.

Corporations are allowed some leeway in the money and capital markets, and it is not uncommon for the debt-to-equity ratio to fluctuate between *x* and *y* over a business cycle. The firm that is at point *y* has lost the flexibility of increasing its debt-to-assets ratio without incurring the penalty of higher capital costs.

Cost of Capital in the Capital Budgeting Decision

The current cost of capital for each source of funds is important when making a capital budgeting decision. Historical costs for past fundings may have very little to do with current costs against which present returns must be measured. When raising new financial capital, a company will tap the various sources of financing over a reasonable time. Regardless of the particular source of funds the company is using for the purchase of an asset, the required rate of return, or discount rate, will be the weighted average cost of capital. As long as the company earns its cost of capital, the common stock value of

---

[5]Market value rather than book value should be used—though in practice, book value is commonly used.

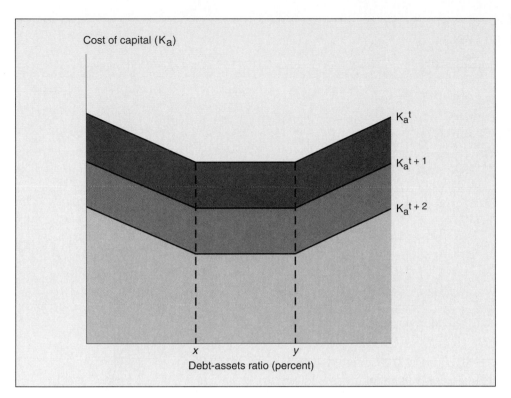

Figure 11–2

Cost of capital over time

the firm will be maintained or will increase, since stockholder expectations are being met. For example, assume the Baker Corporation was considering making an investment in eight projects with the returns and costs shown in Table 11–4.

Table 11–4

Investment projects available to the Baker Corporation

Projects	Expected Returns	Cost ($ millions)
A	16.00%	$10
B	14.00	5
C	13.50	4
D	11.80	20
E	10.65	11
F	9.50	20
G	8.60	15
H	7.00	10
		$95 million

These projects in Table 11–4 could be viewed graphically and merged with the weighted average cost of capital to make a capital budgeting decision, as indicated in Figure 11–3 on page 340.

Notice in Figure 11–3 that the Baker Corporation is considering $95 million in potential projects, but given the weighted average cost of capital of 10.41 percent, it will choose only projects A through E, or $50 million in new investments. Selecting assets

Figure 11–3

Cost of capital and
investment projects for
the Baker Corporation

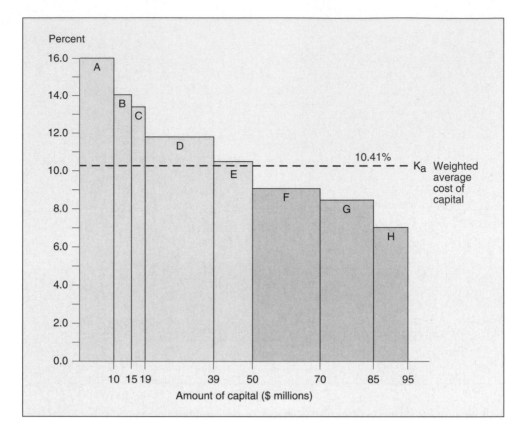

F, G, and H would probably reduce the market value of the common stock because these projects do not provide a return equal to the overall costs of raising funds. The use of the weighted average cost of capital assumes the Baker Corporation is in its optimum capital structure range.

The Marginal Cost of Capital

Nothing guarantees the Baker Corporation that its cost of capital will stay constant for as much money as it wants to raise even if a given capital structure is maintained. If a large amount of financing is desired, the market may demand a higher cost of capital for each amount of funds desired. The point is analogous to the fact that you may be able to go to your relatives and best friends and raise funds for an investment at 10 percent. After you have exhausted the lending or investing power of those closest to you, you will have to look to other sources and the marginal cost of your capital will go up.

As a background for this discussion, the cost of capital table for the Baker Corporation is reproduced again as follows:

		Cost (aftertax)	Weights	Weighted Cost
Debt	K_d	7.05%	30%	2.12%
Preferred stock	K_p	10.94	10	1.09
Common equity (retained earnings)	K_e	12.00	60	7.20
Weighted average cost of capital	K_a			10.41%

EVA Breathes New Life into the Concept of Cost of Capital: Just Ask Eli Lilly & Co.

EVA stands for economic value added and is a concept for financial decision making that was developed by Stern Stewart & Co., a New York City consulting firm, over two decades ago.

Economic value added (EVA) stresses that decisions should be made or projects accepted only if net operating profit after taxes (NOPAT) exceeds the capital costs to finance the investment. For anyone who has ever made an investment decision, the principle behind EVA is well known. When you strip away the fancy wording, EVA merely maintains that you should only make an investment if the return exceeds the cost. Then why all the commotion?

The reason is that it is one thing for managers of corporations to understand the concept, but it is quite another for them to implement it. That is where Joel M. Stern and G. Bennett Stewart III come in. As developers of the concept of EVA, they maintain that they can teach corporate managers how to put a program in place that will ensure that the return on capital exceeds cost and, in the process, stockholder wealth is maximized.

Stern Stewart & Co. now has over 300 EVA clients in the United States and worldwide, including such firms as AT&T, Citicorp, Coca-Cola, Eli Lilly, Georgia Pacific, Kansas City Power & Light, Quaker Oats, Sprint, Sun International, Whirlpool, and the U.S. Postal Service.

Under an EVA program, all decisions from the executive suite to the lowest production level are made with an EVA emphasis. The key issue addressed is whether the project will increase or decrease EVA. EVA is increased when net operating income after taxes exceeds capital costs to finance the project, and decreased when the opposite is true. While one might think that no corporation would undertake a project where costs exceed the return, such is far from the truth.

EVA-draining decisions are sometimes made because the firm does not properly measure return on investment and cost of capital. Also, managers may be wedded to a course of action that is failing, but have not yet recognized the fact, or they may be focused on growth rather than profitability.

One company that has put the concept of EVA to good use is Eli Lilly & Co., the giant pharmaceutical firm that produces such well-established products as Zyprexa (schizophrenia) and Evista (osteoporosis medication).

Prior to the implementation of EVA by Lilly in 1995, the company suffered from confusion about what the firm was trying to maximize. Was it sales, earnings, profit margins, or something else? Since 1995, the target has been on EVA with a strong emphasis on returns exceeding the cost of capital. The bonuses of managers, which have run as high as 50 percent of salary, have also been closely linked to improving EVA.

The stock market has richly rewarded Lilly for its more focused course of action. Prior to the adoption of EVA (between 1990 and 1994) the stock declined from $20 a share to $16. Since 1995, the stock has grown from $16 a share to $52 (June 2006). While it would be naive to attribute all the increase in value to EVA, it was certainly the right medicine at the right time.

finance in action

www.lilly.com

Lilly

We need to review the nature of the firm's capital structure to explain the concept of **marginal cost of capital** as it applies to the firm. Note the firm has 60 percent of the capital structure in the form of equity capital. The equity (ownership) capital is represented by retained earnings. It is assumed that 60 percent is the amount of equity capital the firm must maintain to keep a balance between fixed income securities and ownership interest. But equity capital in the form of retained earnings cannot grow indefinitely as the firm's capital needs expand. Retained earnings is limited to the amount of past and present earnings that can be redeployed into the investment projects of the firm. Let's assume the Baker Corporation has $23.40 million of retained earnings available for investment. Since retained earnings is to represent 60 percent of the capital structure, there is adequate retained earnings to support a capital structure of up to $39 million. More formally, we say:

$$X = \frac{\text{Retained earnings}}{\text{Percent of retained earnings in the capital structure}} \qquad (11\text{--}8)$$

(Where X represents the size of the capital structure that retained earnings will support.)

$$X = \frac{\$23.40 \text{ million}}{.60}$$

$$= \$39 \text{ million}$$

After the first $39 million of capital is raised, retained earnings will no longer be available to provide the 60 percent equity position in the capital structure. Nevertheless lenders and investors will still require that 60 percent of the capital structure be in the form of common equity (ownership) capital. Because of this, *new* common stock will replace retained earnings to provide the 60 percent common equity component for the firm. That is, after $39 million, common equity capital will be in the form of new common stock rather than retained earnings.

In the left-hand portion of Table 11–5, we see the original cost of capital that we have been discussing throughout the chapter. This applies up to $39 million. After $39 million, the concept of marginal cost of capital becomes important. The cost of capital then goes up as shown on the right-hand portion of the table.

Table 11–5   Cost of capital for different amounts of financing

First $39 Million				Next $11 Million			
	A/T Cost	Wts.	Weighted Cost		A/T Cost	Wts.	Weighted Cost
Debt............ K_d	7.05%	.30	2.12%	Debt............ K_d	7.05%	.30	2.12%
Preferred .... K_p	10.94	.10	1.09	Preferred .... K_p	10.94	.10	1.09
Common equity* ... K_e	12.00	.60	7.20	Common equity† ... K_n	12.60	.60	7.56
			$K_a = 10.41\%$				$K_{mc} = 10.77\%$

*Retained earnings.   †New common stock.

K_{mc}, in the bottom right-hand portion of the table, represents the *marginal* cost of capital, and it is 10.77 percent after $39 million. The meaning of K_{mc} is basically the same as K_a; they both represent the cost of capital, but the *mc* subscript after K indicates the (marginal) cost of capital is going up.

The marginal cost of capital has increased after $39 million because common equity is now in the form of new common stock rather than retained earnings. The aftertax (A/T) cost of new common stock is slightly more expensive than retained earnings because of flotation costs (F). The equation for the cost of new common stock was shown earlier in the chapter as Formula 11–7 on page 335 and now we are using it:

$$K_n = \frac{D_1}{P_0 - F} + g = \frac{\$2}{\$40 - \$4} + 7\%$$

$$= \frac{\$2}{\$36} + 7\% = 5.6\% + 7\% = 12.6\%$$

The flotation cost (F) is $4 and the cost of new common stock is 12.60 percent. This is higher than the 12 percent cost of retained earnings that we have been using and causes the increase in the marginal cost of capital.

To carry the example a bit further, we will assume the cost of debt of 7.05 percent applies to the first $15 million of debt the firm raises. After that the aftertax cost of debt will rise to 8.60 percent. Since debt represents 30 percent of the capital structure for the Baker Corporation, the cheaper form of debt can be used to support the capital structure up to $50 million. We derive the $50 million by using Formula 11–9.

$$Z = \frac{\text{Amount of lower-cost debt}}{\text{Percent of debt in the capital structure}} \qquad (11\text{–}9)$$

(Where Z represents the size of the capital structure in which lower-cost debt can be utilized.)

$$Z = \frac{\$15 \text{ million}}{.30}$$

$$= \$50 \text{ million}$$

After the first $50 million of capital is raised, lower-cost debt will no longer be available to provide 30 percent of the capital structure. After $50 million in total financing, the aftertax cost of debt will go up to the previously specified 8.60 percent. The marginal cost of capital for over $50 million in financing is shown in Table 11–6.

Over $50 Million			
	Cost (aftertax)	Weights	Weighted Cost
Debt (higher cost) . . . . K_d	8.60%	.30	2.58%
Preferred stock . . . . K_p	10.94	.10	1.09
Common equity (new common stock) . . . . K_n	12.60	.60	7.56
			K_{mc} = 11.23%

Table 11–6

Cost of capital for increasing amounts of financing

The change in the cost of debt gives way to a new marginal cost of capital (K_{mc}) of 11.23 percent after $50 million of financing. You should observe that the capital structure with over $50 million of financing reflects not only the change in the cost of debt, but also the continued exclusive use of new common stock to represent common equity capital. This change occurred at $39 million, but must be carried on indefinitely as the capital structure expands.

We could continue this process by next indicating a change in the cost of preferred stock, or by continually increasing the cost of debt or new common stock as more capital is used. For now it is sufficient that you merely observe the basic process. To summarize, we have said the Baker Corporation has a basic weighted average cost of capital of 10.41 percent. This value was developed throughout the chapter and was originally presented in Table 11–1. However, as the firm began to substantially expand its capital structure, the weighted average cost of capital increased. This gave way to the term, marginal cost of capital. The first increase or break point was at $39 million in which the marginal cost of capital went up to 10.77 percent as a result of replacing retained earnings with new common stock. The second increase or break point was at $50 million in which the marginal cost of capital increased to 11.23 percent as a result of the utilization of more expensive debt. The changes are summarized below.

Amount of Financing	Marginal Cost of Capital
0–$39 million.....................	10.41%
$39–50 million....................	10.77
Over $50 million	11.23

In previously presented Figure 11–3 on page 340, we showed returns from investments A through H. In Figure 11–4, we reproduce the returns originally shown in Figure 11–3 but include the concept of marginal cost of capital. Observe the increasing cost of capital (dotted lines) in relationship to the decreasing returns (straight lines).

Figure 11–4

Marginal cost of capital and Baker Corporation projects

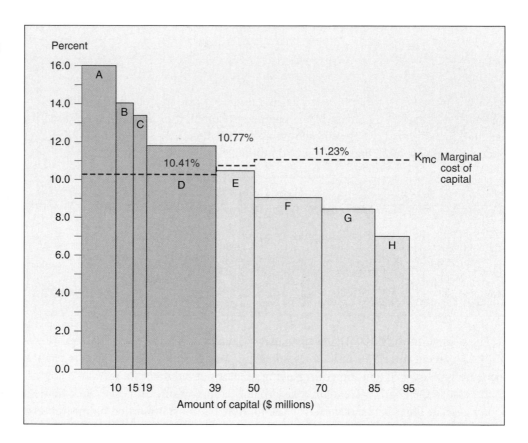

In Figure 11–3 the Baker Corporation was justified in choosing projects A through E for a capital expenditure of $50 million. This is no longer the case in Figure 11–4. Because of the increasing marginal cost of capital, the returns exceed the cost of capital only up to $39 million and now only projects A through D are acceptable.

Although the concept of marginal cost of capital is very important, for most of our capital budgeting decisions in the next chapter, we will assume we are operating on the initial flat part of the marginal cost of capital curve in Figure 11–4, and most of our decisions can be made based on the initial weighted average cost of capital.

Summary

The cost of capital for the firm is determined by computing the costs of various sources of financing and weighting them in proportion to their representation in the capital structure. The cost of each component in the capital structure is closely associated with the valuation of that source, which we studied in the prior chapter. For debt and preferred stock, the cost is directly related to the current yield, with debt adjusted downward to reflect the tax-deductible nature of interest.

For common stock, the cost of retained earnings (K_e) is the current dividend yield on the security plus an anticipated rate of growth for the future. Minor adjustments are made to the formula to determine the cost of new common stock. A summary of Baker Corporation's capital costs is presented in Table 11–7.

Table 11–7   Cost of components in the capital structure

1. Cost of debt...................	$K_d = \text{Yield}(1 - T) = 7.05\%$	$\text{Yield} = 10.84\%$ $T = \text{Corporate tax rate, } 35\%$
2. Cost of preferred stock	$K_p = \dfrac{D_p}{P_p - F} = 10.94\%$	$D_p = \text{Preferred dividend, } \$10.50$ $P_p = \text{Price of preferred stock, } \$100$ $F = \text{Flotation costs, } \$4$
3. Cost of common equity (retained earnings)	$K_e = \dfrac{D_1}{P_0} + g = 12\%$	$D_1 = \text{First year common dividend, } \$2$ $P_0 = \text{Price of common stock, } \$40$ $g = \text{Growth rate, } 7\%$
4. Cost of new common stock	$K_n = \dfrac{D_1}{P_0 - F} + g = 12.60\%$	Same as above, with $F = \text{flotation costs, } \$4$

We weigh the elements in the capital structure in accordance with our desire to achieve a minimum overall cost. While debt is usually the "cheapest" form of financing, excessive debt use may increase the financial risk of the firm and drive up the costs of all sources of financing. The wise financial manager attempts to ascertain what debt component will result in the lowest overall cost of capital. Once this has been determined, the weighted average cost of capital is the discount rate we use in present-valuing future flows to ensure we are earning at least the cost of financing.

The marginal cost of capital is also introduced to explain what happens to a company's cost of capital as it tries to finance a large amount of funds. First the company will use up retained earnings, and the cost of financing will rise as higher-cost new common stock is substituted for retained earnings in order to maintain the optimum capital structure with the appropriate debt-to-equity ratio. Larger amounts of financial capital can also cause the individual means of financing to rise by raising interest rates or by depressing the price of the stock because more is sold than the market wants to absorb.

Review of Formulas

1. $K_d \text{ (cost of debt)} = Y(1 - T)$ (11–2)
    Y is yield
    T is corporate tax rate

2. K_p (cost of preferred stock) $= \dfrac{D_p}{P_p - F}$ (11–3)

    D_p is the annual dividend on preferred stock
    P_p is the price of preferred stock
    F is flotation, or selling, cost

3. K_e (cost of common equity) $= \dfrac{D_1}{P_0} + g$ (11–4)

    D_1 is dividend at the end of the first year (or period)
    P_0 is the price of the stock today
    g is growth rate in dividends

4. K_j (required return on common stock) $= R_f + \beta(K_m - R_f)$ (11–5)
    R_f is risk-free rate of return
    β is beta coefficient
    K_m is return in the market as measured by the appropriate index

5. K_e (cost of common equity in the form of retained earnings)

    $= \dfrac{D_1}{P_0} + g$ (11–6)

    D_1 is dividend at the end of the first year (or period)
    P_0 is price of the stock today
    g is growth rate in dividends

6. K_n (cost of new common stock) $= \dfrac{D_1}{P_0 - F} + g$ (11–7)

    Same as above with:
    F as flotation, or selling, cost

7. X (size of capital structure that retained earnings will support) $= \dfrac{\text{Retained earnings}}{\text{\% of retained earnings in the capital structure}}$ (11–8)

8. Z (size of capital structure that lower-cost debt will support) $= \dfrac{\text{Amount of lower-cost debt}}{\text{\% of debt in the capital structure}}$ (11–9)

List of Terms

Discussion Questions

1. Why do we use the overall cost of capital for investment decisions even when only one source of capital will be used (e.g., debt)?

2. How does the cost of a source of capital relate to the valuation concepts presented previously in Chapter 10?

3. In computing the cost of capital, do we use the historical costs of existing debt and equity or the current costs as determined in the market? Why?

4. Why is the cost of debt less than the cost of preferred stock if both securities are priced to yield 10 percent in the market?

5. What are the two sources of equity (ownership) capital for the firm?

6. Explain why retained earnings have an associated opportunity cost.

7. Why is the cost of retained earnings the equivalent of the firm's own required rate of return on common stock (K_e)?

8. Why is the cost of issuing new common stock (K_n) higher than the cost of retained earnings (K_e)?

9. How are the weights determined to arrive at the optimal weighted average cost of capital?

10. Explain the traditional, U-shaped approach to the cost of capital.

11. It has often been said that if the company can't earn a rate of return greater than the cost of capital it should not make investments. Explain.

12. What effect would inflation have on a company's cost of capital? (Hint: Think about how inflation influences interest rates, stock prices, corporate profits, and growth.)

13. What is the concept of marginal cost of capital?

Practice Problems and Solutions

Approximate yield to maturity and cost of debt

Weighted average cost of capital

1. *a.* A $1,000 par value bond issued by Conseco Electronics has 16 years to maturity. The bond pays $78 a year in interest and is selling for $880. What is the approximate yield to maturity?

    b. If the firm is in a 30 percent tax bracket, what is the aftertax cost of the debt?

2. *a.* Assume the following capital structure for the Morgan Corp.

Debt	35%
Preferred stock	15%
Common equity	50%

    The following facts are also provided:

Bond yield to maturity	9%
Corporate tax rate	35%
Dividend, preferred stock	$8.50
Price, preferred stock	$100
Flotation cost, preferred stock	$2
Dividend, common stock	$1.20
Price, common stock	$30
Growth rate, common stock	9%

    Compute the weighted average cost of capital

    b. If there is $30 million in retained earnings, at what dollar value will the marginal cost of capital go up? If the flotation cost on common stock is $1.50, what will be the cost of new common stock?

Solutions

1. *a.* Approximate yield to maturity (Y′) =

$$\frac{\text{Annual interest payment} + \dfrac{\text{Principal payment} - \text{Price of bond}}{\text{Number of years to maturity}}}{.6\ (\text{Price of bond}) + .4\ (\text{Principal payment})}$$

For the bond under discussion, the approximate yield to maturity (Y′) would be:

$$Y' = \frac{\$78 + \dfrac{\$1,000 - 880}{16}}{.6(\$880) + .4(\$1,000)}$$

$$= \frac{\$78 + \dfrac{\$120}{16}}{\$528 + \$400}$$

$$= \frac{\$78 + 7.50}{\$928} = \frac{\$85.50}{\$928} = 9.21\%$$

b. K_d (aftertax cost of debt) = Y (yield)(1 − T)
$$= 9.21\% \ (1 - .30)$$
$$= 9.21\% \ (.70)$$
$$= 6.45\%$$

2. *a.* First compute the cost of the components in the capital structure.

$$K_d \ (\text{aftertax cost of debt}) = \text{Yield} \ (1 - T) \qquad (11\text{--}2)$$
$$= 9\% \ (1 - .35) = 5.85\%$$

$$K_p \ (\text{cost of preferred stock}) = \frac{D_p}{P_p - F} \qquad (11\text{--}3)$$

D_p = Dividend, preferred stock = $8.50
P_p = Price, preferred stock = $100
F = Flotation cost, preferred stock = $2

$$K_p = \frac{\$8.50}{\$100 - \$2} = \frac{\$8.50}{\$98} = 8.67\%$$

K_e (cost of preferred equity in the form of retained earnings) $= \dfrac{D_1}{P_0} + g$ (11–6)

D_1 = Dividend, common stock = $1.20
P_0 = Price, common stock = $30
g = Growth rate, common stock = 9%

$$K_e = \frac{\$1.20}{\$30} + 9\% = 4\% + 9\% = 13\%$$

Now, combine these with the weights in the capital structure to compute the weighted average cost of capital.

		Cost	Weights	Weighted Cost
Debt.	K_d	5.85%	35%	2.05%
Preferred stock	K_p	8.67	15	1.30
Common equity (retained earnings)	K_e	13.00	50	6.50
Weighted average cost of capital (K_a)				9.85%

b. The marginal cost of capital will go up when there is no longer enough retained earnings to support the capital structure. This is point X.

Solve for X

$$X = \frac{\text{Retained earnings}}{\text{Percent of retained earnings in the capital structure}}$$

$$= \frac{\$30 \text{ million}}{.50} = \$60 \text{ million}$$

At this point, new common stock will be *used* instead of retained earnings in the capital structure. The cost of the new common stock is:

$$K_n = \frac{D_1}{P_0 - F} + g \qquad (11\text{–}7)$$

$$K_n = \text{Cost of new common stock}$$

The only new term is F:

$D_1 = \$1.20$
$P_0 = \$30$
$F = $ Flotation cost, new common stock $\$1.50$
$g = 9\%$

$$K_n = \frac{\$1.20}{\$30 - \$1.50} + 9\% = \frac{\$1.20}{\$28.50} + 9\% = 4.21\% + 9\% = 13.21\%$$

All problems are available in Homework Manager. Please see the preface for more information.   **Problems**

1. In March 2007 Hertz Pain Relievers bought a massage machine that provided a return of 8 percent. It was financed by debt costing 7 percent. In August 2007, Mr. Hertz came up with a heating compound that would have a return of 14 percent. The Chief Financial Officer, Mr. Smith, told him it was impractical because it would require the issuance of common stock at a cost of 16 percent to finance the purchase. Is the company following a logical approach to using cost of capital?

    Cost of capital

2. Speedy Delivery Systems can buy a piece of equipment that is anticipated to provide an 8 percent return and can be financed at 5 percent with debt. Later in the year, the firm turns down an opportunity to buy a new machine that would yield a 15 percent return but would cost 17 percent to finance through common equity. Assume debt and common equity each represent 50 percent of the firm's capital structure.

    Cost of capital

    a. Compute the weighted average cost of capital.

    b. Which project(s) should be accepted?

3. Telecom Systems can issue debt yielding 8 percent. The company is in a 35 percent bracket. What is its aftertax cost of debt?

    Aftertax cost of debt

Aftertax cost of debt

4. Calculate the aftertax cost of debt under each of the following conditions.

	Yield	Corporate Tax Rate
a.	6.0%	16%
b.	12.6	35
c.	9.4	24

Aftertax cost of debt

5. The Goodsmith Charitable Foundation, which is tax-exempt, issued debt last year at 8 percent to help finance a new playground facility in Los Angeles. This year the cost of debt is 20 percent higher; that is, firms that paid 10 percent for debt last year will be paying 12 percent this year.

   a. If the Goodsmith Charitable Foundation borrowed money this year, what would the aftertax cost of debt be, based on their cost last year and the 20 percent increase?

   b. If the receipts of the foundation were found to be taxable by the IRS (at a rate of 35 percent because of involvement in political activities), what would the aftertax cost of the debt be?

Aftertax cost of debt

6. Royal Jewelers Inc. has an aftertax cost of debt of 6 percent. With a tax rate of 40 percent, what can you assume the yield on the debt is?

Approximate yield to maturity and cost of debt

7. Airborne Airlines, Inc., has a $1,000 par value bond outstanding with 25 years to maturity. The bond carries an annual interest payment of $78 and is currently selling for $875. Airborne is in the 30 percent tax bracket. The firm wishes to know what the aftertax cost of a new bond issue is likely to be. The yield to maturity on the new issue will be the same as the yield to maturity on the old issue because the risk and maturity date will be similar.

   a. Compute the approximate yield to maturity (Formula 11–1 on page 329) on the old issue and use this as the yield for the new issue.

   b. Make the appropriate tax adjustment to determine the aftertax cost of debt.

Approximate yield to maturity and cost of debt

8. Russell Container Corporation has a $1,000 par value bond outstanding with 20 years to maturity. The bond carries an annual interest payment of $95 and is currently selling for $920 per bond. Russell Corp. is in a 25 percent tax bracket. The firm wishes to know what the aftertax cost of a new bond issue is likely to be. The yield to maturity on the new issue will be the same as the yield to maturity on the old issue because the risk and maturity date will be similar.

   a. Compute the approximate yield to maturity (Formula 11–1) on the old issue and use this as the yield for the new issue.

   b. Make the appropriate tax adjustment to determine the aftertax cost of debt.

Changing rates and cost of debt

9. For Russell Container Corporation, described in problem 8, assume that the yield on the bonds goes up by 1 percentage point and that the tax rate is now 35 percent.

   a. What is the new aftertax cost of debt?

   b. Has the aftertax cost of debt gone up or down from problem 8? Explain why.

Real-world example and cost of debt

10. MediaOne Group is planning to issue debt that will mature in the year 2027. In many respects the issue is similar to currently outstanding debt of the corporation. Using Table 11–2 on page 330, identify:

   a. The yield to maturity on similarly outstanding debt for the firm, in terms of maturity.

b. Assume that because the new debt will be issued at par, the required yield to maturity will be 0.15 percent higher than the value determined in part *a*. Add this factor to the answer in *a*. (New issues at par sometimes require a slightly higher yield than old issues that are trading below par. There is less leverage and there are fewer tax advantages.)

c. If the firm is in a 30 percent tax bracket, what is the aftertax cost of debt?

11. Medco Corporation can sell preferred stock for $80 with an estimated flotation cost of $3. It is anticipated that the preferred stock will pay $6 per share in dividends.

    Cost of preferred stock

a. Compute the cost of preferred stock for Medco Corp.

b. Do we need to make a tax adjustment for the issuing firm?

12. The Meredith Corporation issued $100 par value preferred stock 10 years ago. The stock provided an 8 percent yield at the time of issue. The preferred stock is now selling for $75. What is the current yield of cost of preferred stock? (Disregard flotation costs.)

    Cost of preferred stock

13. The treasurer of Riley Coal Co. is asked to compute the cost of fixed income securities for her corporation. Even before making the calculations, she assumes the aftertax cost of debt is at least 2 percent less than that for preferred stock. Based on the facts below, is she correct?

    Comparison of the costs of debt and preferred stock

    Debt can be issued at a yield of 10.6 percent, and the corporate tax rate is 35 percent. Preferred stock will be priced at $50 and pay a dividend of $4.40. The flotation cost on the preferred stock is $2.

14. Barton Electronics wants you to calculate its cost of common stock. During the next 12 months, the company expects to pay dividends (D_1) of $1.20 per share, and the current price of its common stock is $30 per share. The expected growth rate is 9 percent.

    Costs of retained earnings and new common stock

a. Compute the cost of retained earnings (K_e). Use Formula 11–6 on page 334.

b. If a $2 flotation cost is involved, compute the cost of new common stock (K_n). Use Formula 11–7 on page 335.

15. Compute K_e and K_n under the following circumstances:

    Costs of retained earnings and new common stock

a. $D_1 = \$4.60$, $P_0 = \$60$, $g = 6\%$, $F = \$3.00$.

b. $D_1 = \$0.25$, $P_0 = \$20$, $g = 9\%$, $F = \$1.50$.

c. E_1 (earnings at the end of period one) = $6, payout ratio equals 30 percent, $P_0 = \$24$, $g = 4.5\%$, $F = \$1.60$.

d. D_0 (dividend at the beginning of the first period) = $3, growth rate for dividends and earnings (g) = 8%, $P_0 = \$50$, $F = \$3$.

16. O'Neal's Men's Shops, Inc., specializes in large-size clothing. Business has been good, as indicated by the six-year growth in earnings per share. The earnings have grown from $1.00 to $1.87.

    Growth rates and common stock valuation

a. Use Appendix A at the back of the text to determine the compound annual rate of growth in earnings ($n = 6$).

b. Based on the growth rate determined in part *a*, project earnings for next year (E_1). (Round to two places to the right of the decimal point.)

c.   Assume the dividend payout ratio is 40 percent. Compute (D_1). (Round to two places to the right of the decimal point).

d.   The current price of the stock is $18. Using the growth rate (g) from part *a* and D_1 from part *c,* compute K_e.

e.   If the flotation cost is $1.50, compute the cost of new common stock (K_n).

Weighted average cost of capital

17.   United Business Forms' capital structure is as follows:

Debt.	35%
Preferred stock	15
Common equity	50

The aftertax cost of debt is 7 percent, the cost of preferred stock is 10 percent, and the cost of common equity (in the form of retained earnings) is 13 percent.

Calculate United Business Forms' weighted average cost of capital in a manner similar to Table 11–1 on page 328.

Weighted average cost of capital

18.   As an alternative to the capital structure shown in Problem 17 for United Business Forms, an outside consultant has suggested the following modifications.

Debt.	65%
Preferred stock	5
Common equity	30

Under this new, more debt-oriented arrangement, the aftertax cost of debt is 9.8 percent; the cost of preferred stock is 12 percent; and the cost of common equity (in the form of retained earnings) is 15.5 percent.

Recalculate United Business Forms' weighted average cost of capital. Which plan is optimal in terms of minimizing the weighted average cost of capital?

Weighted average cost of capital

19.   Sauer Milk, Inc. wants to determine the minimum cost of capital point for the firm. Assume it is considering the following financial plans:

	Cost (aftertax)	Weights
Plan A		
Debt	5.0%	20%
Preferred stock.	10.0	10
Common equity	14.0	70
Plan B		
Debt	5.5%	30%
Preferred stock.	10.5	10
Common equity	15.0	60
Plan C		
Debt	6.0%	40%
Preferred stock.	10.7	10
Common equity	15.8	50
Plan D		
Debt	8.0%	50%
Preferred stock.	11.2	10
Common equity	17.5	40

a. Which of the four plans has the lowest weighted average cost of capital? (Round to two places to the right of decimal point.)

b. Briefly discuss the results from Plan C and Plan D, and why one is better than the other.

20. Given the following information, calculate the weighted average cost of capital for Hamilton Corp. Line up the calculations in the order shown in Table 11–1.

Weighted average cost of capital

Percent of capital structure:

Debt	30%
Preferred stock	15
Common equity	55

Additional information:

Bond coupon rate	13%
Bond yield to maturity	11%
Dividend, expected common	$3.00
Dividend, preferred	$10.00
Price, common	$50.00
Price, preferred	$98.00
Flotation cost, preferred	$5.50
Growth rate	8%
Corporate tax rate	30%

21. Given the following information, calculate the weighted average cost of capital for the Hadley Corporation. Line up the calculations in the order shown in Table 11–1.

Weighted average cost of capital

Percent of capital structure:

Preferred stock	10%
Common equity	60
Debt	30

Additional information:

Corporate tax rate	34%
Dividend, preferred	$9.00
Dividend expected, common	$3.50
Price, preferred	$102.00
Growth rate	6%
Bond yield	10%
Flotation cost, preferred	$3.20
Price, common	$70.00

22. Brook's Window Shields, Inc., is trying to calculate its cost of capital for use in a capital budgeting decision. Mr. Glass, the vice-president of finance, has given you the following information and has asked you to compute the weighted average cost of capital.

Changes in costs and weighted average cost of capital

The company currently has outstanding a bond with an 11.2 percent coupon rate and another bond with a 7.5 percent rate. The firm has been informed by its investment banker that bonds of equal risk and credit rating are now selling to yield 12.4 percent.

The common stock has a price of $54 and an expected dividend (D_1) of $2.70 per share. The firm's historical growth rate of earnings and dividends per share has been 14.5 percent, but security analysts on Wall Street expect this growth to slow to 12 percent in the future years.

The preferred stock is selling at $50 per share and carries a dividend of $4.75 per share. The corporate tax rate is 35 percent. The flotation cost is 2.8 percent of the selling price for preferred stock. The optimum capital structure is 35 percent debt, 10 percent preferred stock, and 55 percent common equity in the form of retained earnings.

Compute the cost of capital for the individual components in the capital structure, and then calculate the weighted average cost of capital (similar to Table 11–1).

Changes in cost and weighted average cost of capital

23. A-Rod Manufacturing Company is trying to calculate its cost of capital for use in making a capital budgeting decision. Mr. Jeter, the vice-president of finance, has given you the following information and has asked you to compute the weighted average cost of capital.

The company currently has outstanding a bond with a 10.6 percent coupon rate and another bond with an 8.2 percent rate. The firm has been informed by its investment banker that bonds of equal risk and credit rating are now selling to yield 11.5 percent. The common stock has a price of $60 and an expected dividend (D_1) of $1.80 per share. The historical growth pattern (g) for dividends is as follows:

$1.35
1.49
1.64
1.80

Compute the historical growth rate, round it to the nearest whole number, and use it for g.

The preferred stock is selling at $80 per share and pays a dividend of $7.60 per share. The corporate tax rate is 30 percent. The flotation cost is 2.5 percent of the selling price for preferred stock. The optimum capital structure for the firm is 25 percent debt, 10 percent preferred stock, and 65 percent common equity in the form of retained earnings.

Compute the cost of capital for the individual components in the capital structure, and then calculate the weighted average cost of capital (similar to Table 11–1).

Impact of credit ratings on cost of capital

24. Northwest Utility Company faces increasing needs for capital. Fortunately, it has an Aa3 credit rating. The corporate tax rate is 35 percent. Northwest's treasurer is trying to determine the corporation's current weighted average cost of capital in order to assess the profitability of capital budgeting projects.

Historically, the corporation's earnings and dividends per share have increased about 6.2 percent annually and this should continue in the future. Northwest's common stock is selling at $60 per share, and the company will pay a $4.50 per share dividend (D_1).

The company's $100 preferred stock has been yielding 8 percent in the current market. Flotation costs for the company have been estimated by its investment banker to be $2.00 for preferred stock.

The company's optimum capital structure is 50 percent debt, 10 percent preferred stock, and 40 percent common equity in the form of retained earnings. Refer to the table below on bond issues for comparative yields on bonds of equal risk to Northwest.

Data on Bond Issues

Issue	Moody's Rating	Price	Yield to Maturity
Utilities:			
Southwest Electric Power—7¼ 2023	Aa2	$ 875.18	8.24%
Pacific Bell—7⅜ 2025	Aa3	887.25	8.43
Pennsylvania Power & Light—8½ 2022	A2	950.66	8.99
Industrials:			
Johnson & Johnson—6¾ 2023	Aaa	840.24	8.14
Dillard's Department Stores—7⅛ 2023	A2	920.92	8.44
Marriott Corp.—10 2012	B2	1,015.10	9.99

Compute the answers to the following questions from the information given.

a. Cost of debt, K_d (use the accompanying table—relate to the utility bond credit rating for yield).

b. Cost of preferred stock, K_p.

c. Cost of common equity in the form of retained earnings, K_e.

d. Weighted average cost of capital.

25. Delta Corporation has the following capital structure:

	Cost (aftertax)	Weights	Weighted Cost
Debt	6.1%	25%	1.53%
Preferred stock (K_p).	7.6	10	.76
Common equity (K_e) (retained earnings)	15.1	65	9.82
Weighted average cost of capital (K_a)			12.11%

Marginal cost of capital

a. If the firm has $26 million in retained earnings, at what size capital structure will the firm run out of retained earnings?

b. The 7.1 percent cost of debt referred to above applies only to the first $13 million of debt. After that the cost of debt will go up. At what size capital structure will there be a change in the cost of debt?

26. The Nolan Corporation finds that it is necessary to determine its marginal cost of capital. Nolan's current capital structure calls for 45 percent debt, 15 percent preferred stock, and 40 percent common equity. Initially common equity will be in the form of retained earnings (K_e) and then new common stock (K_n). The costs of the various sources of financing are as follows: debt, 5.6 percent; preferred stock, 9 percent; retained earning, 12 percent; and new common stock, 13.2 percent.

Marginal cost of capital

a. What is the initial weighted average cost of capital? (Include debt, preferred stock, and common equity in the form of retained earnings, K_e.)

b. If the firm has $12 million in retained earnings, at what size capital structure will the firm run out of retained earnings?

c.   What will the marginal cost of capital be immediately after that point? (Equity will remain at 40 percent of the capital structure, but will all be in the form of new common stock, K_n.)

d.   The 5.6 percent cost of debt referred to above applies only to the first $18 million of debt. After that the cost of debt will be 7.2 percent. At what size capital structure will there be a change in the cost of debt?

e.   What will the marginal cost of capital be immediately after that point? (Consider the facts in both parts c and d.)

Marginal cost
of capital

27.   The McGee Corporation finds it is necessary to determine its marginal cost of capital. McGee's current capital structure calls for 40 percent debt, 5 percent preferred stock, and 55 percent common equity. Initially, common equity will be in the form of retained earnings (K_e) and then new common stock (K_n). The costs of the various sources of financing are as follows: debt, 7.4 percent; preferred stock, 10.0 percent; retained earnings, 13.0 percent; and new common stock, 14.4 percent.

a.   What is the initial weighted average cost of capital? (Include debt, preferred stock, and common equity in the form of retained earnings, K_e.)

b.   If the firm has $27.5 million in retained earnings, at what size capital structure will the firm run out of retained earnings?

c.   What will the marginal cost of capital be immediately after that point? (Equity will remain at 55 percent of the capital structure, but will all be in the form of new common stock, K_n.)

d.   The 7.4 percent cost of debt referred to above applies only to the first $32 million of debt. After that the cost of debt will be 8.6 percent. At what size capital structure will there be a change in the cost of debt?

e.   What will the marginal cost of capital be immediately after that point? (Consider the facts in both parts c and d.)

COMPREHENSIVE PROBLEM

Southern Textiles
(marginal cost of
capital and
investment returns)

Southern Textiles is in the process of expanding its productive capacity to introduce a new line of products. Current plans call for a possible expenditure of $100 million on four projects of equal size ($25 million), but different returns. Project A will increase the firm's processed yarn capacity and has an expected return of 15 percent after taxes. Project B will increase the capacity for woven fabrics and carries a return of 13.5 percent. Project C, a venture into synthetic fibers, is expected to earn 11.2 percent, and Project D, an investment into dye and textile chemicals, is expected to show a 10.5 percent return.

The firm's capital structure consists of 40 percent debt and 60 percent common equity and this will continue in the future. There is no preferred stock.

Southern Textiles has $15 million in retained earnings. After a capital structure with $15 million in retained earnings is reached (in which retained earnings represent 60 percent of the financing), all additional equity financing must come in the form of new common stock.

Common stock is selling for $30 per share and underwriting costs are estimated at $3 if new shares are issued. Dividends for the next year will be $1.50 per share ($D_1$), and earnings and dividends have grown consistently at 9 percent per year.

The yield on comparative bonds has been hovering at 11 percent. The investment banker feels that the first $20 million of bonds could be sold to yield 11 percent while additional debt might require a 2 percent premium and be sold to yield 13 percent. The corporate tax rate is 34 percent.

a.   Based on the two sources of financing, what is the initial weighted average cost of capital? (Use K_d and K_e.)

b.   At what size capital structure will the firm run out of retained earnings?

c.   What will the marginal cost of capital be immediately after that point?

d.   At what size capital structure will there be a change in the cost of debt?

e.   What will the marginal cost of capital be immediately after that point?

f.   Based on the information about potential returns on investments in the first paragraph and information on marginal cost of capital (in parts *a, c,* and *e*), how large a capital investment budget should the firm use?

g.   Graph the answer determined in part *f.*

COMPREHENSIVE PROBLEM

Garner Data Systems is a very large company with common stock listed on the New York Stock Exchange and bonds traded over-the-counter. As of the current balance sheet, it has three bond issues outstanding:

Garner Data Systems (cost of capital with changing financial needs)

	Expiration
$50 million of 9% series	2019
$100 million of 6% series	2016
$150 million of 4% series	2010

The vice-president of finance is planning to sell $150 million of bonds to replace the debt due to expire in 2007. At present, market yields on similar Baa bonds are 11.2 percent. Garner also has $60 million of 6.9 percent noncallable preferred stock outstanding, and it has no intentions of selling any preferred stock at any time in the future. The preferred stock is currently priced at $68 per share, and its dividend per share is $6.30.

The company has had very volatile earnings, but its dividends per share have had a very stable growth rate of 8.5 percent and this will continue. The expected dividend (D_1) is $2.10 per share, and the common stock is selling for $60 per share. The company's investment banker has quoted the following flotation costs to Garner: $1.80 per share for preferred stock and $3 per share for common stock.

On the advice of its investment banker, Garner has kept its debt at 50 percent of assets and its equity at 50 percent. Garner sees no need to sell either common or preferred stock in the foreseeable future as it has generated enough internal funds for its investment needs when these funds are combined with debt financing. Garner's corporate tax rate is 35 percent.

Compute the cost of capital for the following:

a. Bond (debt) (K_d).

b. Preferred stock (K_p).

c. Common equity in the form of retained earnings (K_e).

d. New common stock (K_n).

e. Weighted average cost of capital.

WEB EXERCISE

In Table 11–3, Intel was shown to have a low debt ratio. Let's learn more about this company. Go to its Web site at www.intel.com, and follow the steps below:

1. Click on "About Intel" and then click on "Investor Relations."

2. Scroll down and click on the latest annual report.

3. Then click on the line below "Financial Statements."

4. You should see "Selected Financial Data."

5. *a.* Compute the $ change in "Total Assets" over the last five years.

   b. Do the same computation for "Stockholders' Equity."

   c. Do the same computation for "Long-Term Debt and Put Warrants."

   d. In a brief paragraph, describe the change in long-term obligations (debt) that has taken place relative to the change in total assets and stockholders' equity. Does it appear to be large or small?

Note: From time to time, companies redesign their Web sites and occasionally a topic we have listed may have been deleted, updated, or moved into a different location. If you click on the site map or site index, you will be introduced to a table of contents which should aid you in finding the topic you are looking for.

S&P PROBLEMS   www.mhhe.com/edumarketinsight

STANDARD &POOR'S

1. Log onto the S&P Market Insight Web site, www.mhhe.com/edumarketinsight.

2. Click on "Commentary," which is the third box below the Market Insight title. The second major heading on the left side is Trends and Projections. Click on the current "Trends and Projections."

3. This is a quarterly economic summary for the U.S. economy and it is filled with charts and tables.

4. Find the graphs depicting interest rate behavior over the last several years.

5. What has happened to interest rates on government securities during this time period and how will this affect the cost of debt capital for the average U.S. company?

6. Find the graph for the "S&P 500 Stock Price Index." What has happened to common stock prices during this time period?

7. Consider the impact of the change in stock prices on the dividend yield. Will the dividend yield go up or down with the change in the stock price? Considering

only the impact of the dividend yield on the cost of common stock, what happened to the cost of common stock during this time period?

8. In general, how has the change in interest rates and common stock prices affected the overall cost of capital?

S & P   P R O B L E M S   www.mhhe.com/edumarketinsight

1. Log onto the S&P Market Insight Web site, www.mhhe.com/edumarketinsight.

    STANDARD &POOR'S

2. Click on "Company," which is the first box below the Market Insight title.
3. Type Johnson and Johnson's ticker symbol "JNJ" in the box and click on Go.
4. Scroll down the left margin and click on "Excel Analytics." At the top of the left margin you will see the second item listed as Ann. Balance Sheet.
5. Click on "Ann. Balance Sheet" and find long-term debt and total common equity for the last five years. Add the two together to get total capital. Calculate the weights between debt and equity that you would use in a weighted average cost of capital calculation.
6. What are the weights for debt and equity for the last five years? Have they remained stable? Comment on the stability or lack of stability and how it would affect the company's cost of capital.

A P P E N D I X | 11A

Cost of Capital and the Capital Asset Pricing Model (Optional)

The **capital asset pricing model** (CAPM) relates the risk-return trade-offs of individual assets to market returns. Common stock returns over time have generally been used to test this model since stock prices are widely available and efficiently priced, as are market indexes of stock performance. In theory the CAPM encompasses all assets, but in practice it is difficult to measure returns on all types of assets or to find an all-encompassing market index. For our purposes we will use common stock returns to explain the model and occasionally we will generalize about other assets.

The Capital Asset Pricing Model

The basic form of the CAPM is a linear relationship between returns on individual stocks and stock market returns over time. By using least squares regression analysis, the return on an individual stock, K_j, is expressed in Formula 11A–1.

$$K_j = \alpha + \beta K_m + e \qquad (11A{-}1)$$

where

K_j = Return on individual common stock of a company
α = Alpha, the intercept on the y-axis
β = Beta, the coefficient
K_m = Return on the stock market (an index of stock returns is used, usually the Standard & Poor's 500 Index)
e = Error term of the regression equation

www.mhhe.com/bh12e

As indicated in Table 11A–1 below and Figure 11A–1, this equation uses historical data to generate the beta coefficient (β), a measurement of the return performance of a given stock versus the return performance of the market. Assume that we want to calculate a beta for Parts Associates, Inc. (PAI), and that we have the performance data for that company and the market shown in Table 11A–1. The relationship between PAI and the market appears graphically in Figure 11A–1.

Table 11A–1

Performance of PAI and the market

Year	Rate of Return on Stock	
	PAI	Market
1	12.0%	10.0%
2	16.0	18.0
3	20.0	16.0
4	16.0	10.0
5	6.0	8.0
Mean return	14.0%	12.4%
Standard deviation	4.73%	3.87%

The alpha term in Figure 11A–1 of 2.8 percent is the y intercept of the linear regression. It is the expected return on PAI stock if returns on the market are zero. However, if the returns on the market are expected to approximate the historical rate of 11.6 percent, the expected return on PAI would be $K_j = 2.8 + 0.9(11.6) = 13.2$ percent. This maintains the historical relationship. If the returns on the market are expected to rise to 18 percent next year, expected return on PAI would be $K_j = 2.8 + 0.9(18.0) = 19$ percent.

Notice that we are talking in terms of expectations. The CAPM is an expectational (ex ante) model, and there is no guarantee historical data will reoccur. One area of empirical testing involves the stability and predictability of the beta coefficient based on historical data. Research has indicated that betas are more useful in a portfolio context (for groupings of stocks) because the betas of individual stocks are less stable from period to period than portfolio betas. In addition, research indicates betas of individual common stocks have the tendency to approach 1.0 over time.

The Security Market Line

The capital asset pricing model evolved from Formula 11A–1 into a **market risk premium** model where the basic assumption is that, for investors to take more risk, they must be compensated by larger expected returns. Investors should also not accept returns that are less than they can get from a riskless asset. For CAPM purposes it is assumed that short-term U.S. Treasury bills may be considered a riskless asset.[1] When viewed in this context, an investor must achieve an extra return above that obtainable

---

[1]A number of studies have also indicated that longer-term government securities may appropriately represent R_f (the risk-free rate).

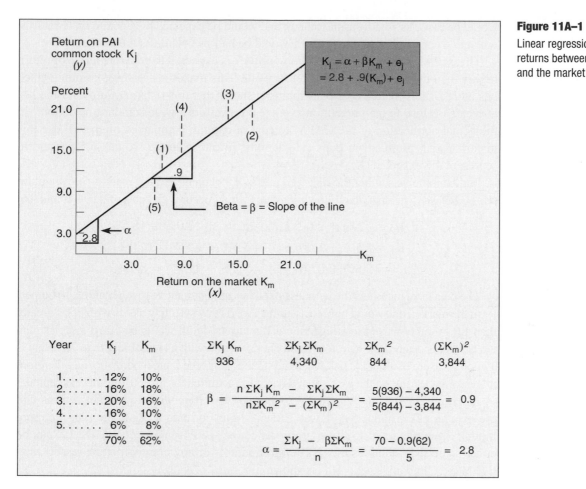

Figure 11A–1

Linear regression of returns between PAI and the market

from a Treasury bill in order to induce the assumption of more risk. This brings us to the more common and theoretically useful model:

$$K_j = R_f + \beta(K_m - R_f) \qquad\qquad (11A\text{--}2)$$

where

$$
\begin{aligned}
R_f &= \text{Risk-free rate of return} \\
\beta &= \text{Beta coefficient from Formula 11A--1} \\
K_m &= \text{Return on the market index} \\
K_m - R_f &= \text{Premium or excess return of the market versus the risk-free} \\
&\quad\ \text{rate (since the market is riskier than } R_f\text{, the assumption is that} \\
&\quad\ \text{the expected } K_m \text{ will be greater than } R_f) \\
\beta(K_m - R_f) &= \text{Expected return above the risk-free rate for the stock of} \\
&\quad\ \text{Company j, given the level of risk}
\end{aligned}
$$

The model centers on "beta," the coefficient of the premium demanded by an investor to invest in an individual stock. For each individual security, **beta** measures the sensitivity (volatility) of the security's return to the market. By definition, the market has a beta of 1.0, so that if an individual company's beta is 1.0, it can expect to have returns as volatile as the market and total returns equal to the market. A company with a beta of 2.0

www.mhhe.com/bh12e

would be twice as volatile as the market and would be expected to generate more returns, whereas a company with a beta of 0.5 would be half as volatile as the market.

The term $(K_m - R_f)$ indicates common stock is expected to generate a rate of return higher than the return on a U.S. Treasury bill. This makes sense since common stock has more risk. Research by Roger Ibbotson shows that this risk premium over the last 79 years is close to 6.5 percent on average but exhibits a wide standard deviation.[2] In the actual application of the CAPM to cost of capital, companies often will use this historical risk premium in their calculations. In our example we use 6.5 percent to represent the expected $(K_m - R_f)$.

For example, assuming the risk-free rate is 5.5 percent and the market risk premium $(K_m - R_f)$ is 6.5 percent, the following returns would occur with betas of 2.0, 1.0, and 0.5:

$$K_2 = 5.5\% + 2.0(6.5\%) = 5.5\% + 13.0\% = 18.5\%$$
$$K_1 = 5.5\% + 1.0(6.5\%) = 5.5\% + 6.5\% = 12.0\%$$
$$K_{.5} = 5.5\% + 0.5(6.5\%) = 5.5\% + 3.25\% = 8.75\%$$

The beta term measures the riskiness of an investment relative to the market. To outperform the market, one would have to assume more risk by selecting assets with betas greater than 1.0. Another way of looking at the risk-return trade-off would be that if less risk than the market is desired, an investor would choose assets with a beta of less than 1.0. Beta is a good measure of a stock's risk when the stock is combined into a portfolio, and therefore it has some bearing on the assets that a company acquires for its portfolio of real capital.

In Figure 11A–1, individual stock returns were compared to market returns and the beta from Formula 11A–1 was shown. From Formula 11A–2, the risk-premium model, a generalized risk-return graph called the **security market line** (SML) can be constructed that identifies the risk-return trade-off of any common stock (asset) relative to the company's beta. This is shown in Figure 11A–2.

Figure 11A–2

The security market line (SML)

---

[2]Ibbotson Associates, *Stocks, Bonds, Bills and Inflation: 2005 Yearbook* (Chicago: Ibbotson Associates and Capital Market Research Center, 2005).

The required return for all securities can be expressed as the risk-free rate plus a premium for risk. Thus we see that a stock with a beta of 1.0 would have a risk premium of 6.5 percent added to the risk-free rate of 5.5 percent to provide a required return of 12 percent. Since a beta of 1.0 implies risk equal to the stock market, the return is also at the overall market rate. If the beta is 2.0, twice the market risk premium of 6.5 percent must be earned, and we add 13 percent to the risk-free rate of 5.5 percent to determine the required return of 18.5 percent. For a beta of 0.5, the required return is 8.75 percent.

Cost of Capital Considerations

When calculating the cost of capital for common stock, remember that K_e is equal to the expected total return from the dividend yield and capital gains.

$$K_e = \frac{D_1}{P_0} + g$$

K_e is the return required by investors based on expectations of future dividends and growth. The SML provides the same information, but in a market-related risk-return model. As required returns rise, prices must fall to adjust to the new equilibrium return level, and as required returns fall, prices rise. Stock markets are generally efficient, and when stock prices are in equilibrium, the K_e derived from the dividend model will be equal to K_j derived from the SML.

The SML helps us to identify several circumstances that can cause the cost of capital to change. Figure 11–2 in Chapter 11 examined required rates of returns over time with changing interest rates and stock prices. Figure 11A–3 does basically the same thing, only through the SML format.

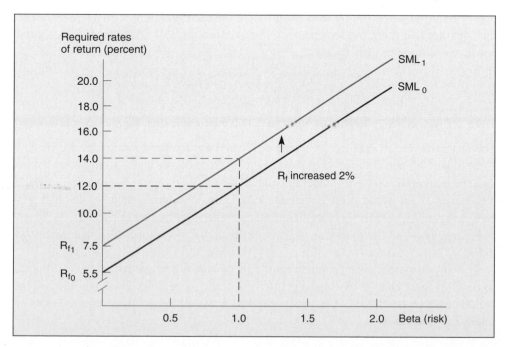

Figure 11A–3

The security market line and changing interest rates

When interest rates increase from the initial period (R_{f1} versus R_{f0}), the security market line in the next period is parallel to SML_0, but higher. What this means is that required rates of return have risen for every level of risk, as investors desire to maintain their risk premium over the risk-free rate.

One very important variable influencing interest rates is the rate of inflation. As inflation increases, lenders try to maintain their real dollar purchasing power, so they increase the required interest rates to offset inflation. The risk-free rate can be thought of as:

$$R_f = RR + IP$$

where

> RR is the real rate of return on a riskless government security when inflation is zero.
>
> IP is an inflation premium that compensates lenders (investors) for loss of purchasing power.

An upward shift in the SML indicates that the prices of all assets will shift downward as interest rates move up. In Chapter 10, "Valuation and Rates of Return," this was demonstrated in the discussion that showed that when market interest rates went up, bond prices adjusted downward to make up for the lower coupon rate (interest payment) on the old bonds.

Another factor affecting the cost of capital is a change in risk preferences by investors. As investors become more pessimistic about the economy, they require larger premiums for assuming risks. Even though the historical average market risk premium may be close to 6.5 percent, this is not stable and investors' changing attitudes can have a big impact on the market risk premium. For example, the 1987 stock market crash on October 19 (a 22.6 percent decline in one day) had to be somewhat influenced by investors' quick moves to a more risk-averse attitude. This risk aversion shows up in higher required stock returns and lower stock prices. For example, if investors raise their market risk premium to 8 percent, the required rates of return from the original equations will increase as follows:

$$K_2 = 5.5\% + 2.0(8.0\%) = 5.5\% + 16.0\% = 21.5\%$$
$$K_1 = 5.5\% + 1.0(8.0\%) = 5.5\% + 8.0\% = 13.5\%$$
$$K_{.5} = 5.5\% + 0.5(8.0\%) = 5.5\% + 4.0\% = 9.5\%$$

The change in the market risk premium will cause the required market return (beta = 1.00) to be 13.5 percent instead of the 12 percent from Figure 11A–2. Any asset riskier than the market would have a larger increase in the required return. For example, a stock with a beta of 2.0 would need to generate a 21.5 percent return, instead of the 18.5 percent in Figure 11A–2. The overall shape of the new security market line (SML_1) is shown in Figure 11A–4 on the following page. Note the higher slope for SML_1, in comparison to SML_0.

In many instances rising interest rates and pessimistic investors go hand in hand, so the SML may change its slope and intercept at the same time. This combined effect would cause severe drops in the prices of risky assets and much larger required rates of return for such assets.

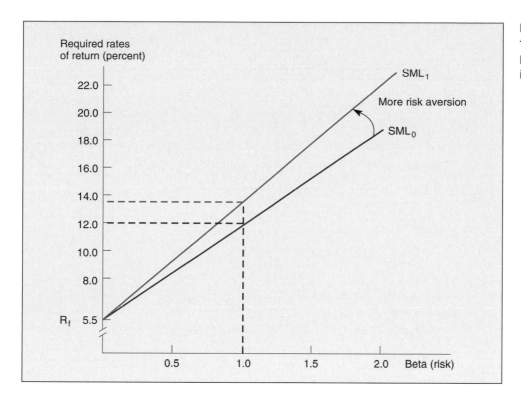

Figure 11A–4

The security market line and changing investor expectations

The capital asset pricing model and the security market line have been presented to further your understanding of market-related events that impact the firm's cost of capital, such as market returns and risk, changing interest rates, and changing risk preferences.

While the capital asset pricing model has received criticism because of the difficulties of dealing with the betas of individual securities and because of the problems involved in consistently constructing the appropriate slope of the SML to represent reality, it provides some interesting insights into risk-return measurement.

List of Terms

capital asset pricing model   359   **beta**   361
market risk premium   360   **security market line**   362

Discussion Questions

11A–1.   How does the capital asset pricing model help explain changing costs of capital?

11A–2.   How does the SML react to changes in the rate of interest, changes in the rate of inflation, and changing investor expectations?

Problems

Capital asset
pricing model

11A–1.   Assume that R_f = 6 percent and K_m = 10 percent. Compute K_j for the
following betas, using Formula 11A–2.

a.   0.7

b.   1.4

c.   1.7

Capital asset
pricing model

11A–2.   In the preceding problem, assume an increase in interest rates changes R_f to
7.0 percent, and the market risk premium ($K_m - R_f$) changes to 6.5 percent.
Compute K_j for the three betas of 0.7, 1.4, and 1.7.

12

The Capital Budgeting Decision

The decision on capital outlays is among the most significant a firm has to make. A decision to build a new plant or expand into a foreign market may influence the performance of the firm over the next decade. The airline industry has shown a tendency to expand in excess of its needs, while other industries have insufficient capacity. The auto industry has often miscalculated its product mix and has had to shift down from one car size to another at an enormous expense.

The capital budgeting decision involves the planning of expenditures for a project with a life of at least one year, and usually considerably longer. In the public utilities sector, a time horizon of 25 years is not unusual. The capital expenditure decision requires extensive planning to ensure that engineering and marketing information is available, product design is completed, necessary patents are acquired, and the capital markets are tapped for the necessary funds. Throughout this chapter we will use techniques developed under the discussion of the time value of money to equate future cash flows to the present, while using the cost of capital as the basic discount rate.

As the time horizon moves farther into the future, uncertainty becomes a greater hazard. The manager is uncertain about annual costs and inflows, product life, interest rates, economic conditions, and technological change. A good example of the vagueness of the marketplace can be observed in the pocket calculator industry going back to the 1970s. A number of firms tooled up in the early 1970s in the hope of being first to break through the $100 price range for pocket calculators, assuming that penetration of the $100 barrier would bring a larger market share and high profitability. However, technological advancement, price cutting, and the appearance of Texas Instruments in the consumer market drove prices down by 60 to 90 percent and made the $100 pocket calculator a museum piece. Rapid Data Systems, the first entry into the under-$100 market, went into bankruptcy. The same type of change, though less dramatic, can be viewed in the personal computer industry over the last 20 years. IBM and Apple took the early lead in product development and had no difficulty selling their products in the $2,000 to $5,000 range. As Compaq, Dell, and foreign competitors moved into the market, prices not only dropped by 50 percent, but also consumer demand for quality went up. Not all new developments are so perilous, and a number of techniques, which will be treated in the next chapter, have been devised to cope with the impact of uncertainty on decision making.

It should be pointed out that capital budgeting is not only important to people in finance or accounting, it is essential to people throughout the business organization. For example, a marketing or production manager who is proposing a new product must be familiar with the capital budgeting procedures of the firm. If he or she is not familiar with the concepts presented in this chapter, the best idea in the world may not be approved because it has not been properly evaluated and presented. You must not only be familiar with your product, but also with its financial viability.

In this chapter capital budgeting is studied under the following major topical headings: administrative considerations, accounting flows versus cash flows, methods of ranking investment proposals, selection strategy, capital rationing, combining cash flow analysis and selection strategy, and the replacement decision. Later in the chapter, taxes and their impact on depreciation and capital budgeting decisions are emphasized.

Administrative Considerations

A good capital budgeting program requires that a number of steps be taken in the decision-making process.

1. Search for and discovery of investment opportunities.
2. Collection of data.
3. Evaluation and decision making.
4. Reevaluation and adjustment.

The search for new opportunities is often the least emphasized, though perhaps the most important, of the four steps. The collection of data should go beyond engineering data and market surveys and should attempt to capture the relative likelihood of the occurrence of various events. The probabilities of increases or slumps in product demand may be evaluated from statistical analysis, while other outcomes may be estimated subjectively.

After all data have been collected and evaluated, the final decision must be made. Generally determinations involving relatively small amounts of money will be made at the department or division level, while major expenditures can be approved only by top management. A constant monitoring of the results of a given decision may indicate that a new set of probabilities must be developed, based on first-year experience, and the initial decision to choose Product A over Product B must be reevaluated and perhaps reversed. The preceding factors are illustrated in Figure 12–1.

Accounting Flows versus Cash Flows

In most capital budgeting decisions the emphasis is on **cash flow**, rather than reported income. Let us consider the logic of using cash flow in the capital budgeting process. Because depreciation does not represent an actual expenditure of funds in arriving

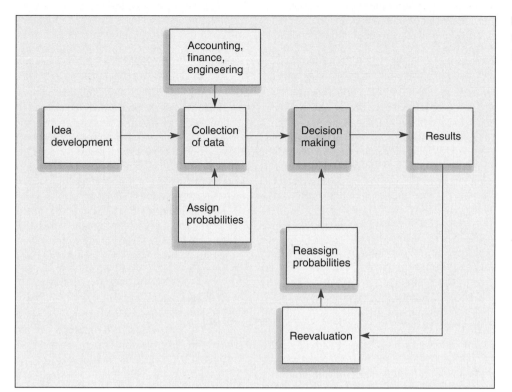

Figure 12–1

Capital budgeting procedures

at profit, it is added back to profit to determine the amount of cash flow generated.[1] Assume the Alston Corporation has $50,000 of new equipment to be depreciated at $5,000 per year. The firm has $20,000 in earnings before depreciation and taxes and pays 35 percent in taxes. The information is presented in Table 12–1 to illustrate the key points involved.

Earnings before depreciation and taxes (cash inflow)	$20,000
Depreciation (noncash expense)	5,000
Earnings before taxes	15,000
Taxes (cash outflow)	5,250
Earnings after taxes	9,750
Depreciation	+ 5,000
Cash flow	$14,750

Table 12–1

Cash flow for Alston Corporation

The firm shows $9,750 in earnings after taxes, but it adds back the noncash deduction of $5,000 in depreciation to arrive at a cash flow figure of $14,750. The logic of

---

[1]As explained in Chapter 2, depreciation is not a new source of funds (except in tax savings) but represents a noncash outlay to be added back.

Bang—Bang, You're Dead

Northrop Grumman used to be a supplier of individual military weapons (guns, planes, and so on). Through capital budgeting expenditures and acquisitions, it has reinvented itself as an integrater of military systems—linking data from satellites and radar to weapons mounted on fighter jets, warships, and guided missiles.

For its sophisticated retooling, it was selected as the *Forbes* magazine "Company of the Year" in the January 6, 2003, issue. Whether you think Northrop is a contributor or a detriment to society, there is no question that it has fulfilled the requirements of the first box of Figure 12–1 of this chapter, "Idea development." As stated by CEO Kent Kresa, "My God, this is the new Northrop Grumman. No more point-and-shoot; targets move too quickly for that. The modern battlefield needs a hot link between the sensor and the shooter."*

Here's the idea as described in *Forbes*. A Northrop Grumman Global Hawk buzzing at 60,000 feet sends intelligence data to a laser-guided targeting device on the ground, which coordinates with an F-35 Joint Strike Fighter jet flying on a fuselage made by Northrop, all of it coordinated by computers and software linked together by Northrop's systems integration unit. Borrowing a catchphrase from the computer business, the weapons designers say that their systems are made for "networkcentric warfare." The connections are as important as the firepower at the end.

Enough high-tech talk for now. Let's converse in terms we financiers all understand. In the great bear market of 2000–2002, this company's stock went the opposite way and increased in value by over 50 percent and it continues to do well. Part of this can be attributed to a favorable environment for defense stocks, and part to good management and astute capital budgeting decisions. Those good decisions were carried on from formerly quoted CEO Kresa to his successor, Roger Sugar, who is no high-tech slouch himself with a PhD in electrical engineering.

The Northrop Grumman empire has been enhanced by recent acquisitions of Westinghouse Defense (1994), Logicom (1997), Data Procurement Corp. (1999), Litton Industries (2001), and TRW (2002).

The icing on the cake for the reinvented firm is the 90,000-ton, 1,100 foot-long *Ronald Reagan,* a ship Northrop Grumman took the lead in designing and building.

_____

*Seth Lubove, lead story in *Forbes* "Platinum List," January 6, 2002, pp. 106–108.

adding back depreciation becomes even greater if we consider the impact of $20,000 in depreciation for the Alston Corp. (Table 12–2). Net earnings before and after taxes are zero, but the company has $20,000 cash in the bank.

Table 12–2

Revised cash flow for Alston Corporation

Earnings before depreciation and taxes	$20,000
Depreciation	20,000
Earnings before taxes	0
Taxes	0
Earnings after taxes.	0
Depreciation	+20,000
Cash flow.	$20,000

To the capital budgeting specialist, the use of cash flow figures is well accepted. However, top management does not always take a similar viewpoint. Assume you are the president of a firm listed on the New York Stock Exchange and must select between two alternatives. Proposal A will provide zero in aftertax earnings and $100,000 in cash flow, while Proposal B, calling for no depreciation, will provide $50,000 in after-tax earnings and cash flow. As president of a publicly traded firm, you have security analysts constantly penciling in their projections of your earnings for the next quarter, and you fear your stock may drop dramatically if earnings are too low by even a small amount. Although Proposal A is superior, you may be more sensitive to aftertax earnings than to cash flow and you may therefore select Proposal B. Perhaps you are overly concerned about the short-term impact of a decision rather than the long-term economic benefits that might accrue.

The student must be sensitive to executives' concessions to short-term pressures. Nevertheless in the material that follows, the emphasis is on the use of proper evaluation techniques to make the best economic choices and assure long-term wealth maximization.

Three widely used methods for evaluating capital expenditures will be considered, along with the shortcomings and advantages of each.

1. Payback method.
2. Internal rate of return.
3. Net present value.

The first method, while not conceptually sound, is often used. Approaches 2 and 3 are more acceptable, and one or the other should be applied to most situations.

Methods of Ranking Investment Proposals

Payback Method

Under the **payback** method, we compute the time required to recoup the initial investment. Assume we are called on to select between Investments A and B in Table 12–3.

Table 12–3
Investment alternatives

	Cash Inflows (of $10,000 investment)	
Year	Investment A	Investment B
1	$5,000	$1,500
2	5,000	2,000
3	2,000	2,500
4		5,000
5		5,000

The payback period for Investment A is 2 years, while Investment B requires 3.8 years. In the latter case, we recover $6,000 in the first three years, leaving us with the need for another $4,000 to recoup the full $10,000 investment. Since the fourth year has a total inflow of $5,000, $4,000 represents 0.8 of that value. Thus the payback period for Investment B is 3.8 years.

In using the payback method to select Investment A, two important considerations are ignored. First there is no consideration of inflows after the cutoff period. The $2,000 in year 3 for Investment A in Table 12–3 is ignored, as is the $5,000 in year 5 for Investment B. Even if the $5,000 were $50,000, it would have no impact on the decision under the payback method.

Second, the method fails to consider the concept of the time value of money. If we had two $10,000 investments with the following inflow patterns, the payback method would rank them equally.

Year	Early Returns	Late Returns
1	$9,000	$1,000
2	1,000	9,000
3	1,000	1,000

Although both investments have a payback period of two years, the first alternative is clearly superior because the $9,000 comes in the first year rather than the second.

The payback method does have some features that help to explain its use by U.S. corporations. It is easy to understand, and it emphasizes liquidity. An investment must recoup the initial investment quickly or it will not qualify (most corporations use a maximum time horizon of three to five years). A rapid payback may be particularly important to firms in industries characterized by rapid technological developments.

Nevertheless the payback method, concentrating as it does on only the initial years of investment, fails to discern the optimum or most economic solution to a capital budgeting problem. The analyst is therefore required to consider more theoretically correct methods.

Internal Rate of Return

The **internal rate of return (IRR)** calls for determining the yield on an investment, that is, calculating the interest rate that equates the cash outflows (cost) of an investment with the subsequent cash inflows. The simplest case would be an investment of $100 that provides $120 after one year, or a 20 percent internal rate of return. For more complicated situations, we use Appendix B (present value of a single amount) and Appendix D (present value of an annuity) at the back of the book, and the techniques described in Chapter 9, "The Time Value of Money." For example, a $1,000 investment returning an annuity of $244 per year for five years provides an internal rate of return of 7 percent, as indicated by the following calculations.

1. First divide the investment (present value) by the annuity.

$$\frac{\text{(Investment)}}{\text{(Annuity)}} = \frac{\$1,000}{\$244} = 4.1 \ (\text{PV}_{\text{IFA}})$$

2. Then proceed to Appendix D (present value of an annuity). The factor of 4.1 for five years indicates a yield of 7 percent.

Whenever an annuity is being evaluated, annuity interest factors (PV_{IFA}) can be used to find the final IRR solution. If an uneven cash inflow is involved, we are not so lucky. We need to use a trial and error method. The first question is, Where do we start? What interest rate should we pick for our first trial? Assume we are once again called on to evaluate the two investment alternatives in Table 12–3, only this time using the internal rate of return to rank the two projects. Because neither proposal represents a precise annuity stream, we must use the trial and error approach to determine an answer. We begin with Investment A.

Cash Inflows
(of $10,000 investment)

Year	Investment A	Investment B
1	$5,000	$1,500
2	5,000	2,000
3	2,000	2,500
4		5,000
5		5,000

1. To find a beginning value to start our first trial, average the inflows as if we were really getting an annuity.

$$\$ 5,000$$
$$5,000$$
$$\underline{2,000}$$
$$\$12,000 \div 3 = \$4,000$$

2. Then divide the investment by the "assumed" annuity value in step 1.

$$\frac{\text{(Investment)}}{\text{(Annuity)}} = \frac{\$10,000}{\$4,000} = 2.5 \ (\text{PV}_{\text{IFA}})$$

3. Proceed to Appendix D to arrive at a *first approximation* of the internal rate of return, using:

$$\text{PV}_{\text{IFA}} \text{ factor} = 2.5$$
$$n(\text{period}) = 3$$

The factor falls between 9 and 10 percent. This is only a first approximation—our actual answer will be closer to 10 percent or higher because our method of averaging cash flows theoretically moved receipts from the first two years into the last year. This averaging understates the actual internal rate of return. The same method would overstate the IRR for Investment B because it would move cash from the last two years into the first three years. Since we know that cash flows in the early years are worth more and increase our return, we can usually gauge whether our first approximation is overstated or understated.

4. We now enter into a trial and error process to arrive at an answer. Because these cash flows are uneven rather than an annuity, we need to use Appendix B. We will begin with 10 percent and then try 12 percent.

Year	10%		Year	12%	
1	$5,000 × 0.909 =	$ 4,545	1	$5,000 × 0.893 =	$4,465
2	5,000 × 0.826 =	4,130	2	5,000 × 0.797 =	3,985
3	2,000 × 0.751 =	1,502	3	2,000 × 0.712 =	1,424
		$10,177			$9,874

At 10%, the present value of the inflows exceeds $10,000—we therefore use a higher discount rate.

At 12%, the present value of the inflows is less than $10,000—thus the discount rate is too high.

The answer must fall between 10 percent and 12 percent, indicating an approximate answer of 11 percent.

If we want to be more accurate, the results can be *interpolated*. Because the internal rate of return is determined when the present value of the inflows (PV_I) equals the present value of the outflows (PV_0), we need to find a discount rate that equates the PV_Is to the cost of $10,000 ($PV_0$). The total difference in present values between 10 percent and 12 percent is $303.

$10,177	PV_I @ 10%		$10,177	PV_I @ 10%
−9,874	PV_I @ 12%		−10,000	(cost)
$ 303			$ 177	

The solution at 10 percent is $177 away from $10,000. Actually the solution is ($177/$303) percent of the way between 10 and 12 percent. Since there is a 2 percentage point difference between the two rates used to evaluate the cash inflows, we need to multiply the fraction by 2 percent and then add our answer to 10 percent for the final answer of:

$$10\% + (\$177/\$303)(2\%) = 11.17\% \text{ IRR}$$

In Investment B the same process will yield an answer of 14.33 percent. (Approximately the same answers can be found through the use of a financially oriented calculator.)

The use of the internal rate of return calls for the prudent selection of Investment B in preference to Investment A, the exact opposite of the conclusion reached under the payback method.

	Investment A	Investment B	Selection
Payback method............	2 years	3.8 years	Quicker payback: Investment A
Internal rate of return........	11.17%	14.33%	Higher yield: Investment B

The final selection of any project under the internal rate of return method will also depend on the yield exceeding some minimum cost standard, such as the cost of capital to the firm.

Net Present Value

The final method of investment selection is to determine the **net present value** of an investment. This is done by discounting back the inflows over the life of the investment to determine whether they equal or exceed the required investment. The basic discount rate is usually the cost of capital to the firm. Thus inflows that arrive in later years must provide a return that at least equals the cost of financing those returns. If we once again evaluate Investments A and B—using an assumed cost of capital, or a discount rate, of 10 percent—we arrive at the following figures for net present value.

$10,000 Investment, 10% Discount Rate						
Year	**Investment A**			Year	**Investment B**	
1	$5,000 × 0.909 =	$ 4,545		1	$1,500 × 0.909 =	$ 1,364
2	5,000 × 0.826 =	4,130		2	2,000 × 0.826 =	1,652
3	2,000 × 0.751 =	1,502		3	2,500 × 0.751 =	1,878
		$10,177		4	5,000 × 0.683 =	3,415
				5	5,000 × 0.621 =	3,105
						$11,414
Present value of inflows		$10,177		Present value of inflows		$11,414
Present value of outflows		−10,000		Present value of outflows		−10,000
Net present value		$177		Net present value............		$ 1,414

While both proposals appear to be acceptable, Investment B has a considerably higher net present value than Investment A.[2] Under most circumstances the net present value and internal rate of return methods give theoretically correct answers, and the subsequent discussion will be restricted to these two approaches. A summary of the various conclusions reached under the three methods is presented in Table 12–4.

	Investment A	Investment B	Selection
Payback method	2 years	3.8 years	Quicker payback: Investment A
Internal rate of return	11.17%	14.33%	Higher yield: Investment B
Net present value	$177	$1,414	Higher net present value: Investment B

Table 12–4
Capital budgeting results

Selection Strategy

In both the internal rate of return and net present value methods, the profitability must equal or exceed the cost of capital for the project to be potentially acceptable. However, other distinctions are necessary—namely, whether the projects are *mutually exclusive or not*. If investments are **mutually exclusive**, the selection of one alternative will preclude the selection of any other alternative. Assume we are going to build a specialized assembly plant, and four major international cities are under consideration, only one of which will be picked. In this situation we select the alternative with the highest acceptable yield or the highest net present value and disregard all others. Even if certain other locations provide a marginal return in excess of the cost of capital, assumed to be 10 percent, they will be rejected. In the table below, the possible alternatives are presented.

Mutually Exclusive Alternatives	IRR	Net Present Value
Bangkok	15%	$300
Beijing	12	200
Mexico City	11	100
Cost of capital	*10*	—
Singapore	9	(100)

Among the mutually exclusive alternatives, only Bangkok would be selected. If the alternatives were not mutually exclusive (for example, much-needed multiple retail outlets), we would accept all of the alternatives that provide a return in excess of our cost of capital, and only Singapore would be rejected.

Applying this logic to Investments A and B in the prior discussion and assuming a cost of capital of 10 percent, only Investment B would be accepted if the alternatives

---

[2]A further possible refinement under the net present value method is to compute a profitability index.

$$\text{Profitability index} - \frac{\text{Present value of the inflows}}{\text{Present value of the outflows}}$$

For Investment A the profitability index is 1.0177 ($10,177/$10,000) and for Investment B it is 1.1414 ($11,414/$10,000). The profitability index can be helpful in comparing returns from different-size investments by placing them on a common measuring standard. This was not necessary in this example.

were mutually exclusive, while both would clearly qualify if they were not mutually exclusive.

	Investment A	Investment B	Accepted If Mutually Exclusive	Accepted If Not Mutually Exclusive
Internal rate of return	11.17%	14.33%	B	A, B
Net present value	$177	$1,414	B	A, B

The discussion to this point has assumed the internal rate of return and net present value methods will call for the same decision. Although this is generally true, there are exceptions. Two rules may be stated:

1. Both methods will accept or reject the same investments based on minimum return or cost of capital criteria. If an investment has a positive net present value, it will also have an internal rate of return in excess of the cost of capital.

2. In certain limited cases, however, the two methods may give different answers in selecting the best investment from a range of acceptable alternatives.

Reinvestment Assumption

It is only under this second state of events that a preference for one method over the other must be established. A prime characteristic of the internal rate of return is the **reinvestment assumption** that all inflows can be reinvested at the yield from a given investment. For example, in the case of the aforementioned Investment A yielding 11.17 percent, the assumption is made that the dollar amounts coming in each year can be reinvested at that rate. For Investment B, with a 14.33 percent internal rate of return, the new funds are assumed to be reinvested at this high rate. The relationships are presented in Table 12–5.

Table 12–5   The reinvestment assumption—internal rate of return ($10,000 investment)

For investments with a very high IRR, it may be unrealistic to assume that reinvestment can occur at an equally high rate. The net present value method, depicted in Table 12–6 on page 377, makes the more conservative assumption that each inflow can be reinvested at the cost of capital or discount rate.

Table 12–6 The reinvestment assumption—net present value ($10,000 investment)

The reinvestment assumption under the net present value method allows for a certain consistency. Inflows from each project are assumed to have the same (though conservative) investment opportunity. Although this may not be an accurate picture for all firms, net present value is generally the preferred method.

Modified Internal Rate of Return   You should also be aware that there is an alternative methodology that combines the reinvestment assumption of the net present value method (cost of capital) with the internal rate of return. This process is termed the **modified internal rate of return (MIRR)**. The analyst searches for the discount rate that will equate the future value of the inflows, each growing at the cost of capital, with the investment.

In terms of a formula, we show:

$$\text{Investment} = \frac{\text{Terminal value of inflows}}{(\text{MIRR})} \qquad (12\text{--}1)$$

The terminal value of the inflows is equal to the sum of the future value of each inflow reinvested at the cost of capital. MIRR is the modified internal rate of return (discount rate) that equates the terminal (final) value of the inflows with the investment. As an example, assume $10,000 will produce the following inflows for the next three years:

Year	Inflows
1..........	$6,000
2..........	5,000
3..........	2,850

The cost of capital is 10 percent.

First, determine the terminal value of the inflows at a growth rate equal to the cost of capital. The assumption is that the inflows will come at the end of each period.

Terminal Value (end of year 3)			
	Periods of Growth	FV Factor (10%)	Future Value
Year 1	$6,000	2	1.21	$ 7,260
Year 2	5,000	1	1.10	5,500
Year 3	2,850	0	1.00	2,850
Terminal Value				$15,610

To determine the modified internal rate of return, we calculate the yield on the investment. The formula to help determine yield is Formula 12–2. PV is the investment value and FV is the terminal value of the inflows.

$$PV_{IF} = \frac{PV}{FV} = \text{(Appendix B)} \qquad (12\text{–}2)$$

$$= \frac{\$10,000}{\$15,610} = .641$$

We go to Appendix B for three periods and a tabular value of .641. We see the yield or modified internal rate of return is 16 percent. Had we computed the conventional internal rate of return used throughout the chapter, the answer would have been approximately 21 percent, which is based on reinvestment at the internal rate of return.

The modified internal rate of return, using the more realistic assumption of reinvestment at the cost of capital, gives a more conservative, perhaps better, answer. For that reason, you should be familiar with it. However in the balance of the chapter, when the internal rate of return is called for, we will use the traditional internal rate of return rather than the modified internal rate of return because of the former's wider usage. (However, Problem 19 at the end of the chapter does call for determining the modified internal rate of return.)

Capital Rationing

At times management may place an artificial constraint on the amount of funds that can be invested in a given period. This is known as **capital rationing**. The executive planning committee may emerge from a lengthy capital budgeting session to announce that only $5 million may be spent on new capital projects this year. Although $5 million may represent a large sum, it is still an artificially determined constraint and not the product of marginal analysis, in which the return for each proposal is related to the cost of capital for the firm, and projects with positive net present values are accepted.

A firm may adopt a posture of capital rationing because it is fearful of too much growth or hesitant to use external sources of financing (perhaps there is a fear of debt). In a strictly economic sense, capital rationing hinders a firm from achieving maximum profitability. With capital rationing, as indicated in Table 12–7, acceptable projects must be ranked, and only those with the highest positive net present value are accepted.

Table 12–7
Capital rationing

	Project	Investment	Total Investment	Net Present Value
Capital rationing solution	A	$2,000,000		$400,000
	B	2,000,000		380,000
	C	1,000,000	$5,000,000	150,000
	D	1,000,000		100,000
Best solution	E	800,000		40,000
	F	800,000		(30,000)

Under capital rationing, only Projects A through C, calling for $5 million in investment, will be accepted. Although Projects D and E have returns exceeding the cost of funds, as evidenced by a positive net present value, they will not be accepted with the capital rationing assumption.

An interesting way to summarize the characteristics of an investment is through the use of the **net present value profile**. The profile allows us to graphically portray the net present value of a project at different discount rates. Let's apply the profile to the investments we have been discussing. The projects are summarized again below.

Net Present Value Profile

	Cash Inflows (of $10,000 investment)	
Year	Investment A	Investment B
1	$5,000	$1,500
2	5,000	2,000
3	2,000	2,500
4		5,000
5		5,000

To apply the net present value profile, you need to know three characteristics about an investment:

1. *The net present value at a zero discount rate.* That is easy to determine. A zero discount rate means no discount rate. The values simply retain their original value. For Investment A the net present value would be $2,000 ($5,000 + $5,000 + $2,000 − $10,000). For Investment B the answer is $6,000 ($1,500 + $2,000 + $2,500 + $5,000 + $5,000 − $10,000).

2. *The net present value as determined by a normal discount rate* (such as the cost of capital). For these two investments, we use a discount rate of 10 percent. As previously summarized in Table 12–4 on page 375, the net present values for the two investments at that discount rate are $177 for Investment A and $1,414 for Investment B.

3. *The internal rate of return for the investments.* Once again referring to Table 12–4, we see the internal rate of return is 11.17 percent for Investment A and 14.33 percent for Investment B. The reader should also realize the internal rate of return is the discount rate that allows the project to have a net present value of zero. This characteristic will become more apparent when we discuss our graphic display.

We summarize the information about discount rates and net present values for each investment below.

Investment A		Investment B	
Discount Rate	Net Present Value	Discount Rate	Net Present Value
0	$2,000	0	$6,000
10%	177	10%	1,414
11.17% (IRR)	0	14.33% (IRR)	0

Note that in Figure 12–2, we have graphed the three points for each investment. For Investment A we showed a $2,000 net present value at a zero discount rate, a $177 net present value at a 10 percent discount rate, and a zero net present value at an 11.17 percent discount rate. We then connected the points. The same procedure was applied to Investment B. The reader can also visually approximate what the net present value for the investment projects would be at other discount rates (such as 5 percent).

Figure 12–2

Net present value profile

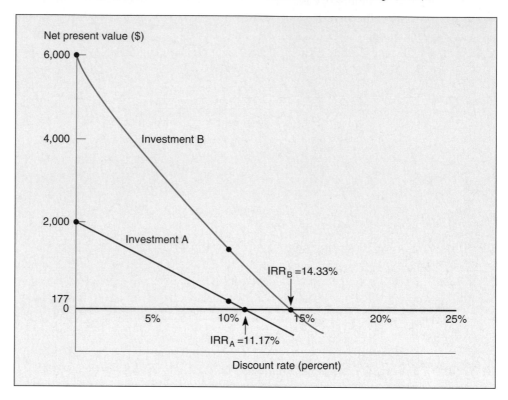

In the current example, the net present value of Investment B was superior to Investment A at every point. This is not always the case in comparing various projects. To illustrate let's introduce a new project, Investment C, and then compare it with Investment B.

Investment C	
($10,000 Investment)	
Year	**Cash Inflows**
1	$9,000
2	3,000
3	1,200

Characteristics of Investment C

1. The net present value at a zero discount rate for this project is $3,200 ($9,000 + $3,000 + $1,200 − $10,000).

2. The net present value at a 10 percent discount rate is $1,560.

3. The internal rate of return is 22.51 percent.

Comparing Investment B to Investment C in Figure 12–3, we observe that at low discount rates, Investment B has a higher net present value than Investment C. However, at high discount rates, Investment C has a higher net present value than Investment B. The actual crossover point can be viewed as approximately 8.7 percent. At lower rates (below 8.7 percent), you would choose Investment B. At higher rates (above 8.7 percent), you would select Investment C. Since the cost of capital is presumed to be 10 percent, you would probably prefer Investment C.

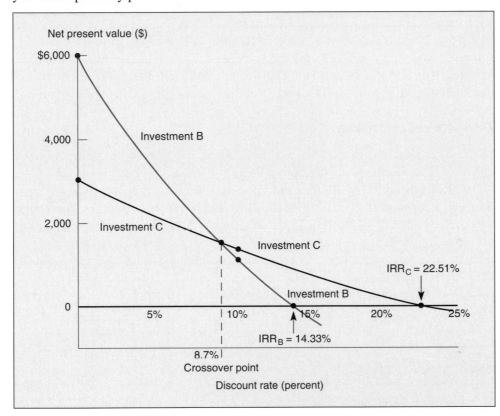

Figure 12–3

Net present value profile with crossover

Why does Investment B do well compared to Investment C at low discount rates and relatively poorly compared to Investment C at high discount rates? This difference is related to the timing of inflows. Let's examine the inflows as reproduced in the following table.

	Cash Inflows (of $10,000 investment)	
Year	Investment B	Investment C
1	$1,500	$9,000
2	2,000	3,000
3	2,500	1,200
4	5,000	
5	5,000	

Investment B has heavy late inflows ($5,000 in both the fourth and fifth years) and these are more strongly penalized by high discount rates. Investment C has extremely high early inflows and these hold up well with high discount rates.

As previously mentioned in the chapter, if the investments are nonmutually exclusive or there is no capital rationing, we would probably accept both Investments B and C at discount rates below 14.33 percent, because they both would have positive net present values. If we can select only one, the decision may well turn on the discount rate. Observe in Figure 12–3 at a discount rate of 5 percent we would select Investment B, at 10 percent we would select Investment C, and so on. The net present value profile helps us make such decisions. Now back to basic capital budgeting issues.

Combining Cash Flow Analysis and Selection Strategy

Many of the points that we have covered thus far will be reviewed in the context of a capital budgeting decision, in which we determine the annual cash flows from an investment and compare them to the initial outlay. To be able to analyze a wide variety of cash flow patterns, we shall first consider the types of allowable depreciation.

The Rules of Depreciation

Through recent tax legislation, assets are classified according to nine categories that determine the allowable rate of depreciation write-off. Each class is referred to as a "MACRS" category; **MACRS** stands for **modified accelerated cost recovery system**. Some references are also made to **ADR**, which stands for **asset depreciation range**, or the expected physical life of the asset or class of assets. Most assets can be written off more rapidly than the midpoint of their ADR. For example, an asset may have a midpoint of its ADR of four years, which means the middle of its expected useful life is four years; this asset might be written off over three years. Table 12–8 on page 383 shows the various categories for depreciation, linking the depreciation write-off period to the midpoint of the ADR.

It is not necessary that you become an expert in determining the category of an asset. In problems at the end of this material you will be given enough information to easily make a determination.

Each of the nine categories in Table 12–8 has its own rate of depreciation that can be applied to the purchase price of the asset. We will direct our attention to the first six categories in Table 12–8, which apply to assets normally used in business transactions. The last three categories relate to real estate investments and, for purposes of simplicity, will not be covered.

The rates of depreciation that apply to the first six classes in Table 12–8 are shown in Table 12–9 also on page 383.[3] The rates shown in Table 12–9 are developed with the use of the half-year convention, which treats all property as if it were put in service in midyear. The half-year convention is also extended to the sale or retirement of an asset. Thus for three-year MACRS depreciation, there are four years of depreciation to be taken, as demonstrated below:

Year 1	½ year
Year 2	1 year
Year 3	1 year
Year 4	½ year

3-year MACRS depreciation

---

[3]The depreciation rates were temporarily increased under the *Job Creation and Worker Assistance Act of 2002.* Since this provision is only applicable for assets purchased after September 10, 2001, and before September 11, 2004, it is not considered here.

Table 12–8

Categories for
depreciation write-off

Class	
3-year MACRS	All property with ADR midpoints of four years or less. Autos and light trucks are excluded from this category.
5-year MACRS	Property with ADR midpoints of more than 4, but less than 10 years. Key assets in this category include automobiles, light trucks, and technological equipment such as computers and research-related properties.
7-year MACRS	Property with ADR midpoints of 10 years or more, but less than 16 years. Most types of manufacturing equipment would fall into this category, as would office furniture and fixtures.
10-year MACRS	Property with ADR midpoints of 16 years or more, but less than 20 years. Petroleum refining products, railroad tank cars, and manufactured homes fall into this group.
15-year MACRS	Property with ADR midpoints of 20 years or more, but less than 25 years. Land improvement, pipeline distribution, telephone distribution, and sewage treatment plants all belong in this category.
20-year MACRS	Property with ADR midpoints of 25 years or more (with the exception of real estate, which is treated separately). Key investments in this category include electric and gas utility property and sewer pipes.
27.5-year MACRS	Residential rental property if 80% or more of the gross rental income is from nontransient dwelling units (e.g., an apartment building); low-income housing.
31.5-year MACRS	Nonresidential real property is real property that has no ADR class life or whose class life is 27.5 years or more.
39-year MACRS	Nonresidential real property placed in service after May 12, 1993.

Table 12–9

Depreciation
percentages (expressed
in decimals)

Depreciation Year	3-Year MACRS	5-Year MACRS	7-Year MACRS	10-Year MACRS	15-Year MACRS	20-Year MACRS
1	.333	.200	.143	.100	.050	.038
2	.445	.320	.245	.180	.095	.072
3	.148	.192	.175	.144	.086	.067
4	.074	.115	.125	.115	.077	.062
5		.115	.089	.092	.069	.057
6		.058	.089	.074	.062	.053
7			.089	.066	.059	.045
8			.045	.066	.059	.045
9				.065	.059	.045
10				.065	.059	.045
11				.033	.059	.045
12					.059	.045
13					.059	.045
14					.059	.045
15					.059	.045
16					.030	.045
17						.045
18						.045
19						.045
20						.045
21						.017
	1.000	1.000	1.000	1.000	1.000	1.000

For five-year depreciation, there are six years to be taken, and so on.

Let's return to Table 12–9 on the bottom of the prior page, and assume you purchase a $50,000 asset that falls in the five-year MACRS category. How much would your depreciation be for the next six years? (Don't forget that we get an extra year because of the half-year convention.) The depreciation schedule is shown in Table 12–10.

Table 12–10
Depreciation schedule

(1) Year	(2) Depreciation Base	(3) Percentage Depreciation (Table 12–9)	(4) Annual Depreciation
1	$50,000	.200	$10,000
2	50,000	.320	16,000
3	50,000	.192	9,600
4	50,000	.115	5,750
5	50,000	.115	5,750
6	50,000	.058	2,900
		Total Depreciation	$50,000

The Tax Rate

In analyzing investment decisions, a corporate tax rate must be considered. As mentioned in Chapter 2, the rate has been changed four times since 1980, and it is almost certain to be changed again in the future. Although the maximum quoted federal corporate tax rate is now in the mid–30 percent range, very few pay this rate. Smaller corporations and those with big tax breaks for research and development, new asset purchases, or natural resource development may only pay taxes at a 15 to 20 percent rate. Larger corporations with foreign tax obligations and special state levies may pay effective total taxes of 40 percent or more. In the following examples, we shall use a rate of 35 percent, but remember, the rate varies from situation to situation and from time period to time period. In the problems at the back of the chapter, you will be given a variety of tax rates with which to work.

Actual Investment Decision

Assume in the $50,000 depreciation analysis shown in Table 12–10 above that we are given additional facts and asked to make an investment decision about whether an asset should be purchased or not. We shall assume we are purchasing a piece of machinery that will have a six-year productive life. It will produce income of $18,500 for the first three years before deductions for depreciation and taxes. In the last three years, the income before depreciation and taxes will be $12,000. Furthermore, we will assume a corporate tax rate of 35 percent and a cost of capital of 10 percent for the analysis. The annual cash flow related to the machinery is presented in Table 12–11. For each year we subtract depreciation from "earnings before depreciation and taxes" to arrive at earnings before taxes. We then subtract the taxes to determine earnings after taxes. Finally depreciation is added to earnings after taxes to arrive at cash flow. The cash flow starts at $15,525 in the first year and ends at $8,815 in the last year.

Table 12–11 Cash flow related to the purchase of machinery

	Year 1	Year 2	Year 3	Year 4	Year 5	Year 6
Earnings before depreciation and taxes (EBDT)	$18,500	$18,500	$18,500	$12,000	$12,000	$12,000
Depreciation (from Table 12–10)	10,000	16,000	9,600	5,750	5,750	2,900
Earnings before taxes	8,500	2,500	8,900	6,250	6,250	9,100
Taxes (35%)	2,975	875	3,115	2,188	2,188	3,185
Earnings after taxes	5,525	1,625	5,785	4,062	4,062	5,915
+ Depreciation	10,000	16,000	9,600	5,750	5,750	2,900
Cash flow	$15,525	$17,625	$15,385	$ 9,812	$ 9,812	$ 8,815

Having determined the annual cash flows, we now are in a position to discount the values back to the present at the previously specified cost of capital, 10 percent. The analysis is presented in Table 12–12. At the bottom of the same table, the present value of the inflows is compared to the present value of the outflows (simply the cost of the asset) to arrive at a net present value of $7,991. On the basis of the analysis, it appears that the asset should be purchased.

Table 12–12

Net present value analysis

Year	Cash Flow (inflows)	Present Value Factor (10%)	Present Value
1	$15,525	.909	$14,112
2	17,625	.826	14,558
3	15,385	.751	11,554
4	9,812	.683	6,702
5	9,812	.621	6,093
6	8,815	.564	4,972
			$57,991
Present value of inflows			$57,991
Present value of outflows (cost)			50,000
Net present value			$ 7,991

The Replacement Decision

So far our analysis has centered on an investment that is being considered as a net addition to the present plant and equipment. However, many investment decisions occur because of new technology, and these are considered **replacement decisions**. The financial manager often needs to determine whether a new machine with advanced technology can do the job better than the machine being used at present.

These replacement decisions include several additions to the basic investment situation. For example we need to include the sale of the old machine in our analysis. This sale will produce a cash inflow that partially offsets the purchase price of the new machine. In addition the sale of the old machine will usually have tax consequences. Some of the cash inflow from the sale will be taxable if the old machine is sold for more than book value. If it is sold for less than book value, this will be considered a loss and will provide a tax benefit.

The replacement decision can be analyzed by using a total analysis of both the old and new machines or by using an incremental analysis that emphasizes the changes in cash flows between the old and the new machines. We will emphasize the incremental approach.

Assume the Bradley Corporation purchased a computer two years ago for $120,000. The asset is being depreciated under the five-year MACRS schedule shown in Table 12–9, which implies a six-year write-off because of the half-year convention. We will assume the old computer can be sold for $37,600. A new computer will cost $180,000 and will also be written off using the five-year MACRS schedule in Table 12–9.

The new computer will provide cost savings and operating benefits, compared to the old computer, of $42,000 per year for the next six years. These cost savings and operating benefits are the equivalent of increased earnings before depreciation and taxes. The firm has a 35 percent tax rate and a 10 percent cost of capital. First we need to determine the net cost of the new computer. We will take the purchase price of the new computer ($180,000) and subtract the cash inflow from the sale of the old computer.

Sale of Old Asset

The cash inflow from the sale of the old computer is based on the sales price as well as the related tax factors. To determine these tax factors, we first compute the book value of the old computer and compare this figure to the sales price to determine if there is a taxable gain or loss. The book value of the old computer is shown in Table 12–13.

Table 12–13

Book value of old computer

Year	Depreciation Base	Percentage Depreciation (Table 12–9)	Annual Depreciation
1	$120,000	.200	$ 24,000
2	120,000	.320	38,400
Total depreciation to date			$ 62,400
Purchase price			$120,000
Total depreciation to date			62,400
Book value			$ 57,600

Since the book value of the old computer is $57,600 and the sales price (previously given) is $37,600, there will be a $20,000 loss.

Book value	$57,600
Sales price	37,600
Tax loss on sale	$20,000

This loss can be written off against other income for the corporation.[4] The Bradley Corporation has a 35 percent tax rate, so the tax write-off is worth $7,000.

---

[4]Note that had there been a capital gain instead of a loss, it would have been automatically taxed at the corporation's normal tax rate.

Tax loss on sale	$20,000
Tax rate.	35%
Tax benefit	$ 7,000

We now add the tax benefit to the sale price to arrive at the cash inflow from the sale of the old computer.

Sale price of old computer	$37,600
Tax benefit from sale.	7,000
Cash inflow from sale of old computer	$44,600

The computation of the cash inflow figure from the old computer allows us to compute the net cost of the new computer. The purchase price of $180,000, minus the cash inflow from the sale of the old computer, provides a value of $135,400 as indicated in Table 12–14.

Price of new computer	$180,000	
− Cash flow from sale of old computer	44,600	
Net cost of new computer.	$135,400	

Table 12–14
Net cost of new computer

The question then becomes: Are the incremental gains from the new computer compared to those of the old computer large enough to justify the net cost of $135,400? We will assume that both will be operative over the next six years, although the old computer will run out of depreciation in four more years. We will base our cash flow analysis on (*a*) the incremental gain in depreciation and the related tax shield benefits and (*b*) cost savings.

Incremental Depreciation

The annual depreciation on the new computer will be:

Year	Depreciation Base	Percentage Depreciation (Table 12–9)	Annual Depreciation
1	$180,000	.200	$ 36,000
2	180,000	.320	57,600
3	180,000	.192	34,560
4	180,000	.115	20,700
5	180,000	.115	20,700
6	180,000	.058	10,440
			$180,000

The annual depreciation on the old computer for the remaining four years would be:

Year*	Depreciation Base	Percentage Depreciation (Table 12–9)	Annual Depreciation
1	$120,000	.192	$23,040
2	120,000	.115	13,800
3	120,000	.115	13,800
4	120,000	.058	6,960

*The next four years represent the last four years for the old computer, which is already two years old.

In Table 12–15, we bring together the depreciation on the old and new computers to determine **incremental depreciation** and the related tax shield benefits. Since depreciation shields other income from being taxed, the benefits of the tax shield are worth the amount being depreciated times the tax rate. For example in year 1, $12,960 (third column below) in incremental depreciation will keep $12,960 from being taxed, and with the firm in a 35 percent tax bracket, this represents a tax savings of $4,536. The same type of analysis applies to each subsequent year.

Table 12–15

Analysis of incremental depreciation benefits

(1) Year	(2) Depreciation on New Computer	(3) Depreciation on Old Computer	(4) Incremental Depreciation	(5) Tax Rate	(6) Tax Shield Benefits
1	$36,000	$23,040	$12,960	.35	$ 4,536
2	57,600	13,800	43,800	.35	15,330
3	34,560	13,800	20,760	.35	7,266
4	20,700	6,960	13,740	.35	4,809
5	20,700		20,700	.35	7,245
6	10,440		10,440	.35	3,654

Cost Savings

The second type of benefit relates to cost savings from the new computer. As previously stated these savings are assumed to be $42,000 for the next six years. The aftertax benefits are shown in Table 12–16.

Table 12–16

Analysis of incremental cost savings benefits

(1) Year	(2) Cost Savings	(3) 1 − Tax Rate	(4) Aftertax Savings
1	$42,000	.65	$27,300
2	42,000	.65	27,300
3	42,000	.65	27,300
4	42,000	.65	27,300
5	42,000	.65	27,300
6	42,000	.65	27,300

As indicated in Table 12–16, we take the cost savings in column 2 and multiply by one minus the tax rate. This indicates the value of the savings on an aftertax basis.

We now combine the incremental tax shield benefits from depreciation (Table 12–15) and the aftertax cost savings (Table 12–16) to arrive at total annual benefits in Table 12–17 (column 4). These benefits are discounted to the present at a 10 percent cost of capital. The present value of the inflows is $150,950 as indicated at the bottom of column 6 in Table 12–17.

We now are in a position to compare the present value of incremental benefits of $150,950 from Table 12–17 to the net cost of the new computer of $135,400 from Table 12–14. The answer of $15,550 is shown in the middle part of the next page.

Table 12–17
Present value of the total
incremental benefits

(1) Year	(2) Tax Shield Benefits from Depreciation (from Table 12–15)	(3) Aftertax Cost Savings (from Table 12–16)	(4) Total Annual Benefits	(5) Present Value Factor (10%)	(6) Present Value
1	$ 4,536	$27,300	$31,836	.909	$ 28,939
2	15,330	27,300	42,630	.826	35,212
3	7,266	27,300	34,566	.751	25,959
4	4,809	27,300	32,109	.683	21,930
5	7,245	27,300	34,545	.621	21,452
6	3,654	27,300	30,954	.564	17,458
		Present value of incremental benefits			$150,950

Present value of incremental benefits	$150,950
Net cost of new computer	135,400
Net present value.	$ 15,550

Clearly there is a positive net present value, and the purchase of the computer should be recommended on the basis of the financial analysis.

Capital Budgeting Practices Utilized by Smaller, Privately Held Businesses

**finance in
action**

While the techniques described in this chapter are intended to be used by the modern, sophisticated business manager, not everyone uses them. It is, however, true that survey studies of large business firms over the past decade have shown an increasing acceptance of such concepts as discounted cash flow (as represented by the internal rate of return or net present value methods) and weighted average cost of capital.

But what about people who do capital budgeting analyses for smaller, privately held business firms? There have been extensive surveys done and only a relatively small percentage of these firms (generally less than 20 percent) use discounted cash flow methods. For example, Runyon* found only 14.4 percent of his questionnaire respondents in small business firms used the internal rate of return or net present value approach. The rest used the payback method or some other unsophisticated approach.

Why do large business firms use theoretically correct approaches, while small business firms do not? There are two primary reasons. The first is that the small business manager is likely to be less sophisticated and educated in financial matters than the employee of a larger corporation. The small businessperson's skills are more likely to be in designing products, meeting customer demands, and hiring and satisfying employees.

But rather than be too critical, we should also realize the second reason why small business owners might be using the payback method or similar less sophisticated techniques. Small business owners must deal primarily with bankers or finance companies rather than stockholders or bondholders. When small business owners approach a banker for a loan to finance a capital investment, they should be prepared to demonstrate their capacity to repay the loan within a set period of time rather than quote their internal rate of return or net present value. That is the reason the payback method is often used, and the payback period required often is "the maturity the bank will allow on the loan."

*L. R. Runyon, "Capital Budgeting Decision Making in Small Firms," *Journal of Business Research* 11 (September 1983), pp. 389–97.

Elective Expensing	The authors have stressed throughout the chapter the importance of taking deductions as early in the life of the asset as possible. Since a tax deduction produces cash flow, the earlier you can get the cash flow the better. Businesses can actually write off tangible property, such as equipment, furniture, tools, and computers, *in the year* they are purchased for up to $100,000. This is clearly superior to depreciating the asset where the write-off must take place over a number of years. This feature of **elective expensing** is primarily beneficial to small businesses because the allowance is phased out dollar for dollar when total property purchases exceed $200,000 in a year. Thus a business that purchases $300,000 in assets for the year no longer has this option.

Summary

The capital budgeting decision involves the planning of expenditures for a project with a life of at least one year and usually considerably longer. Although top management is often anxious about the impact of their decisions on short-term reported income, the planning of capital expenditures dictates a longer time horizon.

Because capital budgeting deals with actual dollars rather than reported earnings, cash flow instead of operating income is used in the decision.

Three primary methods are used to analyze capital investment proposals: the payback method, the internal rate of return, and the net present value. The first method is unsound, while the last two are acceptable, with net present value deserving our greatest attention. The net present value method uses the cost of capital as the discount rate. In using the cost of capital as the discount, or hurdle, rate, we affirm that a project must at least earn the cost of funding to be acceptable as an investment.

As demonstrated in the chapter, the two forms of benefits attributed to an investment are (*a*) aftertax operating benefits and (*b*) the tax shield benefits of depreciation. The present value of these inflows must exceed the investment for a project to be acceptable.

List of Terms

cash flow   368
payback   371
internal rate of return (IRR)   372
net present value   374
mutually exclusive   375
reinvestment assumption   376
modified internal rate of return   377
capital rationing   378

net present value profile   379
modified accelerated cost recovery
 system (MACRS)   382
asset depreciation range (ADR)   382
replacement decision   385
incremental depreciation   388
elective expensing   390

Discussion Questions

1. What are the important administrative considerations in the capital budgeting process?

2. Why does capital budgeting rely on analysis of cash flows rather than on net income?

3. What are the weaknesses of the payback method?

4. What is normally used as the discount rate in the net present value method?

5. What does the term *mutually exclusive investments* mean?

6. How does the modified internal rate of return include concepts from both the traditional internal rate of return and the net present value methods?

7. If a corporation has projects that will earn more than the cost of capital, should it ration capital?

8. What is the net present value profile? What three points should be determined to graph the profile?

9. How does an asset's ADR (asset depreciation range) relate to its MACRS category?

Practice Problems and Solutions

Cash flow

MACRS

depreciation and

net present value

1. Systems Software has earnings before depreciation and taxes of $180,000, depreciation of $60,000, and a tax rate of 35 percent. Compute its cash flow.

2. Archer Chemical Corp. is considering purchasing new equipment that falls under the three-year MACRS category. The cost is $200,000. Earnings before depreciation and taxes for the next four years will be:

Year 1	$ 90,000
Year 2	105,000
Year 3	85,000
Year 4	35,000

The firm is in a 30 percent tax bracket and has a 12 percent cost of capital. Should it purchase the new equipment?

Solutions

1.

Earnings before depreciation and taxes	$180,000
Depreciation	60,000
Earnings before taxes.	$120,000
Taxes @ 35 percent	42,000
Earnings after taxes	$ 78,000
Depreciation	60,000
Cash flow	$138,000

2. First determine annual depreciation based on the $200,000 purchase price. Use table 12–9 on page 383 for the annual depreciation rate for three-year MACRS depreciation.

Year	Depreciation Base	Percentage Depreciation (Table 12–9)	Annual Depreciation
1	$200,000	.333	$66,600
2	200,000	.445	89,000
3	200,000	.148	29,600
4	200,000	.074	14,800

Then determine the annual cash flow for each year.

	Year 1	Year 2	Year 3	Year 4
Earnings before depreciation and taxes	$90,000	$105,000	$85,000	$35,000
Depreciation	66,600	89,000	29,600	14,800
Earnings before taxes	23,400	16,000	55,400	20,200
Taxes @ 30%	7,020	4,800	16,620	6,060
Earnings after taxes	16,380	11,200	38,780	14,140
Depreciation	66,600	89,000	29,600	14,800
Cash flow	$82,980	$100,200	$68,380	$28,940

Finally, determine the present value of the cash flows and compare that to the $200,000 cost to determine the net present value.

Year	Cash Flow (inflows)	Present Value Factor (12%)	Present Value
1	$82,980	.893	$ 74,101
2	100,200	.797	79,859
3	68,380	.712	48,687
4	28,940	.636	18,406
			$221,053

Present value of inflows	$221,053
Present value of outflows (cost)	200,000
Net present value	$ 21,053

The net present value is positive and the new equipment should be purchased.

Problems

All problems are available in Homework Manager. Please see the preface for more information.

Cash flow

1. Assume a corporation has earnings before depreciation and taxes of $100,000, and depreciation of $50,000, and that it has a 30 percent tax bracket. Compute its cash flow using the format below.

Earnings before depreciation and taxes	_____
Depreciation	_____
Earnings before taxes	_____
Taxes @ 30%	_____
Earnings after taxes	_____
Depreciation	_____

Cash flow

2. *a.* In Problem 1, how much would *cash flow* be if there were only $10,000 in depreciation? All other factors are the same.

b. How much *cash flow* is lost due to the reduced depreciation between Problems 1 and 2*a*?

Cash flow

3. Assume a firm has earnings before depreciation and taxes of $500,000 and no depreciation. It is in a 40 percent tax bracket.

a. Compute its cash flow.

b. Assume it has $500,000 in depreciation. Recompute its cash flow.

c. How large a cash flow benefit did the depreciation provide?

4. Al Quick, the president of a New York Stock Exchange–listed firm, is very short term oriented and interested in the immediate consequences of his decisions. Assume a project that will provide an increase of $2 million in cash flow because of favorable tax consequences, but carries a two-cent decline in earning per share because of a write-off against first quarter earnings. What decision might Mr. Quick make?

Cash flow versus earnings

5. Assume a $50,000 investment and the following cash flows for two alternatives.

Payback method

Year	Investment A	Investment B
1.........	$10,000	$20,000
2.........	11,000	25,000
3.........	13,000	15,000
4.........	16,000	
5.........	30,000	

Which alternative would you select under the payback method?

6. Referring back to Problem 5, if the inflow in the fifth year for Investment A were $30,000,000 instead of $30,000, would your answer change under the payback method?

Payback method

7. The Short-Line Railroad is considering a $100,000 investment in either of two companies. The cash flows are as follows:

Payback method

Year	Electric Co.	Water Works
1...........	$70,000	$15,000
2...........	15,000	15,000
3...........	15,000	70,000
4–10........	10,000	10,000

   a. Using the payback method, what will the decision be?

   b. Explain why the answer in part *a* can be misleading.

8. Diaz Camera Company is considering two investments, both of which cost $10,000. The cash flows are as follows:

Payback and net present value

Year	Project A	Project B
1.........	$6,000	$5,000
2.........	4,000	3,000
3.........	3,000	8,000

   a. Which of the two projects should be chosen based on the payback method?

   b. Which of the two projects should be chosen based on the net present value method? Assume a cost of capital of 10 percent.

   c. Should a firm normally have more confidence in answer *a* or answer *b*?

9. You buy a new piece of equipment for $11,778, and you receive a cash inflow of $2,000 per year for 10 years. What is the internal rate of return?

Internal rate of return

10. King's Department Store is contemplating the purchase of a new machine at a cost of $13,869. The machine will provide $3,000 per year in cash flow for six years. King's has a cost of capital of 12 percent. Using the internal rate of return method, evaluate this project and indicate whether it should be undertaken.

Internal rate of return

Internal rate of return

11. Home Security Systems is analyzing the purchase of manufacturing equipment that will cost $40,000. The annual cash inflows for the next three years will be:

Year	Cash Flow
1.........	$20,000
2.........	18,000
3.........	13,000

   a. Determine the internal rate of return using interpolation.

   b. With a cost of capital of 12 percent, should the machine be purchased?

Net present value method

12. Altman Hydraulic Corporation will invest $160,000 in a project that will produce the cash flow shown below. The cost of capital is 11 percent. Should the project be undertaken? Use the net present value method. (Note that the third year's cash flow is negative.)

Year	Cash Flow
1.........	$ 54,000
2.........	66,000
3.........	(60,000)
4.........	57,000
5.........	120,000

Net present value method

13. Hamilton Control Systems will invest $90,000 in a temporary project that will generate the following cash inflows for the next three years.

Year	Cash Flow
1.........	$23,000
2.........	38,000
3.........	60,000

The firm will be required to spend $15,000 to close down the project at the end of three years. If the cost of capital is 10 percent, should the investment be undertaken? Use the net present value method.

Net present value method

14. Cellular Labs will invest $150,000 in a project that will not begin to produce returns until after the third year. From the end of the 3rd year until the end of the 12th year (10 periods), the annual cash flow will be $40,000. If the cost of capital is 12 percent, should this project be undertaken?

Net present value and internal rate of return methods

15. The Hudson Corporation makes an investment of $14,400 that provides the following cash flow:

Year	Cash Flow
1.........	$7,000
2.........	7,000
3.........	4,000

   a. What is the net present value at an 11 percent discount rate?

   b. What is the internal rate of return? Use the interpolation procedure shown in this chapter.

   c. In this problem would you make the same decision under both parts *a* and *b*?

16. The Pan American Bottling Co. is considering the purchase of a new machine that would increase the speed of bottling and save money. The net cost of this machine is $45,000. The annual cash flows have the following projections:

Year	Cash Flow
1...........	$15,000
2...........	20,000
3...........	25,000
4...........	10,000
5...........	5,000

Net present value and internal rate of return methods

a. If the cost of capital is 10 percent, what is the net present value of selecting a new machine?

b. What is the internal rate of return?

c. Should the project be accepted? Why?

17. You are asked to evaluate the following two projects for the Norton Corporation. Using the net present value method, combined with the profitability index approach described in footnote 2 on page 375 of this chapter, which project would you select? Use a discount rate of 10 percent.

Use of profitability index

Project X (Videotapes of the Weather Report) ($10,000 investment)		Project Y (Slow-Motion Replays of Commercials) ($30,000 investment)	
Year	Cash Flow	Year	Cash Flow
1..........	$5,000	1..........	$15,000
2..........	3,000	2..........	8,000
3..........	4,000	3..........	9,000
4..........	3,600	4..........	11,000

18. Turner Video will invest $48,500 in a project. The firm's cost of capital is 9 percent. The investment will provide the following inflows.

Reinvestment rate assumption in capital budgeting

Year	Inflow
1..........	$10,000
2..........	12,000
3..........	16,000
4..........	20,000
5..........	24,000

The internal rate of return is 14 percent.

a. If the reinvestment assumption of the net present value method is used, what will be the total value of the inflows after five years? (Assume the inflows come at the end of each year.)

b. If the reinvestment assumption of the internal rate of return method is used, what will be the total value of the inflows after five years?

c. Generally is one investment assumption likely to be better than another?

Modified internal
rate of return

19. The Caffeine Coffee Company uses the modified internal rate of return. The firm has a cost of capital of 12 percent. The project being analyzed is as follows ($27,000 investment):

Year	Cash Flow
1.........	$15,000
2.........	12,000
3.........	9,000

a. What is the modified internal rate of return? An approximation from Appendix B is adequate. (You do not need to interpolate.)

b. Assume the traditional internal rate of return on the investment is 17.5 percent. Explain why your answer in part *a* would be lower.

Capital
rationing and
mutually exclusive
investments

✗ 20. The Suboptimal Glass Company uses a process of capital rationing in its decision making. The firm's cost of capital is 13 percent. It will only invest $60,000 this year. It has determined the internal rate of return for each of the following projects.

Project	Project Size	Internal Rate of Return
A..........	$10,000	15%
B..........	30,000	14
C..........	25,000	16.5
D..........	10,000	17
E..........	10,000	23
F..........	20,000	11
G..........	15,000	16

a. Pick out the projects that the firm should accept.

b. If Projects D and E are mutually exclusive, how would that affect your overall answer? That is, which projects would you accept in spending $60,000?

Net present value
profile

21. Keller Construction is considering two new investments. Project E calls for the purchase of earthmoving equipment. Project H represents an investment in a hydraulic lift. Keller wishes to use a net present value profile in comparing the projects. The investment and cash flow patterns are as follows:

Project E ($20,000 investment)		Project H ($20,000 investment)	
Year	Cash Flow	Year	Cash Flow
1.........	$5,000	1.........	$16,000
2.........	6,000	2.........	5,000
3.........	7,000	3.........	4,000
4.........	10,000		

a. Determine the net present value of the projects based on a zero discount rate.

b. Determine the net present value of the projects based on a 9 percent discount rate.

c. The internal rate of return on Project E is 13.25 percent, and the internal rate of return on Project H is 16.30 percent. Graph a net present value profile for the two investments similar to Figure 12–3 on page 381. (Use a scale up to $8,000 on the vertical axis, with $2,000 increments. Use a scale up to 20 percent on the horizontal axis, with 5 percent increments.)

d.   If the two projects are not mutually exclusive, what would your acceptance or rejection decision be if the cost of capital (discount rate) is 8 percent? (Use the net present value profile for your decision; no actual numbers are necessary.)

e.   If the two projects are mutually exclusive (the selection of one precludes the selection of the other), what would be your decision if the cost of capital is (1) 6 percent, (2) 13 percent, (3) 18 percent? Once again, use the net present value profile for your answer.

22. Davis Chili Company is considering an investment of $15,000, which produces the following inflows.

Net present value profile

Year	Cash Flow
1.........	$8,000
2.........	7,000
3.........	4,000

You are going to use the net present value profile to approximate the value for the internal rate of return. Please follow these steps:

a.   Determine the net present value of the project based on a zero discount rate.

b.   Determine the net present value of the project based on a 10 percent discount rate.

c.   Determine the net present value of the project based on a 20 percent discount rate (it will be negative).

d.   Draw a net present value profile for the investment and observe the discount rate at which the net present value is zero. This is an approximation of the internal rate of return based on the interpolation procedure presented in this chapter. Compare your answers in parts *d* and *e*.

e.   Actually compute the internal rate of return based on the interpolation procedure presented in this chapter. Compare your answers in parts *d* and *e*.

✗ 23. Telstar Communications is going to purchase an asset for $300,000 that will produce $140,000 per year for the next four years in earnings before depreciation and taxes. The asset will be depreciated using the three-year MACRS depreciation schedule in Table 12–9 on page 383. (This represents four years of depreciation based on the half-year convention.) The firm is in a 35 percent tax bracket. Fill in the schedule below for the next four years.

MACRS depreciation and cash flow

Earnings before depreciation and taxes	_____
Depreciation	_____
Earnings before taxes	_____
Taxes	_____
Earnings after taxes	_____
+ Depreciation	_____
Cash flow	_____

MACRS
depreciation
categories

24. Assume $60,000 is going to be invested in each of the following assets. Using Tables 12–8 and 12–9, indicate the dollar amount of the first year's depreciation.

   a. Office furniture.

   b. Automobile.

   c. Electric and gas utility property.

   d. Sewage treatment plant.

MACRS
depreciation and
net present value

25. The Summitt Petroleum Corporation will purchase an asset that qualifies for three-year MACRS depreciation. The cost is $80,000 and the asset will provide the following stream of earnings before depreciation and taxes for the next four years:

Year 1	$36,000
Year 2	40,000
Year 3	31,000
Year 4	19,000

The firm is in a 35 percent tax bracket and has an 11 percent cost of capital. Should it purchase the asset? Use the net present value method.

MACRS
depreciation and
net present value

26. Propulsion Labs will acquire new equipment that falls under the five-year MACRS category. The cost is $200,000. If the equipment is purchased, the following earnings before depreciation and taxes will be generated for the next six years.

Year 1	$75,000
Year 2	70,000
Year 3	55,000
Year 4	35,000
Year 5	25,000
Year 6	21,000

The firm is in a 30 percent tax bracket and has a 14 percent cost of capital. Should Propulsion Labs purchase the equipment? Use the net present value method.

MACRS
depreciation and
net present value

27. Universal Electronics is considering the purchase of manufacturing equipment with a 10-year midpoint in its asset depreciation range (ADR). Carefully refer to Table 12–8 to determine in what depreciation category the asset falls. (Hint: It is not 10 years.) The asset will cost $90,000 and it will produce earnings before depreciation and taxes of $32,000 per year for three years, and then $12,000 a year for seven more years. The firm has a tax rate of 34 percent. With a cost of capital of 11 percent, should it purchase the asset? Use the net present value method. In doing your analysis, if you have years in which there is no depreciation, merely enter a zero for depreciation.

Working capital
requirements in
capital budgeting

28. The Bagwell Company has a proposed contract with the First Military Base Facility of Texas. The initial investment in land and equipment will be $90,000. Of this amount, $60,000 is subject to five-year MACRS depreciation. The balance is in nondepreciable property (land). The contract covers a six-year period. At the end of six years the nondepreciable assets will be sold for $30,000. The depreciated assets will have zero resale value.

The contract will require an additional investment of $40,000 in working capital at the beginning of the first year and, of this amount, $20,000 will be returned to the Bagwell Company after six years.

The investment will produce $32,000 in income before depreciation and taxes for each of the six years. The corporation is in a 35 percent tax bracket and has a 10 percent cost of capital.

Should the investment be undertaken? Use the net present value method.

29. An asset was purchased three years ago for $120,000. It falls into the five-year category for MACRS depreciation. The firm is in a 35 percent tax bracket. Compute the following:

    a. Tax loss on the sale and the related tax benefit if the asset is sold now for $12,560.

    b. Gain and related tax on the sale if the asset is sold now for $51,060. (Refer to footnote 4 on page 386 in the chapter.)

Tax losses and gains in capital budgeting

30. DataPoint Engineering is considering the purchase of a new piece of equipment for $220,000. It has an eight-year midpoint of its asset depreciation range (ADR). It will require an additional initial investment of $120,000 in nondepreciable working capital. Thirty thousand dollars of this investment will be recovered after the sixth year and will provide additional cash flow for that year. Income before depreciation and taxes for the next six years will be:

Capital budgeting with cost of capital computation

Year	Amount
1.........	$170,000
2.........	150,000
3.........	120,000
4.........	105,000
5.........	90,000
6.........	80,000

The tax rate is 30 percent. The cost of capital must be computed based on the following (round the final value to the nearest whole number):

		Cost (aftertax)	Weights
Debt	K_d	6.5%	30%
Preferred stock..........................	K_p	10.2	10
Common equity (retained earnings)	K_e	15.0	60

    a. Determine the annual depreciation schedule.

    b. Determine annual cash flow. Include recovered working capital in the sixth year.

    c. Determine the weighted average cost of capital.

    d. Determine the net present value. Should DataPoint purchase the new equipment?

31. Hercules Exercising Equipment Co. purchased a computerized measuring device two years ago for $60,000. The equipment falls into the five-year category for MACRS depreciation and can currently be sold for $23,800.

Replacement decision analysis

A new piece of equipment will cost $150,000. It also falls into the five-year category for MACRS depreciation.

Assume the new equipment would provide the following stream of added cost savings for the next six years.

Year	Cost Savings
1.........	$57,000
2.........	49,000
3.........	47,000
4.........	45,000
5.........	42,000
6.........	31,000

The firm's tax rate is 35 percent and the cost of capital is 12 percent.

a. What is the book value of the old equipment?

b. What is the tax loss on the sale of the old equipment?

c. What is the tax benefit from the sale?

d. What is the cash inflow from the sale of the old equipment?

e. What is the net cost of the new equipment? (Include the inflow from the sale of the old equipment.)

f. Determine the depreciation schedule for the new equipment.

g. Determine the depreciation schedule for the remaining years of the old equipment.

h. Determine the incremental depreciation between the old and new equipment and the related tax shield benefits.

i. Compute the aftertax benefits of the cost savings.

j. Add the depreciation tax shield benefits and the aftertax cost savings, and determine the present value. (See Table 12–17 on page 389 as an example.)

k. Compare the present value of the incremental benefits (*j*) to the net cost of the new equipment (*e*). Should the replacement be undertaken?

COMPREHENSIVE PROBLEM

Lancaster Corporation

(replacement decision analysis)

The Lancaster Corporation purchased a piece of equipment three years ago for $250,000. It has an asset depreciation range (ADR) midpoint of eight years. The old equipment can be sold for $97,920.

A new piece of equipment can be purchased for $360,000. It also has an ADR of eight years.

Assume the old and new equipment would provide the following operating gains (or losses) over the next six years.

Year	New Equipment	Old Equipment
1.........	$100,000	$36,000
2.........	86,000	26,000
3.........	80,000	19,000
4.........	72,000	18,000
5.........	62,000	16,000
6.........	43,000	(9,000)

The firm has a 36 percent tax rate and a 9 percent cost of capital. Should the new equipment be purchased to replace the old equipment?

WEB EXERCISE

Northrop Grumman was referred to in a box early in the chapter as being innovative and progressive in its capital budgeting decisions. Go to its Web site at www. northropgrumman.com, and follow the steps below:

1. Under "About Us," click on "Northrop Grumman Today." Based on the information provided, write a one-paragraph description about the company. Obviously, you can not include all of the facts.

2. Under "Investor Relations," select "Financial Info," and then "Fundamentals." Record the following:
    a. Recent price.
    b. 52-week high.
    c. 52-week low.
    d. 52-week price percent change.
    e. YTD price percent change.

    What is the general pattern of the stock movement? Keep in mind the overall market might affect the price movement for Northrop Grumman.

3. A key statistic for a major New York Stock Exchange company is institutional holdings (ownership by banks, mutual funds, pension funds, etc. as opposed to individuals.) A value over 60 percent is considered strong. Record the "Percentage of Shares Outstanding Held by Institutions." Does the value appear to be strong?

Note: From time to time, companies redesign their Web sites and occasionally a topic we have listed may have been deleted, updated, or moved into a different location. If you click on the site map or site index, you will be introduced to a table of contents that should aid you in finding the topic you are looking for.

S&P PROBLEMS   www.mhhe.com/edumarketinsight

1. Log onto the S&P Market Insight Web site, www.mhhe.com/edumarketinsight.
2. Click on "Commentary," which is the third box below the Market Insight title. The second major heading on the left side is Trends and Projections. Click on the current "Trends and Projections."
3. This is a quarterly economic summary for the U.S. economy and it is filled with charts and tables. Please find the graphs showing Industrial Production and Capacity Utilization. If you don't find these graphs, cycle back through the archival files for preceding months until you do.

STANDARD
&POOR'S

www.mhhe.com/bh12e

4. Next find the graph for Capital Spending. Capital Spending measures the amount of money that U.S. corporations spend on plant and equipment. In other words, this graph sums up the capital budgeting decisions of corporate America.

5. Find the graphs for corporate profits for the total economy and interest rates.

6. Examine all the graphs and discuss how economic activity has affected capital budgeting decisions during the periods on the graphs.

S & P   P R O B L E M S   www.mhhe.com/edumarketinsight

STANDARD & POOR'S

1. Log onto the S&P Market Insight Web site, www.mhhe.com/edumarketinsight.

2. Click on "Company," which is the first box below the Market Insight title.

3. Type Apple Computer's ticker symbol "AAPL" in the box and click on Go.

4. Scroll down the left margin and click on "Excel Analytics." At the top of the left margin you will see the second item listed as Ann. Balance Sheet.

5. Click on "Annual Balance Sheet" and find net plant and equipment. Calculate the dollar change in net plant and equipment and the percentage change in net plant and equipment for the years given.

6. Now close the balance sheet and under Excel Analytics find the annual ratio spreadsheet. What has happened to the return on assets and return on investment since the introduction of the iPod.

7. What are your conclusions about Apple's capital budgeting decisions over the last five years?

13

Risk and Capital Budgeting

chapter concepts

1 The concept of risk is based on uncertainty about future outcomes.

2 Most investors are risk-averse, which means they dislike uncertainty.

3 Because investors dislike uncertainty, they will require higher rates of return from risky projects.

4 Simulation models and decision trees can be used to help assess the risk of an investment.

5 Not only must the risk of an individual project be considered, but also how the project affects the total risk of the firm.

No one area is more essential to financial decision making than the evaluation and management of risk. The price of a firm's stock is to a large degree influenced by the amount of risk investors perceive to be inherent in the firm. A company is constantly trying to achieve the appropriate mix between profitability and risk to satisfy those with a stake in its affairs and to achieve wealth maximization for shareholders.

The difficulty is not in finding viable investment alternatives but in determining an appropriate position on the risk-return scale. Would a firm prefer a 20 percent potential return on an untried and new product or a safe 8 percent return on an extension of its current product line? The question can only be answered in terms of profitability, the risk position of the firm, and management and stockholder disposition toward risk.

Nobody knows the definition of risk better that Pfizer, Inc., the international drug company. Although

it has developed such acclaimed drugs as Lipitor, Viagra, and Zoloft, its stock price dropped by almost 50 percent between 2001 and 2005. While its mission is to better the health of the world's citizenry, a 2005 *BusinessWeek* article said the public's opinion of the drug industry these days "seems only one step above that of the tobacco industry."[1] This characterization traces back to the massive litigations against drug companies, as well as the industry's resistance to allowing cheaper drugs from Canada and elsewhere into the U.S. market. To fight the negative image, Pfizer is the fourth largest advertiser in the United States (trailing only such giants as General Motors, Procter & Gamble, and Time Warner).

Its next hope for a blockbuster drug is torcetrapid, a compound that is aimed at raising HDL or "good" cholesterol to complement the company's most successful product, Lipitor, which lowers bad cholesterol. Pfizer has already spent 800 million dollars for

---

[1]"Pfizer's Funk," *BusinessWeek,* February 28, 2005, pp. 72–82.

research on torcetrapid, which may or may not someday pass FDA approval and produce a profit. The dice are now being rolled.

In this chapter we examine definitions of risk, its measurement and its incorporation into the *capital budgeting* process, and the basic tenets of portfolio theory.

Definition of Risk in Capital Budgeting

Risk may be defined in terms of the variability of possible outcomes from a given investment. If funds are invested in a 30-day U.S. government obligation, the outcome is certain and there is no variability—hence no risk. If we invest the same funds in a gold-mining expedition to the deepest wilds of Africa, the variability of possible outcomes is great and we say the project is replete with risk.

The student should observe that risk is measured not only in terms of losses but also in terms of uncertainty.[2] We say gold mining carries a high degree of risk not just because you may lose your money but also because there is a wide range of possible outcomes. Observe in Figure 13–1 examples of three investments with different risk characteristics.

Figure 13–1

Variability and risk

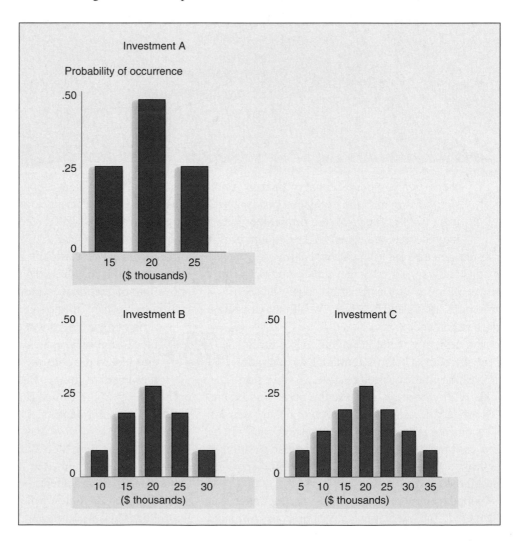

---

[2]We use the term *uncertainty* in its normal sense, rather than in the more formalized sense in which it is sometimes used in decision theory to indicate that insufficient evidence is available to estimate a probability distribution.

Note that in each case the distributions are centered on the same expected value ($20,000), but the variability (risk) increases as we move from Investment A to Investment C. Because you may gain or lose the most in Investment C, it is clearly the riskiest of the three.

The Concept of Risk-Averse

A basic assumption in financial theory is that most investors and managers are **risk-averse**—that is, for a given situation they would prefer relative certainty to uncertainty. In Figure 13–1 on the prior page, they would prefer Investment A over Investments B and C, although all three investments have the same expected value of $20,000. You are probably risk-averse too. Assume you have saved $1,000 toward your last year in college and are challenged to flip a coin, double or nothing. Heads, you end up with $2,000; tails, you are broke. Given that you are not enrolled at the University of Nevada at Las Vegas or that you are not an inveterate gambler, you will probably stay with your certain $1,000.

This is not to say investors or businesspeople are unwilling to take risks—but rather that they will require a higher expected value or return for risky investments. In Figure 13–2, we compare a low-risk proposal with an expected value of $20,000 to a high-risk proposal with an expected value of $30,000. The higher expected return may compensate the investor for absorbing greater risk.

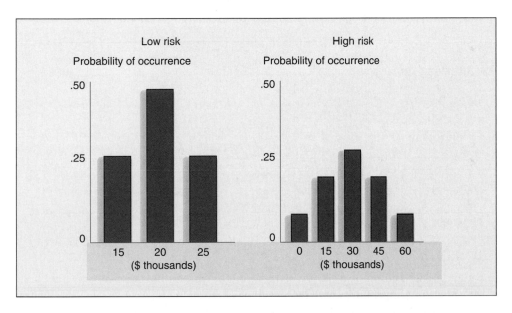

Figure 13–2
Risk-return trade-off

Actual Measurement of Risk

A number of basic statistical devices may be used to measure the extent of risk inherent in any given situation. Assume we are examining an investment with the possible outcomes and probability of outcomes shown in Table 13–1.

Table 13–1
Probability distribution of outcomes

Outcome	Probability of Outcome	Assumptions
$300	.2	Pessimistic
600	.6	Moderately successful
900	.2	Optimistic

The probabilities in Table 13–1 may be based on past experience, industry ratios and trends, interviews with company executives, and sophisticated simulation techniques. The probability values may be easy to determine for the introduction of a mechanical stamping process in which the manufacturer has 10 years of past data, but difficult to assess for a new product in a foreign market. In any event we force ourselves into a valuable analytical process.

Based on the data in Table 13–1, we compute two important statistical measures—the expected value and the standard deviation. The **expected value** is a weighted average of the outcomes (D) times their probabilities (P).

$$\overline{D} \text{ (expected value)} = \Sigma\, DP \qquad\qquad (13\text{–}1)$$

$$
\begin{array}{rcl}
D & P & DP \\
300 \times .2 = & \$\ 60 \\
600 \times .6 = & 360 \\
900 \times .2 = & \underline{180} \\
& \$600 = \Sigma\, DP
\end{array}
$$

The expected value ($\overline{D}$) is $600. We then compute the **standard deviation**—the measure of dispersion or variability around the expected value:

$$\sigma \text{ (standard deviation)} = \sqrt{\Sigma(D - \overline{D})^2 P} \qquad\qquad (13\text{–}2)$$

The following steps should be taken:

Step 1: Subtract the Expected Value ($\overline{D}$) from Each Outcome (D)			Step 2: Square $(D - \overline{D})$	Step 3: Multiply by P and Sum		Step 4: Determine the Square Root
D	$\overline{D}$	$(D - \overline{D})$	$(D - \overline{D})^2$	P	$(D - \overline{D})^2 P$	
300 −	600 =	−300	90,000	× .20 =	18,000	
600 −	600 =	0	0	× .60 =	0	
900 −	600 =	+300	90,000	× .20 =	$\underline{18,000}$	
					36,000	$\sqrt{36,000} = \$190$

The standard deviation of $190 gives us a rough average measure of how far each of the three outcomes falls away from the expected value. Generally, the larger the standard deviation (or spread of outcomes), the greater is the risk, as indicated in Figure 13–3. The student will note that in Figure 13–3 we compare the standard deviation of three investments with the same expected value of $600. If the expected values of the investments were different (such as $600 versus $6,000), a direct comparison of the standard deviations for each distribution would not be helpful in measuring risk. In Figure 13–4 we show such an occurrence.

Note that the investment in Panel A of Figure 13–4 appears to have a high standard deviation, but not when related to the expected value of the distribution. A standard deviation of $600 on an investment with an expected value of $6,000 may indicate less risk than a standard deviation of $190 on an investment with an expected value of only $600 (Panel B).

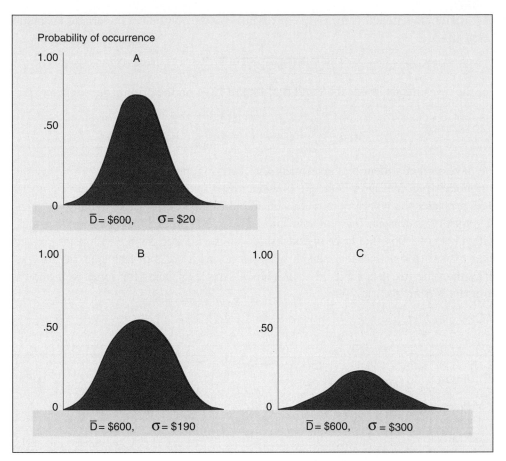

Figure 13–3
Probability distribution with differing degrees of risk

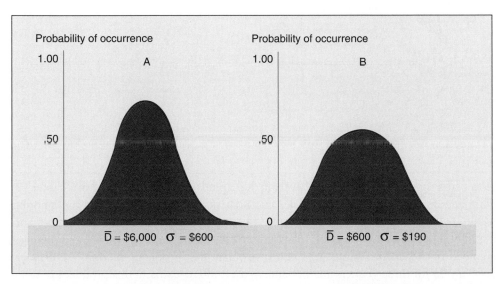

Figure 13–4

We can eliminate the size difficulty by developing a third measure, the **coefficient of variation** (V). This term calls for nothing more difficult than dividing the standard deviation of an investment by the expected value. Generally, the larger the coefficient of variation, the greater is the risk. The formula for the coefficient of variation is numbered 13–3.

$$\text{Coefficient of variation (V)} = \frac{\sigma}{D} \tag{13–3}$$

For the investments in Panels A and B of Figure 13–4 on the prior page, we show:

$$\begin{array}{cc} A & B \\ V = \dfrac{600}{6,000} = .10 & V = \dfrac{190}{600} = .317 \end{array}$$

We have correctly identified investment B as carrying the greater risk.

Another risk measure, **beta** (β), is widely used with portfolios of common stock. Beta measures the volatility of returns on an individual stock relative to the stock market index of returns, such as the Standard & Poor's 500 Stock Index.[3] A common stock with a beta of 1.0 is said to be of equal risk with the market. Stocks with betas greater than 1.0 are riskier than the market, while stocks with betas of less than 1.0 are less risky than the market. Table 13–2 presents a sample of betas for some well-known companies from 2001 to 2006.

Table 13–2

Betas for five-year period (ending January 2006)

Company Name	Beta
Del Monte Foods	.60
Tootsie Roll Industries	.65
Archer Daniels Midland	.70
Peoples Energy	.80
Payless ShoeSource	.90
Olin Corp	.95
Standard & Poor's 500 Index	1.00
Bank of America	1.15
Oracle Corp	1.25
Alcoa	1.45
eBay Inc.	1.50
Merrill Lynch	1.55
Schwab (Charles)	1.80

Risk and the Capital Budgeting Process

How can risk analysis be used effectively in the capital budgeting process? In Chapter 12 we made no distinction between risky and nonrisky events.[4] We showed the amount of the investment and the annual returns—making no comment about the riskiness or likelihood of achieving these returns. We know that enlightened investors and managers need further information. A $1,400 investment that produces "certain" returns of $600 a year for three years is not the same as a $1,400 investment that produces returns

---

[3]Other market measures may also be used.
[4]Our assumption was that the risk factor could be considered constant for various investments.

with an expected value of $600 for three years, but with a high coefficient of variation. Investors, being risk-averse by nature, will apply a stiffer test to the second investment. How can this new criterion be applied to the capital budgeting process?

Risk-Adjusted Discount Rate

A favored approach to adjust for risk is to use different discount rates for proposals with different risk levels. Thus we use **risk-adjusted discount rates**. A project that carries a normal amount of risk and does not change the overall risk composure of the firm should be discounted at the cost of capital. Investments carrying greater than normal risk will be discounted at a higher rate, and so on. In Figure 13–5 we show a possible risk–discount rate trade-off scheme. Risk is assumed to be measured by the coefficient of variation (V).

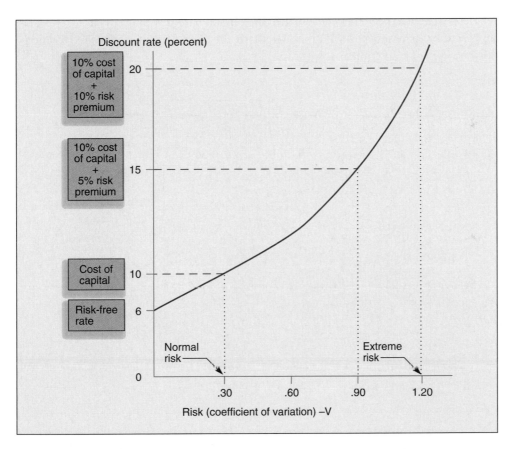

Figure 13–5

Relationship of risk to discount rate

The normal risk for the firm is represented by a coefficient of variation of 0.30 on the bottom of Figure 13–5. An investment with this risk would be discounted at the firm's normal cost of capital of 10 percent. As the firm selects riskier projects, for example, with a V of 0.90, a risk premium of 5 percent is added to compensate for an increase in V of 0.60 (from .30 to .90). If the company selects a project with a coefficient of variation of 1.20, it will add another 5 percent risk premium for this additional

V of 0.30. This is an example of being increasingly risk-averse at higher levels of risk and potential return.

Increasing Risk over Time

Our ability to forecast accurately diminishes as we forecast farther out in time. As the time horizon becomes longer, more uncertainty enters the forecast. The decline in oil prices sharply curtailed the search for petroleum and left many drillers in serious financial condition in the 1980s after years of expanding drilling activity. Conversely, the users of petroleum products were hurt in 1990 when the conflict in the Middle East caused oil prices to skyrocket. Airlines and auto manufacturers had to reevaluate decisions made many years ago that were based on more stable energy prices. September 11, 2001, coupled with the Iraqi war of the mid-decade dealt another blow to the already fragile economy. By summer of 2006, signs of improvement were modestly visible. These unexpected events create a higher standard deviation in cash flows and increase the risk associated with long-lived projects. Figure 13–6 depicts the relationship between risk and time.

Figure 13–6

Risk over time

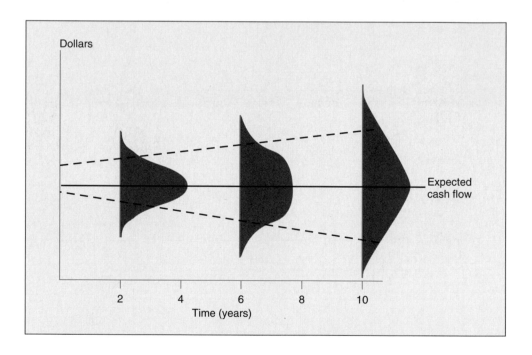

Even though a forecast of cash flows shows a constant expected value, Figure 13–6 indicates that the range of outcomes and probabilities increases as we move from year 2 to year 10. The standard deviations increase for each forecast of cash flow. If cash flows were forecast as easily for each period, all distributions would look like the first one for year 2. Using progressively higher discount rates to compensate for risk tends to penalize late flows more than early flows, and this is consistent with the notion that risk is greater for longer-term cash flows than for near-term cash flows.

Qualitative Measures

Rather than relate the discount rate—or required return—to the coefficient of variation or possibly the beta, management may wish to set up risk classes based on qualitative considerations. Examples are presented in Table 13–3. Once again we are equating the discount rate to the perceived risk.

	Discount Rate
Low or no risk (repair to old machinery)	6%
Moderate risk (new equipment)	8
Normal risk (addition to normal product line)	10
Risky (new product in related market)	12
High risk (completely new market)	16
Highest risk (new product in foreign market)	20

Table 13–3

Risk categories and associated discount rates

Example—Risk-Adjusted Discount Rate   In Chapter 12 we compared two $10,000 investment alternatives and indicated that each had a positive net present value (at a 10 percent cost of capital). The analysis is reproduced in Table 13–4.

Year	Investment A (10% discount rate)	Year	Investment B (10% discount rate)
1	$5,000 × 0.909 = $ 4,545	1	$1,500 × 0.909 = $ 1,364
2	5,000 × 0.826 = 4,130	2	2,000 × 0.826 = 1,652
3	2,000 × 0.751 = 1,502	3	2,500 × 0.751 = 1,878
	$10,177	4	5,000 × 0.683 = 3,415
		5	5,000 × 0.621 = 3,105
			$11,414
Present value of inflows	$10,177	Present value of inflows	$11,414
Investment	−10,000	Investment	−10,000
Net present value	$ 177	Net present value	$ 1,414

Table 13–4

Capital budgeting analysis

Though both proposals are acceptable, if they were mutually exclusive, only Investment B would be undertaken. But what if we add a risk dimension to the problem? Assume Investment A calls for an addition to the normal product line and is assigned a discount rate of 10 percent. Further assume that Investment B represents a new product in a foreign market and must carry a 20 percent discount rate to adjust for the large risk component. As indicated in Table 13–5 on page 412, our answers are reversed and Investment A is now the only acceptable alternative.

Other methods besides the risk-adjusted discount rate approach are also used to evaluate risk in the capital budgeting process. The spectrum runs from a seat-of-the-pants "executive preference" approach to sophisticated computer-based statistical analysis.

Table 13–5

Capital budgeting decision adjusted for risk

Year	Investment A (10% discount rate)	Year	Investment B (20% discount rate)
1	$5,000 × 0.909 = $ 4,545	1	$1,500 × 0.833= $ 1,250
2	5,000 × 0.826 = 4,130	2	2,000 × 0.694 = 1,388
3	2,000 × 0.751 = 1,502	3	2,500 × 0.579 = 1,448
		4	5,000 × 0.482 = 2,410
		5	5,000 × 0.402 = 2,010
	$10,177		$ 8,506
Present value of inflows	$10,177	Present value of inflows	$ 8,506
Investment	−10,000	Investment	−10,000
Net present value	$ 177	Net present value	$(1,494)

All methods, however, include a common approach—that is, they must recognize the riskiness of a given investment proposal and make an appropriate adjustment for risk.[5]

Simulation Models

Computers make it possible to simulate various economic and financial outcomes, using a large number of variables. Thus **simulation** is one way of dealing with the uncertainty involved in forecasting the outcomes of capital budgeting projects or other types of decisions. A Monte Carlo simulation model uses random variables for inputs. By programming the computer to randomly select inputs from probability distributions, the outcomes generated by a simulation are distributed about a mean, and instead of generating one return or net present value, a range of outcomes with standard deviations is provided. A simulation model relies on repetition of the same random process as many as several hundred times. Since the inputs are representative of what one might encounter in the real world, many possible combinations of returns are generated.

One of the benefits of simulation is its ability to test various possible combinations of events. This sensitivity testing allows the planner to ask "what if" questions, such as: What will happen to the returns on this project if oil prices go up? Go down? What effect will a 2 percent increase in interest rates have on the net present value of this project? The analyst can use the simulation process to test possible changes in economic policy, sales levels, inflation, or any other variable included in the modeling process. Some simulation models are driven by sales forecasts with assumptions to derive income statements and balance sheets. Others generate probability acceptance curves for capital budgeting decisions by informing the analyst about the probabilities of having a positive net present value.

---

[5]As an example, each value might be penalized for lack of certainty (adjusted for risk) and then a risk-free discount rate might be applied to the resultant values. This is termed the *certainty equivalent approach*. In practice, the expected value for a given year is multiplied by a percentage figure indicating the degree of certainty and then translated back to the present at a risk-free discount rate (less than the cost of capital). Items with a high degree of certainty are multiplied by 100 percent, less certain items by 75 percent, and so on down the scale.

For example, each distribution in Figure 13–7 will have a value picked randomly and used for one simulation. The simulation will be run many times, each time selecting a new random variable to generate the final probability distribution for the net present value (at the bottom of Figure 13–7). For that probability distribution, the expected values are on the horizontal axis and the probability of occurrence is on the vertical axis. The outcomes also suggest something about the riskiness of the project, which is indicated by the overall dispersion.

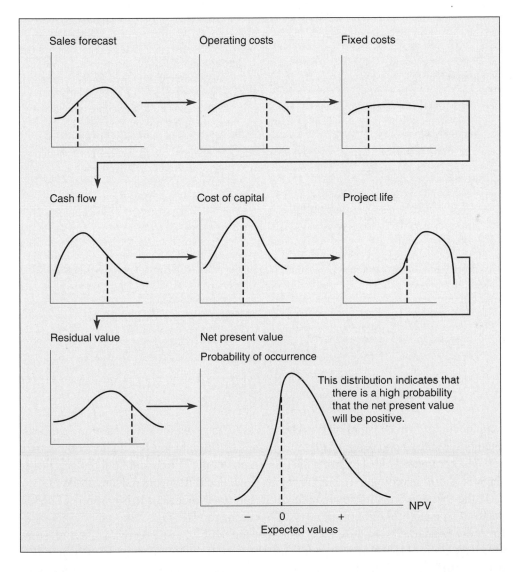

Figure 13–7
Simulation flow chart

Decision Trees

Decision trees help lay out the sequence of decisions that can be made and present a tabular or graphical comparison resembling the branches of a tree, which highlights the differences between investment choices. In Figure 13–8 on page 415, we examine a

How Much Risk Is in Your Genes?

An IPO is an initial public offering (stock sold to the public for the first time).

In recent years, the IPO rage has been for companies engaged in genomics, the study of the human gene system. In the early 2000s, it was announced that scientists had created the map of where genes are located in the body and how the DNA in those genes is structured. The next step is to figure out how all the genes work and interact, and what drugs can be developed to treat genetic conditions. The National Human Genome Research Institute estimates that genetic errors are responsible for 3,000 to 4,000 different hereditary diseases, and that genes play a role in such diseases as cancer and heart disease.

It is anticipated that in the next generation or two, by being treated for genetic diseases that are identified at birth, people may begin living for 150 to 200 years. Assuming a person's descendants have two children every 25 years, a person born in the year 2050 and living 200 years would have 512 children, grandchildren, and great-grandchildren at their funeral. The obituary alone would read like a small town telephone directory.

The government is currently worried about meeting Social Security obligations for the baby boom generation (those born immediately after World War II). These baby boomers will be retiring in the next 5 to 10 years and have a life expectancy of 75 to 77 years of age. If they retire at age 65, the baby boomers will be on Social Security for 10 to 12 years. What about the people born after the new genetic technology is in effect? If they live to age 200, under the current rules they would draw Social Security for 135 years (talk about a burden to the working population!). Also, how would you like to pay for your parents' nursing home care for the next 135 to 140 years?

Nevertheless, investors are very excited about genetic technology companies such as Genecor International, Lexicon Genetics, Celera Genomics Group, Deltagen, Inc., Marvell Technology, Ciena, and many others.

In no other area could the potential returns be greater than in genetic research, but the potential risks include an extremely short shelf life (even with patents) due to the rapid development and intensity of the research; ethical and moral issues relating to cloning and restricted diversity; and leaked genetic information being used against people in employment situations and the purchase of health insurance.

A final risk is the extremely fragile business model that many of the genomics companies have. Most are put together very quickly and the word "profit" is foreign to many of them. Unlike an established drug company such as Pfizer or Merck, many of these companies are truly beginners in the world of business and finance.

Source: Tina Sheesley, "Genomics Films Map Out IPO Blueprint for Success," *The Wall Street Journal,* July 6, 2000, pp. C1 and C20.

semiconductor firm considering two choices: (*a*) expanding the production of semiconductors for sale to end users of these tiny chips or (*b*) entering the highly competitive personal computer market by using the firm's technology. The cost of both projects is the same $60 million (column 4), but the net present value (NPV) and risk are different.

If the firm expands its semiconductor capacity (Project A), it is assured of some demand so a high likelihood of a positive rate of return exists. The market demand for these products is volatile over time, but long-run growth seems to be a reasonable expectation. If the firm expands into the personal computer market (Project B), it faces stiff competition from many existing firms. It stands to lose more money if expected sales are low than it would under option A, but it will make more if sales are high. Even though Project B has a higher expected NPV than Project A (last column in Figure 13–8), its extra risk does not make for an easy choice. More analysis would have to be done before management made the final decision between these two projects. Nevertheless the decision tree provides an important analytical process.

Figure 13–8   Decision trees

	(1)	(2)	(3)	(4)	(5)	(6)
	Expected Sales	Probability	Present Value of Cash Flow from Sales ($ millions)	Initial Cost ($ millions)	NPV (3) − (4) ($ millions)	Expected NPV (2) × (5) ($ millions)
Expand semiconductor capacity	High	.50	$100	$60	$40	$20.00
	Moderate	.25	75	60	15	3.75
	Low	.25	40	60	(20)	(5.00)
A					Expected NPV =	$18.75
						($ millions)
Start						
B						
Enter personal computer market	High	.20	$200	$60	$140	$28.00
	Moderate	.50	75	60	15	7.50
	Low	.30	25	60	(35)	(10.50)
					Expected NPV =	$25.00
						($ millions)

The Portfolio Effect

Up to this point, we have been primarily concerned with the risk inherent in an *individual* investment proposal. While this approach is useful, we also need to consider the impact of a given investment on the overall risk of the firm—the **portfolio effect**. For example, we might undertake an investment in the building products industry that appears to carry a high degree of risk—but if our primary business is the manufacture of electronic components for industrial use, we may diminish the overall risk exposure of the firm. Why? Because electronic component sales expand when the economy does well and falter in a recession. The building products industry reacts in the opposite fashion—performing poorly in boom periods and generally reacting well in recessionary periods. By investing in the building products industry, an electronic components manufacturer could smooth the cyclical fluctuations inherent in its business and reduce overall risk exposure, as indicated in Figure 13–9 on page 416.

The risk-reduction phenomenon is demonstrated by a less dispersed probability distribution in panel C. We say the standard deviation for the entire company (the portfolio of investments) has been reduced.

Portfolio Risk

Whether or not a given investment will change the overall risk of the firm depends on its relationships to other investments. If one airline purchases another, there is very little risk reduction. Highly correlated investments—that is, projects that move in the same direction in good times as well as bad—do little or nothing to diversify away risk. Projects moving in opposite directions (building products and electronic components) are referred to as being negatively correlated and provide a high degree of risk reduction.

Figure 13–9

Portfolio considerations in evaluating risk

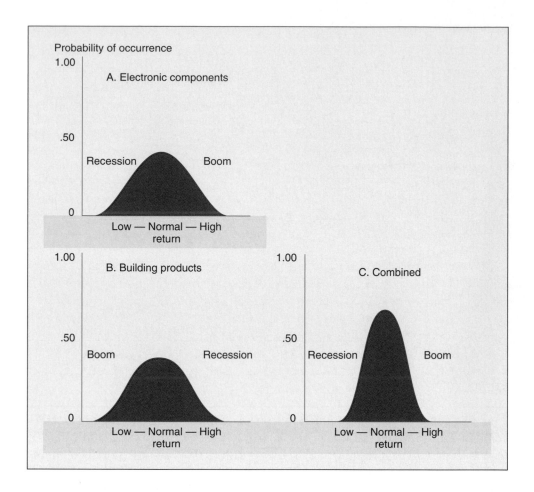

Finally, projects that are totally uncorrelated provide some overall reduction in portfolio risk—though not as much as negatively correlated investments. For example, if a beer manufacturer purchases a textile firm, the projects are neither positively nor negatively correlated; but the purchase will reduce the overall risk of the firm simply through the "law of large numbers." If you have enough unrelated projects going on at one time, good and bad events will probably even out.

The extent of correlation among projects is represented by a new term called the **coefficient of correlation**—a measure that may take on values anywhere from −1 to +1.[6] Examples are presented in Table 13–6.

Table 13–6

Measures of correlation

Coefficient of Correlation	Condition	Example	Impact on Risk
−1	Negative correlation	Electronic components, building products	Large risk reduction
0	No correlation	Beer, textile	Some risk reduction
+1	Positive correlation	Two airlines	No risk reduction

[6]Coefficient of correlation is not to be confused with coefficient of variation, a term used earlier in this chapter.

In the real world, few investment combinations take on values as extreme as −1 or +1, or for that matter exactly 0. The more likely case is a point somewhere between, such as −.2 negative correlation or +.3 positive correlation, as indicated along the continuum in Figure 13–10.

Figure 13–10
Levels of risk reduction as measured by the coefficient of correlation

The fact that risk can be reduced by combining risky assets with low or negatively correlated assets can be seen in the example of Conglomerate, Inc., in Table 13–7. Conglomerate has fairly average returns and standard deviations of returns. The company is considering the purchase of one of two separate but large companies with sales and assets equal to its own. Management is struggling with the decision since both companies have a 14 percent rate of return, which is 2 percentage points higher than that of Conglomerate, and they have the same standard deviation of returns as that of Conglomerate, at 2.82 percent. This information is presented in the first three columns of Table 13–7.

Table 13–7   Rates of return for Conglomerate, Inc., and two merger candidates

Year	(1) Conglomerate, Inc.	(2) Positive Correlation, Inc. +1.0	(3) Negative Correlation, Inc. −.9	(1) + (2) Conglomerate, Inc. + Positive Correlation, Inc.	(1) + (3) Conglomerate, Inc. + Negative Correlation, Inc.
1	14%	16%	10%	15%	12%
2	10	12	16	11	13
3	8	10	18	9	13
4	12	14	14	13	13
5	16	18	12	17	14
Mean return	12%	14%	14%	13%	13%
Standard deviation of returns (σ)	2.82%	2.82%	2.82%	2.82%	.63%
Correlation coefficients with Conglomerate, Inc.				+1.0	−.9

Since management desires to reduce risk (σ) and to increase returns at the same time, it decides to analyze the results of each combination.[7] These are shown in the last two columns in Table 13–7. A combination with Positive Correlation, Inc., increases

---

[7]In Chapter 20 you will evaluate a merger situation in which there is no increase in earnings, only a reduction in the standard deviation. Because the lower risk may mean a higher price-earnings ratio, this could be beneficial.

the mean return for Conglomerate, Inc., to 13 percent but maintains the same standard deviation of returns (no risk reduction) because the coefficient of correlation is +1.0 and no diversification benefits are achieved. A combination with Negative Correlation, Inc., also increases the mean return to 13 percent, but it reduces the standard deviation of returns to 0.63 percent, a significant reduction in risk. This occurs because of the offsetting relationship of returns between the two companies, as evidenced by the coefficient of correlation of −.9 (bottom row of Table 13–7). When one company has high returns, the other has low returns, and vice versa. Thus, a merger with Negative Correlation, Inc., appears to be the best decision.

Evaluation of Combinations

The firm should evaluate all possible combinations of projects, determining which will provide the best trade-off between risk and return. In Figure 13–11 we see a number of alternatives that might be available to a given firm. Each point represents a combination of different possible investments. For example, point F might represent a semiconductor manufacturer combining three different types of semiconductors, plus two types of computers, and two products in unrelated fields. In choosing between the various points or combinations, management should have two primary objectives:

1. Achieve the highest possible return at a given risk level.
2. Provide the lowest possible risk at a given return level.

Figure 13–11

Risk-return trade-offs

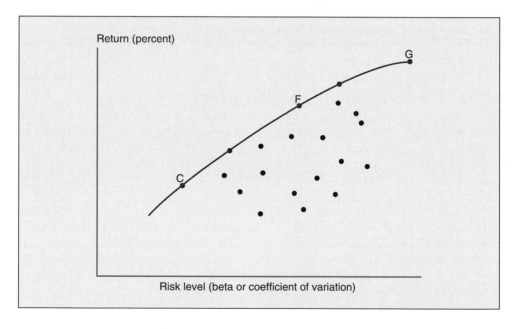

All the best opportunities will fall along the leftmost sector of the diagram (line C–F–G). Each point on the line satisfies the two objectives of the firm. Any point to the right is less desirable.

After we have developed our best risk-return line, known in the financial literature as the **"efficient frontier,"** we must determine where on the line our firm should be. There is no universally correct answer. To the extent we are willing to take large risks for superior returns, we will opt for some point on the upper portion of the line—such as G. However, a more conservative selection might be C.

The firm must be sensitive to the wishes and demands of shareholders. To the extent that unnecessary or undesirable risks are taken, a higher discount rate and lower valuation may be assigned to the stock in the market. Higher profits, resulting from risky ventures, could have a result that is the opposite from that intended. In raising the coefficient of variation, or beta, we could be lowering the overall valuation of the firm.

The Share Price Effect

The aversion of investors to nonpredictability (and the associated risk) is confirmed by observing the relative valuation given to cyclical stocks versus highly predictable growth stocks in the market. Metals, autos, and housing stocks generally trade at an earnings multiplier well below that for industries with level, predictable performance, such as drugs, soft drinks, and even alcohol or cigarettes. Each company must carefully analyze its own situation to determine the appropriate trade-off between risk and return. The changing desires and objectives of investors tend to make the task somewhat more difficult.

Summary

Risk may be defined as the potential variability of the outcomes from an investment. The less predictable the outcomes, the greater is the risk. Both management and investors tend to be risk-averse—that is, all things being equal, they would prefer to take less risk, rather than greater risk.

The most commonly employed method to adjust for risk in the capital budgeting process is to alter the discount rate based on the perceived risk level. High-risk projects will carry a risk premium, producing a discount rate well in excess of the cost of capital.

In assessing the risk components in a given project, management may rely on simulation techniques to generate probabilities of possible outcomes and decision trees to help isolate the key variables to be evaluated.

Management must consider not only the risk inherent in a given project, but also the impact of a new project on the overall risk of the firm (the portfolio effect). Negatively correlated projects have the most favorable effect on smoothing business cycle fluctuations. The firm may wish to consider all combinations and variations of possible projects and to select only those that provide a total risk-return trade-off consistent with its goals.

Review of Formulas

1. $\overline{D}$ (expected value) $= \Sigma\, DP$ (13–1)
   D is outcome
   P is probability of outcome
2. σ (standard deviation) $= \sqrt{\Sigma(D - \overline{D})^2 P}$ (13–2)
   D is outcome
   $\overline{D}$ is expected value
   P is probability of outcome
3. V (coefficient of variation) $= \dfrac{\sigma}{\overline{D}}$ (13–3)

   σ is standard deviation
   $\overline{D}$ is expected value

List of Terms

risk 404	risk-adjusted discount rate 409
risk-averse 405	simulation 412
expected value 406	decision trees 413
standard deviation 406	portfolio effect 415
coefficient of variation 407	coefficient of correlation 416
beta 408	efficient frontier 418

Discussion Questions

1. If corporate managers are risk-averse, does this mean they will not take risks? Explain.

2. Discuss the concept of risk and how it might be measured.

3. When is the coefficient of variation a better measure of risk than the standard deviation?

4. Explain how the concept of risk can be incorporated into the capital budgeting process.

5. If risk is to be analyzed in a qualitative way, place the following investment decisions in order from the lowest risk to the highest risk:

   a. New equipment.

   b. New market.

   c. Repair of old machinery.

   d. New product in a foreign market.

   e. New product in a related market.

   f. Addition to a new product line.

6. Assume a company, correlated with the economy, is evaluating six projects, of which two are positively correlated with the economy, two are negatively correlated, and two are not correlated with it at all. Which two projects would you select to minimize the company's overall risk?

7. Assume a firm has several hundred possible investments and that it wants to analyze the risk-return trade-off for portfolios of 20 projects. How should it proceed with the evaluation?

8. Explain the effect of the risk-return trade-off on the market value of common stock.

9. What is the purpose of using simulation analysis?

Practice Problems and Solutions

Coefficient of variation

1. Hanson Auto Supplies is examining the following probability distribution. What is the coefficient of variation?

Cash Flow	Probability
$20	.30
40	.40
60	.30

2. Hanson Auto Supply in the prior problem uses the risk-adjusted discount rate and relates the discount rate to the coefficient of variation as follows:

Risk-adjusted discount rate decision

Coefficient of Variation	Discount Rate
0–.30	8%
.31–.60	10
.61–.90	12
.91–1.20...............	16

It will invest $120 and receive the expected value of cash flows you computed in problem 1 of $40. Assume those cash flows of $40 will be earned for the next 5 years and are discounted back at the appropriate discount rate based on the coefficient of variation computed in problem 1. What is the net present value?

Solutions

1. The formula for the coefficient of variation (V) is:

$$V = \frac{\sigma}{\overline{D}} \qquad (13\text{–}3)$$

First compute the expected value ($\overline{D}$)

$$\overline{D} = \Sigma \, DP \qquad (13\text{–}1)$$

D = Cash flow or outcome (in 000s)

P = Probability

D	P	DP
$20	.30	6
40	.40	16
60	.30	18
		$40 = \Sigma DP$

$$\overline{D} = \$40$$

Then compute the standard deviation (σ)

$$\sigma = \sqrt{\Sigma(D - \overline{D})^2 P} \qquad (13\text{–}2)$$

D	$\overline{D}$	(D – $\overline{D}$)	(D – $\overline{D}$)²	P	(D – $\overline{D}$)²P
20	40	−20	400	.30	120
40	0	0	0	.40	0
60	40	+20	400	.30	120
					$240 = \Sigma(D - \overline{D})^2 P$

$$\sigma = \sqrt{\Sigma(D - \overline{D})^2 P} = \sqrt{240} = 15.5$$

Next divide the standard deviation (σ) by the expected value ($\overline{D}$) to determine the coefficient of variation (V).

$$V = \frac{\sigma}{\overline{D}} = \frac{15.5}{40} = .3875 \qquad (13\text{–}3)$$

2. First you must determine the appropriate discount rate based on the coefficient of variation. The coefficient of variation computed in the solution to problem 1 is .3875. Using the table for this problem, the discount rate should be 10 percent since .3875 falls between .31–.60.

Now take the present value of an annuity of $40 (thousand) for 5 years and compare it to the investment of $120 (thousand). The interest rate is the risk-adjusted discount rate of 10 percent identified above. The $40 (thousand) is considered an annuity because it is an equal amount each year. This is not always the case, but eases the computation for this example.

PV of the Annuity

$$PV_A = A \times PV_{IFA} \ (n = 5, i = 10\%) \qquad \text{Appendix D}$$
$$PV_A = \$40 \times 3.791 = \$151.64 \ (\text{thousand})$$

PV of cash flows (inflows)	$151.64 (thousand)
Investment	120.00 (thousand)
Net present value	$ 31.64 (thousand)

The investment has a positive net present value of $31.64 (thousand).

Problems

All problems are available in Homework Manager. Please see the preface for more information.

Expected value and standard deviation

1. Lowe Technology Corp. is evaluating the introduction of a new product. The possible levels of unit sales and the probabilities of their occurrence are given.

Possible Market Reaction	Sales in Units	Probabilities
Low response	20	.10
Moderate response	40	.20
High response	65	.40
Very high response	80	.30

a. What is the expected value of unit sales for the new product?

b. What is the standard deviation of unit sales?

Coefficient of variation

2. Shack Homebuilders, Limited, is evaluating a new promotional campaign that could increase home sales. Possible outcomes and probabilities of the outcomes are shown below. Compute the coefficient of variation.

Possible Outcomes	Additional Sales in Units	Probabilities
Ineffective campaign	40	.20
Normal response	60	.50
Extremely effective	140	.30

Coefficient of variation

3. Sam Sung is evaluating a new advertising program that could increase electronics sales. Possible outcomes and probabilities of the outcomes are shown below. Compute the coefficient of variation.

Possible Outcomes	Additional Sales in Units	Probabilities
Ineffective campaign	80	.20
Normal response	124	.50
Extremely effective	340	.30

4. Possible outcomes for three investment alternatives and their probabilities of occurrence are given below.

	Alternative 1		Alternative 2		Alternative 3	
	Outcomes	Probability	Outcomes	Probability	Outcomes	Probability
Failure	50	.2	90	.3	80	.4
Acceptable.....	80	.4	160	.5	200	.5
Successful	120	.4	200	.2	400	.1

Rank the three alternatives in terms of risk from lowest to highest (compute the coefficient of variation).

5. Five investment alternatives have the following returns and standard deviations of returns.

Alternatives	Returns: Expected Value	Standard Deviation
A	$ 1,200	$ 300
B	800	600
C	5,000	450
D	1,000	430
E	60,000	13,200

Using the coefficient of variation, rank the five alternatives from lowest risk to highest risk.

6. Five investment alternatives have the following returns and standard deviations of returns.

Alternative	Returns: Expected Value	Standard Deviation
A	$ 1,000	$ 590
B	3,000	600
C	3,000	750
D	5,000	2,300
E	10,000	800

Using the coefficient of variation, rank the five alternatives from lowest risk to highest risk.

7. In Problem 6, if you were to choose between Alternatives B and C only, would you need to use the coefficient of variation? Why?

8. Sensor Technology wishes to determine its coefficient of variation as a company over time. The firm projects the following data (in millions of dollars):

Year	Profits: Expected Value	Standard Deviation
1	$ 90	$ 31
3	120	52
6	150	83
9	200	146

a. Compute the coefficient of variation (V) for each time period.

b. Does the risk (V) appear to be increasing over a period of time? If so, why might this be the case?

Risk-averse

9. Tim Trepid is highly risk-averse while Mike Macho actually enjoys taking a risk.

    a.   Which one of the following four investments should Tim choose? Compute coefficients of variation to help you in your choice.

Investments	Returns: Expected Value	Standard Deviation
Buy stocks	$ 8,800	$ 5,600
Buy bonds	7,000	2,060
Buy commodity futures	16,900	22,100
Buy options	11,600	12,400

    b.   Which one of the four investments should Mike choose?

Risk-averse

10. Wildcat Oil Company was set up to take large risks and is willing to take the greatest risk possible. Richmond Construction Company is more typical of the average corporation and is risk-averse.

    a.   Which of the following four projects should Wildcat Oil Company choose? Compute the coefficients of variation to help you make your decision.

    b.   Which one of the four projects should Richmond Construction Company choose based on the same criteria of using the coefficient of variation?

Projects	Returns: Expected Value	Standard Deviation
A	$262,000	$138,000
B	674,000	403,000
C	88,000	108,000
D	125,000	207,000

Coefficient of variation and investment decision

11. Kyle's Shoe Stores, Inc., is considering opening an additional suburban outlet. An aftertax expected cash flow of $100 per week is anticipated from two stores that are being evaluated. Both stores have positive net present values.

    Which store site would you select based on the distribution of these cash flows? Use the coefficient of variation as your measure of risk.

Site A		Site B	
Probability	Cash Flows	Probability	Cash Flows
.2	50	.1	20
.3	100	.2	50
.3	110	.4	100
.2	135	.2	150
		.1	180

Risk-adjusted discount rate

12. Micro Systems is evaluating a $50,000 project with the following cash flows.

Years	Cash Flows
1	$ 9,000
2	12,000
3	18,000
4	16,000
5	24,000

The coefficient of variation for the project is .726.

Based on the following table of risk-adjusted discount rates, should the project be undertaken? Select the appropriate discount rate and then compute the net present value.

Coefficient of Variation	Discount Rate
0–.25	6%
.26–.50	8
.51–.75	12
.76–1.00	16
1.01–1.25	20

13. Payne Medical Labs is evaluating two new products to introduce into the marketplace. Product 1 (a new form of plaster cast) is relatively low in risk for this business and will carry a 10 percent discount rate. Product 2 (a knee joint support brace) has a less predictable outcome and will require a higher discount rate of 15 percent. Either investment will require an initial capital outlay of $90,000. The inflows from projected business over the next five years are given below. Which product should be selected, using net present value analysis?

Risk-adjusted discount rate

Year	Product 1	Product 2
1	$25,000	$16,000
2	30,000	22,000
3	38,000	34,000
4	31,000	29,000
5	19,000	70,000

14. Fill in the table below from Appendix B. Does a high discount rate have a greater or lesser effect on long-term inflows compared to recent ones?

Discount rate and timing

	Discount Rate	
Years	6%	18%
1	_____	_____
10	_____	_____
20	_____	_____

15. Debby's Dance Studios is considering the purchase of new sound equipment that will enhance the popularity of its aerobics dancing. The equipment will cost $25,000. Debby is not sure how many members the new equipment will attract, but she estimates that her increased annual cash flows for each of the next five years will have the following probability distribution. Debby's cost of capital is 11 percent.

Expected value with net present value

Cash Flow	Probability
$3,600	.2
5,000	.3
7,400	.4
9,800	.1

   a. What is the expected value of the cash flow? The value you compute will apply to each of the five years.

   b. What is the expected net present value?

   c. Should Debby buy the new equipment?

Deferred cash flows
and risk-adjusted
discount rate

16. Highland Mining and Minerals Co. is considering the purchase of two gold
mines. Only one investment will be made. The Australian gold mine will
cost $1,600,000 and will produce $300,000 per year in years 5 through 15
and $500,000 per year in years 16 through 25. The U.S. gold mine will cost
$2,000,000 and will produce $250,000 per year for the next 25 years. The cost
of capital is 10 percent.

   a. Which investment should be made? (Note: In looking up present value
   factors for this problem, you need to work with the concept of a deferred
   annuity for the Australian mine. The returns in years 5 through 15
   actually represent 11 years; the returns in years 16 through 25 represent
   10 years.)

   b. If the Australian mine justifies an extra 5 percent premium over the normal
   cost of capital because of its riskiness and the relative uncertainty of cash
   flows, does the investment decision change?

Coefficient of
variation and
investment decision

17. Mr. Sam Golff desires to invest a portion of his assets in rental property.
He has narrowed his choices down to two apartment complexes, Palmer
Heights and Crenshaw Village. After conferring with the present owners,
Mr. Golff has developed the following estimates of the cash flows for these
properties.

Palmer Heights		**Crenshaw Village**	
Yearly Aftertax Cash Inflow (in thousands)	**Probability**	**Yearly Aftertax Cash Inflow (in thousands)**	**Probability**
$10	.1	$15	.2
15	.2	20	.3
30	.4	30	.4
45	.2	40	.1
50	.1		

   a. Find the expected cash flow from each apartment complex.

   b. What is the coefficient of variation for each apartment complex?

   c. Which apartment complex has more risk?

Risk-adjusted
discount rate

18. Referring to Problem 17, Mr. Golff is likely to hold the complex of his choice
for 25 years, and he will use this time period for decision-making purposes.
Either apartment complex can be acquired for $200,000. Mr. Golff uses a risk-
adjusted discount rate when considering investments. His scale is related to the
coefficient of variation.

Coefficient of Variation	**Discount Rate**	
0–0.20	5%	
0.21–0.40	9	(cost of capital)
0.41–0.60	13	
Over 0.90	16	

a. Compute the risk-adjusted net present values for Palmer Heights and Crenshaw Village. You can get the coefficient of correlation and cash flow figures (in thousands) from the previous problem.

b. Which investment should Mr. Golff accept if the two investments are mutually exclusive? If the investments are not mutually exclusive and no capital rationing is involved, how would your decision be affected?

19. Allison's Dresswear Manufacturers is preparing a strategy for the fall season. One alternative is to expand its traditional ensemble of wool sweaters. A second option would be to enter the cashmere sweater market with a new line of high-quality designer label products. The marketing department has determined that the wool and cashmere sweater lines offer the following probability of outcomes and related cash flows.

Decision-tree analysis

	Expand Wool Sweaters Line		Enter Cashmere Sweaters Line	
Expected Sales	Probability	Present Value of Cash Flows from Sales	Probability	Present Value of Cash Flows from Sales
Fantastic	.2	$180,000	.4	$300,000
Moderate	.6	130,000	.2	230,000
Low	.2	85,000	.4	0

The initial cost to expand the wool sweater line is $110,000. To enter the cashmere sweater line the initial cost in designs, inventory, and equipment is $125,000.

a. Diagram a complete decision tree of possible outcomes similar to Figure 13–8 on page 415. Note that you are dealing with thousands of dollars rather than millions. Take the analysis all the way through the process of computing expected NPV (last column for each investment).

b. Given the analysis in part *a*, would you automatically make the investment indicated?

20. When returns from a project can be assumed to be normally distributed, such as those shown in Figure 13–6 on page 410 (represented by a symmetrical, bell-shaped curve), the areas under the curve can be determined from statistical tables based on standard deviations. For example, 68.26 percent of the distribution will fall within one standard deviation of the expected value ($\overline{D} \pm 1\sigma$). Similarly 95.44 percent will fall within two standard deviations ($\overline{D} \pm 2\sigma$), and so on. An abbreviated table of areas under the normal curve is shown here.

Probability analysis with a normal curve distribution

Numbers of σ's from Expected Value	+ or −	+ and −
0.5	0.1915	0.3830
1.0	0.3413	0.6826
1.5	0.4332	0.8664
1.96	0.4750	0.9500
2.0	0.4772	0.9544

Assume Project A has an expected value of $30,000 and a standard deviation (σ) of $6,000.

a. What is the probability that the outcome will be between $24,000 and $36,000?

b. What is the probability that the outcome will be between $21,000 and $39,000?

c. What is the probability that the outcome will be at least $18,000?

d. What is the probability that the outcome will be less than $41,760?

e. What is the probability that the outcome will be less than $27,000 or greater than $39,000?

Increasing risk over time

21. The Oklahoma Pipeline Company projects the following pattern of inflows from an investment. The inflows are spread over time to reflect delayed benefits. Each year is independent of the others.

Year 1		Year 5		Year 10	
Cash Inflow	Probability	Cash Inflow	Probability	Cash Inflow	Probability
65	.20	50	.25	40	.30
80	.60	80	.50	80	.40
95	.20	110	.25	120	.30

The expected value for all three years is $80.

a. Compute the standard deviation for each of the three years.

b. Diagram the expected values and standard deviations for each of the three years in a manner similar to Figure 13–6 on page 410.

c. Assuming 6 percent and 12 percent discount rates, complete the table below for present value factors.

Year	PV_{IF} 6%	PV_{IF} 12%	Difference
1	.943	.893	.050
5	_____	_____	_____
10	_____	_____	_____

d. Is the increasing risk over time, as diagrammed in part b, consistent with the larger differences in PV_{IF}s over time as computed in part c?

e. Assume the initial investment is $135. What is the net present value of the investment at a 12 percent discount rate? Should the investment be accepted?

Portfolio effect of a merger

22. Treynor Pie Co. is a food company specializing in high-calorie snack foods. It is seeking to diversify its food business and lower its risks. It is examining three companies—a gourmet restaurant chain, a baby food company, and a nutritional products firm. Each of these companies can be bought at the same multiple of earnings. The following represents information about the companies.

Company	Correlation with Treynor Pie Company	Sales ($ millions)	Expected Earnings ($ millions)	Standard Deviation in Earnings ($ millions)
Treynor Pie Company	+1.0	$100	$8	$2.0
Gourmet restaurant	+ .6	60	6	1.2
Baby food company	+ .2	50	4	1.8
Nutritional products company	− .7	70	5	3.4

a. Using the last two columns, compute the coefficient of variation for each of the four companies. Which company is the least risky? Which company is the most risky?

b. Discuss which of the acquisition candidates is most likely to reduce Treynor Pie Company's risk? Explain why.

23. Transoceanic Airlines is examining a resort motel chain to add to its operation. Prior to the acquisition, the normal expected outcomes for the firm are as follows:

Portfolio effect of a merger

	Outcomes ($ millions)	Probability
Recession	$30	.30
Normal economy	50	.40
Strong economy	70	.30

After the acquisition, the expected outcomes for the firm would be:

	Outcomes ($ millions)	Probability
Recession	$ 10	.30
Normal economy	50	.40
Strong economy	100	.30

a. Compute the expected value, standard deviation, and coefficient of variation prior to the acquisition.

After the acquisition, these values are as follows:

Expected value	53.0 ($ millions)
Standard deviation	34.9 ($ millions)
Coefficient of variation	.658

b. Comment on whether this acquisition appears desirable to you.

c. Do you think the firm's stock price is likely to go up as a result of this acquisition?

d. If the firm were interested in reducing its risk exposure, which of the following three industries would you advise it to consider for an acquisition? Briefly comment on your answer.

(1) Major travel agency

(2) Oil company

(3) Gambling casino

Efficient frontier   24.   Ms. Sharp is looking at a number of different types of investments for her portfolio. She identifies eight possible investments.

	Return	Risk		Return	Risk
(a)	11%	1.5%	(e)	14%	5.0%
(b)	11	2.1	(f)	15	5.0
(c)	13	3.0	(g)	15	5.8
(d)	13	4.2	(h)	16	7.0

a.   Graph the data in a manner similar to Figure 13–11 on page 418. Use the axes below for your data.

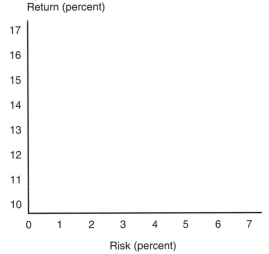

b.   Draw a curved line representing the efficient frontier.

c.   What two objectives do points on the efficient frontier satisfy?

d.   Is there one point on the efficient frontier that is best for all investors?

Certainty   25.   Sheila Goodman recently received her MBA from the Harvard Business School.
equivalent approach   She has joined the family business, Goodman Software Products, Inc., as vice-president of finance.

She believes in adjusting projects for risk. Her father is somewhat skeptical but agrees to go along with her. Her approach is somewhat different than the risk-adjusted discount rate approach, but achieves the same objective.

She suggests that the inflows for each year of a project be adjusted downward for lack of certainty and then be discounted back at a risk-free rate. The theory is that the adjustment penalty makes the inflows the equivalent of riskless inflows, and therefore a risk-free rate is justified.

A table showing the possible coefficient of variation for an inflow and the associated adjustment factor is shown below:

Coefficient of Variation	Adjustment Factor
0–.25	.90
.26–.50	.80
.51–.75	.70
.76–1.00	.60
1.01–1.25	.50

Assume a $150,000 project provides the following inflows with the associated coefficients of variation for each year.

Year	Inflow	Coefficient of Variation
1.........	$30,000	.12
2.........	50,000	.22
3.........	70,000	.46
4.........	55,000	.78
5.........	60,000	1.06

a. Fill in the table below:

Year	Inflow	Coefficient of Variation	Adjustment Factor	Adjusted Inflow
1.........	$30,000	.12	_____	_____
2.........	50,000	.22	_____	_____
3.........	70,000	.46	_____	_____
4.........	55,000	.78	_____	_____
5.........	60,000	1.06	_____	_____

b. If the risk-free rate is 5 percent, should this $120,000 project be accepted? Compute the net present value of the adjusted inflows.

COMPREHENSIVE PROBLEM

Gibson Appliance Co. is a very stable billion-dollar company with a sales growth of about 7 percent per year in good or bad economic conditions. Because of this stability (a coefficient of correlation with the economy of +.4, and a standard deviation of sales of about 5 percent from the mean), Mr. Hoover, the vice-president of finance, thinks the company could absorb a small risky company that could add quite a bit of return without increasing the company's risk very much. He is trying to decide which of the two companies he will buy, using the figures below. Gibson's cost of capital is 12 percent.

Gibson Appliance Co. (portfolio effect of a merger)

Genetic Technology Co. (cost $80 million)		Silicon Microchip Co. (cost $80 million)	
Cash Flow for 10 Years ($ millions)	Probability	Cash Flow for 10 Years ($ millions)	Probability
$ 2	.2	$ 5	.2
8	.3	7	.2
16	.2	18	.3
25	.2	24	.3
40	.1		

a. What is the expected cash flow from both companies?

b. Which company has the lower coefficient of variation?

c. Compute the net present value of each company.

d. Which company would you pick, based on the net present values?

e. Would you change your mind if you added the risk dimensions to the problem? Explain.

f. What if Genetic Technology Co. had a coefficient of correlation with the economy of −.2 and Silicon Microchip Co. had one of +.5? Which of these companies would give you the best portfolio effects for risk reduction?

g. What might be the effect of the acquisitions on the market value of Gibson Appliance Co.'s stock?

COMPREHENSIVE PROBLEM

Kennedy Trucking Company (investment decision based on probability analysis)

Five years ago, Kennedy Trucking Company was considering the purchase of 60 new diesel trucks that were 15 percent more fuel-efficient than the ones the firm was using. Mr. Hoffman, the president, had found that the company uses an average of 10 million gallons of diesel fuel per year at a price of $1.25 per gallon. If he can cut fuel consumption by 15 percent, he will save $1,875,000 per year (1,500,000 gallons times $1.25).

Mr. Hoffman assumed that the price of diesel fuel is an external market force that he cannot control and that any increased costs of fuel will be passed on to the shipper through higher rates endorsed by the Interstate Commerce Commission. If this is true, then fuel efficiency would save more money as the price of diesel fuel rises (at $1.35 per gallon, he would save $2,025,000 in total if he buys the new trucks). Mr. Hoffman has come up with two possible forecasts as shown below—each of which he feels has about a 50 percent chance of coming true. Under assumption number 1, diesel prices will stay relatively low; under assumption number 2, diesel prices will rise considerably. Sixty new trucks will cost Kennedy Trucking $5 million. Under a special provision from the Interstate Commerce Commission, the allowable depreciation will be 25 percent in year 1, 38 percent in year 2, and 37 percent in year 3. The firm has a tax rate of 40 percent and a cost of capital of 10 percent.

a. First compute the yearly expected costs of diesel fuel for both assumption 1 (relatively low prices) and assumption 2 (high prices) from the forecasts below.

Forecast for assumption 1 (low fuel prices):

Probability (same for each year)	Price of Diesel Fuel per Gallon		
	Year 1	Year 2	Year 3
.1	$ .80	$ .90	$1.00
.2	1.00	1.10	1.10
.3	1.10	1.20	1.30
.2	1.30	1.45	1.45
.2	1.40	1.55	1.60

Forecast for assumption 2 (high fuel prices):

Probability (same for each year)	Price of Diesel Fuel per Gallon		
	Year 1	Year 2	Year 3
.1	$1.20	$1.50	$1.70
.3	1.30	1.70	2.00
.4	1.80	2.30	2.50
.2	2.20	2.50	2.80

b. What will be the dollar savings in diesel expenses each year for assumption 1 and for assumption 2?

c. Find the increased cash flow after taxes for both forecasts.

d. Compute the net present value of the truck purchases for each fuel forecast assumption and the combined net present value (that is, weigh the NPVs by .5).

e. If you were Mr. Hoffman, would you go ahead with this capital investment?

f. How sensitive to fuel prices is this capital investment?

WEB EXERCISE

Alcoa was listed in Table 13–2 as a company that has a relativity high beta (a measure of stock price volatility). Alcoa produces aluminum and aluminum products. Go to its Web site at www.alcoa.com, and follow the steps below:

1. Under "About Alcoa," select "Annual Report."

2. Download the latest annual report.

3. Scroll all the way down to "Financial and Corporate Data."

4. Then scroll down to "Selected Financial Data."

5. One of the characteristics of high beta stocks is that they often have volatile earnings performances. Let's check out Alcoa. Compute the year-to-year percentage change in "Diluted-Income from Continuing Operations" for each of the five years. Do the earnings appear to be volatile?

6. Companies with high betas and inconsistent performance are encouraged to keep their debt ratios low (under 50 percent). Compute the ratio of long-term debt to total assets for each of the five years for Alcoa. What does the pattern look like to you?

Note: From time to time, companies redesign their Web sites and occasionally a topic we have listed may have been deleted, updated, or moved into a different location. If you click on the site map or site index, you will be introduced to a table of contents which should aid you in finding the topic you are looking for.

part **5**

Long-Term Financing

RELATED WEB SITES

www.nyse.com

www.nasdaq.com

www.hoovers.com

finance.yahoo.com

www.ceradyne.com

www.ericsson.com

www.3m.com

www.oracle.com

www.cboe.com

The six chapters in this section cover long-term finance with topics such as the capital markets, investment banking, and the various types of securities that companies can sell to raise money. In this section, we highlight Jim Tyree, CEO and chairman of Mesirow Financial, a financial conglomerate in Chicago with offices in 29 locations across the country and in Puerto Rico. Mesirow is a company with over 1,000 employees and more than $27 billion in advisory or managed assets. Mesirow has six divisions specializing in Investment Management, Investment Services, Insurance Services, Investment Banking, Consulting, and Real Estate. The Investment Management division includes services for hedge funds, private equity, investment advisories, fixed income investments, and currency management.

Jim Tyree came to Mesirow Financial in 1900 fresh out of Illinois State University's MBA. program. Two years before he had completed his bachelor's degree while working his way through college. He completed his CPA even though he had majored in finance and had a minor in economics. He had a great balance of theory, practice, and analytical skills and he used them all to become chair-

man and chief executive officer of Mesirow Financial in 1994. He had started at Mesirow Financial as an assistant to Richard Mesirow, the son of the founder, and after two years he ended up running the Investment Banking group before he was 30 years of age. Within a couple of years he had created the Capital Markets division where he founded the firm's Private Equity division. Within six years of arriving at Mesirow the areas he ran accounted for over 25 percent of the company's revenue. He was promoted to partner when he was 32 years old, and the rest is history.

Tyree has been innovative in the way he has connected the many different businesses that Mesirow operates. He believes that in order to be a great company, you need to offer quality service to your clients and that you are better off to focus on fewer clients using more services than many clients using a single service. Knowing and serving your customers' needs is very important in the cross selling of services.

As a private employee-owned company, the fruits of everyone's labor enhance the book value of the firm. With revenues of close to $300 million in 2005 and capital of $165 million, Mesirow is not a big player compared to Merrill Lynch, but its hedge funds group (Advanced Strategies) is one of

Jim Tyree—Mesirow Financial
Courtesy of Mesirow Financial

the largest in the country, and the rest of their services are targeted at high-wealth individuals and institutions who value a high degree of personal attention.

Jim Tyree is an avid sports fan, and the Chicago White Sox winning the World Series made one of his lifelong dreams come true. Now if the Chicago Bulls could win another title that would be the frosting on his cake.

Capital Markets

1 The capital markets are made up of securities that have a life of one year or longer (often much longer).

2 The primary participants raising funds in the capital markets are the U.S. Treasury; other agencies of the federal, state, and local governments; and corporations.

3 The United States is a three-sector economy in which households,

corporations, and governmental units allocate funds among themselves.

4 Securities markets consist of physical and electronic markets.

5 Security markets are considered to be efficient when prices adjust rapidly to new information.

6 Security legislation is intended to protect investors against fraud, manipulation, and illegal insider trading.

Security markets comprise a myriad of securities from government bonds to corporate common stock. These markets are influenced by many variables such as interest rates, investors' confidence, economic growth, global crises, and more. These influences were all present during the last decade. U.S. and world markets suffered from sluggish economies, worldwide terrorism, diminished consumer confidence, and the war in Iraq. The capital markets recovered from the currency devaluations of the late 1990s in Thailand, Malaysia, and Korea, and these countries' economies were growing again in the mid-2000s. Russia, a country that had defaulted on its sovereign debt in 1998, still seems to be unable to achieve the political democracy and stability the West had hoped for, but the Russian economy is growing, in large part due to its role as one of the world's largest oil producers. The euro, the currency of the European Union, is doing well and is now a formidable competitor to the U.S. dollar in world currency markets.

The recession of 2001, coupled with the stock market bubble of 1999–2000, resulted in falling stock markets, but bond prices rose as interest rates fell to their lowest level since the 1950s and 1960s as the Federal Reserve Board stimulated the economy with a monetary policy relying on artificially low interest rates. The three-year decline in the U.S. stock markets from 2000 through 2002 was punctuated by a rebound in 2003 followed by modest growth in 2004 and 2005. The 9/11 terrorist attacks on New York City, had a devastating effect on Wall Street with thousands of financial employees laid off and earnings plummeting. To make matters worse, investor confidence in corporate accounting statements suffered from the many accounting scandals such as those of Enron, WorldCom, Tyco, Global Crossing, and others. In general, the U.S. economy has recovered and maintained a relatively high growth in GDP despite Hurricane Katrina and its devastation of New Orleans and the resultant spike in oil prices. This is history, but it shows that the markets have to deal with these types of events and provide a place for governments and corporations to raise capital under all types of conditions.

Domestic and global events all impact the world's securities markets. Corporations come to these international markets for short-term sources of funds or long-term capital. When the markets are good, money is cheap and easy to find, and when the markets are bad, money is hard to find and often relatively expensive. The world economic markets often move back and forth between the two extremes.

Security markets are generally separated into short-term and long-term markets. The short-term markets comprise securities with maturities of one year or less and are referred to as **money markets**. The securities most commonly traded in these markets, such as Treasury bills, commercial paper, and negotiable certificates of deposit, were previously discussed under working capital and cash management in Chapter 7 and will not be covered again.

The long-term markets are called **capital markets** and consist of securities having maturities greater than one year. The most common corporate securities in this category are bonds, common stock, preferred stock, and convertible securities. These securities are found on the firm's balance sheet under the designation long-term liabilities and equities. Taken together, these long-term securities comprise the firm's capital structure.

In this chapter, we will be looking at how the capital markets are organized and integrated into the corporate and economic system of the United States. Capital markets are becoming increasingly international as suppliers of financial capital seek out the best risk-return opportunities from among the major industrialized countries in the global economy.

The globalization of capital markets is particularly important for large U.S. multinational corporations that use these markets to raise capital for both domestic and international operations. We start with a global overview of markets and then discuss the U.S. capital markets more fully.

International Capital Markets

As discussed in the introduction, international capital markets have increased in importance during the last decade and continue to become larger, more efficient, and more competitive in the new millennium. Since the early 1990s, the Iron Curtain has collapsed, giving rise to free markets in these formerly communist countries; the two Germanys were reunited; and at the beginning of 1993, the European Community implemented a more competitive and tariff-free Europe. In 1994, the North American Free Trade Agreement (NAFTA) was established between the United States, Canada, and Mexico. In addition to these events, the Asian countries, led by China, continue to expand their economic growth. All these events have combined to create an international demand and need for capital worldwide, and the U.S. markets—while still the most important—will be challenged by the Euro-zone countries.

International money and capital markets will be affected for years by the European Monetary Union (EMU), which began in January 1999. This economic and political trading bloc of 20 countries has created a new economic order for Europe.

The new European Central Bank is in charge of monetary policy for the whole Eurozone and will have to learn to use the right regional economic indicators in adjusting monetary policy. In 2002 the euro became the only official currency in the Eurozone, with liquidity and size second only to the U.S. dollar. Companies are now selling bonds and stocks denominated in euro currency, not French francs, Italian lira, German deutsche marks, or the other local currencies. The impact on the Euro-bond market will continue to be large as the European Central Bank issues bonds, notes, and bills denominated in the new euro currency. Eventually we can expect to have stock and bond indexes tracking the performance of a combined group of common stocks and bonds from these countries.

The European Union is an emerging economic trading bloc. It will be interesting to see if these countries can put aside their nationalistic tendencies and become one cohesive economic community. Results since 2002 have been bumpy, as countries such as Germany, France, and Italy have struggled to stay within the economic guidelines set down for member nations.

Companies search the international markets for opportunities to raise debt capital at the lowest cost. Many corporations list their common stock the world over to increase liquidity for their stockholders and to provide opportunities for the potential sale of new stock in foreign countries. While these developments are also very important to investors (suppliers of capital), our focus in this chapter is primarily on corporations.

By the end of 2004 foreign investors had made net investments in the United States totaling $12.5 trillion while the United States had made net investments totaling $10.0 trillion in foreign countries. Subtracting these two figures indicates that foreign countries have invested $2.5 trillion more in the United States than the United States has invested in the rest of the world. This is not surprising since the U.S. dollar is the world's international currency, and the United States is one of the most politically stable countries in the world. About 5.1 percent of foreign investment ($640 billion) has been invested in U.S. government securities, which has helped fund the large fiscal deficits the United States has been running. Most of the rest has gone into corporate bonds, common stock, and direct investment in U.S. companies.[1] On the other hand, U.S. investors have made $3.3 trillion of direct investments in foreign companies and about $3.4 trillion of investments in foreign bonds and stocks.[2] The United States has not helped foreign governments finance their deficits. Table 14–1 provides the dollars and percentage breakdowns of the international investments between the United States and the rest of the world at the end of 2004.

---

[1]There is also a catchall category called "other."
[2]Here, there is also an "other" category.

Net U.S. Assets Owned by Foreigners	2004 Year-end ($ billions)	Percent of Total
Foreign direct investment in U.S. at market value	$ 2,686.890	21.47%
Foreign official assets in the United States	1,981.992	15.84
U.S. Treasury securities and U.S. currency	639.716	5.11
U.S. corporate bonds	2,059.250	16.45
U.S. corporate stocks	1,928.547	15.41
Deposits in U.S. banks	2,304.640	18.41
U.S. currency	332.735	2.66
Other.	581.258	4.64
Total net U.S. assets owned by foreigners	$12,515.028	100.00%
Net Foreign Assets Owned by United States		
U.S. direct investment abroad at market value	$ 3,287.373	32.96%
U.S. Treasury official reserves + other U.S. government assets	189.591	1.90
U.S. govt. assets other than official reserves.	83.566	0.84
Foreign bonds.	916.655	9.19
Foreign stocks.	2,520.063	25.27
Claims by U.S. banks	2,174.009	21.80
Claim by U.S. nonbanking concerns	801.536	8.04
Total net foreign assets owned by United States	$ 9,972.793	100.00%
Net international investment position of the United States.	−$ 2,542.235	

Source: Bureau of Economic Analysis, "Table 1—International Position of the United States at Year-end 2003 and 2004."

Table 14–1
International investments

Competition for Funds in the U.S. Capital Markets

Let's return to the United States. In order to put U.S. corporate securities into perspective, it is necessary to look at other securities available in the capital markets. The federal government, government agencies, state governments, and local municipalities all compete with one another and corporations for a limited supply of financial capital. The capital markets serve as a way of allocating the available capital to the most efficient user. Therefore the ultimate investor must choose among many kinds of securities, both corporate and noncorporate. Before investors part with their money, they desire to maximize their return for any given level of risk, and thus the expected return from the universe of securities acts as an allocating mechanism in the markets.

Government Securities

U.S. Government Securities   In accordance with government fiscal policy, the U.S. Treasury manages the federal government's debt in order to balance the flow of funds into and out of the U.S. Treasury. When deficits are incurred, the Treasury can sell short-term or long-term securities to finance the shortfall and when surpluses occur, the government can retire debt. When the U.S. government collects more in taxes than it is spending, it doesn't need to borrow and this frees up capital for the other sectors of the economy.

Federally Sponsored Credit Agencies   The **federally sponsored credit agencies** are governmental units that issue their securities on a separate basis from those securities sold directly by the U.S. Treasury. Although the U.S. Treasury does not directly back these securities, none of these issues has ever failed. The Federal Home Loan Banks (FHLB) and the Federal National Mortgage Association (Fannie Mae) are both involved in lending to the housing market. Fannie Mae is included as a government-sponsored agency even though it is currently a privately run corporation. It still maintains a quasi-agency relationship with the United States government, based on its original government charter. Two other large federal agencies are the Farm Credit Banks and the Student Loan Marketing Association.

State and Local Securities   State and local issues are referred to as **municipal securities** or tax-exempt offerings. Interest payments from securities issued by state and local governments are exempt from federal income taxes and income taxes levied by the state of issue. (For example, if the state of California issues a bond that is bought by someone living in the state of California, the interest is not taxable by California. However if someone living in the state of California buys a bond issued by the state of New York, the interest will be taxable by California.) Because these securities are exempt from federal taxes, they tend to be purchased by investors in high marginal tax brackets. Unlike the federal government, most state governments are required by law to balance their budgets and so bonds issued by municipal governments or state entities are usually supported by revenue-generating projects such as sewers, college dormitories, and toll roads.

Corporate Securities

Corporate Bonds   One misconception held by many investors is that the market for common stocks dominates the corporate bond markets in size. This is far from the truth. Bonds are debt instruments that have a fixed life and must be repaid at maturity. As bonds come due and are paid off, the corporation normally replaces this debt with new bonds. For this reason, corporate bonds have traditionally made up the majority of external financing by corporations.

In general, when interest rates are expected to rise, financial managers try to lock in long-term financing at a low cost and balance the company's debt structure with more long-term debt and less short-term debt. The amount of long-term debt a corporation chooses to employ as a percentage of total capital is also a function of several options. Management must decide about its willingness to accept risk and examine the amount of financing available from other sources, such as internal cash flow, common stock, and preferred stock.

Preferred Stock   Preferred stock is the least used of all long-term corporate securities. The major reason for the small amount of financing with preferred stock is that the dividend is not tax-deductible to the corporation, as is bond interest. Corporations who are at their maximum debt limit issue much of the preferred stock that is sold. These companies may also suffer from low common stock prices or want to issue preferred stock that may some day be convertible into common stock.

Common Stock   Companies seeking new equity capital sell common stock. As explained in the next chapter on investment banking, common stock is either sold as a new issue in an initial public offering (IPO) or as a secondary offering. A secondary offering means that shares are already being publicly traded in the markets and the new offering will be at least the second time the company has sold common stock to the public. Also, when companies *purchase* their own shares in the market because they have excess cash, these shares are shown on the company's balance sheet as treasury stock. Because common stock has no maturity date like bonds, new common stock is never sold to replace old stock in the way that new bonds are used to refund old bonds.

Internal versus External Sources of Funds   So far we have discussed how corporations raise funds externally through long-term financing using bonds, common stock, and preferred stock. Another extremely important source of funds to the corporation is **internally generated funds** as represented by retained earnings and cash flow added back from depreciation. On average, during the last 20 years corporations raised about 40 percent of their funds internally and 60 percent of their funds externally through the sale of new securities.

What about the composition of internal funds actually making up the 40 percent of financing? The composition of internal funds is a function of corporate profitability, the dividends paid and the resultant retained earnings, and the depreciation tax shield firms get from making additions to plant and equipment. As companies invest heavily in new plant and equipment, depreciation can rise significantly in the following years, which will have a positive impact on internally generated funds. Figure 14–1 shows the relative importance of depreciation and retained earnings in providing internal financing.

Figure 14–1   Internally generated funds: Depreciation and retained earnings

Note: Does not include any adjustments for inflation.
Source: www.bea.gov.

During the period covered in Figure 14–1, retained earnings provided about 21 percent of the internal funds while the depreciation tax shield provided the remaining 79 percent. In times of recession when corporate net income falls, retained earnings declines as a percentage of internal funds while the opposite is true during economic expansions. During the recession of 2001, retained earnings only provided 14.2 percent of internal funds while in the boom year of 1995 they accounted for 28 percent of interal funds.

The Supply of Capital Funds

Having discussed the major users of capital in the U.S. economy, we turn our attention to the suppliers of capital. In a **three-sector economy**, consisting of business, government, and households, the major supplier of funds for investment is the household sector. Corporations and the federal government have traditionally been net demanders of funds. Figure 14–2 below diagrams the flow of funds through our basic three-sector economy.

Figure 14–3 presents a chart showing the percentage of funds provided by the major suppliers of funds to the credit markets at the end of 2004. The figure shows that households provided 4.68 percent of the funds directly to the credit markets, but we

Figure 14–2

Flow of funds through the economy

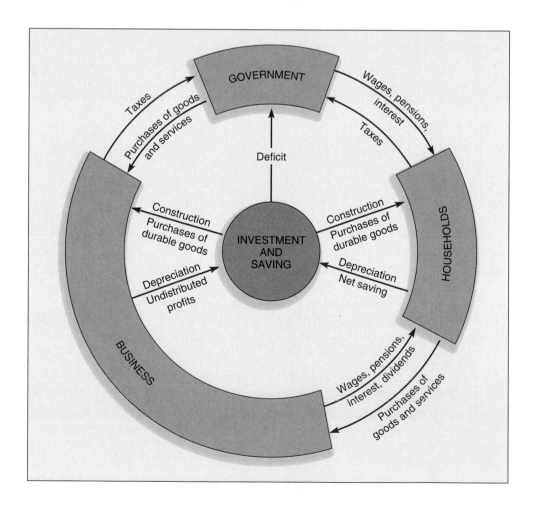

The Capital Markets Punish General Motors

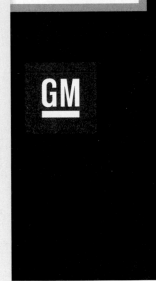

General Motors has been losing market share for many years and the result of lower sales is lower profits and even losses. In addition, GM is saddled with heavy pension fund costs and health care costs for both its workers and retirees, which reduces its profit margins. All three negatives create a recipe for disaster and/or bankruptcy. So far GM is bending but not breaking under the weight of these combined forces.

In GM's case it is unfortunate that this financial crisis has caused it to sell two of its last profitable divisions. During the last decade, GM has sold off Hughes and EDS for billions of dollars to shore up its pension funds. In late 2005 it announced that it would sell off 60 percent of GMAC Commercial Holding Corporation, its commercial mortgage division. The sale will raise $11 billion in funds from the buying investor group that will use a $3 billion revolving loan, a $3 billion term loan, and asset-backed securities to finance the deal. The investing syndicate includes Citigroup, Credit Suisse First Boston, Deutsche Bank, Goldman Sachs & Co., JPMorgan Chase, Royal Bank of Scotland, and the private equity group of Kohlberg Kravis Roberts & Co. Additionally GM announced the group would also buy a majority stake in GMAC, the firm's automotive financing division.

The reason for these asset sales by GM can best be summed up by a quote from *The Wall Street Journal.*

> GM's sales come as it struggles with access to capital since being downgraded to speculative-grade status amid a declining North American market share. The spinoffs are designed to achieve investment-grade status.*

This is an example of how the capital markets allocate capital. Even a giant like General Motors is not immune from the discipline of the markets. When you don't perform, investors won't lend you long-term funds or buy your equity unless you are willing to pay a high cost of capital. In short, GM's poor financial and operating performance has raised its cost of capital to very high levels.

---

*Tom Sullivan of Dow Jones Newswires, "Investors to Borrow $6B in loans for GMAC Commercial," 11-07-1229 ET Copyright © 2005 Dow Jones & Company, Inc.

need to consider that insurance and pension funds (9.66 percent), commercial banks and credit unions (29.84 percent), and mutual funds (.26 percent) all get most of their funds from households. These institutions act as financial intermediaries by funneling individuals' money into the credit and equity markets. The reason that mutual fund contributions were almost nonexistent as a source of funds in 2004 was because individuals took $129 billion out of their money market mutual funds during the year searching for higher returns. Mortgage money is largely accounted for by asset-backed issuers of securities (11.18 percent), federally related mortgage pools (1.92 percent), and government-sponsored agencies (1.67 percent). Foreign suppliers of credit funds are the second largest supplier of funds to the U.S. credit markets, providing 27.26 percent of the funds. Given that the United States has been running balance of trade deficits of over $300 billion dollars for the last several years, some of this money also is finding its way back into the U.S. economy.

As households receive wages and transfer payments from the government and wages and dividends from corporations, they generally save some portion of their income. These savings are usually funneled to **financial intermediaries** that, in turn, make investments in the capital markets with the funds received from the household sector. This is known as indirect investment. The types of financial institutions that channel funds into the capital markets are specialized and diverse. Funds may flow into commercial banks, mutual savings banks, and credit unions. Households may

Figure 14–3

Suppliers of funds to credit markets (Year-end 2004)

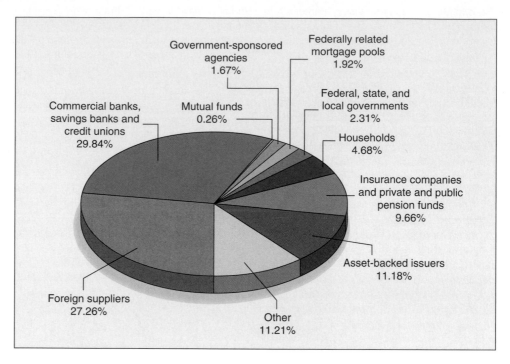

also purchase mutual fund shares, invest in life insurance, or participate in some form of private pension plan or profit sharing. All these financial institutions act as intermediaries; they help make the flow of funds from one sector of the economy to another very efficient and competitive. Without intermediaries, the cost of funds would be higher, and the efficient allocation of funds to the best users at the lowest cost would not occur.

The Role of the Security Markets

Security markets exist to aid the allocation of capital among households, corporations, and governmental units, with financial institutions acting as intermediaries. Just as financial institutions specialize in their services and investments, the capital markets are divided into many functional subsets, with each specific market serving a certain type of security. For example, the common stocks of some of the largest corporations are traded on the New York Stock Exchange, whereas government securities are traded by government security dealers in the over-the-counter markets.

Once a security is sold for the first time as an original offering, the security trades in its appropriate market among all kinds of investors. This trading activity is known as **secondary trading**, since funds flow among investors, rather than to the corporation. Secondary trading provides liquidity to investors and keeps prices competitive among alternative security investments. It is very important to the functioning of the financial markets.

Security markets provide liquidity in two ways. First, they enable corporations to raise funds by selling new issues of securities rapidly at fair, competitive prices. Second, they allow the investor who purchases securities to sell them with relative ease and speed and thereby turn a paper asset into cash. Ask yourself the question, "Would I buy securities if there were no place to sell them?" You would probably think twice before committing funds to an illiquid investment. Without markets, corporations and governmental units would not be able to raise the large amounts of capital necessary for economic growth.

The Organization of the Security Markets

The structure of the security markets has changed drastically in the last years of the 20th century and the beginning of this century, and it is expected to continue evolving into global electronic markets. These changes include mergers or alliances between exchanges, the transformation of member exchanges into public companies, and the elimination of trading on the exchange floor. Other changes such as decimalization of price quotes have impacted the efficiency of the markets and their profitability. Many of the changes are being driven by technology, which is creating low-cost competition for the traditional markets such as the New York Stock Exchange.

In this section we present the current organization of the markets and provide updates on significant events of the last few years. Historically, the markets have been divided into organized exchanges, which were floor-traded auction markets conducted by brokers, and over-the-counter markets (OTC), which were traded through dealers using electronic quotes. During the last decade, the increased popularity of electronic trading has lowered the cost of trading and put pressure on both the New York Stock Exchange and the NASDAQ Market to lower costs and increase efficiency.

The New York Stock Exchange

Traditionally, stock exchanges have had a central location where buyers and sellers gathered to trade securities. The **New York Stock Exchange (NYSE)** is located on Wall Street in New York City and brokers meet to buy and sell securities through a bid (buy price) and ask (sell price) market, called an auction market. Buyers and sellers of the securities are not actually present on the floor of the exchange but are represented by brokers who act as their agents. These brokers are registered members of the exchange and own seats which give them on-floor trading privileges. The NYSE is a national exchange, and has an elected board of directors comprised of public directors and industry directors, each representing approximately half of the total.

Size and Liquidity   The NYSE is the largest and most important of all global stock exchanges. Companies with shares listed on the New York Stock Exchange include ExxonMobil, Coca-Cola, IBM, Johnson & Johnson, and thousands of other well-known companies including foreign firms such as Nokia, DaimlerChrysler, and Sony. Because of these large companies, the NYSE had an average daily trading volume of over 1.5 billion shares in 2005. This provides a tremendous amount of liquidity. The volume comparison between the NYSE and the NASDAQ Market can be seen in Table 14–2 on the following page. Interestingly enough, the NYSE became a publicly traded company in 2006, so one can now buy shares of the NYSE Group, Inc.

Table 14–2 NYSE and NASDAQ trading* (As of July 2005)

	Average Daily Volume NYSE (shares, mil.)	Average Daily Volume NYSE (% change)	Average Daily Volume NASDAQ† (shares, mil.)	Average Daily Volume NASDAQ† (% change)	Average Daily Value NYSE ($ bil.)	Average Daily Value NYSE (% change)	Average Daily Value NASDAQ† ($ bil.)	Average Daily Value NASDAQ† (% change)
2005	1,582	9%	1,415	12%	$54.7	19%	$35.3	30%
2004	1,457	4	1,259	−13	46.1	20	27.2	1
2003	1,398	−3	1,449	−16	38.5	−6	26.8	−6
2002	1,441	16	1,722	−8	40.9	−3	28.5	−35
2001	1,240	19	1,874	7	42.3	−4	44.1	−46
2000	1,042	29	1,757	63	43.9	24	80.9	86
1999	809	20	1,076	34	35.5	22	43.5	90
1998	674	28	802	24	29.0	27	22.9	29
1997	527	28	648	19	22.8	43	17.7	36
1996	412	19	544	36	16.0	31	13.0	37
1995	346	19	401	36	12.2	26	9.5	65
1994	291	10	295	12	9.7	8	5.8	8
1993	265	31	263	38	9.0	31	5.3	52
1992	202	13	191	17	6.9	14	3.5	28
1990	157	249%	132	389%	$ 5.2	253%	$ 1.8	560%

*Year average, except for current year average through the end of July. Sources: NASDAQ data 1990–1997 from *NASDAQ Fact Book*; 1980, 1999–2002 directly from NASDAQ.

†NASDAQ share volume and value of trading figures are inflated because of dealer trading. While on the NYSE (an auction market) public investors typically trade directly with each other, on NASDAQ (a dealer market) public investors typically trade with dealers.

Source: www.nysedata.com/factbook.

Listing Requirements   Let's go back to the topic at hand. In order to be traded on the NYSE, a company must apply for listing, and the requirements of the NYSE are much more stringent than the other markets. **Listing requirements** set minimum standards for earnings, net tangible assets, market value of publicly held shares, number of common shares owned by the public, and monthly trading volume. For those interested in the specifics of listing requirements, we refer you to the Web Exercise at the end of the chapter. Corporations that want to be listed on the public markets have decided that public availability of the stock on a stock market will benefit their shareholders. The benefits include providing liquidity to owners and allowing the company a more viable means for raising external capital for growth and expansion. The company must pay the exchange an initial listing fee, annual listing fees based on shares outstanding, and additional fees based on the number of shares traded each year.

The NYSE and the SEC both have the authority to remove (delist) or suspend a security from trading when the company fails to meet certain criteria. There is much latitude in these decisions, but generally a company's security may be considered for delisting if the company falls seriously below any of the minimum initial listing standards.

Decimalization   Traditionally the NYSE quoted its shares in fractions based on eighths ($\frac{1}{8}$, $\frac{1}{4}$, $\frac{3}{8}$, $\frac{1}{2}$, $\frac{5}{8}$, $\frac{3}{4}$, and $\frac{7}{8}$). As the fractions were divided into smaller and smaller units such as $\frac{1}{64}$ and $\frac{1}{128}$, the calculations became mind numbing for investors. To make the quotations more readable and understandable for the investing public, the Securities and Exchange Commission mandated the switch to listing quotations in decimals. The **decimalization** of the quotes began in August 2000 and has impacted the trading profits and liquidity. The NYSE states that the average spread (the difference between the bid and ask price) for NYSE stocks is between $.03 and $.05 per share which is a steep reduction from spreads of $.10 to $.15 in the 1990s. While there have been many complaints from professional traders about lost profits, the system has withstood the test of time and seems to be working well.

Electronic Trading   If you can't beat them, buy them. That is what the New York Stock Exchange did in 2005 when it bought the second leading ECN (electronic communications network), Archipelago, because their own electronic trading platform was not competitive and they were losing market share to the NASDAQ market. While the NYSE states that they will keep both floor trading and electronic markets, the bet is that electronic markets will dominate because of their speed, efficiency, and low cost execution.

International Merger   In June of 2006, the New York Stock Exchange announced an intended move that should have a major impact as far as one can see into the future. It is going to merge with Euronext, the European exchange operator. The $20 billion merger will create the first ever Trans-Atlantic linkup of stock and derivative markets.

The combined company (NYSE Euronext) will be the world's largest publicly traded exchange company, trading a wide range of stocks and derivatives through the New York Stock Exchange; on the electronic Euronext Liffe exchange in London; and on the stock exchanges of Paris, Lisbon, Brussels, and Amsterdam. The deal represents the ultimate move toward internationalization.

The deal will also put the merged company in competition with the Chicago Mercantile Exchange and the Chicago Board of Trade for derivatives business.

The NASDAQ Market

Unlike the New York Stock Exchange, NASDAQ is strictly an electronic market without any pretense of a physical location. NASDAQ is an acronym for National Association of Security Dealers Automated Quotation.

NASDAQ has traditionally been considered an over-the-counter market because it lacked the seal of "exchange status" granted by the SEC. Most likely, NASDAQ will be granted exchange status by the SEC and it will then have the same legal status as the NYSE.

The National Market and Small-Cap Market   NASDAQ is the largest **screen-based market** in the United States. Screen based means that there is no physical location, but trading is based on computers and other communication mediums. Over the years it has moved to the forefront of electronic trading and with the acquisition of Instinet it is expected to stay at the head of the pack. As the first market to use computerized quotation systems it attracted small technology companies which often grew into giants and continued to trade on the NASDAQ Market. It is still the favorite market for large technology companies such as Microsoft, Intel, Cisco Systems, Oracle, and others. Over 30 percent of the Nasdaq Index consists of technology stocks. During the 1990s, there were many Internet companies that raised capital by selling shares to the public with follow-up trading on the NASDAQ Market. If you examine Table 14–2 on page 446, you can see the "stock market bubble" in technology stocks quite easily. In 2000 the average daily volume for NASDAQ was $80.9 billion per day (second column from the right, six lines down). If you examine the period before and after 2000, you can see that 2000 was the peak year.

The Nasdaq Small-Cap Market includes small companies with a national market such as Cobra Electronics or First Citizens BanCorp, or small regional companies that are traded in local markets by local people. Many companies in this market are closely held by their founders and there are few shares available. This is especially true of small local banks and insurance companies.

The American Stock Exchange

Like the New York Stock Exchange, the **American Stock Exchange (AMEX)** has a central location on Wall Street. After several years of being affiliated with NASDAQ, the AMEX became a separately managed exchange on December 31, 2004. It currently has about 800 common stocks listed but it should be pointed out that its listing requirements are less stringent than both the NYSE and NASDAQ markets. It is one of the largest options exchanges and is a major exchange for Exchange Traded Funds which are funds structured to represent various securities indexes such as the S&P500 and the Lehman bond index. Exchange Traded funds trade like common stocks rather than like mutual funds.

Regional Stock Exchanges

Regional stock exchanges exist outside of New York and trade primarily in issues of large national companies. Some of the smaller exchanges, such as those in Boston and Cincinnati, are more regional in the sense that many of the companies listed are headquartered or do their principal business in the region in which the exchange is located. The regional exchanges can trade common stock of the same companies that are traded on the New York Stock Exchange. This **dual trading** accounts for over 90 percent of the stocks traded on the Chicago and Pacific regional exchanges. The consolidated tape reports the prices and volume of all shares listed on the NYSE and trade on the regional exchanges, NASDAQ, and the NYSE.

Foreign Exchanges

As the industrialized world has grown, capital markets around the world have increased in size and importance. As a sign of the international capital markets, large U.S. international companies—such as IBM, Intel, and McDonald's—trade on the Tokyo and Frankfurt stock exchanges; and many foreign companies trade on the New York Stock Exchange—such as Sony and TDK of Japan, Royal Dutch Petroleum and Phillips G.N.V. of the Netherlands, and BMW and Siemens of Germany.

Table 14–3 lists the major global stock markets by country, alphabetically. Not all are large but most are flourishing, with growing volume, new listings, and increased interest by investors worldwide. This pattern of international trading is enhanced by the proposed merger on the New York Stock Exchange and Euronext, previously discussed in the chapter.

Table 14–3
Global stock markets

Australia	Hong Kong	Singapore/Malaysia
Austria	Italy	Spain
Belgium	Japan	Sweden
Canada	Mexico	Switzerland
Denmark	Netherlands	United Kingdom
France	Norway	United States
Germany		

Electronic Communication Networks (ECNs)

A recent addition to the security markets are electronic communications networks. **Electronic communication networks**, or ECNs, are electronic trading systems that automatically match buy and sell orders at specified prices. ECNs are also known as alternative trading systems (ATS), have been given Securities and Exchange Commission approval to be more fully integrated into the national market system, and can choose to act as a broker dealer or as an exchange. An ECN's subscribers can include retail and institutional investors, market markers, and broker dealers.

ECNs lower the cost of trading by creating better and faster executions, more price transparency, and trading after the traditional exchanges close. This is known as "after-hours trading." One of the major advantages of the ECNs is that they can trade 24 hours per day. Unfortunately, the volume in after-market trading is very low and individual investors who trade in this market are subject to price volatility and low liquidity. However, because ECNs usually take orders at a set price to buy and sell and then match orders, the order process takes some of the risk out of after-hours markets. At one time there were nine major ECNs but in recent years Instinet and Archipelago have been the dominant platforms and others have specialized in certain market niches.

National Association of Securities Dealers (NASD)

The **National Association of Securities Dealers** is the world's largest private-sector regulator of financial services. It is responsible for regulating the brokers and dealers on all domestic markets. As it states, "By law, every securities firm doing business with the American public must register with NASD. Today, about 5,160 brokerage firms and more than 663,935 stockbrokers and registered representatives fall under our jurisdiction. We register securities firms, write rules to govern their behavior, examine them for compliance and, when necessary, bring enforcement actions against those who break those rules."[3]

Market Efficiency

There are several concepts of **market efficiency** and there are many degrees of efficiency, depending on which market we are talking about. Markets in general are efficient when: (1) Prices adjust rapidly to new information; (2) There is a continuous market, in which each successive trade is made at a price close to the previous price (the faster that the price responds to new information and the smaller the differences in price changes, the more efficient the market); and (3) The market can absorb large dollar amounts of securities without destabilizing the prices.

A key variable affecting efficiency is the certainty of the income stream. The more certain the expected income, the less volatile price movements will be. Fixed income securities, with known maturities, have reasonably efficient markets. The most efficient market is that for U.S. government securities, with the short-term Treasury bill market being exemplary. Corporate bond markets are somewhat efficient, but less so than government bond markets. A question that is still widely debated and researched by academics is the degree of efficiency for common stock. We do know that trading common stock in the United States has become cheaper and more efficient with the advent of decimalization, ECNs, and online brokerages.

The Efficient Market Hypothesis

If stock markets are efficient, it is very difficult for investors to select portfolios of common stocks that can outperform the stock market in general. The efficient market hypothesis is stated in three forms—the weak, semistrong, and strong.

The weak form simply states that past price information is unrelated to future prices, and that trends cannot be predicted and taken advantage of by investors. The semistrong form states that prices currently reflect all *public* information. Most of the research in this area focuses on changes in public information and on the measurement of how rapidly prices converge to a new equilibrium after new information has been released. The strong form states that all information, *both private and public,* is immediately reflected in stock prices.

Generally researchers have indicated that markets are somewhat efficient in the weak and semistrong sense, but not in the strong sense (private, insider information is valuable—though generally illegal to use for quick profits).

Our objective in bringing up this subject is to make you aware that much current research is focused on the measurement of market efficiency. As communications

---

[3]"NASDAQ Online."

systems advance, information gets disseminated faster and more accurately. Further-more, securities laws are forcing fuller disclosure of corporate data. It would appear that our security markets are generally efficient, but far from perfect, in digesting information and adjusting stock prices.

Organized securities markets are regulated by the Securities and Exchange Commission (SEC) and by the self-regulation of the exchanges. The OTC market is controlled by the National Association of Securities Dealers. Three major laws govern the sale and subsequent trading of securities. The Securities Act of 1933 pertains to new issues of securities, while the Securities Exchange Act of 1934 deals with trading in the securities markets. Another major piece of legislation is the Securities Acts Amendments of 1975, whose main emphasis is on a national securities market. The primary purpose of these laws is to protect unwary investors from fraud and manipulation and to make the markets more competitive and efficient by forcing corporations to make relevant investment information public.

Regulation of the Security Markets

Securities Act of 1933

The **Securities Act of 1933** was enacted after congressional investigations of the abuses present in the securities markets during the 1929 crash. Its primary purpose was to provide full disclosure of all pertinent investment information whenever a corporation sold a new issue of securities. For this reason, it is sometimes referred to as the truth-in-securities act. The Securities Act of 1933 has several important features, which follow:

1. All offerings except government bonds and bank stocks that are to be sold in more than one state must be registered with the SEC.[4]

2. The registration statement must be filed 20 days in advance of the date of sale and must include detailed corporate information.[5] If the SEC finds the information misleading, incomplete, or inaccurate, it will delay the offering until the registration statement is corrected. The SEC in no way certifies that the security is fairly priced, but only that the information seems to be accurate.

3. All new issues of securities must be accompanied by a prospectus containing the same information appearing in the registration statement. Usually included in the prospectus are a list of directors and officers; their salaries, stock options, and shareholdings; financial reports certified by a CPA; a list of the underwriters; the purpose and use of the funds to be provided from the sales of securities; and any other reasonable information that investors may need before they can wisely invest their money. A preliminary prospectus may be distributed to potential buyers before the offering date, but it will not contain the offering price or the underwriting fees. It is called a "red herring" because stamped on the front in red letters are the words *preliminary prospectus*.

---

[4]Actually the SEC was not established until 1934. References to the SEC in this section refer to 1934 to the present. The FTC performed these functions in 1933.
[5]Shelf registration, which was initiated by the SEC in 1982, changes this provision somewhat. Shelf registration is discussed in Chapter 15.

4. For the first time, officers of the company and other experts preparing the prospectus or the registration statement could be sued for penalties and recovery of realized losses if any information presented was fraudulent, factually wrong, or omitted.

Securities Exchange Act of 1934

This act created the **Securities and Exchange Commission** to enforce the securities laws. The SEC was empowered to regulate the securities markets and those companies listed on the exchanges. Specifically, the major points of the **Securities Exchange Act of 1934** are:

1. Guidelines for insider trading were established. Insiders must hold securities for at least six months before they can sell them. This is to prevent them from taking quick advantage of information that could result in a short-term profit. All short-term profits are payable to the corporation.[6] Insiders were at first generally thought to be officers, directors, employees, or relatives. In the late 1960s, however, the SEC widened its interpretation to include anyone having information that was not public knowledge. This could include security analysts, loan officers, large institutional holders, and many others who had business dealings with the firm.

2. The Federal Reserve's Board of Governors became responsible for setting margin requirements to determine how much credit would be available to purchasers of securities.

3. Manipulation of securities by conspiracies among investors was prohibited.

4. The SEC was given control over the proxy procedures of corporations (a proxy is an absent stockholder's vote).

5. In its regulation of companies traded on the markets, the SEC required that certain reports be filed periodically. Corporations must file quarterly financial statements and annual 10K reports with the SEC and send annual reports to stockholders. The 10K report has more financial data than the annual report and can be very useful to an investor or a loan officer. Most companies will now send 10K reports to stockholders on request.

6. The act required all security exchanges to register with the SEC. In this capacity, the SEC supervises and regulates many pertinent organizational aspects of exchanges, such as the mechanics of listing and trading.

Securities Acts Amendments of 1975

The major focus of the **Securities Acts Amendments of 1975** was to direct the SEC to supervise the development of a national securities market. No exact structure was put forth, but the law did assume that any national market would make extensive use of computers and electronic communication devices. In addition the law prohibited fixed commissions on public transactions and also prohibited banks, insurance companies, and other financial institutions from buying stock exchange memberships to save commission costs for their own institutional transactions. This act is a worthwhile addition to the securities laws, since it fosters greater competition and more efficient prices. Much progress has already been made on the national market system as mandated by this act. While it has taken over 25 years, we

---

[6]In the mid-1980s, Congress and the SEC passed legislation to make the penalty three times the size of the gain.

are finally seeing the coming together of markets through the Intermarket Trading System, the computerization of markets as demonstrated by the Electronic Communication Networks (ECNs), and a much more competitive market system than we had in 1975.

Sarbanes-Oxley Act of 2002

The **Sarbanes-Oxley Act of 2002** was previously discussed in Chapters 1 and 2, so only limited coverage will be provided here. Although it is not directly related to security trading as the first three acts are, you should still be familiar with it.

After the debacles related to false financial reporting and the associated negative impact on stock values in the early 2000s, Congress passed the Sarbanes-Oxley Act. Among the major provisions are the authorization of an independent private-sector board to oversee the accounting profession, the creation of new penalties and long prison terms for corporate fraud and document destruction, restrictions on accounting firms from providing consulting services to audit clients, and other similar provisions.

When Pleading Ignorance Didn't Work: The Case of Bernie Ebbers and WorldCom, Inc.

**finance in
action**

Former WorldCom Chief Executive Bernie Ebbers was convicted of participating in the largest accounting fraud in U.S. history in March 2005. Members of the firm were accused of cooking the books of the telecommunications giant (for $11 billion).

In the process, the company booked highly questionable revenue, which was financed by debt obligations it had no chance of ever collecting because the debtor was going out of business. Furthermore, the company claimed as capital expenditures everyday expenses used in the operations of the business. By claiming the funds as capital expenditures, WorldCom could write off the amount over many years instead of having to take the painful full deduction in the year the money was spent (see Accounting 101).

Through such deceitful practices, WorldCom was able to create on its books billions of dollars of profits that never existed. Slow to catch on, federal regulators allowed the firm to generate higher and higher earnings per share and value for its stock. The ill-gotten stock value was, in turn, used to buy up other telecommunication companies in the ever-increasing pyramid scheme. WorldCom grew to a market capitalization of $180 billion before its fraudulent activities were uncovered.

When Mr. Ebbers was faced with a nine-count indictment by the New York Feds, he used the "Aw, shucks" defense. He claimed he had no expert knowledge of accounting and

knew nothing about the fraud that was taking place on his watch. However, the judge ruled that he could not have merely turned a blind eye to highly suspicious activity even if he didn't know accounting (hope this doesn't apply to students in this course). The judge suggested that it defied common sense for a hands-on executive like Mr. Ebbers, who had cut off free coffee for employees to save $4 million, to then go on and miss bogus adjustments to the books that sometimes neared a billion dollars in a single quarter. Kenneth Lay, the CEO of Enron, was convicted on the same type of charges in 2006.

In his defense, Mr. Ebbers's lawyers claimed his main accuser, Chief Financial Officer Scott Sullivan, was using cocaine while all the financial malfeasance was going on and could not be trusted as a creditable witness. (Sullivan turned state's evidence against Ebbers to try to save his own questionable soul.)

The Ebbers legal team also claimed federal prosecutors had home court advantage in being able to try the case in New York instead of Ebbers's and WorldCom's home state of Mississippi (sounds a little like NCAA tournament talk). They promised to appeal the case partially on the basis of improper jurisdiction in the trial.

Having said all this, there is one clear message that came out of the Ebbers case and will serve as a warning to all Fortune 500 CEOs in the future. The "Aw, shucks, I didn't know" defense no longer works.

Perhaps most important of all, the act holds corporate executives legally accountable for the accuracy of their firm's financial statements. When the CEO must sign off along with the chief financial officer (CFO), the monitoring starts to get very serious. The president of the firm can no longer use as an excuse the fact that he or she did not know what was going on.

Summary

In the capital markets, corporations compete for funds not only among themselves but also with governmental units of all kinds. The U.S. Treasury raises funds to finance the federal government deficit; federal agencies such as the Student Loan Marketing Association are continually raising long-term funds; and state and local governments raise funds for public works such as sewers, roads, and university dormitories. Corporations account for a significant percentage of all funds raised in the capital market, and most of that is obtained through the sale of corporate debt.

We also depicted a three-sector economy consisting of households, corporations, and governmental units, and showed how funds flow through the capital markets from suppliers of funds to the ultimate users. This process is highly dependent on the efficiency of the financial institutions that act as intermediaries in channeling the funds to the most productive users.

Security markets are divided into organized exchanges and over-the-counter markets. The New York Stock Exchange is the largest of the organized exchanges. We explored some of its major characteristics, such as its relative size, the liquidity it provides corporations and investors, and its requirements for listing securities. We also discussed the functions of the NASDAQ and how the NYSE is becoming more like the NASDAQ in terms of its electronic trading. Foreign markets are also becoming increasingly important to U.S. multinational firms.

Throughout this chapter we have tried to present the concept of efficient markets doing an important job in allocating financial capital. The existing markets provide liquidity for both the corporation and the investor, and they are efficient in adjusting to new information. Reducing the trading spread between the bid and asked prices has reduced costs for investors and has most likely helped make the market more efficient in terms of fair pricing.

Because of the laws governing the markets, much information is available for investors, and this in itself creates more competitive prices. In the future, we expect even more efficient markets, with a national market system using the best of both the NYSE and OTC trading systems.

List of Terms

money markets   437
capital markets   437
federally sponsored credit
    agencies   440
municipal securities   440
internally generated funds   441
three-sector economy   442

financial intermediaries   443
secondary trading   444
New York Stock Exchange
    (NYSE)   445
listing requirements   447
decimalization   447
screen-based market   448

Discussion Questions

1. In addition to U.S. corporations, what government groups compete for funds in the U.S. capital markets?

2. Are federally sponsored credit agency issues directly backed by the U.S. Treasury?

3. What is a key tax characteristic associated with state and local (municipal) securities?

4. What are three forms of corporate securities discussed in the chapter?

5. Do corporations rely more on external or internal funds as sources of financing?

6. Explain the role of financial intermediaries in the flow of funds through the three-sector economy.

7. What is the difference between organized exchanges and over-the-counter markets?

8. How would you define efficient security markets?

9. The efficient market hypothesis is interpreted in a weak form, a semistrong form, and a strong form. How can we differentiate its various forms?

10. What was the primary purpose of the Securities Act of 1933?

11. What act of Congress created the Securities and Exchange Commission?

12. What was the purpose of the Sarbanes-Oxley Act of 2002?

W E B   E X E R C I S E

This chapter on capital markets focuses on long-term financing and the various stock markets. Each stock market has its own listing requirements and this exercise will look at the New York Stock Exchange listing requirements and listing fees. Students interested in repeating this exercise for Nasdaq may easily find the same information at www.nasdaq.com.

Go to the New York Stock Exchange's Web site at www.nyse.com.

1. Click on "Listing on the NYSE" along the left margin.

2. Then click on "Listing Standards."

3. Then click on "U.S. Listing Standards," and answer the following questions.

   a. How many round lot holders are required to be listed?

   b. How many total shareholders (use the first number)?

   c. What market value is required for public companies?

   d. What are the earnings requirements to be listed (use the first number)?

   e. What revenue for the most recent fiscal year is required? Look under "Pure Valuation" on the same page.

Note: From time to time, companies redesign their Web sites and occasionally a topic we have listed may have been deleted, updated, or moved into a different location. If you click on the site map or site index, you will be introduced to a table of contents which should aid you in finding the topic you are looking for.

S & P   P R O B L E M S   www.mhhe.com/edumarketinsight

STANDARD &POOR'S

1. Log onto the S&P Market Insight Web site, www.mhhe.com/edumarketinsight.

2. Click on "Commentary," which is the third box below the Market Insight title. The second major heading on the left side is Trends and Projections. Click on the current "Trends and Projections."

3. This is a quarterly economic summary for the U.S. economy and it is filled with charts and tables.

4. You may already be familiar with sections of Trends and Projections if you did the S&P problems in Chapters 11 and 12.

5. As a supplement to this chapter, please read the whole summary at this time to update yourself on the recent events affecting the capital markets. Be prepared to discuss them in class.

15

Investment Banking
Public and Private Placement

chapter concepts

1. Investment bankers are intermediaries between corporations in need of funds and the investing public.

2. Investment bankers, rather than corporations, normally take the risk of successfully distributing corporate securities.

3. Investment bankers also advise corporations on potential mergers

and acquisitions and other important matters.

4. Corporations turn to investment bankers and others in making the critical decision about whether to go public (distribute their securities in the public markets) or stay private.

5. Leveraged buyouts rely heavily on debt in the restructuring of a corporation.

T he late 1990s may well go down in history as that period when investors went wild over companies that had anything to do with the Internet. It seemed that if a company had "dot-com" or "Internet" in its title or was connected to the Internet because of its business model, it could easily raise capital without having any cash flow or earnings. In some cases, companies with 5 or 10 million dollars in sales were able to raise capital that was 5 or 10 times their level of sales. Investors were willing to bid the stocks of these companies to very high levels, based on expectations of high growth for long periods of time.

Amazon.com, the Internet book company, became a public company in 1998, as did eBay, the Internet auction company. Actually, eBay was one of those rare Internet companies that made money, and the demand for shares of its initial public offering was 10 times greater than the shares available for sale. Goldman Sachs, its managing investment banker,

priced the shares at $18 per share for the 3.5 million shares available for sale on the day of the offering. The opening price for eBay common stock was $53.50 per share. It never traded at its anticipated offering price of $18.

Amazon and eBay are examples of two winners. Amazon's stock price soared to new highs and split three times, so an initial investor would have 12 shares for each share purchased. While Amazon peaked out at $113 at the end of 1999 and fell to $5.50 per share in late 2001, it was trading at a respectable price of $50 per share in January 2006.

eBay was by all measures more successful than Amazon, and because of stock splits, an original investor would have 24 shares of eBay for each original share purchased. After accounting for splits, the stock traded as high as $765 per original share by March 2000. Then the stock's price fell by 79 percent before the end of that year. Since then, eBay's stock has more than recovered its losses. For the record,

100 shares of eBay purchased at the first-day price of $53.50 per share ($5,350) would now represent 2,400 shares at $47 for a total of $112,800. Both Amazon and eBay had business strategies that worked. They made profits because they met real market needs, but many other "new economy" companies went out of business or were acquired at low prices by other companies.

Sometimes markets focus on fads and new ideas. One idea that caught on was the Linux operating language for computers. Linux is a free computer operating system designed for networks and is sustained and improved by thousands of computer programmers around the world who donate their programming skills. The Linux operating system continues to make inroads in corporate America and is the choice of many computer programmers and software developers. This Linux craze played out in the initial public offering (IPO) markets in 1999.

On December 8, 1999, VA Linux Systems went public at an offering price of $30 per share and increased in price by 698 percent on the first day it was sold to the public. This was a record price increase for an IPO and was slightly ahead of the Cobalt Networks 482 percent gain on November 4, 1999. Cobalt was a hardware company specializing in network servers running on the Linux operation system. Another example was FreeMarkets, Inc., which went public the day after VA Linux, and soared from a $48 offering price to $280 on the first day. During a period of less than 17 months, between November 1998 and March 2000, 20 companies went public with a first-day price increase of more than 300 percent. Not a single company had 300 percent first-day returns in the previous 20 years, and none have done so since then either. These speculative bubbles came to a grinding halt in March 2000. Investors became impatient with the lack of earnings and cash flow, and investment bankers started to withdraw and postpone Internet offerings because of sagging demand. Prices of many previously issued offerings plummeted.

The Role of Investment Banking

The **investment banker** is the link between the corporation in need of funds and the investor. As a middleman, the investment banker is responsible for designing and packaging a security offering and selling the securities to the public. The investment banking fraternity has long been thought of as an elite group—with appropriate memberships in the country club, the yacht club, and other such venerable institutions. However, several changes have occurred in the investment banking industry over the last 10 years.

Concentration of Capital   Competition has become the new way of doing business, in which the fittest survive and prosper, while others drop out of the game. Raising capital has become an international proposition and firms need to be very large to compete. This concentration of capital allows large firms to take additional risks and satisfy the needs of an ever increasingly hungry capital market. There have been international consolidations underway for some time with foreign banks buying U.S. firms and U.S. banks buying foreign firms.

The high level of global concentration is shown in Table 15–1 with the top 10 underwriters controlling 58.3 percent of the global market for stocks and bonds (Part A).

Part B separates the global investment banking market into equity and debt components. Many students are surprised to see that the debt market is much larger than the equity market. After all, equity IPOs receive more exposure in the press than do debt issues. However, unlike stocks, debt issuances mature periodically. Most companies must then reissue the debt. In other words, much of the debt market is driven by corporate refinancing of existing debt. In Part C on page 460, we view market leaders in various sectors of the market.

Table 15–1

Underwriters, markets, and rankings

PART A   GLOBAL STOCKS AND BONDS

(U.S. public, Rule 144a, domestic and international equity and euro-market issues, ranked by 2005 proceeds)

	2005			2004	
Manager	**Proceeds (billions)**	**No. of Issues**	**Market Share**	**Proceeds (billions)**	**Rank**
Citigroup	$564.7	1,856	8.7%	$539.9	1
Lehman Brothers	420.8	1,249	6.5	377.2	5
Deutsche Bank AG	418.1	1,398	6.4	343.4	7
J.P. Morgan	414.6	1,553	6.4	395.6	3
Morgan Stanley	383.5	1,238	5.9	416.3	2
Merrill Lynch	343.2	1,450	5.3	385.7	4
Credit Suisse First Boston	337.3	1,138	5.2	366.5	6
UBS	323.5	1,188	5.0	303.6	8
Goldman Sachs	310.2	819	4.8	291.1	9
Barclays Capital	269.7	853	4.1	191.8	12
Top 10 Totals	$3,785.6	12,742	58.3%	$3,611.2	–
Industry Total	$6,511.3	20,118	100.0%	$5,767.0	–

PART B   GLOBAL EQUITY AND EQUITY-RELATED

(U.S. public, Rule 144a, domestic and international equity and equity-related markets)

	Amount	Market Share	
Manager	**(billions)**	**2005**	**2004**
Citigroup	$50.1	9.6%	9.3%
Goldman Sachs	47.9	9.2	10.0
Morgan Stanley	45.1	8.7	10.6
UBS	41.8	8.0	7.3
Merrill Lynch	39.2	7.5	8.4
J.P. Morgan	35.8	6.9	6.0
Credit Suisse F.B.	28.4	5.5	5.0
Deutsche Bank	27.7	5.3	5.2
Lehman Brothers	26.5	5.1	4.1
Nomura	13.5	2.6	3.2
Top 10 Totals	$356.1	68.4%	69.1%
Industry Total	$520.7	100.0%	100.0%

PART B CONTINUED: GLOBAL DEBT

(U.S. public, Rule 144a and euro-market issues.)

	Amount	Market Share	
Manager	**(billions)**	**2005**	**2004**
Citigroup	$514.5	8.6%	9.4%
Lehman Brothers	394.3	6.6	6.8
Deutsche Bank	390.8	6.5	6.0
J.P. Morgan	378.7	6.3	7.0
Morgan Stanley	338.4	5.7	6.9
Credit Suisse F.B.	309.0	5.2	6.5
Merrill Lynch	304.4	5.1	6.5
UBS	281.7	4.7	5.1
Barclays Capital	268.6	4.5	3.6
Goldman Sachs	262.3	4.4	4.6
Top 10 Totals	$3,442.7	57.6%	62.4%
Industry Totals	$5,991.4	100.0%	100.0%

PART C   WHO'S NO. 1?

(Leading stock and bond underwriters, by 2005 proceeds)

Market Sector	No. 1 Ranked Manager	2005 Mkt. Share	Change from 2004 (pct. pts.)
Global Debt, Stock & Stock-Related	Citigroup	8.7%	−0.70
U.S. Debt, Stock & Stock-Related	Citigroup	10.1	−0.90
Stocks			
Global Common Stock	Citigroup	9.5	−1.10
Global Convertible Offerings	J.P. Morgan	14.6	5.00
Global Common Stock—U.S. Issuers	Morgan Stanley	12.1	−3.30
Global Conv. Offerings—U.S. Issuers	Goldman Sachs	15.7	4.90
Bonds			
U.S. Asset-backed Securities	Citigroup	8.6	−1.10
U.S. Investment Grade Corporate Debt	Citigroup	16.5	−3.90
U.S. High Yield Corporate Debt	J.P. Morgan	13.0	1.60
U.S. Mortgage-backed Securities	Bear Stearns	10.7	−1.70
Syndicated Loans			
U.S. Syndicated Loans	J.P. Morgan	28.1	−4.00

The Gramm-Leach-Bliley Act Repeals the Glass-Steagall Act   The Glass-Steagall Act, passed after the great crash of 1929 and bank runs of the early 1930s, required U.S. banks to separate their commercial banking operations and investment banking operations into two different entities. Banks like J.P. Morgan were forced to sell off Morgan Stanley. Congress took this position because they thought the risk of the securities business impaired bank capital and put the banking system at risk of default. Over the last decade it became clear that U.S. commercial and investment banks were at a competitive disadvantage against large European and Japanese banks, who were not hobbled by these restrictions. Foreign banks were universal banks and could offer traditional banking services as well as insurance, securities brokerage, and investment banking.

In 1999 the U.S. Congress passed the Gramm-Leach-Bliley Act, which repealed Depression-era laws that had separated banking, brokerage, insurance, and investment banking. The Federal Reserve and the Treasury, however, still have the power to impose restrictions on the activities of banks. Recently, the Fed and Treasury have been concerned that banks' investments into risky venture capital companies may impair their capital. The Fed has effectively banned some banks from participating in this merchant banking activity unless they set aside reserves equal to 50 percent of their capital. This allows the strong banks to participate in the venture capital market but forces the weak ones to sit on the sidelines.

The Gramm-Leach-Bliley Act allowed Citigroup to keep its commercial banking (CitiBank), insurance (Travelers), investment banking (Smith Barney), and other financial services as part of one company. Ever since CitiBank and Travelers Insurance merged to form Citigroup, the U.S. banking community has been imitating the model. However Citigroup later sold Travelers noncommercial insurance business but kept the Travelers umbrella logo as their own. Bank American bought investment banker Robertson Stevens,

Chase Manhattan bought Hambrecht and Quist; but in September 2000 Chase and J.P. Morgan merged and several years later the combined J.P. Morgan Chase bought Bank One. As you can see from Table 15–1 on page 459, J.P. Morgan was ranked number four on the domestic list (Part A). To have a traditional old-line commercial bank this high up on the list signifies the transformation that has occurred in the investment banking industry.

Investment Banking Competitors   The tables demonstrate the segmented nature of the market and the different leaders in the market. Goldman Sachs is ranked number nine in Part A of Table 15–1, but it leads U.S. issuers in global convertible bond offerings as shown in Part C of Table 15-1. Bear Sterns does not even make the top ten in Part A, but it leads the market in U.S. mortgage-backed securities issuances. Citigroup wins five spots in Part C, J.P. Morgan wins three spots, and Morgan Stanley wins one.

As you can see throughout this discussion, the competition is quite intense. Being a leader in one sector helps a firm's overall reputation, but does not ensure success in other areas. Some investment bankers purposefully go after a given line of business (such as U.S. mortgage-backed securities) because they have climbed up the learning curve and have special expertise in that area. This may encourage their competitors to back off to some extent.

As a middleman in the distribution of securities, the investment banker has a number of key roles. These functions are described below.

Underwriter   In most cases the investment banker is a risk taker. The investment banker will contract to buy securities from the corporation and resell them to other security dealers and the public. By giving a "firm commitment" to purchase the securities from the corporation, the investment banker is said to **underwrite** any risks that might be associated with a new issue. While the risk may be fairly low in handling a bond offering for ExxonMobil or General Electric in a stable market, such may not be the case in selling the shares of a lesser-known firm in a very volatile market environment.

Though most large, well-established investment bankers would not consider managing a public offering without assuming the risk of distribution, smaller investment houses may handle distributions for relatively unknown corporations on a **"best-efforts,"** or commission, basis. Some issuing companies even choose to sell their own securities directly. Both the "best-efforts" and "direct" methods account for a relatively small portion of total offerings.

Market Maker   During distribution and for a limited time afterward, the investment banker may make a market in a given security—that is, engage in the buying and selling of the security to ensure a liquid market. The investment banker may also provide research on the firm to encourage active investor interest.

Advisor   The investment banker may advise clients on a continuing basis about the types of securities to be sold, the number of shares or units for distribution, and the timing of the sale. A company considering a stock issuance to the public may be persuaded, in counsel with an investment banker, to borrow the funds from an insurance company or, if stock is to be sold, to wait for two more quarters of earnings

Enumeration of Functions

before going to the market. The investment banker also provides important advisory services in the area of mergers and acquisitions, leveraged buyouts, and corporate restructuring.

Agency Functions   The investment banker may act as an **agent** for a corporation that wishes to place its securities privately with an insurance company, a pension fund, or a wealthy individual. In this instance the investment banker will shop around among potential investors and negotiate the best possible deal for the corporation.

The Distribution Process

The actual distribution process requires the active participation of a number of parties. The principal or **managing investment banker** will call on other investment banking houses to share the burden of risk and to aid in the distribution. To this end, they will form an **underwriting syndicate** comprising as few as 2 or as many as 100 investment banking houses. In Figure 15–1 we see a typical case in which a hypothetical firm, the Maxwell Corporation, wishes to issue 250,000 additional shares of stock with Merrill Lynch as the managing underwriter and an underwriting syndicate of 15 firms.

Figure 15–1

Distribution process in investment banking

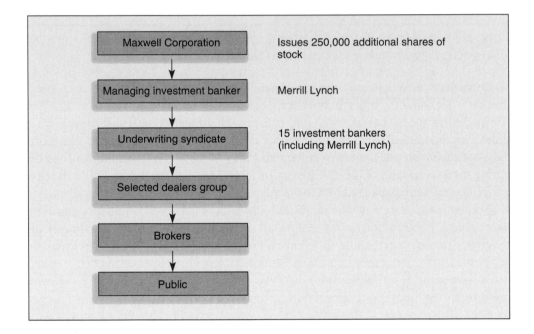

The underwriting syndicate will purchase shares from the Maxwell Corporation and distribute them through the channels of distribution. Syndicate members will act as wholesalers in distributing the shares to brokers and dealers who will eventually sell the shares to the public. Large investment banking houses may be vertically integrated, acting as underwriter-dealer-brokers and capturing all fees and commissions.

The Spread   The **underwriting spread** represents the total compensation for those who participate in the distribution process. If the public or retail price is $21.50 and the managing investment banker pays a price of $20.00 to the issuing company, we say there is a total spread of $1.50. The $1.50 may be divided up among the participants, as indicated in Figure 15–2.

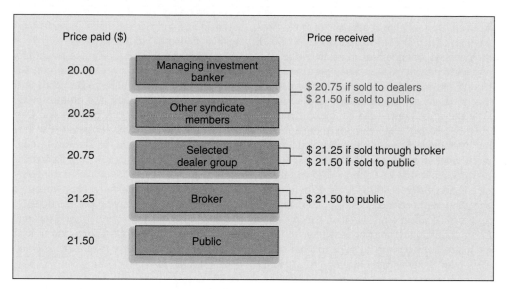

Figure 15–2
Allocation of underwriting spread

Price paid ($) / Price received

20.00 — Managing investment banker
$ 20.75 if sold to dealers
$ 21.50 if sold to public

20.25 — Other syndicate members

20.75 — Selected dealer group
$ 21.25 if sold through broker
$ 21.50 if sold to public

21.25 — Broker
$ 21.50 to public

21.50 — Public

Note that the lower a party falls in the distribution process, the higher the price for shares. The managing investment banker pays $20, while dealers pay $20.75. Also, the farther down the line the securities are resold, the higher is the potential profit. If the managing investment banker resells to dealers, he makes 75 cents per share; if he resells to the public, he makes $1.50.

The total spread of $1.50 in the present case represents 7 percent of the offering price ($1.50/$21.50). Generally, the larger the dollar value of an issue, the smaller the spread is as a percentage of the offering price. Percentage figures on underwriting spreads for U.S. corporations are presented in Table 15–2. This table actually illustrates that the smaller the issue, the higher the fees percentagewise, and also that equity capital is more expensive than debt capital. The higher equity spreads reflect the fact that there is more uncertainty with common stock than for other types of capital.

Table 15–2
Underwriting compensation as a percentage of proceeds

	Spread	
Size of Issue ($ millions)	Common Stock	Debt
Under 0.5	11.3%	7.4%
0.5–0.9	9.7	7.2
1.0–1.9	8.6	7.0
2.0–4.9	7.4	4.2
5.0–9.9	6.7	1.5
10.0–19.9	6.2	1.0
20.0–49.9	4.9	1.0
50.0 and over	2.3	0.8

Source: Securities and Exchange Commission data.

The Investment Banker and the Roadshow

Company management pays the investment banker to develop the market and create demand for its stock. One of the most important functions of the investment banker is to find institutional buyers for the new shares. To do this, the banker often takes company management on a "pre-offering *roadshow*" to market the company. They are called roadshows because members of management travel to major U.S. and international cities to make presentations. During the roadshow, management presents the company's business plan, its estimated financial statements, and its management's operating philosophy. The performance is one part finance and one part showbiz. The investment banker must coach the management team (usually the chairman, chief executive officer, and the chief financial officer) in the presentation of the company's story. This coaching may include using a presentation coach, simulating question and answer sessions, and giving instructions on what to say and what not to say under Security and Exchange regulations.

There have been more than a few IPOs withdrawn from the market because management failed to impress the audience of financial investors. A good roadshow will help create more demand for the stock than the available number of shares being sold. When this happens, the successful offering usually rises above its offering price on the day of the IPO.

In 2005, the SEC issued rules to address electronic road shows over the Internet. The rules are intended to allow wider access to road shows and to encourage greater media scrutiny and reporting on road shows. Over the years, the SEC has struggled with how much companies should be allowed to communicate prior to a stock offering. Restricting how much information companies can release around stock issuances may protect unsophisticated investors from buying overpriced IPOs. However, restricting the information that small investors receive may also place them at an information disadvantage relative to sophisticated institutions.

Since the Maxwell Corporation stock issue is for $5.375 million (250,000 shares × $21.50), the 7 percent spread is in line with SEC figures in Table 15–2. It should be noted that the issuer bears not only the "give-up" expense of the spread in the underwriting process but also out-of-pocket costs related to legal and accounting fees, printing expenses, and so forth. As indicated in Table 15–3, when the spread plus the out-of-pocket costs are considered, the total cost of a small issue is rather high but decreases as the issue size increases. Of course substantial benefits may still be received.

Table 15–3

Total costs to issue stock (percentage of total proceeds)

Size of Issue ($ millions)	Common Stock		
	Spread	Out-of-Pocket Cost*	Total Expense
Under 0.5	11.3%	7.3%	18.6%
0.5–0.9	9.7	4.9	14.6
1.0–1.9	8.6	3.0	11.6
2.0–4.9	7.4	1.7	9.1
5.0–9.9	6.7	1.0	7.7
10.0–19.9	6.2	0.6	6.8
20.0–49.9	4.9	0.8	5.7
50.0 and over	2.3	0.3	2.6

*Out-of-pocket cost of debts is approximately the same.
Source: Securities and Exchange Commission data.

Because the syndicate members purchase the stock for redistribution in the marketing channels, they must be careful about the pricing of the stock. When a stock is sold to the public for the first time (i.e., the firm is going public), the managing investment banker will do an in-depth analysis of the company to determine its value. The study will include an analysis of the firm's industry, financial characteristics, and anticipated earnings and dividend-paying capability. Based on valuation techniques that the underwriter deems to be appropriate, a price will be tentatively assigned and will be compared to that enjoyed by similar firms in a given industry. If the industry's average price-earnings ratio is 20, the firm should not stray too far from this norm. Anticipated public demand will also be a major factor in pricing a new issue.

The great majority of the issues handled by investment bankers are, however, additional issues of stocks or bonds for companies already trading publicly. When additional shares are to be issued, the investment bankers will generally set the price at slightly below the current market value. This process, known as **underpricing**, will help ensure a receptive market for the securities.

At times an investment banker will also deal in large blocks of securities for existing stockholders. Because the number of shares may be too large to trade in normal channels, the investment banker will manage the issue and underprice the stock below current prices to the public. Such a process is known as a secondary offering, in contrast to a primary offering, in which new corporate securities are sold to the public for the first time.

Dilution

A problem a company faces when issuing additional securities is the actual or perceived **dilution of earnings** effect on shares currently outstanding. In the case of the Maxwell Corporation, the 250,000 new shares may represent a 10 percent increment to shares currently in existence. Perhaps the firm had earnings of $5 million on 2,500,000 shares before the offering, indicating earnings per share of $2. With 250,000 new shares to be issued, earnings per share will temporarily slip to $1.82 ($5,000,000 ÷ 2,750,000).

The proceeds from the sale of new shares may well be expected to provide the increased earnings necessary to bring earnings back to at least $2. While financial theory dictates that a new equity issue should not be undertaken if it diminishes the overall wealth of current stockholders, there may be a perceived time lag in the recovery of earnings per share as a result of the increased shares outstanding. For this reason, there may be a temporary weakness in a stock when an issue of additional shares is proposed. In most cases this is overcome with time.

Market Stabilization

Another problem may set in when the actual public distribution begins—namely, unanticipated weakness in the stock or bond market. Since the sales group normally has made a firm commitment to purchase stock at a given price for redistribution, it is essential that the price of the stock remain relatively strong. Syndicate members, committed to purchasing the stock at $20 or better, could be in trouble if the sale price falls to $19 or $18. The managing investment banker is generally responsible for stabilizing the offering during the distribution period and may accomplish this by repurchasing securities as the market price moves below the initial public offering price of $21.50 in this example.

The period of **market stabilization** usually lasts two or three days after the initial offering, but it may extend up to 30 days for difficult-to-distribute securities. In a very poor market environment, stabilization may be virtually impossible to achieve. As a classic example, when past Federal Reserve Board Chairman Paul Volcker announced an extreme credit-tightening policy in October 1979, newly underwritten, high-quality IBM bond prices fell dramatically, and Salomon Brothers and other investment bankers got trapped into approximately $10 million in losses. The bonds later recovered in value, but the investment bankers had already taken their losses.

Manipulation of prices in security markets is normally illegal. Market stabilization or underwriter price support is a rare exception to the general market manipulation prohibition. Temporary market stabilization is accepted as necessary for smoothly functioning new-issue markets.

Aftermarket

The investment banker is also interested in how well the underwritten security behaves after the distribution period because the banker's ultimate reputation rests on bringing strong securities to the market. This is particularly true of initial public offerings.

Exhaustive research shows that initial public offerings tend to perform well in the immediate **aftermarket**. Between 1960 and 2001 there were approximately 14,800 initial public offerings in the United States. The average first-day return for these stocks was 18.4 percent, and IPOs tended to continue to perform well during the following several months. In many other countries, the initial aftermarket returns are even higher. Studies covering over 11,700 IPOs from 37 other countries show initial returns that average almost 35 percent. In fact, IPOs are underpriced in every country where stocks are publicly traded.

After the first few months, initial public offerings appear to lose their luster. After the first day of trading, IPO returns are approximately 3.4 percent lower than returns for similar sized firms over the first full year of trading. Over the first three years of public trading, IPOs underperform similar sized firms by more than 5 percent per year. On average, IPOs appear to be a good deal for investors who purchase shares from the underwriter at the offering and quickly sell them. After the first day of trading most companies underperform the market for several years.

Shelf Registration

In February 1982, the Securities and Exchange Commission began allowing a new filing process called shelf registration under SEC Rule 415. **Shelf registration** permits large companies, such as IBM or Citigroup, to file one comprehensive registration statement that outlines the firm's financing plans for up to the next two years. Then, when market conditions seem appropriate, the firm can issue the securities without further SEC approval. Future issues are thought to be sitting on the shelf, waiting for the appropriate time to appear.

Shelf registration is at variance with the traditional requirement that security issuers file a detailed registration statement for SEC review and approval every time they plan a sale. Whether investors are deprived of important "current" information as a result of shelf registration is difficult to judge. While shelf registration was started on an experimental basis by the SEC in 1982, it has now become a permanent part of the underwriting process. Shelf registration has been most frequently used with debt issues, with relatively less utilization in the equity markets (corporations do not wish to announce equity dilution in advance).

Shelf registration has contributed to the concentrated nature of the investment banking business, previously discussed. The strong firms are acquiring more and more business and, in some cases, are less dependent on large syndications to handle debt issues. Only investment banking firms with a big capital base and substantial expertise are in a position to benefit from this registration process.

Our discussion to this point has assumed the firm was distributing stocks or bonds in the public markets (as explained in Chapter 14). However, many companies, by choice or circumstance, prefer to remain private—restricting their financial activities to direct negotiations with bankers, insurance companies, and so forth. Let us evaluate the advantages and the disadvantages of **public placement** versus private financing and then explore the avenues open to a privately financed firm.

Public versus Private Financing

Advantages of Being Public

First of all, the corporation may tap the security markets for a greater amount of funds by selling securities directly to the public. With over 80 million individual stockholders in the country, combined with thousands of institutional investors, the greatest pool of funds is channeled toward publicly traded securities. Furthermore, the attendant prestige of a public security may be helpful in bank negotiations, executive recruitment, and the marketing of products. Some corporations listed on the New York Stock Exchange actually allow stockholders a discount on the purchase of their products.

Stockholders of a heretofore private corporation may also sell part of their holdings if the corporation decides to go public. A million-share offering may contain 500,000 authorized but unissued corporate shares and 500,000 existing stockholder shares. The stockholder is able to achieve a higher degree of liquidity and to diversify his or her portfolio. A publicly traded stock with an established price may also be helpful for estate planning.

Finally, going public allows the firm to play the merger game, using marketable securities for the purchase of other firms. A public company can purchase another firm using its own stock as currency, whereas a private firm might be forced to buy using cash. The high visibility of a public offering may even make the acquiring firm a potential recipient of attractive offers for its own securities. (This may not be viewed as an advantage by firms that do not wish to be acquired.)

Disadvantages of Being Public

The company must make all information available to the public through SEC and state filings. Not only is this tedious, time-consuming, and expensive, but also important corporate information on profit margins and product lines must be divulged. The president must adapt to being a public relations representative to all interested members of the securities industry.

Another disadvantage of being public is the tremendous pressure for short-term performance placed on the firm by security analysts and large institutional investors. Quarter-to-quarter earnings reports can become more important to top management than providing a long-run stewardship for the company. A capital budgeting decision calling for the selection of Alternative A—carrying a million dollars higher net present value than Alternative B—may be discarded in favor of the latter because Alternative B adds two cents more to next quarter's earnings per share.

In a number of cases, the blessings of having a publicly quoted security may become quite the opposite. Although a security may have had an enthusiastic reception in a strong "new-issues" market, such as that of 1967–68, 1981–83, or 1998–99, a dramatic erosion in value may later occur, causing embarrassment and anxiety for stockholders and employees.

As was evidenced in Table 15–3, there can be a high cost to going public. For small firms, the underwriting spread and the out-of-pocket costs can run in the 15–18 percent range. Moreover, after going public the firm faces higher compliance costs because of various public disclosure requirements. In response to the collapse of Enron Corporation and its accounting firm, Arthur Andersen and Co., Congress passed the Sarbanes-Oxley Act of 2002. Sarbanes-Oxley created several costly new requirements. For example, the management of public companies must now report on internal controls for financial reporting. Then, the firm's external auditor must render an opinion on the effectiveness of these controls. For many small companies, the additional costs of designing and implementing new internal controls to certify Sarbanes-Oxley compliance has made the cost of being a public company too high. As a result, many private companies have chosen to remain private, and some public companies have taken steps to convert to private status.

Public Offerings   ### A Classic Example of Instant Wealth—EDS Goes Public

In September 1968, Ross Perot took EDS public, and within one month he found himself worth $300 million. This was no small accomplishment for a man who, six years earlier, had been an IBM salesman with only a few thousand dollars in the bank and a degree from the Naval Academy.

The original EDS offering—managed by P. W. Presprich, a New York investment banker—was priced at 118 times current earnings (the norm at the time was 10 to 12 times earnings). After one month in the hot new-issues market of 1966–68, the stock was trading at over 200 times earnings. A company with earnings of only $1.5 million had a market value well over $300 million, exceeding many of *Fortune*'s 500 largest companies. By 1970 EDS had a total market value of $1.5 billion. All of this was accomplished by a firm with a few hundred employees.

It is interesting to note that Perot's main concern in the initial pricing of his stock was not to set too low a value. In the strong new-issues market of the period, too many computer issues, which had been underpriced when they first crossed the tape, quickly doubled or tripled in price. Perot considered this an irrevocable loss to original shareholders, who initially sold large blocks of their holdings. He was determined to avoid this by fully pricing his stock and trading only a small percentage of the total capitalization on the initial offering (only 650,000 shares out of 11.5 million). Even at a price-earnings ratio of 118 at initial trading, the stock jumped from $16.50 to $23 in one day.[1]

In the bear markets of the 1970s, EDS suffered more than most companies, and its stock price declined from a high of $161 per share in 1970 to a low of $12 1/2 in 1974. Total market value retreated from a high of $1.5 billion to about $200 million. After the stock price recovered over the next decade, Perot sold EDS to General Motors Corporation in 1984 for $2.5 billion, and stockholders received Class E common stock of General Motors. Perot became the largest single shareholder of General Motors through his ownership of Class E shares and was elected to the board of directors. By 1986 GM tired of Perot's criticism of corporate policy and, in a very controversial move, bought out his shares of stock and he resigned from the board. By 1992, this hard-driving Texan was a candidate for the U.S. presidency and won 19 percent of the total vote as an independent.

A number of years later, Perot was still active in politics, but General Motors made EDS an independent company again. After a decade of ownership originated at a purchase price of $2.5 billion, GM spun off EDS as a company valued at $24 billion.

Perhaps Ross Perot didn't get rich quite as fast as many of the Internet cowboys, but at least he still has a few billion dollars in cash. He also created a company that had $20.1 billion in revenues in 2005, with a total market value that ranged between $9.7 and $13.3 billion during 2005. Time will tell how many of today's quick winners are still around 35 years from now.

Internet Capital Group—A Second Example

The Internet Capital Group partners with companies in the B2B (business-to-business) markets and especially those companies that specialize in infrastructure companies and market makers in the B2B auction markets. The Group provides capital to these firms, taking an equity position and sometimes even a controlling position. If the companies they own do well, Internet Capital Group does well. In a sense, Internet Capital behaves somewhat like an Internet mutual fund. Its performance mirrors the performance of the companies it owns. Its ticker symbol is ICGE.

On December 15, 1999, Internet Capital raised $1,431,450,000 through a combined offering of common stock, convertible bonds, and private equity as shown in Figure 15–3 on page 470. The offering of 6.9 million shares of common stock at

---

[1]A. M. Louis, "Fastest Richest Texan Ever," *Fortune,* November 1968, pp. 168–70.

Figure 15–3

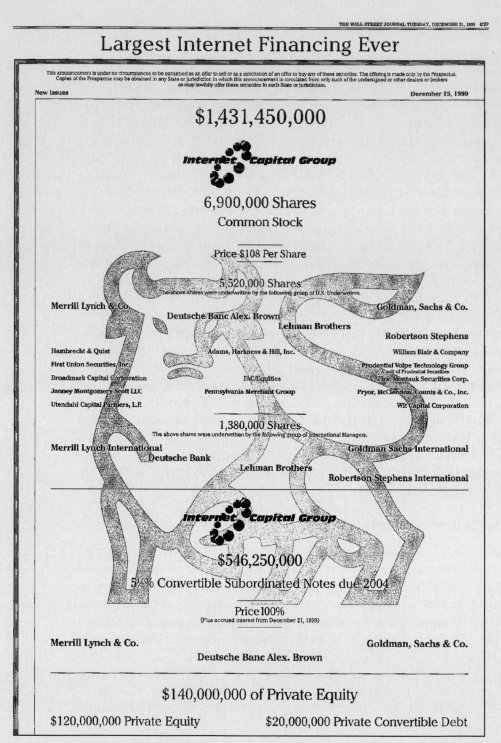

$108 per share raised $745 million; the convertible bond offering raised $546 million; and the private equity component raised $140 million.

Merrill Lynch was the lead investment banker and is named toward the top left-hand portion of the advertisement (sometimes called a tombstone advertisement) in Figure 15–3. The offering was co-managed by Goldman, Sachs & Co., whose name appears on the same line in the right-hand corner. In the United States 16 other investment-banking underwriters joined these two firms, and the advertisement provides some information about the syndicate. The amount of shares that each underwriter is allocated to sell decreases with the type size of its listing in the advertisement. Those in large type have more shares to sell than those underwriters listed in smaller type. Usually the firm listed in the lower bottom right corner of the advertisement represents the smallest allocation of shares. In the case of the international portion of the offering, Deutsche Bank, Lehman Brothers, and Robertson Stephens International joined Merrill Lynch and Goldman Sachs (names shown above the first straight line in the figure).

Let's move the clock forward. Internet Capital reported in its 2004 financial statements that it had $52 million in revenue with a net loss of $135 million. The firm had refinanced some of its debt for 29 cents on the dollar, and the stock's price had fallen to 20 cents per share in April of that year. Because NASDAQ requires companies to maintain a minimum bid of $1 to avoid being delisted, on May 10, 2004 the company initiated a 1-for-20 reverse stock split, which raised the price to $4. Following the reverse split, a shareholder who had purchased 100 shares in Internet Capital at $108 each in 1999 had seen his investment fall in value from $10,800 to $20 (5 shares worth $4.00 each). Figure 15–4, a stock price graph below, tells the whole story and should be a reminder that doing your homework when analyzing companies is a good idea. The

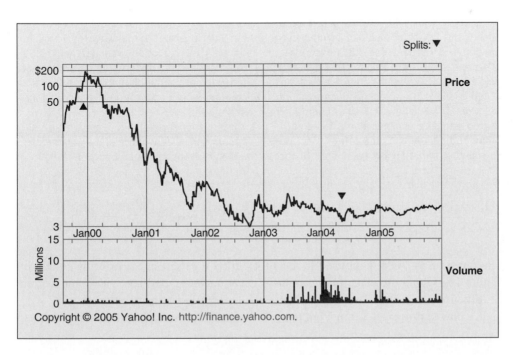

Figure 15–4

Internet Capital Group stock price (as of January 13, 2006)

Tulip Auctions and the Google IPO

While traditional investment banking relies on institutional relationships, there is a move afoot to do some initial public offerings on the Internet using auctions. Most individual investors (especially those with less than million-dollar accounts) find it very difficult to acquire shares in a traditional IPO. Shares are typically allocated to mutual funds, pension funds, and other institutional investors who have connections with the investment bankers. Often, these institutions are repeat customers who participate in most of an underwriter's offerings. While this is obviously bad for small investors, firms that are going public also have concerns with the traditional distribution system. They wonder whose interest the underwriter is looking out for? Are they looking out for the issuer? Or is the banker looking out for the interests of the institutional investors who are the banker's repeat customers?

In 1998, William Hambrecht founded WR Hambrecht & Co., which helped pioneer U.S. stock auctions. During 1999 Hambrecht brought three companies public, which included a small winery and two high-flying Internet-based companies. Hambrecht's OpenIPO® auctions are based on the method developed to auction Dutch tulip bulbs in the 17th century. In a "Dutch" auction, prices are determined after all prospective buyers have placed bids. Then one price is set for all buyers. That price is the highest price at which all the securities can be sold to the bidders. No investor pays more than his bid price, but many will receive securities at a price that is less than their bid. Dutch auctions are commonly used to sell U.S. Treasury securities, and about 150 auctions of Treasuries are held each year. One of the attractive features of Dutch auctions is that connections don't matter. Mom-and-Pop investors can compete for shares alongside big institutional investors.

In August 2004, Google Inc. went public using a variation on the Dutch auction.

Google's IPO was, by far, the largest auction-based offering ever. The auction rules ensured that small investors could participate because orders as small as 5 shares were accepted. In traditional IPOs, allocations of less than 100 shares are rare, although most deals have no official minimum. Google's IPO did not go off without a hitch. The company originally estimated a selling range between $108 and $135 per share, but the eventual issue price was only $85 per share. Noting this fact, many Wall Street bankers and professional investors declared the IPO auction a failure. Of course, there is no evidence that a traditional IPO would have yielded a higher initial selling price, and Google paid underwriting fees of only 2.8 percent, which is less than the norm. On the first day of trading, Google's price rose in the aftermarket to $100.34, an 18 percent gain that is about average for IPOs. By January 2006, Google's price had risen above $300 per share.

In 2005, Chicago investment research firm Morningstar Inc. chose to go public using Hambrecht's OpenIPO system. However, traditional Wall Street underwriters strongly discouraged Morningstar from using the auction format. After all, the traditional underwriting method is extremely profitable for underwriters and institutional investors. Institutional investors clearly did not receive preferential treatment in the Morningstar IPO. Investment behemoth Fidelity Investments received no shares in the IPO. Its $17.50 bid for 2.2 million Morningstar shares was too low. The auction clearing price was set at $18.50. Morningstar paid underwriting fees of less than 2 percent of the offering proceeds, much less than would be expected in a traditional offering.

Internet-based auctions may eventually capture a significant share of the underwriting market, but that time is probably still far off.

real question is, What happened to the $1.4 billion it raised in the offering shown in Figure 15–3? Only management can answer that question, perhaps with some degree of difficulty.

We now shift our attention from public offerings to private placements.

Private placement refers to the selling of securities directly to insurance companies, pension funds, and wealthy individuals, rather than through the security markets. This financing device may be employed by a growing firm that wishes to avoid or defer an initial public stock offering or by a publicly traded company that wishes to incorporate private funds into its financing package. Private placements have increased in popularity to such an extent that privately placed debt now exceeds 50 percent of all long-term corporate debt outstanding.[2]

The advantages of private placement are worthy of note. First, there is no lengthy, expensive registration process with the SEC. Second, the firm has greater flexibility in negotiating with one or a handful of insurance companies, pension funds, or bankers than is possible in a public offering. Because there is no SEC registration or underwriting, the initial costs of a private placement may be considerably lower than those of a public issue. However, the interest rate on bonds is usually higher to compensate the investor for holding a less liquid obligation.

Private Placement

Going Private and Leveraged Buyouts

Throughout the years, there have always been some public firms **going private**. In the 1970s, a number of firms gave up their public listings to be private, but these were usually small firms. Management figured it could save several hundred thousand dollars a year in annual report expenses, legal and auditing fees, and security analysts meetings—a significant amount for a small company.

In the 1980s, 1990s, and mid-2000s, however, very large corporations began going private and not just to save several hundred thousand dollars. More likely they had a long-term strategy in mind.

There are basically two ways to accomplish going private. In the most frequent method, a publicly owned company is purchased by a private company or a private equity fund. Private equity funds typically are partnerships formed specifically to buy nonpublic companies. An alternative avenue for going private is for a company to repurchase all publicly traded shares from stockholders. Both methods have been in vogue and are usually accomplished through the use of a leveraged buyout. In a **leveraged buyout**, either the management or some other investor group borrows the needed cash to repurchase all the shares of the company. After the repurchase, the company exists with substantial debt and heavy interest expense.

Usually management of the private company must sell assets to reduce the debt load, and a corporate **restructuring** occurs, wherein divisions and products are sold and assets redeployed into new, higher-return areas. As specialists in the valuation of assets, investment bankers try to determine the "breakup value" of a large company. This is its value if all its divisions were divided up and sold separately. Over the long run, these strategies can be rewarding, and these companies may again become publicly owned. For example, Beatrice Foods went private in 1986

[2]M. Carey, S. Prowse, J. Rhea, and G. Udell, 1993. "The Economics of the Private Placement Markets: A New Look." *Financial Markets, Institutions, and Instruments,* pp. 1–66.

for $6.2 billion. One year later, it sold various pieces of the company—Avis, Coke Bottling, International Playtex, and other assets worth $6 billion and still had assets left valued at $4 billion for a public offering. Leslie Fay, an apparel firm, bought its shares for $58 million in 1982 and a number of years later resold them to the public for $360 million.

However, not all leveraged buyouts have worked as planned. Because they are based on the heavy use of debt, any shortfall in a company's performance after the buyout can prove disastrous. In 1990 Chase Manhattan Corporation, a major lender in the leveraged buyout market, was desperately selling part of its $4.6 billion leveraged buyout portfolio at a deep discount in hopes of avoiding future problems.

International Investment Banking Deals

Privatization

The last decade could very well be called the era of privatization. Note in Table 15–4, a listing of previously foreign government-owned companies that were partially or fully sold to private investors. Ownership of companies like General Motors, Intel, and Boeing by private individuals, mutual funds, pension funds, and other investors has been a common practice in the United States for over 100 years. However, in many countries—especially socialist and communist countries—the auto industry, steel industry, aerospace industry, and virtually all other major industries, have been owned by the state. With the collapse of the USSR, many of the former communist countries such as Poland, Hungary, and the Czech Republic began to privatize their industries with public offerings of common stock. The process of **privatization** involves investment bankers taking companies public, but instead of selling companies formerly owned by individuals, the companies sold had been previously owned by governments.

Many other countries such as Britain and France had started the process of privatization years before the 1990s. In fact, the wave of privatizations had previously covered Western Europe, Eastern Europe, Latin America, and Asia. For example, the Japanese government owned Nippon Telephone and Telegraph (NTT) until 1987 when they sold shares of stock in the company to the public. The deals presented in Table 15–4 represent a very interesting history of the largest privatization deals in many countries around the world.

Table 15–4 The big international deals

Country	Company	Business	Year	Sale Price ($ billions)	Percent Private	Major Buyers
The Americas						
Argentina	YPF	Oil and gas	1993	$ 2,500	80%	Public offering
Bolivia	Corani (part of Ende)	Power plant	1995	58	51	Dominion Energy (U.S.)
Brazil	Cia. Siderurgica Nacional	Steelmaker	1993	1,056	100	Banco Bamerindus, Grupo Vicunha, Banco Gradesco, Banco Itau, Docenave (Brazil)
Canada	Petro-Canada	Oil and gas	1991	1,980	80	Public offering
Chile	CTC	Telecom.	1988	115	100	Bond Corp. (Aus)
Colombia	Banco de Colombia	Banking	1994	490	99	Group led by Jaime Gilinski (Col.)
Cuba	Etecsa	Telecom.	1994	706	49	Grupo Domos (Mex.)
Jamaica	Telecommunications of Jamaica	Telecom.	1987	61	72	Cable & Wireless (U.K.)
Mexico	Telmex	Telecom.	1990	7,000	100	Grupo Carso (Mex.), SBC Communications (U.S.), France Cable et Radio (France)
Panama	Cementos Bayaro	Cement	1994	60	100	Cemex (Mexico)
Peru	ENTEL-CPT	Telecom.	1994	2,000	35	Telefonica de Espana (Spain)
Venezuela	Cia. Anonima Nacional Telefonas de Venezuela	Telecom.	1991	1,900	40	Group led by GTE (U.S.)
Western Europe						
Austria	OMV	Energy	1987	736	50	Public offering
Belgium	ASLK-CGER	Banking	1993	1,200	50	Fortis (Neth./Belgium)
France	Elf-Aquitaine	Oil	1994	6,220	90	Public offering
Germany	VEBA	Energy, telecomm., and chems.	1984	1,670	100	Public offering
Greece	AGET Heracles General Cement	Cement	1992	560	70	Calcestruzzi (Italy) and National Bank of Greece (Greece)
Italy	Istituto Nazionale delle Assicurazicni	Insurance	1994	4,150	66	Public offering
The Netherlands	Koninklijke PTT Nederland	Telecom.	1994	3,750	30	Public offering
Spain	Repsol	Oil, gas, and chemicals	1989	4,160	80	Public offering
Sweden	Pharmacia	Pharmaceuticals	1994	1,200	87	Public offering, Volvo
United Kingdom	British Telecom	Telecom.	1984	21,990	~100	Public offering

(continues)

Table 15–4 (concluded)

Country	Company	Business	Year	Sale Price ($ billions)	Percent Private	Major Buyers
Eastern Europe						
Estonia	Viru Hotell	Hotel	1994	$ 12	100%	Estonia/Finnish Investment Group
Hungary	MATAV	Telecom.	1993	875	5	Consortium of Deutsche Telekom (Ger.) and Ameritech (U.S.)
Latvia	Latvijas Universala Banka	Banking	1995	23	50	Clients, employees, public (Latvia)
Lithuania	Klaipeda Tobacco Factory	Tobacco products	1993	13	100	Philip Morris (U.S.)
Poland	FSM	Automaker	1994	1,230	90	Fiat (Italy)
Russia	Lukoil	Oil company	1994	3,900	62	N.A.
Asia						
Australia	Commonwealth Bank of Australia	Banking	1991	2,280	50	Public offering
China	Huaneng International	Power	1994	555	N/A	Public offering
Indonesia	Indosat	Telecom.	1994	1,120	35	Public offering
Japan	NTT	Telecom.	1987	73,490	35	Public offering
New Zealand	Telecom. New Zealand	Telecom.	1990	2,460	100	BellAtlantic/Ameritech (U.S.)
The Philippines	Petron	Oil refining and distribution	1993	931	60	Saudi Aramco (Saud.)
Singapore	Singapore Telecommunications	Telecom.	1993	N.A.	11	Public offering
South Korea	Korea Electric Power	Electric utility	1989	1,930	22	Individual investors
Taiwan	China Steel	Steelmaker	1989	3,020	52	Public offering
Thailand	PTT Exploration & Production	Petroleum	1994	258	29	Public offering

Summary

The investment banker acts as an intermediary between corporations in need of funds and those investors having funds, such as the investing public, pension funds, and mutual funds, to name a few. Of course the investment banker charges a fee to the corporation selling securities and the fee is based on the size of the offering, the risk associated with the company, and whether the security is equity or debt.

The role of the investment banker is critical to the distribution of securities in the U.S. economy. The investment banker serves as an underwriter or the risk taker by purchasing securities from the issuing corporation and redistributing them to the public; he or she may continue to maintain a market in the distributed securities long after they have been sold to the public. The investment banking firm can also help a company sell a new issue on a "best-efforts" basis. As corporations become larger and more global, they need larger investment banks and this has caused consolidation in the investment banking industry. A few large investment banks that are able to take down large blocks of securities and compete in international markets now dominate the industry.

Investment bankers also serve as important advisors to corporations by providing advice on mergers, acquisitions, foreign capital markets, and leveraged buyouts, and also on resisting hostile takeover attempts. The fees earned for this advice can be substantial.

The advantages of selling securities in the public markets must be weighed against the disadvantages. While going public may give the corporation and major stockholders greater access to funds, as well as additional prestige, these advantages quickly disappear in a down market. Furthermore the corporation must open its books to the public and orient itself to the short-term emphasis of investors.

Companies may decide to go from public to private. This trend was evident in the late 1980s, 1990s, and mid-2000s with many large companies going private through leveraged buyouts. However, a number of these companies again publicly distributed their shares a year or two later, generating large profits for their owners in the process.

List of Terms

investment banker 458	market stabilization 466
underwrite 461	aftermarket 466
"best-efforts" basis 461	shelf registration 466
agent 462	public placement 467
managing investment	private placement 473
banker 462	going private 473
underwriting syndicate 462	leveraged buyout 473
underwriting spread 462	restructuring 473
underpricing 465	privatization 474
dilution of earnings 465	

Discussion Questions

1. In what way is an investment banker a risk taker?
2. What is the purpose of market stabilization activities during the distribution process?

3. Discuss how an underwriting syndicate decreases risk for each underwriter and at the same time facilitates the distribution process.

4. Discuss the reason for the differences between underwriting spreads for stocks and bonds.

5. Explain how the price of a new security issue is determined.

6. What is shelf registration? How does it differ from the traditional requirements for security offerings?

7. Comment on the market performance of U.S. companies going public, specifically on the first day of trading and after three years.

8. Discuss the benefits accruing to a company that is traded in the public securities markets.

9. What are the disadvantages to being public?

10. If a company were looking for capital by way of a private placement, where would it look for funds?

11. How does a leveraged buyout work? What does the debt structure of the firm normally look like after a leveraged buyout? What might be done to reduce the debt?

12. How might a leveraged buyout eventually lead to high returns for a company?

13. What is privatization?

Practice Problems and Solutions

Dilution effect of new issue

1. Dawson Motor Company has 6 million shares outstanding with total earnings of $12 million. The company is considering issuing 1.5 million new shares.

   a. What will be the immediate dilution in earnings per share?

   b. If the new shares can be sold at $25 per share and the proceeds will earn 12 percent, will there still be dilution? Based on the new EPS, should the new shares be issued?

Underwriting costs

2. Gallagher Corp. will issue 300,000 shares at a retail (public) price of $40. The company will receive $37.90 per share and incur $160,000 in out-of-pocket expenses.

   a. What is the percentage spread?

   b. What percent of the total value of the issue (based on the retail price) are the out-of-pocket costs?

Solutions

1. a. Earnings per share before the stock issue:

$$\frac{\$12,000,000}{6,000,000} = \$2.00$$

Earnings per share after the stock issue

$$\frac{\$12,000,000}{7,500,000} = \$1.60$$

$2.00	Before
1.60	After
$ .40	Dilution

b.   New income $= 12\% \times (1.5$ million shares $\times \$25) = 12\% \times 37,500,000$
                     $= \$4,500,000$

Total income $= \$12,000,000 + \$4,500,000 - \$16,500,000$

Earnings per share based on the additional income included in total income.

$$\text{EPS} = \frac{\$16,500,000}{7,500,000} = \$2.20$$

There is no longer dilution. Earnings per share will grow from the initial amount of $2.00 to $2.20. The new shares should be issued.

2. a.   Percentage spread $= \dfrac{\$\text{ Spread}}{\text{Public price}}$

$\$$ Spread $=$ Public price $-$ Net to corporation

$\$2.10 = \$40 - 37.90$

Percentage spread $= \dfrac{\$2.10}{\$40} = 5.25\%$

b.   Retail (public) price $ 40
       Number of new shares $\times$ 300,000
       Total retail value $12,000,000

$\dfrac{\text{Out-of pocket costs}}{\text{Total retail value}} = \dfrac{\$160,000}{\$12,000,000} = 1.33\%$

All problems are available in Homework Manager. Please see the preface for more information.   ## Problems

1.   The Hamilton Corporation currently has 4 million shares of stock outstanding and will report earnings of $6,000,000 in the current year. The company is considering the issuance of 1 million additional shares that will net $30 per share to the corporation.   *Dilution effect of stock issue*

     a.   What is the immediate dilution potential for this new stock issue?

     b.   Assume the Hamilton Corporation can earn 10.5 percent on the proceeds of the stock issue in time to include them in the current year's results. Should the new issue be undertaken based on earnings per share?

2.   In Problem 1, if the one million additional shares can only be issued at $23 per share and the company can earn 6.0 percent on the proceeds, should the new issue be undertaken based on earnings per share?   *Dilution effect of stock issue*

3.   American Health Systems currently has 6,000,000 shares of stock outstanding and will report earnings of $15 million in the current year. The company is considering the issuance of 1,500,000 additional shares that will net $50 per share to the corporation.   *Dilution effect of stock issue*

     a.   What is the immediate dilution potential for this new stock issue?

     b.   Assume that American Health Systems can earn 12 percent on the proceeds of the stock issue in time to include them in the current year's results. Should the new issue be undertaken based on earnings per share?

Dilution effect of stock issue

4. In Problem 3, if the 1,500,000 additional shares can only be issued at $28 per share and the company can earn 10 percent on the proceeds, should the new issue be undertaken based on earnings per share?

Dilution and pricing effect of stock issue

5. Jordan Broadcasting Company is going public at $40 net per share to the company. There also are founding stockholders that are selling part of their shares at the same price. Prior to the offering, the firm had $24 million in earnings divided over eight million shares. The public offering will be for five million shares; three million will be new corporate shares and two million will be shares currently owned by the founding stockholders.

    a. What is the immediate dilution based on the new corporate shares that are being offered?

    b. If the stock has a P/E of 23 immediately after the offering, what will the stock price be?

    c. Should the founding stockholders be pleased with the $40 they received for their shares?

Underwriting spread ✗

6. Assume Fisher Food Products is thinking about three different size offerings for the issuance of additional shares.

Size of Offer	Public Price	Net to Corporation
a. $ 1.6 million	$40	$36.70
b. 6.0 million	40	37.28
c. 25.0 million	40	38.12

    What is the percentage underwriting spread for each size offer? What principle does this demonstrate?

Underwriting spread

7. Walton and Company is the managing investment banker for a major new under writing. The price of the stock to the investment banker is $18 per share. Other syndicate members may buy the stock for $18.25. The price to the selected dealers group is $18.80, with a price to brokers of $19.20. Finally, the price to the public is $19.50.

    a. If Walton and Company sells its shares to the dealers group, what will the percentage return be?

    b. If Walton and Company performs the dealer's function also and sells to brokers, what will the percentage return be?

    c. If Walton and Company fully integrates its operation and sells directly to the public, what will its percentage return be?

Underwriting spread

8. The Wrigley Corporation needs to raise $30 million. The investment banking firm of Tinkers, Evers, & Chance will handle the transaction.

    a. If stock is utilized, 2,000,000 shares will be sold to the public at $15.70 per share. The corporation will receive a net price of $15 per share. What is the percentage underwriting spread per share?

    b. If bonds are utilized, slightly over 30,000 bonds will be sold to the public at $1,001 per bond. The corporation will receive a net price of $992 per bond.

What is the percentage of underwriting spread per bond? (Relate the dollar spread to the public price.)

c.   Which alternative has the larger percentage of spread? Is this the normal relationship between the two types of issues?

9.   Kevin's Bacon Company Inc. has earnings of $6 million with 2,000,000 shares outstanding before a public distribution. Five hundred thousand shares will be included in the sale, of which 300,000 are new corporate shares, and 200,000 are shares currently owned by Ann Fry, the founder and CEO. The 200,000 shares that Ann is selling are referred to as a secondary offering and all proceeds will go to her.

Secondary offering

The net price for the offering will be $15.50 and the corporate proceeds are expected to produce $1.5 million in corporate earnings.

a.   What were the corporation's earnings per share before the offering?

b.   What are the corporation's earnings per share expected to be after the offering?

10.   Becker Brothers is the managing underwriter for a 1-million-share issue by Jay's Hamburger Heaven. Becker Brothers is "handling" 10 percent of the issue. Its price is $25 per share and the price to the public is $26.40.

Market Stabilization and risk

Becker also provides the market stabilization function. During the issuance, the market for the stock turns soft, and Becker is forced to purchase 40,000 shares in the open market at an average price of $25.75. They later sell the shares at an average value of $23.

Compute Becker Brothers' overall gain or loss from managing the issue.

11.   Trump Card Co. will issue stock at a retail (public) price of $30. The company will receive $27.60 per share.

Underwriting costs

a.   What is the spread on the issue in percentage terms?

b.   If the firm demands receiving a new price only $1.50 below the public price suggested in part *a*, What will the spread be in percentage terms?

c.   To hold the spread down to 3 percent based on the public price in part *a*, what net amount should Trump Card Co. receive?

✗ 12.   Winston Sporting Goods is considering a public offering of common stock. Its investment banker has informed the company that the retail price will be $18 per share for 600,000 shares. The company will receive $16.50 per share and will incur $150,000 in registration, accounting, and printing fees.

Underwriting costs

a.   What is the spread on this issue in percentage terms? What are the total expenses of the issue as a percentage of total value (at retail)?

b.   If the firm wanted to net $18 million from this issue, how many shares must be sold?

13.   Rodgers Homebuilding is about to go public. The investment banking firm of Leland Webber and Company is attempting to price the issue. The home-building industry generally trades at a 20 percent discount below the P/E ratio on the Standard & Poor's 500 Stock Index. Assume that index currently

P/E ratio for new public issue

has a P/E ratio of 25. Rodgers can be compared to the homebuilding industry as follows:

	Rodgers	Homebuilding Industry
Growth rate in earnings per share	12 percent	10 percent
Consistency of performance.	Increased earnings 4 out of 5 years	increased earnings 3 out of 5 years
Debt to total assets.	55 percent	40 percent
Turnover of product.	Slightly below average	Average
Quality of management	High	Average

Assume, in assessing the initial P/E ratio, the investment banker will first determine the appropriate industry P/E based on the Standard & Poor's 500 Index. Then ½ point will be added to the P/E ratio for each case in which Rodgers is superior to the industry norm, and ½ point will be deducted for an inferior comparison. On this basis, what should the initial P/E be for Rodgers Homebuilding?

Dividend valuation model for new public issue

14. The investment banking firm of Einstein & Co. will use a dividend valuation model to appraise the shares of the Modern Physics Corporation. Dividends (D_1) at the end of the current year will be $1.44. The growth rate (g) is 8 percent and the discount rate (K_e) is 12 percent.

   a. Using Formula 10–9 on page 297 in Chapter 10, what should be the price of the stock to the public?

   b. If there is a 6 percent total underwriting spread on the stock, how much will the issuing corporation receive?

   c. If the issuing corporation requires a net price of $34.50 (proceeds to the corporation) and there is a 6 percent underwriting spread, what should be the price of the stock to the public? (Round to two places to the right of the decimal point.)

Comparison of private and public debt offering

15. The Landers Corporation needs to raise $1 million of debt on a 25-year issue. If it places the bonds privately, the interest rate will be 11 percent. Thirty thousand dollars in out-of-pocket costs will be incurred. For a public issue, the interest rate will be 10 percent, and the underwriting spread will be 4 percent. There will be $100,000 in out-of-pocket costs. Assume interest on the debt is paid semiannually, and the debt will be outstanding for the full 25-year period, at which time it will be repaid.

   Which plan offers the higher net present value? For each plan, compare the net amount of funds initially available—inflow—to the present value of future payments of interest and principal to determine net present value. Assume the stated discount rate is 12 percent annually. Use 6 percent semiannually throughout the analysis. (Disregard taxes.)

Features associated with a stock distribution

16. Midland Corporation has a net income of $15 million and 6 million shares outstanding. Its common stock is currently selling for $40 per share. Midland plans to sell common stock to set up a major new production facility with a net cost of $21,660,000. The production facility will not produce a profit for one year, and then it is expected to earn a 15 percent return on the investment. Stanley Morgan and Co., an investment banking firm, plans to sell the issue to the public for $38 per share with a spread of 5 percent.

a. How many shares of stock must be sold to net $21,660,000? (Note: No out-of-pocket costs must be considered in this problem.)

b. Why is the investment banker selling the stock at less than its current market price?

c. What are the earnings per share (EPS) and the price-earnings ratio before the issue (based on a stock price of $40)? What will be the price per share immediately after the sale of stock if the P/E stays constant?

d. Compute the EPS and the price (P/E stays constant) after the new production facility begins to produce a profit.

e. Are the shareholders better off because of the sale of stock and the resultant investment? What other financing strategy could the company have tried to increase earnings per share?

17. The Presley Corporation is about to go public. It currently has aftertax earnings of $7,500,000 and 2,500,000 shares are owned by the present stockholders (the Presley family). The new public issue will represent 600,000 new shares. The new shares will be priced to the public at $20 per share, with a 5 percent spread on the offering price. There will also be $200,000 in out-of-pocket costs to the corporation.

Dilution and rates of return

a. Compute the net proceeds to the Presley Corporation.

b. Compute the earnings per share immediately before the stock issue.

c. Compute the earnings per share immediately after the stock issue.

d. Determine what rate of return must be earned on the net proceeds to the corporation so there will not be a dilution in earnings per share during the year of going public.

e. Determine what rate of return must be earned on the proceeds to the corporation so there will be a 5 percent increase in earnings per share during the year of going public.

18. Tyson Iron Works is about to go public. It currently has aftertax earnings of $4,500,000, and 300,000 shares are owned by the present stockholders. The new public issue will represent 400,000 new shares. The new shares will be priced to the public at $15 per share with a 4 percent spread on the offering price. There will also be $160,000 in out-of-pocket costs to the corporation.

Dilution and rates of return

a. Compute the net proceeds to Tyson Iron Works.

b. Compute the earnings per share immediately before the stock issue.

c. Compute the earnings per share immediately after the stock issue.

d. Determine what rate of return must be earned on the net proceeds to the corporation so there will not be a dilution in earnings per share during the year of going public.

e. Determine what rate of return must be earned on the proceeds to the corporation so there will be a 10 percent increase in earnings per share during the year of going public.

19. I. B. Michaels has a chance to participate in a new public offering by Hi-Tech Micro Computers. His broker informs him that demand for the 500,000 shares to be issued is very strong. His broker's firm is assigned 15,000 shares in the

Aftermarket for new public issue

distribution and will allow Michaels, a relatively good customer, 1.5 percent of its 15,000 share allocation.

The initial offering price is $30 per share. There is a strong aftermarket, and the stock goes to $33 one week after issue. After the first full month after issue, Mr. Michaels is pleased to observe his shares are selling for $34.75. He is content to place his shares in a lockbox and eventually use their anticipated increased value to help send his son to college many years in the future. However, one year after the distribution, he looks up the shares in *The Wall Street Journal* and finds they are trading at $28.75.

    a.   Compute the total dollar profit or loss on Mr. Michaels's shares one week, one month, and one year after the purchase. In each case compute the profit or loss against the initial purchase price.

    b.   Also compute this percentage gain or loss from the initial $30 price and compare this to the results that might be expected in an investment of this nature based on prior research. Assume the overall stock market was basically unchanged during the period of observation.

    c.   Why might a new public issue be expected to have a strong aftermarket?

Leveraged buyout 20. The management of Mitchell Labs decided to go private in 2002 by buying in all 3 million of its outstanding shares at $19.50 per share. By 2006, management had restructured the company by selling off the petroleum research division for $13 million, the fiber technology division for $9.5 million, and the synthetic products division for $21 million. Because these divisions had been only marginally profitable, Mitchell Labs is a stronger company after the restructuring. Mitchell is now able to concentrate exclusively on contract research and will generate earnings per share of $1.25 this year. Investment bankers have contacted the firm and indicated that if it reentered the public market, the 3 million shares it purchased to go private could now be reissued to the public at a P/E ratio of 16 times earnings per share.

    a.   What was the initial cost to Mitchell Labs to go private?

    b.   What is the total value to the company from (1) the proceeds of the divisions that were sold, as well as (2) the current value of the 3 million shares (based on current earnings and an anticipated P/E of 16)?

    c.   What is the percentage return to the management of Mitchell Labs from the restructuring? Use answers from parts *a* and *b* to determine this value.

COMPREHENSIVE PROBLEM

Bailey Corporation (impact of new public offering)

The Bailey Corporation, a manufacturer of medical supplies and equipment, is planning to sell its shares to the general public for the first time. The firm's investment banker, Robert Merrill and Company, is working with Bailey Corporation in determining a number of items. Information on the Bailey Corporation follows:

BAILEY CORPORATION
Income Statement
For the Year 200X

Sales (all on credit)	$42,680,000
Cost of goods sold	32,240,000
Gross profit	10,440,000
Selling and administrative expenses	4,558,000
Operating profit	5,882,000
Interest expense	600,000
Net income before taxes	5,282,000
Taxes	2,120,000
Net income	$ 3,162,000

BAILEY CORPORATION
Balance Sheet
As of December 31, 200X

Assets

Current assets

Cash	$ 250,000
Marketable securities	130,000
Accounts receivable	6,000,000
Inventory	8,300,000
Total current assets	14,680,000
Net plant and equipment	13,970,000
Total assets	$28,650,000

Liabilities and Stockholders' Equity

Current liabilities:

Accounts payable	$ 3,800,000
Notes payable	3,550,000
Total current liabilities	7,350,000
Long-term liabilities	5,620,000
Total liabilities	$12,970,000

Stockholders' equity:

Common stock (1,800,000 shares at $1 par)	$ 1,800,000
Capital in excess of par	6,300,000
Retained earnings	7,580,000
Total stockholders' equity	15,680,000
Total liabilities and stockholders' equity	$28,650,000

---

a. Assume that 800,000 new corporate shares will be issued to the general public. What will earnings per share be immediately after the public offering? (Round to two places to the right of the decimal point.) Based on the price-earnings ratio of 12, what will the initial price of the stock be? Use earnings per share after the distribution in the calculation.

b. Assuming an underwriting spread of 5 percent and out-of-pocket costs of $300,000, what will net proceeds to the corporation be?

c. What return must the corporation earn on the net proceeds to equal the earnings per share before the offering? How does this compare with current return on the total assets on the balance sheet?

d. Now assume that, of the initial 800,000 share distribution, 400,000 belong to current stockholders and 400,000 are new shares, and the latter will be added to the 1,800,000 shares currently outstanding. What will earnings per share be immediately after the public offering? What will the initial market price of the stock be? Assume a price-earnings ratio of 12 and use earnings per share after the distribution in the calculation.

e. Assuming an underwriting spread of 5 percent and out-of-pocket costs of $300,000, what will net proceeds to the corporation be?

f. What return must the corporation now earn on the net proceeds to equal earnings per share before the offering? How does this compare with current return on the total assets on the balance sheet?

WEB EXERCISE

Initial public offerings (IPOs) were covered in the chapter. Let's take a closer look at two actual issues. Go to www.hoovers.com/global/ipoc/index.xhtml.

1. For the first two issues under "latest pricing," do the following steps all the way through, one company at a time.
2. Click on and write down the company name.
3. Write a short paragraph about what the company does or its products.
4. Scroll down and record the date the company went public.
5. Write down the actual offer price.
6. Click on "More Information" and write down the number of shares offered in millions. Compute the percent this represents of post-offering shares.
7. Record the name of the first underwriter listed for the offering.

Note: From time to time, companies redesign their Web sites and occasionally a topic we have listed may have been deleted, updated, or moved into a different location. If you click on the site map or site index, you will be introduced to a table of contents which should aid you in finding the topic you are looking for.

S&P PROBLEMS   www.mhhe.com/edumarketinsight

STANDARD &POOR'S

1. Log onto the S&P Market Insight Web site, www.mhhe.com/edumarketinsight.
2. Click on "Company," which is the first box below the Market Insight title.
3. Type Goldman Sachs' ticker symbol "GS" in the box and click on Go.
4. Scroll down the left margin and click on "S&P Stock Reports." When the screen opens, click on the first stock report. You will have a four-page report summarizing the activities of Goldman Sachs.

5. The purpose of this exercise is to familiarize you with one of the world's premier investment banking companies. Please read the full report being careful to notice the following:

   a. What has happened to revenues and earnings over the years covered? Why do you think this has happened?

   b. Do you see any cyclicality to the revenue stream and if so can you explain what might cause that?

   c. Has the stock price kept up with the earnings per share of the company?

6. In the Business Summary section please describe the various segments of the business where Goldman Sachs makes their money.

7. Now go back to the first screen and click on "Wall Street Consensus." What do Wall Street analysts predict is in store for this industry during the coming year?

8. As an optional piece of this problem (for the very curious student who has a strong interest in the financial services industry), close the window and go back to the top of the page. Click on "Industry" and find the Investment Banking and Brokerage industry in the box directly under Industry. Go to S&P Industry Surveys and click on "Investment Services" where you will find a comprehensive overview of the industry.

Long-Term Debt and Lease Financing

16

For those who invest in the highly rated bonds of firms such as General Electric, IBM, and Procter & Gamble, there is very little to worry about. You get a higher return than you could get on U.S. Government securities while still being able to sleep soundly at night.

However, for those who invest in bonds of companies in telecommunications or the airline industry, sleep may not come so easily. Take the case of U.S. Airways. The company began its close-to-death spiral not long after

astute investor Warren Buffet sank $358 million into the firm. It has twice gone bankrupt in the current decade. Even after dumping half its employees, cutting $2 billion in expenses, and unloading its pension plan, it still managed to lose $611 million in 2004.[1] Although its merger with America West may help, U.S. Airways' original bond investors still stand to lose a large portion of their investment.

In this chapter, you will learn more about corporate debt, both from a corporate finance and investor viewpoint.

---

[1]"Unready for Takeoff," *Forbes,* June 20, 2005, p. 64.

Corporate debt has increased dramatically in the last three decades. This growth is related to rapid business expansion, the inflationary impact on the economy, and, at times, inadequate funds generated from the internal operations of business firms. The expansion of the U.S. economy has placed pressure on U.S. corporations to raise capital and will continue to do so. In this context a new set of rules has been developed for evaluating corporate bond issues. Some deterioration in borrowing qualifications has occurred. In 1977, the average U.S. manufacturing corporation had its interest payments covered by operating earnings at a rate of eight times (operating earnings were eight times as great as interest). By the year 2006, the ratio had been cut to less than half that amount. Figure 16–1 indicates the long-term trend is down, but it is also cyclically dependent on the economy. The recession of 1990–1991 pushed times interest earned to its lowest level over the time period, but it recovered in the subsequent economic expansion. With the declining interest-paying capabilities of some U.S. corporations, the debt contract between corporate borrowers and lenders has become increasingly important.

The Expanding Role of Debt

Figure 16–1   Times interest earned for Standard & Poor's industrials

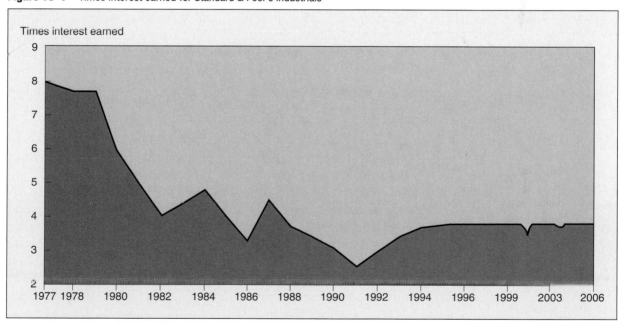

The corporate bond represents the basic long-term debt instrument for most large U.S. corporations. The bond agreement specifies such basic items as the par value, the coupon rate, and the maturity date.

The Debt Contract

Par Value   This is the initial value of the bond. The **par value** is sometimes referred to as the principal or face value. Most corporate bonds are initially traded in $1,000 units.

Coupon Rate   This is the actual interest rate on the bond, usually payable in semi-annual installments. To the extent that interest rates in the market go above or below the coupon rate after the bond has been issued, the market price of the bond will change from the par value.

Maturity Date   The **maturity date** is the final date on which repayment of the bond principal is due.

The bond agreement is supplemented by a much longer document termed a bond **indenture**. The indenture, often containing over 100 pages of complicated legal wording, covers every detail surrounding the bond issue—including collateral pledged, methods of repayment, restrictions on the corporation, and procedures for initiating claims against the corporation. The corporation appoints a financially independent trustee to administer the provisions of the bond indenture under the guidelines of the Trust Indenture Act of 1939. Let's examine two items of interest in any bond agreement: the security provisions of the bond and the methods of repayment.

Security Provisions

A **secured debt** is one in which specific assets are pledged to bondholders in the event of default. Only infrequently are pledged assets actually sold and the proceeds distributed to bondholders. Typically the defaulting corporation is reorganized and existing claims are partially satisfied by issuing new securities to the participating parties. The stronger and better secured the initial claim, the higher the quality of the new security to be received in exchange. When a defaulting corporation is reorganized for failure to meet obligations, existing management may be terminated and, in extreme cases, held legally responsible for any imprudent actions.

A number of terms are used to denote collateralized or secured debt. Under a **mortgage agreement**, real property (plant and equipment) is pledged as security for the loan. A mortgage may be senior or junior in nature, with senior requiring satisfaction of claims before payment is given to junior debt. Bondholders may also attach an **after-acquired property clause**, requiring that any new property be placed under the original mortgage.

The student should realize not all secured debt will carry every protective feature, but rather represents a carefully negotiated position including some safeguards and rejecting others. Generally, the greater the protection offered a given class of bondholders, the lower is the interest rate on the bond. Bondholders are willing to assume some degree of risk to receive a higher yield.

Unsecured Debt

A number of corporations issue debt that is not secured by a specific claim to assets. In Wall Street jargon, the name **debenture** refers to a long-term, unsecured corporate bond. Among the major participants in debenture offerings are such prestigious firms as ExxonMobil, IBM, Dow Chemical, and Intel. Because of the legal problems associated with "specific" asset claims in a secured bond offering, the trend is to issue unsecured debt—allowing the bondholder a general claim against the corporation—rather than a specific lien against an asset.

Even unsecured debt may be divided between high-ranking and subordinated debt. A **subordinated debenture** is an unsecured bond in which payment to the holder will occur only after designated senior debenture holders are satisfied. The hierarchy of creditor obligations for secured as well as unsecured debt is presented in Figure 16–2, along with consideration of the position of stockholders. For a further discussion of payment of claims and the hierarchy of obligations, the reader should see Appendix 16A, "Financial Alternatives for Distressed Firms," which also covers bankruptcy considerations.

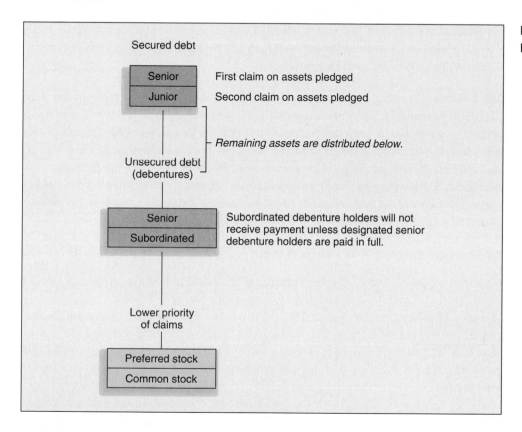

Figure 16–2
Priority of claims

Methods of Repayment

The method of repayment for bond issues may not always call for one lump-sum disbursement at the maturity date. Some Canadian and British government bonds are perpetual in nature. More interestingly, West Shore Railroad 4 percent bonds are not scheduled to mature until 2361 (approximately 355 years in the future). Nevertheless most bonds have some orderly or preplanned system of repayment. In addition to the simplest arrangement— a single-sum payment at maturity—bonds may be retired by serial payments, through sinking-fund provisions, through conversion, or by a call feature.

Serial Payments   Bonds with **serial payment** provisions are paid off in installments over the life of the issue. Each bond has its own predetermined date of maturity and receives interest only to that point. Although the total issue may span over 20 years, 15 or 20 different maturity dates may be assigned specific dollar amounts.

Sinking-Fund Provision   A less structured but more popular method of debt retirement is through the use of a **sinking fund**. Under this arrangement semiannual or annual contributions are made by the corporation into a fund administered by a trustee for purposes of debt retirement. The trustee takes the proceeds and purchases bonds from willing sellers. If no willing sellers are available, a lottery system may be used among outstanding bondholders.

Conversion   A more subtle method of reducing debt outstanding is to provide for debt conversion into common stock. Although this feature is exercised at the option of the bondholder, a number of incentives or penalties may be utilized to encourage conversion. The mechanics of convertible bond trading are discussed at length in Chapter 19, "Convertibles, Warrants, and Derivatives."

Call Feature   A **call provision** allows the corporation to retire or force in the debt issue before maturity. The corporation will pay a premium over par value of 5 to 10 percent —a bargain value to the corporation if bond prices are up. Modern call provisions usually do not take effect until the bond has been outstanding at least 5 to 10 years. Often the call provision declines over time, usually by 0.5 to 1 percent per year after the call period begins. A corporation may decide to call in outstanding debt issues when interest rates on new securities are considerably lower than those on previously issued debt (let's get the high-cost, old debt off the books).

An Example: Dillard's 7.875 Percent Bond

Now that we have covered the key features of the bond indenture, let us examine an existing bond. Table 16–1 presents an excerpt from *Mergent Bond Record* (formerly *Moody's Bond Record*) for March 2006, and we find that Dillard Department Stores, one of the largest retailers in the world, has a 7.875 debenture due in 2023. As of March 2006, the bond carried a Moody's rating of B2. More specific features of this bond are found in Table 16–2 on page 494, which is an excerpt from *Mergent's Industrial Manual*.

As we can see in Table 16–2, the 7.875 percent bond had an original authorized offering of $100 million. The trustee is Chase Manhattan Bank, and it is the trustee's obligation to make sure Dillard's adheres to the indenture.

The information in Table 16–2 also provides other pertinent information found in the indenture, such as the interest payment dates (January 1 and July 1), denominations of each bond, security provisions, call features, and high and low bond prices.

Bond Prices, Yields, and Ratings

The financial manager must be sensitive to interest rate changes and price movements in the bond market. The treasurer's interpretation of market conditions will influence the timing of new issues, the coupon rate offered, and the maturity date. In case the student of finance thinks bonds maintain stable long-term price patterns, he or she need merely consider bond pricing during the five-year period 1967–72. When the market interest rate on outstanding 30-year, Aaa corporate bonds went from 5.10 percent to 8.10 percent, the average price of existing bonds dropped 36 percent. A conservative investor would be quite disillusioned to see a $1,000, 5.10 percent bond now quoted

Table 16–1 Mergent Bond Record

U.S. CORPORATE BONDS
<Box—Dove 77

CUSIP	ISSUE	MOODY'S® RATING	INTEREST DATES	CURRENT CALL PRICE	CALL DATE	SINK FUND PROV	CURRENT PRICE		YIELD TO MAT.	2005 HIGH	2005 LOW	AMT. OUTST. MIL. $	ISSUED	ISSUED PRICE
25243YAF	Diageo Cap PLC nt 3.375 03/20/08	A2	M&S 20	—		No	97.13	bid	4.40	103.66	0.00	1000	03/18/03	99.25
25244SAA	Diageo Fin BV global nt 3 12/15/06	A2	J&D 15	—		No	98.26	bid	4.05	102.68	98.26	500	12/10/03	99.97
25244SAB	nt 3.875 04/01/11	A2	A&O 01	—		No	96.13	bid	4.61	99.48	92.81	500	03/30/04	99.17
25243QAB	Diageo PLC nt 3.5 11/19/07	A2	M&N 19	—		No	97.95	bid	4.32	106.33	97.57	1000	11/12/02	99.79
252500AA	Dialog Corp Plc sr sub nt ser a 11 11/15/07	B3	M&N 15	—	fr 11/15/05	No	0.00	·	—	104.13	0.00	180	02/20/98	0.00
252646AC	Diamond Hldgs PLC uks$ sr nt 10 02/01/08	Caa2	F&A 01	—	fr 02/01/06	No	0.00	·	—	102.04	0.00	135	05/12/98	0.00
25271CAG	Diamond Offshore Drilling Inc sr nt 5.15 09/01/14	Baa2	M&S 01	—		No	105.22	bid	4.48	105.22	104.10	250	02/11/05	0.00
252747AE	Diamond Shamrock Inc deb 7.25 06/15/10	Baa3	J&D 15	—		No	100.34	bid	7.17	111.97	99.67	25	06/01/95	100.00
252747AD	deb 8.75 06/15/15	Baa3	J&D 15	—		No	111.16	bid	7.25	124.25	108.23	75	02/06/95	100.00
252747AF	deb 7.65 07/01/26	Baa3	J&D 01	—		No	122.84	bid	5.90	126.51	96.86	100	06/20/96	99.84
252759AL	Diamond St Tel Co deb 8.375 09/15/19	Aa3	M&S 15	—		No	105.90	bid	7.74	140.07	101.19	15	10/02/89	100.00
252759AP	deb 7 12/01/23	Aa3	J&D 01	—		No	112.34	bid	5.97	120.40	95.18	20	12/01/93	98.75
252759AM	deb 8.625 10/15/31	Aa3	A&O 15	100.00	fr 12/01/13	No	106.75	bid	8.10	147.57	100.03	15	10/22/91	99.39
252768AC	Diamond Triumph Auto Glass Inc sr nt 9.25 04/01/08	Caa1	A&O 01	—	fr 04/01/05	No	90.50	bid	12.75	92.75	88.50	100	04/27/00	0.00
254063AG	Dillard Dept Stores Inc deb 9.5 09/01/09	B2	M&S 01	—		No	109.25	bid	7.09	117.00	0.00	50	09/06/89	99.64
254063AR	deb 7.875 01/01/23	B2	J&J 01	—		No	104.00	bid	7.50	107.50	0.00	100	01/06/93	98.64
254063AU	deb 7.75 07/15/26	B2	J&J 15	—		No	104.00	bid	7.41	105.50	0.00	100	07/12/96	99.42
254063AS	nt 6.875 06/01/05	B2	J&D 01	—		No	100.50	bid	4.46	104.75	0.00	100	05/24/95	99.18
254063AT	nt 7.375 06/01/06	B2	J&D 01	—		No	103.25	bid	4.57	106.00	0.00	100	06/04/96	99.78
254063AV	nt 7.15 02/01/07	B2	F&A 01	—		No	103.50	bid	5.16	105.75	0.00	100	01/30/97	99.79
254063AM	nt 9.125 08/01/11	B2	F&A 01	—		No	112.50	bid	6.73	115.25	0.00	100	08/02/91	99.36
254063AQ	nt 7.85 10/01/12	B2	A&O 01	—		No	107.75	bid	6.56	112.25	0.00	100	10/02/92	100.00
254063AX	nt 6.625 01/15/18	B2	J&J 15	—		No	97.75	bid	6.88	101.00	0.00	100	01/07/98	99.77
254063AW	nt 7.75 05/15/27	B2	M&N 15	—		No	104.00	bid	7.42	106.00	0.00	100	05/12/97	100.00
254067AW	Dillard's Inc. (United States) global nt 0.0 05/15/27	B2	—	—		No	—		—	0.00	0.00	100	05/12/97	100.00
254067AJ	sub deb 7.5 08/01/38	B3	—	—		No	—		—	0.00	0.00	200	08/05/98	0.00
254067AH	Dillards Inc deb 7.13 08/01/18	B2	F&A 01	—		No	100.00	bid	7.13	104.00	0.00	200	07/30/98	100.00
254067AG	nt 6.69 08/01/07	B2	F&A 15	—		No	102.75	bid	5.45	105.00	0.00	200	07/30/98	99.97
254067AA	nt 6.3 02/15/08	B2	F&A 15	—		No	101.25	bid	5.83	104.00	0.00	100	02/19/98	99.95
254067AM	nt 6.625 11/15/08	B2	M&N 15	—		No	103.75	bid	5.49	105.00	0.00	100	11/10/98	99.75
254067AN	nt 7 12/01/28	B2	J&D 01	—		No	96.75	bid	7.26	99.00	0.00	150	12/01/98	100.00
254394AE	Dimon Inc sr nt 9.625 10/15/11	B1	A&O 15	104.81	fr 10/15/06	No	111.50	bid	7.44	112.00	101.50	200	11/20/01	0.00
254394AJ	Dimon Inc sr nt 7.75 06/01/13	B1	J&D 01	103.88	fr 06/01/08	No	112.00	bid	5.93	119.85	91.50	125	01/12/04	0.00
25459HAB	Directv Hldgs LLC sr nt 8.375 03/15/13	Ba2	M&S 15	104.19	fr 03/15/08	No	107.75	bid	7.13	113.25	107.75	1400	08/19/03	0.00
254687AM	Disney Walt Co global sr nt 6.75 03/30/06	Baa1	M&S 30	—		No	102.90	bid	3.78	109.86	102.43	1300	03/22/96	99.86
254687AH	sr deb 7.55 07/15/93	A3	J&J 15	103.02	fr 07/15/23	No	113.86	bid	6.91	129.20	107.67	300	07/21/93	100.00
999926@A	Dixons Group PLC gbp$ bd 6.125 11/15/12	Baa1	Nov 15	—		No	95.54	bid	6.86	107.58	94.33	300	11/05/02	99.59
23326LAA	DLI Acquisition Corp sr unit 8.00 02/01/12	B3	F&A 01	104.00	fr 02/01/08	No	98.50	bid	8.28	100.00	98.50	175	01/19/05	99.34
256006AD	Doane Pet Care Co sr nt 10.75 03/01/10	B3	M&S 01	105.38	fr 07/21/07	No	108.00	bid	8.78	109.00	102.50	213	05/07/03	0.00
256006AA	Doane Pet Care Co sr sub nt 9.75 05/15/07	Caa2	M&N 15	—	fr 05/15/05	No	99.50	bid	10.01	100.75	87.00	150	04/09/99	0.00
256067AC	Dobson Cellular Sys Inc 1st priority sr secd nt fltg rt rule 144a 7.4925 11/01/11	B2	M&N 01	102.00	fr 11/01/06	No	102.50	bid	7.03	100.75	101.25	250	10/26/04	100.00
256067AA	1st priority sr secd nt rule 144a 8.375 11/01/11	B2	M&N 01	104.00	fr 11/01/08	No	102.25	bid	7.94	107.50	100.00	250	10/26/04	100.00
256067AD	2nd priority sr secd nt rule 144a 9.875 11/01/12	B3	M&N 01	105.00	fr 11/01/08	No	102.25	bid	9.47	106.25	97.75	325	10/26/04	100.00
256069AE	Dobson Communications Corp sr nt 10.875 07/01/10	Ca	J&J 01	105.44	fr 07/01/05	No	89.25	bid	13.65	110.75	69.50	300	07/27/00	0.00
256072AD	sr nt 8.875 10/01/13	Ca	A&O 01	104.44	fr 10/01/08	No	79.25	bid	12.62	123.20	60.50	650	12/01/03	0.00
256605AJ	Dole Food Co Inc sr nt 7.25 05/01/09	B2	M&N 01	—		No	106.00	bid	5.61	111.50	97.61	400	06/10/02	0.00
256605AN	Dole Food Co Inc sr nt 7.25 06/15/10	B2	J&D 15	103.63	fr 06/15/07	No	100.50	bid	7.14	114.31	0.00	400	06/15/00	0.00
256605AP	sr nt 8.875 03/15/11	B2	M&S 15	104.44	fr 03/15/07	No	108.25	bid	7.19	118.20	101.25	475	07/25/03	0.00
256605AD	Dole Food Inc deb 7.875 07/15/13	B2	J&J 15	—		No	106.75	bid	6.83	113.00	95.51	175	07/27/93	99.37
256666AE	Dollar Finl Group Inc sr nt 9.75 11/15/11	B3	M&N 15	104.88	fr 11/15/07	No	106.00	bid	8.59	122.18	100.00	240	01/20/04	0.00
256669AC	Dollar Gen Corp nt 8.625 06/15/10	Ba2	J&D 15	—		No	112.50	bid	5.86	115.00	0.00	200	08/09/00	0.00
257072AB	Dome Corp putable adj demand bd fltg rt ser 91 5.75 08/31/16	Aa2	Monthly	—	fr 10/01/05	No	100.15	bid	5.73	249.59	97.87	12.6	08/30/91	100.00
257469AC	Dominion Res Inc rmkd nt ser e 7.195 09/15/14	Baa1	M&S 15	—	fr 09/15/05	No	112.79	bid	5.49	117.62	99.25	250	09/06/00	99.97
25746UAS	sr nt fltg rt ser b 2004 3.09438 05/15/06	Baa1	F,M,A&N 15	—		No	100.11	bid	3.00	100.15	90.52	100	01/12/04	100.00
25746UAJ	sr nt ser 2002 b 6.25 06/30/12	Baa1	J&D 30	—		No	106.84	bid	5.13	110.43	93.44	500	06/24/02	99.81
257469AF	sr nt ser 2002 c 5.7 09/17/12	Baa1	M&S 17	—		No	103.83	bid	5.09	107.25	89.89	520	09/09/02	99.93
257469AH	sr nt ser 2002 d 5.125 12/15/09	Baa1	J&D 15	—		No	101.29	bid	4.82	105.47	91.81	300	12/09/02	99.55
257469AG	sr nt ser 2002 e 6.75 12/15/32	Baa1	J&D 15	—		No	108.36	bid	6.19	116.84	89.35	300	12/09/02	99.76
25746UAA	sr nt ser a 8.125 06/15/10	Baa1	J&D 15	—		No	114.52	bid	4.98	119.68	105.79	700	06/21/00	99.90
25746UAR	sr nt ser a 2004 5.2 01/15/16	Baa1	J&J 15	—		No	98.50	bid	5.38	113.84	97.02	200	01/12/04	99.97
25746UAB	sr nt ser b 7.625 07/15/05	Baa1	J&J 15	—		No	101.07	bid	3.92	110.82	98.13	700	07/10/00	99.87
25746UAL	sr nt ser b 4.125 02/15/08	Baa1	F&A 15	—		No	98.99	bid	4.50	104.91	0.00	400	02/10/03	99.67
25746UAM	sr nt ser c 5 03/15/13	Baa1	M&S 15	—		No	98.70	bid	5.20	103.87	0.00	300	03/03/03	99.80
25746UAN	sr nt ser e 6.3 03/15/33	Baa1	M&S 15	—		No	104.67	bid	5.99	111.51	93.18	300	03/03/03	99.97
257469AJ	sr nt ser f 5.25 08/01/33	Baa1	F&A 01	—		No	99.66	bid	5.27	109.75	96.37	510	07/21/03	99.16
25746UAD	sr nt ser g 3.66 11/15/06	Baa1	F,M,A&N 15	—		No	99.09	bid	4.24	100.27	98.95	412.305	11/10/04	100.25
25754QAF	Dominos Inc sr sub nt 8.25 07/01/11	B2	J&J 01	104.13	fr 07/01/07	No	105.00	bid	7.27	111.00	103.50	284.9	12/11/03	0.00
257561AT	Domtar Inc deb 9.5 08/01/16	Baa3	F&A 01	—		No	126.80	bid	6.29	147.43	124.09	125	07/26/96	99.65
257561AS	nt 8.75 08/01/06	Baa3	F&A 01	—		No	106.11	bid	4.05	119.77	105.88	150	07/26/96	99.74
257561AV	nt 5.375 12/01/13	Baa3	J&D 01	—		No	94.31	bid	6.21	114.46	93.68	350	11/13/03	99.26
257561AU	sr nt 7.875 10/15/11	Baa3	A&O 15	—		No	109.89	bid	6.06	126.03	109.29	600	10/11/01	98.69
257661AM	Donaldson Lufkin & Jenrette Inc sr nt 6.875 11/01/05	Aa3	M&N 01	—		No	100.11	bid	0.17	111.61	100.00	1000	10/08/98	99.22
257661AE	nt 6.5 04/01/08	Aa3	A&O 01	—		No	105.65	bid	4.49	116.11	105.27	150	03/18/98	99.58
257661AF	nt 6.5 06/01/08	Aa3	J&D 01	—		No	105.90	bid	4.51	117.36	105.22	500	06/03/98	99.59
257867AC	Donnelley R R & Sons Co deb 8.875 04/15/21	Baa1	A&O 15	—		No	128.46	bid	6.22	133.25	118.06	80.966	04/18/91	99.73
257867AG	deb 6.625 04/15/29	Baa1	A&O 15	—		No	112.73	bid	5.73	113.17	99.91	200	04/13/99	98.98
257867AF	deb 8.82 04/15/31	Baa1	A&O 15	—		No	165.74	bid	4.74	166.39	163.21	69.034	05/28/98	0.00
257867AH	nt 5 11/15/06	Baa1	M&N 15	—		No	101.43	bid	4.09	106.37	101.29	225	11/08/01	99.47
257867AK	nt 3.75 04/01/09	Baa1	A&O 01	—		No	96.60	bid	4.68	99.67	96.10	399.975	03/29/04	0.00
257867AM	nt 4.95 04/01/14	Baa1	A&O 01	—		No	98.56	bid	5.15	106.33	97.60	598.5	08/06/04	0.00
257867AJ	sr nt rule 144a 3.75 04/01/09	Baa1	A&O 01	—		No	97.60	bid	4.40	104.79	97.09	0.025	03/03/04	99.85
257867AL	sr nt rule 144a 4.95 04/01/14	Baa1	A&O 01	—		No	103.77	bid	4.45	110.88	100.75	1.5	03/03/04	99.61
258040AA	Donohue Forest Products sr nt 7.625 05/15/07	Ba3	M&N 15	—		No	101.56	bid	6.84	114.88	101.20	200	05/13/97	99.73
25811PAG	Doral Financial Corp. secd nt 7.1 04/26/17	Baa2	Monthly	—		No	—	·	—	0.00	0.00	40	04/04/02	97.98
25811PAH	secd nt 7.15 04/26/22	Baa2	Monthly	—		No	—	·	—	0.00	0.00	30	04/04/02	97.98
25811PAF	sr nt 7 04/26/12	Baa2	Monthly	—		No	—	·	—	0.00	0.00	30	04/04/02	97.98
25811PAE	Doral Finl Corp sr nt 7.65 03/26/16	Baa2	Monthly	102.00	fr 03/26/11	No	103.01	bid	7.27	115.01	102.32	100	03/27/01	97.83
25811PAJ	sr nt fltg rt 1.985 12/07/05	Baa2	M,J,S&D 07	—		No	98.91	bid	3.58	99.77	97.38	115	06/02/04	100.00
25811PAK	sr nt fltg rt 3.5 07/20/07	Baa2	J,A,J&O 20	—		No	99.64	bid	3.66	100.94	91.05	625	07/15/04	100.00
259603AA	Douglas Dynamics LLC / Douglas Dynamics Fin Co sr nt rule 144a 7.75 01/15/12	B3	J&J 15	103.38	fr 01/15/09	No	98.00	bid	8.12	102.75	98.00	150	12/10/04	100.00
260003AC	Dover Corp deb 6.65 06/01/28	A1	J&D 01	—		No	115.59	bid	5.55	129.16	101.64	200	06/04/98	99.56
260003AA	nt 6.45 11/15/05	A1	M&N 15	—		No	101.86	bid	3.45	111.94	101.66	200	11/09/95	99.48
260003AB	nt 6.25 06/01/08	A1	J&D 01	—		No	105.14	bid	4.51	116.81	104.61	150	06/04/98	99.93

Notes: Moody's® ratings are subject to change. Because of the possible time lapse between Moody's® assignment or change of a rating and your use of this monthly publication, we suggest you verify the current rating of any security or issuer in which you are interested. For standard abbreviations and symbols, see page 6.

Source: *Mergent Bond Record*, March 2006, p. 77.

Table 16–2

Dillard's Bond Offering

DILLARD'S 7.875% BONDS DUE JANUARY 1, 2023

Moody's Rating: B2
Indenture Date: January 1, 1993
Authorized: $100,000,000
Outstanding: $100,000,000
Security of Obligation: A direct unsecured obligation
Interest Payable: January 1, July 1
Grace Period: 30 days
Trustee: Chase Manhattan Bank
Call Feature: Noncallable
Trading Exchange: OTC

Price Range

Year	High	Low
2005	91.188	86.325
2004	94.205	89.075
2003	93.165	88.125
2002	95.500	87.250
2001	88.660	69.520
2000	93.000	61.875
1999	110.375	92.250
1998	114.000	108.875
1997	112.325	98.250

Source: Mergent Industrial Manual, 2006.

---

at $640.[2] Though most bonds are virtually certain to be redeemed at their face value at maturity ($1,000 in this case), this is small consolation to the bondholder who has many decades to wait. At times, bonds also greatly increase in value, such as they did in 1984–85, 1990–92, 1994–95, and 2003.

As indicated in the paragraph above and in Chapter 10, the price of a bond is directly tied to current interest rates. One exception to this rule was discussed at the beginning of the chapter; that is, when survival becomes a key factor in pricing and valuation. We will look at the more normal case where interest rates are the key factor in determining price.

A bond paying 5.10 percent ($51 a year) will fare quite poorly when the going market rate is 8.10 percent ($81 a year). To maintain a market in the older issue, the price is adjusted downward to reflect current market demands. The longer the life of the issue, the greater the influence of interest rate changes on the price of the bond.[3] The same process will work in reverse if interest rates go down. A 30-year, $1,000 bond initially issued to yield 8.10 percent would go up to $1,500 if interest rates declined to 5.10 percent (assuming the bond is not callable). A further illustration of interest rate effects on bond prices is presented in Table 16–3 for a bond paying 12 percent interest. Observe that not only interest rates in the market but also years to maturity have a strong influence on bond prices.

---

[2]Bond prices are generally quoted as a percentage of original par value. In this case the quote would read 64.
[3]This is known as Malkiel's second theory of bonds. In fact it is only completely true when the coupon rate of the bond equals or is greater than the original discount rate.

Table 16–3
Bond price table

Interest Rates and Bond Prices (the bond pays 12% interest)				
Rate in the Market (%)—Yield to Maturity*				
Years to Maturity	**8%**	**10%**	**12%**	**14%**	**16%**
1	$1,038.16	$1,018.54	$1,000	$981.48	$963.98
15	1,345.52	1,153.32	1,000	875.54	774.48
25	1,429.92	1,182.36	1,000	862.06	754.98

*The prices in the table are based on semiannual interest, but you enter the table with annual values.

From 1945 through the early 1980s, the pattern had been for long-term interest rates to move upward (Figure 16–3). However, long-term interest rates have generally been declining since 1982.

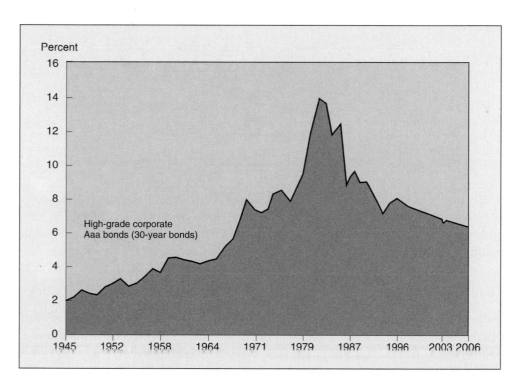

Figure 16–3
Long-term yields on debt

Bond Yields

Bond yields are quoted three different ways: **coupon rate, current yield,** and **yield to maturity.** We will apply each to a $1,000 par value bond paying $100 per year interest for 10 years. The bond is currently priced at $900.

Coupon Rate (Nominal Yield)   Stated interest payment divided by the par value.

$$\frac{\$100}{\$1,000} = 10\%$$

Current Yield   Stated interest payment divided by the current price of the bond.

$$\frac{\$100}{\$900} = 11.11\%$$

Yield to Maturity   The yield to maturity is the interest rate that will equate future interest payments and the payment at maturity (principal payment) to the current market price. This represents the concept of the internal rate of return. In the present case, an interest rate of approximately 11.70 percent will equate interest payments of $100 for 10 years and a final payment of $1,000 to the current price of $900. A simple formula may be used to approximate yield to maturity.[4] This formula was initially presented in Chapter 10.

$$\text{Approximate yield to maturity } (Y') = \frac{\text{Annual interest payment} + \dfrac{\text{Principal payment} - \text{Price of the bond}}{\text{Number of years to maturity}}}{0.6 \text{ (Price of the bond)} + 0.4 \text{ (Principal payment)}} \tag{16-1}$$

$$Y' = \frac{\$100 + \dfrac{\$1,000 - 900}{10}}{0.6(\$900) + 0.4(\$1,000)}$$

$$= \frac{\$100 + \dfrac{\$100}{10}}{\$540 + \$400}$$

$$Y' = \frac{\$100 + \$10}{\$940} = \frac{\$110}{\$940} = \boxed{11.70\%}$$

Extensive bond tables indicating yield to maturity are also available. Calculators and computers may also be used to determine yield to maturity. When financial analysts speak of bond yields, the general assumption is that they are speaking of yield to maturity. This is deemed to be the most significant measure of return.

Bond Ratings

STANDARD &POOR'S

Both the issuing corporation and the investor are concerned about the rating their bond is assigned by the two major bond rating agencies—Moody's Investor Service and Standard & Poor's Corporation. The higher the rating assigned a given issue, the lower the required interest payments are to satisfy potential investors. This is because highly rated bonds carry lower risk. A major industrial corporation may be able to issue a 30-year bond at 6.5 to 7 percent yield to maturity because it is rated Aaa, whereas a smaller, regional firm may only qualify for a B rating and be forced to pay 9 or 10 percent.

---

[4]The exact answer can be found through the procedures in Appendix 10B covering financial calculators.

As an example of **bond rating** systems, Moody's Investor Service provides the following nine categories of ranking:

Aaa Aa A Baa Ba B Caa Ca C

The first two categories of bond ratings represent the highest quality (for example, IBM and Procter & Gamble); the next two, medium to high quality; and so on. Beginning in 1982, Moody's began applying numerical modifiers to categories Aa through B: 1 is the highest in a category, 2 is the midrange, and 3 is the lowest. Thus, a rating of Aa2 means the bond is in the midrange of Aa. Standard & Poor's has a similar letter system with + and − modifiers.

Bonds receive ratings based on the corporation's ability to make interest payments, its consistency of performance, its size, its debt-equity ratio, its working capital position, and a number of other factors. The yield spread between higher- and lower-rated bonds changes with the economy. If investors are pessimistic about economic events, they will accept as much as 3 percent less return to go into securities of very high quality, whereas in more normal times the spread may be only 1.5 percent.

Examining Actual Bond Ratings

Three actual bond offerings are presented in Table 16–4 to illustrate the various terms we have used.

Name	Coupon	Type of Bond	Rating	Price	Yield to Maturity
United Technologies	8.75%	Debenture, due 2021	A2	$1,150.30	6.10%
First Union Corp. (North Carolina)	7.50	Subordinate bonds, due 2035	A1	1,199.20	6.27
Beverly Enterprises	8.625	Mortgage bonds, due 2010	Ba2	945.00	9.21

Source: Mergent Bond Guide, January 2006.

Table 16–4

Outstanding bond issues (January 2006)

Recall that the true return on a bond is measured by yield to maturity (the last column of Table 16–4). The United Technologies bonds are unsecured, as indicated by the term *debenture.* The bonds are rated A2, or middle investment grade, and carry a price of $1,150.30. This price is higher than the par value or $1,000.00, because the interest rate at time of issue (8.75 percent coupon) is higher than the demanded yield to maturity of 6.10 percent in January 2006 for bonds of equal quality and maturity. The First Union Corporation bonds are subordinated bonds with a rating of A1 and a yield to maturity of 6.27 percent. The Beverly Enterprises bonds are secured by a mortgage and rated Ba2, based on the corporation's overall outlook. Because they are relatively low in quality, they pay a yield to maturity of 9.21 percent (in spite of the fact they are secured in nature). The bonds in Table 16–4 can be refunded if the companies desire. The meaning and benefits of refunding will be made clear in the following section.

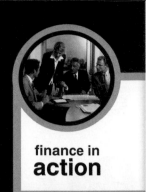

GM's Bond Rating Drop

In the first week of May 2005, General Motors saw its bond rating by Moody's (and Standard and Poor's) drop from Baa to Ba. This meant it no longer was in the top four categories of bond ratings (Aaa to Baa). The top four rated categories are considered investment grade and highly desired by bond issuers. Many mutual funds, trust funds, and endowments are restricted to only buying investment grade securities. Once a firm falls out of the investment grade designation, it is considered a "junk" bond. In the case of GM, when it hit the junk bond rating category (along with Ford), the required yield on its bonds went from 8.25 percent to 8.75 percent. While half a percentage point might not seem like much, it is when a firm has billions of dollars of bonds outstanding.

Why the downgrade by the bond rating agencies? First of all, GM announced that it would show a loss for the first quarter of 2005. Also, escalating gas prices in the spring of 2005 were cutting into SUV sales. Overall, the projection for industry sales of this larger vehicle were cut from 2.8 million to 2.4 million as gas prices spiraled from $1.75 to $3.00 a gallon.

As if to add injury to insult, GM's pension fund was judged to be underfunded by financial analysts, and labor unions were asking for greater job security and increased benefits. Furthermore, popular imports from Japan, Germany, Korea, and elsewhere were cutting into GM's market share.

Lastly, GM had committed to pay a $2 per share cash dividend to its common stockholders over the last few years, and any reduction in the dividend was sure to cause a further reduction in the stock price (which had already fallen from $42 to $25). Although bondholders have a superior claim to common stockholders in the distribution of funds, top management at GM had to remain sensitive to the desires of common stockholders or face the danger of being removed from office.

As often happens, the unfortunate plight of GM caught a shrewd investor's attention. Hollywood and Las Vegas's 80-year-old mogul, Kirk Kerkorian, put out a bid to buy 28 million shares of GM at $31 a share and acquired 9 percent ownership of the company. At the time of the offer, GM's shares were selling at the lowest value since 1991 at $25 a share.

Kerkorian is known as a turnaround artist of the highest order, and the common stock price shot up to $36 by August 2005. During the first few months of Kerkorian's major move, GM initiated the "You pay what we pay" promotional program in which nonemployee customers paid the same price for new automobiles as full-time employees. It also improved its relationship and bargaining position with labor unions and announced exciting new models of smaller SUVs and other vehicles.

How all of these activities will ultimately affect GM's bond rating remains to be seen. If it can follow through with plans for its future, this "fallen angel" may once again return to an investment grade status. If not, continued downgrades and ever-increasing required interest rates will be part of its future.

The Refunding Decision

Assume you are the financial vice-president for a corporation that has issued bonds at 11.75 percent, only to witness a drop in interest rates to 9.5 percent. If you believe interest rates will rise rather than sink further, you may wish to redeem the expensive 11.75 percent bonds and issue new debt at the prevailing 9.5 percent rate. This process is labeled a **refunding** operation. It is made feasible by the call provision that enables a corporation to buy back bonds at close to par, rather than at high market values, when interest rates are declining.

A Capital Budgeting Problem

The refunding decision involves outflows in the form of financing costs related to redeeming and reissuing securities, and inflows represented by savings in annual interest costs and tax savings. In the present case, we shall assume the corporation issued $10 million worth of 11.75 percent debt with a 25-year maturity and the debt has been on the books for five years. The corporation now has the opportunity to buy back the old debt at 10 percent above par (the call premium) and to issue new debt at 9.5 percent interest with a 20-year life. The underwriting cost for the old issue was $125,000, and the underwriting cost for the new issue is $200,000. We shall also assume the corporation is in the 35 percent tax bracket and uses a 6 percent discount rate for refunding decisions. Since the savings from a refunding decision are certain—unlike the savings from most other capital budgeting decisions—we use the aftertax cost of new debt as the discount rate, rather than the more generalized cost of capital.[5] Actually, in this case, the aftertax cost of new debt is 9.5 percent $(1 - \text{Tax rate})$, or $9.5\% \times 0.65 = 6.18\%$. We round to 6 percent. The facts in this example are restated as follows.

Restatement of facts

	Old Issue	New Issue
Size	$10,000,000	$10,000,000
Interest rate	11.75%	9.5%
Total life................	25 years	20 years
Remaining life	20 years	20 years
Call premium	10%	—
Underwriting costs	$125,000	$200,000

Tax bracket	35%
Discount rate	6%

Let's go through the capital budgeting process of defining our outflows and inflows and determining the net present value.

Step A—Outflow Considerations

1. *Payment of call premium*—The first outflow is the 10 percent call premium on $10 million, or $1 million. This prepayment penalty is necessary to call in the original issue. Being an *out-of-pocket* tax-deductible expense, the $1 million cash expenditure will cost us only $650,000 on an aftertax basis. We multiply the expense by $(1 - \text{Tax rate})$ to get the aftertax cost.

$$\$1,000,000 \ (1 - T) = \$1,000,000 \ (1 - 0.35) = \$650,000$$

$$\text{Net cost of call premium} = \$650.000$$

2. *Underwriting cost on new issue*—The second outflow is the $200,000 underwriting cost on the new issue. The actual cost is somewhat less because the payment is tax-deductible, though the write-off must be spread over the life of the bond. While the actual $200,000 is being spent now, equal tax deductions of $10,000 a year will occur over the next 20 years (in a manner similar to depreciation).

---

[5]A minority opinion would be that there is sufficient similarity between the bond refunding decision and other capital budgeting decisions to disallow any specialized treatment. Also note that although the bondholders must still bear some risk of default, for which they are compensated, the corporation assumes no risk.

The tax savings from a *noncash* write-off are equal to the amount times the tax rate. For a company in the 35 percent tax bracket, $10,000 of annual tax deductions will provide $3,500 of tax savings each year for the next 20 years. The present value of these savings is the present value of a $3,500 annuity for 20 years at 6 percent interest:

$$\$3,500 \times 11.470 \ (n = 20, i = 6\%) = \$40,145$$

The net cost of underwriting the new issue is the actual expenditure now, minus the present value of future tax savings as indicated below.

Actual expenditure..............	$200,000
− PV of future tax savings	40,145
Net cost of underwriting expense on the new issue.......	$159,855

Step B—Inflow Considerations

The major inflows in the refunding decision are related to the reduction of annual interest expense and the immediate write-off of the underwriting cost on the old issue.

3. *Cost savings in lower interest rates*—The corporation will enjoy a 2.25 percentage point drop in interest rates, from 11.75 percent to 9.50 percent, on $10 million of bonds.

11.75% × $10,000,000	$1,175,000
9.50% × $10,000,000	950,000
Savings	$ 225,000

Since we are in the 35 percent tax bracket, this is equivalent to $146,250 of aftertax benefits per year for 20 years. We have taken the savings and multiplied by one minus the tax rate to get the annual aftertax benefits.

$$\$225,000 \ (1 - T)$$
$$\$225,000 \ (1 - 0.35)$$
$$\$146,250$$

Applying a 6 percent discount rate for a 20-year annuity:

$$\$146,250 \times 11.470 \ (n = 20, i = 6\%) = \$1,677,488$$

Cost savings in lower interest rates $1,677,488

4. *Underwriting cost on old issue*—There is a further cost savings related to immediately writing off the remaining underwriting costs on the old bonds. Note that the initial amount of $125,000 was spent five years ago and was to be written off for tax purposes over 25 years at $5,000 per year. Since five years have passed, $100,000 of old underwriting costs have not been amortized as indicated in the following:

Original amount	$125,000
Written off over five years................	25,000
Unamortized old underwriting costs	$100,000

A tax benefit is associated with the immediate write-off of old underwriting costs, which we shall consider shortly.

Note, however, that this is not a total gain. We would have gotten the $100,000 additional write-off eventually if we had not called in the old bonds. By calling them in now, we simply take the write-off sooner. If we extended the write-off over the remaining life of the bonds, we would have taken $5,000 a year for 20 years. Discounting this value, we show:

$$\$5,000 \times 11.470 \ (n = 20, i = 6\%) = \$57,350$$

Thus, we are getting a write-off of $100,000 now, rather than a present value of future write-offs of $57,350. The gain in immediate tax write-offs is $42,650. The tax savings from a *noncash* tax write-off equal the amount times the tax rate. Since we are in the 35 percent tax bracket, our savings from this write-off are $14,928. The following calculations, which were discussed above, are necessary to arrive at $14,928.

Immediate write-off	$100,000
− PV of future write-off	57,350
Gain from immediate write-off	$ 42,650

$$\$42,650(T)$$
$$\$42,650(.35) = \$14,928$$

Net gain from the underwriting on the old issue $14,928

Step C—Net Present Value

We now compare our outflows and our inflows from the prior pages.

Outflows		Inflows	
1. Net cost of call premium	$650,000	3. Cost savings in lower interest rates	$1,677,488
2. Net cost of underwriting expense on new issue	159,855	4. Net gain from underwriting cost on old issue	14,928
	$809,855		$1,692,416

Present value of inflows	$1,692,416
Present value of outflows	809,855
Net present value	$ 882,561

The refunding decision has a positive net present value, suggesting that interest rates have dropped to a sufficiently low level to indicate refunding is in order. The only question is, Will interest rates go lower—indicating an even better time for refunding? There is no easy answer. Conditions in the financial markets must be carefully considered.

A number of other factors could be plugged into the problem. For example, there could be overlapping time periods in the refunding procedure when both issues are outstanding and the firm is paying double interest (hopefully for less than a month). The dollar amount in these cases, however, tends to be small and is not included in the analysis.

In working problems, the student should have minimum difficulty if he or she follows the four suggested calculations. In each of the four calculations we had the following tax implications:

1. Payment of call premium—the cost equals the amount times (1 − Tax rate) for this *cash tax-deductible expense.*

2. Underwriting costs on new issue—we pay an amount now and then amortize it over the life of the bond for tax purposes. This subsequent amortization is similar to depreciation and represents a *noncash write-off* of a tax-deductible expense. The tax saving from the amortization is equal to the amount times the tax rate.

3. Cost savings in lower interest rates—cost savings are like any form of income, and we will retain the cost savings times (1 − Tax rate).

4. Underwriting cost on old issue—once again, the writing off of underwriting costs represents a *noncash write-off* of a tax-deductible expense. The tax savings from the amortization are equal to the amount times the tax rate.

Other Forms of Bond Financing

As interest rates continued to show increasing volatility in the 1980s and early 1990s, two innovative forms of bond financing became very popular and remain so today. We shall examine the zero-coupon rate bond and the floating rate bond.

The **zero-coupon rate bond,** as the name implies, does not pay interest. It is, however, sold at a deep discount from face value. The return to the investor is the difference between the investor's cost and the face value received at the end of the life of the bond. For example, in early 1982, BankAmerica Corporation offered $1,000 zero-coupon rate bonds with maturities of 5, 8, and 10 years. The 5-year bonds were sold for $500, the 8-year bonds for $333.33, and the 10-year bonds for $250. All three provided an initial yield to maturity (through gain in value) of approximately 14.75 percent. A dramatic case of a zero-coupon bond was an issue offered by PepsiCo, Inc., in 1982, in which the maturities ranged from 6 to 30 years. The 30-year $1,000 par value issue could be purchased for $26.43, providing a yield of approximately 12.75 percent. The purchase price per bond of $26.43 represented only 2.643 percent of the par value. A million dollars worth of these 30-year bonds could be initially purchased for a mere $26,430.

The advantage to the corporation is that there is immediate cash inflow to the corporation, without any outflow until the bonds mature. Furthermore, the difference between the initial bond price and the maturity value may be amortized for tax purposes by the corporation over the life of the bond. This means the corporation will be taking annual deductions without current cash outflow.

From the investor's viewpoint, the zero-coupon bonds allow him or her to lock in a multiplier of the initial investment. For example, investors may know they will get three times their investment after a specified number of years. The major drawback is that the annual increase in the value of bonds is taxable as ordinary income as it accrues, even though the bondholder does not get any cash flow until maturity. For this reason most investors in zero-coupon rate bonds have tax-exempt or tax-deferred status (pension funds, foundations, charitable organizations, individual retirement accounts, and the like).

The prices of the bonds tend to be highly volatile because of changes in interest rates. Even though the bonds provide no annual interest payment, there is still an initial yield to maturity that may prove to be too high or too low with changes in the marketplace.

The bonds of the first two companies listed in Table 16–5 are examples of zero-coupon bonds. The bonds sell at a considerable discount from par value of $1,000 since both have some time remaining until maturity. Note in the price column that the PepsiCo Capital Resources bonds are selling at the larger discount due to the long time to their maturity.

	Rating	Coupon	Maturity	Price	Yield to Maturity
Zero-Coupon Bonds					
PepsiCo Capital Resources	A1	0.00%	2112	$ 623.18	6.61%
Honeywell International	A2	0.00	2010	713.25	7.01
Floating Rate Bonds					
CIT Group Holdings	Aa3	6.51	2011	1,000.75	6.50
Source: Mergent Bond Guide, Selected issues, 2006.					

Table 16–5

Zero-coupon and floating rate bonds

A second type of innovative bond issue is the **floating rate bond** (long popular in European capital markets). In this case, instead of a change in the price of the bond, the interest rate paid on the bond changes with market conditions (usually monthly or quarterly). Thus, a bond that was initially issued to pay 9 percent may lower the interest payments to 6 percent during some years and raise them to 12 percent in others. The interest rate is usually tied to some overall market rate, such as the yield on Treasury bonds (perhaps 120 percent of the going yield on long-term Treasury bonds).

An example of a floating rate bond is the CIT Group Holdings, Inc., bond presented at the bottom of Table 16–5. Notice that the price of $1,000.75 is close to the $1,000 par value since the coupon adjusts with changes in market rates.

The advantage to investors in floating rate bonds is that they have a constant (or almost constant) market value for the security, even though interest rates vary. An exception is that floating rate bonds often have broad limits that interest payments cannot exceed. For example, the interest rate on a 9 percent initial offering may not be allowed to go over 16 percent or below 4 percent. If long-term interest rates dictated an interest payment of 20 percent, the payment would still remain at 16 percent. This could cause some short-term loss in market value. To date, floating rate bonds have been relatively free of this problem.

Zero-coupon rate bonds and floating rate bonds still represent a relatively small percentage of the total market of new debt offerings. Nevertheless, they should be part of a basic understanding of long-term debt instruments.

The financial manager must consider whether debt will contribute to or detract from the firm's operations. In certain industries, such as airlines, very heavy debt utilization is a way of life, whereas in other industries (drugs, photographic equipment) reliance is placed on other forms of capital.

Advantages and Disadvantages of Debt

Benefits of Debt

The advantages of debt may be enumerated as:

1. Interest payments are tax-deductible. Because the maximum corporate tax rate is in the mid-30 percent range, the effective aftertax cost of interest is approximately two-thirds of the dollar amount expended.

2. The financial obligation is clearly specified and of a fixed nature (with the exception of floating rate bonds). Contrast this with selling an ownership interest in which stockholders have open-ended participation in profits; however, the amount of profits is unknown.

3. In an inflationary economy, debt may be paid back with "cheaper dollars." A $1,000 bond obligation may be repaid in 10 or 20 years with dollars that have shrunk in value by 50 or 60 percent. In terms of "real dollars," or purchasing power equivalents, one might argue that the corporation should be asked to repay something in excess of $2,000. Presumably, high interest rates in inflationary periods compensate the lender for loss in purchasing power, but this is not always the case.

4. The use of debt, up to a prudent point, may lower the cost of capital to the firm. To the extent that debt does not strain the risk position of the firm, its low aftertax cost may aid in reducing the weighted overall cost of financing to the firm.

Drawbacks of Debt

Finally, we must consider the disadvantages of debt:

1. Interest and principal payment obligations are set by contract and must be met, regardless of the economic position of the firm.

2. Indenture agreements may place burdensome restrictions on the firm, such as maintenance of working capital at a given level, limits on future debt offerings, and guidelines for dividend policy. Although bondholders generally do not have the right to vote, they may take virtual control of the firm if important indenture provisions are not met.

3. Utilized beyond a given point, debt may depress outstanding common stock values.

Eurobond Market

A market with an increasing presence in world capital markets is that in Eurobonds. A **Eurobond** may be defined as a bond payable in the borrower's currency but sold outside the borrower's country. The Eurobond is usually sold by an international syndicate of investment bankers and includes bonds sold by companies in Switzerland, Japan, the Netherlands, Germany, the United States, and Britain, to name the most popular countries. An example might be a bond of a U.S. company, payable in dollars and sold in London, Paris, Tokyo, or Frankfurt. Disclosure requirements in the Eurobond market are less demanding than those of the Securities and Exchange Commission or other domestic regulatory agencies. Examples of several Eurobonds are presented in Table 16–6.

Table 16–6

Examples of Eurobonds

	Rating	Coupon	Maturity	Amount Outstanding ($ millions)	Currency Denomination*
Petro-Canada	Baa1	9.25%	2021	300.0	C$
Procter & Gamble Co.	Aa2	10.88	2010	200.0	U.S.$
Sony Corporation	Aa3	1.40	2009	300.0	Yen

*C$ is Canadian dollar.
Source: Mergent Bond Record, Selected issues, 2006.

Leasing as a Form of Debt

When a corporation contracts to lease an oil tanker or a computer and signs a non-cancelable, long-term agreement, the transaction has all the characteristics of a debt obligation. Long-term leasing was not recognized as a debt obligation in the early post–World War II period, but since the mid-60s there has been a strong movement by the accounting profession to force companies to fully divulge all information about leasing obligations and to indicate the equivalent debt characteristics.

This position was made official for financial reporting purposes as a result of *Statement of Financial Accounting Standards (SFAS) No. 13,* issued by the Financial Accounting Standards Board (FASB) in November 1976. This statement said certain types of leases must be shown as long-term obligations on the financial statements of the firm. Before *SFAS No. 13,* lease obligations could merely be divulged in footnotes to financial statements, and large lease obligations did not have to be included in the debt structure (except for the upcoming payment). Consider the case of Firm ABC, whose balance sheet is shown in Table 16–7.

Table 16–7

Balance sheet ($ millions)

Current assets.	$ 50	Current liabilities	$ 50
Fixed assets	150	Long-term liabilities	50
		Total liabilities	100
		Stockholders' equity.	100
		Total liabilities and	
Total assets	$200	stockholders' equity	$200

Before the issuance of *SFAS No. 13,* a footnote to the financial statements might have indicated a lease obligation of $12 million a year for the next 15 years, with a present value of $100 million. With the issuance of *SFAS No. 13,* this information was moved directly to the balance sheet, as indicated in Table 16–8.

Table 16–8

Revised balance sheet ($ millions)

Current assets.	$ 50	Current liabilities	$ 50
Fixed assets	150	Long-term liabilities	50
Leased property		Obligation under	
under capital lease*	100	capital lease*	100
		Total liabilities	200
		Stockholders' equity.	100
		Total liabilities and	
Total assets	$300	stockholders' equity	$300

*See discussion below concerning this table.

We see that both a new asset and a new liability have been created, as indicated by the asterisks. The essence of this treatment is that a long-term, noncancelable lease is tantamount to purchasing the asset with borrowed funds, and this should be reflected on the balance sheet. Note that between the original balance sheet (Table 16–7) and the revised balance sheet (Table 16–8), the total-debt-to-total-assets ratio has gone from 50 percent to 66.7 percent.

$$\textit{Original:} \quad \frac{\text{Total debt}}{\text{Total assets}} = \frac{\$100 \text{ million}}{\$200 \text{ million}} = 50\%$$

$$\textit{Revised:} \quad \frac{\text{Total debt}}{\text{Total assets}} = \frac{\$200 \text{ million}}{\$300 \text{ million}} = 66.7\%$$

Though this represents a substantial increase in the ratio, the impact on the firm's credit rating or stock price may be minimal. To the extent that the financial markets are efficient, the information was already known by analysts who took the data from footnotes or other sources and made their own adjustments. Nevertheless, corporate financial officers fought long, hard, and unsuccessfully to keep the lease obligation off the balance sheet. They tend to be much less convinced about the efficiency of the marketplace.

Capital Lease versus Operating Lease

Not all leases must be capitalized (present-valued) and placed on the balance sheet. This treatment is necessary only when substantially all the benefits and risks of ownership are transferred in a lease. Under these circumstances, we have a **capital lease** (also referred to as a financing lease). Identification as a capital lease and the attendant financial treatment are required whenever any one of the four following conditions is present:

1. The arrangement transfers ownership of the property to the lessee (the leasing party) by the end of the lease term.
2. The lease contains a bargain purchase price at the end of the lease. The option price will have to be sufficiently low so exercise of the option appears reasonably certain.
3. The lease term is equal to 75 percent or more of the estimated life of the leased property.
4. The present value of the minimum lease payments equals 90 percent or more of the fair value of the leased property at the inception of the lease.[6]

A lease that does not meet any of these four criteria is not regarded as a capital lease, but as an **operating lease**. An operating lease is usually short-term and is often cancelable at the option of the lessee. Furthermore, the lessor (the owner of the asset) may provide for the maintenance and upkeep of the asset, since he or she is likely to get it back. An operating lease does not require the *capitalization,* or presentation, of the full obligation on the balance sheet. Operating leases are used most frequently with such assets as automobiles and office equipment, while capital leases are used with oil drilling equipment, airplanes and rail equipment, certain forms of real estate, and other long-term assets. The greatest volume of leasing obligations is represented by capital leases.

---

[6]The discount rate used for this test is the leasing firm's new cost of borrowing or the lessor's (the firm that owns the asset) implied rate of return under the lease. The lower of the two must be used when both are known.

Income Statement Effect

The capital lease calls not only for present-valuing the lease obligation on the balance sheet but also for treating the arrangement for income statement purposes as if it were somewhat similar to a purchase-borrowing arrangement. Thus, under a capital lease, the intangible asset account previously shown in Table 16–8 on page 505 as "Leased property under capital lease" is amortized, or written off, over the life of the lease with an annual expense deduction. Also, the liability account shown in Table 16–8 as "Obligation under capital lease" is written off through regular amortization, with an implied interest expense on the remaining balance. Thus, for financial reporting purposes the annual deductions are amortization of the asset, plus the implied interest expense on the remaining present value of the liability. Though the actual development of these values and accounting rules is best deferred to an accounting course, the finance student should understand the close similarity between a capital lease and borrowing to purchase an asset, for financial reporting purposes.

An operating lease, on the other hand, usually calls for an annual expense deduction equal to the lease payment, with no specific amortization, as is indicated in Appendix 16B, "Lease versus Purchase Decision," at the end of this chapter.

Advantages of Leasing

Why is leasing so popular? It has emerged as a trillion-dollar industry, with such firms as Clark Equipment, GECapital, and U.S. Leasing International providing an enormous amount of financing. Major reasons for the popularity of leasing include the following:

1. The lessee may lack sufficient funds or the credit capability to purchase the asset from a manufacturer, who is willing, however, to accept a lease arrangement or to arrange a lease obligation with a third party.

2. The provisions of a lease obligation may be substantially less restrictive than those of a bond indenture.

3. There may be no down payment requirement, as would generally be the case in the purchase of an asset (leasing allows for a larger indirect loan).

4. The lessor may possess particular expertise in a given industry—allowing for expert product selection, maintenance, and eventual resale. Through this process, the negative effects of obsolescence may be reduced.

5. Creditor claims on certain types of leases, such as real estate, are restricted in bankruptcy and reorganization proceedings. Leases on chattels (non-real estate items) have no such limitation.

There are also some tax factors to be considered. Where one party to a lease is in a higher tax bracket than the other party, certain tax advantages, such as depreciation write-off or research-related tax credits, may be better utilized. For example, a wealthy party may purchase an asset for tax purposes, then lease the asset to another party in a lower tax bracket for actual use. Also, lease payments on the use of land are tax-deductible, whereas land ownership does not allow a similar deduction for depreciation.

Finally, a firm may wish to engage in a sale-leaseback arrangement, in which assets already owned by the lessee are sold to the lessor and then leased back. This process provides the lessee with an infusion of capital, while allowing the lessee to continue to use the asset. Even though the dollar costs of a leasing arrangement are often higher than the dollar costs of owning an asset, the advantages cited above may outweigh the direct cost factors.

Summary

Corporate bonds may be secured by a lien on a specific asset or may carry an unsecured designation, indicating the bondholder possesses a general claim against the corporation. A special discussion of the hierarchy of claims for firms in financial distress is presented in Appendix 16A.

Both the issuing corporation and the investor are concerned about the rating their bond is assigned by the two major bond rating agencies—Moody's Investor Service and Standard & Poor's Corporation. The higher the rating assigned a given issue, the lower the required interest payments needed to satisfy potential investors. This is because highly rated bonds carry lower risk.

Bond refundings may take place when interest rates are going down. The financial manager must consider whether the savings in interest will compensate for the additional cost of calling in the old issue and selling a new one.

The zero-coupon rate bond, as the name implies, does not pay interest. It is, however, sold at a deep discount from face value. The return to the investor is the difference between the investor's cost and the face value received at the end of the life of the bond.

A second type of innovative bond issue is the floating rate bond. In this case, instead of a change in the price of the bond, the interest rate paid on the bond changes with market conditions (usually monthly or quarterly).

When a corporation contracts to lease an oil tanker or a computer and signs a noncancelable, long-term agreement, the transaction has all the characteristics of a debt obligation, and should be recognized as such on the financial statements of the firm.

List of Terms

par value 489	call provision 492
maturity date 490	coupon rate 495
indenture 490	current yield 495
secured debt 490	yield to maturity 495
mortgage agreement 490	bond rating 497
after-acquired property	refunding 498
clause 490	zero-coupon rate bond 502
debenture 490	floating rate bond 503
subordinated debenture 491	Eurobond 504
serial payment 491	capital lease 506
sinking fund 492	operating lease 506

Discussion Questions

1. Corporate debt has been expanding very dramatically in the last three decades. What has been the impact on interest coverage, particularly since 1977?

2. What are some specific features of bond agreements?

3. What is the difference between a bond agreement and a bond indenture?

4. Discuss the relationship between the coupon rate (original interest rate at time of issue) on a bond and its security provisions.

5. Take the following list of securities and arrange them in order of their priority of claims:

Preferred stock	Senior debenture
Subordinated debenture	Senior secured debt
Common stock	Junior secured debt

6. What method of "bond repayment" reduces debt and increases the amount of common stock outstanding?

7. What is the purpose of serial repayments and sinking funds?

8. Under what circumstances would a call on a bond be exercised by a corporation? What is the purpose of a deferred call?

9. Discuss the relationship between bond prices and interest rates. What impact do changing interest rates have on the price of long-term bonds versus short-term bonds?

10. What is the difference between the following yields: coupon rate, current yield, yield to maturity?

11. How does the bond rating affect the interest rate paid by a corporation on its bonds?

12. Bonds of different risk classes will have a spread between their interest rates. Is this spread always the same? Why?

13. Explain how the bond refunding problem is similar to a capital budgeting decision.

14. What cost of capital is generally used in evaluating a bond refunding decision? Why?

15. Explain how the zero-coupon rate bond provides return to the investor. What are the advantages to the corporation?

16. Explain how floating rate bonds can save the investor from potential embarrassments in portfolio valuations.

17. Discuss the advantages and disadvantages of debt.

18. What is a Eurobond?

19. What do we mean by capitalizing lease payments?

20. Explain the close parallel between a capital lease and the borrow–purchase decision from the viewpoint of both the balance sheet and the income statement.

---

1. The Gorden Corporation has a bond outstanding with $85 annual interest payments, a market price of $860, and a maturity date in seven years.
    Compute the following:

    a. The coupon rate.

    b. The current yield.

    c. The yield to maturity.

Practice Problems and Solutions

Bond yields

Refunding decision

2.   The Hudson Corporation has a $15 million bond obligation outstanding which it is considering refunding. Though the bonds were initially issued at 9 percent, the interest rates on similar issues have declined to 7.2 percent. The bonds were originally issued for 15 years and have 10 years remaining. The new issue would be for 10 years. There is a 9 percent call premium on the old issue. The underwriting cost on the new $15,000,000 issue is $200,000, and the underwriting cost on the old issue was $450,000. The company is in a 30 percent tax bracket, and it will use a 5 percent discount rate (rounded aftertax cost of debt) to analyze the refunding decision.

Should the old issue be refunded with new debt?

Solutions

1. *a.* $85 interest/$1,000 par = 8.5% coupon rate

    b. $85 interest/$860 market price = $9.88% current yield

    c.   Approximate yield to maturity = (Y′)

$$Y' = \frac{\text{Annual interest payment} + \dfrac{\text{Principal payment} - \text{Price of bond}}{\text{Number of years to maturity}}}{0.6\,(\text{Price of bond}) + 0.4\,(\text{Principal payment})}$$

$$= \frac{\$85 + \dfrac{\$1,000 - 860}{7}}{.6(\$860) + .4(\$1,000)}$$

$$= \frac{\$85 + \dfrac{\$140}{7}}{\$516 + \$400}$$

$$= \frac{\$85 + 20}{\$916} = \frac{\$105}{916} = 11.46\%$$

2.   **Outflows**

     1.   Payment of call premium (cost)

$$\$15,000,000 \times 9\% = \$1,350,000$$
$$\$1,350,000 \times (1 - .30) = \$945,000$$

     2.   Underwriting cost on new issue

Actual expenditure $200,000
Amortization of cost ($200,000/10) .30
$20,000 × (.30) = $6,000 tax savings per year
PV of future tax savings (n = 10, i = 5%)   Appendix D
$6,000 × 7.722 = $46,332

Actual expenditure	$200,000
− PV of future tax savings	46,332
Net cost of underwriting expense on new issue	$153,668

Inflows

3. Cost savings in lower interest rates

9% (interest on old bonds) × $15,000,000 = ...	$1,350,000	per year
7.2% (interest on new bonds) × $15,000,000 = ...	1,080,000	per year
Savings per year	$270,000	
Savings per year after tax $270,000 (1 − .3)	$189,000	
PV of future savings (n = 10, i = 5 %)		Appendix D
$189,000 × 7.722 = ...	$1,459,458	

4. Underwriting cost on old issue

Original amount.	$450,000
Annual write-off $450,000/15 = ...	30,000
Amount written off over initial 5 years at $30,000 per year	$150,000
Unamortized old underwriting cost.	$300,000

PV of future write-off of $30,000 per year:

n = 10 (years remaining i = 5%   Appendix D

PV = 30,000 × 7.722 = $231,660

Take the difference between the unamortized old underwriting costs of $300,000 and the PV of the future write-off of $231,600.

Immediate write-off of unamortized old underwriting costs	$300,000
−PV of future write-off	231,660
Net gain from immediate write-off.	$ 68,340
Multiply this figure by the tax rate to get the net tax benefit	$ 68,340
of the immediate write-off	.30
	$ 20,502

Summarize the inflows and outflows to get the net present value

Outflows		**Inflows**	
1. Net cost of call premium	$945,000	3. Cost savings in lower interest rates.	$1,459,458
2. Net cost of underwriting expense on new issue	153,668	4. Net gain from underwriting expense on old issue	20,502
	$1,098,668		$1,479,960
		Present value of inflows	$1,479,960
		Present value of outflows	1,098,668
		Net present value	$ 381,292

Due to the positive net present value, the old issue should be refunded.

Problems

All problems are available in Homework Manager. Please see the preface for more information.

(Assume the par value of the bonds in the following problems is $1,000 unless otherwise specified.)

Bond yields

1. Garland Corporation has a bond outstanding with a $90 annual interest payment, a market price of $820, and a maturity date in five years.
   Find the following:
   a. The coupon rate.
   b. The current rate.
   c. The approximate yield to maturity.

Bond yields

2. Preston Corporation has a bond outstanding with a $110 annual interest payment, a market price of $1,200, and a maturity date in 10 years.
   Find the following:
   a. The coupon rate.
   b. The current rate.
   c. The approximate yield to maturity.

Bond yields

3. An investor must choose between two bonds:
   Bond A pays $80 annual interest and has a market value of $800. It has 10 years to maturity.
   Bond B pays $85 annual interest and has a market value of $900. It has two years to maturity.
   a. Compute the current yield on both bonds.
   b. Which bond should he select based on your answer to part *a*?
   c. A drawback of current yield is that it does not consider the total life of the bond. For example, the approximate yield to maturity on Bond A is 11.36 percent. What is the approximate yield to maturity on Bond B?
   d. Has your answer changed between parts *b* and *c* of this question in terms of which bond to select?

Bond yields   ✗

4. An investor must choose between two bonds:
   Bond A pays $92 annual interest and has a market value of $875. It has 10 years to maturity. Bond B pays $82 annual interest and has a market value of $900. It has two years to maturity.
   a. Compute the current yield on both bonds.
   b. Which bond should she select based on your answer to part *a*?
   c. A drawback of current yield is that it does not consider the total life of the bond. For example, the approximate yield to maturity on Bond A is 11.30 percent. What is the approximate yield to maturity on Bond B?
   d. Has your answer changed between parts *b* and *c* of this question in terms of which bond to select?

Secured vs. unsecured debt

5. Match the yield to maturity in column 2 with the security provisions (or lack thereof) in column 1. Higher returns tend to go with greater risk.

	(1)		(2)
a.	Debenture...............	a.	7.79%
b.	Secured debt	b.	9.17%
c.	Subordinated debenture ..	c.	8.67%

6. The Florida Investment Fund buys 90 bonds of the Gator Corporation through a broker. The bonds pay 8 percent annual interest. The yield to maturity (market rate of interest) is 10 percent. The bonds have a 25-year maturity.

    Using an assumption of semiannual interest payments:

    a. Compute the price of a bond (refer to "Semiannual interest and bond prices" in Chapter 10 for review if necessary).

    b. Compute the total value of the 90 bonds.

    Bond value

7. Cox Media Corporation pays an 11 percent coupon rate on debentures that are due in 20 years. The current yield to maturity on bonds of similar risk is 8 percent. The bonds are currently callable at $1,060. The theoretical value of the bonds will be equal to the present value of the expected cash flow from the bonds.

    a. Find the theoretical market value of the bonds using semiannual analysis.

    b. Do you think the bonds will sell for the price you arrived at in part *a*? Why?

    Bond value

8. The yield to maturity for 15-year bonds is as follows for four different bond rating categories.

    Effect of bond rating change

    | Aaa 9.4% .... | Aa2 10.0% |
    | Aa1 9.6% .... | Aa3 10.2% |

    The bonds of Falter Corporation were rated as Aa1 and issued at par a few weeks ago. The bonds have just been downgraded to Aa2. Determine the new price of the bonds, assuming a 15-year maturity and semiannual interest payments. (Refer to page 292 in Chapter 10 for a review if necessary.)

9. Twenty-five-year B-rated bonds of Katz Copying Machines were initially issued at a 12 percent yield. After 10 years the bonds have been upgraded to Aa2. Such bonds are currently yielding 10 percent. Use Table 16–3 on page 495 to determine the price of the bonds with 15 years remaining to maturity. (You do not need the bond ratings to enter the table; just use the basic facts of the problem.)

    Interest rates and bond ratings

10. A previously issued A2, 15-year industrial bond provides a return one-fourth higher than the prime interest rate of 8 percent. Previously issued A2 public utility bonds provide a yield of three-eighths of a percentage point higher than previously issued A2 industrial bonds of equal quality. Finally, new issues of A2 public utility bonds pay one-fourth of a percentage point more than previously issued A2 public utility bonds.

    What should be the interest rate on a newly issued A2 public utility bond?

    Interest rates and bond ratings

11. A 20-year, $1,000 par value, zero-coupon rate bond is to be issued to yield 11 percent.

    Zero-coupon rate bond

    a. What should be the initial price of the bond? (Take the present value of $1,000 for 20 years at 11 percent, using Appendix B.)

    b. If immediately upon issue, interest rates dropped to 9 percent, what would be the value of the zero-coupon rate bond?

c. If immediately upon issue, interest rates increased to 13 percent, what would be the value of the zero-coupon rate bond?

Zero-coupon bond yield

12. What is the effective yield to maturity on a zero-coupon bond that sells for $116 and will mature in 25 years at $1,000? (Compute PV_{IF} and go to Appendix B for the 25-year figure to find the answer, or compute FV_{IF} and go to Appendix A for the 25-year figure. Either approach will work.)

Floating rate bond

13. You buy a 7 percent, 30-year, $1,000 par value, floating rate bond in 2001. By the year 2007, rates on bonds of similar risk are up to 9 percent. What is your one best guess as to the value of the bond?

Effect of inflation on purchasing power of bond

14. Twelve years ago, the Archer Corporation borrowed $6,000,000. Since then, cumulative inflation has been 80 percent (a compound rate of approximately 5 percent per year).

a. When the firm repays the original $6,000,000 loan this year, what will be the effective purchasing power of the $6,000,000? (Hint: Divide the loan amount by one plus cumulative inflation.)

b. To maintain the original $6,000,000 purchasing power, how much should the lender be repaid? (Hint: Multiply the loan amount by one plus cumulative inflation.)

c. If the lender knows he will receive only $6,000,000 in payment after 12 years, how might he be compensated for the loss in purchasing power? A descriptive answer is acceptable.

Profit potential associated with margin

15. A $1,000 par value bond was issued 25 years ago at a 12 percent coupon rate. It currently has 15 years remaining to maturity. Interest rates on similar debt obligations are now 8 percent.

a. What is the current price of the bond? (Look up the answer in Table 16–3.)

b. Assume Ms. Russell bought the bond three years ago when it had a price of $1,070. What is her dollar profit based on the bond's current price?

c. Further assume Ms. Russell paid 30 percent of the purchase price in cash and borrowed the rest (known as buying on margin). She used the interest payments from the bond to cover the interest costs on the loan. How much of the purchase price of $1,070 did Ms. Russell pay in cash?

d. What is Ms. Russell's percentage return on her cash investment? Divide the answer to part b by the answer to part c.

e. Explain why her return is so high.

Loss exposure and profit potential

16. A $1,000 par value bond was issued 25 years ago at a 7 percent coupon rate. It currently has 10 years remaining to maturity. Interest rates on similar debt obligations are now 12 percent.

a. Compute the current price of the bond using an assumption of semiannual payments.

b. If Mr. Robinson initially bought the bond at par value, what is his percentage loss (or gain)?

c. Now assume Mrs. Pinson buys the bond at its current market value and holds it to maturity, what will her percentage return be?

d. Although the same dollar amounts are involved in part b and c, explain why the percentage gain is larger than the percentage loss.

✗ 17. The Bowman Corporation has a $20 million bond obligation outstanding, which it is considering refunding. Though the bonds were initially issued at 12 percent, the interest rates on similar issues have declined to 10.5 percent. The bonds were originally issued for 20 years and have 15 years remaining. The new issue would be for 15 years. There is an 8 percent call premium on the old issue. The underwriting cost on the new $20,000,000 issue is $570,000, and the underwriting cost on the old issue was $400,000. The company is in a 35 percent tax bracket, and it will use a 7 percent discount rate (rounded aftertax cost of debt) to analyze the refunding decision.

Should the old issue be refunded with new debt?

Refunding decision

18. The Robinson Corporation has $50 million of bonds outstanding that were issued at a coupon rate of 11¾ percent seven years ago. Interest rates have fallen to 10¾ percent. Mr. Brooks, the vice-president of finance, does not expect rates to fall any further. The bonds have 18 years left to maturity, and Mr. Brooks would like to refund the bonds with a new issue of equal amount also having 18 years to maturity. The Robinson Corporation has a tax rate of 35 percent. The underwriting cost on the old issue was 2.5 percent of the total bond value. The underwriting cost on the new issue will be 1.8 percent of the total bond value. The original bond indenture contained a five-year protection against a call, with a 9.5 percent call premium starting in the sixth year and scheduled to decline by one-half percent each year thereafter. (Consider the bond to be seven years old for purposes of computing the premium.) Assume the discount rate is equal to the aftertax cost of new debt rounded up to the nearest whole number. Should the Robinson Corporation refund the old issue?

Refunding decision

19. In Problem 18, what would be the aftertax cost of the call premium at the end of year 13 (in dollar value)?

Call premium

20. The Deluxe Corporation has just signed a 120-month lease on an asset with a 15-year life. The minimum lease payments are $2,000 per month ($24,000 per year) and are to be discounted back to the present at a 7 percent annual discount rate. The estimated fair value of the property is $175,000.

Should the lease be recorded as a capital lease or an operating lease?

Capital lease or operating lease

21. The Ellis Corporation has heavy lease commitments. Prior to *SFAS No. 13,* it merely footnoted lease obligations in the balance sheet, which appeared as follows.

Balance sheet effect of leases

In $ millions		In $ millions	
Current assets	$ 50	Current liabilities	$ 10
Fixed assets	50	Long-term liabilities	30
		Total liabilities	$ 40
		Stockholders' equity.	60
		Total liabilities and	
Total assets	$100	stockholders' equity	$100

The footnotes stated that the company had $10 million in annual capital lease obligations for the next 20 years.

a. Discount these annual lease obligations back to the present at a 6 percent discount rate (round to the nearest million dollars).

b. Construct a revised balance sheet that includes lease obligations, as in Table 16–8 on page 505.

c. Compute total debt to total assets on the original and revised balance sheets.

d. Compute total debt to equity on the original and revised balance sheets.

e. In an efficient capital market environment, should the consequences of *SFAS No. 13,* as viewed in the answers to parts *c* and *d*, change stock prices and credit ratings?

f. Comment on management's perception of market efficiency (the viewpoint of the financial officer).

Determining size of lease payments   22.   The Hardaway Corporation plans to lease a $900,000 asset to the O'Neil Corporation. The lease will be for 10 years.

a. If the Hardaway Corporation desires a 12 percent return on its investment, how much should the lease payments be?

b. If the Hardaway Corporation is able to take a 10 percent deduction from the purchase price of $900,000 and will pass the benefits along to the O'Neil Corporation in the form of lower lease payments (related to the Hardaway Corporation's lower initial net cost), how much should the revised lease payments be? Continue to assume the Hardaway Corporation desires a 12 percent return on the 10-year lease.

COMPREHENSIVE PROBLEM

Broadband, Inc. Bond prices, refunding

Barton Simpson, the chief financial officer of Broadband, Inc., could hardly believe the change in interest rates that had taken place over the last few months. The interest rate on A2 rated bonds was now 6 percent. The $30 million, 15-year bond issue that his firm has outstanding was initially issued at 9 percent five years ago.

Because interest rates had gone down so much, he was considering refunding the bond issue. The old issue had a call premium of 8 percent. The underwriting cost on the old issue had been 3 percent of par and on the new issue, it would be 5 percent of par. The tax rate would be 30 percent and a 4 percent discount rate would be applied for the refunding decision. The new bond would have a 10-year life.

Before Barton used the 8 percent call provision to reacquire the old bonds, he wanted to make sure he could not buy them back cheaper in the open market.

a. First compute the price of the old bonds in the open market. Use the valuation procedures for a bond that were discussed in Chapter 10 (use annual analysis). Determine the price of a single $1,000 par value bond.

b. Compare the price in part *a* to the 8 percent call premium over par value. Which appears to be more attractive in terms of reacquiring the old bonds?

c. Now do the standard bond refunding analysis as discussed in this chapter. Is the refunding financially feasible?

d. In terms of the refunding decision, how should Barton be influenced if he thinks interest rates might go down even more?

WEB EXERCISE

We will examine the debt ratios for two airlines.

1. First go to finance.yahoo.com.
2. In the "Get Quotes" box, enter LUV for Southwest Airlines.
3. Scroll down along the left margin and click on "Balance Sheet."
4. Compute the ratio of Long-Term debt to Total Stockholders' Equity for the three years shown. Do the same thing for Total Liabilities to Total Stockholders' Equity.
5. Go back to the homepage and follow the same process for JetBlue Airways Corp. (JBLU).
6. Write a paragraph summary of the two airlines' debt ratios. Which company is in better condition?

Note: From time to time, companies redesign their Web sites and occasionally a topic we have listed may have been deleted, updated, or moved into a different location. If you click on the site map or site index, you will be introduced to a table of contents which should aid you in finding the topic you are looking for.

S&P PROBLEMS   www.mhhe.com/edumarketinsight

STANDARD &POOR'S

1. Log onto the S&P Market Insight Web site, www.mhhe.com/edumarketinsight.
2. Click on "Company," which is the first box below the Market Insight title.
3. Type American Airlines' ticker symbol "AMR1" in the box and click on Go.
4. Scroll down the left margin and click on "Excel Analytics." At the top of the left margin you will see the second item listed as Annual Balance Sheet.
5. Click on "Ann. Balance Sheet" and scroll down to the liabilities section. Over the years covered, what percentage has debt increased from the first year in the report to the most current year?
6. What has happened to the category called "Other Debt"?
7. How much have total liabilities increased over the period in dollar terms?
8. Compare total liabilities to total assets. What percentage of total assets is financed by debt?
9. Under the current liabilities section look at the category called "Long-term debt due in one year." What has happened to this number over the years?
10. Without looking at the income statement, determine what has been going on with profitability by examining the retained earnings account and the total equity account.

11. Can you explain what is happening with Net Plant and Equipment?
12. Please repeat the exercise using Southwest Airlines (LUV) and then compare the two companies.

APPENDIX | 16A

Financial Alternatives for Distressed Firms

A firm may be in financial distress because of **technical insolvency** or bankruptcy. The first term refers to a firm's inability to pay its bills as they come due. Thus, a firm may be technically insolvent, even though it has a positive net worth; there simply may not be sufficient liquid assets to meet current obligations. The second term, **bankruptcy**, indicates the market value of a firm's assets are less than its liabilities and the firm has a negative net worth. Under the law, either technical insolvency or bankruptcy may be adjudged as a financial failure of the business firm.

Many firms do not fall into either category but are still suffering from extreme financial difficulties. Perhaps they are rapidly approaching a situation in which they cannot pay their bills or their net worth will soon be negative.

Firms in the types of financial difficulty discussed in the first two paragraphs may participate in out-of-court settlements or in-court settlements through formal bankruptcy proceedings under the National Bankruptcy Act.

Out-of-court settlements, where possible, allow the firm and its creditors to bypass certain lengthy and expensive legal procedures. If an agreement cannot be reached on a voluntary basis between a firm and its creditors, in-court procedures will be necessary.

Out-of-Court Settlement

Out-of-court settlements may take many forms. Four alternatives will be examined. The first is an **extension**, in which creditors agree to allow the firm more time to meet its financial obligations. A new repayment schedule will be developed, subject to the acceptance of the creditors.

A second alternative is a **composition**, under which creditors agree to accept a fractional settlement of their original claim. They may be willing to do this because they believe the firm is unable to meet its total obligations and they wish to avoid formal bankruptcy procedures. In the case of either a proposed extension or a composition, some creditors may not agree to go along with the arrangements. If their claims are relatively small, major creditors may allow them to be paid off immediately in full to hold the agreement together. If their claims are large, no out-of-court settlement may be possible, and formal bankruptcy proceedings may be necessary.

A third type of out-of-court settlement may take the form of a **creditor committee** established to run the business. Here the parties involved assume management can no longer effectively conduct the affairs of the firm. Once the creditors' claims have been partially or fully settled, a new management team may be brought in to replace the creditor committee. The outgoing management may be willing to accept the imposition of a creditor committee only when formal bankruptcy proceedings appear likely and they wish to avoid that stigma. Sometimes creditors are unwilling to form such a committee because they fear lawsuits from other dissatisfied creditors or from common or preferred stockholders.

A fourth type of out-of-court settlement is an **assignment**, in which assets are liquidated without going through formal court action. To effect an assignment, creditors must agree on liquidation values and the relative priority of claims. This is not an easy task.

In actuality, there may be combinations of two or more of the above-described out-of-court procedures. For example, there may be an extension as well as a composition, or a creditor committee may help to establish one or more of the alternatives.

In-Court Settlements—Formal Bankruptcy

When it is apparent an out-of-court settlement cannot be reached, the next step is formal bankruptcy. Bankruptcy proceedings may be initiated voluntarily by the company or, alternatively, by creditors.

Once the firm falls under formal bankruptcy proceedings, a referee is appointed by the court to oversee the activities. The referee becomes the arbitrator of the proceedings, whose actions and decisions are final, subject only to review by the court. A trustee will also be selected to properly determine the assets and liabilities of the firm and to carry out a plan of reorganization or liquidation for the firm.

Reorganization   If the firm is to be reorganized (under the Bankruptcy Act's Chapter 11 restructuring), the plan must prove to be fair and feasible. An **internal reorganization** calls for an evaluation of current management and operating policies. If current management is shown to be incompetent, it will probably be discharged and replaced by new management. An evaluation and possible redesign of the current capital structure is also necessary. If the firm is top-heavy with debt (as is normally the case), alternate securities, such as preferred or common stock, may replace part of the debt.[1] Any restructuring must be fair to all parties involved.

An **external reorganization**, in which a merger partner is found for the firm, may also be considered. The surviving firm must be deemed strong enough to carry out the financial and management obligations of the joint entities. Old creditors and stockholders may be asked to make concessions to ensure that a feasible arrangement is established. Their motivation is that they hope to come out further ahead than if such a reorganization were not undertaken. Ideally the firm should be merged with a strong firm in its own industry, although this is not always possible. The savings and loan and banking industries have been particularly adept at merging weaker firms with stronger firms within the industry.

Liquidation   A **liquidation** or sale of assets may be recommended when an internal or external reorganization does not appear possible and it is determined that the assets of the firm are worth more in liquidation than through a reorganization. Priority of claims becomes extremely important in a liquidation, because it is unlikely that all parties will be fully satisfied in their demands.

---

[1]Another possibility is income bonds, in which interest is payable only if earned.

The priority of claims in a bankruptcy liquidation is as follows:

1. Cost of administering the bankruptcy procedures (lawyers get in line first).
2. Wages due workers if earned within three months of filing the bankruptcy petition. The maximum amount is $600 per worker.
3. Taxes due at the federal, state, or local level.
4. Secured creditors to the extent that designated assets are sold to meet their claims. Secured claims that exceed the sales value of the pledged assets are placed in the same category as other general creditor claims.
5. General or unsecured creditors are next in line. Examples of claims in this category are those held by debenture (unsecured bond) holders, trade creditors, and bankers who have made unsecured loans.

   There may be senior and subordinated positions within category 5, indicating that subordinated debt holders must turn over their claims to senior debt holders until complete restitution is made to the higher-ranked category. Subordinated debenture holders may keep the balance if anything is left over after that payment.
6. Preferred stockholders.
7. Common stockholders.

The priority of claims 4 through 7 is similar to that presented in Figure 16–2 on page 491 of the chapter.

Let us examine a typical situation to determine "who" should receive "what" under a liquidation in bankruptcy. Assume the Mitchell Corporation has a book value and liquidation value as shown in Table 16A–1. Liabilities and stockholders' claims are also presented.

Table 16A–1

Financial data for the Mitchell Corporation

Assets	Book Value	Liquidation Value
Accounts receivable	$ 200,000	$160,000
Inventory	410,000	240,000
Machinery and equipment	240,000	100,000
Building and plant	450,000	200,000
	$1,300,000	$700,000

Liabilities and Stockholders' Claims	
Liabilities:	
Accounts payable	$ 300,000
First lien, secured by machinery and equipment*	200,000
Senior unsecured debt	400,000
Subordinated debentures	200,000
Total liabilities	1,100,000
Stockholders' claims:	
Preferred stock	50,000
Common stock	150,000
Total stockholders' claims	200,000
Total liabilities and stockholders' claims	$1,300,000

*A lien represents a potential claim against property. The lien holder has a secured interest in the property.

We see that the liquidation value of the assets is far less than the book value ($700,000 versus $1.3 million). Also, the liquidation value of the assets will not cover the total value of liabilities ($700,000 compared to $1.1 million). Since all liability claims will not be met, it is evident that lower-ranked preferred stockholders and common stockholders will receive nothing.

Before a specific allocation is made to the creditors (those with liability claims), the three highest priority levels in bankruptcy must first be covered. That would include the cost of administering the proceedings, allowable past wages due to workers, and overdue taxes. For the Mitchell Corporation, we shall assume these total $100,000. Since the liquidation value of assets was $700,000, that would leave $600,000 to cover creditor demands, as indicated in the left-hand column of Table 16A–2.

Table 16A–2   Asset values and claims

Assets		Creditor Claims	
Asset values in liquidation..........	$700,000	Accounts payable.................	$ 300,000
Administrative costs, wages, and taxes....................	100,000	First lien, secured by machinery and equipment........	200,000
Remaining asset values	$600,000	Senior unsecured debt.............	400,000
		Subordinated debentures...........	200,000
		Total liabilities...................	$1,100,000

Before we attempt to allocate the values in the left-hand column of Table 16A–2 to the right-hand column, we must first identify any creditor claims that are secured by the pledge of a specific asset. In the present case, there is a first lien on the machinery and equipment of $200,000. Referring back to Table 16A–1, we observe that the machinery and equipment has a liquidation value of only $100,000. The secured debt holders will receive $100,000, with the balance of their claim placed in the same category as the unsecured debt holders. In Table 16A–3, we show asset values available for unsatisfied secured claims and unsecured debt (top portion) and the extent of the remaining claims (bottom portion).

Asset values:	
Asset values in liquidation.....................	$ 700,000
Administrative costs, wages, and taxes	100,000
Remaining asset values	600,000
Payment to secured creditors.................	−100,000
Amount available to unsatisfied secured claims and unsecured debt	$ 500,000
Remaining claims of unsatisfied secured debt and unsecured debt:	
Secured debt (unsatisfied first lien)	$ 100,000
Accounts payable........................	300,000
Senior unsecured debt....................	400,000
Subordinated debentures	200,000
	$1,000,000

Table 16A–3

Asset values available for unsatisfied secured claims and unsecured debt holders—and their remaining claims

In comparing the available asset values and claims in Table 16A–3, it appears that the settlement on the remaining claims should be at a 50 percent rate ($500,000/$1,000,000). The allocation will take place in the manner presented in Table 16A–4.

Table 16A–4

Allocation procedures for unsatisfied secured claims and unsecured debt

(1) Category	(2) Amount of Claim	(3) Initial Allocation (50%)	(4) Amount Received
Secured debt (unsatisfied 1st lien)	$ 100,000	$ 50,000	$ 50,000
Accounts payable	300,000	150,000	150,000
Senior unsecured debt	400,000	200,000	300,000
Subordinated debentures	200,000	100,000	0
	$1,000,000	$500,000	$500,000

Each category receives 50 percent as an initial allocation. However, the subordinated debenture holders must transfer their $100,000 initial allocation to the senior debt holders in recognition of their preferential position. The secured debt holders and those having accounts payable claims are not part of the senior-subordinated arrangement and, thus, hold their initial allocation position.

Finally, in Table 16A–5, we show the total amounts of claims, the amount received, and the percent of the claim that was satisfied.

Table 16A–5

Payments and percent of claims

(1) Category	(2) Total Amount of Claim	(3) Amount Received	(4) Percent of Claim
Secured debt (1st lien)	$200,000	$150,000	75%
Accounts payable	300,000	150,000	50
Senior unsecured debt	400,000	300,000	75
Subordinated debentures	200,000	0	0

The $150,000 in column (3) for secured debt represents the $100,000 from the sale of machinery and equipment, and $50,000 from the allocation process in Table 16A–4. The secured debt holders and senior unsecured debt holders come out on top in terms of percent of claim satisfied (it is coincidental that they are equal). Furthermore, the subordinated debt holders and, as previously mentioned, the preferred and common stockholders receive nothing. Naturally, allocations in bankruptcy will vary from circumstance to circumstance. Working problem 16A–1 will help to reinforce many of the liquidation procedure concepts discussed in this section.

List of Terms

16A–1.   What is the difference between technical insolvency and bankruptcy?

16A–2.   What are four types of out-of-court settlements? Briefly describe each.

16A–3.   What is the difference between an internal reorganization and an external reorganization under formal bankruptcy procedures?

16A–4.   What are the first three priority items under liquidation in bankruptcy?

16A–1.   The trustee in the bankruptcy settlement for Titanic Boat Co. lists the following book values and liquidation values for the assets of the corporation. Liabilities and stockholders' claims are also shown.

Assets

	Book Value	Liquidation Value
Accounts receivable	$1,400,000	$1,200,000
Inventory	1,800,000	900,000
Machinery and equipment	1,100,000	600,000
Building and plant	4,200,000	2,500,000
Total assets	$8,500,000	$5,200,000

Liabilities and Stockholders' Claims

Liabilities:	
Accounts payable	$2,800,000
First lien, secured by machinery and equipment	900,000
Senior unsecured debt	2,200,000
Subordinated debenture	1,700,000
Total liabilities	7,600,000
Stockholders' claims:	
Preferred stock	250,000
Common stock	650,000
Total stockholders' claims	900,000
Total liabilities and stockholders' claims	$8,500,000

a.   Compute the difference between the liquidation value of the assets and the liabilities.

b.   Based on the answer to part *a,* will preferred stock or common stock participate in the distribution?

c.   Assuming the administrative costs of bankruptcy, workers' allowable wages, and unpaid taxes add up to $400,000, what is the total of remaining asset value available to cover secured and unsecured claims?

d.   After the machinery and equipment are sold to partially cover the first lien secured claim, how much will be available from the remaining asset liquidation values to cover unsatisfied secured claims and unsecured debt?

e.   List the remaining asset claims of unsatisfied secured debt holders and unsecured debt holders in a manner similar to that shown at the bottom portion of Table 16A–3.

f. Compute a ratio of your answers in part *d* and part *e*. This will indicate the initial allocation ratio.

g. List the remaining claims (unsatisfied secured and unsecured) and make an initial allocation and final allocation similar to that shown in Table 16A–4. Subordinated debenture holders may keep the balance after full payment is made to senior debt holders.

h. Show the relationship of amount received to total amount of claim in a similar fashion to that of Table 16A–5 on page 522. (Remember to use the sales liquidation value for machinery and equipment plus the allocation amount in part *g* to arrive at the total received on secured debt.)

APPENDIX | 16B

Lease versus Purchase Decision

The classic lease versus purchase decision does not fit a *capital* leasing decision given the existence of *SFAS No. 13* and the similar financial accounting and tax treatment accorded to a capital lease and borrowing to purchase. Nevertheless, the classic lease versus purchase decision is still appropriate for the short-term *operating lease*.

Assume a firm is considering the purchase of a $6,000 asset in the three-year MACRS category (with a four-year write-off) or entering into two sequential operating leases, for two years each. Under the operating leases, the annual payments would be $1,400 on the first lease and $2,600 on the second lease. If a firm purchased the asset, it would pay $1,893 annually to amortize a $6,000 loan over four years at 10 percent interest. This is based on the use of Appendix D for the present value of an annuity.

$$A = \frac{PV_A}{PV_{IFA}} = \frac{\$6,000}{3.170} = \$1,893 \ (n = 4, i = 10\%)$$

The firm is in a 30 percent tax bracket. In doing our analysis, we look first at the aftertax costs of the operating lease arrangements in Table 16B–1. The tax shield in column (2) indicates the amount the lease payments will save us in taxes. In column (3) we see the net aftertax cost of the lease arrangement.

Table 16B–1
Aftertax cost of operating leases

Year	(1) Payment	(2) Tax Shield 30% of (1)	(3) Aftertax Cost
1.........	$1,400	$420	$ 980
2.........	1,400	420	980
3.........	2,000	700	1,820
4.........	2,600	780	1,820

For the borrowing and purchasing decision, we must consider not only the amount of the payment but also separate out those items that are tax-deductible. First we consider interest and then depreciation.

In Table 16B–2, we show an amortization table to pay off a $6,000 loan over four years at 10 percent interest with $1,893 annual payments. In column (1) we show the beginning balance for each year. This is followed by the annual payment in column (2). We then show the amount of interest we will pay on the beginning balance at a 10 percent rate in column (3). In column (4) we subtract the interest payment from the annual payment to determine how much is applied directly to the repayment of principal. In column (5) we subtract the repayment of principal from the beginning balance to get the year-end balance.

Year	(1) Beginning Balance	(2) Annual Payment	(3) Annual Interest 10% of (1)	(4) Repayment of Principal (2) − (3)	(5) Ending Balance (1) − (4)
1.........	$6,000	$1,893	$600	$1,293	$4,707
2.........	4,707	1,893	471	1,422	3,285
3.........	3,285	1,893	329	1,564	1,721
4.........	1,721	1,893	172	1,721	0

Table 16B–2
Amortization table

After determining our interest payment schedule, we look at the depreciation schedule that would apply to the borrow–purchase decision. Using the three-year MACRS depreciation category (with the associated four-year write-off), the asset is depreciated at the rates indicated in Table 16B–3.

Year	Depreciation Base	Depreciation Percentage	Depreciation
1.........	$6,000	.333	$1,998
2.........	6,000	.445	2,670
3.........	6,000	.148	888
4.........	6,000	.074	444
			$6,000

Table 16B–3
Depreciation schedule

We now bring our interest and depreciation schedules together in Table 16B–4 to determine the aftertax cost, or cash outflow, associated with the borrow–purchase decision.

Year	(1) Payment	(2) Interest	(3) Depreciation	(4) Total Tax Deductions (2) + (3)	(5) Tax Shield 30% × (4)	(6) Net Aftertax Cost (1) − (5)
1........	$1,893	$600	$1,998	$2,598	$779	$1,114
2........	1,893	471	2,670	3,141	942	951
3........	1,893	329	888	1,217	365	1,528
4........	1,893	172	444	616	185	1,708

Table 16B–4
Aftertax cost of borrow–purchase

The interest and depreciation charges are tax-deductible expenses and provide a tax shield against other income. The total deductions in column (4) are multiplied by the tax rate of 30 percent to show the tax shield benefits in column (5). In column (6), we subtract the tax shield from the payments to get the net aftertax cost, or cash outflow.

Finally, we compare the cash outflows from leasing to the cash outflows from borrowing and purchasing. To consider the time value of money, we discount the annual values at an interest rate of 7 percent. This is the aftertax cost of debt to the firm, and it is computed by multiplying the interest rate of 10 percent by (1–Tax rate). Because the costs associated with both leasing and borrowing are contractual and certain, we use the aftertax cost of debt as the discount rate, rather than the normal cost of capital. The overall analysis is presented in Table 16B–5.

Table 16B–5   Net present value comparison

Year	Aftertax Cost of Leasing	Present Value Factor at 7%	Present Value	Aftertax Cost of Borrow– Purchase	Present Value Factor at 7%	Present Value
1..........	$ 980	0.935	$ 916	$1,114	0.935	$1,042
2..........	980	0.873	856	951	0.873	830
3..........	1,820	0.816	1,485	1,528	0.816	1,247
4..........	1,820	0.763	1,389	1,708	0.763	1,303
			$4,646			$4,422

The borrow–purchase alternative has a lower present value of aftertax costs ($4,422 versus $4,646), which would appear to make it the more desirable alternative. However, many of the previously discussed qualitative factors that support leasing must also be considered in the decision-making process.

Problem

Lease versus purchase decision

16B–1.   Howell Auto Parts is considering whether to borrow funds and purchase an asset or to lease the asset under an operating lease arrangement. If the company purchases the asset, the cost will be $10,000. It can borrow funds for four years at 12 percent interest. The firm will use the three-year MACRS depreciation category (with the associated four-year write-off). Assume a tax rate of 35 percent.

The other alternative is to sign two operating leases, one with payments of $2,600 for the first two years, and the other with payments of $4,600 for the last two years. In your analysis, round all values to the nearest dollar.

  a.   Compute the aftertax cost of the leases for the four years.

  b.   Compute the annual payment for the loan (round to the nearest dollar).

  c.   Compute the amortization schedule for the loan. (Disregard a small difference from a zero balance at the end of the loan—due to rounding.)

  d.   Determine the depreciation schedule (see Table 12–9).

  e.   Compute the aftertax cost of the borrow–purchase alternative.

  f.   Compute the present value of the aftertax cost of the two alternatives. Use a discount rate of 8 percent.

  g.   Which alternative should be selected, based on minimizing the present value of aftertax costs?

17

Common and Preferred Stock Financing

527

chapter concepts

1 Common stockholders are the owners of the corporation and therefore have a claim to undistributed income, the right to elect the board of directors, and other privileges.

2 Cumulative voting provides minority stockholders with the potential for some representation on the board of directors.

3 A rights offering gives current stockholders a first option to purchase new shares.

4 Poison pills and other similar provisions may make it difficult for outsiders to take over a corporation against management's wishes.

5 Preferred stock is an intermediate type of security that falls somewhere between debt and common stock.

The ultimate ownership of the firm resides in **common stock**, whether it is in the form of all outstanding shares of a closely held corporation or one share of IBM. In terms of legal distinctions, it is the common stockholder alone who directly controls the business. While control of the company is legally in the shareholders' hands, it is practically wielded by management on an everyday basis. It is also important to realize that a large creditor may exert tremendous pressure on a firm to meet certain standards of financial performance, even though the creditor has no voting power.

Often in small companies the founders control the company, but as small companies grow, they attract attention, sell more shares of stock, and the founders' percentage of ownership is diluted. One such small company is Ceradyne, a manufacturer of ceramics for the automotive industry, the dental industry, and the military. In 2001 Ceradyne had sales of $45 million dollars and was growing at a modest rate. However after September 11, 2001, the world changed and the

United States went to war in Iraq. One of Ceradyne's products was ceramic body armor and as the war progressed, body armor became more in demand. Order after order followed from the U.S. government and Ceradyne's sales grew to $101 million in 2003, to $215 million in 2004, and close to $370 million in 2005. According to Standard and Poor's, its five-year sales growth rate between 2001 and 2005 was 42 percent and its net income grew 59 percent. Ceradyne's stock price went from $4.89 on January 3, 2002, to $50 on January 18, 2006.

The demands on Ceradyne's manufacturing capability were enormous for a company so small, and in 2004 the company borrowed $109 million in long-term debt to increase its production capabilities. By December 2005, it needed more capital for expansion and so the firm went to the stock market with a secondary offering of 1.8 million shares of common stock. At an offering price of $43.31, the sale of stock provided almost $78 million in equity. At the same time Ceradyne sold $110 million of senior subordinated convertible notes due in 2035. The idea is that at sometime in the future, the stock price will continue to rise and these notes will be converted into common stock. If that happens, Ceradyne will not have to come up with the cash to pay off the notes.

The total amount raised was $188 million, which almost equaled the firm's sales for the previous year and over half of its sales for the year 2005. The additional capital allowed Ceradyne to add new plant and equipment to meet the increasing demand for its products. It also allowed the company to add the necessary working capital in the form of inventory, and to finance the increasing accounts receivable balances. This offering balanced the sale of stock (equity) and bonds (liabilities) and kept the balance sheet ratios relatively stable. The stock offering allowed Ceradyne to also issue bonds, because without the stock offering the bond offering alone would have created too much leverage and increased the financial risk of the company. The question now is what happens to Ceradyne once the war in Iraq is over. Will demand for diesel engines and orthodontia material offset the decline in sales of ceramic body armor? Will the firm use some of its capital to expand into other areas of business that use ceramic materials? You can check out its progress at www.ceradyne.com.

In this chapter we will also look closely at preferred stock. Preferred stock plays a secondary role in financing the corporate enterprise. It represents a hybrid security, combining some of the features of debt and common stock. Though preferred stockholders do not have an ownership interest in the firm, they do have a priority of claims to dividends that is superior to that of common stockholders.

To understand the rights and characteristics of the different means of financing, we shall examine the powers accorded to shareholders under each arrangement. In the case of common stock, everything revolves around three key rights: the residual claim to income, the voting right, and the right to purchase new shares. We shall examine each of these in detail and then consider the rights of preferred stockholders.

Common Stockholders' Claim to Income

All income that is not paid out to creditors or preferred stockholders automatically belongs to common stockholders. Thus we say they have a **residual claim to income**. This is true regardless of whether these residual funds are actually paid out in dividends or retained in the corporation. A firm that earns $10 million before capital costs and pays $1 million in interest to bondholders and a like amount in dividends to preferred stockholders will have $8 million available for common stockholders.[1] Perhaps half of that will be paid out as common stock dividends and the balance will be reinvested in the business for the benefit of stockholders, with the hope of providing even greater income, dividends, and price appreciation in the future.

Of course, it should be pointed out the common stockholder does not have a legal or enforceable claim to dividends. Whereas a bondholder may force the corporation into bankruptcy for failure to make interest payments, the common stockholder must accept circumstances as they are or attempt to change management if a new dividend policy is desired.

Occasionally a company will have several classes of common stock outstanding that carry different rights to dividends and income. For example, Dow Jones & Company,

---

[1] Tax consequences related to interest payments are ignored for the present.

Google, and Ford Motor Company have two separate classes of common stock that differentiate the shares of founders from other stockholders and grant preferential rights to founders' shares.

Although there are over 80 million common stockholders in the United States, increasingly ownership is being held by large institutional interests, such as pension funds, mutual funds, or bank trust departments, rather than individual investors. As would be expected, management has become more sensitive to these large stockholders who may side with corporate raiders in voting their shares for or against merger offers or takeover attempts (these topics are covered in Chapter 20). Table 17–1 presents a list of major companies with high percentages of common stock owned by institutions at the end of June 2005. Institutional investors owned 78.18 percent of General Motors, 60.33 percent of Coca-Cola, and 34.34 percent of Wal-Mart Stores.

Company Name	Institutional Ownership	Ownership in Shares (000s)
General Motors Corp.	78.18%	442,110
Hewlett-Packard Co.	71.76	2,056,049
Motorola, Inc.	68.97	1,702,975
Bristol-Myers Squibb Co.	68.53	1,329,721
Amazon.com	68.04	281,987
Minnesota Mining & Manufacturing	67.36	525,639
Disney	67.20	1,350,736
PepsiCo, Inc.	66.89	1,111,102
e-Bay	65.28	885,958
Johnson & Johnson	64.85	1,929,357
Du Pont Co.	60.59	602,762
Coca-Cola Co.	60.33	1,434,347
Procter & Gamble	59.26	1,465,443
General Electric	55.59	5,893,027
Microsoft	55.48	5,905,401
International Business Machines	53.88	859,802
ExxonMobil	50.57	3,146,795
Wal-Mart Stores	34.34	1,429,649

Source: Data is 2nd Quarter 2005 and taken from various issues of *Value Line Investment Survey.*

Table 17–1

Institutional ownership of U.S. companies

The Voting Right

Because common stockholders are the owners of a firm, they are accorded the right to vote in the election of the board of directors and on all other major issues. Common stockholders may cast their ballots as they see fit on a given issue, or assign a **proxy**, or "power to cast their ballot," to management or some outside contesting group. As mentioned in the previous section, some corporations have different classes of common stock with unequal voting rights.

There is also the issue of "founders' stock." Perhaps the Ford Motor Company is the biggest and best example of such stock. Class B shares were used to differentiate between the original **founders' shares** and those shares sold to the public. The founders wanted to preserve partial control of the company while at the same time raise new capital for expansion. The regular common stock (no specific class) has one vote per share and is entitled to elect 60 percent of the board of directors, and the Class B shares have one vote per share but are entitled, as a class of shareholders, to elect 40 percent of the board of directors. Class B stock is reserved solely for Ford family members or their descendants, trusts, or appointed interests. The Ford family has a very important position in Henry Ford's company without owning more than about 3½ percent of the current outstanding stock. Both common and Class B stockowners share in dividends equally, and no stock dividends may be given unless to both common and Class B stockholders in proportion to their ownership. Class B is convertible into regular common stock on a share-for-share basis.

While common stockholders and the different classes of common stock that they own may, at times, have different voting rights, they do have a vote. Bondholders and preferred stockholders may vote only when a violation of their corporate agreement exists and a subsequent acceleration of their rights takes place. For example, Continental Illinois Corporation was on the edge of bankruptcy in 1984, and failed to pay dividends on one series of preferred stock for five quarters from July 1, 1984, to September 30, 1985. The preferred stockholder agreement stated that failure to pay dividends for six consecutive quarters would result in the preferred stockholders being able to elect two directors to the board to represent their interests. Continental Illinois declared a preferred dividend in November 1985 and paid all current and past dividends on the preferred stock, thus avoiding the special voting privileges for preferred stockholders. The bank continued to recover and instituted dividends on common stock in 1990. In 1994 Continental was again in a healthy financial condition but much smaller than in 1984 and was bought by BankAmerica to become the California bank's corporate banking center.

Cumulative Voting

The most important voting matter is the election of the board of directors. As indicated in Chapter 1, the board has primary responsibility for the stewardship of the corporation. If illegal or imprudent decisions are made, the board can be held legally accountable. Furthermore, members of the board of directors normally serve on a number of important subcommittees of the corporation, such as the audit committee, the long-range financial planning committee, and the salary and compensation committee. The board may be elected through the familiar majority rule system or by cumulative voting. Under **majority voting**, any group of stockholders owning over 50 percent of the common stock may elect all of the directors. Under **cumulative voting**, it is possible for those who hold less than a 50 percent interest to elect some of the directors. The provision for some minority interests on the board is important to those who, at times, wish to challenge the prerogatives of management.

The type of voting has become more important to stockholders and management with the threat of takeovers, leveraged buyouts, and other challenges to management's control of the firm. In many cases large minority stockholders, seeking a voice in the operations and direction of the company, desire seats on the board of directors. To further their goals several have gotten stockholders to vote on the issue of cumulative voting at the annual meeting.

Apple's New Board Member

Computer pioneer and Apple CEO Steve Jobs had this to say about Apple's newest board member. "Al brings an incredible wealth of knowledge and wisdom to Apple from having helped run the largest organization in the world—the United States Government—as a Congressman, Senator, and our 45th Vice-President. Al is also an avid Mac user and does his own video editing in Final Cut Pro."

If you are thinking Al Gore, you are correct. While in Congress, Gore popularized the term "Information Highway" and was a strong advocate of wiring every classroom in the country to the Internet. He also has academic credentials with a BA in Government from Harvard University and currently serves as a visiting professor at UCLA, Fisk University, and Middle Tennessee State University. He also serves in an advisory capacity to Google, Inc.

In polishing the apple just a little, Mr. Gore said, "Steve and his team have done an incredible job in making Apple once again the best in the world." Of course, Mr. Gore has to remain aware of the fiduciary responsibility he has to the stockholders of Apple. An impressive resumé used to be the basis for corporate directorships but no longer is. The corporation and its directors are frequently sued by dissident stockholders and must demonstrate they acted in a well-informed and prudent manner. Superstar status alone is not an appropriate defense in the courtroom.

In return for the responsibilities they take on for large public corporations, outside directors are normally paid $75,000 to $150,000 a year in director's fees and may have other stock-related incentives as well. They normally attend four major board meetings a year and also serve on various committees.

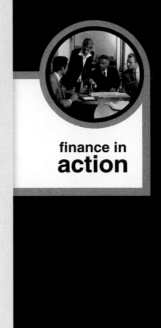

finance in action

How does this cumulative voting process work? A stockholder gets one vote for each share of stock he or she owns, times one vote for each director to be elected. The stockholder may then accumulate votes in favor of a specified number of directors.

Assume there are 10,000 shares outstanding, you own 1,001, and nine directors are to be elected. Your total number of votes under a cumulative election system is:

Number of shares owned	1,001
Number of directors to be elected	9
Number of votes	9,009

Let us assume you cast all your votes for the one director of your choice. With nine directors to be elected, there is no way for the owners of the remaining shares to exclude you from electing a person to one of the top nine positions. If you own 1,001 shares, the majority interest could control a maximum of 8,999 shares. This would entitle them to 80,991 votes.

Number of shares owned (majority)	8,999
Number of directors to be elected	9
Number of votes (majority)	80,991

These 80,991 votes cannot be spread thinly enough over nine candidates to stop you from electing your one director. If they are spread evenly, each of the majority's nine choices will receive 8,999 votes (80,991/9). Your choice is assured 9,009 votes as previously indicated. Because the nine top vote-getters win, you will claim one position. Note that candidates do not run head-on against each other (such as Place A or Place B on the ballot), but rather that the top nine candidates are accorded directorships.

To determine the number of shares needed to elect a given number of directors under cumulative voting, the following formula is used:

$$\text{Shares required} = \frac{\text{Number of directors desired} \times \text{Total number of shares outstanding}}{\text{Total number of directors to be elected} + 1} + 1 \qquad (17\text{–}1)$$

The formula reaffirms that in the previous instance, 1,001 shares would elect one director.

$$\frac{1 \times 10,000}{9 + 1} + 1 = \frac{10,000}{10} + 1 = 1,001$$

If three director positions out of nine are desired, 3,001 shares are necessary.

$$\frac{3 \times 10,000}{9 + 1} + 1 = \frac{30,000}{10} + 1 = 3,001$$

Note that, with approximately 30 percent of the shares outstanding, a minority interest can control one-third of the board. If instead of cumulative voting a majority rule system were utilized, a minority interest could elect no one. The group that controlled 5,001 or more shares out of 10,000 would elect every director.

As a restatement of the problem: If we know the number of minority shares outstanding under cumulative voting and wish to determine the number of directors that can be elected, we use the formula:

$$\frac{\text{Number of directors that can be elected}}{} = \frac{(\text{Shares owned} - 1) \times (\text{Total number of directors to be elected} + 1)}{(\text{Total number of shares outstanding})} \qquad (17\text{–}2)$$

Plugging 3,001 shares into the formula, we show:

$$\frac{(3,001 - 1)(9 + 1)}{10,000} = \frac{3,000(10)}{10,000} = 3$$

If the formula yields an uneven number of directors, such as 3.3 or 3.8, you always round down to the nearest whole number (i.e., 3).

It is not surprising that 22 states require cumulative voting in preference to majority rule, that 18 consider it permissible as part of the corporate charter, and that only 10 make no provision for its use. Such consumer-oriented states as California, Illinois, and Michigan require cumulative voting procedures.

The Right to Purchase New Shares

In addition to a claim to residual income and the right to vote for directors, the common stockholders may also enjoy a privileged position in the offering of new securities. If the corporate charter contains a **preemptive right** provision, holders of common stock must be given the first option to purchase new shares. While only two states specifically require the use of preemptive rights, most other states allow for the inclusion of a **rights offering** in the corporation charter.

The preemptive right provision ensures that management cannot subvert the position of present stockholders by selling shares to outside interests without first offering them to current shareholders. If such protection were not afforded, a 20 percent stockholder might find his or her interest reduced to 10 percent through the distribution of new shares to outsiders. Not only would voting rights be diluted, but proportionate claims to earnings per share would be reduced.

The Use of Rights in Financing

Many corporations also engage in a preemptive rights offering to tap a built-in market for new securities—the current investors. Rights offerings are used by many U.S. companies, and are especially popular as a fund-raising method in Europe. It is quite common in European markets for companies to ask their existing shareholders to help finance expansion. For example, Telephon A.B. Ericsson, a Swedish company, had a $3 billion rights offering to raise new funds.

To illustrate the use of rights, let's take a look at the Watson Corporation, which has 9 million shares outstanding and a current market price of $40 per share (the total market value is $360 million). Watson needs to raise $30 million for new plant and equipment and will sell 1 million new shares at $30 per share.[2] As part of the process, it will use a rights offering in which each old shareholder receives a first option to participate in the purchase of new shares.

Each old shareholder will receive one right for each share of stock owned and may combine a specified number of rights plus $30 cash to buy a new share of stock. Let us consider these questions:

1. How many rights should be necessary to purchase one new share of stock?
2. What is the monetary value of these rights?

Rights Required   Since 9 million shares are currently outstanding and 1 million new shares will be issued, the ratio of old to new shares is 9 to 1. On this basis, the old stockholder may combine nine rights plus $30 cash to purchase one new share of stock.

A stockholder with 90 shares of stock would receive an equivalent number of rights, which could be applied to the purchase of 10 shares of stock at $30 per share. As indicated later in the discussion, stockholders may choose to sell their rights, rather than exercise them in the purchase of new shares.

Monetary Value of a Right   Anything that contributes toward the privilege of purchasing a considerably higher priced stock for $30 per share must have some market value. Consider the following two-step analysis.

Nine old shares sold at $40 per share, or for $360; now one new share will be introduced for $30. Thus, we have a total market value of $390 spread over 10 shares. After the rights offering has been completed, the average value of a share is theoretically equal to $39.[3]

Nine old shares sold at $40 per share	$360
One new share will sell at $30 per share	30
Total value of 10 shares	$390
Average value of one share	$ 39

---

[2]If this were not a rights offering, the discount from the current market price would be much smaller. The new shares might sell for $38 or $39.
[3]A number of variables may intervene to change the value. This is a "best" approximation.

The rights offering thus entitles the holder to buy a stock that should carry a value of $39 (after the transactions have been completed) for $30. With a differential between the anticipated price and the subscription price of $9 and nine rights required to participate in the purchase of one share, the value of a right in this case is $1.

Average value of one share	$39
Subscription price	30
Differential.	$ 9
Rights required to buy one share	9
Value of a right	$ 1

Formulas have been developed to determine the value of a right under any circumstance. Before they are presented, let us examine two new terms that will be part of the calculations—*rights-on* and *ex-rights*. When a rights offering is announced, a stock initially trades **rights-on**; that is, if you buy the stock, you will also acquire a right toward a future purchase of the stock. After a certain period (say four weeks) the stock goes **ex-rights**—when you buy the stock you no longer get a right toward future purchase of stock. Consider the following:

	Date	Value of Stock	Value of Right
March 1:	Stock trades rights-on	$40	$1 (part of $40)
April 1:	Stock trades ex-rights.	39	$1
April 30:	End of subscription period	39	—

Once the ex-rights period is reached, the stock will go down by the theoretical value of the right. The remaining value ($39) is the ex-rights value. Though there is a time period remaining between the ex-rights date (April 1) and the end of the subscription period (April 30), the market assumes the dilution has already occurred. Thus, the ex-rights value reflects the same value as can be expected when the new, underpriced $30 stock issue is sold. In effect, it projects the future impact of the cheaper shares on the stock price.

The formula for the value of the right when the stock is trading rights-on is:

$$R = \frac{M_0 - S}{N + 1} \tag{17–3}$$

where

M_0 = Market value—rights-on, $40
S = Subscription price, $30
N = Number of rights required to purchase a new share of stock; in this case, 9

$$\frac{\$40 - \$30}{9 + 1} = \frac{\$10}{10} = \$1$$

Using Formula 17–3 we determined that the value of a right in the Watson Corporation offering was $1. An alternative formula giving precisely the same answer is:

$$R = \frac{M_e - S}{N} \tag{17–4}$$

The only new term is M_e, the market value of the stock when the shares are trading ex-rights. It is $39. We show:

$$R = \frac{\$39 - \$30}{9} = \frac{\$9}{9} = \$1$$

These are all theoretical relationships, which may be altered somewhat in reality. If there is great enthusiasm for the new issue, the market value of the right may exceed the initial theoretical value (perhaps the right will trade for 1.375).

Effect of Rights on Stockholder's Position

At first glance a rights offering appears to bring great benefits to stockholders. But is this really the case? Does a shareholder really benefit from being able to buy a stock that is initially $40 (and later $39) for $30? Don't answer too quickly!

Think of it this way: Assume 100 people own shares of stock in a corporation and one day decide to sell new shares to themselves at 25 percent below current value. They cannot really enhance their wealth by selling their own stock more cheaply to themselves. What is gained by purchasing inexpensive new shares is lost by diluting existing outstanding shares.

Take the case of Stockholder A, who owns nine shares before the rights offering and also has $30 in cash. His holdings would appear as follows:

Nine old shares at $40	$360
Cash	30
Total value	$390

If he receives and exercises nine rights to buy one new share at $30, his portfolio will contain:

Ten shares at $39 (diluted value)	$390
Cash	0
Total value	$390

Clearly he is no better off. A second alternative would be for him to sell his rights in the market and stay with his position of owning only nine shares and holding cash. The outcome is shown below.

Nine shares at $39 (diluted value)	$351
Proceeds from sale of nine rights	9
Cash	30
Total value	$390

As indicated above, whether he chooses to exercise his rights or not, the stock will still go down to a lower value (others are still diluting). Once again, his overall value remains constant. The value received for the rights ($9) exactly equals the extent of dilution in the value of the original nine shares.

The only foolish action would be for the stockholder to regard the rights as worthless securities. He would then suffer the pains of dilution without the offset from the sale of the rights.

Nine shares at $39 (diluted value)	$351
Cash	30
Total value	$381

Empirical evidence indicates this careless activity occurs 1 to 2 percent of the time.

Desirable Features of Rights Offerings

The student may ask, If the stockholder is no better off in terms of total valuation, why undertake a rights offering? There are a number of possible advantages.

As previously indicated, by giving current stockholders a first option to purchase new shares, we protect their current position in regard to voting rights and claims to earnings. Of equal importance, the use of a rights offering gives the firm a built-in market for new security issues. Because of this built-in base, distribution costs are likely to be lower than under a straight public issue in which investment bankers must underwrite the full risk of distribution.[4]

Also, a rights offering may generate more interest in the market than would a straight public issue. There is a market not only for the stock but also for the rights. Because the subscription price is normally set 15 to 25 percent below current value, there is the "nonreal" appearance of a bargain, creating further interest in the offering.

A last advantage of a rights offering over a straight stock issue is that stock purchased through a rights offering carries lower margin requirements. The **margin requirement** specifies the amount of cash or equity that must be deposited with a brokerage house or a bank, with the balance of funds eligible for borrowing. Though not all investors wish to purchase on margin, those who do so prefer to put down a minimum amount. While normal stock purchases may require a 50 percent margin (half cash, half borrowed), stock purchased under a rights offering may be bought with as little as 25 percent down, depending on the current requirements of the Federal Reserve Board.

Poison Pills

During the last two decades, a new wrinkle was added to the meaning of rights when firms began receiving merger and acquisition proposals from companies interested in acquiring voting control of the firm. The management of many firms did not want to give up control of the company, and so they devised a method of making the firm very unattractive to a potential acquisition-minded company. As you can tell from our discussion of voting provisions, for a company using majority voting, a corporate raider needs to control only slightly over 50 percent of the voting shares to exercise total control. Management of companies considered potential takeover targets began to develop defensive tactics in fending off these unwanted takeovers. One widely used strategy is called the *poison pill.*

---

[4]Though investment bankers generally participate in a rights offering as well, their fees are less because of the smaller risk factor.

A **poison pill** may be a rights offer made to existing shareholders of Company X with the sole purpose of making it more difficult for another firm to acquire Company X. Most poison pills have a trigger point. When a potential buyer accumulates a given percentage of the common stock (for example, 25 percent), the other shareholders may receive rights to purchase additional shares from the company, generally at very low prices. If the rights are exercised by shareholders, this increases the total shares outstanding and dilutes the potential buyer's ownership percentage. Poison pill strategies often do not have to be voted on by shareholders to be put into place. At International Paper Company, however, the poison pill issue was put on the proxy ballot and 76 percent of the voting shareholders sided with management to maintain the poison pill defense. This was surprising, because many institutional investors are opposed to the pill. They believe it lowers the potential for maximizing shareholder value by discouraging potential high takeover bids.

American Depository Receipts

American Depository Receipts (ADRs) are certificates that have a legal claim on an ownership interest in a foreign company's common stock. The shares of the foreign company are purchased and put in trust in a foreign branch of a major U.S. bank. The bank, in turn, receives and can issue depository receipts to the American shareholders of the foreign firm. These ADRs (depository receipts) allow foreign shares to be traded in the United States much like common stock. ADRs have been around for a long time and they are sometimes referred to as American Depository Shares (ADSs).

Since foreign companies want to tap into the world's largest capital market, the United States, they need to offer securities for sale in the United States that can be traded by investors and have the same liquidity features as U.S. securities. ADRs imitate common stock traded on the New York Stock Exchange. Foreign companies such as Nestlé (Swiss), Heineken (Dutch), and Sony (Japanese), that have common stock trading on their home exchanges in Zurich, Amsterdam, and Tokyo, may issue ADRs in the United States. An American investor (or any foreign investor) can buy American Depository Shares of several hundred foreign companies listed on the New York Stock Exchange or the over-the-counter Nasdaq market.

There are many advantages to American Depository Shares for the U.S. investor. The annual reports and financial statements are presented in English according to generally accepted accounting principles. Dividends are paid in dollars and are more easily collected than if the actual shares of the foreign stock were owned. Although ADRs are considered to be more liquid, less expensive, and easier to trade than buying foreign companies' stock directly on that firm's home exchange, there are some drawbacks.

Even though the ADRs are traded in the U.S. market in dollars, they are still traded in their own country in their local currency. This means that the investor in ADRs is subject to a foreign currency risk if the exchange rates between the two countries change. Also, most foreign companies do not report their financial results as often as U.S. companies. Furthermore, there is an information lag as foreign companies need to translate their reports into English. By the time the reports are translated, some of the information has already been absorbed in the local markets and by international traders.

Telephon A.B. Ericsson Rights Offering

Telephon A.B. Ericsson of Sweden is one of the world's largest manufacturers of telephone equipment and cellular phones. It competes internationally for its share of the world's markets in these products against Motorola, Nokia, Siemens, Alcatel, and others. In 1995 the company had been growing rapidly and was in need of new equity capital for expansion. It launched a $1 billion rights offering from its existing shareholders that was successful.

In August 2002, the story was a little different. The worldwide wireless phone market collapsed due to overcapacity and there were high debt loads among the world's telephone companies. Customers of Ericsson's such as AT&T, WorldCom, Verizon, Vodafone, Sprint PCS, and many others spent so much money during the late 1990s buying airwaves from governments around the world that they had no money left to increase their capacity. In addition the recession and stock market collapse of 2000–2002 caused consumers to reduce their demand for cell phones. Ericsson's stock price fell from a high of around $25 to less than $.50 per share. The company was losing money and needed capital to survive what might be several more years of slow sales.

True to form, Ericsson returned to the stock market with a rights offering worth $3.14 billion in U.S. dollars. Each shareholder would receive one right to buy one share of Class B common stock for every Class A or B share currently held. Ericsson intended to sell a maximum of 7,908,754,111 new shares of common stock through this rights offering and expected that about two-thirds of the shares would be sold outside the United States. The rights offering was also available to ADR owners in the United States who held claims on Class B shares. The very low price of the shares ($.40 per share) and the large number of new shares required to raise the necessary capital of $3.1 billion, caused a large dilution in earnings per share.

When all was said and done, the offering was very successful. It was about 37 percent oversubscribed, which meant there was more demand for the shares than supply, and this was good news for Ericsson. It intended to use some of the proceeds to pay down debt that was coming due in 2003, and the rest would be put into working capital while the firm tried to get its costs in line with its revenues. After the rights offering, Ericsson performed a 10 for 1 reverse stock split that reduced the number of shares by a divisor of 10. In other words, for every billion shares outstanding there would now be only 100 million outstanding, and in response the stock price would be expected to rise 10 times. An investor that owned 1,000 shares at $.40 would now own 100 shares at $4.00. In fact the stock more than doubled after the rights offering as investors breathed a sigh of relief that Ericsson would live to play the telecommunications game for yet another day. Investors who exercised their rights and still owned the stock in January 2006 would have shares at $34 for a return of 750 percent (a $30 profit).

Preferred Stock Financing

Having discussed bonds in Chapter 16 and common stock in this chapter, we are prepared to look at an intermediate or hybrid form of security known as **preferred stock**. You may question the validity of the term *preferred*, for preferred stock does not possess any of the most desirable characteristics of debt or common stock. In the case of debt, bondholders have a contractual claim against the corporation for the payment of interest and may throw the corporation into bankruptcy if payment is not forthcoming. Common stockholders are the owners of the firm and have a residual claim to all income not paid out to others. Preferred stockholders are merely entitled to receive a stipulated dividend and, generally, must receive the dividend before the payment of dividends to common stockholders. However, their right to annual dividends is not mandatory for the corporation, as is true of interest on debt, and the corporation may forgo preferred dividends when this is deemed necessary.

For example, XYZ Corporation might issue 9 percent preferred stock with a $100 par value. Under normal circumstances, the corporation would pay the $9 per share dividend. Let us also assume it has $1,000 bonds carrying 9.2 percent interest and shares of common stock with a market value of $50, normally paying a $1 cash dividend. The 9.2 percent interest must be paid on the bonds. The $9 preferred dividend has to be paid before the $1 dividend on common stock, but both may be waived without threat of bankruptcy. The common stockholder is the last in line to receive payment, but the stockholder's potential participation is unlimited. Instead of getting a $1 dividend, the investor may someday receive many times that much in dividends and also capital appreciation in stock value.

Justification for Preferred Stock

Because preferred stock has few unique characteristics, why might the corporation issue it and, equally important, why are investors willing to purchase the security?

Most corporations that issue preferred stock do so to achieve a balance in their capital structure. It is a means of expanding the capital base of the firm without diluting the common stock ownership position or incurring contractual debt obligations.

Even here, there may be a drawback. While interest payments on debt are tax deductible, preferred stock dividends are not. Thus, the interest cost on 10 percent debt may be only 6.5 to 7 percent on an aftertax cost basis, while the aftertax cost on 10 percent preferred stock would be the stated amount. A firm issuing the preferred stock may be willing to pay the higher aftertax cost to assure investors it has a balanced capital structure, and because preferred stock may have a positive effect on the costs of the other sources of funds in the capital structure.

Investor Interest   Primary purchasers of preferred stock are corporate investors, insurance companies, and pension funds. To the corporate investor, preferred stock offers a very attractive advantage over bonds. The tax law provides that any corporation that receives either preferred or common dividends from another corporation must add only 30 percent of such dividends to its taxable income. Thus, 70 percent of such dividends are exempt from taxation. On a preferred stock issue paying a 10 percent dividend, only 30 percent would be taxable. By contrast, all the interest of bonds is taxable to the recipient except for municipal bond interest.

If we take 2005 figures for A-rated utility bond yields and utility preferred stock yields in Table 17–2 and adjust them for aftertax yields to a *corporate* investor, the advantage of preferred stock ownership to these investors is evident. Since interest on bonds receives no preferential tax treatment, the aftertax bond yield must be adjusted by the investing corporation's marginal tax rate as shown on page 540

Year	Moody's A-Rated Utility Bonds	Moody's A-Rated Utility Preferred Stock Yields	Yield Spread (Bonds–Preferred stock)
2000	8.25	7.00	1.25
2001	7.76	7.29	0.47
2002	7.37	7.28	0.09
2003	6.58	6.88	−0.30
2004	6.16	6.62	−0.46
2005	5.61	6.26	−0.65

Source: Data is taken from *Mergent Bond Record*, December 2005.

Table 17–2

Before-tax yields on Moody's A-rated utility bonds and utility preferred stock

In this example we shall use a rate of 35 percent and 2005 data from Table 17–2.

$$\text{Aftertax bond yield} = \text{Before-tax bond yield} \times (1 - \text{Tax rate})$$
$$= 5.61\% \, (1 - .35)$$
$$= 3.65\%$$

The bondholder will receive 3.65% as an aftertax yield.

For preferred stock the adjustment includes the advantageous 30 percent tax provision. Also under the 2003 tax laws, the tax rate on dividends is only 15 percent. The computation for aftertax return for preferred stock is as follows:

$$\text{Aftertax preferred yield} = \text{Before-tax preferred stock yield} \times [1 - (\text{Tax rate})(.30)]$$
$$= 6.26\% \times [1 - (.15)(.30)]$$
$$= 6.26\% \times (1 - .045)$$
$$= 6.26\% \times (.955)$$
$$= 5.98\%$$

The aftertax yield on preferred stock is higher than the aftertax bond yield (5.98 percent versus 3.65 percent).

Summary of Tax Considerations   Tax considerations for preferred stock work in two opposite directions. First, they make the aftertax cost of debt cheaper than preferred stock to the issuing corporation because interest is deductible to the payer. (This is true even though the quoted rate may be higher.) Second, tax considerations generally make the receipt of preferred dividends more valuable than corporate bond interest to corporate investors because 70 percent of the dividend is exempt from taxation.

Provisions Associated with Preferred Stock

A preferred stock issue contains a number of stipulations and provisions that define the stockholder's claim to income and assets.

1. Cumulative Dividends   Most issues are **cumulative preferred stock** and have a cumulative claim to dividends. That is, if preferred stock dividends are not paid in any one year, they accumulate and must be paid in total before common stockholders can receive dividends. If preferred stock carries a $10 cash dividend and the company does not pay dividends for three years, preferred stockholders must receive the full $30 before common stockholders can receive anything.

The cumulative dividend feature makes a corporation very aware of its obligation to preferred stockholders. When a financially troubled corporation has missed a number of dividend payments under a cumulative arrangement, there may be a financial recapitalization of the corporation in which preferred stockholders receive new securities in place of the dividend that is in arrears (unpaid). Assume the corporation has now missed five years of dividends under a $10 a year obligation and the company still remains in a poor cash position. Preferred stockholders may be offered $50 or more in new common stock or bonds as forgiveness of the missed dividend payments. Preferred stockholders may be willing to cooperate in order to receive some potential benefit for the future.

2. Conversion Feature   Like certain forms of debt, preferred stock may be convertible into common shares. Thus, $100 in preferred stock may be convertible into a specified number of shares of common stock at the option of the holder. One new wrinkle on convertible preferreds is the use of **convertible exchangeable preferreds** that allow the company to force conversion from convertible preferred stock into convertible debt. This can be used to allow the company to take advantage of falling interest rates or to allow the company to change preferred dividends into tax-deductible interest payments when it is to the company's advantage to do so. The topic of convertibility is discussed at length in Chapter 19, "Convertibles, Warrants, and Derivatives."

3. Call Feature   Also, preferred stock, like debt, may be callable; that is, the corporation may retire the security before maturity at some small premium over par. This, of course, accrues to the advantage of the corporation and to the disadvantage of the preferred stockholder. A preferred issue carrying a call provision will be accorded a slightly higher yield than a similar issue without this feature. The same type of refunding decision applied to debt obligations in Chapter 16 could also be applied to preferred stock.

4. Participation Provision   A small percentage of preferred stock issues are **participating preferreds**; that is, they may participate over and above the quoted yield when the corporation is enjoying a particularly good year. Once the common stock dividend equals the preferred stock dividend, the two classes of securities may share equally in additional payouts.

5. Floating Rate   Beginning in the 1980s, a few preferred stock issuers made the dividend adjustable in nature and this stock is classified as **floating rate preferred stock**. These issuers include such firms as Alcoa and BankAmerica Corporation. Typically the dividend is changed on a quarterly basis, based on current market conditions. Because the dividend rate only changes quarterly, there is still some possibility of a small price change between dividend adjustment dates. Nevertheless, it is less than the price change for regular preferred stock.

Investors that participate in floating rate preferred stock do so for two reasons: to minimize the risk of price changes and to take advantage of the tax benefits associated with preferred stock corporate ownership. The price stability actually makes floating rate preferred stock the equivalent of a safe short-term investment even though preferred stock is normally thought of as long term in nature.

6. Dutch Auction Preferred Stock   Dutch auction preferred stock is similar to floating rate preferred stock—but is a short-term instrument. The security matures every seven weeks and is sold (reauctioned) at a subsequent bidding. The concept of Dutch auction means the stock is issued to the bidder willing to accept the lowest yield and then to the next lowest bidder and so on until all the preferred stock is sold. This is much like the Treasury bill auctions held by the Federal Reserve Bank. This auction process at short-term intervals allows investors to keep up with the changing interest rates in the short-term market. Some corporate investors like Dutch auction preferred stock because it allows them to invest at short-term rates and take advantage of the tax benefits available to them with preferred stock investments.

7. Par Value   A final important feature associated with preferred stock is par value. Unlike the par value of common stock, which is often only a small percentage of the actual value, the par value of preferred stock is set at the anticipated market value at the time of issue. The par value establishes the amount due to preferred stockholders in the event of liquidation. Also, the par value of preferred stock determines the base against which the percentage or dollar return on preferred stock is computed. Thus, 10 percent preferred stock would indicate $10 a year in preferred dividends if the par value were $100, but only $5 annually if the par value were $50.

Comparing Features of Common and Preferred Stock and Debt

In Table 17–3, we compare the characteristics of common stock, preferred stock, and bonds. The student should consider the comparative advantages and disadvantages of each.

In terms of the risk-return features of these three classes of securities and also of the other investments discussed earlier in Chapter 7, we might expect the risk-return patterns depicted in Figure 17–1. The lowest return is obtained from savings accounts, and the highest return and risk are generally associated with common stock. In between, we note that short-term instruments generally, though not always, provide lower returns than longer-term instruments. We also observe that government securities pay lower returns than issues originated by corporations, because of the lower risk involved. Next on the scale after government issues is preferred stock. This hybrid form of security generally pays a lower return than even well-secured corporate debt instruments, because of the 70 percent tax-exempt status of preferred stock dividends to corporate purchasers. Thus, the focus on preferred stock is not just on risk-return trade-offs but also on aftertax return.[5]

Table 17–3   Features of alternative security issues

	Common Stock	Preferred Stock	Bonds
1. Ownership and control of the firm	Belongs to common stockholders through voting rights and residual claim to income	Limited rights when dividends are missed	Limited rights under default in interest payment
2. Obligations to provide return	None	Must receive payment before common stockholders	Contractual obligation
3. Claim to assets in bankruptcy	Lowest claim of any security holder	Bondholders and creditors must be satisfied first	Highest claim
4. Cost of distribution	Highest	Moderate	Lowest
5. Risk-return trade-off	Highest risk, highest return (at least in theory)	Moderate risk, moderate return	Lowest risk, moderate return
6. Tax status of payment by corporation	Not deductible	Not deductible	Tax-deductible Cost = Interest payment × (1 − Tax rate)
7. Tax status of payment to recipient	70 percent of dividend to another corporation is tax-exempt	Same as common stock	Municipal bond interest is tax-exempt

---

[5]In a strict sense, preferred stock does not belong on the straight line because of its unique tax characteristics.

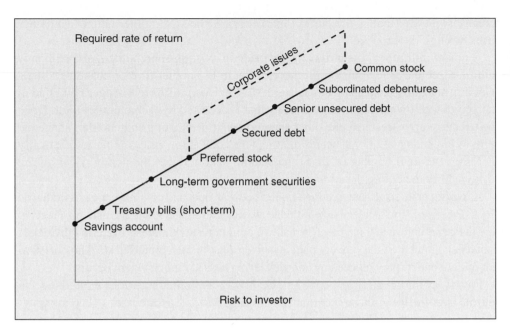

Figure 17–1

Risk and expected
return for various
security classes

Next, we observe increasingly high return requirements on debt, based on the presence or absence of security provisions and the priority of claims on unsecured debt. At the top of the scale is common stock. Because of its lowest priority of claim in the corporation and its volatile price movement, it has the highest demanded return.

Though extensive research has tended to validate these general patterns,[6] short-term or even intermediate-term reversals have occurred, in which investments with lower risk have outperformed investments at the higher end of the risk scale.

Summary

Common stock ownership carries three primary rights or privileges. First, there is a residual claim to income. All funds not paid out to other classes of securities automatically belong to the common stockholder; the firm may then choose to pay out these residual funds in dividends or to reinvest them for the benefit of common stockholders.

Because common stockholders are the ultimate owners of the firm, they alone have the privilege of voting. To expand the role of minority stockholders, many corporations use a system of cumulative voting, in which each stockholder has voting power equal to the number of shares owned times the number of directors to be elected. By cumulating votes for a small number of selected directors, minority stockholders are able to have representation on the board.

Common stockholders may also enjoy a first option to purchase new shares. This privilege is extended through the procedure known as a rights offering. A shareholder receives one right for each share of stock owned and may combine a certain number of rights, plus cash, to purchase a new share. While the cash or subscription price is

---

[6]Ibbotson Associates, *Stocks, Bonds, Bills and Inflation: 2000 Yearbook* (Chicago: Ibbotson Associates Capital Management Research Center, 2002).

usually somewhat below the current market price, the stockholder neither gains nor loses through the process.

A poison pill represents a rights offer made to existing shareholders of a company with the sole purpose of making it more difficult for another firm or outsiders to take over a firm against management's wishes. Most poison pills have a trigger point tied to the percentage ownership in the company that is acquired by the potential suitor. Once the trigger point is reached, the other shareholders (the existing shareholders) have the right to buy many additional shares of company stock at low prices. This automatically increases the total number of shares outstanding and reduces the voting power of the firm wishing to acquire the company.

A hybrid, or intermediate, security, falling between debt and common stock, is preferred stock. Preferred stockholders are entitled to receive a stipulated dividend and must receive this dividend before any payment is made to common stockholders. Preferred dividends usually accumulate if they are not paid in a given year, though preferred stockholders cannot initiate bankruptcy proceedings or seek legal redress if nonpayment occurs.

Finally, common stock, preferred stock, bonds, and other securities tend to receive returns over the long run in accordance with risk, with corporate issues generally paying a higher return than government securities.

Review of Formulas

1. $\text{Shares required} = \dfrac{\text{Number of directors desired} \times \text{Total number of shares outstanding}}{\text{Total number of directors to be elected} + 1} + 1$ (17–1)

2. $\dfrac{\text{Number of directors}}{\text{that can be elected}} = \dfrac{(\text{Shares owned} - 1) \times (\text{Total number of directors to be elected} + 1)}{(\text{Total number of shares outstanding})}$ (17–2)

3. $R = \dfrac{M_0 - S}{N + 1}$ (17–3)

   R is the value of a right
   M_0 is the market value of the stock—rights-on (stock carries a right)
   S is the subscription price
   N is the number of rights required to purchase a new share of stock

4. $R = \dfrac{M_e - S}{N}$ (17–4)

   R is the value of a right
   M_e is the market value of stock—ex-rights (stock no longer carries a right)
   S is the subscription price
   N is the number of rights required to purchase a new share of stock

List of Terms

common stock   527
residual claim to income   528
proxy   529
founders' shares   529

majority voting   530
cumulative voting   530
preemptive right   532
rights offering   532

Discussion Questions

1. Why has corporate management become increasingly sensitive to the desires of large institutional investors?

2. Why might a corporation use a special category such as founders' stock in issuing common stock?

3. What is the purpose of cumulative voting? Are there any disadvantages to management?

4. How does the preemptive right protect stockholders from dilution?

5. If common stockholders are the *owners* of the company, why do they have the last claim on assets and a residual claim on income?

6. During a rights offering, the underlying stock is said to sell "rights-on" and "ex-rights." Explain the meaning of these terms and their significance to current stockholders and potential stockholders.

7. Why might management use a poison pill strategy?

8. Preferred stock is often referred to as a hybrid security. What is meant by this term as applied to preferred stock?

9. What is the most likely explanation for the use of preferred stock from a corporate viewpoint?

10. Why is the cumulative feature of preferred stock particularly important to preferred stockholders?

11. A small amount of preferred stock is participating. What would your reaction be if someone said common stock is also participating?

12. What is an advantage of floating rate preferred stock for the risk-averse investor?

13. Put an X by the security that has the feature best related to the following considerations. You may wish to refer to Table 17–3.

	Common Stock	Preferred Stock	Bonds
a. Ownership and control of the firm			
b. Obligation to provide return			
c. Claims to assets in bankruptcy			
d. High cost of distribution			
e. Highest return			
f. Highest risk			
g. Tax-deductible payment			
h. Payment partially tax-exempt to corporate recipient			

Practice Problems and Solutions

Cumulative voting

1. *a.* George Kelly wishes to elect 5 of the 13 directors on the Data Processing Corp. board. There are 98,000 shares of the company's stock outstanding. How many shares will be required to accomplish this goal?

   b. Jennifer Wallace owns 60,001 shares of stock in the Newcastle Corp. There are 12 directors to be elected with 195,000 shares outstanding. How many directors can Jennifer elect?

Rights offering

2. Dunn Resources has issued rights to its shareholders. The subscription price is $60. Four rights are needed along with the subscription price of $60 to buy one new share. The stock is selling for $72 rights-on.

   a. What is the value of one right?

   b. After the stock goes ex-rights, what will the new stock price be?

Solutions

1. *a.*
$$\text{Shares required} = \frac{\text{(Number of directors desired)} \times \text{(Total number of shares outstanding)}}{\text{Total number of directors to be elected} + 1}$$

$$= \frac{5 \times 98,000}{13 + 1} + 1$$

$$= \frac{490,000}{14} + 1$$

$$= 35,000 + 1 = 35,001 \text{ shares}$$

   b.
$$\frac{\text{Number of directors}}{\text{that can be elected}} = \frac{\text{(Shares owned} - 1) \times \text{(Total number of directors to be elected} + 1)}{\text{Total number of shares outstanding}}$$

$$= \frac{(60,001 - 1) \times (12 + 1)}{195,000}$$

$$= \frac{60,000 \times 13}{195,000} = \frac{780,000}{195,000} = 4 \text{ directors}$$

2. *a.* $R = \dfrac{M_0 - S}{N + 1}$

   R = Value of a right

   M_0 = Market value rights-on. This is the value before the effect of the right offering, $72.

   S = Subscription price $60.

   N = Number of rights necessary to purchase a new share 4.

   $R = \dfrac{\$72 - 60}{4 + 1} = \dfrac{\$12}{5} = \$2.40$

   b. The market value of the stock ex-rights (after the effect of the rights offering) is equal to M_0 (the market value before the rights offering) minus the value of a right (R).

   $M_e = M_0 - R$

   M_e = Market value of the stock ex-rights

$$M_0 = \$72$$
$$R = \$2.40$$
$$M_e = \$72 - \$2.40 = \$69.60$$

All problems are available in Homework Manager. Please see the preface for more information.   **Problems**

1. Diploma Mills has $30 million in earnings, pays $4.25 million in interest to bondholders, and $2.95 million in dividends to preferred stockholders.
   a. What are the common stockholders' residual claims to earnings?
   b. What are the common stockholders' legal, enforceable claims to dividends?

   Residual claims to earnings

2. Russell Stover wishes to know how many shares are necessary to elect 4 directors out of 11 directors up for election for the Tasty Candy Company board. There are 75,000 shares outstanding. (Use Formula 17–1 on page 532 to determine the answer.)

   Cumulative voting

3. Dr. Phil wishes to know how many shares are necessary to elect 6 directors out of 15 directors up for election for the board of the Winfrey Publishing Company. There are 400,000 shares outstanding. (Use Formula 17–1 on page 532 to determine the answer.)

   Cumulative voting

4. Mr. R.C. Cola owns 7,001 shares of Softdrinks, Inc. There are 10 seats on the company board of directors, and the company has a total of 77,000 shares outstanding. Softdrinks, Inc., utilizes cumulative voting.

   Can Mr. Cola elect himself to the board when the vote to elect 10 directors is held next week? (Use Formula 17–2 on page 532 to determine if he can elect one director.)

   Cumulative voting

5. Betsy Ross owns 918 shares in the Hanson Fabrics Company. There are 13 directors to be elected. Thirty-one thousand shares are outstanding. The firm has adopted cumulative voting.
   a. How many total votes can be cast?
   b. How many votes does Betsy control?
   c. What percentage of the total votes does she control?

   Cumulative voting

6. The Beasley Corporation has been experiencing declining earnings, but has just announced a 50 percent salary increase for its top executives. A dissident group of stockholders wants to oust the existing board of directors. There are currently 11 directors and 30,000 shares of stock outstanding. Mr. Wright, the president of the company, has the full support of the existing board. The dissident stock-holders control proxies for 10,001 shares. Mr. Wright is worried about losing his job.
   a. Under cumulative voting procedures, how many directors can the dissident stockholders elect with the proxies they now hold? How many directors could they elect under majority rule with these proxies?
   b. How many shares (or proxies) are needed to elect six directors under cumulative voting?

   Dissident stockholder group and cumulative voting

Dissident stockholder group and cumulative voting

7. Midland Petroleum is holding a stockholders' meeting next month. Ms. Ramsey is the president of the company and has the support of the existing board of directors. All 11 members of the board are up for reelection. Mr. Clark is a dissident stockholder. He controls proxies for 40,001 shares. Ms. Ramsey and her friends on the board control 60,001 shares. Other stockholders, whose loyalties are unknown, will be voting the remaining 19,998 shares. The company uses cumulative voting.

    a. How many directors can Mr. Clark be sure of electing?

    b. How many directors can Ms. Ramsey and her friends be sure of electing?

    c. How many directors could Mr. Clark elect if he obtains all the proxies for the uncommitted votes? (Uneven values must be rounded down to the nearest whole number regardless of the amount.) Will he control the board?

Cumulative voting

8. In Problem 7, if nine directors were to be elected, and Ms. Ramsey and her friends had 60,001 shares and Mr. Clark had 40,001 shares plus half the uncommitted votes, how many directors could Mr. Clark elect?

Strategies under cumulative voting

9. Mr. Michaels controls proxies for 38,000 of the 70,000 outstanding shares of Northern Airlines. Mr. Baker heads a dissident group that controls the remaining 32,000 shares. There are seven board members to be elected and cumulative voting rules apply. Michaels does not understand cumulative voting and plans to cast 100,000 of his 266,000 (38,000 × 7) votes for his brother-in-law, Scott. His remaining votes will be spread evenly for three other candidates.

    How many directors can Baker elect if Michaels acts as described above? Use logical numerical analysis rather than a set formula to answer the question. Baker has 224,000 votes (32,000 × 7).

Different classes of voting stock

10. Rust Pipe Co. was established in 1991. Four years later the company went public. At that time, Robert Rust, the original owner, decided to establish two classes of stock. The first represents Class A founders' stock and is entitled to 10 votes per share. The normally traded common stock, designated as Class B, is entitled to one vote per share. In late 2007, Mr. Steele was considering purchasing shares in Rust Pipe Co. While he knew the existence of founders' shares were not often present in other companies, he decided to buy the shares anyway because of a new technology Rust Pipe had developed to improve the flow of liquids through pipes.

    Of the 1,200,000 total shares currently outstanding, the original founder's family owns 51,325 shares. What is the percentage of the founder's family votes to Class B votes?

Rights offering

11. Prime Bankcorp has issued rights to its shareholders. The subscription price is $50 and five rights are needed along with the subscription price to buy one of the new shares. The stock is selling for $59 rights-on.

    a. What would be the value of one right?

    b. If the stock goes ex-rights, what would the new stock price be?

12. Computer Graphics has announced a rights offering for its shareholders. Carol Stevens owns 1,200 shares of Computer Graphics stock. Four rights plus $60

cash are needed to buy one of the new shares. The stock is currently selling for $72 rights-on.

Procedures associated with a rights offering

    a.   What is the value of a right?

    b.   How many of the new shares could Carol buy if she exercised all her rights? How much cash would this require?

    c.   Carol doesn't know if she wants to exercise her rights or sell them. Would either alternative have a more positive effect on her wealth?

13. Todd Winningham IV has $4,000 to invest. He has been looking at Gallagher Tennis Clubs, Inc., common stock. Gallagher has issued a rights offering to its common stockholders. Six rights plus $38 cash will buy one new share. Gallagher's stock is selling for $50 ex-rights.

Investing in rights

    a.   How many rights could Todd buy with his $4,000? Alternatively, how many shares of stock could he buy with the same $4,000 at $50 per share?

    b.   If Todd invests his $4,000 in Gallagher rights and the price of Gallagher stock rises to $59 per share ex-rights, what would his dollar profit on the rights be? (First compute profits per right.)

    c.   If Todd invests his $4,000 in Gallagher stock and the price of the stock rises to $59 per share ex-rights, what would his total dollar profit be?

    d.   What would be the answer to part *b* if the price of Gallagher's stock falls to $30 per share ex-rights instead of rising to $59?

    e.   What would be the answer to part *c* if the price of Gallagher's stock falls to $30 per share ex-rights?

14. Mr. and Mrs. Anderson own five shares of Magic Tricks Corporation's common stock. The market value of the stock is $60. The Andersons also have $48 in cash. They have just received word of a rights offering. One new share of stock can be purchased at $48 for each five shares currently owned (based on five rights).

Effect of rights on stockholder position

    a.   What is the value of a right?

    b.   What is the value of the Andersons' portfolio before the rights offering? (Portfolio in this question represents stock plus cash.)

    c.   If the Andersons participate in the rights offering, what will be the value of their portfolio, based on the diluted value (ex-rights) of the stock?

    d.   If they sell their five rights but keep their stock at its diluted value and hold on to their cash, what will be the value of their portfolio?

15. Walker Machine Tools has 5 million shares of common stock outstanding. The current market price of Walker common stock is $42 per share rights-on. The company's net income this year is $15 million. A rights offering has been announced in which 500,000 new shares will be sold at $36.50 per share. The subscription price plus 10 rights is needed to buy one of the new shares.

Relation of rights to EPS and the price-earnings ratio

    a.   What are the earnings per share and price-earnings ratio before the new shares are sold via the rights offering?

    b.   What would the earnings per share be immediately after the rights offering? What would the price-earnings ratio be immediately after the rights offering? (Assume there is no change in the market value of the stock, except for the change when the stock begins trading ex-rights.) Round answers to two places after the decimal point.

Aftertax comparison of preferred stock and other investments

16. The Omega Corporation has some excess cash that it would like to invest in marketable securities for a long-term hold. Its vice-president of finance is considering three investments (Omega Corporation is in a 35 percent tax bracket and the tax rate on dividends is 15 percent). Which one should she select based on aftertax return: (*a*) Treasury bonds at a 9 percent yield; (*b*) corporate bonds at a 12 percent yield; or (*c*) preferred stock at a 10 percent yield?

Preferred stock dividends in arrears

17. National Health Corporation (NHC) has a cumulative preferred stock issue outstanding, which has a stated annual dividend of $9 per share. The company has been losing money and has not paid preferred dividends for the last five years. There are 300,000 shares of preferred stock outstanding and 600,000 shares of common stock.

   a. How much is the company behind in preferred dividends?

   b. If NHC earns $11,000,000 in the coming year after taxes but before dividends, and this is all paid out to the preferred stockholders, how much will the company be in arrears (behind in payments)? Keep in mind that the coming year would represent the sixth year.

   c. How much, if any, would be available in common stock dividends in the coming year if $11,000,000 is earned as explained in part *b*?

Preferred stock ⚡ dividends in arrears

18. Robbins Petroleum Company is four years in arrears on cumulative preferred stock dividends. There are 850,000 preferred shares outstanding, and the annual dividend is $6.50 per share. The vice-president of finance sees no real hope of paying the dividends in arrears. She is devising a plan to compensate the preferred stockholders for 90 percent of the dividends in arrears.

   a. How much should the compensation be?

   b. Robbins will compensate the preferred stockholders in the form of bonds paying 12 percent interest in a market environment in which the going rate of interest is 14 percent for similar bonds. The bonds will have a 15-year maturity. Using the bond valuation table in Chapter 16 (Table 16–3), indicate the market value of a $1,000 par value bond.

   c. Based on market value, how many bonds must be issued to provide the compensation determined in part *a*? (Round to the nearest whole number.)

Preferred stock dividends in arrears and valuing common stock

19. Enterprise Storage Company has 400,000 shares of cumulative preferred stock outstanding, which has a stated dividend of $4.75. It is six years in arrears in its dividend payments.

   a. How much in total dollars is the company behind in its payments?

   b. The firm proposes to offer new common stock to the preferred stockholders to wipe out the deficit.

   The common stock will pay the following dividends over the next four years:

D_1	$1.25
D_2	1.50
D_3	1.75
D_4	2.00

The company anticipates earnings per share after four years will be $4.05 with a P/E ratio of 12/12.

The common stock will be valued as the present value of future dividends plus the present value of the future stock price after four years. The discount rate used by the investment banker is 10 percent. Round to two places to the right of the decimal point. What is the calculated value of the common stock?

c. How many shares of common stock must be issued at the value computed in part *b* to eliminate the deficit (arrearage) computed in part *a*? Round to the nearest whole number.

20. The treasurer of Kelly Bottling Company (a corporation) currently has $100,000 invested in preferred stock yielding 8 percent. He appreciates the tax advantages of preferred stock and is considering buying $100,000 more with borrowed funds. The cost of the borrowed funds is 10 percent. He suggests this proposal to his board of directors. They are somewhat concerned by the fact that the treasurer will be paying 2 percent more for funds than the company will be earning on the investment. Kelly Bottling is in a 34 percent tax bracket, with dividends taxed at 15 percent.

Borrowing funds to purchase preferred stock

a. Compute the amount of the aftertax income from the additional preferred stock if it is purchased.

b. Compute the aftertax borrowing cost to purchase the additional preferred stock. That is, multiply the interest cost times $(1 - T)$.

c. Should the treasurer proceed with his proposal?

d. If interest rate and dividend yields in the market go up six months after a decision to purchase is made, what impact will this have on the outcome?

21. Barnes Air Conditioning, Inc., has two classes of preferred stock: floating rate preferred stock and straight (normal) preferred stock. Both issues have a par value of $100. The floating rate preferred stock pays an annual dividend yield of 6 percent, and the straight preferred stock pays 7 percent. Since the issuance of the two securities, interest rates have gone up by 2 percent for each issue. Both securities will pay their year-end dividend today.

Floating rate preferred stock

a. What is the price of the floating rate preferred stock likely to be?

b. What is the price of the straight preferred stock likely to be? Refer back to Chapter 10 and use Formula 10–4 on page 294 to answer this question.

COMPREHENSIVE PROBLEM

The Crandall Corporation currently has 100,000 shares outstanding that are selling at $50 per share. It needs to raise $900,00. Net income after taxes is $500,000. Its vice-president of finance and its investment banker have decided on a rights offering, but are not sure how much to discount the subscription price from the current market value. Discounts of 10 percent, 20 percent, and 40 percent have been suggested. Common stock is the sole means of financing for the Crandall Corporation.

Crandall Corporation (rights offering and the impact on shareholders)

a. For each discount, determine the subscription price, the number of shares to be issued, and the number of rights required to purchase one share. (Round to one place after the decimal point where necessary.)

b. Determine the value of one right under each of the plans. (Round to two places after the decimal point.)

c. Compute the earnings per share before and immediately after the rights offering under a 10 percent discount from the market price.

d. By what percentage has the number of shares outstanding increased?

e. Stockholder X has 100 shares before the rights offering and participated by buying 20 new shares. Compute his total claim to earnings both before and after the rights offering (that is, multiply shares by the earnings per share figures computed in part *c*).

f. Should Stockholder X be satisfied with this claim over a longer period of time?

COMPREHENSIVE PROBLEM

Electro Cardio
Systems, Inc.
(poison pill
strategy)

Dr. Robert Grossman founded Electro Cardio Systems, Inc. (ECS), in 1998. The principal purpose of the firm was to engage in research and development of heart pump devices. Although the firm did not show a profit until 2003, by 2007 it reported after-tax earnings of $1,200,000. The company had gone public in 2001 at $10 a share. Investors were initially interested in buying the stock because of its future prospects. By year-end 2007, the stock was trading at $42 per share because the firm had made good on its promise to produce lifesaving heart pumps and, in the process, was now making reasonable earnings. With 850,000 shares outstanding, earnings per share were $1.41.

Dr. Grossman and the members of the board of directors were initially pleased when another firm, Parker Medical Products, began buying their stock. John Parker, the chairman and CEO of Parker Medical Products, was thought to be a shrewd investor and his company's purchase of 50,000 shares of ECS was taken as an affirmation of the success of the heart pump research firm.

However, when Parker bought another 50,000 shares, Dr. Grossman and members of the board of directors of ECS became concerned that John Parker and his firm might be trying to take over ECS.

Upon talking to his attorney, Dr. Grossman was reminded that ECS had a poison pill provision that took effect when any outside investor accumulated 25 percent or more of the shares outstanding. Current stockholders, excluding the potential takeover company, were given the privilege of buying up to 500,000 new shares of ECS at 80 percent of current market value. Thus, new shares would be restricted to friendly interests.

The attorney also found that Dr. Grossman and "friendly" members of the board of directors currently owned 175,000 shares of ECS.

a. How many more shares would Parker Medical Products need to purchase before the poison pill provision would go into effect? Given the current price of ECS stock of $42, what would be the cost to Parker to get up to that level?

b. ECS's ultimate fear was that Parker Medical Products would gain over a 50 percent interest in ECS's outstanding shares. What would be the additional cost to Parker to get 50 percent (plus 1 share) of the stock outstanding of ECS at the current market price of ECS stock? In answering this question, assume Parker had previously accumulated the 25 percent position discussed in question *a*.

c. Now assume that Parker exceeds the number of shares you computed in part *b* and gets all the way up to accumulating 625,000 shares of ECS. Under the poison pill provision, how many shares must "friendly" shareholders purchase to thwart a takeover attempt by Parker? What will be the total cost? Keep in mind that friendly interests already own 175,000 shares of ECS and to maintain control, they must own one more share than Parker.

d. Would you say the poison pill is an effective deterrent in this case? Is the poison pill in the best interest of the general stockholders (those not associated with the company)?

WEB EXERCISE

3M (Minnesota Mining & Manufacturing Co.) was listed in Table 17–1 as one of the companies having a large percentage of institutional ownership. Institutional ownership represents stock held by nonindividuals such as pension funds, mutual funds, or bank trust departments. Let's learn more about the company.

Go to 3M's Web site, www.3m.com, and follow the steps below:

1. Click on "About 3M."
2. Click on "Stock Information" under "Investor Relations."
3. Click on "Financial Information."
4. Write down the following:
    a. Recent price
    b. "52-week High"
    c. "52-week Low"
    d. "52-week Change"
    e. "Average Daily Volume last 10 days"
5. On the same page, click on "Ratios" toward the bottom of the page. The average firm in 3M's industry of diversified chemicals has the following ratios. How does 3M compare?
    a. Price to Earnings   22.0x
    b. Price to Revenue   2.5x
    c. Price to Book   5.0x
    d. Net Profit   14.0%
    e. Current Ratio   1.6x

Note: From time to time, companies redesign their Web sites and occasionally a topic we have listed may have been deleted, updated, or moved into a different location. If you click on the site map or site index, you will be introduced to a table of contents which should aid you in finding the topic you are looking for.

www.mhhe.com/bh12e

Dividend Policy and Retained Earnings

18

chapter concepts

1 The board of directors and corporate management must decide what to do with the firm's annual earnings: pay them out in dividends or retain them for reinvestment in future projects.

2 Dividends may have a positive or negative information content for shareholders. Dividend policy can also provide information about where the firm is on its life cycle curve.

3 Many other factors also influence dividend policy, such as legal rules, the cash position of the firm, and the tax position of shareholders.

4 Stock dividends and stock splits provide common stockholders with new shares, but their value must be carefully assessed.

5 Some firms make a decision to repurchase their shares in the market rather than increase dividends.

One of the best performing companies in the stock market in the current decade is a cigarette company. Its stock even went up 20 percent in the six months after 9/11 as the stock market was falling apart. No way, you say! Guess again. It goes by an alias, but don't be confused. Altria Group, Inc., is the name for Philip Morris, the producer of Marlboro, Benson & Hedges, Merit, Virginia Slims, and other tobacco products. Fifty percent of the cigarettes sold in the United States are Philip Morris products.

It not only produces cigarettes for U.S. consumption, but exports them throughout the world. Twenty-five percent of the total world consumption of cigarettes is in China, with its population of over a billion people, and Philip Morris is happy to accommodate them. The firm is in the process of signing a licensing agreement with the Chinese government which will allow them to sell two billion (not million) Marlboro cigarettes annually in that country.

Of course, Philip Morris is constantly under attack by lawyers and state and federal regulators for selling a product that may cause cancer and heart disease. So, why the popularity of Philip Morris (i.e., the Altria Group) in the stock market? Well, for one reason, it's branching out beyond tobacco products. The firm owns a controlling interest in Kraft Foods and also sells such products as Jell-O, Kool-Aid, Oscar Mayer hot dogs, Miracle Whip salad dressing, and so on.

However, far more important than its diversification policy is the firm's dividend policy. It is one of the highest paying dividend stocks on the New York Stock Exchange. Its dividend per share was $3.20 in 2006 for a dividend yield (dividends/stock price) of 4.7 percent. Of equal importance, it has raised its dividend every year for the last 35 years.

Of course, paying high dividends is not the right strategy for every company, particularly young, growth companies that need to retain the funds to create growth. Read on to find out more.

In theory, CEOs and board members concerned about dividends should ask, "How can the best use of the funds be made?" The rate of return that the corporation can achieve on retained earnings for the benefit of stockholders must be compared to what stockholders could earn if the funds were paid to them in dividends. This is known as the **marginal principle of retained earnings**. Each potential project to be financed by internally generated funds must provide a higher rate of return than the stockholder could achieve on other investments. We speak of this as the opportunity cost of using stockholder funds.

Life Cycle Growth and Dividends

One of the major influences on dividends is the corporate growth rate in sales and the subsequent return on assets. Figure 18–1 shows a corporate **life cycle** and the corresponding dividend policy that is most likely to be found at each stage. A small firm in the initial stages of development (Stage I) pays no dividends because it needs all its profits (if there are any) for reinvestment in new productive assets. If the firm is successful in the marketplace, the demand for its products will create growth in

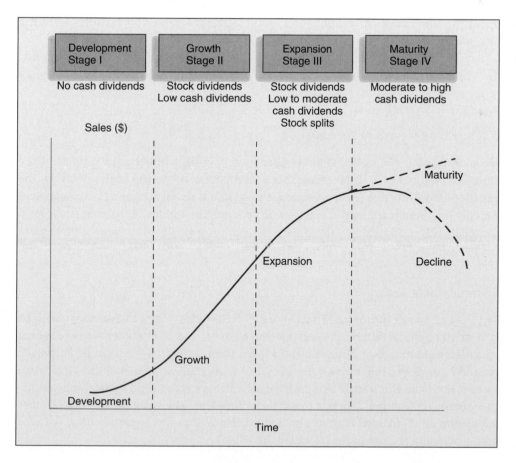

Figure 18–1

Life cycle growth and dividend policy

sales, earnings, and assets, and the firm will move into Stage II. At this stage sales and returns on assets will be growing at an increasing rate, and earnings will still be reinvested. In the early part of Stage II, stock dividends (distribution of additional shares) may be instituted and, in the latter part of Stage II, low cash dividends may be started to inform investors that the firm is profitable but cash is needed for internal investments.

After the growth period the firm enters Stage III. The expansion of sales continues, but at a decreasing rate, and returns on investment may decline as more competition enters the market and tries to take away the firm's market share. During this period the firm is more and more capable of paying cash dividends, as the asset expansion rate slows and external funds become more readily available. Stock dividends and stock splits are still common in the expansion phase, and the dividend payout ratio usually increases from a low level of 5 to 15 percent of earnings to a moderate level of 20 to 30 percent of earnings. Finally, at Stage IV, maturity, the firm maintains a stable growth rate in sales similar to that of the economy as a whole; and, when risk premiums are considered, its returns on assets level out to those of the industry and the economy. In unfortunate cases firms suffer declines in sales if product innovation and diversification have not occurred over the years. In Stage IV, assuming maturity rather than decline, dividends might range from 35 to 40 percent of earnings. These percentages will be different from industry to industry, depending on the individual characteristics of the company, such as operating and financial leverage and the volatility of sales and earnings over the business cycle.

As the chapter continues, more will be said about stock dividends, stock splits, the availability of external funds, and other variables that affect the dividend policy of the firm.

Dividends as a Passive Variable

In the preceding analysis, dividends were used as a passive decision variable: They are to be paid out only if the corporation cannot make better use of the funds for the benefit of stockholders. The active decision variable is retained earnings. Management decides how much retained earnings will be spent for internal corporate needs, and the residual (the amount left after internal expenditures) is paid to the stockholders in cash dividends.

An Incomplete Theory

The only problem with the **residual theory of dividends** is that we have not recognized how stockholders feel about receiving dividends. If the stockholders' only concern is achieving the highest return on their investment, either in the form of *corporate retained earnings remaining in the business or as current dividends paid out,* then there is no issue. But if stockholders have a preference for current funds, for example, over retained earnings, then our theory is incomplete. The issue is not only whether reinvestment of retained earnings or dividends provides the highest return, but also how stockholders react to the two alternatives.

While some researchers maintain that stockholders are indifferent to the division of funds between retained earnings and dividends[1] (holding investment opportunities constant), others disagree.[2] Though there is no conclusive proof one way or the other, the judgment of most researchers is that investors have some preference between dividends and retained earnings.

Arguments for the Relevance of Dividends

A strong case can be made for the relevance of dividends because they resolve uncertainty in the minds of investors. Though retained earnings reinvested in the business theoretically belong to common stockholders, there is still an air of uncertainty about their eventual translation into dividends. Thus, it can be hypothesized that stockholders might apply a higher discount rate (K_e) and assign a lower valuation to funds that are retained in the business as opposed to those that are paid out.[3]

It is also argued that dividends may be viewed more favorably than retained earnings because of the **information content of dividends**. In essence the corporation is telling the stockholder, "We are having a good year, and we wish to share the benefits with you." If the dividend per share is raised, then the information content of the dividend increase is quite positive while a reduction in the dividend generally has negative information content. Even though the corporation may be able to generate the same or higher returns with the funds than the stockholder and perhaps provide even greater dividends in the future, some researchers find that "in an uncertain world in which verbal statements can be ignored or misinterpreted, dividend action does provide a clearcut means of making a statement that speaks louder than a thousand words."[4]

The primary contention in arguing for the relevance of dividend policy is that stockholders' needs and preferences go beyond the marginal principle of retained earnings. The issue is not only who can best utilize the funds (the corporation or the stockholder) but also what are the stockholders' preferences. In practice it appears that most corporations adhere to the following logic. First investment opportunities relative to a required return (marginal analysis) are determined. This is then tempered by some subjective notion of stockholders' desires. Corporations with unusual growth prospects and high rates of return on internal investments generally pay a relatively low dividend (or no dividend). For the more mature firm, an analysis of both investment opportunities and stockholder preferences may indicate that a higher rate of payout is necessary. Examples of dividend policies of selected major U.S. corporations are presented in Table 18 1 on page 558. Notice that the high-growth firms have a propensity to retain earnings rather than pay dividends, while the slow-growth firms have a rather large payout ratio. The normal payout has been approximately 35–40 percent of aftertax earnings in the post–World War II period.

---

[1]Merton H. Miller and Franco Modigliani, "Dividend Policy, Growth and Valuation of Shares," *Journal of Business* 34 (October 1961), pp. 411–33. Under conditions of perfect capital markets with an absence of taxes and flotation costs, it is argued that the sum of discounted value per share after dividend payments equals the total valuation before dividend payments.

[2]Myron J. Gordon, "Optimum Investment and Financing Policy," *Journal of Finance* 18 (May 1963), pp. 264–72; and John Lintner, "Dividends, Earnings, Leverage, Stock Prices, and the Supply of Capital to the Corporation," *Review of Economics and Statistics* 44 (August 1962), pp. 243–69.

[3]Ibid.

[4]Ezra Solomon, *The Theory of Financial Management* (New York: Columbia University Press, 1963).

Table 18–1

Corporate dividend policy

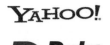

	Historical Growth in EPS (2001–2005)	Estimated Growth in EPS* (2008–2010)	Dividend Payment as a Percent of Aftertax Earnings (2005)
Category 1—Rapid Growth			
Oracle	12%	15%	0%
Amgen	20	16	0
Doubleclick, Inc.	25	34	0
Priceline.com	35	32	0
Yahoo! Inc.	40	29	0
Category 2—Slow Growth			
CH Energy Group	−3%	4%	83%
Cinergy	1	5	71
Duke Energy	0	5	41
Edison International	7	3	45
Southern Co.	2	6	70

*Estimated growth from various issues of *Value Line Investment Survey.*

Dividend Stability

In considering stockholder desires in dividend policy, a primary factor is the maintenance of stability in dividend payments. Thus corporate management must not only ask, "How many profitable investments do we have this year?" It must also ask, "What has been the pattern of dividend payments in the last few years?" Though earnings may change from year to year, the dollar amount of cash dividends tends to be much more stable, increasing in value only as new permanent levels of income are achieved. Note in Figure 18–2 the considerably greater volatility of aftertax profits (earnings) compared to dividends for U.S. manufacturing corporations.

By maintaining a record of relatively stable dividends, corporate management hopes to lower the discount rate (K_e) applied to future dividends of the firm, thus raising the value of the firm. The operative rule appears to be that a stockholder would much prefer to receive $1 a year for three years, rather than 75 cents for the first year, $1.50 for the second year, and 75 cents for the third year—for the same total of $3. Once again, we temper our policy of marginal analysis of retained earnings to include a notion of stockholder preference, with the emphasis on stability of dividends.

Other Factors Influencing Dividend Policy

Corporate management must also consider the legal basis of dividends, the cash flow position of the firm, and the corporation's access to capital markets. Other factors that must be considered include management's desire for control and the tax and financial positions of shareholders. Each is briefly discussed.

Legal Rules

Most states forbid firms to pay dividends that would impair the initial capital contributions to the firm. For this reason dividends may be distributed only from past and current earnings. To pay dividends in excess of this amount would mean the corpora-

Figure 18–2   Corporate profits and dividends for nonfinancial firms

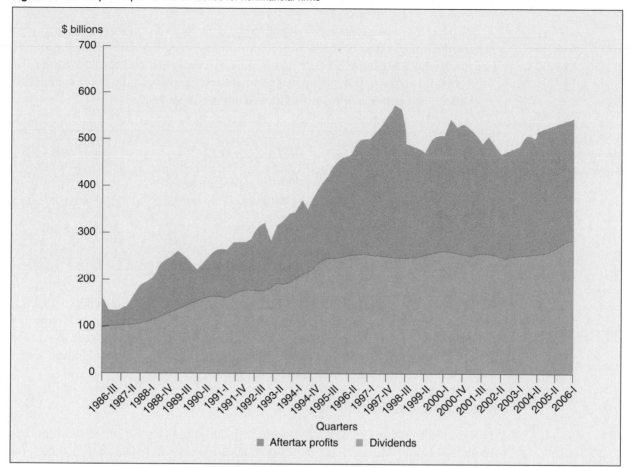

tion is returning to investors their original capital contribution (raiding the capital). If the ABC Company has the following statement of net worth, the maximum dividend payment would be $20 million.

Common stock (1 million shares at $10 par value)*	$10,000,000
Retained earnings	20,000,000
Net worth	$30,000,000

*If there is a "paid-in capital in excess of par" account, some states will allow additional dividend payments while others will not. To simplify the problem for now, paid-in capital in excess of par is not considered.

Why all the concern about impairing permanent capital? Since the firm is going to pay dividends only to those who contributed capital in the first place, what is the problem? Clearly there is no abuse to the stockholders, but what about the creditors? They have extended credit on the assumption that a given capital base would remain intact throughout the life of the loan. While they may not object to the payment of dividends from past and current earnings, they must have the protection of keeping contributed capital in place.[5]

Even the laws against having dividends exceed the total of past and current earnings (retained earnings) may be inadequate to protect creditors. Because retained earnings are merely an accounting concept and in no way certify the current liquidity of the firm, a company paying dividends equal to retained earnings may, in certain cases, jeopardize the operation of the firm. Let us examine Table 18–2.

Table 18–2

Dividend policy considerations

Cash	$ 500,000	Debt	$10,000,000
Accounts receivable	4,500,000	Common stock	10,000,000
Inventory	15,000,000	Retained earnings	15,000,000
Plant and equipment	15,000,000		$35,000,000
	$35,000,000		
	Current earnings	$ 1,500,000	
	Potential dividends	$15,000,000	

Theoretically, management could pay up to $15,000,000 in dividends by selling assets even though current earnings are only $1,500,000. In most cases such frivolous action would not be taken; but the mere possibility encourages creditors to closely watch the balance sheets of corporate debtors and, at times, to impose additional limits on dividend payments as a condition for the granting of credit.

Cash Position of the Firm

Not only do retained earnings fail to portray the liquidity position of the firm, but there are also limitations to the use of current earnings as an indicator of liquidity. As described in Chapter 4, "Financial Forecasting," a growth firm producing the greatest gains in earnings may be in the poorest cash position. As sales and earnings expand rapidly, there is an accompanying buildup in receivables and inventory that may far outstrip cash flow generated through earnings. Note that the cash balance of $500,000 in Table 18–2 represents only one-third of the current earnings of $1,500,000. A firm must do a complete funds flow analysis before establishing a dividend policy.

Access to Capital Markets

The medium-to-large-size firm with a good record of performance may have relatively easy access to the financial markets. A company in such a position may be willing to pay dividends now, knowing it can sell new common stock or bonds in the future if funds are needed. Some corporations may even issue debt or stock now and use part of the proceeds to ensure the maintenance of current dividends. Though this policy seems at variance with the concept of a dividend as a reward, management may justify its action on the basis of maintaining stable dividends. In the era of the late 1990s and

---

[5]Of course, on liquidation of the corporation, the contributed capital to the firm may be returned to common stockholders after creditor obligations are met. Normally stockholders who need to recoup all or part of their contributed capital sell their shares to someone else.

2000s, only a relatively small percentage of firms had sufficient ease of entry to the capital markets to modify their dividend policy in this regard.

Desire for Control

Management must also consider the effect of the dividend policy on its collective ability to maintain control. The directors and officers of a small, closely held firm may be hesitant to pay any dividends for fear of diluting the cash position of the firm.

A larger firm, with a broad base of shareholders, may face a different type of threat in regard to dividend policy. Stockholders, spoiled by a past record of dividend payments, may demand the ouster of management if dividends are withheld.

Tax Position of Shareholders

The tax position of shareholders was once a major consideration, but it is no more. Prior to the Jobs and Growth Tax Relief Act of 2003, dividends were taxed at a maximum rate of 38.6 percent and capital gains (achieved from the increase in the value of a security) at a maximum rate of 20 percent. Wealthy, high income tax bracket investors had a preference for stocks that had the potential to generate capital gains rather than dividends because of the tax rate differential.

With the passage of the 2003 Tax Act, dividends and capital gains are now taxed at a maximum rate of 15 percent for high income taxpayers. It should be pointed out that only *long-term* capital gains (assets held over a year) are taxed at the maximum rate of 15 percent. Short-term capital gains are taxed at the taxpayer's normal rate (up to a maximum in the high 30 percent range). For our purposes, in this discussion and in the problems at the end of the chapter, we shall assume capital gains are long term.

Those in lower tax brackets are now taxed at five percent on both types of income (except in 2008 when lower income taxpayers will not be taxed at all on dividends or capital gains). The 2003 Tax Act provisions are intended to end after 2008, but are likely to be continued well into the future.

Clearly, the 2003 tax legislation makes high dividend paying stocks, such as public utilities, more attractive than they were in the past now that the tax rate differential has been eliminated.

Given that we have examined the many factors that influence dividend policy, let us track the actual procedures for announcing and paying a dividend. Though dividends are quoted on an annual basis, the payments actually take place over four quarters during the year. For example, in 2006 H.J. Heinz Corp. paid an annual cash dividend of $1.20. This meant stockholders received $0.30 in dividends each quarter. If we divide the annual dividend per share by the current stock price, the result is called the **dividend yield**, which is the percentage return provided by the cash dividend based on the current market price. Because Heinz's stock was selling $36.00 per share in early 2006, the dividend yield at the time was 3.33 percent ($1.20/$36.00). Also because Heinz had expected earnings per share of $2.60 for 2006, the **dividend payout ratio** was 46.2 percent ($1.20/$2.60).

Three key dates are associated with the declaration of a quarterly dividend: the ex-dividend date, the holder-of-record date, and the payment date.

Dividend Payment Procedures

Bill Gates: What Have You Done for Me Lately?

When Bill Gates, the founder and chairman of the board of Microsoft, walked out of a movie theater in December 2004, people stopped eating their popcorn long enough to give him a big thank you and pat on the back. At first the richest man on the face of the earth was surprised, but he quickly figured out that praise could be traced back to the $3 per share special cash dividend his company was about to pay.* With a $28 stock price at the time, that translated into a 10.71 percent one time payout to stockholders. The company was intent on continuing its $.32 regular annual dividend for an additional 1.14 percent yield or a total dividend yield of 11.85 percent for 2004.

There were two primary reasons for Bill Gates and Microsoft paying the huge $3 per share special dividend. One was that Microsoft, the king of stock options for employees during the 1990s and early 2000s, had stopped granting them. This corporate policy can be traced to new accounting rules requiring that stock options be expensed at the time of issue, potentially sharply cutting into earnings for Microsoft and other options-granting companies. Instead of giving stock options to high performing individuals (most of whom are stockholders), the company decided to give them a very large cash dividend. Of course, all other stockholders benefited as well.

A second reason for the special $3 cash dividend was the huge cash hoard that Microsoft had built up through a decade and a half of enormous profitability. At the time of the payout, Microsoft was sitting on $64.6 billion in cash and marketable securities, which represented 70 percent of total assets. The firm had already undertaken all the profitable ventures it could possibly pursue and was being told by the U.S. Justice Department to slow down its anticompetitive activities. To a certain extent, breakneck future growth was not a legal option.

In order to reduce the cash hoard, the company paid out the $3 special dividend on 10 billion shares or $30 billion in extra dividends. This reduced the cash balance to $34.4 billion. But by 2005, the cash balance was once again growing by $1 billion a month due to the cash generating capacity of its Windows operating system and its Office productivity software.

A new cash balance of $50 to $60 billion was not out of the question in the not too distant future, and employees and stockholders were asking Bill Gates, "What have you done for me lately?" The question was particularly relevant because the stock had been stuck in the $22–$28 range for the last three years.

———
*Jay Greene, "BusinessWeek Online," July 28, 2005.

We begin with the **holder-of-record date**. On this date the firm examines its books to determine who is entitled to a cash dividend. To have your name included on the corporate books, you must have bought or owned the stock before the **ex-dividend date**, which is two business days before the holder-of-record date. If you bought the stock on the ex-dividend date or later, your name will eventually be transferred to the corporate books, but you bought the stock without the current quarterly dividend privilege. Thus we say you bought the stock ex-dividend.[6] As an example, a stock with a holder-of-record date of March 4 will go ex-dividend on March 2. You must buy the stock by March 1 (three days before the holder-of-record date and a day before the ex-dividend date) to get the dividend. Investors are very conscious of the date on which the stock goes ex-dividend, and the value of the stock will go down by the value of the quarterly dividend on the ex-dividend date (all other things being equal). Finally, in our example, we might assume the **dividend payment date** is April 1 and checks will go out to entitled stockholders on or about this time.

———
[6]In this case the old stockholder will receive the dividend.

A **stock dividend** represents a distribution of additional shares to common stockholders. The typical size of such dividends is in the 10 percent range, so a stockholder with 10 shares might receive 1 new share in the form of a stock dividend. Larger distributions of 20 to 25 percent or more are usually considered to have the characteristics of a stock split, a topic to be discussed later in the chapter.

Stock Dividend

Accounting Considerations for a Stock Dividend

Assume that before the declaration of a stock dividend, the XYZ Corporation has the net worth position indicated in Table 18–3.

Capital accounts		
	Common stock (1,000,000 shares at $10 par)	$10,000,000
	Capital in excess of par	5,000,000
	Retained earnings	15,000,000
	Net worth	$30,000,000

Table 18–3

XYZ Corporation's financial position before stock dividend

If a 10 percent stock dividend is declared, shares outstanding will increase by 100,000 (10 percent times 1 million shares). An accounting transfer will occur between retained earnings and the two capital stock accounts based on the market value of the stock dividend. If the stock is selling at $15 a share, we will assign $1 million to common stock (100,000 shares times $10 par) and $500,000 to capital in excess of par. The latter value is based on 100,000 new shares times ($15 − $10), or $5. In the calculation in parentheses, we subtracted par value from market value. The net worth position of XYZ after the transfer is shown in Table 18–4.

Capital accounts		
	Common stock (1,100,000 shares at $10 par)	$11,000,000
	Capital in excess of par	5,500,000
	Retained earnings	13,500,000
	Net worth	$30,000,000

Table 18–4

XYZ Corporation's financial position after stock dividend

Value to the Investor

An appropriate question might be: Is a stock dividend of real value to the investor? Suppose your finance class collectively purchased $1,000 worth of assets and issued 10 shares of stock to each class member. Three days later it is announced that each stockholder will receive an extra share. Has anyone benefited from the stock dividend? Of course not! The asset base remains the same ($1,000), and your proportionate ownership in the business is unchanged (everyone got the same new share). You merely have more paper to tell you what you already knew.

The same logic is essentially true in the corporate setting. In the case of the XYZ Corporation, shown in Tables 18–3 and 18–4, we assumed 1 million shares were outstanding before the stock dividend and 1.1 million shares afterward. Now let us assume the corporation had aftertax earnings of $6.6 million. Without the stock dividend, earnings per share would be $6.60, and with the dividend $6.00.

$$\text{Earnings per share} = \frac{\text{Earnings after taxes}}{\text{Shares outstanding}}$$

Without stock dividend:

$$= \frac{\$6.6 \text{ million}}{1 \text{ million shares}} = \$6.60$$

With stock dividend:

$$= \frac{\$6.6 \text{ million}}{1.1 \text{ million shares}} = \$6.00$$
$$\text{(10\% decline)}$$

Earnings per share have gone down by exactly the same percentage that shares outstanding increased. For further illustration, assuming that Stockholder A had 10 shares before the stock dividend and 11 afterward, what are his or her total claims to earnings? As expected, they remain the same, at $66.

$$\text{Claim to earnings} = \text{Shares} \times \text{Earnings per share}$$

Without stock dividend: $10 \times \$6.60 = \$66$
With stock dividend: $11 \times \$6.00 = \$66$

Taking the analogy one step further, assuming the stock sold at 20 times earnings before and after the stock dividend, what is the total market value of the portfolio in each case?

$$\text{Total market value} = \text{Shares} \times (\text{Price-earnings ratio} \times \text{Earnings per share})$$

Without stock dividend:

$$10 \times (20 \times \$6.60)$$
$$10 \times \$132 = \$1,320$$

With stock dividend:

$$11 \times (20 \times \$6.00)$$
$$11 \times \$120 = \$1,320$$

The total market value is unchanged. Note that if the stockholder sells the 11th share to acquire cash, his or her stock portfolio will be worth $120 less than it was before the stock dividend.

Possible Value of Stock Dividends

There are limited circumstances under which a stock dividend may be more than a financial sleight of hand. If, at the time a stock dividend is declared, the cash dividend per share remains constant, the stockholder will receive greater total cash dividends. Assume the annual cash dividend for the XYZ Corporation will remain $1 per share even though earnings per share decline from $6.60 to $6.00. In this instance a stockholder going from 10 to 11 shares as the result of a stock dividend has a $1 increase in total dividends. The overall value of his total shares may then increase in response to larger dividends.

Use of Stock Dividends

Stock dividends are most frequently used by growth companies such as Oracle or eBay as a form of "informational content" in explaining the retention of funds for reinvestment purposes. This was indicated in the discussion of the life cycle of the firm earlier in the chapter. A corporation president may state, "Instead of doing more in the way of cash dividends, we are providing a stock dividend. The funds remaining in the corporation will be used for highly profitable investment opportunities." The market reaction to such an approach may be neutral or slightly positive.

Another use of stock dividends may be to camouflage the inability of the corporation to pay cash dividends and to cover up the ineffectiveness of management in generating cash flow. The president may proclaim, "Though we are unable to pay cash dividends, we wish to reward you with a 15 percent stock dividend." Well-informed investors are likely to react negatively.

Stock Splits

A **stock split** is similar to a stock dividend, only more shares are distributed. For example, a two-for-one stock split would double the number of shares outstanding. In general, the rules of the New York Stock Exchange and the Financial Accounting Standards Board encourage distributions in excess of 20 to 25 percent to be handled as stock splits.

The accounting treatment for a stock split is somewhat different from that for a stock dividend, in that there is no transfer of funds from retained earnings to the capital accounts but merely a reduction in par value and a proportionate increase in the number of shares outstanding. For example, a two-for-one stock split for the XYZ Corporation would necessitate the accounting adjustments shown in Table 18–5.

In this case all adjustments are in the common stock account. Because the number of shares is doubled and the par value halved, the market price of the stock should drop proportionately. There has been much discussion in the financial literature about the

Table 18–5
XYZ Corporation before and after stock split

Before	
Common stock (1 million shares at $10 par)	$10,000,000
Capital in excess of par	5,000,000
Retained earnings	15,000,000
	$30,000,000
After	
Common stock (2 million shares at $5 par)	$10,000,000
Capital in excess of par	5,000,000
Retained earnings	15,000,000
	$30,000,000

impact of a split on overall stock value. While there might be some positive benefit, that benefit is virtually impossible to capture after the split has been announced. Perhaps a $66 stock will drop only to $36 after a two-for-one split, but one must act very early in the process to benefit.

The primary purpose of a stock split is to lower the price of a security into a more popular trading range. A stock selling for over $100 per share may be excluded from consideration by many small investors. Splits are also popular because only stronger companies that have witnessed substantial growth in market price are in a position to participate in them.

Reverse Stock Splits

In the bear market of the early 2000s, the **reverse stock split** became popular. In this case, a firm exchanges fewer shares for existing shares with the intent of increasing the stock price. An example might be a one-for-four reverse stock split in which you would get one new share in place of four old shares. A stockholder who held 100 shares would now own 25. With total earnings unaffected by the reverse stock split, earnings per share should increase fourfold because there would be only one-fourth as many shares outstanding.

It is also hoped that the stock price will increase fourfold. Perhaps, you originally had 100 shares at $2 per share and now you have 25 shares at $8. The stock price does not always increase by a commensurate amount. Keep in mind that a reverse stock split is normally used by firms whose stock has plummeted in value. The announcement of a reverse stock split may represent further evidence that the firm is having problems.

One useful purpose of a reverse stock split is to attempt to place a stock's value at a level that is acceptable to the New York Stock Exchange, the American Stock Exchange, or the NASDAQ for trading purposes. All three will delist a stock if its value remains under $1 for an extended period of time (such as six months).

As an example, Lucent Technologies was in danger of being delisted from the New York Stock Exchange in late 2002 because its stock had been in a $.40–.70 range for a number of months. After a 3-for-1 reverse stock split, the stock's price settled in at $1.50. At least for a while, Lucent was out of danger of being delisted. Of course, if the stock price falls again, Lucent will have to try a second reverse split and may not be as fortunate the second time around.

Firms such as Millicom, Storage Access (now BluePoint Data Storage), Diversinet, and Total Entertainment also utilized reverse stock splits in an attempt to maintain their listing status in the current decade.

Repurchase of Stock as an Alternative to Dividends

A firm with excess cash may choose to make a **corporate stock repurchase** of its own shares in the market, rather than pay a cash dividend. For this reason, the stock repurchase decision may be thought of as an alternative to the payment of cash dividends.

The benefits to the stockholder are equal under either alternative, at least in theory. For purposes of our study, the Morgan Corporation's financial position is described by the data in Table 18–6.

Table 18–6

Financial data of
Morgan Corporation

Earnings after taxes	$3,000,000
Shares	1,000,000
Earnings per share	$3
Price-earnings ratio	10
Market price per share	$30
Excess cash	$2,000,000

Assume the firm is considering a repurchase of its own shares in the market.

The firm has $2 million in excess cash, and it wishes to compare the value to stockholders of a $2 cash dividend (on the million shares outstanding) as opposed to spending the funds to repurchase shares in the market. If the cash dividend is paid, the shareholder will have $30 in stock and the $2 cash dividend. On the other hand, the $2 million may be used to repurchase shares at slightly over market value (to induce sale).[7] The overall benefit to stockholders is that earnings per share will go up as the number of shares outstanding is decreased. If the price-earnings ratio of the stock remains constant, then the price of the stock should also go up. If a purchase price of $32 is used to induce sale, then 62,500 shares will be purchased.

$$\frac{\text{Excess funds}}{\text{Purchase price per share}} = \frac{\$2,000,000}{\$32} = 62,500 \text{ shares}$$

Total shares outstanding are reduced to 937,500 (1,000,000 − 62,500). Revised earnings per share for the Morgan Corporation become:

$$\frac{\text{Earnings after taxes}}{\text{Shares}} = \frac{\$3,000,000}{937,500} = \$3.20$$

Since the price-earnings ratio for the stock is 10, the market value of the stock should go to $32. Thus we see that the consequences of the two alternatives are presumed to be the same as shown in the following:

(1) **Funds Used for Cash Dividend**	(2) **Funds Used to Repurchase Stock**
Market value per share $30	
Cash dividend per share 2	
$32	Market value per share $32

Prior to the Tax Act of 2003, the stock price increase of $2 received preferential capital gains tax treatment over the $2 cash dividend, but this is no longer the case. Both are now taxed at the same rate, though the capital gains tax can be deferred until the stock is sold.[8]

In either instance the total value is presumed to be $32. Theoretically, the stockholder would be indifferent with respect to the two alternatives.

---

[7]To derive the desired equality between the two alternatives, the purchase price for the new shares should equal the current market price plus the proposed cash dividend under the first alternative ($30 + $2 = $32).
[8]Some would argue that the capital gains tax can be completely avoided. If you hold the stock until you die, there is no capital gains tax on your estate. An estate tax will have to be paid on property valued over $2 million, but that is different from a capital gains tax. (The $2 million exemption will increase over time.)

Other Reasons for Repurchase

In addition to using the repurchase decision as an alternative to cash dividends, corporate management may acquire its own shares in the market, because it believes they are selling at a low price. A corporation president who sees his firm's stock decline by 25 to 30 percent over a six-month period may determine the stock is the best investment available to the corporation.

By repurchasing shares the corporation can maintain a constant demand for its own securities and, perhaps, stave off further decline. Stock repurchases by corporations were partially credited with stabilizing the stock market after the 508-point crash on October 19, 1987.

In Table 18–7, we see some recent stock repurchases announced by major U.S. corporations. In many cases companies may take years to complete stock repurchases, and they may time the repurchase depending on stock price behavior.

Table 18–7

Recent examples of share repurchase announcements

Company	Amount ($ billion)	Date Announced
Citigroup	15.0	4/12/05
IBM	5.0	4/26/05
Merrill Lynch	4.0	4/19/05
PepsiCo	3.0	2/28/05
Duke Energy	2.5	2/25/05
Genentech	2.0	6/15/05
Air Products	0.5	3/18/05
Liberty Mutual	0.2	6/22/05

Reacquired shares may also be used for employee stock options or as part of a tender offer in a merger. A firm may also reacquire part of its shares as a protective device against being taken over as a merger candidate.

Dividend Reinvestment Plans

Years ago, many companies started **dividend reinvestment plans** for their shareholders. These plans take various forms, but basically they provide the investor with an opportunity to buy additional shares of stock with the cash dividend paid by the company. Some plans will sell treasury stock or authorized but unissued shares to the stockholders. With this type of plan, the company is the beneficiary of increased cash flow, since dividends paid are returned to the company for reinvestment in common stock. These types of plans have been very popular with cash-short public utilities, and often public utilities will allow shareholders a 5 percent discount from market value at the time of purchase. This is justified because no investment banking or underwriting fees need be paid.

Under a second popular dividend reinvestment plan, the company's transfer agent, usually a bank, buys shares of stock in the market for the stockholder. This plan provides no cash flow for the company; but it is a service to the shareholder, who benefits from much lower transaction costs, the right to own fractional shares, and more flexibility in choosing between cash and common stock. Usually a shareholder can also add cash payments of between $500 and $1,000 per month to his or her dividend payments and receive the same lower transaction costs. Shareholder accounts are kept at the bank, and quarterly statements are provided.

Summary

In choosing either to pay a dividend to stockholders or to reinvest the funds in the company, management's first consideration is whether the firm will be able to earn a higher return for the stockholders. However, we must temper this "highest return theory" with a consideration of stockholder preferences and the firm's need for earnings retention and growth as presented in the life cycle growth curve.

Dividends provide information content to shareholders. An increase in the dividend is generally interpreted as a positive signal while dividend cuts are negative, and shareholders generally prefer dividend stability. The dividend payout ratio (dividends/earnings) often signals where a firm is in its life cycle stage. During the initial stages, dividends will be small or nonexistent, while in the later stages, dividends normally increase.

Other factors influencing dividend policy are legal rules relating to maximum payments, the cash position of the firm, the firm's access to capital markets, and management's desire for control.

An alternative (or a supplement) to cash dividends may be the use of stock dividends and stock splits. While neither of these financing devices directly changes the intrinsic value of the stockholders' position, they may provide communication to stockholders and bring the stock price into a more acceptable trading range. A stock dividend may take on actual value when total cash dividends are allowed to increase. Nevertheless, the alert investor will watch for abuses of stock dividends—situations in which the corporation indicates that something of great value is occurring when, in fact, the new shares that are created merely represent the same proportionate interest for each shareholder.

List of Terms

marginal principle of retained earnings   555
life cycle   555
residual theory of dividends   556
information content of dividends   557
dividend yield   561
dividend payout ratio   561
holder-of-record date   562

ex-dividend date   562
dividend payment date   562
stock dividend   563
stock split   565
reverse stock split   566
corporate stock repurchase   566
dividend reinvestment plans   568

Discussion Questions

1. How does the marginal principle of retained earnings relate to the returns that a stockholder may make in other investments?
2. Discuss the difference between a passive and an active dividend policy.
3. How does the stockholder, in general, feel about the relevance of dividends?
4. Explain the relationship between a company's growth possibilities and its dividend policy.
5. Since initial contributed capital theoretically belongs to the stockholders, why are there legal restrictions on paying out the funds to the stockholders?

6. Discuss how desire for control may influence a firm's willingness to pay dividends.

7. If you buy stock on the ex-dividend date, will you receive the upcoming quarterly dividend?

8. How is a stock split (versus a stock dividend) treated on the financial statements of a corporation?

9. Why might a stock dividend or a stock split be of limited value to an investor?

10. Does it make sense for a corporation to repurchase its own stock? Explain.

11. What advantages to the corporation and the stockholder do dividend reinvestment plans offer?

Practice Problems and Solutions

Stock dividend

1. United Equipment Corp. shows the following capital accounts before a 10 percent stock dividend.

Common stock (200,000 shares at $5 par)	$1,000,000
Capital in excess of par	600,000
Retained earnings	2,400,000
Net worth.	$4,000,000

The firm's shares have a market price of $20. Show the revised capital accounts after the 10 percent stock dividend.

Effect of stock dividend on the stockholders

2. a. Assume United Equipment Corp. in the problem above had total earnings of $400,000 before the stock dividend. It also had a P/E ratio of 10. What were the EPS and stock price before the stock dividend?

b. After the stock dividend, what will earnings per share and the stock price be? Assume the P/E ratio stays at 10.

c. Albert Gonzales owned 100 shares before and 110 after the stock dividend. What is the value of his portfolio (total holdings) before and after the stock dividend? Is he any better off as a result of the stock dividend?

Solutions

1. Revised capital accounts after the 10 percent stock dividend.

*Common stock (220,000 shares at $5 par)	$1,100,000
†Capital in excess of par.	900,000
‡Retained earnings.	2,000,000
Net worth	$4,000,000

*20,000 more shares are added to common stock.

†Added capital in excess of par is equal to the number of new shares times the (market price minus par value).

$$20,000 \times (\$20 - \$5) = 20,000 \times \$15 = \$300,000$$

This value is added to the initial value of capital in excess of par to arrive at total capital in excess of par.

$$\$300,000 + 600,000 = \$900,000$$

‡The retained earnings shown above is equal to the initial retained earnings value minus the addition to common stock of $100,000 and the addition to 'capital in excess of par' of $300,000.

$$\$2,400,000 - \$100,000 - \$300,000 = \$2,000,000$$

2. *a.* EPS before the stock dividend = Earnings/Shares = $400,000/200,000 = $2
Stock price before the stock dividend = P/E ratio × EPS = 10 × $2 = $20

b. EPS after the stock dividend = Earnings/Shares = $400,000/220,000 = $1.82
Stock price after the stock dividend = 10 × $1.82 = $18.20

c. Value of portfolio before the stock dividend:

$$100 \text{ shares} \times \$20 \text{ stock price} = \$2,000$$

Value of portfolio after the stock dividend:

$$110 \text{ shares} \times 18.20 \text{ stock price} = \$2,002$$

The only difference between the before and after stock price is due to rounding ($2,000 vs. $2,002). Albert Gonzales is no better off.

All problems are available in Homework Manager. Please see the preface for more information.   **Problems**

1. Neil Diamond Brokers, Inc., reported earnings per share of $4.00 and paid $.90 in dividends. What is the payout ratio?   Payout ratio

2. Sewell Enterprises earned $160 million last year and retained $100 million. What is the payout ratio?   Payout ratio

3. Biogen, Inc., earned $850 million last year and had a 30 percent payout ratio. How much did the firm add to its retained earnings?   Payout ratio

4. Polycom Systems earned $480 million last year and paid out 20 percent of earnings in dividends.   Dividends, retained earnings, and yield

    a. By how much did the company's retained earnings increase?

    b. With 100 million shares outstanding and stock price of $80, what was the dividend yield? (Hint: First compute dividends per share.)

5. The following companies have different financial statistics. What dividend policies would you recommend for them? Explain your reasons.   Growth and dividend policy

	Turtle Co.	Hare Corp.
Growth rate in sales and earnings	5%	20%
Cash as a percentage of total assets	15	2

6. Carnegie Mellon and Produce Co. has $120,000,000 in stockholders' equity. Forty million dollars is listed as common stock and the balance is in retained earnings. The firm has $250,000,000 in total assets and 3 percent of this value is in cash. Earnings for the year are $20,000,000 and are included in retained earnings.   Limits on dividends

    a. What is the legal limit on current dividends?

    b. What is the practical limit based on liquidity?

    c. If the company pays out the amount in part *b,* what is the dividend payout ratio? (Compute this based on total dollars rather than on a per share basis because the number of shares is not given.)

$$\text{Payout ratio} = \text{Dividends/Earnings}$$

Life cycle growth and dividends

7. A financial analyst is attempting to assess the future dividend policy of Environmental Systems by examining its life cycle. She anticipates no payout of earnings in the form of cash dividends during the development stage (I). During the growth stage (II), she anticipates 10 percent of earnings will be distributed as dividends. As the firm progresses to the expansion stage (III), the payout ratio will go up to 30 percent, and eventually reach 50 percent during the maturity stage (IV).

a. Assuming earnings per share will be as follows during each of the four stages, indicate the cash dividend per share (if any) during each stage.

Stage I	$ .15
Stage II	1.80
Stage III	2.60
Stage IV	3.10

b. Assume in Stage IV that an investor owns 275 shares and is in a 31 percent tax bracket; what will be the investor's aftertax income from the cash dividend?

c. In what two stages is the firm most likely to utilize stock dividends or stock splits?

Stock split and stock dividend

8. Austin Power Company has the following balance sheet:

Assets	
Cash..	$ 50,000
Accounts receivable.................................	250,000
Fixed assets.......................................	700,000
Total assets...................................	$1,000,000

Liabilities		
	Accounts payable..........................	$ 250,000
	Notes payable.............................	50,000
	Common stock 100,000 shares @ $2 par........	200,000
Capital	Capital in excess of par	100,000
accounts	Retained earnings	400,000
		$1,000,000

The firm has a market price of $11 a share.

a. Show the effect on the capital account(s) of a two-for-one stock split.

b. Show the effect on the capital account of a 10 percent stock dividend. Part *b* is separate from part *a*. In part *b* do not assume the stock split has taken place.

c. Based on the balance in retained earnings, which of the two dividend plans is more restrictive on future cash dividends?

Policy on payout ratio

9. In doing a five-year analysis of future dividends, the Dawson Corporation is considering the following two plans. The values represent dividends per share.

Year	Plan A	Plan B
1..........	$1.50	$ .50
2.........	1.50	2.00
3.........	1.50	.20
4.........	1.60	4.00
5.........	1.60	1.70

  a. How much in total dividends per share will be paid under each plan over the five years?

  b. Mr. Bright, the vice-president of finance, suggests that stockholders often prefer a stable dividend policy to a highly variable one. He will assume that stockholders apply a lower discount rate to dividends that are stable. The discount rate to be used for Plan A is 10 percent; the discount rate for plan B is 12 percent. Which plan will provide the higher present value for the future dividends? (Round to two places to the right of the decimal point.)

10. The stock of North American Dandruff Company is selling at $80 per share. The firm pays a dividend of $2.50 per share.

  a. What is the dividend yield?

  b. If the firm has a payout rate of 50 percent, what is the firm's P/E ratio?

Dividend yield

11. The shares of Charles Darwin Fitness Centers sell for $60. The firm has a P/E ratio of 20. Forty percent of earnings are paid out in dividends. What is the firm's dividend yield?

Dividend yield

12. Ms. Reeves is in a 35 percent marginal tax bracket. If she receives $2.40 in cash dividends, how much in taxes (per share) will she pay? (Recall the 15 percent rule.)

Dividends and taxation

13. Chuck Wagon owns 200 shares of Western Transportation Company stock, which he bought for $17 per share. He is in a 35 percent tax bracket. It is the first week in December, and he has already received the full cash dividend for the year of $.90 per share. For his tax bracket, dividends are taxed at 15 percent. The stock is currently selling for 32⅛. He has decided to sell the stock and after paying broker commissions, his net proceeds will be $32 per share. His tax rate on capital gains is also 15 percent (the capital gains are long term).

  How much in total taxes will Chuck Wagon pay this year for his investment in Western Transportation Company? Consider dividend income as well as capital gains.

Dividends and taxation

14. The Ohio Freight Company's common stock is selling for $40 the day before the stock goes ex-dividend. The annual dividend yield is 6.7 percent, and dividends are distributed quarterly. Based solely on the impact of the cash dividend, by how much should the stock go down on the ex-dividend date? What will the new price of the stock be?

Ex-dividends date and stock price

15. The Western Pipe Company has the following capital section in its balance sheet. Its stock is currently selling for $5 per share.

Stock dividend and cash dividend

Common stock (50,000 shares at $1 par)	$ 50,000
Capital in excess of par.	50,000
Retained earnings.	100,000
	$200,000

  The firm intends to first declare a 10 percent stock dividend and then pay a 20-cent cash dividend (which also causes a reduction of retained earnings). Show the capital section of the balance sheet after the first transaction and then after the second transaction.

Cash dividend
policy

16. Phillips Rock and Mud is trying to determine the maximum amount of cash dividends it can pay this year. Assume its balance sheet is as follows:

Assets	
Cash......................................	$ 312,500
Accounts receivable.........................	800,000
Fixed assets................................	987,500
Total assets.............................	$2,100,000

Liabilities and Stockholders' Equity	
Accounts payable...........................	$ 445,000
Long term payable	280,000
Common stock (250,000 shares at $2 par)	500,000
Retained earnings	875,000
Total liabilities and stockholders' equity	$2,100,000

   a. From a legal perspective, what is the maximum amount of dividends per share the firm could pay? Is this realistic?

   b. In terms of cash availability, what is the maximum amount of dividends per share the firm could pay?

   c. Assume the firm earned 16 percent return on stockholders' equity last year. If the board wishes to pay out 60 percent of earnings in the form of dividends, how much will dividends per share be? (Round to two places to the right of the decimal point.)

Dividends and
stockholder wealth
maximization

17. The Warner Corporation has earnings of $750,000 with 300,000 shares outstanding. Its P/E ratio is 16. The firm is holding $400,000 of funds to invest or pay out in dividends. If the funds are retained, the aftertax return on investment will be 15 percent, and this will add to present earnings. The 15 percent is the normal return anticipated for the corporation and the P/E ratio would remain unchanged. If the funds are paid out in the form of dividends, the P/E ratio will increase by 10 percent because the stockholders have a preference for dividends over retained earnings. Which plan will maximize the market value of the stock?

Dividend valuation
model and wealth
maximization

18. Omni Telecom is trying to decide whether to increase its cash dividend immediately or use the funds to increase its future growth rate. It will use the dividend valuation model originally presented in Chapter 10 for purposes of analysis. The model was shown as Formula 10–9 on page 298 and is reproduced below (with a slight addition in definition of terms).

$$P_0 = \frac{D_1}{K_e - g}$$

P_0 = Price of the stock today

D_1 = Dividend at the end of the first year
$\qquad D_0 \times (1 + g)$

D_0 = Dividend today

K_e = Required rate of return

g = Constant growth rate in dividends

D_0 is currently $2.00, K_e is 10 percent, and g is 5 percent.

Under Plan A, D_0 would be *immediately* increased to $2.20 and K_e and g will remain unchanged.

Under Plan B, D_0 will remain at $2.00 but g will go up to 6 percent and K_e will remain unchanged.

a. Compute P_0 (price of the stock today) under Plan A. Note D_1 will be equal to $D_0 \times (1 + g)$, or $2.20 (1.05). K_e will equal 10 percent and g will equal 5 percent.

b. Compute P_0 (price of the stock today) under Plan B. Note D_1 will be equal to $D_0 \times (1 + g)$, or $2.00 (1.06). K_e will be equal to 10 percent and g will be equal to 6 percent.

c. Which plan will produce the higher value?

19. Wilson Pharmaceuticals' stock has done very well in the market during the last three years. It has risen from $45 to $70 per share. The firm's current statement of stockholders' equity is as follows:

Common stock (4 million shares issued at par value of $10 per share)	$ 40,000,000
Paid-in capital in excess of par	15,000,000
Retained earnings.	45,000,000
Net worth.	$100,000,000

Stock split and its effects

a. What changes would occur in the statement of stockholders' equity after a two-for-one stock split?

b. What changes would occur in the statement of stockholders' equity after a three-for-one stock split?

c. Assume that Wilson earned $14 million. What would be its earnings per share before and after the two-for-one stock split? After the three-for-one stock split?

d. What would be the price per share after the two-for-one stock split? After the three-for-one stock split? (Assume that the price-earnings ratio of 20 stays the same.)

e. Should a stock split change the price-earnings ratio for Wilson?

20. Ace Products sells marked playing cards to blackjack dealers. It has not paid a dividend in many years, but is currently contemplating some kind of dividend. The capital accounts for the firm are as follows:

Stock dividend and its effect

Common stock (2,000,000 shares at $5 par)	$10,000,000
Capital in excess of par*	6,000,000
Retained earnings	24,000,000
Net worth.	$40,000,000

*The increase in capital in excess of par as a result of a stock dividend is equal to the new shares created times (Market price − Par Value).

The company's stock is selling for $20 per share. The company had total earnings of $4,000,000 during the year. With 2,000,000 shares outstanding, earnings per share were $2.00. The firm has a P/E ratio of 10.

a. What adjustments would have to be made to the capital accounts for a 10 percent stock dividend? Show the new capital accounts.

b. What adjustments would be made to EPS and the stock price? (Assume the P/E ratio remains constant.)

c. How many shares would an investor end up with if he or she originally had 100 shares?

d. What is the investor's total investment worth before and after the stock dividend if the P/E ratio remains constant? (There may be a $1 to $2 difference due to rounding.)

e. Has Ace Products pulled a magic trick, or has it given the investor something of value? Explain.

Stock dividend and cash dividend

21. Health Systems, Inc. is considering a 15 percent stock dividend. The capital accounts are as follows:

Common stock (3,000,000 shares at $10 par)	$30,000,000
Capital in excess of par*	·15,000,000
Retained earnings	45,000,000
Net worth	$90,000,000

*The increase in capital in excess of par as a result of a stock dividend is equal to the shares created times (Market price − Par value).

The company's stock is selling for $35 per share. The company had total earnings of $7,500,000 with 3,000,000 shares outstanding and earnings per share were $2.50. The firm has a P/E ratio of 14.

a. What adjustments would have to be made to the capital accounts for a 15 percent stock dividend? Show the new capital accounts.

b. What adjustments would be made to EPS and the stock price? (Assume the P/E ratio remains constant.)

c. How many shares would an investor have if he or she originally had 100?

d. What is the investor's total investment worth before and after the stock dividend if the P/E ratio remains constant? (There may be a slight difference due to rounding.)

e. Assume Mr. Heart, the president of Health Systems, wishes to benefit stockholders by keeping the cash dividend at a previous level of $1.05 in spite of the fact that the stockholders how have 15 percent more shares. Because the cash dividend is not reduced, the stock price is assumed to remain at $35.

What is an investor's total investment worth after the stock dividend if he/she had 100 shares before the stock dividend?

f. Under the scenario described in part e, is the investor better off?

g. As a final question, what is the dividend yield on this stock under the scenario described in part e?

Reverse stock split

22. Double Vision Optical Company has had a lot of complaints from customers of late and its stock price is now only $2 per share. It is going to employ a one-for-six reverse stock split to increase the stock value. Assume Johnnie Walker owns 120 shares.

    a. How many shares will he own after the reverse stock split?

    b. What is the anticipated price of the stock after the reverse stock split?

    c. Because investors often have a negative reaction to a reverse stock split, assume the stock only goes up to 80 percent of the value computed in part *b*. What will the stock's price be?

    d. How has the total value of Johnnie Walker's holdings changed from before the reverse stock split to after the reverse stock split (based on the stock value computed in part *c*)? To get the total value before and after the split, multiply the shares held times the stock price.

23. The Carlton Corporation has $4 million in earnings after taxes and 1 million shares outstanding. The stock trades at a P/E ratio of 20. The firm has $3 million in excess cash.   *Cash dividend versus stock repurchase*

    a. Compute the current price of the stock.

    b. If the $3 million is used to pay dividends, how much will dividends per share be?

    c. If the $3 million is used to repurchase shares in the market at a price of $83 per share, how many shares will be acquired? (Round to the nearest share.)

    d. What will the new earnings per share be? (Round to two places to the right of the decimal.)

    e. If the P/E ratio remains constant, what will the price of the securities be? By how much, in terms of dollars, did the repurchase increase the stock price?

    f. Has the stockholder's total wealth changed as a result of the stock repurchase as opposed to receiving the cash dividends?

    g. What are some reasons a corporation may wish to repurchase its own shares in the market?

24. The Hastings Sugar Corporation has the following pattern of net income each year, and associated capital expenditure projects. The firm can earn a higher return on the projects than the stockholders could earn if the funds were paid out in the form of dividends.   *Retaining funds versus paying them out*

Year	Net Income	Profitable Capital Expenditure
1	$10 million	$ 7 million
2	15 million	11 million
3	9 million	6 million
4	12 million	7 million
5	14 million	8 million

    The Hastings Corporation has 2 million shares outstanding (the following questions are separate from each other).

    a. If the marginal principle of retained earnings is applied, how much in total cash dividends will be paid over the five years?

    b. If the firm simply uses a payout ratio of 40 percent of net income, how much in total cash dividends will be paid?

c. If the firm pays a 10 percent stock dividend in years 2 through 5, and also pays a cash dividend of $2.40 per share for each of the five years, how much in total dividends will be paid?

d. Assume the payout ratio in each year is to be 30 percent of net income and the firm will pay a 20 percent stock dividend in years 2 through 5; how much will dividends per share for each year be?

COMPREHENSIVE PROBLEM

Modern Furniture Company (Dividend payments versus stock repurchases)

Modern Furniture Company had finally arrived at the point where it had a sufficient excess cash flow of $4.8 million to consider paying a dividend. It had 3 million shares of stock outstanding and was considering paying a cash dividend of $1.60 per share. The firm's total earnings were $12 million, providing $4.00 in earnings per share. The stock traded in the market at $88.00 per share.

However, Al Rosen, the chief financial officer, was not sure that paying a cash dividend was the best route to go. He had recently read a number of articles in *The Wall Street Journal* about the advantages of stock repurchases and before he made a recommendation to the CEO and board of directors, he decided to do a number of calculations.

a. What is the firm's P/E ratio?

b. If the firm paid the cash dividend, what would be its dividend yield and dividend payout ratio per share?

c. If a stockholder held 100 shares of stock and received the cash dividend, what would be the total value of his portfolio (stock plus dividends)?

d. Assume instead of paying the cash dividend, the firm used the $4.8 million of excess funds to purchase shares at slightly over the current market value of $88 at a price of $89.60. How many shares could be repurchased? (Round to the nearest share.)

e. What would the new earnings per share be under the stock repurchase alternative? (Round to three places to the right of the decimal point.)

f. If the P/E ratio stayed the same under the stock repurchase alternative, what would be the stock value per share? If a stockholder owned 100 shares, what would now be the total value of his portfolio? (This answer should be approximately the same as the answer to part *c.*)

WEB EXERCISE

Oracle was referred to as a profitable, rapid-growth company in this chapter. This presumably justifies the firm not paying a cash dividend, but a stock dividend instead. Go to its Web site, www.oracle.com, and follow the steps below:

1. Click on "Investors."

2. Click on "Detailed Financials" under "Investor Relations."

3. Select the most recent full year.

4. Scroll down and use the data to compute the following ratios for the most recent year, and compare them to the stock analysts' target numbers for the company.

		Target
a.	Net income/Total revenue	12%
b.	Operating income/Total revenue	25%
c.	Cost of services/Total revenue (the lower the better)	40%
d.	Provision for income taxes/Income before provision for income taxes (the lower the better)	32%

5. Write a one-paragraph summary about Oracle's ability to beat the analysts' targets in step 4. Do not automatically assume the firm will be able to beat the target numbers as Oracle is in a highly competitive environment. Some years it will beat the target numbers and other years it will not.

Note: From time to time, companies redesign their Web sites and occasionally a topic we have listed may have been deleted, updated, or moved into a different location. If you click on the site map or site index, you will be introduced to a table of contents which should aid you in finding the topic you are looking for.

S&P PROBLEMS
www.mhhe.com/edumarketinsight

1. Log onto the S&P Market Insight Web site, www.mhhe.com/edumarketinsight.

2. Click on "Company," which is the first box below the Market Insight title.

3. Type the ExxonMobil ticker symbol "XOM" in the box and click on Go.

4. Scroll down the left margin and click on "Stock Reports" and then after the window reopens, click on the stock report on the first line.

5. Look at the quarterly dividends on the bottom right corner of the first page of the report. Notice the dividend payment process. Quarterly earnings statements and dividend payments are relatively consistent from year to year. Given the time of year right now, estimate when the next dividend will be declared, the exdividend date, the stockholder of record date, and the actual payment date.

6. Scroll down to the bottom of the second page and find the per share data section at the top of the 10-year table. If you were a stockholder, would you expect a higher or lower dividend in the next period or do you expect the dividend to stay the same? Why?

7. In the same section, examine the payout ratio over the 10-year time period. What is the payment pattern? Make an educated guess as to why the dividend payout ratio follows the pattern that it does.

8. Now repeat the exercise using Adobe Systems (ADBE).

9. What can you say about the dividend life cycle that might explain the difference between these two companies' dividend policies?

Convertibles, Warrants, and Derivatives

19

chapter concepts

1 Convertible securities can be converted to common stock at the option of the owner.

2 Because these securities can be converted to common stock, they may move with the value of common stock.

3 Interest rates on convertibles are lower than those on straight debt issues.

4 Warrants are similar to convertibles in that they give the warrant holder the right to acquire common stock.

5 Accountants require that the potential effect of convertibles and warrants on earnings per share be reported on the income statement.

6 Derivative securities such as options and futures can be used by corporate financial managers for hedging activities.

There are as many types of securities as there are innovative corporate treasurers or forward looking portfolio managers. As we have discussed in the previous chapters, corporate financial managers usually raise long-term capital by selling common stock, preferred stock, or bonds. Occasionally a company will issue convertible securities, which are a hybrid security combining the features of debt and common equity. Sometimes to sweeten a straight debt offering, the financial manager may attach warrants to a bond offering. Warrants are a type of derivative security because they derive their value from the underlying common stock price. Other derivative securities introduced in this chapter are options and futures contracts.

Convertible bonds and convertible preferred stock are not used on a regular basis by corporations raising funds, but are used occasionally to diversify a company's capital structure. New issues of convertible bonds run in streaks as chief financial officers (CFOs) and corporate treasurers try to take advantage of interest rate forecasts and lock in low cost debt. For example, according to the Value Line Convertible Survey, in 2005 there were 113 new convertible bonds issued worth $39.1 billion dollars. This is a small amount compared to nonconvertible debt and new stock offerings. When CFOs expect interest rates to rise, they are more likely to lock in low cost debt capital before interest rates go up. Convertible securities offer the chief financial officer an alternative source of financing that combines the features of common stock and debt.

On February 1, 2006, AAR Corp. sold $150 million of convertible senior notes due in 2026 paying 1.75 percent interest. AAR Corp. stated that the funds would be used for the purpose of repaying some short-term debt, to make payments under lease agreements, to repurchase some securitized accounts receivables, and for future acquisitions.

Continental Airlines

AAR Corp. specializes in aviation support services and is located in Wood Dale, Illinois, close to O'Hare Airport. It provides aircraft and engine parts and services on a just-in-time basis. The firm has a wide variety of customers such as American Airlines, Continental Airlines, Delta Air Lines, United Airlines, and most other major and regional airlines. It also serves cargo carriers such as FedEx and UPS and manufacturers such as Boeing, General Electric, and Northrop Grumman.

A **convertible security** is a bond or share of preferred stock that can be converted, at the option of the holder, into common stock. Thus the owner has a fixed income security that can be transferred into common stock if and when the affairs of the firm indicate such a conversion is desirable. Even though convertible securities are most often converted into common stock, some convertible preferred stock is exchangeable, in turn, into convertible bonds, which are then convertible into common stock. Additionally, when a company is merged with another company, sometimes the convertible securities of the acquired company may become convertible into common stock of the surviving company. While these departures from the norm are interesting, in this chapter we focus on convertible bonds (debentures) that result in the potential for common stock ownership and recognize that the same principles apply to other forms of convertibles.

Convertible Securities

When a convertible debenture is initially issued, a **conversion ratio** to common stock is specified. The ratio indicates the number of shares of common stock into which the debentures may be converted. Assume that in 2007 the Williams Company issued $10 million of 25-year, 6 percent convertible debentures, with each $1,000 bond convertible into 20 shares of common stock. The conversion ratio of 20 may also be expressed in terms of a **conversion price**. To arrive at the conversion price, we divide the par value of the bond by the conversion ratio of 20. In the case of the Williams Company, the conversion price is $50. Conversely the conversion ratio may also be found by dividing the par value by the conversion price ($1,000/$50 = 20).

Value of the Convertible Bond

As a first consideration in evaluating a convertible bond, we must examine the value of the conversion privilege. In the above case, we might assume that the common stock is selling at $45 per share, so the total **conversion value** is $900 ($45 × 20). Nevertheless, the bond may sell for par or face value ($1,000) in anticipation of future developments in the common stock and because interest payments are being received on the bonds. With the bond selling for $1,000 and a $900 conversion value, the bond would have a $100 **conversion premium**, representing the dollar difference between market value and conversion value. The conversion premium generally will be influenced by the expectations of future performance of the common stock. If investors are optimistic about the prospects of the common stock, the premium may be large.

If the price of the common stock really takes off and goes to $60 per share, the conversion privilege becomes quite valuable. The bonds, which are convertible into 20 shares, will go up to at least $1,200 and perhaps more. Note that you do not have to convert to common immediately, but may enjoy the price movement of the convertible in concert with the price of the common.

What happens if the common stock goes in the opposite direction? Assume that instead of going from $45 to $60 the common stock simply drops from $45 to $25—what will happen to the value of the convertible debentures? We know the value of a convertible bond will go down in response to the drop in the common stock, but will it fall all the way to its conversion value of $500 (20 × $25 per share)? The answer is clearly no, because the debenture still has value as an interest-bearing security. If the going market rate of interest in straight debt issues of similar maturity (25 years) and quality is 8 percent, we would say the debenture has a pure bond value of $785.46.[1] The **pure bond value** equals the value of a bond that has no conversion features but has the same risk as the convertible bond being evaluated. Thus a convertible bond has a **floor value**,[2] but no upside limitation. The price pattern for the convertible bond is depicted in Figure 19–1.

Figure 19–1

Price movement pattern for a convertible bond

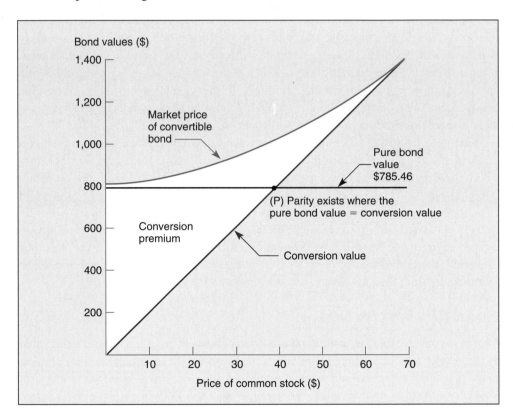

We see the effect on the convertible bond price as the common stock price, shown along the X-axis, is assumed to change. Note that the floor (pure bond) value for the convertible is well above the conversion value when the common stock price is very low. As the common stock price moves to higher levels, the convertible bond price moves together with the conversion value. Where the pure bond value equals the conversion value, we have the parity point (P).

---

[1]Based on discounting procedures covered in Chapter 10, "Valuation and Rates of Return." Semiannual interest payments are assumed.
[2]The floor value can change if interest rates in the market change. For ease of presentation, we shall assume they are constant for now.

Representative information on outstanding convertible bonds is presented in Table 19–1. Many of the bonds listed in Table 19–1 are good examples of what is meant by floor value. Notice that for the bonds of AudioCodes, Chiron Corp., Digital River, Medtronic, and Novell (conversion values all noted in red), the conversion value is less than the pure bond value. All five of these bonds are trading to the left of the parity point (P) on Figure 19–1. For these bonds the pure bond value is more important than the conversion value.

Table 19–1   Pricing pattern for convertible bonds outstanding, 2006 January prices

Issue, Coupon, and Maturity	Conversion Value ($)	Market Value of Bond ($)	Pure Bond Value ($)	Conversion Premium	Downside Risk*	Yield to Maturity on Bond
American Tower 3.25s2010	$2,360.20	$2,439.80	$830.00	3.37%	193.95%	1.50%
Anadarko Petroleum 0s2021	1,017.20	987.50	990.00	−2.92	−0.25	NMF**
AudioCodes Ltd. 2s2024	683.10	950.20	810.00	39.10	17.31	2.30%
Chiron Corp 2.75s2034	667.70	978.80	890.00	46.59	9.98	2.90
Digital River 1.25s2024	754.60	1,000.00	830.00	32.52	20.48	1.20
Genzyme 1.25s2023	1,022.20	1,115.10	890.00	9.09	25.29	0.60
Medtronic 1.25s2021	943.90	995.00	970.00	5.41	2.58	1.30
Novell 0.5s2024	775.90	962.20	780.00	24.01	23.36	0.70
Reebok 2s2024	1,142.30	1,131.50	890.00	−0.95	27.13	1.20
Red Hat 0.5s2024	1,126.90	1,228.70	810.00	9.03	51.69	NMF
Sirius Satellite Radio 3.25s2011	1,184.90	1,386.00	610.00	16.97	127.21	2.00%

*(Bond value − Pure bond value)/Pure bond value.
**NMF—not meaningful

Source: Value Line Convertible Survey, January 23, 2006

If we look in the downside risk column in Table 19–1 we see Medtronic's convertible bond has a downside risk of 2.58 percent, and because its market price is only $25 dollars above the pure bond value, a drop in the common stock price would have little impact on the market price of the bond. On the other hand, if we look at American Tower, the first bond in the list, its downside risk is 193.95 percent because the market price is $1,609.80 above its pure bond value. If the American Tower common stock price would decline, the floor value won't protect the convertible bond price from a major price drop.

The Chiron bond due in 2034 demonstrates that the market price can be set at a large premium to both the conversion value and the pure bond value. In this case, Chiron's market price is 46.6 percent above the conversion value and almost 10 percent above the pure bond value. Because the bond has such a long term to maturity, investors have a long time before they have to decide whether to convert the bond into common stock or to take the par value at maturity. They have a long-term option on the stock price for which they are willing to pay a $311.10 premium over the conversion value ($978.80 − 667.70).

The other bonds in Table 19–1 (Genzyme, Reebok, Red Hat, and Sirius) have conversion values and market prices above their pure bond value, indicating that the ability to convert the bond to common stock is more valuable than the interest payments in determining the market price of the bond. In the case of Sirius Satellite Radio, the market value of $1,386 is greater than the pure bond value by $776, and we can assume that the market price of the bond is being supported by a rising common stock price and not the pure bond value. Now that Howard Stern broadcasts on Sirius, investors may have raised their expectations for the future of the company.

Is This Fool's Gold?

Have we repealed the old risk-return trade-off principle—to get superior returns, we must take larger than normal risks? With convertible bonds, we appear to limit our risk while maximizing our return potential.

Although there is some truth to this statement, there are many qualifications. For example, once convertible debentures begin going up in value, say to $1,100 or $1,200, the downside protection becomes pretty meaningless. In the case of the Williams Company in our earlier example in Figure 19–1 on page 582, the floor is at $785.46. If an investor were to buy the convertible bond at $1,200, he or she would be exposed to $414.54 in potential losses (hardly adequate protection for a true risk averter). Also if interest rates in the market rise, the floor value, or pure bond value, could fall, creating more downside risk.

A second drawback with convertible bonds is that the purchaser is invariably asked to accept below-market rates of interest on the debt instrument. The interest rate on convertibles is generally one-third below that for instruments in a similar risk class at time of issue. In the sophisticated environment of the bond and stock markets, one seldom gets an additional benefit without having to suffer a corresponding disadvantage.

The student will also recall that the purchaser of a convertible bond normally pays a premium over the conversion value. For example, if a $1,000 bond were convertible into 20 shares of common stock at $45 per share, a $100 conversion premium might be involved initially. If the same $1,000 were invested directly in common stock at $45 per share, 22.2 shares could be purchased. In this case, if the shares go up in value, we have 2.2 more shares on which to garner a profit.

Lastly, convertibles may suffer from the attachment of a call provision giving the corporation the option of redeeming the bonds at a specified price above par ($1,000) in the future. In a subsequent section, we will see how the corporation can use this device to force the conversion of the bonds into common stock.

None of these negatives is meant to detract from the fact that convertibles carry some inherently attractive features if they are purchased with appropriate objectives in mind. If the investor wants downside protection, he or she should search out convertible bonds trading below par, perhaps within 10 to 15 percent of the floor value. Though a fairly large move in the stock may be necessary to generate upside profit, the investor has the desired protection and some hope for capital appreciation.

Advantages and Disadvantages to the Corporation

Having established the fundamental characteristics of the convertible security from the *investor* viewpoint, let us now turn the coin over and examine the factors a corporate financial officer must consider in weighing the advisability of a convertible offer for the firm.

Not only has it been established that the interest rate paid on convertible issues is lower than that paid on a straight debt instrument, but also the convertible feature may be the only device for allowing smaller corporations access to the bond market. For small risky companies, investor acceptance of new debt may be contingent on a special sweetener, such as the ability to convert to common stock.

Convertible debentures are also attractive to a corporation that believes its stock is currently undervalued. You will recall in the case of the Williams Company, $1,000 bonds were convertible into 20 shares of common stock at a conversion price of $50. Since the common stock had a current price of $45 and new shares of stock might be sold at only $44,[3] the corporation effectively received $6 over current market price, assuming future conversion. Of course, one can also argue that if the firm had delayed the issuance of common stock or convertibles for a year or two, the stock might have gone up from $45 to $60 and new common stock might have been sold at this lofty price.

To translate this to overall numbers for the firm, if a corporation needs $10 million in funds and offers straight stock now at a net price of $44, it must issue 227,273 shares ($10 million shares/$44). With convertibles, the number of shares potentially issued is only 200,000 shares ($10 million/$50). Finally if no stock or convertible bonds are issued now and the stock goes up to a level at which new shares can be offered at a net price of $60, only 166,667 shares will be required ($10 million/$60).

Table 19–2 demonstrates the company's ability to sell stock at premium prices through the use of convertible bonds. The table represents a composite picture of convertible bonds outstanding during recent times. The typical convertible bond had a 20 percent conversion premium at issue (last line of table).

Yield to maturity	3.0%
Years to maturity	20.0
Size	$100 million
Investment value grade	Ba Moody's rating
Initial premium over conversion value	20.0%

Table 19–2
Characteristics of convertible bonds

The table also provides other information on yield to maturity, years to maturity, size, and investment rating. Notice that the average size of convertibles is quite small, with an average offering of only $100 million per issue. This is because many small companies with less than a top-grade credit rating are primary issuers of convertible bonds.

Another matter of concern to the corporation is the accounting treatment accorded to convertibles. In the funny-money days of the conglomerate merger movement decades ago, corporate management often chose convertible securities over common stock, because the convertibles had a nondilutive effect on earnings per share. As is indicated in a later section on reporting earnings for convertibles, the rules were changed, and this is no longer the case. Convertibles are dilutive.

Inherent in a convertible issue is the presumed ability of the corporation to force the security holder to convert the present instrument to common stock. We will examine this process.

---

[3]There is always a bit of underpricing to ensure the success of a new offering.

Forcing Conversion

How does a corporation, desirous of shifting outstanding debt to common stock, force conversion? The principal device is the call provision. As previously indicated, when the value of the common stock goes up, the convertible security will move in a similar fashion. Table 19–3 further indicates that convertible bonds may go up substantially in value. Some particularly successful convertibles trade at many times the initial value of $1,000 as shown in the "Current Market Price" column of Table 19–3.

Table 19–3   Successful convertible bonds not yet called

Issue, Coupon, and Maturity	Current Market Price ($)	Current Call Price ($)	Current Yield (%)	Common Stock Dividend Yield (%)
Elan Corp. 6.5s2008	$2,246.30	$1,000.00	2.89%	0.0%
Equinix 2.5s2024	1,242.40	1,000.00	2.01	0.0
GTECH Holdings 1.75s2021	2,409.50	1,000.00	0.73	1.0
Harris Corp. 2.75s2021	2,087.60	1,000.00	1.32	0.2
Komag 2s2024	1,574.70	1,011.43	1.27	0.0
Legg Mason Inc. 0s2031	1,481.30	NCB*	0.00	0.6
Pan American Silver 5.25s2009	2,102.50	1,000.00	2.50%	0.0
St Mary Land & Exploration 6.25s2022 . .	3,076.30	1,000.00	2.03	0.8
Schlumberger 1.5s2023	1,494.00	NCB*	1.00	0.0
Sierra Health Services 2.25s2023	4,230.80	NCB*	0.53	0.0
Sirius Satellite Radio 3.5s2008	4,862.50	NCB*	0.72	0.0
Walter Industries, Inc. 3.75s2024	2,845.70	1,011.30	1.32	0.3

*Noncallable bond.

Source: Value Line Convertible Bond Survey, January 2006; *Mergent Bond Record,* January 2006

Schlumberger

If one of these companies wanted to call in the bonds (pay off the bonds before maturity) to force conversion to common stock, this is how it would work. As an example we will use the Walter Industries 3.75 percent coupon bonds due in 2024 listed at the bottom of Table 19–3. At the time of issue, the corporation established a future privilege for calling the bond at 5 percent above par value—thus the $1,000 debenture was initially redeemable at $1,050. Most bonds have an initial 5 to 10 percent call premium, which declines over time. As the stock price of Walter Industries has gone up, the bond has risen in value to $2,845.70 per bond. The call price has declined annually from its initial call value of $1,050 to its current level of $1,011.30. Additionally, an owner of this bond is entitled to a conversion ratio of 56.03 shares of common stock (valued at $48.92 per share) worth $2,740.99. If the bond is called the owner has the choice of 56.03 shares or the call price of $1,011.30. If the conversion value is above the call price when the bond is called, any rational investor would take the shares of stock rather than the cash payout. In the case of Walter Industries, the 56.03 shares of stock are worth approximately $1,730 more than the call price ($2,740.99 − $1,011.30). This demonstrates the derivation of the term **forced conversion**. By calling the bond, Walter Industries would force bondholders to convert their debt to equity. This would improve the composition of the company's balance sheet by decreasing the debt-to-asset ratio.

It would also help their cash flow. Walter has $175 million of bonds outstanding and since each bond pays interest of 3.75 percent, Walter would save interest expense of $6,562,500 each year. The dividend on the common stock is only .3 percent or $.16 per share. The bonds will convert into approximately 980,000 shares of stock which would require a dividend of $156,800. When comparing the current yield on the bond to the dividend yield on the common stock, *all things being equal,* investors generally do not want to convert unless the dividend yield is higher than the yield on the bond, but may be forced to when the conversion value is much higher than the call value.

Notice that four of the bonds in Table 19–3 are noncallable (NCB). This means that the company does not get the right to call the bonds before maturity. That doesn't mean that the bondholders can't convert to stock if they so choose. Three of these companies with noncallable bonds (Schlumberger, Sierra Health Services, and Sirius Satellite Radio) pay no dividends on their common stock and so bondholders have no motivation to convert since they are getting interest payments by owning the bonds. Only when the dividend payments on the common stock exceed the interest payments on the bond would bondholders consider converting their bonds. Even then, they have to consider that interest payments are legally guaranteed while dividend payments are not.

The fourth noncallable bond (Legg Mason) is a zero-coupon bond and has no cash interest payment. In this case the dividend on the common stock could entice some bondholders to convert the bond into stock before the maturity date. If Legg Mason raises the dividend on the common stock, there will be more motivation to convert the bond to common stock.

Conversion may also be encouraged through a **step-up in the conversion price** over time. When the bond is issued, the contract may specify the conversion provisions as shown below.

	Conversion Price	Conversion Ratio
First five years	$40	25.0 shares
Next three years	45	22.2 shares
Next two years	50	20.0 shares
Next five years	55	18.2 shares

At the end of each time period, there is a strong inducement to convert rather than accept an adjustment to a higher conversion price and a lower conversion ratio.

Accounting Considerations with Convertibles

Before 1969, the full impact of the conversion privilege as it applied to convertible securities, warrants (long-term options to buy stock), and other dilutive securities was not adequately reflected in reported earnings per share. Since all of these securities may generate additional common stock in the future, the potential effect of this dilution (the addition of new shares to the capital structures) should be considered. The accounting profession has applied many different measures to earnings per share over the years, most recently replacing the concepts of primary earnings per share and fully diluted earnings per share with **basic earnings per share** and **diluted earnings per share**. In 1997, the Financial Accounting Standards Board issued "Earnings per Share" *Statement of Financial Accounting Standards No. 128,* which covered the adjustments that must be made when reporting earnings per share.

If we examine the financial statements of the XYZ Corporation in Table 19–4, we find that the earnings per share reported is not adjusted for convertible securities and is referred to as basic earnings per share.

Table 19–4

XYZ Corporation

1. Capital section of balance sheet:

Common stock (1 million shares at $10 par)	$10,000,000
4.5% convertible debentures (10,000 debentures of $1,000; convertible into 40 shares per bond, or a total of 400,000 shares)	10,000,000
Retained earnings	20,000,000
Net worth	$40,000,000

2. Condensed income statement:

Earnings before interest and taxes	$ 2,950,000
Interest (4.5% of $10 million of convertibles)	450,000
Earnings before taxes	2,500,000
Taxes (40%)	1,000,000
Earnings after taxes	$ 1,500,000

3. Basic earnings per share:

$$\frac{\text{Earnings after taxes}}{\text{Shares of common stock}} = \frac{\$1,500,000}{1,000,000} = \$1.50 \tag{19–1}$$

Diluted earnings per share adjusts for all potential dilution from the issuance of any new shares of common stock arising from convertible bonds, convertible preferred stocks, warrants, or any other options outstanding. The comparison of basic and diluted earnings per share gives the analyst or investor a measure of the potential effects of these securities.

We get diluted earnings per share for the XYZ Corporation by assuming that 400,000 new shares will be created from potential conversion, while at the same time allowing for the reduction in interest payments that would occur as a result of the conversion of the debt to common stock. Since before-tax interest payments on the convertibles are $450,000, the aftertax interest cost ($270,000) will be saved and can be added back to income. Aftertax interest cost is determined by multiplying interest payments by one minus the tax rate, or $450,000 (1 − .40) = $270,000. Making the appropriate adjustments to the numerator and denominator, we show adjusted earnings per share:

$$\frac{\text{Diluted earnings}}{\text{per share}} = \frac{\text{Adjusted earnings after taxes}}{\text{Shares outstanding} + \text{All convertible securities[4]}} \tag{19–2}$$

$$= \frac{\overset{\substack{\text{Reported} \\ \text{earnings}}}{\$1,500,000} + \overset{\substack{\text{Interest} \\ \text{savings}}}{\$270,000}}{1,000,000 + 400,000} = \frac{\$1,770,000}{1,400,000} = \$1.26$$

We see a $0.24 reduction from the basic earnings per share figure of $1.50. The new figure is the value that a sophisticated security analyst would utilize.

---

[4]Other types of securities that create common stock, such as warrants and options, would also be included.

A **warrant** is an option to buy a stated number of shares of common stock at a specified price (the exercise price) over a given time period. For example, the warrant of Coastal Bankshares shown in Table 19–5, fourth column, allows the holder to buy 1 share of common stock at $5.00 per share from Coastal Bankshares. The warrant of SpectraSite allows the holder to buy 2 shares of SpectraSite common stock at an exercise price of $16.00 per share until its expiration on February 10, 2010. This is a very successful company whose stock price has grown rapidly since it issued the warrants. A third warrant of Expedia allows the owner of the warrant to buy one-half share of common stock at an exercise price of $31.22. These examples show that not all warrants allow a one-for-one purchase of common stock for one warrant.

Financing through Warrants

Table 19–5   Relationships determining warrant prices

Firm, Places of Warrant Listing, Stock Listing, and Expiration Date	Warrant Price	Stock Price	Exercise Price	Number of Shares	Intrinsic Value ($)	Speculative Premium ($)
Arena Resources ASE, OTC 8/09/08	$ 18.50	$27.80	$ 7.32	1.00	20.48	−1.98
Chart Industries OTC, OTC 9/15/10	30.00	63.55	32.97	1.00	30.58	−0.58
Coastal Bankshares OTC, OTC 2/13/10	0.46	5.96	5.00	1.00	0.96	−0.50
Expedia OTC, OTC 2/4/09	4.99	21.65	31.22	0.50	0.00	4.99
Magellan Health Services OTC, OTC 1/5/11	7.65	31.31	30.46	1.00	0.85	6.80
Redback Networks OTC, OTC 8/29/08	7.00	14.01	9.50	1.00	4.51	2.49
SpectraSite OTC, OTC 2/10/10	149.00	80.87	16.00	2.00	129.74	19.26
Vertical Health Solutions OTC, OTC 4/20/08	1.25	0.51	1.22	1.00	0.00	1.25

OTC = Over-The-Counter, NYSE = New York Stock Exchange.
Source: Value Line Convertibles Survey, February 24, 2003.

Warrants are sometimes issued as a **financial sweetener** in a bond offering, and they may enable the firm to issue debt when this would not be otherwise feasible because of a low quality rating or a high interest rate environment. The warrants are usually detachable from the bond issue, have their own market price, and are generally traded on the New York Stock Exchange or over-the-counter. After warrants are detached, the initial debt to which they were attached remains in existence as a stand-alone bond. Often the bond price will fall and the bond yield will rise once the warrants are detached.

Because a warrant is dependent on the market movement of the underlying common stock and has no "security value" as such, it is highly speculative. If the common stock of the firm is volatile, the value of the warrants may change dramatically.

In prior time periods, Tri-Continental Corporation warrants went from ⅓₂ to 75¾, while United Airlines warrants moved from 4½ to 126. Of course this is not a one-way street, as holders of LTV warrants will attest as they saw their holdings dip from 83 to 2¼.

Valuation of Warrants

Because the value of a warrant is closely tied to the underlying stock price, we can develop a formula for the **intrinsic value** of a warrant.

$$I = (M - E) \times N \qquad (19\text{--}3)$$

where

I = Intrinsic value of a warrant
M = Market value of common stock (stock price)
E = Exercise price of a warrant
N = Number of shares each warrant entitles the holder to purchase

Using the prior data from Table 19–5 on page 589, we see that Redback Networks common stock was trading at $14.01 per share. Each warrant carried with it the option to purchase one share of Redback common stock at an **exercise price** of $9.50 per share until August 29, 2008. Using Formula 19–3, the intrinsic value is $4.51 or ($14.1 − 9.50) × 1. Since the warrant had time to run and was an effective vehicle for speculative trading, it was selling at $7.00 per warrant. This is $2.49 more than its intrinsic value.

Investors are willing to pay a speculative premium because a small percentage gain in the stock price may generate large percentage increases in the warrant price. Formula 19–4 demonstrates the calculation of the **speculative premium**.

$$S = W - I \qquad (19\text{--}4)$$

where:

S = Speculative premium
W = Warrant price
I = Intrinsic value

For Redback Networks we use the formula to show the calculation of the previously stated speculative premium of $2.49.

$$S = W - I$$
$$\$2.49 = \$7.00 - \$4.51$$

We see that even the two stocks in Table 19–5 that have no intrinsic value (Expedia and Vertical Health Solutions) still have a warrant price. Investors are willing to pay $1.25 for Vertical Health Solutions warrants even though the stock price is below the exercise price by $.71 ($.51 vs. $1.22). An investor who pays $1.25 for this warrant would have to see the stock rise in price to $2.47 ($1.25 + $1.22) before breaking even on the investment. In a rising stock market with good earnings momentum, a company's stock price could double or triple in two years and thereby reward the owner of the warrant. SpectraSite is an example of this kind of performance.

It is opportunities like these, however, that entice investors to buy bonds with warrants attached. Bond investors are willing to accept lower interest rates when warrants are attached because they know that the warrants have potential value that could be far in excess of the interest rate on the bond. This expectation of potential profit is what makes warrants financial sweeteners.

The typical relationship between the warrant price and intrinsic value of a warrant is depicted in Figure 19–2. We assume the warrant entitles the holder to purchase one new share of common at $20. Although the intrinsic value of the warrant is theoretically negative at a common stock price between 0 and 20, the warrant still carries some value in the market. Also observe that the difference between the market price of the warrant and its intrinsic value is diminished at the upper ranges of value. Two reasons may be offered for the declining premium.

Figure 19–2

Market price relationships for a warrant

First the speculator loses the ability to use leverage to generate high returns as the price of the stock goes up. When the price of the stock is relatively low, say, $25, and the warrant is in the $5 range, a 10-point movement in the stock could mean a 200 percent gain in the value of the warrant, as indicated in the left-hand panel of Table 19–6.

Table 19–6

Leverage in valuing warrants

At the upper levels of stock value, much of this leverage is lost. At a stock value of $50 and a warrant value of approximately $30, a 10-point movement in the stock would produce only a 33 percent gain in the warrant as indicated in the right-hand panel of Table 19–6.

Another reason speculators pay a very low premium at higher stock prices is that there is less downside protection. A warrant selling at $30 when the stock price is $50 is more vulnerable to downside movement than is a $5 to $10 warrant when the stock is in the $20s.

Use of Warrants in Corporate Finance

Let us examine the suitability of warrants for corporate financing purposes. As previously indicated, warrants may allow for the issuance of debt under difficult circumstances. While a straight debt issue may not be acceptable or may be accepted only at extremely high rates, the same security may be well received because detachable warrants are included. Warrants may also be included as an add-on in a merger or acquisition agreement. A firm might offer $20 million in cash plus 10,000 warrants in exchange for all the outstanding shares of the acquisition candidate. Warrants may also be issued in a corporate reorganization or bankruptcy to offer the shareholders a chance to recover some of their investment if the restructuring goes well.

The use of warrants has traditionally been associated with aggressive high-flying firms such as speculative real estate companies, airlines, and conglomerates. However, in the 1970s staid and venerable American Telephone & Telegraph came out with a $1.57 billion debt offering, sweetened by the use of warrants.

As a financing device for creating new common stock, warrants may not be as desirable as convertible securities. A corporation with convertible debentures outstanding may force the conversion of debt to common stock through a call, while no similar device is available to the firm with warrants. The only possible inducement might be a step-up in exercise price—whereby the warrant holder pays a progressively higher option price if he does not exercise by a given date.

Accounting Considerations with Warrants

As with convertible securities, the potential dilutive effect of warrants must be considered. All warrants are included in computing diluted earnings per share.[5] The accountant must compute the number of new shares that could be created by the exercise of all warrants, with the provision that the total can be reduced by the assumed use of the cash proceeds to purchase a partially offsetting amount of shares at the market price. Assume that warrants to purchase 10,000 shares at $20 are outstanding and that the current price of the stock is $50. We show the following:

1. New shares created   10,000
2. Reduction of shares from cash proceeds (computed below)   4,000
    Cash proceeds—10,000 shares at $20 = $200,000
    Current price of stock—$50
      Assumed reduction in shares outstanding from
      cash proceeds = $200,000/$50 − 4,000
3. Assumed net increase in shares from exercise
    of warrants (10,000 − 4,000)   6,000

---

[5]Under most circumstances, if the market price is below the option price, dilution need not be considered; see *APB Opinion 15,* par. 35.

In computing earnings per share, we will add 6,000 shares to the denominator, with no adjustment to the numerator. This of course will lead to some dilution in earnings per share. Its importance must be interpreted by the financial manager and security analyst.

There are many types of derivative securities but those that are most important to a basic financial management course are options and futures contracts.[6] **Derivative securities** have value derived from an underlying security. In the case of equity options, the value is derived by the underlying common stock. Futures contracts on government bonds or Treasury bills derive their value from those government securities, and futures contracts on oil or wheat have those commodities as determinants of their basic values. Our intent here is to present basic conceptual material that introduces you to derivative securities.

Derivative Securities

Options

Options give the owner the right, but not the obligation, to buy or sell an underlying security at a set price for a given period of time. Companies often reward their most valuable employees with stock options as part of their compensation. An employee stock option is very similar to a warrant. An employee may be given an option to buy 10,000 shares of stock from the company at $25 per share. The employee stock option can have a life of 5 to 10 years and is supposed to motivate employees to focus on stockholder value. After all, if the stock goes to $100 per share over the life of the option, the employee could buy 10,000 shares of stock from the company for $250,000, sell the stock for $1 million (10,000 × $100) and pocket a taxable profit of $750,000. This is a phenomenon that has driven employee compensation for many companies.[7] Employee stock options are worth understanding; you never know when you might get offered a bonus package consisting of an employee stock option.

A **call option** is similar to an employee stock option in that it is an option to buy securities at a set price for a specific period of time, but it is usually traded between individual investors and not exercisable from the company. The Chicago Board Options Exchange is the foremost market for trading options. In a standardized call option, the writer of the call option guarantees that he or she will sell you 100 shares of stock at a set price. For this guarantee, the buyer of the call option pays the call writer a premium, perhaps $1 or $2 per share. If the option allows an investor to buy the stock at $40 per share and the stock closes at $38 on the expiration date, then the call writer keeps the premium and the call buyer loses his or her investment. On the other hand if the stock closes at $45 per share, the owner of the call has the right to pay the call writer $40 per share for the 100 shares and the writer must deliver the 100 shares. There are also other ways to close out the position at a profit that go beyond the scope of this discussion.

A **put option** is an option to sell securities to the option writer at a set price for a specific period of time. A put works just the opposite of a call. The put writer guarantees to buy the shares from you at a set price. The put buyer generally thinks that there is

---

[6]Warrants, which were discussed in the prior section, are also a form of derivatives.
[7]However, when misused, employee stock options have come under heavy criticism.

a good probability that the underlying stock will fall in price and he or she wants to hedge the risk of loss by giving the put writer a premium for the guarantee of transferring the stock at a set price. For example if the put owner has an option to "put" (sell) the stock at $80 per share, the option would only be exercised if the stock price was less than $80. If the stock went to $65, the owner of the put could sell 100 shares to the writer of the put for $80 per share ($8,000). A profit of $1,500 would be garnered. Puts are often used as hedges against falling security prices and the financial manager who is in charge of the corporate pension fund could use this tactic to insure the pension portfolio from declining in value.

Futures

Futures contracts give the owner the right but not the obligation to buy or sell the underlying security or commodity at a future date. Futures contracts are very common for commodities and interest rate securities, especially government bonds. One characteristic of futures contracts is that the contract requires a very small down payment (margin) to control the futures contract. Often the down payment is five percent of the value of the underlying value of the securities or commodities. The major futures exchanges are the Chicago Board of Trade (CBOT) and the Chicago Mercantile Exchange (CME).

Let us suppose that Southwest Airlines was concerned that the price of oil might rise over the next six months. It could buy futures contracts on oil to be delivered six months from now at a price of $60 per barrel. If the price were $70 per barrel six months from now, it would exercise its right to buy oil at $60 per barrel, or $10 cheaper, than the market price at that time. All this is done on paper, but the $10 profit is real. Southwest Airlines actually hedged its fuel prices until the end of 2008. While other airlines were losing money in 2005–2006, Southwest was still making a profit. A similar strategy could be used by Pillsbury or General Mills to lock in the price of the wheat they buy to make flour. Using futures contracts guarantees the price for both the farmer who might sell the futures contract and the manufacturer who buys the futures contract. Futures contracts have varying time periods and the participants usually have monthly choices out to one year. With futures contracts you do not take physical possession of the item; the gains or losses are all settled on paper.

Other futures contracts that are commonly used to hedge corporate financial strategies are interest rate futures or foreign currency futures. One common financial futures strategy is to hedge against interest rate movements. Perhaps you are building a new plant and you intend to pay for the plant by borrowing money through a mortgage. In the short term, the treasurer has negotiated a one-year construction loan at a floating rate. When the plant is complete, the treasurer will borrow the full amount from a mortgage banker on a 30-year loan and repay the construction loan. If interest rates go up during the next 12 months, the treasurer will pay more money for the loan. To hedge rising interest rates, the treasurer can use a financial futures contract to either lock in a rate or to profit from an increase in rates. If rates go up, the treasurer can take the profit on the financial futures contract and use the profit to offset higher interest costs.

Strategies on using options and futures are usually taught in an advanced finance course. For those of you wanting to accelerate your learning, we suggest that you use the Web Exercise at the end of the chapter.

Summary

A number of security devices related to the debt and common stock of the firm are popular. Each security offers downside protection or upside potential, or a combination of these features.

A convertible security is a bond or share of preferred stock that can be converted into common stock at the option of the holder. Thus the holder has a fixed income security that will not go below a minimum amount because of the interest or dividend payment feature and, at the same time, he or she has a security that is potentially convertible to common stock. If the common stock goes up in value, the convertible security will appreciate as well. From a corporate viewpoint, the firm may force conversion to common stock through a call feature and thus achieve a balanced capital structure. Interest rates on convertibles are usually lower than those on straight debt issues.

A warrant is an option to buy a stated number of shares of stock at a specified price over a given time period. The warrant has a large potential for appreciation if the stock goes up in value. Warrants are used primarily as sweeteners for debt instruments or as add-ons in merger tender offers or bankruptcy proceedings. When warrants are exercised, the basic debt instrument to which they may be attached is not eliminated, as is the case for a convertible debenture. The potential dilutive effect of warrants and convertible securities must be considered in computing earnings per share.

Derivative securities such as options and futures can be used to hedge risk such as the decline in the value of a pension fund portfolio, an oil price shock, an interest rate change, or a currency fluctuation. An option is the right, but not the obligation, to buy or sell a security at a set price for a fixed period of time. An employee stock option is one type of option contract and so are calls and puts. A call option is an option to buy while a put option is an option to sell. A futures contract is the agreement that provides for sale or purchase of a specific amount of a commodity or financial product at a designated time in the future at a given price.

Review of Formulas

1. Basic earnings per share $= \dfrac{\text{Earnings after taxes}}{\text{Shares of common stock}}$ (19–1)

2. $\dfrac{\text{Diluted earnings}}{\text{per share}} = \dfrac{\text{Adjusted earnings after taxes}}{\text{Shares outstanding} + \text{All convertible securities*}}$ (19–2)

*Other types of securities that create common stock, such as warrants and options, would also be included.

3. Intrinsic value of a warrant

$$I = (M - E) \times N \qquad (19\text{–}3)$$

where

I = Intrinsic value of a warrant
M = Market value of common stock
E = Exercise price of a warrant
N = Number of shares each warrant entitles the holder to purchase

4. Speculative premium of a warrant

$$S = W - I \qquad (19\text{–}4)$$

where
S = Speculative premium
W = Warrant price
I = Intrinsic value

List of Terms

Discussion Questions

1. What are the basic advantages to the corporation of issuing convertible securities?

2. Why are investors willing to pay a premium over the theoretical value (pure bond value or conversion value)?

3. Why is it said that convertible securities have a floor price?

4. The price of Haltom Corporation 5¼ 2019 convertible bonds is $1,380. For the Williams Corporation, the 6⅛ 2018 convertible bonds are selling at $725.

   a. Explain what factors might cause their prices to be different from their par values of $1,000.

   b. What will happen to each bond's value if long-term interest rates decline?

5. How can a company force conversion of a convertible bond?

6. What is meant by a step-up in the conversion price?

7. Explain the difference between basic earnings per share and diluted earnings per share.

8. Explain how convertible bonds and warrants are similar and different.

9. Explain why warrants are issued. (Why are they used in corporate finance?)

10. What are the reasons that warrants often sell above their intrinsic value?

11. What is the difference between a call option and a put option?

12. Suggest two areas where the use of futures contracts is most common. What percent of the value of the underlying security is typical as a down payment in a futures contract?

13. You buy a stock option with an exercise price of $50. The cost of the option is $4. If the stock ends up at $56, indicate whether you have a profit or loss with a call option? With a put option?

Practice Problems and Solutions

1. Scientific Instruments has a $1,000 par value convertible bond outstanding with a conversion ratio of 25. The common stock is selling for $45. The convertible bond is selling for $1,165.70.

    Features of a convertible bond

    a. What is the conversion value?

    b. What is the conversion premium?

    c. What is the conversion price?

    d. If the common stock price falls to $20, and the pure bond price is $780, will the bond sell for greater than its conversion value?

2. Eaton Hotel Corp. has warrants outstanding that allow the warrant holder to purchase 1.3 shares of stock per warrant at $9 per share (exercise price). The common stock is currently selling for $14.50, and the warrant is selling for $9.75.

    Value of warrants

    a. What is the intrinsic (minimum value) of the warrant?

    b. What is the speculative premium on this warrant?

    c. If the common stock price goes up to $19 and the speculative premium goes down to $1.50, what will be the price of the warrant?

Solutions

1. *a.* Conversion value = Stock price × Conversion ratio = $45 × 25 = $1,125

    b. Conversion premium = Convertible bond price − Conversion value

    $$= \$1,165.70 - \$1,125.00 = \$40.70$$

    c. Conversion price = Par value/Conversion ratio = $1,000/25 = $40

    d. First compute the new conversion value

    Conversion value = Stock price × Conversion ratio = $20 × 25 = $500

    The newly computed conversion value ($500) is below the pure bond value ($780), so the bond will definitely sell at a price above the conversion value.

2. *a.* Intrinsic value

    $$I - (M - E) \times N$$

    Where

    $$I = \text{Intrinsic value of a warrant}$$
    $$M = \text{Market value of common stock} \qquad \$14.50$$
    $$E = \text{Exercise price of a warrant} \qquad \$9.00$$
    $$N = \text{Number of shares each warrant entitles}$$
    $$\qquad \text{the holder to purchase} \qquad 1.3$$
    $$I = (\$14.50 - \$9.00) \times 1.3 = \$5.50 \times 1.3 = \$7.15$$

    b. Speculative premium

    $$S = W - I$$

    Where

    $$S = \text{Speculative premium}$$
    $$W = \text{Warrant price} \qquad \$9.75$$
    $$I = \text{Intrinsic value} \qquad \$7.15$$
    $$S = \$9.75 - \$7.15 = \$2.60$$

c. First compute the new intrinsic value

$$I = (M - E) \times N$$
$$I = (\$19 - \$9) \times 1.3 = \$10 \times 1.3 = \$13$$

Then add the new speculative premium of $1.50 to the intrinsic value of $13 to get the price of the warrant.
   The warrant price is $13 + $1.50 = $14.50

Problems

▄▀▄ ™ All problems are available in Homework Manager. Please see the preface for more information.

Value of warrants

1. National Motors, Inc., has warrants outstanding that allow the holder to purchase 1.5 shares of stock per warrant at $28 per share (exercise price). Thus, each individual share can be purchased at $28 with the warrant. The common stock is currently selling for $35. The warrant is selling for $14.
    a. What is the intrinsic (minimum) value of this warrant?
    b. What is the speculative premium on this warrant?
    c. What should happen to the speculative premium as the expiration date approaches?

Breakeven on warrants

2. The warrants of Airbus Transportation Corporation allow the holder to buy a share of stock at $13.25 and are selling for $3.75. The stock price is currently $10.65. To what price must the stock go for the warrant purchaser to at least be assured of breaking even?

(Assume all bonds in the following problems have a par value of $1,000.)

Features of convertible bond

3. DNA Labs, Inc. has a $1,000 convertible bond outstanding that can be converted into 40 shares of common stock. The common stock is currently selling for $26.75 a share, and the convertible bond is selling for $1,118.50.
    a. What is the conversion value of the bond?
    b. What is the conversion premium?
    c. What is the conversion price?

Features of convertible bond

4. O'Reilly Moving Company has a $1,000 par value convertible bond outstanding that can be converted into 25 shares of common stock. The common stock is currently selling for $36.25 a share, and the convertible bond is selling for $970.
    a. What is the conversion value of the bond?
    b. What is the conversion premium?
    c. What is the conversion price?

Price of a convertible bond

5. The bonds of Stein Company have a conversion premium of $35. Their conversion price is $20. The common stock price is $18.50. What is the price of the convertible bond?

Price of a convertible bond

6. The bonds of Generic Labs, Inc., have a conversion premium of $75. Their conversion price is $25. The common stock price is $21.50. What is the price of the convertible bond?

Conversion premium for a bond

7. Sherwood Forest Products has a convertible bond quoted on the NYSE bond market at 95. (Bond quotes represent percentage of par value. Thus, 70 represents

$700, 80 represents $800, and so on.) It matures in 10 years and carries a coupon rate of 6½ percent. The conversion ratio is 25, and the common stock is currently selling for $35 per share on the NYSE.

a.   Compute the conversion premium.

b.   At what price does the common stock need to sell for the conversion value to be equal to the current bond price?

8.   Pittsburgh Steel Company has a convertible bond outstanding, trading in the marketplace at $930. The par value is $1,000, the coupon rate is 8 percent, and the bond matures in 25 years. The conversion price is $50 and the company's common stock is selling for $44 per share. Interest is paid semiannually.

a.   What is the conversion value?

b.   If similar bonds which are not convertible are currently yielding 10 percent, what is the pure bond value of this convertible bond? (Use semiannual analysis as described in Chapter 10.)

Conversion value and pure bond value

9.   In Problem 8, if the interest rate on similar bonds which are not convertible goes up from 10 percent to 12 percent, what will be the new pure bond value of the Pittsburgh Steel Company bonds? Assume the Pittsburgh Steel Company bonds have the same coupon rate of 8 percent as described in Problem 8 and that 25 years remain to maturity. Use semiannual analysis.

Pure bond value and change in interest rates

10.   The Olsen Mining Company has been very successful in the last five years. Its $1,000 par value convertible bonds have a conversion ratio of 32. The bonds have a quoted interest rate of 5 percent a year. The firm's common stock is currently selling for $39.50 per share. The current bond price has a conversion premium of $10 over the conversion value.

Current yield on a convertible bond

a.   What is the current price of the bond?

b.   What is the current yield on the bond (annual interest divided by the bond's market price)?

c.   If the common stock price goes down to $21.50 and the conversion premium goes up to $100, what will be the new current yield on the bond?

11.   Standard Olive Company of California has a convertible bond outstanding with a coupon rate of 9 percent and a maturity date of 15 years. It is rated Aa, and competitive, nonconvertible bonds of the same risk class carry a 10 percent return. The conversion ratio is 25. Currently the common stock is selling for $30 per share on the New York Stock Exchange.

Conversion value versus pure bond value

a.   What is the conversion price?

b.   What is the conversion value?

c.   Compute the pure bond value. (Use semiannual analysis.)

d.   Draw a graph that includes the pure bond value and the conversion value but not the convertible bond price. For the stock price on the horizontal axis, use 10, 20, 30, 40, 50, and 60.

e.   Which will influence the bond price more—the pure bond value or the conversion value?

Call feature with a
convertible bond

12. Swift Shoe Co. has convertible bonds outstanding that are callable at $1,080. The bonds are convertible into 22 shares of common stock. The stock is currently selling for $59.25 per share.

a. If the firm announces it is going to call the bonds at $1,080, what action are bondholders likely to take, and why?

b. Assume that instead of the call feature, the firm has the right to drop the conversion ratio from 22 down to 20 after 5 years and down to 18 after 10 years. If the bonds have been outstanding for four years and 11 months, what will the price of the bonds be if the stock price is $60? Assume the bonds carry no conversion premium.

c. Further assume that you anticipate that the common stock price will be up to $63.50 in two months. Considering the conversion feature, should you convert now or continue to hold the bond for at least two more months?

Convertible bond
and rates of return

13. Vernon Glass Company has $20 million in 10 percent convertible bonds outstanding. The conversion ratio is 50, the stock price is $19, and the bond matures in 10 years. The bonds are currently selling at a conversion premium of $70 over their conversion value.

If the price of the common stock rises to $25 on this date next year, what would your rate of return be if you bought a convertible bond today and sold it in one year? Assume on this date next year, the conversion premium has shrunk from $70 to $15.

Price appreciation
with a warrant

14. Assume you can buy a warrant for $5 that gives you the option to buy one share of common stock at $15 per share. The stock is currently selling at $18 per share.

a. What is the intrinsic value of the warrant?

b. What is the speculative premium on the warrant?

c. If the stock rises to $27 per share and the warrant sells at its theoretical value without a premium, what will be the percentage increase in the stock price and the warrant price if you buy the stock and the warrant at the prices stated above? Explain this relationship.

Profit potential
with a warrant

15. The Gifford Investment Company bought 100 Cable Corporation warrants one year ago and would like to exercise them today. The warrants were purchased at $30 each, and they expire when trading ends today. (Assume there is no speculative premium left.) Cable Corp. common stock is selling today for $60 per share. The exercise price is $36, and each warrant entitles the holder to purchase two shares of stock, each at the exercise price.

a. If the warrants are exercised today, what would Gifford's *total* profit or loss be?

b. What is Gifford's percentage rate of return?

Comparing returns
on warrants and
common stock

16. Assume in Problem 15 that Cable Corporation common stock was selling for $50 per share when Gifford Investment Company bought the warrants.

a. What was the intrinsic value of a warrant at that time?

b. What was the speculative premium per warrant when the warrants were purchased? The purchase price, as indicated above, was $30.

   c. What would Gifford's total dollar profit or loss have been had they invested the $3,000 directly in Cable Corporation's common stock one year ago at $50 per share? Recall the current value is $60 per share.

   d. What would the percentage rate of return be on this common stock investment? Compare this to the rate of return on the warrant computed in problem 15*b*.

17. Mr. John Hailey has $1,000 to invest in the market. He is considering the purchase of 50 shares of Comet Airlines at $20 per share. His broker suggests that he may wish to consider purchasing warrants instead. The warrants are selling for $5, and each warrant allows him to purchase one share of Comet Airlines common stock at $18 per share.

   a. How many warrants can Mr. Hailey purchase for the same $1,000?

   b. If the price of the stock goes to $30, what would be his total dollar and percentage returns on the stock?

   c. At the time the stock goes to $30, the speculative premium on the warrant goes to 0 (though the market value of the warrant goes up). What would be Mr. Hailey's total dollar and percentage returns on the warrant?

   d. Assuming that the speculative premium remains $3.50 over the intrinsic value, how far would the price of the stock have to fall from $30 before the warrant has no value?

18. Online Network, Inc., has had net income of $600,000 in the current fiscal year. There are 100,000 shares of common stock outstanding along with convertible bonds, which have a total face value of $1.4 million. The $1.4 million is represented by 1,400 different $1,000 bonds. Each $1,000 bond pays 5 percent interest. The conversion ratio is 20. The firm is in a 30 percent tax bracket.

   a. Calculate basic earnings per share.

   b. Calculate diluted earnings per share.

19. Myers Drugs, Inc., has 2 million shares of stock outstanding. Earnings after taxes are $6 million. Myers also has warrants outstanding which allow the holder to buy 100,000 shares of stock at $15 per share. The stock is currently selling for $50 per share.

   a. Compute basic earnings per share.

   b. Compute diluted earnings per share considering the possible impact of the warrants. Use the following formula:

$$\frac{\text{Earnings after taxes}}{\text{Shares outstanding} + \text{Assumed net increase in shares from the warrants}}$$

20. Tulsa Drilling Company has $1 million in 11 percent convertible bonds outstanding. Each bond has a $1,000 par value. The conversion ratio is 40, the stock price is $32, and the bonds mature in 10 years. The bonds are currently selling at a conversion premium of $70 over the conversion value.

   a. If the price of Tulsa Drilling Company common stock rises to $42 on this date next year, what would your rate of return be if you bought a convertible bond today and sold it in one year? Assume that on this date next year, the conversion premium has shrunk from $70 to $20.

Return calculations with warrants

Earnings per share with warrants

Earnings per share with convertibles

Conversion value and changing pure bond value

b.   Assume the yield on similar nonconvertible bonds has fallen to 8 percent at the time of sale. What would the pure bond value be at that point? (Use semiannual analysis.) Would the pure bond value have a significant effect on valuation then?

Falling stock prices and pure bond value

21. Manpower Electric Company has 7 percent convertible bonds outstanding. Each bond has a $1,000 par value. The conversion ratio is 25, the stock price $38, and the bonds mature in 16 years.

a.   What is the conversion value of the bond?

b.   Assume after one year, the common stock price falls to $27.50. What is the conversion value of the bond?

c.   Also, assume after one year, interest rates go up to 10 percent on similar bonds. There are 15 years left to maturity. What is the pure value of the bond? Use semiannual analysis.

d.   Will the conversion value of the bond (part *b*) or the pure value of the bond (part *c*) have a stronger influence on its price in the market?

e.   If the bond trades in the market at its pure bond value, what would be the conversion premium (stated as a percentage of the conversion value)?

COMPREHENSIVE PROBLEM

Fondren Exploration, Ltd.

(rates of return on convertible bond investments)

Fondren Exploration, Ltd., has 1,000 convertible bonds ($1,000 par value) outstanding, each of which may be converted to 50 shares of stock. The $1 million worth of bonds has 25 years to maturity. The current price of the stock is $26 per share. The firm's net income in the most recent fiscal year was $270,000. The bonds pay 12 percent interest. The corporation has 150,000 shares of common stock outstanding. Current market rates on long-term nonconvertible bonds of equal quality are 14 percent. A 35 percent tax rate is assumed.

a.   Compute diluted earnings per share.

b.   Assume the bonds currently sell at a 5 percent conversion premium over conversion value (based on a stock price of $26). However, as the price of the stock increases from $26 to $37 due to new events, there will be an increase in the bond price, and a zero conversion premium. Under these circumstances, determine the rate of return on a convertible bond investment that is part of this price change, based on the appreciation in value.

c.   Now assume the stock price is $16 per share because a competitor introduced a new product. Would the conversion value be greater than the pure bond value, based on the interest rates stated above? (See Table 16–3 in Chapter 16 to get the bond value without having to go through the actual computation.)

d.   Referring to part *c,* if the convertible traded at a 15 percent premium over the conversion value, would the convertible be priced above the pure bond value?

e.   If long-term interest rates in the market go down to 10 percent while the stock price is at $23, with a 6 percent conversion premium, what would the difference be between the market price of the convertible bond and the pure bond value? Assume 25 years to maturity, and once again use Table 16–3 for part of your answer.

f. If Fondren were able to retire the convertibles and replace them with 50,000 shares of common stock selling at $26 per share and paying a 5 percent dividend yield (dividend-to-price ratio), would the aftertax cash outflow related to the original convertibles be greater or less than the cash outflow related to the stock?

COMPREHENSIVE PROBLEM

United Technology Corporation (UTC) has $40 million of convertible bonds outstanding (40,000 bonds at $1,000 par value) with a coupon rate of 11 percent. Interest rates are currently 8 percent for bonds of equal risk. The bonds have 15 years left to maturity. The bonds may be called at a 9 percent premium over par. They are convertible into 30 shares of common stock. The tax rate for the company is 25 percent.

United Technology Corp.

(a call decision with convertible bonds)

The firm's common stock is currently selling for $41 and it pays a dividend of $3.50 per share. The expected income for the company is $38 million with 6 million shares outstanding.

Thoroughly analyze the bond and determine whether the firm should call the bond at the 9 percent call premium. In your analysis, consider the following:

a. The impact of the call on basic and diluted earnings per share (assume the call forces conversion).

b. The consequences of your decision on financing flexibility.

c. The net change in cash outflows to the company as a result of the call and conversion.

WEB EXERCISE

In this Web exercise we use the Chicago Board Options Exchange Web site to cover options. While we will stay with basic coverage of the material, this Web site is capable of taking you into much more complex areas of derivative securities than the textbook.

Go to www.cboe.com and click on "Products."

1. What are the first five products offered?

2. Continue to scroll down the page until you get to "LEAPS." What does the title stand for? How long a life may a LEAP have?

3. Go to "Strategies." Click on "Equity Options."

    a. If you thought an (underlying) stock price was going up, what strategy would you use? One answer is all that is necessary.

    b. If you thought an (underlying) stock price was going down, what strategy would you use? One sentence is all that is necessary.

Note: From time to time, companies redesign their Web sites and occasionally a topic we have listed may have been deleted, updated, or moved into a different location. If you click on the site map or site index, you will be introduced to a table of contents which should aid you in finding the topic you are looking for.

part 6

Expanding the Perspective of Corporate Finance

RELATED WEB SITES

finance.yahoo.com

www.opic.gov

news makers

The last section of this book discusses the two topics of mergers and international finance. Richard Parsons, chairman and CEO of Time Warner, presides over an international media company that sells magazines (*Time*), operates HBO and Turner Broadcasting, produces movies (Warner Bros. Entertainment and New Line Cinema), provides cable service (Time Warner Cable), and owns AOL. Many of these divisions were acquired through mergers or purchases. Additionally, Time Warner is an international company with about 75 percent of its revenues coming from the United States and the rest coming from the United Kingdom, Germany, France, Canada, Japan and other countries.

Richard Parsons has had a varied career. He worked as a lawyer for Nelson Rockefeller and went with Mr. Rockefeller to Washington in 1974 when Rockefeller served as vice president of the United States. He came back to New York where he was a lawyer with the Wall Street firm, Patterson and Belknap. He moved on to become president of Dime Savings Bank and was elected to the board of directors of Time Warner in 1991. In 1995 he became president of Time Warner and helped to negotiate the company's merger with AOL, the largest merger in the history of the United States. Unfortunately, AOL was valued at a sky-high price during the Internet stock bubble and eventually AOL Time Warner dropped AOL from its name and wrote down over $60 billion of AOL assets. In 2002 Richard Parsons became chairman of the board and CEO of Time Warner. Ted Turner, who was a large shareholder through his sale of Turner Broadcasting to Time Warner, lost almost $8 billion in the value of his Time Warner stock as the price of the shares declined from over $90 in 2000 to $10 in 2003. By 2006 the stock had recovered to $17 per share.

Richard Parsons graduated from the University of Hawaii and was a member of the varsity basketball team. Another of his distinctions is having the highest score on the New York State Bar exam in 1971 after earning a degree from Albany Law School. Parsons, like many executives, serves on many boards and committees. President Bush selected him to cochair a commission on Social Security in 2001, and he also helped work on the transition team for Michael Bloomberg after he was elected mayor of New York City. He is chairman of the Apollo Theatre

Richard Parsons– Time Warner
AP/Wide World Photos

Foundation and is on the boards of trustees for Howard University, the Museum of Modern Art in New York, and the Museum of Natural History. He is also on the board of directors of Citigroup and Estée Lauder.

External Growth through Mergers

20

chapter concepts

1 Firms engage in mergers for financial motives and to increase operating efficiency.

2 Companies may be acquired through cash purchases or by one company exchanging its shares for another company's shares.

3 The potential impact of the merger on earnings per share and stock value must be carefully assessed.

4 The diversification benefits of a merger should be evaluated.

5 Some buyouts are unfriendly and are strongly opposed by the potential candidates.

A new twist to mergers is that of U.S. companies acquiring foreign firms to penetrate the firms' markets. Few companies have been more impressive in this activity than Citigroup, which acquired Mexico's second largest bank, Banamex, for $15 billion in 2001.

Not only did the merger give Citigroup a major presence in Mexico, but it helped make the powerful New York banking firm the leading contender for Hispanic banking business in the United States. There are 45 million Hispanics in the United States and the market is not only growing but is a lucrative one as well.

New arrivals in the United States from Mexico must be approached in Spanish, while those who have been in the United States for an extended period of time can normally communicate in either English or Spanish. Not all major banks have learned these rules.

Citigroup was smart enough to allow its Mexican subsidiary to retain its original name of Banamex, and the firm was contributing $1 billion to Citigroup's bottom line one year after the merger.

The merger worked out so well that Citigroup decided to extend its Hispanic reach by acquiring San Francisco–based Golden State Bancorp for $5.8 billion in May of 2002. The firm has 353 branches in California and Nevada where a third of all U.S. Hispanics live. Although the merger is not an exclusive play for Hispanic business, the implications for market penetration in the Hispanic community are obvious. California-based Bank of America and Wells Fargo could only sit back and watch as the New York banking giant moved into their territory.

Mergers also have had a presence in a number of other industries. Particularly evident were the telecommunications and public utility industries where mergers were announced between AT&T and SBC Communications; Sprint and Nextel; and Verizon Communications and MCI, Inc. These mergers were largely the result of deregulation, which created an environment in which companies felt the need to be larger and have greater power. With the severe decline in the telecom industry's profits in the early 2000s, not all of these mergers have had their intended results.

Another area of increased merger activity was the pharmaceutical industry. Drug company giant Pfizer acquired Warner-Lambert, as well as Pharmacia. Another important merger in the industry was between SmithKline Beecham and Glaxo Wellcome. Johnson & Johnson also made a number of key acquisitions. There is no doubt that the high cost and risk involved in bringing new drugs to the market in this industry have caused companies to combine their resources.

The energy sector has also been active in the merger game with combinations between Exxon and Mobil, British Petroleum and Amoco, as well as Chevron and Texaco. There are two factors encouraging consolidation in this industry—the hazardous risk of finding new sources of energy and the unsettling presence of volatile oil prices.

Mergers have also had significant impact in aerospace, entertainment, consumer products, food processing, and any and all forms of technology industries. For an historical perspective, please note the largest completed or announced mergers in the United States (and world) in Table 20–1.

Buyer	Acquired Company	Cost ($ billions)	Year
1. America Online	Time Warner	$183	2000
2. Vodaphone Airtouch	Mannesmann	149	2000
3. Bell Atlantic	GTE	85	2000
4. SBC Communications	Ameritech	81	1999
5. Exxon	Mobil	79	1998
6. Vodaphone	AirTouch	74	1999
7. Pfizer	Warner-Lambert	73	2000
8. Travelers	Citicorp	71	1998
9. AT&T	MediaOne Group	63	2000
10. Procter & Gamble	Gillette	61	2005

Table 20–1
Largest acquisitions ever

In the following sections, we more fully examine the motives for business combinations; the establishment of negotiated terms of exchange, with the associated accounting implications; and the stock market effect of mergers (including unfriendly takeovers).

Motives for Business Combinations

A business combination may take the form of either a merger or a consolidation. A **merger** is defined as a combination of two or more companies in which the resulting firm maintains the identity of the acquiring company. In a **consolidation** two or more companies are combined to form a new entity. A consolidation might be utilized when the firms are of equal size and market power. For purposes of our discussion, the primary emphasis will be on mergers, though virtually all of the principles presented could apply to consolidations as well.

Financial Motives

The motives for mergers and consolidations are both financial and nonfinancial in nature. We examine the financial motives first. As discussed in Chapter 13, a merger allows the acquiring firm to enjoy a potentially desirable **portfolio effect** by achieving risk reduction while perhaps maintaining the firm's rate of return. If two firms that benefit from opposite phases of the business cycle combine, their variability in performance may be reduced. Risk-averse investors may then discount the future performance of the merged firm at a lower rate and thus assign it a higher valuation than that assigned to the separate firms. The same point can be made in regard to multinational mergers. Through merger, a firm that has holdings in diverse economic and political climates can enjoy some reduction in the risks that derive from foreign exchange translation, government politics, military takeovers, and localized recessions.

While the portfolio diversification effect of a merger is intellectually appealing—with each firm becoming a mini–mutual fund unto itself—the practicalities of the situation can become quite complicated. No doubt one of the major forces of merger movements in prior decades was the desire of the conglomerates for diversification. The lessons we have learned from the LTVs, the Littons, and others is that too much diversification can strain the operating capabilities of the firm.

As one form of evidence on the lack of success of some of these earlier mergers, the ratio of divestitures[1] to new acquisitions was only 11 percent in 1967, but it rose to over 50 percent generations later. As examples, Sears spent the early 1990s shedding itself of its Allstate insurance division and also Dean Witter, its entry into the stock brokerage business. Eastman Kodak sold off its chemical holdings during the same time period. The stock market reaction to divestitures may actually be positive when it can be shown that management is freeing itself from an unwanted or unprofitable division.[2]

A second financial motive is the improved financing posture that a merger can create as a result of expansion. Larger firms may enjoy greater access to financial markets and thus be in a better position to raise debt and equity capital. Such firms may also be able to attract larger and more prestigious investment bankers to handle future financing.

Greater financing capability may also be inherent in the merger itself. This is likely to be the case if the acquired firm has a strong cash position or a low debt-equity ratio that can be used to expand borrowing by the acquiring company.

A final financial motive is the **tax loss carryforward** that might be available in a merger if one of the firms has previously sustained a tax loss.

In the example on page 609, we assume Firm A acquires Firm B, which has a $220,000 tax loss carryforward. We look at Firm A's financial position before and after the merger. The assumption is that the firm has a 40 percent tax rate.

The tax shield value of a carryforward to Firm A is equal to the loss involved times the tax rate ($220,000 $\times$ 40 percent = $88,000). Based on the carryforward, the company can reduce its total taxes from $120,000 to $32,000, and thus it could pay $88,000 for the carryforward alone (this is on a nondiscounted basis).

---

[1]A divestiture is a spin-off or a sell-off of a subsidiary or a division.
[2]J. Fred Weston, "Divestitures: Mistakes or Learning," *Journal of Applied Corporate Finance* 4 (Summer 1989), pp. 68–76.

	2004	2005	2006	Total Values
Firm A (without merger):				
Before-tax income	$100,000	$100,000	$100,000	$300,000
Taxes (40%)	40,000	40,000	40,000	120,000
Income available to stockholders	$ 60,000	$ 60,000	$ 60,000	$180,000
Firm A (with merger and associated tax benefits):				
Before-tax income	$100,000	$100,000	$100,000	$300,000
Tax loss carryforward	100,000	100,000	20,000	220,000
Net taxable income	0	0	80,000	80,000
Taxes (40%)	0	0	32,000	32,000
Income available to stockholders	$100,000	$100,000	$ 68,000*	$268,000

*Before-tax income minus taxes ($100,000 − $32,000 = $68,000).

As would be expected, income available to stockholders also has gone up by $88,000 ($268,000 − $180,000 = $88,000). Of course Firm B's anticipated operating gains and losses for future years must also be considered in analyzing the deal.

Nonfinancial Motives

The nonfinancial motives for mergers and consolidations include the desire to expand management and marketing capabilities as well as the acquisition of new products.

While mergers may be directed toward either **horizontal integration** (that is, the acquisition of competitors) or **vertical integration** (the acquisition of buyers or sellers of goods and services to the company), antitrust policy generally precludes the elimination of competition. For this reason mergers are often with companies in allied but not directly related fields. The pure conglomerate merger of industries in totally unrelated industries is still undertaken, but less frequently than in the past.

Perhaps the greatest management motive for a merger is the possible synergistic effect. **Synergy** is said to occur when the whole is greater than the sum of the parts. This "2 + 2 = 5" effect may be the result of eliminating overlapping functions in production and marketing as well as meshing together various engineering capabilities. In terms of planning related to mergers, there is often a tendency to overestimate the possible synergistic benefits that might accrue.

Motives of Selling Stockholders

Most of our discussion has revolved around the motives of the acquiring firm that initiates a merger. Likewise the selling stockholders may be motivated by a desire to receive the acquiring company's stock—which may have greater acceptability or activity in the marketplace than the stock they hold. Also when cash is offered instead of stock, this gives the selling stockholders an opportunity to diversify their holdings into many new investments. As will be discussed later in the chapter, the selling stockholders generally receive an attractive price for their stock that may well exceed its current market or book value.

Are Diversified Firms Winners or Losers?

A generation ago, the corporate conglomerate was thought to be the ideal business model. Firms such as LTV, Litton, and Textron all owned subsidiaries that were in widely different industries.

The advantages of the conglomerate organization were thought to be many. First of all, to the extent that the firm's subsidiaries are noncorrelated or negatively correlated, there is risk reduction. For example, a firm that owns airlines, oil companies, machine tools manufacturers, banks, and hotels is going to be influenced by different factors during the up and down phases of a business cycle. To the extent there is risk reduction and investors are risk-averse (do not like risk), there should be a higher valuation for the firm's stock. Furthermore, the firm should have greater capacity to take on debt because there will be less variability in earnings and cash flow.

Also, there are tax advantages. Losses in one division of the firm can be written off against gains in another. While the same goal of lower taxes could be achieved in a single industry firm through tax loss carrybacks and carryforwards, that is a much more tedious process.

Furthermore, the conglomerate's internal allocation of capital to the most efficient divisions and away from the least efficient divisions may be more effective than the overall stock market in accomplishing the same goal between companies. The managers of a conglomerate are viewing the financial performance of each industry's division on a daily or weekly basis as opposed to the stock market where there is a lag in reporting performance, and not all investors are well informed even when information is available.

But wait a minute! Don't run out and buy stock in a conglomerate just yet. Research has shown that single-line businesses tend to have higher operating profitability than the subsidiary of a conglomerate in the same industry. This is due to greater focus. A conglomerate may represent a "jack of all trades, but a master of none."

Also a failing business cannot have a value below zero if operated on its own, but may have a negative value if it is part of an otherwise profitable conglomerate. Its losses can continue to eat into the profits and value of the nonrelated divisions. Such was the case with Tenneco in the 1990s when the firm's money-losing farm equipment business drained the profits and incentives from its auto parts and chemical divisions.

What about stock market performance? How do conglomerates compare to single industry firms in terms of providing returns to investors? There are enough studies on this topic to fill up a midsize university's library. The results of hundreds of studies ranging from Copeland and Weston (1979, Addison-Wesley) to Comment and Jerrell (1994, *Journal of Financial Economics*) are pretty much a draw.

What is not a draw is the overall value assigned to conglomerates versus single industry firms. There is a diversification discount of 13 percent to 15 percent on average (Berger and Otek, *Journal of Finance,* 1995). This has also been confirmed by later studies. Furthermore, the more unrelated the divisions, the greater the discount.

Take the example of Fortune Brands. It is the successor to American Brands, the successor to the American Tobacco Co. Fortune Brands is involved in four major industries: hardware and home improvement; office products; golf and leisure products; and wine and spirits. Some of its better-known labels across the board are Master Lock, Titleist golf balls, and Jim Beam bourbon (none of you have heard of the latter). The firm no longer has any cigarette products.

True to form, when the imputed value of each division (based on the value of publicly traded companies in the same industry) is added together on a weighted average basis, the total value is approximately 15 percent greater than the stock market value of Fortune Brands (Kelleher, Working Paper, 2003). Thus, we speak of a diversification discount of approximately 15 percent for the conglomerate firm. In this case, the whole (the conglomerate) is less than the sum of the parts.

In addition, officers of the selling company may receive attractive postmerger management contracts as well as directorships in the acquiring firm. In some circumstances they may be allowed to operate the company as a highly autonomous subsidiary after the merger (though this is probably the exception).[3]

A final motive of the selling stockholders may simply be the bias against smaller businesses that has developed in this country and around the world. Real clout in the financial markets may dictate being part of a larger organization. These motives should not be taken as evidence that all or even most officers or directors of smaller firms wish to sell out—a matter that we shall examine further when we discuss negotiated offers versus takeover attempts.

In determining the price that will be paid for a potential acquisition, a number of factors are considered, including earnings, cash flow, dividends, and growth potential. We shall divide our analysis between cash purchases and stock-for-stock exchanges, in which the acquiring company trades stock rather than paying cash for the acquired firm.

Terms of Exchange

Cash Purchases

The cash purchase of another company can be viewed within the context of a capital budgeting decision. Instead of purchasing new plant or machinery, the purchaser has opted to acquire a *going concern*. For example, assume the Invest Corporation is analyzing the acquisition of the Sell Corporation for $1 million. The Sell Corporation has expected cash flow (aftertax earnings plus depreciation) of $100,000 per year for the next 5 years and $150,000 per year for the 6th through the 20th years. Furthermore, the synergistic benefits of the merger (in this case, combining production facilities) will add $10,000 per year to cash flow. Finally, the Sell Corporation has a $50,000 tax loss carryforward that can be used immediately by the Invest Corporation. Assuming a 40 percent tax rate, the $50,000 loss carryforward will shield $20,000 of profit from taxes immediately. The Invest Corporation has a 10 percent cost of capital, and this is assumed to remain stable with the merger. Our analysis would be as follows:

Cash outflow:

Purchase price	$1,000,000
Less tax shield benefit from tax loss carryforward ($50,000 × 40%)	20,000
Net cash outflow	$ 980,000

Cash inflows:

Years 1–5: $100,000 Cash inflow
                 10,000 Synergistic benefit
            $110,000 Total cash inflow

Present value of $110,000 × 3.791	$ 417,010

Years 6–20: $150,000 Cash inflow
                 10,000 Synergistic benefit
            $160,000 Total cash inflow

Present value of $160,000 × 4.723	755,680
Total present value of inflows	$1,172,690

---

[3]This is most likely to happen when the acquiring firm is a foreign company.

The present value factor for the first five years (3.791) is based on n = 5, i = 10 percent, and can be found in Appendix D. For the 6th through the 20th years, we take the present value factor in Appendix D for n = 20, i = 10 percent, and subtract the present value factor for n = 5, i = 10 percent. This allows us to isolate the 6th through the 20th years with a factor of 4.723 (8.514 − 3.791).

Finally, the net present value of the investment is:

Total present value of inflows	$1,172,690
Net cash outflow.	980,000
Net present value	$192,690

The acquisition appears to represent a desirable alternative for the expenditure of cash, with a positive net present value of $192,690.

In the market environment of the last two decades, some firms could be purchased at a value below the replacement costs of their assets and thus represented a potentially desirable capital investment. As an extreme example, Anaconda Copper had an asset replacement value of $1.3 billion when the firm was purchased by Atlantic Richfield for $684 million in the 1980s. With the stock market gains of the 1990s, such bargain purchases were more difficult to achieve.

Stock-for-Stock Exchange

On a stock-for-stock exchange, we use a somewhat different analytical approach, emphasizing the earnings per share impact of exchanging securities (and ultimately the market valuation of those earnings). The analysis is made primarily from the viewpoint of the acquiring firm. The shareholders of the acquired firm are concerned mainly about the initial price they are paid for their shares and about the outlook for the acquiring firm.

Assume that Expand Corporation is considering the acquisition of Small Corporation. Significant financial information on the firms before the merger is provided in Table 20–2.

Table 20–2

Financial data on potential merging firms

	Small Corporation	Expand Corporation
Total earnings	$200,000	$500,000
Number of shares of stock outstanding	50,000	200,000
Earnings per share	$4.00	$2.50
Price-earnings ratio (P/E)	7.5×	12×
Market price per share	$30.00	$30.00

We begin our analysis with the assumption that one share of Expand Corporation ($30) will be traded for one share of Small Corporation ($30). In actuality, Small Corporation will probably demand more than $30 per share because the acquired firm usually gets a premium over the current market value. We will later consider the impact of paying such a premium.

If 50,000 new shares of Expand Corporation are traded in exchange for all the old shares of Small Corporation, Expand Corporation will then have 250,000 shares outstanding. At the same time, its claim to earnings will go to $700,000 when the two firms are combined. Postmerger earnings per share will be $2.80 for the Expand Corporation, as indicated in Table 20–3.

Table 20–3
Postmerger earnings per share

A number of observations are worthy of note. First the earnings per share of Expand Corporation have increased as a result of the merger, rising from $2.50 to $2.80. This has occurred because Expand Corporation's P/E ratio of 12 was higher than the 7.5 P/E ratio of Small Corporation at the time of the merger (as previously presented in Table 20–2). Whenever a firm acquires another entity whose P/E ratio is lower than its own, there is an immediate increase in earnings per share.

Of course, if Expand Corporation pays a price higher than Small Corporation's current market value, which is typically the case, it may be paying equal to or more than its own current P/E ratio for Small Corporation. For example, at a price of $48 per share for Small Corporation, Expand Corporation will be paying 12 times Small Corporation's earnings, which is exactly the current P/E ratio of Expand Corporation. Under these circumstances there will be no change in postmerger earnings per share for Expand Corporation.

Endless possibilities can occur in mergers based on stock-for-stock exchanges. Even if the acquiring company increases its immediate earnings per share as a result of the merger, it may slow its future growth rate if it is buying a less aggressive company. Conversely, the acquiring company may dilute immediate postmerger earnings per share but increase its potential growth rate for the future as a result of acquiring a rapidly growing company.

The ultimate test of a merger rests with its ability to maximize the market value of the acquiring firm. This is sometimes a difficult goal to achieve but is the measure of the success of a merger.

Portfolio Effect

Inherent in all of our discussion is the importance of the merger's portfolio effect on the risk-return posture of the firm. The reduction or increase in risk may influence the P/E ratio as much as the change in the growth rate. To the extent that we are diminishing the overall risk of the firm in a merger, the postmerger P/E ratio and market value may increase even if the potential earnings growth is unchanged. Business risk reduction may be achieved through acquiring another firm that is influenced by a set of factors in the business cycle opposite from those that influence the acquiring firm, while financial risk reduction may be achieved by restructuring the postmerger financial arrangements to include less debt.

Perhaps Expand Corporation may be diversifying from a heavy manufacturing industry into the real estate/housing industry. While heavy manufacturing industries move with the business cycle, the real estate/housing industry tends to be countercyclical. Even though the expected value of earnings per share may remain relatively constant as a result of the merger, the standard deviation of possible outcomes may decline as a result of risk reduction through diversification, as is indicated in Figure 20–1.

Figure 20–1

Risk-reduction portfolio benefits

We see that the expected value of the earnings per share has remained constant at $2.50 in this instance but the standard deviation has gone down. Because there is less risk in the corporation, the investor may be willing to assign a higher valuation, thus increasing the price-earnings ratio.

Accounting Considerations in Mergers and Acquisitions

The role of financial accounting has significance in the area of mergers and acquisitions. Prior to 2001, there were competing accounting methods for recording mergers and acquisitions. The first method was a **pooling of interests**, under which the financial statements of the firms were combined, subject to minor adjustments, and no goodwill was credited.

To qualify for a pooling of interests, certain criteria had to be met, such as:

1. The acquiring corporation issues only common stock, with rights identical to its old outstanding voting stock, in exchange for substantially all of the other company's voting stock.
2. The acquired firm's stockholders maintain an ownership position in the surviving firm.
3. The combined entity does not intend to dispose of a significant portion of the assets of the combined companies within two years.
4. The combination is effected in a single transaction.

Goodwill may be created when the second type of merger recording—a purchase of assets—is used. Because of the criteria described above (particularly items 1 and 2), a purchase of assets treatment, rather than a pooling of interests treatment, was generally necessary when the tender offer is in cash, bonds, preferred stock, or common stock with restricted rights. Before June 2001, under a **purchase of assets** accounting treatment, any excess of purchase price over book value must be recorded as goodwill and written off over a maximum period of 40 years. If a company purchases a firm with a $4 million book value (net worth) for $6 million, $2 million of goodwill is created on the books of the acquiring company, and it must be written off over a maximum period of 40 years. This would cause a $50,000-per-year reduction in reported earnings ($2 million/40 years). Under a pooling of interests accounting treatment, you will recall, goodwill is not created.

The writing off of goodwill had a devastating effect on postmerger earnings per share for many mergers and was feared by the acquiring firm's management.

In a historic move in June of 2001, the Financial Accounting Standards Board put *SFAS 141* and *SFAS 142* in place. The impact of the standards was to eliminate pooling of interests accounting and to greatly change the way goodwill is treated under the purchase of assets method. No longer must merger-related goodwill be amortized over a maximum period of 40 years, but rather it is placed on the balance sheet of the acquiring firm at the time of acquisition and not subsequently written down unless it is impaired. Norman N. Strauss, national director of accounting standards at Ernst and Young and a member of FASB's emerging issues task force, said, "The elimination of pooling [and the associated change in goodwill treatment] is one of the most significant and dramatic changes in accounting treatment in years."[4]

Although goodwill is no longer amortized, it still must be carefully evaluated. In fact, the reporting obligations related to goodwill are now much more substantial than in the past. At least once a year goodwill must be tested to see if it has been impaired. The question becomes, "Is the fair value of goodwill greater or less than its current book value?" This can be determined by taking the present value of future cash flows, subtracting out liabilities, and arriving at a value. If goodwill is impaired (less than book value), part of it must be immediately written down against operating income.

In writing the new merger reporting requirements, the FASB was generous in one respect. It allowed reporting companies to take a one time write-down of all past goodwill impairment at the time of adoption by the firm (the January 1, 2002, calendar year for most companies). This feature not only gave the firm a one-time opportunity to clear the slate, but the impairment was treated as a "change in accounting principles" and not directly charged to operating results. This is significant because impairment charges (after 2002) come directly out of reported income.

Negotiated versus Tendered Offers

Traditionally, mergers have been negotiated in a friendly atmosphere between officers and directors of the participating corporations. Product lines, quality of assets, and future growth prospects are discussed, and eventually an exchange ratio is hammered out and reported to the investment community and the financial press.

A not so friendly offer has been developed, the **takeover tender offer**, in which a company attempts to acquire a target firm against its will. One of the most notorious examples was the announced intent of American Express to take over McGraw-Hill. At that time the stock of McGraw-Hill was selling at $26 per share. The initial American Express

---

[4]N. B. Strauss, from S. R. Moehrle and J. A. Reynolas-Moehrle, "Say Goodbye to Pooling and Goodwill Amortization," *Journal of Accountancy* (September 2001), pp. 31–38.

offer was for $34, and eventually the offer went up to $40. McGraw-Hill fought off the offer by maintaining that American Express would obstruct the independent character required of a publisher. McGraw-Hill discouraged the unwelcome offer from American Express, but many small McGraw-Hill stockholders sued the publisher, claiming calling off the merger caused them to lose an opportunity to advance the cash value of their holdings.

Not all companies can fend off the unwanted advances of suitors. An entire vocabulary has developed on Wall Street around the concept of the target takeover. For example the **Saturday night special** refers to a surprise offer made just before the market closes for the weekend and takes the target company's officers by surprise. By the time the officers can react, the impact of the offer has already occurred. Perhaps a stock is trading at $20 and an unfriendly offer comes in at $28. Though the offer may please the company's stockholders, its management faces the dangers of seeing the company going down the wrong path in a merger and perhaps being personally ousted.

To avoid an unfriendly takeover, management may turn to a **white knight** for salvation. A white knight represents a third firm that management calls on to help it avoid the initial unwanted tender offer. The biggest white knight on record was Chevron, which acquired Gulf Oil and saved the firm from an unwanted tender offer from T. Boone Pickens and Mesa Petroleum.[5]

Many firms that wish to avoid takeovers have moved their corporate offices to states that have tough prenotification and protection provisions in regard to takeover offers. Other companies have bought portions of their own shares to restrict the amount of stock available for a takeover or have encouraged employees to buy stock under corporate pension plans. Other protective measures include increasing dividends to keep stockholders happy and staggering the election of members of the boards of directors to make outside power plays more difficult to initiate. Possible target companies have also bought up other companies to increase their own size and make themselves more expensive and less vulnerable. One of the key rules for avoiding a targeted takeover is to never get caught with too large a cash position. A firm with large cash balances serves as an ideal target for a leveraged takeover. The acquiring company can negotiate a bank loan based on the target company's assets and then go into the marketplace to make a cash tender offer. For example, CIT Financial left itself wide open when it sold a banking subsidiary for $425 million. At that point CIT had cash balances equal to $20 per share for shares that had a market value in the $30 to $40 range. RCA bought the company for $65 per share.

Also, the poison pill, discussed at some length in Chapter 17, is an effective device for protection. It may give those in an entrenched position the ability to accumulate new shares at well below the market price in order to increase their percentage of ownership. This privilege is usually triggered when an unwanted outside group accumulates a certain percentage of the shares outstanding (such as 25 percent).

While a takeover bid may not appeal to management, it may be enticing to stockholders, as previously indicated. Herein lies the basic problem. The bidding may get so high that stockholders demand action. The desire of management to maintain the status quo can conflict with the objective of stockholder wealth maximization.

---

[5]The situation was reversed for T. Boone Pickens and Mesa Petroleum in 1995 as they fell victim to unfriendly takeover offers.

Why CEOs Like the Merger Game

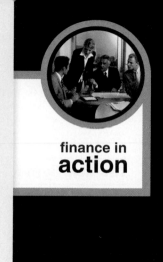

finance in action

When Procter & Gamble bought out Gillette in a $62 billion deal in 2005, some felt sorry for James Kilts, the top man at Gillette, who would soon be out of a job. The tears could have been spared. As it turned out, Mr. Kilts walked away from the deal with $153 million in profits on the Gillette stock options he owned.

Employees did not fare nearly as well. Procter & Gamble announced 6,000 jobs would be eliminated after the merger. Mitchell Marks, a San Francisco strategy consultant and specialist on mergers, said, "People think they are joining a company for the long haul, and boom, the rug is pulled out from under them because the CEO wants a quick payday."*

David Yermack, a New York University business professor, expresses a similar sentiment in describing outgoing CEOs in merger deals by saying, "Many of them really dip in and take an extra bonus, an extra augmentation of their contract at the 11th hour, when there is very little ability for the stockholders or even their own directors to do anything about it,"*

In the case of Mr. Kilts, the CEO at Gillette, some thought he had earned his big payday as a result of turning around the fortunes of the company when he took over in 2001. He cut back the firm's debt burden and spent wisely to revitalize key brand names.

However, the big payoff for CEOs in mergers all too often comes after the top executive has misguided the company. Take the case of John Zeglis at AT&T Wireless. The firm went public at $30 a share in 2001, but in 2004 the firm was sold to Cingular Wireless for $15 per share. Mr. Zeglis was CEO during this entire period of falling values, but walked away from the merger with $32 million in added compensation.

---

*Mark Maremart, "No Razor Here: Gillette Chief Executive to Get a Giant Payday," *The Wall Street Journal,* January 31, 2005, pp. A1, A14.

Premium Offers and Stock Price Movements

Few merger candidates are acquired at their current market value. Typically, a **merger premium** of 40 to 60 percent (or more) is paid over the premerger price of the acquired company. For example, Johnson & Johnson bought Neutrogena Corp. at $35.25 per share, a price 70 percent above its premerger value.

It is not surprising that a company that is offered a large premium over its current market value has a major upside movement. The only problem for the investor is that much of this movement may occur before the public announcement of the merger offer.[6] If a firm is selling at $25 per share when informal negotiations begin, it may be $36 by the time an announced offer of $40 is made. Still, there are good profits to be made if the merger goes through.

The only problem with this strategy or of any merger-related investment strategy is that the merger may be called off. In that case the merger candidate's stock, which shot up from $25 to $36, may fall back to $25, and the Johnny-come-lately investor would lose $11 per share. In Table 20–4, we consider the case of three canceled mergers. Of

Johnson&Johnson

Table 20–4 Stock movement of potential acquirees

Acquirer—Potential Acquiree	Preannouncement	One Day after Announcement	One Day after Cancellation
Mead Corp.—Occidental Petroleum	20⅜	33¼	23¼
Olin Corp.—Celanese	16	23¾	16¾
Chicago Rivet—MITE	20¾	28⅛	20¾

---

[6]This upside movement is often the result of insider trading on nonpublished information. While the SEC tries to control this activity, it is quite difficult to do.

course, if a new suitor comes along shortly after cancellation (or causes the original cancellation), the price may quickly rebound.

Two-Step Buyout

A merger ploy that has been undertaken in the recent merger movement is the **two-step buyout**. Under this plan the acquiring company attempts to gain control by offering a very high cash price for 51 percent of the shares outstanding. At the same time, it announces a second, lower price that will be paid later, either in cash, stock, or bonds. As an example, an acquiring company may offer stockholders of a takeover target company a $70 cash offer that can be executed in the next 20 days (for 51 percent of the shares outstanding). Subsequent to that time period, the selling stockholders will receive $57.50 in preferred stock for each share.

This buyout procedure accomplishes two purposes. First, it provides a strong inducement to stockholders to quickly react to the offer. Those who delay must accept a lower price. Second, it allows the acquiring company to pay a lower total price than if a single offer is made. In the example above, a single offer may have been made for $68 a share. Assume 1 million shares are outstanding. The single offer has a total price tag of $68,000,000, while the two-step offer would have called for only $63,875,000.

Single offer:

> 1,000,000 shares at $68 = $68,000,000

Two-step offer:

> 510,000 shares (51%) at $70.00 = $35,700,000
>
> 490,000 shares (49%) at $57.50 =   28,175,000
>
> $63,875,000

An example of a two-step buyout was the Mobil Oil attempt to acquire 51 percent of Marathon Oil shares at a price of $126 in cash, with a subsequent offer to buy the rest of the shares for $90 face value debentures. In this case Marathon Oil decided to sell to U.S. Steel, which also made a two-step offer of $125 in cash or $100 in notes to later sellers. Incidentally, before the bidding began, Marathon Oil was selling for $60 a share.

The SEC has continued to keep a close eye on the two-step buyout. Government regulators fear that smaller stockholders may not be sophisticated enough to compete with arbitrageurs or institutional investors in rapidly tendering shares to ensure receipt of the higher price. The SEC has emphasized the need for a pro rata processing of stockholder orders, in which each stockholder receives an equal percentage of shares tendered.

Similar measures to the two-step buyout are likely to develop in the future as companies continue to look for more attractive ways to acquire other companies. Such new activity can be expected in the mergers and acquisitions area where some of the finest minds in the investment banking and legal community are continually at work.

Summary

Corporations may seek external growth through mergers to reduce risk, to improve access to the financial markets through increased size, or to obtain tax carryforward benefits. A merger may also expand the marketing and management capabilities of the firm and allow for new product development. While some mergers promise synergistic benefits (the $2 + 2 = 5$ effect), this can be an elusive feature, with initial expectations exceeding subsequent realities.

The *cash* purchase of another corporation takes on many of the characteristics of a classical capital budgeting decision. In a *stock-for-stock* exchange, there is often a trade-off between immediate gain or dilution in earnings per share and future growth. If a firm buys another firm with a P/E ratio lower than its own, there is an immediate increase in earnings per share, but the long-term earnings growth prospects must also be considered. The ultimate objective of a merger, as is true of any financial decision, is stockholder wealth maximization, and the immediate and delayed effects of the merger must be evaluated in this context.

To the extent that we are diminishing the overall risk of the firm in a merger, the postmerger P/E ratio and market value may increase even if the potential earnings growth is unchanged. Business risk reduction may be achieved through acquiring another firm that is influenced by a set of factors in the business cycle opposite from those that influence our own firm, while financial risk reduction may be achieved by restructuring the postmerger financial arrangements to include less debt.

In the recent merger movement, the unsolicited tender offer for a target company has gained in popularity. Offers are made at values well in excess of the current market price, and management of the target company becomes trapped in the dilemma of maintaining its current position versus agreeing to the wishes of the acquiring company, and even the target company's own stockholders.

List of Terms

merger 607	goodwill 614
consolidation 607	purchase of assets 614
portfolio effect 608	takeover tender offer 615
tax loss carryforward 608	Saturday night special 616
horizontal integration 609	white knight 616
vertical integration 609	merger premium 617
synergy 609	two-step buyout 618
pooling of interests 614	

Discussion Questions

1. Name three industries in which mergers have been prominent.
2. What is the difference between a merger and a consolidation?
3. Why might the portfolio effect of a merger provide a higher valuation for the participating firms?

4. What is the difference between horizontal integration and vertical integration? How does antitrust policy affect the nature of mergers?

5. What is synergy? What might cause this result? Is there a tendency for management to *over-* or *underestimate* the potential synergistic benefits of a merger?

6. If a firm wishes to achieve immediate appreciation in earnings per share as a result of a merger, how can this be best accomplished in terms of exchange variables? What is a possible drawback to this approach in terms of long-range considerations?

7. It is possible for the postmerger P/E ratio to move in a direction opposite to that of the immediate postmerger earnings per share. Explain why this could happen.

8. How is goodwill now treated in a merger?

9. Suggest some ways in which firms have tried to avoid being part of a target takeover.

10. What is a typical merger premium paid in a merger or acquisition? What effect does this premium have on the market value of the merger candidate and when is most of this movement likely to take place?

11. Why do management and stockholders often have divergent viewpoints about the desirability of a takeover?

12. What is the purpose(s) of the two-step buyout from the viewpoint of the acquiring company?

Practice Problems and Solutions

Tax loss carryforward

1. American Century Corp. is considering acquiring Southern Homes, Inc. Southern Homes has a tax loss carryforward of $240,000. Projected earnings for American Century Corp. are as follows:

	200x	200y	200z	Total Values
Before-tax income.	$80,000	$70,000	$180,000	$330,000
Taxes (30%)	24,000	21,000	54,000	99,000
Income available to stockholders	$56,000	$49,000	$126,000	$231,000

a. How much of American Century's total taxes can be reduced by the tax loss carryforward? Keep in mind its tax rate is 30 percent as shown above.

b. How much will the total income to shareholders be for each year if the acquisition occurs? Use the same approach as that shown on page 609 of the text.

Impact of merger on earnings per share

2. Assume the following financial data for the Rotan Corp. and the Mosley Corp.

	Rotan	Mosley
Total earnings.	$300,000	$600,000
Number of shares of stock outstanding	100,000	300,000
Earnings per share.	$3.00	$2.00
Price-earnings ratio (P/E).	16.7×	25×
Market price per share	$50	$50

If all the shares of Rotan Corp. are exchanged for Mosley Corp. on a share-for-share basis, what will the postmerger earnings per share be for Mosley Corp? Use an approach similar to that in Table 20–3 on page 613.

Solutions

1. *a.* Reduction in taxes due to tax loss carryforward = Loss × Tax rate

    $$= \$240,000 \times .30 = \$72,000$$

    b. Mosley Corp. (with the merger and the associated benefits).

	200x	200y	200z	Total Values
Before-tax income.................	$80,000	$70,000	$180,000	$330,000
Taxes loss carryforward	80,000	70,000	90,000	240,000
Net taxable income.................	0	0	$ 90,000	$ 90,000
Taxes (30%)......................	0	0	27,000	27,000
Income available to stockholders (Before-tax income − Taxes)	$80,000	$70,000	$153,000*	$303,000†

*Before-tax income minus taxes = $180,000 − $27,000 = $153,000
†Before-tax income minus taxes = $330,000 − $27,000 = $303,000

2. **Total earnings:**

Rotan	$300,000
Mosley	600,000
	$900,000

Shares outstanding in surviving corporation:

Old (300,000) + New (100,000) = 400,000

$$\text{New earnings per share for the Mosley Corp.} = \frac{\text{Earnings}}{\text{Shares}} = \frac{\$900,000}{400,000} = \$2.25$$

All problems are available in Homework Manager. Please see the preface for more information.

Problems

1. Boardwalk Corporation desires to expand. It is considering a cash purchase of Park Place Corporation for $2,400,000. Park Place has a $600,000 tax loss carryforward that could be used immediately by Boardwalk, which is paying taxes at the rate of 35 percent. Park Place will provide $300,000 per year in cash flow (aftertax income plus depreciation) for the next 20 years. If Boardwalk Corporation has a cost of capital of 11 percent, should the merger be undertaken?

    Tax loss carryforward

2. Assume that Western Exploration Corp. is considering the acquisition of Ogden Drilling Company. The latter has a $400,000 tax loss carryforward. Projected earnings for the Western Exploration Corp. are as follows:

    Tax loss carryforward

	2005	2006	2007	Total Values
Before-tax income	$160,000	$200,000	$320,000	$680,000
Taxes (40%)......................	64,000	80,000	128,000	272,000
Income available to stockholders	$ 96,000	$120,000	$192,000	$408,000

a. How much will the total taxes of Western Exploration Corp. be reduced as a result of the tax loss carryforward?

b. How much will the total income available to stockholders be for the three years if the acquisition occurs? Use the same format as that in the text.

Cash acquisition with deferred benefits

3. J & J Enterprises is considering a cash acquisition of Patterson Steel Company for $4,000,000. Patterson will provide the following pattern of cash inflows and synergistic benefits for the next 20 years. There is no tax loss carryforward.

	Years		
	1–5	**6–15**	**16–20**
Cash inflow (aftertax)	$440,000	$600,000	$800,000
Synergistic benefits (aftertax)	40,000	60,000	70,000

The cost of capital for the acquiring firm is 12 percent. Should the merger be undertaken? (If you have difficulty with deferred time value of money problems, consult Chapter 9.)

Cash acquisition with deferred benefits

4. Worldwide Scientific Equipment is considering a cash acquisition of Medical Labs for $1.5 million. Medical Labs will provide the following pattern of cash inflows and synergistic benefits for the next 25 years. There is no tax loss carryforward.

	Years		
	1–5	**6–15**	**16–25**
Cash inflow (aftertax)	$100,000	$120,000	$160,000
Synergistic benefits (aftertax)	15,000	25,000	45,000

The cost of capital for the acquiring firm is 9 percent. Should the merger be undertaken?

Impact of merger on earnings per share

5. Assume the following financial data for Rembrandt Paint Co. and Picasso Art Supplies:

	Rembrandt Paint Co.	**Picasso Art Supplies**
Total earnings.	$300,000	$900,000
Number of shares of stock outstanding	100,000	500,000
Earnings per share.	$3.00	$1.80
Price-earnings ratio (P/E).	12×	20×
Market price per share	$36	$36

a. If all the shares of Rembrandt Paint Co. are exchanged for those of Picasso Art Supplies on a share-for-share basis, what will postmerger earnings per share be for Picasso Art Supplies?

b. Explain why the earnings per share of Picasso Art Supplies changed.

c. Can we necessarily assume that Picasso Art Supplies is better off after the merger?

6. Assume the following financial data for Noble Corporation and Barnes Enterprises: Impact of merger on earnings per share

	Noble Corporation	Barnes Enterprises
Total earnings...........................	$1,200,000	$3,600,000
Number of shares of stock outstanding........	600,000	2,400,000
Earnings per share.......................	$2.00	$1.50
Price-earnings ratio (P/E).................	24×	32×
Market price per share...................	$48	$48

    a. If all the shares of Noble Corporation are exchanged for those of Barnes Enterprises on a share-for-share basis, what will postmerger earnings per share be for Barnes Enterprises? Use an approach similar to that in Table 20–3 on page 613.

    b. Explain why the earnings per share of Barnes Enterprises changed.

    c. Can we necessarily assume that Barnes Enterprises is better off after the merger?

7. The Nebraska Corporation is considering acquiring the Lincoln Corporation. The data for the two companies are as follows: Mergers and dilution

	Lincoln Corp.	Nebraska Corp.
Total earnings...........................	$500,000	$2,000,000
Number of shares of stock outstanding........	200,000	1,000,000
Earnings per share.......................	$2.50	$2.00
Price-earnings ratio (P/E).................	16	20
Market price per share...................	$40	$40

    a. The Nebraska Corp. is going to give Lincoln Corp. a 50 percent premium over Lincoln Corp.'s current market value. What price will it pay?

    b. At the price computed in part *a,* what is the total market value of Lincoln Corp.? (Use number of Lincoln Corp. shares times price.)

    c. At the price computed in part *a,* what is the P/E ratio Nebraska Corp. is assigning to Lincoln Corp.

    d. How many shares must Nebraska Corp. issue to buy the Lincoln Corp. at the total value computed in part *b*? (Keep in mind Nebraska Corp.'s price per share is $40.)

    e. Given the answer to part *d,* how many shares will Nebraska Corp. have after the merger?

    f. Add together the total earnings of both corporations and divide by the total shares computed in part *e.* What are the new postmerger earnings per share?

    g. Why has Nebraska Corp's earnings per share gone down?

    h. How can Nebraska Corp. hope to overcome this dilution?

Two-step buyout

8. The Hollings Corporation is considering a two-step buyout of the Norton Corporation. The latter firm has 2 million shares outstanding and its stock price is currently $40 per share. In the two-step buyout, Hollings will offer to buy 51 percent of Norton's shares outstanding for $68 per share in cash, and the balance in a second offer of 980,000 convertible preferred stock shares. Each share of preferred stock would be valued at 45 percent over the current value of Norton's common stock. Mr. Green, a newcomer to the management team at Hollings, suggests that only one offer for all Norton's shares be made at $65.25 per share. Compare the total costs of the two alternatives. Which is better in terms of minimizing costs?

Premium offers and stock price movement

9. Chicago Savings Corp. is planning to make an offer for Ernie's Bank & Trust. The stock of Ernie's Bank & Trust is currently selling for $40 a share.

   a. If the tender offer is planned at a premium of 60 percent over market price, what will be the value offered per share for Ernie's Bank & Trust?

   b. Suppose before the offer is actually announced, the stock price of Ernie's Bank & Trust goes to $56 because of strong merger rumors. If you buy the stock at that price and the merger goes through (at the price computed in part *a*), what will be your percentage gain?

   c. Because there is always the possibility that the merger could be called off after it is announced, you also want to consider your percentage loss if that happens. Assume you buy the stock at $56 and it falls back to its original value after the merger cancellation, what will be your percentage loss?

   d. If there is an 80 percent probability that the merger will go through when you buy the stock at $56 and only a 20 percent chance that it will be called off, does this appear to be a good investment? Compute the expected value of the return on the investment.

Portfolio effect of a merger

10. Assume the Shelton Corporation is considering the acquisition of Cook, Inc. The expected earnings per share for the Shelton Corporation will be $3.00 with or without the merger. However, the standard deviation of the earnings will go from $1.89 to $1.20 with the merger because the two firms are negatively correlated.

   a. Compute the coefficient of variation for the Shelton Corporation before and after the merger. (Consult Chapter 13 to review statistical concepts if necessary.)

   b. Comment on the possible impact on Shelton's postmerger P/E ratio, assuming investors are risk-averse.

Portfolio considerations and risk aversion

11. General Meters is considering two mergers. The first is with Firm A in its own volatile industry, the auto speedometer industry, whereas the second is a merger with Firm B in an industry that moves in the opposite direction (and will tend to level out performance due to negative correlation).

   a. Compute the mean, standard deviation, and coefficient of variation for both investments (refer to Chapter 13 if necessary).

General Meters Merger with Firm A		General Meters Merger with Firm B	
Possible Earnings ($ millions)	Probability	Possible Earnings ($ millions)	Probability
$40	.30	$10	.25
50	.40	50	.50
60	.30	90	.25

b. Assuming investors are risk-averse, which alternative can be expected to bring the higher valuation?

WEB EXERCISE

The merger between Hewlett-Packard and Compaq Computer in 2002 was the largest merger ever between companies in the computer industry. We will examine the combined company, which is still called Hewlett-Packard.

1. Go to finance.yahoo.com.

2. Type "hpq" into the enter symbol box.

3. Scroll down and click on "Income Statement" and print it out, and do the same for the "Balance Sheet."

    By what percent did the following change for the three years under observation?

    a. Total revenue.

    b. Net income.

    c. Total stockholders' equity.

4. Also compute (for each of the three years)

    a. Net income to total revenue.

    b. Net income to tangible net assets.

5. In two paragraphs describe how Hewlett-Packard appears to be doing a few years after the merger.

Note: From time to time, companies redesign their Web sites and occasionally a topic we have listed may have been deleted, updated, or moved into a different location. If you click on the site map or site index, you will be introduced to a table of contents which should aid you in finding the topic you are looking for.

STANDARD &POOR'S

1. Log onto the S&P Market Insight Web site, www.mhhe.com/edumarketinsight.

2. Click on "Company," which is the first box below the Market Insight title.

3. Type Procter and Gamble's ticker symbol "PG" in the box and click on Go.

4. This exercise is simply aimed at showing you a company that has made acquisitions in recent years.

5. Click on "Stock Reports" and then click again on "Stock Reports" once the page opens. Read the report of Procter and Gamble's acquisition of Gillette.

6. How much did they pay for Gillette?

7. What do they expect the synergies (expense savings/cost reductions) to be?

8. By the time you do this assignment, have the financial statements used to analyze Procter and Gamble's profit margins and other measures of profitability improved since the acquisition of Gillette?

21

International Financial Management

Today the world economy is more integrated than ever, and nations are dependent on one another for many valuable and scarce resources. Just as the United States is dependent on China for textiles and Russia for oil, China is dependent on the United States and other Western countries for technology and heavy machinery. The World Trade Organization has made it easier for many countries to trade their goods and services without tariffs and import duties and the economic laws of competitive advantage are at work. Countries like the United States, with a well-educated workforce, provide leading technological products while developing economies such as those in India and China, with large populations and low-cost labor, provide much of the world's labor-intensive goods such as textiles, clothing, and assembled technology products. Additionally the United States, Canada, and Mexico instituted the North American Free Trade Association (NAFTA) which has generated increased trade among those three countries.

This growing interdependence necessitates the development of sound international business relations, which will enhance the prospects for future international cooperation and understanding. It is virtually impossible for any country to isolate itself from the impact of international developments in an integrated world economy. However, world politics continue to play a role in economic development. Many Latin and South American countries are moving towards more socialist economies and are increasing trade with China while maintaining strong ties to their European trading partners. A growing schism between the Middle East and the United States is causing the Saudi Arabian government to purchase more goods from Europe. These crosscurrents have affected trade for centuries and will continue.

We were reminded by the events of September 11, 2001, the war in Iraq, the outbreak of SARS (severe acute respiratory syndrome), the occurrence of tsunamis and hurricanes, and bird flu in 2006 that terrorism, war, infectious disease, and weather can not only cause economic impacts for short periods of time, but can have catastrophic effects on localized economies or specific industries. With financial markets becoming more global, a major impact in one area of the world can affect economies thousands of miles away. The capital markets are so integrated that world events such as a currency crisis, government defaults on sovereign debt, or terrorism can cause stock and bond markets to suffer emotional declines well beyond the expected economic impact of a major event.

Even when stock and bond markets are relatively stable and free of crisis, companies still have to pay attention to the currency markets. These currency markets impact imports and exports between countries and therefore affect sales and earnings of all companies doing business internationally whether the company is Japan's Sony, Germany's Volkswagen, or the United States' Intel. These companies do quite a bit of their business in the three largest and most liquid currencies in the world: the Japanese yen, the euro, and the U.S. dollar.

In 1999, 11 countries from the European Union adopted the **euro** as their currency, which fully replaced their previous domestic currencies in January 2002. Since then, many other countries have joined the European Union, bringing the total to 26 countries. Eventually, their local currencies will become obsolete and most member countries will also begin using the euro as their domestic currency.

Figure 21–1 presents the value of the euro since its inception against the U.S. dollar and the British pound. Even though Great Britain is a member of the European Union, it has

Figure 21–1   1 euro to the U.S. dollar and the British pound

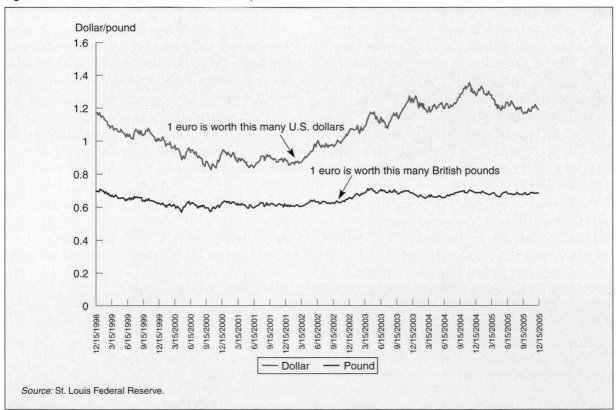

Source: St. Louis Federal Reserve.

not adopted the euro as its domestic currency but remains with the pound. Figure 21–1 shows that the pound does have a fairly stable relationship with the euro as it trades in a narrow band between .6 and .7 pounds per euro. We can see that the euro fell against the U.S. dollar from the beginning of 1999 to February 2002. U.S. companies doing business abroad had to translate their euros into fewer and fewer dollars and so their earnings in dollar terms were negatively affected by the falling euro. This trend then reversed itself. On February 1, 2002, the euro was worth $.86 and by January 3, 2005, it was worth $1.35. This $.49 swing was a 57 percent increase in the value of the euro relative to the dollar or a 57 percent decline in the dollar relative to the euro, depending on which side of the ocean you were on. In March 2005, when U.S. companies began reporting their 2004 year-end earnings, U.S. companies reported an increase in earnings from their European operations as the euro was translated into more dollars. By mid-2006, this pattern was somewhat reversed.

The significance of international business corporations becomes more apparent if we look at the size of foreign sales relative to domestic sales for major American corporations. Table 21–1 shows companies such as Intel with foreign sales of 81 percent, Coca-Cola with foreign sales of 70 percent, and other companies with foreign sales of 40 percent or more.

	Foreign Sales (% of total sales)	Fiscal Year-End
3M	61%	31-Dec-04
Cisco Systems	44	30-Jul-05
Coca-Cola	70	31-Dec-04
General Electric	47	31-Dec-04
IBM	63	31-Dec-04
Intel	81	31-Dec-04
Johnson & Johnson	41	31-Dec-04
McDonald's	66	31-Dec-04
Motorola	40	31-Dec-04
Sun Microsystems	60	30-Jun-05

Source: Each company's annual report.

Table 21–1
International sales of selected U.S. companies

Just as foreign operations affect the performance of American business firms, developments in international financial markets also affect our lifestyles. If you took a fall trip to Europe in October 2002 you would have received about 1.00 euro per dollar. But if you took a second trip in February 2006, your dollar would only get you .84 euros, a decline of 16 percent from several years earlier. On the other hand, Europeans traveling to the United States would benefit by having $1.19 for every euro. These sets of circumstances occur daily throughout the world and often reverse themselves after brief periods of time.

This chapter deals with the dimensions of doing business worldwide. We believe the chapter provides a basis for understanding the complexities of international financial decisions. Such an understanding is important whether you work for a multinational manufacturing firm, a large commercial bank, a major brokerage firm, or any firm involved in international transactions.

The following section of this chapter describes the international business firm and its environment. Then, we examine foreign exchange rates and the variables influencing foreign currency values and strategies for dealing with foreign exchange risk. Finally, we discuss international financing sources, including the Eurodollar market, the Eurobond market, and foreign equity markets.

The Multinational Corporation: Nature and Environment

The focus of international financial management has been the multinational corporation (MNC). One might ask, just what is a **multinational corporation**? Some definitions of a multinational corporation require that a minimum percentage (often 30 percent or more) of a firm's business activities be carried on outside its national borders. For our understanding, however, a firm doing business across its national borders is considered a multinational enterprise. Multinational corporations can take several forms. Four are briefly examined.

Exporter An MNC could produce a product domestically and export some of that production to one or more foreign markets. This is, perhaps, the least risky method—reaping the benefits of foreign demand without committing any long-term investment to that foreign country.

Licensing Agreement A firm with exporting operations may get into trouble when a foreign government imposes or substantially raises an import tariff to a level at which the exporter cannot compete effectively with the local domestic manufacturers. The foreign government may even ban all imports at times. When this happens the exporting firm may grant a license to an independent local producer to use the firm's technology in return for a license fee or a royalty. In essence, then, the MNC will be exporting technology, rather than the product, to that foreign country.

Joint Venture As an alternative to licensing, the MNC may establish a joint venture with a local foreign manufacturer. The legal, political, and economic environments around the globe are more conducive to the joint venture arrangement than any of the other modes of operation. Historical evidence also suggests that a joint venture with a local entrepreneur exposes the firm to the least amount of political risk. This position is preferred by most business firms and by foreign governments as well.

Fully Owned Foreign Subsidiary Although the joint venture form is desirable for many reasons, it may be hard to find a willing and cooperative local entrepreneur with sufficient capital to participate. Under these conditions the MNC may have to go it alone. For political reasons, however, a wholly owned foreign subsidiary is becoming more of a rarity. The reader must keep in mind that whenever we mention a *foreign affiliate* in the ensuing discussion, it could be a joint venture or a fully owned subsidiary.

As the firm crosses its national borders, it faces an environment that is riskier and more complex than its domestic surroundings. Sometimes the social and political environment can be hostile. Despite these difficult challenges, foreign affiliates often are more profitable than domestic businesses. A purely domestic firm faces several basic risks, such as the risk related to maintaining sales and market share, the financial risk of too much leverage, the risk of a poor equity market, and so on. In addition to these types of risks, the foreign affiliate is exposed to foreign exchange risk and political risk. While the foreign affiliate experiences a larger amount of risk than a domestic firm, it actually lowers the portfolio risk of its parent corporation by stabilizing the combined operating cash flows for the MNC. This risk reduction occurs because foreign and domestic economies are less than perfectly correlated.

Foreign business operations are more complex because the host country's economy may be different from the domestic economy. The rate of inflation in many foreign countries is likely to be higher than in the United States. The rules of taxation are different. The structure and operation of financial markets and institutions also vary from country to country, as do financial policies and practices. The presence of a foreign affiliate benefits the host country's economy. Foreign affiliates have been a decisive factor in shaping the pattern of trade, investment, and the flow of technology between nations. They can have a significant positive impact on a host country's economic growth, employment, trade, and balance of payments. This positive contribution, however, is occasionally overshadowed by allegations of wrongdoing. For example, some host countries have charged that foreign affiliates subverted their governments and caused instability of their currencies. The less-developed countries (LDCs) have, at times, alleged that foreign businesses exploit their labor with low wages.

The multinational companies are also under constant criticism in their home countries where labor unions charge the MNCs with exporting jobs, capital, and technology to foreign nations while avoiding their fair share of taxes. Despite all these criticisms, multinational companies have managed to survive and prosper. The MNCs are well positioned to take advantage of imperfections in the global markets. Furthermore, since current global resource distribution favors the MNCs' survival and growth, it may be concluded that multinational corporations are here to stay.

Foreign Exchange Rates

Suppose you are planning to spend a semester in London studying the culture of England. To put your plan into operation you will need British currency, that is, British pounds (£), so you can pay for your expenses during your stay. How many British pounds you can obtain for $1,000 will depend on the exchange rate at that time. The relationship between the values of two currencies is known as the **exchange rate**. The exchange rate between U.S. dollars and British pounds is stated as dollars per pound or pounds per dollar. For example, the quotation of $1.49 per pound is the same as £.67 per dollar (1/$1.49). At this exchange rate you can purchase 670 British pounds with $1,000. *The Wall Street Journal* publishes exchange rates of major foreign currencies each day. Figure 21–2 on page 632 depicts euros, pounds, yen, and pesos because they are used by some of the United States' major trading partners. This figure shows the amount of each currency that one can exchange for one U.S. dollar.

There is no guarantee that any currency will stay strong relative to other currencies and the dollar is no exception. While the dollar has been strong in the past, it has been relatively weak lately since the United States is faced with expanding budget deficits and at the same time a huge imbalance of imports over exports. Financial managers should always pay close attention to exchange rates and any changes that might be forecasted to occur. The relative change in the purchasing power between countries affects imports and exports, interest rates, and other economic variables. During this time period (covered in Figure 21–2), the U.S. foreign trade deficit (more imports than

Figure 21–2   Exchange rates to the dollar

Source: The Federal Reserve Web site: **www.federalreserve.gov**.

exports) increased dramatically. The major reasons for exchange rate movements are discussed in the following sections.

Factors Influencing Exchange Rates

The present international monetary system consists of a mixture of "freely" floating exchange rates and fixed rates. The currencies of the major trading partners of the United States are traded in free markets. In such a market the exchange rate between two currencies is determined by the supply of, and the demand for, those currencies. This activity, however, is subject to intervention by many countries' central banks. Factors that tend to increase the supply or decrease the demand schedule for a given currency will bring down the value of that currency in foreign exchange markets. Similarly the factors that tend to decrease the supply or increase the demand for a currency will raise the value of that currency. Since fluctuations in currency values result in foreign exchange risk, the financial executive must understand the factors causing these changes in currency values. Although the value of a currency is determined by the aggregate supply and demand for that currency, this alone does not help financial managers understand or predict the changes in exchange rates. Fundamental factors, such as inflation, interest rates, balance of payments, and government policies, are quite important in explaining both the short-term and long-term fluctuations of a currency value.

Inflation   A parity between the purchasing powers of two currencies establishes the rate of exchange between the two currencies. Suppose it takes $1.00 to buy one dozen apples in New York and 1.25 euros to buy the same apples in Frankfurt, Germany. Then the rate of exchange between the U.S. dollar and the euro is E1.25/$1.00 or $.80/euro. If prices of apples double in New York while the prices in Frankfurt remain the same, the purchasing power of a dollar in New York should drop 50 percent. Consequently, you will be able to exchange $1.00 for only E.625 in foreign currency markets (or receive $1.60 per euro).

Currency exchange rates tend to vary inversely with their respective purchasing powers to provide the same or similar purchasing power in each country. This is called the **purchasing power parity theory**. When the inflation rate differential between two countries changes, the exchange rate also adjusts to correspond to the relative purchasing powers of the countries.

Interest Rates   Another economic variable that has a significant influence on exchange rates is interest rates. As a student of finance, you should know that investment capital flows in the direction of higher yield for a given level of risk. This flow of short-term capital between money markets occurs because investors seek equilibrium through arbitrage buying and selling. If investors can earn 6 percent interest per year in Country X and 10 percent per year in Country Y, they will prefer to invest in Country Y, provided the inflation rate and risk are the same in both countries. Thus interest rates and exchange rates adjust until the foreign exchange market and the money market reach equilibrium. This interplay between interest rate differentials and exchange rates is called the **interest rate parity theory**.

Balance of Payments   The term **balance of payments** refers to a system of government accounts that catalogs the flow of economic transactions between the residents of one country and the residents of other countries. (The balance of payments statement for the United States is prepared by the U.S. Department of Commerce quarterly and annually.) It resembles the cash flow statement presented in Chapter 2 and tracks the country's exports and imports as well as the flow of capital and gifts. When a country sells (exports) more goods and services to foreign countries than it purchases (imports), it will have a surplus in its balance of trade. Japan, through its aggressive competition in world markets, exports more goods than it imports and has been enjoying a trade surplus for quite some time. Since the foreigners who buy Japanese goods are expected to pay their bills in yen, the demand for yen and, consequently, its value, increases in foreign currency markets. On the other hand, continuous deficits in the balance of payments are expected to depress the value of a currency because such deficits would increase the supply of that currency relative to the demand. This has been the case with the U.S. dollar.

Government Policies   A national government may, through its central bank, intervene in the foreign exchange market, buying and selling currencies as it sees fit to support the value of its currency relative to others. Sometimes a given country may deliberately pursue a policy of maintaining an undervalued currency in order to promote cheap exports. In some countries the currency values are set by government decree. Even in some free market countries, the central banks fix the exchange rates, subject to periodic review and adjustment. Some nations affect the foreign exchange rate indirectly by restricting the flow of funds into and out of the country. Monetary and fiscal policies also affect the currency value in foreign exchange markets. For example, expansionary monetary policy and excessive government spending are primary causes of inflation, and continual use of such policies eventually reduces the value of the country's currency.

Other Factors   A pronounced and extended stock market rally in a country attracts investment capital from other countries, thus creating a huge demand by foreigners for that country's currency. This increased demand is expected to increase the value of that currency. Similarly a significant drop in demand for a country's principal exports worldwide is expected to result in a corresponding decline in the value of its currency. The South African rand is an example from recent history. A precipitous drop in gold prices is cited as the reason for the depreciation of this currency during the last two decades. Political turmoil in a country often drives capital out of the country into stable countries. A mass exodus of capital, due to the fear of political risk, undermines the value of a country's currency in the foreign exchange market. Also, widespread labor strikes that may appear to weaken the nation's economy will depress its currency value.

Although a wide variety of factors that can influence exchange rates has been discussed, a few words of caution are in order. All of these variables will not necessarily influence all currencies to the same degree. Some factors may have an overriding influence on one currency's value, while their influence on another currency may be negligible at that time.

Spot Rates and Forward Rates

When you look into a major financial newspaper (e.g., *The Wall Street Journal*), you will discover that two exchange rates exist simultaneously for most major currencies—the spot rate and the forward rate. The **spot rate** for a currency is the exchange rate at which the currency is traded for immediate delivery. For example, you walk into a local commercial bank and ask for Swiss francs.[1] The banker will indicate the rate at which the franc is selling, say SF 1.3078/$. If you like the rate, you buy 1,307.80 francs with $1,000 and walk out the door. This is a spot market transaction at the retail level. The trading of currencies for future delivery is called a forward market transaction.

Suppose IBM Corporation expects to receive SF 130,429 from a Swiss customer in 30 days. It is not certain, however, what these francs will be worth in dollars in 30 days. To eliminate this uncertainty, IBM calls a bank and offers to sell SF 130,429 for U.S. dollars in 30 days. In their negotiation the two parties may agree on an exchange rate of SF 1.30429/$. This is the same as $0.7667/SF. The 1.30429 quote is in Swiss francs per dollar. The reciprocal or .7667 is in dollars per Swiss franc.

---

[1]While Switzerland is a European country, it prefers to trade in its own currency rather than the euro.

Since the exchange rate is established for future delivery, it is a **forward rate**. After 30 days IBM delivers SF 130,429 to the bank and receives $100,000. The difference between spot and forward exchange rates, expressed in dollars per unit of foreign currency, may be seen in the following typical values.

Rates*	Swiss Franc (SF) ($/SF)	New Zealand Dollar (USD/NZD)
Spot	$0.7646	$0.6627
30-day forward	0.7667	$0.6611
90-day forward	0.7714	$0.6582
180-day forward	0.7787	$0.6543

*As of February 21, 2006.

The forward exchange rate of a currency is slightly different from the spot rate prevailing at that time. Since the forward rate deals with a future time, the expectations regarding the future value of that currency are reflected in the forward rate. Forward rates may be greater than the current spot rate (premium) or less than the current spot rate (discount). The table above shows the forward rates on the Swiss franc were at a premium in relation to the spot rate, while the forward rates for the New Zealand dollar were at a discount from the spot rate. This means the participants in the foreign exchange market expected the Swiss franc to appreciate relative to the U.S. dollar in the future and the New Zealand dollar to depreciate against the dollar. The discount or premium is usually expressed as an annualized percentage deviation from the spot rate. The percentage discount or premium is computed with the following formula:

$$\begin{array}{c} \text{Forward premium} \\ \text{(or discount)} \end{array} = \frac{\text{Forward rate} - \text{Spot rate}}{\text{Spot rate}} \times \frac{12}{\begin{array}{c}\text{Length of} \\ \text{forward contract} \\ \text{(in months)}\end{array}} \times 100 \qquad (21\text{--}1)$$

For example, the 90-day forward contract in Swiss francs, as previously listed, was selling at a 3.557 percent premium:

$$\frac{0.7714 - 0.7646}{0.7646} \times \frac{12}{3} \times 100 = 3.557\% \text{ (premium)}$$

while the 90-day forward contract in New Zealand dollars was trading at a 2.716 percent discount:

$$\frac{0.6582 - 0.6627}{0.6627} \times \frac{12}{3} \times 100 = 2.716\% \text{ (discount)}$$

Normally the forward premium or discount is between 0.1 percent and 6 percent.

The spot and forward transactions are said to occur in the over-the-counter market. Foreign currency dealers (usually large commercial banks) and their customers (importers, exporters, investors, multinational firms, and so on) negotiate the exchange rate, the length of the forward contract, and the commission in a mutually agreeable fashion. Although the length of a typical forward contract may generally vary between one month and six months, contracts for longer maturities are not uncommon. The dealers, however, may require higher returns for longer contracts.

Cross Rates

Because currencies are quoted against the U.S. dollar in *The Wall Street Journal,* sometimes it may be necessary to work out the **cross rates** for other currencies than the dollar. For example, on February 21, 2006, the Swiss franc was selling for $0.7637 and the British pound was selling for $1.7428. The cross rate between the franc and the pound was 2.2820 (francs/pound). In determining this value, we show that one dollar would buy 1.3094 francs (1/0.7637) and a pound was equal to 1.7428 dollars. Thus 1.3094 Swiss francs per *dollar* times 1.7428 *dollars* per pound equaled 2.2820 Swiss francs per pound.

To determine if your answer is correct, you can check a currency cross rate table such as that shown in Table 21–2. There you will see the cross rate between the Swiss franc and the British pound is, in fact, 2.2820 on February 21, 2006. GBP along the side stands for British pound and CHF across the top stands for Swiss franc. Many of the designations are interchangeable in the table.

Table 21–2   Key currency cross rates as of February 21, 2006

Currency	USD	Euro	GBP	JPY	CHF	CAD	AUD	NZD	HKD	SGD
USD	1.0000	0.8384	0.5736	118.560	1.3094	1.1476	1.3557	1.5036	7.7611	1.6299
Euro	1.1921	1.0000	0.6840	141.390	1.5606	1.3681	1.6161	1.7909	9.2531	1.9428
GBP	1.7428	1.4614	1.0000	206.650	2.2820	2.0002	2.3625	2.6175	13.5250	2.8407
JPY	0.0084	0.0071	0.0048	1.000	0.0110	0.0097	0.0114	0.0127	0.0655	0.0137
CHF	0.7637	0.6407	0.4378	90.570	1.0000	0.8763	1.0353	1.1473	5.9200	1.2437
CAD	0.8710	0.7304	0.4996	103.270	1.1403	1.0000	1.1808	1.3079	6.7515	n.a.
AUD	0.7371	0.6182	0.4229	87.440	0.9649	0.8459	1.0000	1.1076	5.7204	1.2017
NZD	0.6646	0.5579	0.3817	78.860	0.8706	0.7633	0.9016	1.0000	5.1578	1.0846
HKD	0.1288	0.1080	0.0739	15.280	16.8640	0.1479	0.1747	0.1937	1.0000	0.2075
SGD	0.6133	0.5142	0.3518	72.670	0.8025	0.7075	0.8315	n.a.	4.7585	1.0000

USD = United States dollar   CHF = Swiss franc   NZD = New Zealand dollar
Euro = European monetary unit   CAD = Canadian dollar   HKD = Hong Kong dollar
GBP = Great Britain pound   AUD = Australian dollar   SGD = Singaporean dollar
JPY = Japanese yen

Source: www.fxstreet.com/nou/graph/netdaniacrossrates.asp.

Managing Foreign Exchange Risk

When the parties associated with a commercial transaction are located in the same country, the transaction is denominated in a single currency. International transactions inevitably involve more than one currency (because the parties are residents of different countries). Since most foreign currency values fluctuate from time to time, the monetary value of an international transaction measured in either the seller's currency or the buyer's currency is likely to change when payment is delayed. As a result, the seller may receive less revenue than expected or the buyer may have to pay more than the expected amount for the merchandise. Thus the term **foreign exchange risk** refers to the possibility of a drop in revenue or an increase in cost in an international transaction due to a change in foreign exchange rates. Importers, exporters, investors, and multinational firms are all exposed to this foreign exchange risk.

The international monetary system has undergone a significant change over the last 30 years. The free trading Western nations basically went from a fixed exchange rate system to a "freely" floating rate system. For the most part, the new system proved its agility and resilience during the most turbulent years of oil price hikes and hyperinflation of the last two decades. The free market exchange rates responded and adjusted well to these adverse conditions. Consequently, the exchange rates fluctuated over a much wider range than before. The increased volatility of exchange markets forced many multinational firms, importers, and exporters to pay more attention to the function of foreign exchange risk management.

The foreign exchange risk of a multinational company is divided into two types of exposure. They are: accounting or translation exposure and transaction exposure. An MNC's foreign assets and liabilities, which are denominated in foreign currency units, are exposed to losses and gains due to changing exchange rates. This is called accounting or **translation exposure**. The amount of loss or gain resulting from this form of exposure and the treatment of it in the parent company's books depend on the accounting rules established by the parent company's government. In the United States, the rules are spelled out in the *Statement of Financial Accounting Standards (SFAS) No. 52*. Under *SFAS 52* all foreign currency–denominated assets and liabilities are converted at the rate of exchange in effect on the date of balance sheet preparation. An unrealized translation gain or loss is held in an equity reserve account while the realized gain or loss is incorporated in the parent's consolidated income statement for that period. Thus *SFAS 52* partially reduces the impact of accounting exposure resulting from the translation of a foreign subsidiary's balance sheet on reported earnings of multinational firms.

However, foreign exchange gains and losses resulting from international transactions, which reflect **transaction exposure**, are shown in the income statement for the current period. As a consequence of these transactional gains and losses, the volatility of reported earnings per share increases. Three different strategies can be used to minimize this transaction exposure.

1. Hedging in the forward exchange market.
2. Hedging in the money market.
3. Hedging in the currency futures market.

Forward Exchange Market Hedge   To see how the transaction exposure can be covered in forward markets, suppose Electricitie de France, an electric company in France, purchases a large generator from the General Electric Company of the United States for 822,400 euros on February 21, 2006, and GE is promised the payment in euros in 90 days. Since GE is now exposed to exchange rate risk by agreeing to receive the payment in euros in the future, it is up to General Electric to find a way to reduce this exposure. One simple method is to hedge the exposure in the forward exchange market with a 90-day forward contract. On February 21, 2006, to establish a forward cover, GE sells a forward contract to deliver the 822,400 euros 90 days from that date in exchange for $1,000,000. On May 22, 2006,[2] GE receives payment from Electricitie de France and delivers the 822,400 euros to the bank that signed the contract. In return the bank delivers $1,000,000 to GE.

---

[2]February 21, 2006, to May 22, 2006, represents 90 days.

Motorola Manages Currency Risk

Motorola is a major electronics company with worldwide sales of over $35 billion in 2005. Over $4 billion of Motorola's sales were to China where the company employs thousands and manufactures cell phones and electronics equipment. Another $2.8 billion of sales are in Germany and many more in other countries around the world. It is not surprising then that Motorola has a currency risk to manage. The five largest currency positions that they manage include the euro, Chinese renminbi, Brazilian real, Canadian dollar, and the Japanese yen. They are either long (own these currencies) or short (have sold these currencies), depending on their expectations for currency movements and the amount of accounts receivable they have outstanding in each currency. In a recent annual report Motorola states:

> As a multinational company, the Company's transactions are denominated in a variety of currencies. The company uses financial instruments to hedge, and therefore attempts to reduce its overall exposure to the effects of currency fluctuations on cash flows. The Company's policy is not to speculate in financial instruments for profit on the exchange rate price fluctuations, trade in currencies for which there are no underlying exposure, or enter into trades for any currency to intentionally increase the underlying exposure. Instruments that are designated as hedges must be effective at reducing the risk associated with the exposure being hedged and must be designated as a hedge at the inception of the contract. Accordingly, changes in market values of hedge instruments must be highly correlated with changes in market values of underlying hedged items both at inception of the hedge and over the life of the hedge contract.

From this statement it is clear that a hedge is not meant to be speculative or make money based on expectations of currency fluctuations but to protect a given cash flow that is known to exist from the sale of goods and services. Many other companies are in this same situation. It is important to distinguish between trading for a profit (speculating) and locking in a profit (hedging). Derivative contracts often get a bad reputation as risky because of financial officers speculating rather that hedging.

Money Market Hedge   A second way to have eliminated transaction exposure in the previous example would have been to borrow money in euros and then convert it to U.S. dollars immediately. When the account receivable from the sale is collected three months later, the loan is cleared with the proceeds. In this case GE's strategy consists of the following steps.

On February 21, 2006:

1. Borrow 822,400 euros—(822,400 euros/1.02) = 806,274.51 euros—at the rate of 8.0 percent per year for three months. You will borrow less than the full amount of 822,400 euros in recognition of the fact that interest must be paid on the loan. Eight percent interest for 90 days translates into 2.0 percent. Thus 822,400 euros is divided by 1.02 to arrive at the size of the loan before the interest payment.

2. Convert the euros into the U.S. dollars in the spot market.

Then on May 22, 2006 (90 days later):

3. Receive the payment of 822,400 euros from Electricitie de France.

4. Clear the loan with the proceeds received from Electricitie de France.

The money market hedge basically calls for matching the exposed asset (account receivable) with a liability (loan payable) in the same currency. Some firms prefer this money market hedge because of the early availability of funds possible with this method.

Currency Futures Market Hedge   Transaction exposure associated with a foreign currency can also be covered in the futures market with a **currency futures contract**. The International Monetary Market (IMM) of the Chicago Mercantile Exchange began trading in futures contracts in foreign currencies on May 16, 1972. Trading in currency futures contracts also made a debut on the London International Financial Futures Exchange (LIFFE) in September 1982. Other markets have also developed around the world. Just as futures contracts are traded in corn, wheat, hogs, and beans, foreign currency futures contracts are traded in these markets. Although the futures market and forward market are similar in concept, they differ in their operations. To illustrate the hedging process in the currency futures market, suppose that in May the Chicago-based LaSalle National Bank considers lending 500,000 pesos to a Mexican subsidiary of a U.S. parent company for seven months. The bank purchases the pesos in the spot market, delivers them to the borrower, and simultaneously hedges its transaction exposure by selling December contracts in pesos for the same amount. In December when the loan is cleared, the bank sells the pesos in the spot market and buys back the December peso contracts. The transactions are illustrated for the spot and futures market in Table 21–3:[3]

Date	Spot Market	Futures Market
May 7	Buys 500,000 pesos at $0.0980/peso = $49,000	Sells 500,000 pesos for December delivery at $0.0954/peso = $47,700
December 7	Sells 500,000 pesos at $.0941/peso = $47.050	Buys 500,000 pesos at $0.0941/peso = $47,050
	Loss $1,950	Gain $650

Table 21–3
Currency futures hedging

While the loan was outstanding, the peso declined in value relative to the U.S. dollar. Had the bank remained unhedged, it would have lost $1,950 in the spot market. By hedging in the futures market, the bank was able to reduce the loss to $1,300. A $650 gain in the futures market was used to cancel some of the $1,950 loss in the spot market.

These are not the only means companies have for protecting themselves against foreign exchange risk. Over the years, multinational companies have developed elaborate foreign asset management programs, which involve such strategies as switching cash and other current assets into strong currencies, while piling up debt and other liabilities in depreciating currencies. Companies also encourage the quick collection of bills in weak currencies by offering sizable discounts, while extending liberal credit in strong currencies.

It is estimated from the *Directory of American Firms Operating in Foreign Countries* that more than 4,500 U.S. firms have one or more foreign affiliates. Several explanations are offered for the moves to foreign soil. First, with the emergence of trading blocs in Europe, American firms feared their goods might face import tariffs in those countries. To avoid such trade barriers, U.S. firms started manufacturing in foreign

Foreign Investment Decisions

---

[3]For purposes of this example, we assumed the peso was trading at a discount in the futures market. Had it been trading at a premium, the hedge would have been even more attractive.

countries. The second factor was the lower production costs overseas. Firms were motivated by the significantly lower wage costs prevailing in foreign countries. Firms in labor-intensive industries, such as textiles and electronics, moved some of their operations to countries where labor was cheap. Third, superior American technology gave U.S. firms an easy access to oil exploration, mining, and manufacturing in many developing nations. A fourth advantage relates to taxes. The U.S.-based multinational firms can postpone payment of U.S. taxes on income earned abroad until such income is actually repatriated (forwarded) to the parent company. This tax deferral provision can be used by an MNC to minimize its tax liability. Some countries, like Israel, Ireland, and South Africa, offer special tax incentives for foreign firms that establish operations there.[4] Although the benefits of lower taxes and lower wage costs and the technological gap have diminished in recent years, the average rate of return on U.S. investments abroad continues to be higher than on U.S. domestic investments.

The decision to invest in a foreign country by a firm operating in an oligopolistic industry is also motivated by strategic considerations. When a competitor undertakes a direct foreign investment, other companies quickly follow with defensive investments in the same foreign country. Foreign investments undertaken by U.S. soft drink companies are classic examples of this competitive reaction. Wherever you find a Coca-Cola subsidiary in a foreign country, you are likely to see a Pepsi affiliate also operating in that country.

Many academicians believe international diversification of risks is also an important motivation for direct foreign investment. The basic premise of portfolio theory in finance is that an investor can reduce the risk level of a portfolio by combining those investments whose returns are less than perfectly positively correlated. In addition to domestic diversification, it is shown in Figure 21–3 that further reduction in investment risk can be achieved by diversifying across national boundaries. International stocks, in Figure 21–3, show a consistently lower standard deviation compared to any given number of U.S. stocks in a portfolio. It is argued, however, that institutional and political constraints, language barriers, and lack of adequate information on foreign investments prevent investors from diversifying across nations. Multinational firms, on the other hand, through their unique position around the world, derive the benefits of international diversification. This argument has been weakened somewhat by the introduction of international mutual funds.

While U.S.-based firms took the lead in establishing overseas subsidiaries during the 1950s and 1960s, European and Japanese firms started this activity in the 1970s and have continued into the new century. The flow of foreign direct investment into the United States has proceeded at a rapid rate. These investments employ millions of people. It is evident that the United States is becoming an attractive site for foreign investment. In addition to the international diversification and strategic considerations, many other factors are responsible for this inflow of foreign capital into the United States. Increased foreign labor costs in some countries and saturated overseas markets in others are partly responsible. In Japan, an acute shortage of land suitable for industrial development and a near total dependence on imported oil prompted some Japanese firms to locate in the United States. In Germany, a large number of paid holidays,

---

[4]Tax advantages for multinational corporations are being challenged in Congress and may be less in the future.

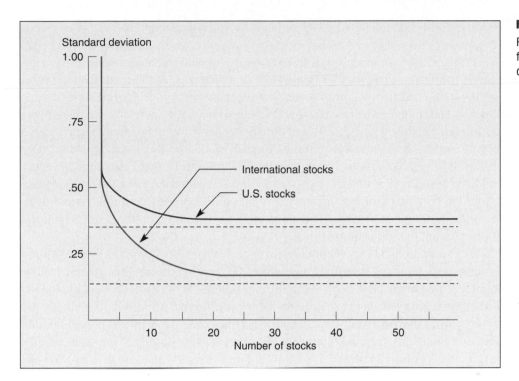

Figure 21–3
Risk reduction
from international
diversification

restrictions limiting labor layoffs, and worker participation in management decision making caused many firms to look favorably at the United States. Political stability, large market size, and access to advanced technology are other primary motivating factors for firms to establish operations in the United States. Also, large U.S. balance of payments deficits have spread hundreds of millions of dollars around the world for potential reinvestment in the United States, particularly by the Japanese.

To some extent foreign investors in the U.S. Treasury bond market have been bank-rolling enormous budget deficits that the government has been running up. When the U.S. government began falling $150 to $200 billion into the red on an annual basis in the 1980s, many analysts thought this would surely mean high inflation, high interest rates, and perhaps a recession. They also were sure there would be a "shortage of capital" for investments because of large government borrowing to finance the deficits. For the most part, foreign investors from Japan, Western Europe, Canada, and elsewhere have bailed the government out by supplying the necessary capital. Of course, this means the United States is more dependent on flows of foreign capital into the country. We must satisfy our "outside" investors or face the unpleasant consequences. During the last two decades, we have gone from being the largest lender in the world to the largest borrower.

Analysis of Political Risk

Business firms tend to make direct investments in foreign countries for a relatively long time. This is because of the time necessary to recover the initial investment. The government may change hands several times during the foreign firm's tenure in that country; and, when a new government takes over, it may not be as friendly or as co-operative as the previous administration. An unfriendly government can interfere with the foreign affiliate in many ways. It may impose foreign exchange restrictions, or the foreign ownership share may be limited to a set percentage of the total. **Repatriation** (transfer) of a subsidiary's profit to the parent company may be blocked, at least temporarily; and, in the extreme case, the government may even **expropriate** (take over) the foreign subsidiary's assets. The multinational company may experience a sizable loss of income or property, or both, as a result of this political interference. Many once well-known U.S. firms, like Anaconda, ITT, and Occidental Petroleum, have lost hundreds of millions of dollars in politically unstable countries. Over the last 30 years, more than 60 percent of U.S. companies doing business abroad suffered some form of politically inflicted damage. Therefore, analysis of foreign political risk is gaining more attention in multinational firms.

The best approach to protection against political risk is to thoroughly investigate the country's political stability long before the firm makes any investment in that country. Companies have been using different methods for assessing political risk. Some firms hire consultants to provide them with a report of political-risk analysis. Others form their own advisory committees (little state departments) consisting of top-level managers from headquarters and foreign subsidiaries. After ascertaining the country's political-risk level, the multinational firm can use one of the following strategies to guard against such risk:

1.   One strategy is to establish a joint venture with a local entrepreneur. By bringing a local partner into the deal, the MNC not only limits its financial exposure but also minimizes antiforeign feelings.

2.   Another risk-management tactic is to enter into a joint venture with firms from other countries. For example, an energy company may pursue its oil production operation in Zaire in association with Royal Dutch Petroleum and Nigerian National Petroleum as partners. The foreign government will be more hesitant to antagonize a number of partner-firms of many nationalities at the same time.

3.   When the perceived political-risk level is high, insurance against such risks can be obtained in advance. **Overseas Private Investment Corporation (OPIC)**, a federal government agency, sells insurance policies to qualified firms. This agency insures against losses due to inconvertibility into dollars of amounts invested in a foreign country. Policies are also available from OPIC to insure against expropriation and against losses due to war or revolution. Many firms have used this service over the years. Greenlaw, Inc., a Florida-based firm, insured its fruit-processing plant in the Dominican Republic through OPIC. Private insurance companies, such as Lloyds of London, American International Group Inc., CIGNA, and others, issue similar policies to cover political risk.

Political-risk umbrella policies do not come cheaply. Coverage for projects in "fairly safe" countries can cost anywhere from 0.3 percent to 12 percent of the insured values per year. Needless to say, the coverage is more expensive or unavailable in troubled countries. OPIC's rates are lower than those of private insurers, and its policies extend for up to 20 years, compared to three years or less for private insurance policies.

When the parties to an international transaction are well known to each other and the countries involved are politically stable, sales are generally made on credit, as is customary in domestic business operations. However, if a foreign importer is relatively new or the political environment is volatile, or both, the possibility of nonpayment by the importer is worrisome for the exporter. To reduce the risk of nonpayment, an exporter may request that the importer furnish a letter of credit. The importer's bank normally issues the **letter of credit**, in which the bank promises to subsequently pay the money for the merchandise. For example, assume Archer Daniels Midland (ADM) is negotiating with a South Korean trading company to export soybean meal. The two parties agree on price, method of shipment, timing of shipment, destination point, and the like. Once the basic terms of sale have been agreed to, the South Korean trading company (importer) applies for a letter of credit from its commercial bank in Seoul. The Korean bank, if it so desires, issues such a letter of credit, which specifies in detail all the steps that must be completed by the American exporter before payment is made. If ADM complies with all specifications in the letter of credit and submits to the Korean bank the proper documentation to prove that it has done so, the Korean bank guarantees the payment on the due date. On that date the American firm is paid by the Korean bank, not by the buyer of the goods. Therefore, all the credit risk to the exporter is absorbed by the importer's bank, which is in a good position to evaluate the creditworthiness of the importing firm.

The exporter who requires cash payment or a letter of credit from foreign buyers of marginal credit standing is likely to lose orders to competitors. Instead of risking the loss of business, American firms can find an alternative way to reduce the risk of nonpayment by foreign customers. This alternative method consists of obtaining export credit insurance. The insurance policy provides assurance to the exporter that should the foreign customer default on payment, the insurance company will pay for the shipment. The **Foreign Credit Insurance Association (FCIA)**, a private association of 60 U.S. insurance firms, provides this kind of insurance to exporting firms.

Funding of Transactions

Assistance in the funding of foreign transactions may take many forms.

Eximbank (Export-Import Bank)   This agency of the U.S. government facilitates the financing of U.S. exports through its various programs. In its direct loan program, the **Eximbank** lends money to foreign purchasers of U.S. goods such as aircraft, electrical equipment, heavy machinery, computers, and the like. The Eximbank also purchases eligible medium-term obligations of foreign buyers of U.S. goods at a discount from face value. In this discount program, private banks and other lenders are able to rediscount (sell at a lower price) promissory notes and drafts acquired from foreign customers of U.S. firms.

Loans from the Parent Company or a Sister Affiliate   An apparent source of funds for a foreign affiliate is its parent company or its sister affiliates. In addition to contributing equity capital, the parent company often provides loans of varying maturities to its foreign affiliate. Although the simplest arrangement is a direct loan from the parent

Financing International Business Operations

to the foreign subsidiary, such a loan is rarely extended because of foreign exchange risk, political risk, and tax treatment. Instead, the loans are often channeled through an intermediary to a foreign affiliate. Parallel loans and fronting loans are two examples of such indirect loan arrangements between a parent company and its foreign affiliate. A typical parallel loan arrangement is depicted in Figure 21–4.

Figure 21–4

A parallel loan arrangement

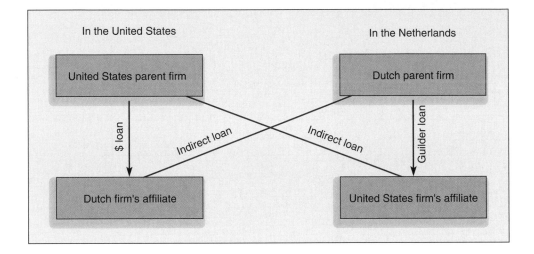

In this illustration of a **parallel loan,** an American firm that wants to lend funds to its Dutch affiliate locates a Dutch parent firm, which needs to transfer funds to its U.S. affiliate. Avoiding the exchange markets, the U.S. parent lends dollars to the Dutch affiliate in the United States, while the Dutch parent lends guilders to the American affiliate in the Netherlands. At maturity the two loans would each be repaid to the original lender. Notice that neither loan carries any foreign exchange risk in this arrangement. In essence both parent firms are providing indirect loans to their affiliates.

A **fronting loan** is simply a parent's loan to its foreign subsidiary channeled through a financial intermediary, usually a large international bank. A schematic of a fronting loan is shown in Figure 21–5.

Figure 21–5

A fronting loan arrangement

In the example the U.S. parent company deposits funds in an Amsterdam bank and that bank lends the same amount to the U.S. firm's affiliate in the Netherlands. In this manner the bank fronts for the parent by extending a risk-free (fully collateralized) loan to the foreign affiliate. In the event of political turmoil, the foreign government is more likely to allow the American subsidiary to repay the loan to a large international bank than to allow the same affiliate to repay the loan to its parent company. Thus the parent company reduces its political risk substantially by using a fronting loan instead of transferring funds directly to its foreign affiliate.

Even though the parent company would prefer that its foreign subsidiary maintain its own financial arrangements, many banks are apprehensive about lending to a foreign affiliate without a parent guarantee. In fact, a large portion of bank lending to foreign affiliates is based on some sort of a guarantee by the parent firm. Usually, because of its multinational reputation, the parent company has a better credit rating than its foreign affiliates. The lender advances funds on the basis of the parent's creditworthiness even though the affiliate is expected to pay back the loan. The terms of a parent guarantee may vary greatly, depending on the closeness of the parent-affiliate ties, parent-lender relations, and the home country's legal jurisdiction.

Eurodollar Loans   The Eurodollar market is an important source of short-term loans for many multinational firms and their foreign affiliates.

Eurodollars are simply U.S. dollars deposited in foreign banks. A substantial portion of these deposits are held by European branches of U.S. commercial banks. About 85 to 90 percent of these deposits are in the form of term deposits with the banks for a specific maturity and at a fixed interest rate. The remaining 10 to 15 percent of these deposits represent negotiable certificates of deposit with maturities varying from one week to five years or longer. However, maturities of three months, six months, and one year are most common in this market.

Since the early 1960s, the Eurodollar market has established itself as a significant part of world credit markets. The participants in these markets are diverse in character and geographically widespread. Hundreds of corporations and banks, mostly from the United States, Canada, Western Europe, and Japan, are regular borrowers and depositors in this market.

U.S. firms have more than doubled their borrowings in the Eurodollar market during the last decade. The lower costs and greater credit availability of this market continue to attract borrowers. The lower borrowing costs in the Eurodollar market are often attributed to the smaller overhead costs for lending banks and the absence of a compensating balance requirement. The lending rate for borrowers in the Eurodollar market is based on the **London Interbank Offered Rate (LIBOR)**, which is the interest rate for large deposits, as discussed in Chapter 8. Interest rates on loans are calculated by adding premiums to this basic rate. The size of this premium varies from 0.25 percent to 0.50 percent, depending on the customer, length of the loan period, size of the loan, and so on. For example, Northern Indiana Public Service Company obtained a $75 million, three-year loan from Merrill Lynch International Bank. The utility company paid 0.375 points above LIBOR for the first two years and 0.50 points above for the final year of the loan. Over the years, borrowing in the Eurodollar market has been one-eighth to seven-eighths of a percentage point cheaper than borrowing at the U.S. prime interest rate. During a recent peak interest rate period in the United States, many cost-conscious domestic borrowers fled to the Eurodollar market. Having seen this trend, in order to stay competitive, some U.S. banks began offering their customers the option of taking a LIBOR-based rate in lieu of the prime rate.

Lending in the Eurodollar market is done almost exclusively by commercial banks. Large Eurocurrency loans are often syndicated by a group of participating banks. The loan agreement is put together by a lead bank, known as the manager, which is usually one of the largest U.S. or European banks. The manager charges the borrower a once-and-for-all fee or commission of 0.25 percent to 1 percent of the loan value. A portion of this fee is kept by the lead bank and the remainder is shared by all the participating banks. The aim of forming a syndicate is to diversify the risk, which would be too large for any single bank to handle by itself. Multicurrency loans and revolving credit arrangements can also be negotiated in the Eurocurrency market to suit borrowers' needs.

Eurobond Market   When long-term funds are needed, borrowing in the Eurobond market is a viable alternative for leading multinational corporations. The **Eurobond** issues are sold simultaneously in several national capital markets, but denominated in a currency different from that of the nation in which the bonds are issued. The most widely used currency in the Eurobond market is the U.S. dollar. Eurobond issues are underwritten by an international syndicate of banks and securities firms. Eurobonds of longer than seven years in maturity generally have a sinking-fund provision.

Disclosure requirements in the Eurobond market are much less stringent than those required by the Securities and Exchange Commission (SEC) in the United States. Furthermore, the registration costs in the Eurobond market are lower than those charged in the United States. In addition, the Eurobond market offers tax flexibility for borrowers and investors alike. All these advantages of Eurobonds enable the borrowers to raise funds at a lower cost. Nevertheless, a caveat may be in order with respect to the effective cost of borrowing in the Eurobond market. When a multinational firm borrows by issuing a foreign currency–denominated debt issue on a long-term basis, it creates transaction exposure, a kind of foreign exchange risk. If the foreign currency appreciates in value during the bond's life, the cost of servicing the debt could be prohibitively high. Many U.S. multinational firms borrowed at an approximately 7 percent coupon interest by selling Eurobonds denominated in deutsche marks and Swiss francs in the late 1980s and early 1990s. Nevertheless, these U.S. firms experienced an average debt service cost of approximately 13 percent, which is almost twice as much as the coupon rate. This increased cost occurred because the U.S. dollar fell with respect to these currencies. Therefore, currency selection for denominating Eurobond issues must be made with extreme care and foresight. To lessen the impact of foreign exchange risk, some recently issued Eurobond issues were denominated in multicurrency units.

International Equity Markets   The entire amount of equity capital comes from the parent company for a *wholly owned* foreign subsidiary, but a majority of foreign affiliates are not owned completely by their parent corporations. In Malaysia, majority ownership of a foreign affiliate must be held by the local citizens. In some other countries, the parent corporations are allowed to own their affiliates completely in the initial stages, but they are required to relinquish partial ownership to local citizens after five or seven years. To avoid nationalistic reactions to wholly owned foreign subsidiaries, such multinational firms as ExxonMobil, General Motors, Ford, and IBM sell shares to worldwide stockholders. It is also believed that widespread foreign ownership of the firm's common stock encourages the loyalty of foreign stockholders and employees

Are International Mergers More Beneficial Than Domestic Mergers?

There is a large amount of literature on the effect of a domestic merger, as opposed to an international merger, on the market value of the acquiring firm. The results for domestic mergers are universally negative in regard to stock returns. As an example, when Bank of America announced it was acquiring Fleet Boston Financial in the fall of 2003, its stock fell from $82 to $73 on the day of announcement because analysts felt it was overpaying for the entrance into the Northeast banking corridor. A full six months later, Bank of America stock was still trading in the $70 range.

The results for acquiring firms in international mergers are quite the opposite. The acquiring firm, on average, tends to show a risk-adjusted return above the market of 1.76 percent on the combined two-day period around the announcement of the merger.* This is far superior to a negative return of 2–3 percent for domestic mergers at announcement.

Why the disparity in results? For domestic mergers, researchers suggest that the acquiring firm's stock may be overvalued and the takeover offer is an attempt to trade inflated stock. The implications of the trade are that management is putting out a sell signal on its own stock, and the market acts accordingly. While this is not always the case, it is a matter of concern among some investors, especially when management pays a high premium for the acquired company and claims questionable benefits for the future.

In the case of international mergers, there is often the potential for greater benefits. In comparison to domestic acquisitions, foreign transactions offer an opportunity for international diversification. While there is increasing integration between world economies, the correlation is still far from perfect. For example, while the U.S. and European economies suffered from slow growth and lack of job creation in the early 2000s, the Chinese economy was moving forward at breakneck speed.

International mergers also offer a company the opportunity to move into a foreign market much more quickly than could be accomplished by internal growth. Such mergers may also offer the opportunities for cost-effective gains in technology, brand-name recognition, and logistics, while also eliminating a foreign competitor.

Furthermore, there may be an opportunity to acquire undervalued assets in foreign acquisitions. The heavy weight of research indicates that U.S. financial markets are efficient and that stocks are correctly priced at any point in time. The foreign markets do not possess this degree of efficiency, particularly in smaller, emerging markets. Without the presence of continual research by security analysts, rigorous reporting requirements, mandated by the governments, and the presence of continuous trading, stocks in emerging or even developed foreign markets may not be correctly priced. A sophisticated MNC may be able to recognize potential undervaluation and capitalize on it. This was particularly true of acquisitions in the Asian markets after the currency crisis of the late 1990s.

By bringing superior marketing and technology skills into an underserved foreign market, there is a further opportunity for gain. However, not all factors are positive in international acquisitions.

In a domestic merger, government approval is much simpler. If the Justice Department and Federal Trade Commission approve the merger, the participating companies are free to move ahead without further government intervention. However, in a foreign acquisition, the host country's government may have to approve the method of transfer and the impact on employees. Unlike in the United States, there is no concept of stockholder wealth maximization.

*Stanley Block, " Are International Mergers' Value Enhancing to Acquirer Shareholders? *Journal of Global Business,* Spring 2005, pp. 73–81.

toward the firm. Thus selling common stock to residents of foreign countries is not only an important financing strategy, but it is also a risk-minimizing strategy for many multinational corporations.

As you have learned in Chapter 14, a well-functioning secondary market is essential to entice investors into owning shares. To attract investors from all over the world, reputable multinational firms list their shares on major stock exchanges around the

HITACHI

SONY

world. Over 450 foreign companies are listed on the New York Stock Exchange, and the American Stock Exchange also lists foreign firms. Several hundred foreign issues are traded in the over-the-counter market. Even more foreign firms would sell stock issues in the United States and list on the NYSE and AMEX were it not for the tough and costly disclosure rules in effect in this country and enforced by the Securities and Exchange Commission. Many foreign corporations, such as Hoechst, Honda, Hitachi, Sony, Magnet Metals Ltd., DeBeers, and the like, accommodate American investors by issuing **American Depository Receipts (ADRs)**. All the American-owned shares of a foreign company are placed in trust in a major U.S. bank. The bank, in turn, will issue its depository receipts to the American stockholders and will maintain a stockholder ledger on these receipts, thus enabling the holders of ADRs to sell or otherwise transfer them as easily as they transfer any American company shares. ADR prices tend to move in a parallel path with the prices of the underlying securities in their home markets.

Looking elsewhere around the world, U.S. firms have listed their shares on the Toronto Stock Exchange and the Montreal Exchange. Similarly, more than 100 U.S. firms have listed their shares on the London Stock Exchange. To obtain exposure in an international financial community, listing securities on world stock exchanges is a step in the right direction for a multinational firm. This international exposure also brings an additional responsibility for the MNC to understand the preferences and needs of heterogeneous groups of investors of various nationalities. The MNC may have to print and circulate its annual financial statements in many languages. Some foreign investors are more risk-averse than their counterparts in the United States and prefer dividend income over less-certain capital gains. Common stock ownership among individuals in countries like Japan and Norway is relatively insignificant, with financial institutions holding substantial amounts of common stock issues. Institutional practices around the globe also vary significantly when it comes to issuing new securities. Unlike the United States, European commercial banks play a dominant role in the securities business. They underwrite stock issues, manage portfolios, vote the stock they hold in trust accounts, and hold directorships on company boards. In Germany the banks also run an over-the-counter market in many stocks.

The International Finance Corporation   Whenever a multinational company has difficulty raising equity capital due to lack of adequate private risk capital in a foreign country, the firm may explore the possibility of selling partial ownership to the **International Finance Corporation (IFC)**. This is a unit of the World Bank Group. The International Finance Corporation was established in 1956, and it is owned by 119 member countries of the World Bank. Its objective is to further economic development by promoting private enterprises in these countries. The profitability of a project and its potential benefit to the host country's economy are the two criteria the IFC uses to decide whether to assist a venture. The IFC participates in private enterprise through buying equity shares of a business, providing long-term loans, or a combination of the two for up to 25 percent of the total capital. The IFC expects the other partners to assume managerial responsibility, and it does not exercise its voting rights as a stockholder. The IFC helps finance new ventures as well as the expansion of existing ones in a variety of industries. Once the venture is well established, the IFC sells its investment position to private investors to free up its capital.

As firms become multinational in scope, the nature of their financial decisions also becomes more complex. A multinational firm has access to more sources of funds than a purely domestic corporation. Interest rates and market conditions vary between the alternative sources of funds, and corporate financial practices may differ significantly between countries. For example, the debt ratios in many foreign countries are higher than those used by U.S. firms. A foreign affiliate of an American firm faces a dilemma in its financing decision: Should it follow the parent firm's norm or that of the host country? Who must decide this? Will it be decided at the corporate headquarters in the United States or by the foreign affiliate? This is a matter of control over financial decisions. Dividend policy is another area of debate. Should the parent company dictate the dividends the foreign affiliate must distribute or should it be left completely to the discretion of the foreign affiliate? Foreign government regulations may also influence the decision. Questions like these do not have clear-cut answers. The complex environment in which the MNCs operate does not permit simple and clear-cut solutions. Obviously, each situation has to be evaluated individually, and specific guidelines for decision making must be established. Such coordination, it is to be hoped, will result in cohesive policies in the areas of working capital management, capital structure, and dividend decisions throughout the MNC network.

Some Unsettled Issues in International Finance

Summary

A significant proportion of earnings for many American companies comes from overseas markets. In general, international business operations have been more profitable than domestic operations, and this higher profitability is one factor that motivates business firms to go overseas to expand their markets. U.S. multinational firms have played a major role in promoting economic development and international trade for several decades, and now foreign firms have started to invest huge amounts of capital in the United States. Brand-name companies such as Sony, Coca-Cola, Heineken, McDonald's, Nestlé, and BMW are famous the world over.

When a domestic business firm crosses its national borders to do business in other countries, it enters a riskier and more complex environment. A multinational firm is exposed to foreign exchange risk in addition to the usual business and financial risks. International business transactions are denominated in foreign currencies and the rate at which one currency unit is converted into another is called the exchange rate. In today's global monetary system, exchange rates of major currencies fluctuate rather freely and on occasion are very volatile. For example on October 7, 1998, the Japanese yen fell over 6 percent versus the U.S. dollar; this was a record one-day movement against the U.S. dollar. These "freely" floating exchange rates expose multinational business firms to foreign exchange risk.

To deal with this foreign currency exposure effectively, the financial executive of a MNC must understand foreign exchange rates and how they are determined. Foreign exchange rates are influenced by differences in inflation rates among countries, differences in interest rates, governmental policies, and by the expectations of the participants in the foreign exchange markets. The international financial manager can reduce the firm's foreign currency exposure by hedging in the forward exchange markets, in the money markets, and in the currency futures market.

Foreign direct investments are usually quite large in size and many of them are exposed to enormous political risk. Although discounted cash flow analysis is applied to screen the projects in the initial stages, strategic considerations and political risk are often the overriding factors in reaching the final decisions about foreign investments. Political risk could involve negative policy decisions by a foreign government that discriminates against foreign firms. Political risk could also be the possibility of a country defaulting on sovereign debt—such as Russia did in 1998—or it could be a country's economic policies that have negative impacts on the economy such as inducing high inflation or a recession, high unemployment, and social unrest. Political events are hard to forecast and this makes analyzing a foreign investment proposal more difficult than analyzing a domestic investment project.

Financing international trade and investments is another important area of international finance that one must understand to raise funds at the lowest cost possible. The multinational firm has access to both the domestic and foreign capital markets. The Export-Import Bank finances American exports to foreign countries. Borrowing in the Eurobond market may appear less expensive at times, but the effect of foreign exchange risk on debt servicing costs must be weighed carefully before borrowing in these markets. Floating common stock in foreign capital markets is also a viable financing alternative for many multinational companies. The International Finance Corporation, which is a subsidiary of the World Bank, also provides debt capital and equity capital to qualified firms. These alternative sources of financing may significantly differ with respect to cost, terms, and conditions. Therefore, the financial executive must carefully locate and use the proper means to finance international business operations.

List of Terms

1. What risks does a foreign affiliate of a multinational firm face in today's business world?

2. What allegations are sometimes made against foreign affiliates of multinational firms and against the multinational firms themselves?

3. List the factors that affect the value of a currency in foreign exchange markets.

4. Explain how exports and imports tend to influence the value of a currency.

5. Differentiate between the spot exchange rate and the forward exchange rate.

6. What is meant by translation exposure in terms of foreign exchange risk?

7. What factors would influence a U.S. business firm to go overseas?

8. What procedure(s) would you recommend for a multinational company in studying exposure to political risk? What actual strategies can be used to guard against such risk?

9. What factors beyond the normal domestic analysis go into a financial feasibility study for a multinational firm?

10. What is a letter of credit?

11. Explain the functions of the following agencies:

    Overseas Private Investment Corporation (OPIC).

    Export–Import Bank (Eximbank).

    Foreign Credit Insurance Association (FCIA).

    International Finance Corporation (IFC).

12. What are the differences between a parallel loan and a fronting loan?

13. What is LIBOR? How does it compare to the U.S. prime rate?

14. What is the danger or concern in floating a Eurobond issue?

15. What are ADRs?

16. Comment on any dilemmas that multinational firms and their foreign affiliates may face in regard to debt ratio limits and dividend payouts.

1. Suppose a Swedish krona is selling for $0.1286 and a Maltan lira is selling for $2.8148. What is the exchange rate (cross rate) of the Swedish krona to the Maltan lira?

2. An investor in the United States bought a one-year New Zealand security valued at 200,000 New Zealand dollars. The U.S. dollar equivalent was $100,000. The New Zealand security earned 15 percent during the year, but the New Zealand dollar depreciated 5 cents against the U.S. dollar during the time period ($0.50/NZD to $0.45/NZD). After transferring the funds back to the United States, what was the investor's return on his $100,000? Determine the total ending value of the New Zealand investment in New Zealand dollars and then translate this value to U.S. dollars by multiplying by $0.45. Then compute the return on the $100,000.

Solutions

1. One dollar is worth 7.776 Swedish krona (1/0.1286) and one Maltan lira is worth 2.8148 dollars. Thus, 7.776 Swedish krona per *dollar* times 2.8148 *dollars* per Maltan lira equals 21.89 Swedish krona per Maltan lira.

2. Initial value × (1 + earnings)

$$200,000 \times 1.15 = 230,000 \text{ New Zealand dollars}$$

$$\text{New Zealand dollars} \times .45 = \text{U.S. dollars equivalent}$$

$$230,000 \times .45 = 103,500 \text{ U.S. dollars equivalent}$$

$$\frac{\$103,500}{\$100,000} \times 100 = 103.50 = 3.50\%$$

Problems

HM™ **All problems are available in Homework Manager. Please see the preface for more information.**

Spot and forward rates

1. *The Wall Street Journal* reported the following spot and forward rates for the Swiss franc ($/SF).

Spot	$0.7876
30-day forward	$0.7918
90-day forward	$0.7968
180-day forward	$0.8039

   a. Was the Swiss franc selling at a discount or premium in the forward market?

   b. What was the 30-day forward premium (or discount)?

   c. What was the 90-day forward premium (or discount)?

   d. Suppose you executed a 90-day forward contract to exchange 100,000 Swiss francs into U.S. dollars. How many dollars would you get 90 days hence?

   e. Assume a Swiss bank entered into a 180-day forward contract with Citicorp to buy $100,000. How many francs will the Swiss bank deliver in six months to get the U.S. dollars?

Cross rates

2. Suppose the Chinese renminbi is selling for $0.1241 and an Irish punt is selling for $1.5662. What is the exchange rate (cross rate) of the Chinese renminbi to the Irish punt? That is, how many Chinese renminbis are equal to an Irish punt?

Cross rates

3. Suppose a Polish zloty is selling for $0.3068 and a British pound is selling for $1.7504. What is the exchange rate (cross rate) of the Polish zloty to the British pound? That is, how many Polish zlotys are equal to a British pound?

Purchasing power theory

4. From the base price level of 100 in 1977, Saudi Arabian and U.S. price levels in 2007 stood at 200 and 404, respectively. If the 1977 $/riyal exchange rate was $0.31/riyal, what should the exchange rate be in 2007? Suggestion: Using purchasing power parity, adjust the exchange rate to compensate for inflation. That is, determine the relative rate of inflation between the United States and Saudi Arabia and multiply this times $/riyal of 0.31.

Continuation of purchasing power theory

5. In Problem 4, if the United States had somehow managed no inflation since 1977, what should the exchange rate be in 2007, using the purchasing power theory?

6. An investor in the United States bought a one-year Singapore security valued at 200,000 Singapore dollars. The U.S. dollar equivalent was $100,000. The Singapore security earned 15 percent during the year, but the Singapore dollar depreciated 5 cents against the U.S. dollar during the same time period ($0.50/SD to $0.45/SD). After transferring the funds back to the United States, what was the investor's return on his $100,000? Determine the total ending value of the Singapore investment in Singapore dollars and then translate this value to U.S. dollars by multiplying by $0.45. Then compute the return on the $100,000.

Adjusting returns for exchange rates

7. A Peruvian investor buys 100 shares of a U.S. stock for $4,000 ($40 per share). Over the course of a year, the stock goes up by $6 per share.

Adjusting returns for exchange rates

   a. If there is a 10 percent gain in the value of the dollar versus the Peruvian sol, what will be the total percentage return to the Peruvian investor? First determine the new dollar value of the investment and multiply this figure by 1.10. Divide this answer by $4,000 and get a percentage value, and then subtract 100 percent to get the percentage return.

   b. Now assume that the stock increases by $7, but that the dollar decreases by 10 percent versus the Peruvian sol. What will be the total percentage return to the Peruvian investor? Use 0.90 in place of 1.10 in this case.

8. You are the vice-president of finance for Exploratory Resources, headquartered in Houston, Texas. In January 2007, your firm's Canadian subsidiary obtained a six-month loan of 100,000 Canadian dollars from a bank in Houston to finance the acquisition of a titanium mine in Quebec province. The loan will also be repaid in Canadian dollars. At the time of the loan, the spot exchange rate was U.S. $0.8180/Canadian dollar and the Canadian currency was selling at a discount in the forward market. The June 2007 contract (Face value = $100,000 per contract) was quoted at U.S. $0.8120/Canadian dollar.

Hedging exchange rate risk

   a. Explain how the Houston bank could lose on this transaction assuming no hedging.

   b. If the bank does hedge with the forward contract, what is the maximum amount it can lose?

9. Ms. Angelo is the chief financial officer of Worldwide Videos located in Los Angeles. In September 2007, the firms's French subsidiary obtained a three-month bank loan of 500,000 euros from a bank in Los Angeles to finance seasonal needs overseas. The loan will be repaid in euros. At the time of the loan, the spot exchange rate was $1.2240/euro and the currency was selling at a discount in the forward market. The December 2007 contract (Face value, 100,000 euros per contract) was quoted at U.S. $1.2195/euro.

Hedging exchange rate risk

   a. If the Los Angeles bank hedges 60 percent of their exposure, what is the maximum amount it could lose based on changes in exchange rates?

   b. If it hedges 100 percent of its exposure, what is the most it could lose?

   c. Under what circumstance, in regard to the euro, is it most likely to want to hedge?

WEB EXERCISE

Chapter 21 deals with international finance and the decisions that companies have to make when operating in a foreign country. The Overseas Private Investment Corporation is a U.S. agency that helps U.S. companies that operate in developing economies. Their Web site has a great deal of information about doing business in a foreign country and excellent links to the 140 countries in which it has relationships.

1. Go to www.opic.gov.
2. Click on the top left item "Development Mission." Describe OPIC's mission.
3. Click on "Insurance, Finance, and Funds."
4. Then click on "OPIC Political Risk Insurance Can Help Protect Your Overseas Investments." Then click on "Small Business" along the left margin.
5. How does OPIC define a small business?
6. Next click on "Products" along the left margin. Then click on "Political Violence" to the right. List the areas for which OPIC compensates for property and income losses.

Note: From time to time, companies redesign their Web sites and occasionally a topic we have listed may have been deleted, updated, or moved into a different location. If you click on the site map or site index, you will be introduced to a table of contents which should aid you in finding the topic you are looking for.

S&P PROBLEMS   www.mhhe.com/edumarketinsight

STANDARD &POOR'S

1. Log onto the S&P Market Insight Web site, www.mhhe.com/edumarketinsight.
2. Click on "Company," which is the first box below the Market Insight title.
3. Type McDonald's ticker symbol "MCD" in the box and click on Go.
4. The purpose of this exercise is to show you a company that has diversified foreign operations and the impact that this can have on profits, growth, and the company's ability to expand.
5. Click on "Edgar" and then click again on the first 10K under "Annual Filings."
6. You will find McDonald's foreign information beginning on approximately page 18 of the Annual Report (and we hope in a similar location in more recent reports). You may have to scroll down to the section for "Revenues" where you will find a table with blue and white lines breaking down international revenues. Following the first revenue table you will find a series of tables breaking down expenses and income by international region.
7. What percentage of sales is derived from the various geographic areas?
8. What percentage of operating benefits comes from the various geographic areas?
9. From your analysis of these pages, where is McDonald's most profitable? Rank profitability by region.

APPENDIX 21A

Cash Flow Analysis and the Foreign Investment Decision

Direct foreign investments are often relatively large. As we mentioned in the chapter, these investments are exposed to some extraordinary risks, such as foreign exchange fluctuations and political interference, which are nonexistent for domestic investments. Therefore, the final decision is often made at the board of directors level after considering the financial feasibility and the strategic importance of the proposed investment. Financial feasibility analysis for foreign investments is basically conducted in the same manner as it is for domestic capital budgets. Certain important differences exist, however, in the treatment of foreign tax credits, foreign exchange risk, and remittance of cash flows. To see how these are handled in foreign investment analysis, let us consider a hypothetical illustration.

Tex Systems, Inc., a Texas-based manufacturer of computer equipment, is considering the establishment of a manufacturing plant in Salaysia, a country in Southeast Asia. The Salaysian plant will be a wholly owned subsidiary of Tex Systems, and its estimated cost is 90 million ringgits (2 ringgits = $1). Based on the exchange rate between ringgits and dollars, the cost in dollars is $45 million. In addition to selling in the local Salaysian market, the proposed subsidiary is expected to export its computers to the neighboring markets in Singapore, Hong Kong, and Thailand. Expected revenues and operating costs are as shown in Table 21A–1. The country's investment climate, which reflects the foreign exchange and political risks, is rated BBB (considered fairly safe)

Table 21A–1 Cash flow analysis of a foreign investment

	Projected Cash Flows (million ringgits unless otherwise stated)					
	Year 1	Year 2	Year 3	Year 4	Year 5	Year 6
Revenues	45.00	50.00	55.00	60.00	65.00	70.00
− Operating expenses	28.00	30.00	30.00	32.00	35.00	35.00
− Depreciation	10.00	10.00	10.00	10.00	10.00	10.00
Earnings before Salaysian taxes	7.00	10.00	15.00	18.00	20.00	25.00
− Salaysian income tax (25%)	1.75	2.50	3.75	4.50	5.00	6.25
Earnings after foreign income taxes	5.25	7.50	11.25	13.50	15.00	18.75
− Dividends repatriated	5.25	7.50	11.25	13.50	15.00	18.75
Gross U.S. taxes (30% of foreign earnings before taxes)	2.10	3.00	4.50	5.40	6.00	7.50
− Foreign tax credit	1.75	2.50	3.75	4.50	5.00	6.25
Net U.S. taxes payable	0.35	0.50	0.75	0.90	1.00	1.25
Aftertax dividend received by Tex Systems	4.90	7.00	10.50	12.60	14.00	17.50
Exchange rate (ringgits/$)	2.00	2.04	2.08	2.12	2.16	2.21
Aftertax dividend (U.S. $)	2.45	3.43	5.05	5.94	6.48	7.92
PV$_{IF}$ (at 20%)	0.833	0.694	0.579	0.482	0.402	0.335
PV of dividends ($)	2.04 +	2.38 +	2.92 +	2.86 +	2.60 +	2.65 = $15.45

by a leading Asian business journal. After considering the investment climate and the nature of the industry, Tex Systems has set a target rate of return of 20 percent for this foreign investment.

Salaysia has a 25 percent corporate income tax rate and has waived the withholding tax on dividends repatriated (forwarded) to the parent company. A dividend payout ratio of 100 percent is assumed for the foreign subsidiary. Tex Systems's marginal tax rate is 30 percent. It was agreed by Tex Systems and the Salaysian government that the subsidiary will be sold to a Salaysian entrepreneur after six years for an estimated 30 million ringgits. The plant will be depreciated over a period of six years using the straight-line method. The cash flows generated through depreciation cannot be remitted to the parent company until the subsidiary is sold to the local private entrepreneur six years from now. The Salaysian government requires the subsidiary to invest the depreciation-generated cash flows in local government bonds yielding an aftertax rate of 15 percent. The depreciation cash flows thus compounded and accumulated can be returned to Tex Systems when the project is terminated. Although the value of ringgits in the foreign exchange market has remained fairly stable for the past three years, the projected budget deficits and trade deficits of Salaysia may result in a gradual devaluation of ringgits against the U.S. dollar at the rate of 2 percent per year for the next six years.

Note that the analysis in Table 21A–1 is primarily done in terms of ringgits. Expenses (operating, depreciation, and Salaysian income taxes) are subtracted from revenues to arrive at earnings after foreign income taxes. These earnings are then repatriated (forwarded) to Tex Systems in the form of dividends. Dividends repatriated thus begin at 5.25 ringgits (in millions) in year 1 and increase to 18.75 ringgits in year 6. The next item, gross U.S. taxes, refers to the unadjusted U.S. tax obligation. As specified, this is equal to 30 percent of foreign earnings before taxes (earnings before Salaysian taxes).[1] For example, gross U.S. taxes in the first year are equal to:

Earnings before Salaysian taxes............	7.00
30% of foreign earnings before taxes........	30%
Gross U.S. taxes.......................	2.10

From gross U.S. taxes, Tex Systems may take a foreign tax credit equal to the amount of Salaysian income tax paid. Gross U.S. taxes minus this foreign tax credit are equal to net U.S. taxes payable. Aftertax dividends received by Tex Systems are equal to dividends repatriated minus U.S. taxes payable. In the first year, the values are:

Dividends repatriated.........................	5.25
Net U.S. taxes payable.......................	−0.35
Aftertax dividends received by Tex Systems........	4.90

The figures for aftertax dividends received by Tex Systems are all stated in ringgits (the analysis up to this point has been in ringgits). These ringgits will now be converted

---

[1]If foreign earnings had not been repatriated, this tax obligation would not be due.

into dollars. The initial exchange rate is 2.00 ringgits per dollar, and this will go up by 2 percent per year.[2] For the first year, 4.90 ringgits will be translated into 2.45 dollars. Since values are stated in millions, this will represent $2.45 million. Aftertax dividends in U.S. dollars grow from $2.45 million in year 1 to $7.92 million in year 6. The last two rows of Table 21A–1 show the present value of these dividends at a 20 percent discount rate. The *total* present value of aftertax dividends received by Tex Systems adds up to $15.45 million. Repatriated dividends will be just one part of the cash flow. The second part consists of depreciation-generated cash flow accumulated and reinvested in Salaysian government bonds at a 15 percent rate per year. The compound value of reinvested depreciation cash flows (10 million ringgits per year) is:

$$\text{10 million ringgits} \times 8.754^* = \text{87.54 million ringgits after six years}$$

*Future value at 15 percent for six years (from Appendix C at end of book).

These 87.54 million ringgits must now be translated into dollars and then discounted back to the present. Since the exchange rate is 2.21 ringgits per dollar in the 6th year (fourth line from the bottom in Table 21A–1), the dollar equivalent of 87.54 million ringgits is:

$$\text{87.54 million ringgits} \div 2.21 = \$39.61 \text{ million}$$

The $39.61 million can now be discounted back to the present, by using the present value factor for six years at 20 percent (Appendix B).

$$\begin{array}{r} \$39.61 \text{ million} \\ \underline{\times \ 0.335 \ PV_{IF}} \\ \$13.27 \text{ million} \end{array}$$

The final benefit to be received is the 30 million ringgits when the plant is sold six years from now.[3] We first convert this to dollars and then take the present value.

$$\text{30 million ringgits} \div 2.21 = \$13.57 \text{ million}$$

The present value of $13.57 million after six years at 20 percent is:

$$\begin{array}{r} \$13.57 \text{ million} \\ \underline{\times \ 0.335 \ PV_{IF}} \\ \$ \ 4.55 \text{ million} \end{array}$$

The present value of all cash inflows in dollars is equal to:

Present value of dividends	$15.45 million
Present value of repatriated accumulated depreciation	13.27
Present value of sales price for plant	4.55
Total present value of inflows	$33.27 million

[2] The 2 percent appreciation means the dollar is equal to an increasing amount of ringgits each year. The dollar is appreciating relative to ringgits, and ringgits are depreciating relative to the dollar. Since Tex Systems's earnings are in ringgits, they are being converted at a less desirable rate each year. Big Tex may eventually decide to hedge its foreign exchange risk exposure.

[3] Capital gains taxes are not a necessary consideration in foreign transactions of this nature.

The cost of the project was initially specified as 90 million ringgits, or $45 million. In the following table, we see the total present value of inflows in dollars is less than the cost, and the project has a negative net present value.

Total present value of inflows	$33.27 million
Cost	45.00
Net present value	($11.73 million)

Problem

Cash flow analysis with a foreign investment

21A–1.   The Office Automation Corporation is considering a foreign investment. The initial cash outlay will be $10 million. The current foreign exchange rate is 2 ugans = $1. Thus the investment in foreign currency will be 20 million ugans. The assets have a useful life of five years and no expected salvage value. The firm uses a straight-line method of depreciation. Sales are expected to be 20 million ugans and operating cash expenses 10 million ugans every year for five years. The foreign income tax rate is 25 percent. The foreign subsidiary will repatriate all aftertax profits to Office Automation in the form of dividends. Furthermore, the depreciation cash flows (equal to each year's depreciation) will be repatriated during the same year they accrue to the foreign subsidiary. The applicable cost of capital that reflects the riskiness of the cash flows is 16 percent. The U.S. tax rate is 40 percent of foreign earnings before taxes.

    a.   Should the Office Automation Corporation undertake the investment if the foreign exchange rate is expected to remain constant during the five-year period?

    b.   Should Office Automation undertake the investment if the foreign exchange rate is expected to be as follows:

Year 0	$1 = 2.0 ugans
Year 1	$1 = 2.2 ugans
Year 2	$1 = 2.4 ugans
Year 3	$1 = 2.7 ugans
Year 4	$1 = 2.9 ugans
Year 5	$1 = 3.2 ugans

APPENDIXES

Appendix A

Future value of $1, FV_{IF} $FV = PV(1 + i)^n$

Percent

Period	1%	2%	3%	4%	5%	6%	7%	8%	9%	10%	11%
1	1.010	1.020	1.030	1.040	1.050	1.060	1.070	1.080	1.090	1.100	1.110
2	1.020	1.040	1.061	1.082	1.103	1.124	1.145	1.166	1.188	1.210	1.232
3	1.030	1.061	1.093	1.125	1.158	1.191	1.225	1.260	1.295	1.331	1.368
4	1.041	1.082	1.126	1.170	1.216	1.262	1.311	1.360	1.412	1.464	1.518
5	1.051	1.104	1.159	1.217	1.276	1.338	1.403	1.469	1.539	1.611	1.685
6	1.062	1.126	1.194	1.265	1.340	1.419	1.501	1.587	1.677	1.772	1.870
7	1.072	1.149	1.230	1.316	1.407	1.504	1.606	1.714	1.828	1.949	2.076
8	1.083	1.172	1.267	1.369	1.477	1.594	1.718	1.851	1.993	2.144	2.305
9	1.094	1.195	1.305	1.423	1.551	1.689	1.838	1.999	2.172	2.358	2.558
10	1.105	1.219	1.344	1.480	1.629	1.791	1.967	2.159	2.367	2.594	2.839
11	1.116	1.243	1.384	1.539	1.710	1.898	2.105	2.332	2.580	2.853	3.152
12	1.127	1.268	1.426	1.601	1.796	2.012	2.252	2.518	2.813	3.138	3.498
13	1.138	1.294	1.469	1.665	1.886	2.133	2.410	2.720	3.066	3.452	3.883
14	1.149	1.319	1.513	1.732	1.980	2.261	2.579	2.937	3.342	3.797	4.310
15	1.161	1.346	1.558	1.801	2.079	2.397	2.759	3.172	3.642	4.177	4.785
16	1.173	1.373	1.605	1.873	2.183	2.540	2.952	3.426	3.970	4.595	5.311
17	1.184	1.400	1.653	1.948	2.292	2.693	3.159	3.700	4.328	5.054	5.895
18	1.196	1.428	1.702	2.026	2.407	2.854	3.380	3.996	4.717	5.560	6.544
19	1.208	1.457	1.754	2.107	2.527	3.026	3.617	4.316	5.142	6.116	7.263
20	1.220	1.486	1.806	2.191	2.653	3.207	3.870	4.661	5.604	6.727	8.062
25	1.282	1.641	2.094	2.666	3.386	4.292	5.427	6.848	8.623	10.835	13.585
30	1.348	1.811	2.427	3.243	4.322	5.743	7.612	10.063	13.268	17.449	22.892
40	1.489	2.208	3.262	4.801	7.040	10.286	14.974	21.725	31.409	45.259	65.001
50	1.645	2.692	4.384	7.107	11.467	18.420	29.457	46.902	74.358	117.39	184.57

Appendix A (concluded)

Future value of $1

							Percent					
Period	**12%**	**13%**	**14%**	**15%**	**16%**	**17%**	**18%**	**19%**	**20%**	**25%**	**30%**
1	1.120	1.130	1.140	1.150	1.160	1.170	1.180	1.190	1.200	1.250	1.300
2	1.254	1.277	1.300	1.323	1.346	1.369	1.392	1.416	1.440	1.563	1.690
3	1.405	1.443	1.482	1.521	1.561	1.602	1.643	1.685	1.728	1.953	2.197
4	1.574	1.630	1.689	1.749	1.811	1.874	1.939	2.005	2.074	2.441	2.856
5	1.762	1.842	1.925	2.011	2.100	2.192	2.288	2.386	2.488	3.052	3.713
6	1.974	2.082	2.195	2.313	2.436	2.565	2.700	2.840	2.986	3.815	4.827
7	2.211	2.353	2.502	2.660	2.826	3.001	3.185	3.379	3.583	4.768	6.276
8	2.476	2.658	2.853	3.059	3.278	3.511	3.759	4.021	4.300	5.960	8.157
9	2.773	3.004	3.252	3.518	3.803	4.108	4.435	4.785	5.160	7.451	10.604
10	3.106	3.395	3.707	4.046	4.411	4.807	5.234	5.696	6.192	9.313	13.786
11	3.479	3.836	4.226	4.652	5.117	5.624	6.176	6.777	7.430	11.642	17.922
12	3.896	4.335	4.818	5.350	5.936	6.580	7.288	8.064	8.916	14.552	23.298
13	4.363	4.898	5.492	6.153	6.886	7.699	8.599	9.596	10.699	18.190	30.288
14	4.887	5.535	6.261	7.076	7.988	9.007	10.147	11.420	12.839	22.737	39.374
15	5.474	6.254	7.138	8.137	9.266	10.539	11.974	13.590	15.407	28.422	51.186
16	6.130	7.067	8.137	9.358	10.748	12.330	14.129	16.172	18.488	35.527	66.542
17	6.866	7.986	9.276	10.761	12.468	14.426	16.672	19.244	22.186	44.409	86.504
18	7.690	9.024	10.575	12.375	14.463	16.879	19.673	22.091	26.623	55.511	112.46
19	8.613	10.197	12.056	14.232	16.777	19.748	23.214	27.252	31.948	69.389	146.19
20	9.646	11.523	13.743	16.367	19.461	23.106	27.393	32.429	38.338	86.736	190.05
25	17.000	21.231	26.462	32.919	40.874	50.658	62.669	77.388	95.396	264.70	705.64
30	29.960	39.116	50.950	66.212	85.850	111.07	143.37	184.68	237.38	807.79	2,620.0
40	93.051	132.78	188.88	267.86	378.72	533.87	750.38	1,051.7	1,469.8	7,523.2	36,119.
50	289.00	450.74	700.23	1,083.7	1,670.7	2,566.2	3,927.4	5,988.9	9,100.4	70,065.	497,929.

Appendix B
Present value of $1, PV_{IF}

$$PV = FV\left[\frac{1}{(1+i)^n}\right]$$

Period	1%	2%	3%	4%	5%	6%	7%	8%	9%	10%	11%	12%
1	0.990	0.980	0.971	0.962	0.952	0.943	0.935	0.926	0.917	0.909	0.901	0.893
2	0.980	0.961	0.943	0.925	0.907	0.890	0.873	0.857	0.842	0.826	0.812	0.797
3	0.971	0.942	0.915	0.889	0.864	0.840	0.816	0.794	0.772	0.751	0.731	0.712
4	0.961	0.924	0.885	0.855	0.823	0.792	0.763	0.735	0.708	0.683	0.659	0.636
5	0.951	0.906	0.863	0.822	0.784	0.747	0.713	0.681	0.650	0.621	0.593	0.567
6	0.942	0.888	0.837	0.790	0.746	0.705	0.666	0.630	0.596	0.564	0.535	0.507
7	0.933	0.871	0.813	0.760	0.711	0.665	0.623	0.583	0.547	0.513	0.482	0.452
8	0.923	0.853	0.789	0.731	0.677	0.627	0.582	0.540	0.502	0.467	0.434	0.404
9	0.914	0.837	0.766	0.703	0.645	0.592	0.544	0.500	0.460	0.424	0.391	0.361
10	0.905	0.820	0.744	0.676	0.614	0.558	0.508	0.463	0.422	0.386	0.352	0.322
11	0.896	0.804	0.722	0.650	0.585	0.527	0.475	0.429	0.388	0.350	0.317	0.287
12	0.887	0.788	0.701	0.625	0.557	0.497	0.444	0.397	0.356	0.319	0.286	0.257
13	0.879	0.773	0.681	0.601	0.530	0.469	0.415	0.368	0.326	0.290	0.258	0.229
14	0.870	0.758	0.661	0.577	0.505	0.442	0.388	0.340	0.299	0.263	0.232	0.205
15	0.861	0.743	0.642	0.555	0.481	0.417	0.362	0.315	0.275	0.239	0.209	0.183
16	0.853	0.728	0.623	0.534	0.458	0.394	0.339	0.292	0.252	0.218	0.188	0.163
17	0.844	0.714	0.605	0.513	0.436	0.371	0.317	0.270	0.231	0.198	0.170	0.146
18	0.836	0.700	0.587	0.494	0.416	0.350	0.296	0.250	0.212	0.180	0.153	0.130
19	0.828	0.686	0.570	0.475	0.396	0.331	0.277	0.232	0.194	0.164	0.138	0.116
20	0.820	0.673	0.554	0.456	0.377	0.312	0.258	0.215	0.178	0.149	0.124	0.104
25	0.780	0.610	0.478	0.375	0.295	0.233	0.184	0.146	0.116	0.092	0.074	0.059
30	0.742	0.552	0.412	0.308	0.231	0.174	0.131	0.099	0.075	0.057	0.044	0.033
40	0.672	0.453	0.307	0.208	0.142	0.097	0.067	0.046	0.032	0.022	0.015	0.011
50	0.608	0.372	0.228	0.141	0.087	0.054	0.034	0.021	0.013	0.009	0.005	0.003

Percent

Appendix B (concluded)
Present value of $1

Period						Percent							
	13%	14%	15%	16%	17%	18%	19%	20%	25%	30%	35%	40%	50%
1	0.885	0.877	0.870	0.862	0.855	0.847	0.840	0.833	0.800	0.769	0.741	0.714	0.667
2	0.783	0.769	0.756	0.743	0.731	0.718	0.706	0.694	0.640	0.592	0.549	0.510	0.444
3	0.693	0.675	0.658	0.641	0.624	0.609	0.593	0.579	0.512	0.455	0.406	0.364	0.296
4	0.613	0.592	0.572	0.552	0.534	0.515	0.499	0.482	0.410	0.350	0.301	0.260	0.198
5	0.543	0.519	0.497	0.476	0.456	0.437	0.419	0.402	0.328	0.269	0.223	0.186	0.132
6	0.480	0.456	0.432	0.410	0.390	0.370	0.352	0.335	0.262	0.207	0.165	0.133	0.088
7	0.425	0.400	0.376	0.354	0.333	0.314	0.296	0.279	0.210	0.159	0.122	0.095	0.059
8	0.376	0.351	0.327	0.305	0.285	0.266	0.249	0.233	0.168	0.123	0.091	0.068	0.039
9	0.333	0.300	0.284	0.263	0.243	0.225	0.209	0.194	0.134	0.094	0.067	0.048	0.026
10	0.295	0.270	0.247	0.227	0.208	0.191	0.176	0.162	0.107	0.073	0.050	0.035	0.017
11	0.261	0.237	0.215	0.195	0.178	0.162	0.148	0.135	0.086	0.056	0.037	0.025	0.012
12	0.231	0.208	0.187	0.168	0.152	0.137	0.124	0.112	0.069	0.043	0.027	0.018	0.008
13	0.204	0.182	0.163	0.145	0.130	0.116	0.104	0.093	0.055	0.033	0.020	0.013	0.005
14	0.181	0.160	0.141	0.125	0.111	0.099	0.088	0.078	0.044	0.025	0.015	0.009	0.003
15	0.160	0.140	0.123	0.108	0.095	0.084	0.074	0.065	0.035	0.020	0.011	0.006	0.002
16	0.141	0.123	0.107	0.093	0.081	0.071	0.062	0.054	0.028	0.015	0.008	0.005	0.002
17	0.125	0.108	0.093	0.080	0.069	0.060	0.052	0.045	0.023	0.012	0.006	0.003	0.001
18	0.111	0.095	0.081	0.069	0.059	0.051	0.044	0.038	0.018	0.009	0.005	0.002	0.001
19	0.098	0.083	0.070	0.060	0.051	0.043	0.037	0.031	0.014	0.007	0.003	0.002	0
20	0.087	0.073	0.061	0.051	0.043	0.037	0.031	0.026	0.012	0.005	0.002	0.001	0
25	0.047	0.038	0.030	0.024	0.020	0.016	0.013	0.010	0.004	0.001	0.001	0	0
30	0.026	0.020	0.015	0.012	0.009	0.007	0.005	0.004	0.001	0	0	0	0
40	0.008	0.005	0.004	0.003	0.002	0.001	0.001	0.001	0	0	0	0	0
50	0.002	0.001	0.001	0.001	0	0	0	0	0	0	0	0	0

Appendix C

Future value of an annuity of $1, FV_{IFA}

$$FV_A = A\left[\frac{(1+i)^n - 1}{i}\right]$$

Percent

Period	1%	2%	3%	4%	5%	6%	7%	8%	9%	10%	11%
1	1.000	1.000	1.000	1.000	1.000	1.000	1.000	1.000	1.000	1.000	1.000
2	2.010	2.020	2.030	2.040	2.050	2.060	2.070	2.080	2.090	2.100	2.110
3	3.030	3.060	3.091	3.122	3.153	3.184	3.215	3.246	3.278	3.310	3.342
4	4.060	4.122	4.184	4.246	4.310	4.375	4.440	4.506	4.573	4.641	4.710
5	5.101	5.204	5.309	5.416	5.526	5.637	5.751	5.867	5.985	6.105	6.228
6	6.152	6.308	6.468	6.633	6.802	6.975	7.153	7.336	7.523	7.716	7.913
7	7.214	7.434	7.662	7.898	8.142	8.394	8.654	8.923	9.200	9.487	9.783
8	8.286	8.583	8.892	9.214	9.549	9.897	10.260	10.637	11.028	11.436	11.859
9	9.369	9.755	10.159	10.583	11.027	11.491	11.978	12.488	13.021	13.579	14.164
10	10.462	10.950	11.464	12.006	12.578	13.181	13.816	14.487	15.193	15.937	16.722
11	11.567	12.169	12.808	13.486	14.207	14.972	15.784	16.645	17.560	18.531	19.561
12	12.683	13.412	14.192	15.026	15.917	16.870	17.888	18.977	20.141	21.384	22.713
13	13.809	14.680	15.618	16.627	17.713	18.882	20.141	21.495	22.953	24.523	26.212
14	14.947	15.974	17.086	18.292	19.599	21.015	22.550	24.215	26.019	27.975	30.095
15	16.097	17.293	18.599	20.024	21.579	23.276	25.129	27.152	29.361	31.772	34.405
16	17.258	18.639	20.157	21.825	23.657	25.673	27.888	30.324	33.003	35.950	39.190
17	18.430	20.012	21.762	23.698	25.840	28.213	30.840	33.750	36.974	40.545	44.501
18	19.615	21.412	23.414	25.645	28.132	30.906	33.999	37.450	41.301	45.599	50.396
19	20.811	22.841	25.117	27.671	30.539	33.760	37.379	41.446	46.018	51.159	56.939
20	22.019	24.297	26.870	29.778	33.066	36.786	40.995	45.762	51.160	57.275	64.203
25	28.243	32.030	36.459	41.646	47.727	54.865	63.249	73.106	84.701	98.347	114.41
30	34.785	40.588	47.575	56.085	66.439	79.058	94.461	113.28	136.31	164.49	199.02
40	48.886	60.402	75.401	95.026	120.80	154.76	199.64	259.06	337.89	442.59	581.83
50	64.463	84.579	112.80	152.67	209.35	290.34	406.53	573.77	815.08	1,163.9	1,668.8

Appendix C (concluded)

Future value of an annuity of $1

Period	12%	13%	14%	15%	16%	17%	18%	19%	20%	25%	30%
1	1.000	1.000	1.000	1.000	1.000	1.000	1.000	1.000	1.000	1.000	1.000
2	2.120	2.130	2.140	2.150	2.160	2.170	2.180	2.190	2.200	2.250	2.300
3	3.374	3.407	3.440	3.473	3.506	3.539	3.572	3.606	3.640	3.813	3.990
4	4.779	4.850	4.921	4.993	5.066	5.141	5.215	5.291	5.368	5.766	6.187
5	6.353	6.480	6.610	6.742	6.877	7.014	7.154	7.297	7.442	8.207	9.043
6	8.115	8.323	8.536	8.754	8.977	9.207	9.442	9.683	9.930	11.259	12.756
7	10.089	10.405	10.730	11.067	11.414	11.772	12.142	12.523	12.916	15.073	17.583
8	12.300	12.757	13.233	13.727	14.240	14.773	15.327	15.902	16.499	19.842	23.858
9	14.776	15.416	16.085	16.786	17.519	18.285	19.086	19.923	20.799	25.802	32.015
10	17.549	18.420	19.337	20.304	21.321	22.393	23.521	24.701	25.959	33.253	42.619
11	20.655	21.814	23.045	24.349	25.733	27.200	28.755	30.404	32.150	42.566	56.405
12	24.133	25.650	27.271	29.002	30.850	32.824	34.931	37.180	39.581	54.208	74.327
13	28.029	29.985	32.089	34.352	36.786	39.404	42.219	45.244	48.497	68.760	97.625
14	32.393	34.883	37.581	40.505	43.672	47.103	50.818	54.841	59.196	86.949	127.91
15	37.280	40.417	43.842	47.580	51.660	56.110	60.965	66.261	72.035	109.69	167.29
16	42.753	46.672	50.980	55.717	60.925	66.649	72.939	79.850	87.442	138.11	218.47
17	48.884	53.739	59.118	65.075	71.673	78.979	87.068	96.022	105.93	173.64	285.01
18	55.750	61.725	68.394	75.836	84.141	93.406	103.74	115.27	128.12	218.05	371.52
19	63.440	70.749	78.969	88.212	98.603	110.29	123.41	138.17	154.74	273.56	483.97
20	72.052	80.947	91.025	102.44	115.38	130.03	146.63	165.42	186.69	342.95	630.17
25	133.33	155.62	181.87	212.79	249.21	292.11	342.60	402.04	471.98	1,054.8	2,348.80
30	241.33	293.20	356.79	434.75	530.31	647.44	790.95	966.7	1,181.9	3,227.2	8,730.0
40	767.09	1,013.7	1,342.0	1,779.1	2,360.8	3,134.5	4,163.21	5,529.8	7,343.9	30,089.	120,393.0
50	2,400.0	3,459.5	4,994.5	7,217.7	10,436.	15,090.	21,813.	31,515.	45,497.	280,256.	1,659,760.

Appendix D

Present value of an annuity of $1, PV_{IFA} $PV_A = A \left[\dfrac{1 - \dfrac{1}{(1+i)^n}}{i} \right]$

Percent

Period	1%	2%	3%	4%	5%	6%	7%	8%	9%	10%	11%	12%
1	0.990	0.980	0.971	0.962	0.952	0.943	0.935	0.926	0.917	0.909	0.901	0.893
2	1.970	1.942	1.913	1.886	1.859	1.833	1.808	1.783	1.759	1.736	1.713	1.690
3	2.941	2.884	2.829	2.775	2.723	2.673	2.624	2.577	2.531	2.487	2.444	2.402
4	3.902	3.808	3.717	3.630	3.546	3.465	3.387	3.312	3.240	3.170	3.102	3.037
5	4.853	4.713	4.580	4.452	4.329	4.212	4.100	3.993	3.890	3.791	3.696	3.605
6	5.795	5.601	5.417	5.242	5.076	4.917	4.767	4.623	4.486	4.355	4.231	4.111
7	6.728	6.472	6.230	6.002	5.786	5.582	5.389	5.206	5.033	4.868	4.712	4.564
8	7.652	7.325	7.020	6.733	6.463	6.210	5.971	5.747	5.535	5.335	5.146	4.968
9	8.566	8.162	7.786	7.435	7.108	6.802	6.515	6.247	5.995	5.759	5.537	5.328
10	9.471	8.983	8.530	8.111	7.722	7.360	7.024	6.710	6.418	6.145	5.889	5.650
11	10.368	9.787	9.253	8.760	8.306	7.887	7.499	7.139	6.805	6.495	6.207	5.938
12	11.255	10.575	9.954	9.385	8.863	8.384	7.943	7.536	7.161	6.814	6.492	6.194
13	12.134	11.348	10.635	9.986	9.394	8.853	8.358	7.904	7.487	7.103	6.750	6.424
14	13.004	12.106	11.296	10.563	9.899	9.295	8.745	8.244	7.786	7.367	6.982	6.628
15	13.865	12.849	11.939	11.118	10.380	9.712	9.108	8.559	8.061	7.606	7.191	6.811
16	14.718	13.578	12.561	11.652	10.838	10.106	9.447	8.851	8.313	7.824	7.379	6.974
17	15.562	14.292	13.166	12.166	11.274	10.477	9.763	9.122	8.544	8.022	7.549	7.102
18	16.398	14.992	13.754	12.659	11.690	10.828	10.059	9.372	8.756	8.201	7.702	7.250
19	17.226	15.678	14.324	13.134	12.085	11.158	10.336	9.604	8.950	8.365	7.839	7.366
20	18.046	16.351	14.877	13.590	12.462	11.470	10.594	9.818	9.129	8.514	7.963	7.469
25	22.023	19.523	17.413	15.622	14.094	12.783	11.654	10.675	9.823	9.077	8.422	7.843
30	25.808	22.396	19.600	17.292	15.372	13.765	12.409	11.258	10.274	9.427	8.694	8.055
40	32.835	27.355	23.115	19.793	17.159	15.046	13.332	11.925	10.757	9.779	8.951	8.244
50	39.196	31.424	25.730	21.482	18.256	15.762	13.801	12.233	10.962	9.915	9.042	8.304

Period	13%	14%	15%	16%	17%	18%	19%	20%	25%	30%	35%	40%	50%
1	0.885	0.877	0.870	0.862	0.855	0.847	0.840	0.833	0.800	0.769	0.741	0.714	0.667
2	1.668	1.647	1.626	1.605	1.585	1.566	1.547	1.528	1.440	1.361	1.289	1.224	1.111
3	2.361	2.322	2.283	2.246	2.210	2.174	2.140	2.106	1.952	1.816	1.696	1.589	1.407
4	2.974	2.914	2.855	2.798	2.743	2.690	2.639	2.589	2.362	2.166	1.997	1.849	1.605
5	3.517	3.433	3.352	3.274	3.199	3.127	3.058	2.991	2.689	2.436	2.220	2.035	1.737
6	3.998	3.889	3.784	3.685	3.589	3.498	3.410	3.326	2.951	2.643	2.385	2.168	1.824
7	4.423	4.288	4.160	4.039	3.922	3.812	3.706	3.605	3.161	2.802	2.508	2.263	1.883
8	4.799	4.639	4.487	4.344	4.207	4.078	3.954	3.837	3.329	2.925	2.598	2.331	1.922
9	5.132	4.946	4.772	4.607	4.451	4.303	4.163	4.031	3.463	3.019	2.665	2.379	1.948
10	5.426	5.216	5.019	4.833	4.659	4.494	4.339	4.192	3.571	3.092	2.715	2.414	1.965
11	5.687	5.453	5.234	5.029	4.836	4.656	4.486	4.327	3.656	3.147	2.752	2.438	1.977
12	5.918	5.660	5.421	5.197	4.988	4.793	4.611	4.439	3.725	3.190	2.779	2.456	1.985
13	6.122	5.842	5.583	5.342	5.118	4.910	4.715	4.533	3.780	3.223	2.799	2.469	1.990
14	6.302	6.002	5.724	5.468	5.229	5.008	4.802	4.611	3.824	3.249	2.814	2.478	1.993
15	6.462	6.142	5.847	5.575	5.324	5.092	4.876	4.675	3.859	3.268	2.825	2.484	1.995
16	6.604	6.265	5.954	5.668	5.405	5.162	4.938	4.730	3.887	3.283	2.834	2.489	1.997
17	6.729	6.373	6.047	5.749	5.475	5.222	4.988	4.775	3.910	3.295	2.840	2.492	1.998
18	6.840	6.467	6.128	5.818	5.534	5.273	5.033	4.812	3.928	3.304	2.844	2.494	1.999
19	6.938	6.550	6.198	5.877	5.584	5.316	5.070	4.843	3.942	3.311	2.848	2.496	1.999
20	7.025	6.623	6.259	5.929	5.628	5.353	5.101	4.870	3.954	3.316	2.850	2.497	1.999
25	7.330	6.873	6.464	6.097	5.766	5.467	5.195	4.948	3.985	3.329	2.856	2.499	2.000
30	7.496	7.003	6.566	6.177	5.829	5.517	5.235	4.979	3.995	3.332	2.857	2.500	2.000
40	7.634	7.105	6.642	6.233	5.871	5.548	5.258	4.997	3.999	3.333	2.857	2.500	2.000
50	7.675	7.133	6.661	6.246	5.880	5.554	5.262	4.999	4.000	3.333	2.857	2.500	2.000

Percent

Selected References

CHAPTER 1

Azarchs, Tanya. "Market Discipline: the Holy Grail." *Journal of Lending and Credit Risk Management* 82 (May 2000), pp. 35–39.

Bitler, Marianne P., and Tobias Moskowitz. "Testing Agency Theory with Entrepreneur Effort and Wealth." *Journal of Finance* 60 (April 2005), pp. 539–76.

Byrd, John; Robert Parrine; and Gunnar Pritsch. "Stockholder-Manager Conflicts and Firm Value." *Financial Analysts Journal* 54 (May–June 1998), pp. 14–30.

Claessens, Stijn; Simon Djankov; Joseph P. H. Fan; and Larry Rees. "Disentangling the Incentive and Entrenchment Effects of Large Shareholdings." *Journal of Finance* 57 (December 2002), pp. 2741–71.

Cooper, Dan, and Glenn Petry. "Corporate Performance and Adherence to Stockholder Wealth-Maximizing Principles." *Financial Management* 23 (Spring 1994), pp. 71–78.

Fairchild, Lisa, and Joanne Li. "Director Quality and Film Performance." *Financial Review* 40 (May 2005), pp. 257–79.

Franks, Julian; Colin Mayer; and Luc Renneborg. "Who Disciplines Management in Poorly Performance Companies?" *Journal of Financial Intermediation* 10 (July–October 2001), pp. 209–48.

Jensen, Michael C. "The Eclipse of the Public Corporation." *Harvard Business Review* 67 (September–October 1989), pp. 61–74.

Kahn, Charles, and Andrew Winton. "Ownership Structure, Speculation, and Shareholder Intervention." *Journal of Finance* 53 (April 1998), pp. 99–129.

LaBaron, Dean. "Our Roles in Corporate Malfeasance." *Financial Analysts Journal* 61 (January–February 2005), pp. 25–26.

McLean, Bethany. "Why Enron Went Bust." *Fortune* 144 (December 24, 2001), pp. 58–68.

Tutano, Peter. "Agency Costs of Corporate Risk Management." *Financial Management* 27 (Spring 1998), pp. 67–77.

CHAPTER 2

Brennan, Michael J. "A Perspective on Accounting and Stock Prices." *Journal of Applied Corporate Finance* 8 (Spring 1995), pp. 43–52.

Bukics, Rose Marie; Marge O'Reilly-Allen; and Chris Schnitter. "Accounting for Differences." *Financial Executive* 16 (March–April 2000), pp. 36–38.

Darrough, Masako, and Aravind Srinivasan. "Do Insiders Manipulate Earnings When They Sell Their Shares in an Initial Pubic Offering?" *Journal of Accounting Research* 43 (March 2005), pp.1–33.

Duelke, Dean W. "The Importance of Accrual Profits." *Journal of Lending and Credit Risk Management* 82 (February 2000), pp. 82–87.

Graziano, Cheryl De Mesa. "XBRL: Streamlining Financial Reporting." *Financial Executive* 18 (November 2002), pp. 52–55.

Lamont, Owen. "Cash Flow and Investment Evidence from Internal Capital Markets." *Journal of Finance* 52 (March 1997), pp. 83–109.

Moehrle, Stephen R. "Is There a Gap in Your Knowledge of GAAP?" *Financial Analysts Journal* 58 (September–October 2002), pp. 43–47.

Ruback, Richard S. "Capital Cash Flows: A Simple Approach to Valuing Risky Cash Flows." *Financial Management* 31 (Summer 2002), pp. 85–103.

Ward, Terry. "Using Information from Cash Flow Statements to Predict Insolvency." *Journal of Commercial Lending* 77 (March 1995), pp. 29–36.

Yu, Fan. "Accounting Transparency and the Term Structure of Credit Spreads." *Journal of Financial Economics* 75 (January 2005), pp. 53–84.

CHAPTER 3

Artz, William A., and Raymond N. Neihengen, Jr. "Analysis of Finance Company Ratios." *Journal of Lending and Credit Risk Management* 80 (September 1997), pp. 32–36.

R

Easley, David; Soeren Hvidkjaer; and Maureen O'Hara. "Is Information Risk a Detriment of Asset Returns?" *Journal of Finance* 57 (October 2002), pp. 2184–2221.

Fama, Eugene F., and Kenneth R. French. "Size and Book-to-Market Factors in Earnings and Returns." *Journal of Finance* 50 (March 1995), pp. 131–55.

Ferguson, Robert, and Ean Leistikow. "Search for the Best Financial Performance Measure: Basics Are Better." *Financial Analysts Journal* 54 (January–February 1998), pp. 81–85.

Firer, Colin. "Driving Financial Performance through the duPont Identity: A Strategic Use of Financial Analysis and Planning." *Financial Practice and Education* 9 (Spring–Summer 1999), pp. 34–45.

Henry, Peter Blair. "Is Disinflation Good for the Stock Market?" *Journal of Finance* 57 (August 2002), pp. 1593–1648.

Marquardt, Carol, and Christine Wiedman. "Earnings Management through Transaction Structuring: Contingent Convertible Debt and Diluted Earnings per Share." *Journal of Accounting Research* 43 (May 2005), pp. 205–43.

Park, Kwangwoo, and Ronald A. Ratti. "Real Activity Inflation, Stock Returns, and Monetary Policy." *Financial Review* 36 (May 2000), pp. 59–78.

Schukat, Ann. "Inside the Retrenchment: Profits Matter." *Fortune* 142 (August 14, 2000), p. 280.

Useem, Jerry. "Backward Looking Accounting." *Fortune* 146 (October 28, 2002), p. 192.

Wang, Zheng. "Financial Ratio Selection for Default-Rating Modeling: A Model-Free Approach and Its Empirical Performance." *Journal of Applied Finance* 14 (Summer–Spring 2004), pp. 20–35.

CHAPTER 4

Butler, Alexander W.; Gustavo Grullon; and James P. Weston. "Can Managers Forecast Aggregate Market Returns?" *Journal of Finance* 60 (April 2005), pp. 963–86.

Chase, Charles W., Jr. "The Realities of Business Forecasting." *The Journal of Business Forecasting Methods and Systems* 14 (Spring 1995), p. 2.

Clement, Michael B., and Senyo Y. Tse. "Financial Analyst Characteristics and Herding Behavior in Forecasting." *Journal of Finance* 60 (February 2005), pp. 307–41.

Kumst, R. M., and P. H. Franses. "The Impact of Seasonal Constants on Forecasting Seasonally Cointegrated Time Series." *Journal of Forecasting* 17 (March 1998), pp. 109–24.

Lam, Kin, and King Chung Lam. "Forecasting for the Generation of Trading Signals in Financial Markets." *Journal of Forecasting* 19 (July 2000), pp. 39–52.

Mahaffy, Dale. "Predictive Intelligence Helps CFOs Forecast Demand." *Financial Executive* 18 (November 2002), pp. 48–50.

Reeves, William. "Essential Tasks for Today's CFOs." *Financial Executive* 18 (November 2002), pp. 28–31.

Strischek, Dev. "Cash Flow Projections for Contractors Revisited." *Journal of Commercial Lending* 77 (June 1995), pp. 17–37.

Tay, Anthony S., and Kenneth F. Wallis. "Density Forecasting: A Survey." *Journal of Forecasting* 19 (January 2000), pp. 235–54.

Tergesen, Anne. "Fearless Forecast." *BusinessWeek* (January 3, 2000), pp. 122–24.

CHAPTER 5

Biais, Bruno, and Catherine Casamatta. "Optimal Leverage and Aggregate Investment." *Journal of Finance* 54 (August 1999), pp. 1291–1323.

Dennis, David J. "The Benefits of High Leverage from Kroger's Leveraged Recap and Safeway's LBO." *Journal of Applied Corporate Finance* 7 (Winter 1995), pp. 38–52.

D'Souze, Juliet, and William L. Megginson. "The Financial and Operating Performance of Privatized Firms during the 1990s." *Journal of Finance* 54 (August 1999), pp. 1397–1438.

Eales, Robert, and Edward Bosworth. "Severity of Loss in the Event of Default in Small Business and Larger Consumer Loans." *Journal of Lending and Credit Risk Management* 80 (May 1998), pp. 58–65.

Fredman, Albert J., and Joseph J. Reising. "Explaining Performance Trends in Leveraged Loan Investment." *Journal of Fixed Income* 11 (September 2001), pp. 83–94.

Holthausen, Robert W., and David F. Larcker. "Performance, Leverage, and Ownership Structure in Reverse LBOs." *Journal of Applied Corporate Finance* 10 (Spring 1997), pp. 8–20.

Hull, Robert M. "Leverage Ratios, Industry Norms, and Stock Price Reaction: An Empirical Investigation of Stock-for-Debt Transactions." *Financial Management* 28 (Summer 1999), pp. 32–45.

Jandik, Tomas, and Anil K. Makhija. "Leverage and the Complexity of Takeovers." *Financial Review* 40 (February 2005), pp. 95–112.

Novaes, Walter. "Managerial Turnover and Leverage under a Takeover Threat." *Journal of Finance* 57 (December 2002), pp. 2619–50.

Sarig, Oded, and James Scott. "The Puzzle of Financial Leverage Clienteles." *Journal of Finance* 40 (December 1985), pp. 1459–67.

CHAPTER 6

Bansel, Ravi, and Hao Zhou. "Term Structure of Interest Rates and Regime Shifts." *Journal of Finance* 57 (October 2002), pp. 1997–2043.

Boudoukh, Jacob; Mathew Richardson; Tom Smith; and Robert F. Whitelaw. "Ex Ante Bond Returns and the Liquidity Preference Hypothesis." *Journal of Finance* 54 (June 1999), pp. 1153–67.

Brown, Cathy. "Getting a Grip: Year 2000 Credit Risk." *Journal of Lending and Commercial Risk Management* 80 (January 1998), pp. 62–68.

Chrystal, K. Alec, and Paul Mizen. "A Dynamic Model of Money, Credit, and Consumption: A Joint Model for the UK Household Sector." *Journal of Money, Credit, and Banking* 37 (February 2005), pp.119–43.

Duffie, Darrell, and Jun Liu. "Floating-Fixed Credit Spread." *Financial Analysts Journal* 57 (May–June 2001), pp. 76–87.

Fass, Greg. "Capital Allocation and Pricing Credit Risk." *Journal of Commercial Lending* 75 (September 1992), pp. 35–53.

Jarrow, Robert A., and Stuart M. Turnbull. "The Intersection of Market and Credit Risk." *Journal of Banking and Finance* 24 (January 2000), pp. 271–99.

Scholtens, Bert, and Dick van Wensveen. "A Critique of the Theory of Financial Intermediation." *Journal of Banking and Finance* 24 (August 2000), pp. 1243–51.

Spitler, Rick. "The New Survival Skills." *ABA Banking Journal* 97 (February 2005), pp. 58–62.

CHAPTER 7

Black, Sandra E., and Philip E. Strahan. "Entrepreneurship and Bank Credit Availability." *Journal of Finance* 57 (December 2002), pp. 2807–34.

Denis, David J., and Vassil T. Mihov. "The Choice Among Bank Debt, Nonbank Private Debt, and Public Debt: Evidence from New Corporate Borrowings." *Journal of Financial Economics* 70 (2003), pp. 3–23.

Diamond, Douglas W., and Raghuram G. Rajan. "Liquidity Shortages and Banking Crises." *Journal of Finance* 60 (April 2005), pp. 615–47.

Grossman, Robert J. "Securitize or Sink." *Journal of Lending and Credit Risk Management* 82 (April 2000), pp. 56–60.

Hill, Claire A. "Securitization: A Low Cost Sweetener for Lemons." *Journal of Applied Corporate Finance* 10 (Spring 1997), pp. 64–71.

Krishnan, C. N. V.; P. H. Ritchken; and J. B. Thomson. "Monitoring and Controlling Bank Risk: Does Risky Debt Help?" *Journal of Finance* 60 (February 2005), pp. 343–78.

Mian, Schzad L., and Clifford W. Smith, Jr. "Accounts Receivable Management Policy: Theory and Evidence." *Journal of Finance* 47 (March 1992), pp. 169–99.

Petersen, Mitchell A., and Raghuram G. Rajan. "Does Distance Still Matter? The Information Revolution and Small Business Lending." *Journal of Finance* 57 (December 2002), pp. 2533–70.

Strischek, Dev. "The Quotable Five C's." *Journal of Lending and Credit Risk Management* 82 (April 2000), pp. 47–49.

Whiting, Richard M. "Promises Finally Kept: Glass-Steagall Repealed and More." *Journal of Lending and Credit Risk Management* 82 (February 2000), pp. 48–52.

CHAPTER 8

Agin, William E. "Websites—Obtaining and Perfecting a Security Interest." *Journal of Lending and Credit Risk Management* 82 (July–August 2000), pp. 78–83.

Behar, Richard. "Banks Cruisin for E-Mail Bruisin." *Fortune* 146 (December 30, 2002), p. 56.

Berger, Allen N.; W. Scott Frame; and Nathan H. Miller. "Credit Scoring and the Availability, Price, and Risk of Small Business Credit." *Journal of Money, Credit, and Banking* 37 (April 2005), pp. 191–222.

Faulkender, Michael. "Hedging or Market Timing? Selecting the Interest Rate Exposure of Corporate Debt." *Journal of Finance* 60 (April 2005), pp. 931–62.

Fisher, Mark, and Christian Gilles. "Around and Around, the Expectations Hypothesis." *Journal of Finance* 53 (February 1998), pp. 365–83.

Hadlock, Charles J., and Christopher M. James. "Do Banks Provide Financial Slack?" *Journal of Finance* 57 (June 2002), pp. 1383–1419.

Hull, Robert M., and Richard Moellenberndt. "Bank Debt Reduction Announcements and Negative Signaling." *Financial Management* 23 (September 1994), pp. 21–30.

James, Christopher, and David Smith. "Are Bankers Still Special? New Evidence on Their New Role in the Capital Raising Process." *Journal of Applied Corporate Finance* 13 (Spring 2000), pp. 64–74.

Maroney, Tyler. "Credit Denied: Dot-Coms Feel the Squeeze." *Fortune* 142 (July 24, 2000), pp. 336–38.

Petersen, Mitchell A. "The Benefits of Lending Relationships: Evidence from Small Business Data." *Journal of Finance* 49 (March 1994), pp. 3–37.

Vardi, Nathan. "The Check Is Not in the Mail." *Forbes* 170 (September 30, 2002), p. 67.

CHAPTER 9

Black, Fischer. "A Simple Discounting Rule." *Financial Management* 17 (Summer 1988), pp. 7–11.

Crosby, Mark, and Glenn Oho. "Inflation and the Capital Stock." *Journal of Money, Credit, and Banking* 32 (May 2000), pp. 237–53.

Schlolnick, Barry. "Interest Rate Asymmetrics in Long-Term Loan and Deposit Markets." *Journal of Financial Services Research* 16 (September 1999), pp. 5–26.

Varchaver, Nicholas. "What's a Life Worth?" *Fortune* 146 (September 16, 2002), pp. 120–28.

CHAPTER 10

Arnold, Tom, and Jerry James. "Finding Firm Value without a Pro Forma Analysis." *Financial Analysts Journal* 56 (March–April 2000), pp. 77–84.

Beaves, Robert G. "A Comment on Interpreting Rates of Return: A Modified Rate-of-Return Approach." *Financial Practice and Education* 4 (Fall–Winter 1994), pp. 136–37.

Denis, David J.; Diane K. Dennis; and Kevin Yost. "Global Diversification, Industrial Diversification, and Firm Values." *Journal of Finance* 57 (October 2002), pp. 1951–79.

Finnerty, John D., and Douglas R. Emery. "The Value of Corporate Control and the Comparable Method of Valuation." *Financial Management* 33 (Spring 2004), pp. 91–99.

Kemley, Deen, and Doran Nissim. "Valuation of the Tax Debt Shield." *Journal of Finance* 57 (October 2002), pp. 2045–73.

Klein, Linda S., and Dogan Tirtirogiu. "Valuation Process and Market Efficiency for U.S. Treasury Bonds." *Financial Management* 26 (Winter 1997), pp. 74–80.

Linsmeier, Thomas J., and Neil D. Pearson. "Value at Risk." *Financial Analysts Journal* 56 (March–April 2000), pp. 57–67.

Sheng-Syan, Chen; Kim Wai Ho; Kueh Hwa Ik; and Cheng-Fee Lee. "How Does Strategic Competition Affect Firm Values?" *Financial Management* 31 (Summer 2002), pp. 67–84.

Zhang, Lu. "The Value Premium." *Journal of Finance* 60 (February 2005), pp. 67–103.

CHAPTER 11

Amihud, Yakov, and Hiam Mendelson. "The Liquidity Route to a Lower Cost of Capital." *Journal of Applied Corporate Finance* 12 (Winter 2000), pp. 8–25.

Barclay, Michael J., and Clifford W. Smith. "The Capital Structure Puzzle: The Evidence Revisited." *Journal of Applied Corporate Finance* 17 (Winter 2005), pp. 8–17.

Botosan, Christine A. "Evidence That Greater Disclosure Lowers the Cost of Equity Capital." *Journal of Applied Corporate Finance* 12 (Winter 2000), pp. 60–69.

Damodaran, Aswath. "Value and Risk: Beyond Betas." *Financial Analysts Journal* 61 (March–April 2005), pp. 38–43.

Martin, John D.; J. William Petty; and Steven P. Rich. "A Survey of EVA and Other Income Models of Firm Performance." *Journal of Finance Literature* 1 (Winter 2005), pp. 1–20.

McDaniel, William R. "Techniques for Including Flotation Costs in Capital Budgeting: Materiality, Generality, and Circularity." *Financial Practice and Education* 4 (Spring–Summer 1994), pp. 139–48.

Modigliani, Franco, and Merton H. Miller. "The Cost of Capital, Corporation Finance and the Theory of Investment." *American Economic Review* 48 (June 1958), pp. 261–96.

Pastor, Lubos, and Robert F. Stambough. "Cost of Equity Capital and Model Mispricing." *Journal of Finance* 54 (February 1999), pp. 67–121.

Roden, Dianne M., and Wilbur G. Lewellen. "Corporate Capital Structure Decisions: Evidence from Leveraged Buyouts." *Financial Management* 24 (Summer 1995), pp. 76–87.

Titman, Sheridan. "The Modigliani and Miller Theorem and the Integration of Financial Markets." *Financial Management* 31 (Spring 2002), pp. 101–15.

CHAPTER 12

Block, Stanley B. "Are There Differences in Capital Budgeting Procedures Between Industries? An Empirical Study." *The Engineering Economist* 50 (Spring 2005), pp. 55–67.

Dixit, Avinash K., and Robert S. Pindyck. "The Options Approach to Capital Investment." *Harvard Business Review* 63 (May–June 1995), pp. 105–15.

Eccles, Robert G., and Philip J. Pyburn. "Creating a Comprehensive System to Measure Performance." *Management Accounting* 74 (October 1992), pp. 41–51.

Kite, Devaun. "Capital Budgeting: Integrating Environmental Impact." *Journal of Cost Management* 9 (Summer 1995), pp. 11–14.

Lipscomb, Joseph. "Real Estate Capital Budgeting." *The Real Estate Appraiser and Analyst* 48 (Summer 1982), pp. 23–31.

Mukherje, Tarun K., and Vineeta L. Hingorani. "Capital-Rationing Decision of Fortune 500 Firms: A Survey." *Financial Practice and Education* 9 (Summer–Spring 1999), pp. 7–15.

Payne, Janet D.; Will Carrington Heath; and Lewis R. Gale. "Comparative Financial Practice in the U.S. and Canada: Capital Budgeting and Risk Assessment Techniques." *Financial Practice and Education* 9 (Spring–Summer 1999), pp. 25–33.

Stein, Jeremy. "Information Production and Capital Allocation: Decentralized versus Hierarchal Firms." *Journal of Finance* (October 2002), pp. 1891–1921.

CHAPTER 13

Ankrim, Ernest M., and Zhuanxin Ding. "Cross-Sectional Volatility and Return Dispersion." *Financial Analysts Journal* 58 (September–October 2002), pp. 67–73.

Bali, Turan G.; Nusret Cakici; Xuemin (Sterling) Yan; and Zhe Zhang. "Does Idiosyncratic Risk Really Matter?" *Journal of Finance* 60 (April 2005), pp. 905–29.

Brooks, Chris, and Ceta Persand. "Model Choice and Value-at-Risk Performance." *Financial Analysts Journal* 58 (September–October 2002), pp. 87–97.

Cochrane, John H. "The Risk and Return of Venture Capital." *Journal of Financial Economics* 75 (January 2005), pp. 3–52.

Lins, Karl V., and Henri Servaes. "Is Corporate Diversification Beneficial in Emerging Markets?" *Financial Management* 31 (Summer 2002), pp. 5–31.

Mayhew, Stewart, and Vassil Mihov. "How Do Exchanges Select Stocks for Option Listing?" *Journal of Finance* 59 (February 2004), pp. 447–72.

Moore, James; Jay Culver; and Bonnie Masterman. "Risk Management for Middle Market Companies." *Journal of Applied Corporate Finance* 12 (Winter 2000), pp. 112–19.

Rubenstein, Mark. "Markowitz Portfolio Selection: A Fifty-Year Retrospective." *Journal of Finance* 57 (June 2002), pp. 1041–45.

Sealy, Tom. "Risk and Assessment in a New World Environment." *Journal of Lending and Credit Risk Management* 82 (June 2000), pp. 18–22.

Solnik, Bruno, and Jacques Roulet. "Dispersion as 'Cross-Sectional Correlation.'" *Financial Analysts Journal* 56 (January–February 2000), pp. 54–61.

Trencher, Jeffrey W. "Risk-Adjusted Performance Measurement." *Journal of Lending and Credit Risk Management* 80 (May 1998), pp. 17–21.

CHAPTER 14

Aggarwal, Reena, and Sandeep Dahiya. "Capital Formation and the Internet." *Journal of Applied Corporate Finance* 13 (Spring 2000), pp. 108–13.

Baker, H. Kent; Gary E. Powell; and Daniel G. Weaver. "Does NYSE Listing Affect Firm Visibility?" *Financial Management* 28 (Summer 1999), pp. 46–54.

Boehmer, Ekkehart; Gideon Saar; and Lei Yu. "Lifting the Veil: An Analysis of Pretrade Transparency at the NYSE." *Journal of Finance* 60 (April 2005), pp. 783–815.

Desai, Hemang; K. Ramesh; S. Ramu Thiagarajan; and Bala V. Valachandran. "An Investigation of the Informational Role of Short Interest in the Nasdaq Market." *Journal of Finance* 57 (October 2002), pp. 2263–87.

Ellis, Katrina; Roni Michaely; and Maureen O'Hara. "The Making of a Dealer Market: From Entry to Equilibrium in the Trading of Nasdaq Stocks." *Journal of Finance* 57 (October 2002), pp. 2289–2316.

Federal Reserve Bulletin, selected issues.

Fox, Justin. "Is the Market Rational?" *Fortune* 146 (December 9, 2002), pp. 116–26.

Hamilton, James L. "Anatomy of Satellite Trading in the National Market System for NYSE-Listed Stocks." *Journal of Financial Research* (Summer 1995), pp. 189–206.

Hughen, J. Christopher, and Cynthia G. McDonald. "Who Are the Noise Traders?" *Journal of Financial Research* 20 (Summer 2005), pp. 281–98.

Jackson, Andrew R. "Trade Generation, Reputation, and Sell-Side Analysts." *Journal of Finance* 60 (April 2005), pp. 673–77.

Modhavan, Ananth. "Trading Mechanisms in Securities Markets." *Journal of Finance* 47 (June 1992), pp. 607–41.

Vickers, Marcia, and Mike France. "How Corrupt Is Wall Street?" *BusinessWeek* (May 13, 2002), pp. 37–42.

CHAPTER 15

Barry, Christopher. "Initial Public Offering Underpricing: The Issuer's View—A Comment." *Journal of Finance* 44 (September 1989), pp. 1099–1103.

Barry, Christopher; Chris Muscarella; and Michael Vetsuypens. "Underwriter Warrants, Underwriter Compensation and Cost of Going Public." *Journal of Financial Economics* 18 (March 1991), pp. 113–35.

Corwin, Shane A., and Paul Schultz. "The Role of IPO Underwriting Syndicates: Pricing, Information Production, and Underwriting Competition." *Journal of Finance* 60 (February 2005), pp. 443–86.

Derrien, Francois. "IPO Pricing in 'Hot' Market Conditions: Who Leaves Money on the Table?" *Journal of Finance* 60 (February 2005), pp. 487–521.

Dunbar, Craig G. "Factors Affecting Investment Bank Initial Public Offering Market Share." *Journal of Financial Economics* 55 (January 2000), pp. 3–41.

Hanley, Kathleen Weiss, and William J. Wilhelm, Jr. "Evidence on the Strategic Allocation of Initial Public Offerings." *Journal of Financial Economics* 37 (February 1995), pp. 239–57.

Lowry, Michelle, and G. William Schwert. "IPO Market Cycles: Bubbles or Sequential Learning?" *Journal of Finance* (June 2002), pp. 1171–1200.

O'Keefe, Brian. "Return of the IPO." *Fortune* (January 7, 2002), pp. 103–5.

Pagano, Marco; Fabio Panetta; and Luigi Zingales. "Why Do Companies Go Public? An Empirical Analysis." *Journal of Finance* 53 (February 1998), pp. 27–64.

Reilly, Frank K. "New Issues Revisited." *Financial Management* 6 (Winter 1977), pp. 28–42.

Ritter, Jay R. "The Long-Term Performance of Initial Public Offerings." *Journal of Finance* 46 (March 1991), pp. 3–27.

Sherman, Ann E. "Underwriter Certification and the Effect of Shelf Registration on Due Diligence." *Financial Management* 28 (Spring 1999), pp. 5–19.

CHAPTER 16

Altman, Edward. "Revisiting the High Yield Debt Market: Mature but Never Dull." *Journal of Applied Corporate Finance* 13 (Spring 2000), pp. 64–74.

Altman, Edward; Andrea Resti; and Andrea Sironi. "Default Recovery Rates in Credit Risk Modeling; A Review of the Literature and Recent Evidence." *Journal of Finance Literature* (Winter 2005), pp. 21–45.

Arslanalp, Serkan, and Peter Blair Henry. "Is Debt Relief Efficient?" *Journal of Finance* 60 (April 2005), pp. 1017–51.

Barclay, Michael J., and Clifford W. Smith, Jr. "The Maturity Structure of Corporate Debt." *Journal of Finance* 50 (June 1995), pp. 609–31.

Dichev, Illa D. "Is the Risk of Bankruptcy a Systematic Risk?" *Journal of Finance* 53 (June 1998), pp. 1131–47.

Graham, John R.; Michael L. Lemmon; and James S. Schallheim. "Debt, Leases, Taxes and Endogenicity of Corporate Tax Status." *Journal of Finance* 53 (February 1998), pp. 99–129.

Hong, Gwangheon, and Arthur Wagna. "An Empirical Study of Bond Market Transactions." *Financial Analysts Journal* 56 (March–April 2000), pp. 32–46.

Kemley, Deen, and Doren Nissim. "Valuation of the Debt Tax Shield." *Journal of Finance* (October 2002), pp. 2045–73.

Leland, Hayne E. "Corporate Debt Value, Bond Covenants, and Optimal Capital Structure." *Journal of Finance* 49 (September 1994), pp. 1213–52.

Revell, Janice. "How Debt Triggers Can Whack a Stock." *Fortune* (March 18, 2002), pp. 147–52.

Rynecki, David. "Stocks or Bonds? Two of the World's Best Investors Duke It Out." *Fortune* (August 12, 2002), pp. 89–92.

Schall, Lawrence D. "Analytic Issues in Lease vs. Purchase Decisions." *Financial Management* 16 (Summer 1987), pp. 17–22.

CHAPTER 17

Brunch, Timothy; William G. Christy; and Vikram Nanda. "Do Films Time Equity Offerings? Evidence from the 1930s and 1940s." *Financial Management* 33 (Spring 2004), pp. 523.

D'Souza, Julie, and John Jacob. "Why Firms Issue Target Stock." *Journal of Financial Economics* 56 (June 2000), pp. 459–83.

Francis, Jack, and Rekesh Bali. "Innovation in Partitioning a Share of Stock." *The Journal of Applied Corporate Finance* 13 (Spring 2000), pp. 128–36.

Gunther, Marc. "Investors of the World Unite." *Fortune* (July 1, 2002), pp. 78–86.

Harper, Joel T., and Jeff Madura. "Sources of Hidden Value and Risk within Tracking Stocks." *Financial Management* (Autumn 2002), pp. 91–109.

Lee, Inmoo. "Do Firms Knowingly Sell Overvalued Equity?" *Journal of Finance* 52 (September 1997), pp. 1439–66.

Logue, Dennis E., and James K. Seward. "The Time Warner Rights Offering and the Destruction of Stockholder Value." *Financial Analysts Journal* 48 (March–April 1992), pp. 37–45.

Moyer, R. Charles; Ramesh Rao; and Phillip M. Sisneros. "Substitutes for Voting Rights: Evidence from Dual Class Recapitalizations." *Financial Management* 21 (Autumn 1992), pp. 35–47.

Narayanan, Ranga. "Insider Trading and the Voluntary Disclosure of Information by Firms." *Journal of Banking and Finance* 24 (March 2000), pp. 395–425.

Paré, Terence P. "How to Know When to Buy Stocks." *Fortune* 126 (Fall 1992), pp. 79–83.

Shum, Connie M.; Wallace N. Davidson III; and John L. Glasscock. "Voting Rights and Market Reaction to Dual Class Common Stock Issues." *Financial Review* 30 (May 1995), pp. 275–87.

Thornton, Emily, and Louis Lavell. "It's Getting Tough to Fill a Boardroom." *BusinessWeek* (July 29, 2002), pp. 80–81.

Xiaoqing, Eleanor Xu. "Venture Capital and Buyout Funds as Alternative Equity Investment Classes." *Journal of Investing* 13 (Winter 2004), pp. 74–82.

CHAPTER 18

Bell, Leonie, and Tim Jenkinson. "New Evidence of the Impact of Dividend Taxation on the Identity of the Marginal Investor." *Journal of Finance* (June 2002), pp. 1321–46.

Bernstein, Peter L. "Dividends and the Frozen Orange Juice Syndrome." *Financial Analysts Journal* 91 (March–April 2005), pp. 25–30.

Conroy, Robert M., and Robert S. Harris. "Stock Splits and Information: The Role of Share Price." *Financial Management* 28 (Autumn 1999), pp. 28–40.

Deshmukh, Sanjay. "The Effect of Asymmetric Information on Dividend Policy." *Quarterly Journal of Business & Economics* 44 (Winter–Spring 2005), pp. 107–27.

Grullon, Gustavo, and Roni Michaely. "Dividends, Share Repurchases, and the Substitution Hypothesis." *Journal of Finance* (Autumn 2002), pp. 1649–84.

Moh'd, Mahmoud A.; Larry G. Perry; and James N. Rimbey. "An Investigation of the Dynamic Relationship between Agency Theory and Dividend Policy." *Financial Review* 30 (May 1995), pp. 367–85.

Popper, Margaret. "For Cold, Hard Cash, Focus on Dividends." *BusinessWeek* (August 12, 2002), p. 107.

Rozeff, Michael S. "Stock Splits: Evidence from Mutual Funds." *Journal of Finance* 53 (February 1998), pp. 335–49.

Wu, Chunci, and Xu-Ming Wang. "The Predictive Ability of Dividend and Earnings Yields for Long-Term Stock Returns." *Financial Review* 36 (May 2000), pp. 97–124.

CHAPTER 19

Arak, Marcelle, and L. Ann Martin. "Convertible Bonds: How Much Equity, How Much Debt?" *Financial Analysts Journal* 61 (March–April 2005), pp. 44–50.

Fields, L. Paige, and William T. Moore. "Equity Valuation Effect of Forced Warrant Exercise." *Journal of Financial Research* 18 (Summer 1995), pp. 157–70.

Fox, Justin. "The Only Option for Stock Options, That Is." *Fortune* (August 12, 2002), pp. 110–12.

Ganshaw, Trevor, and Deick Dillon. "Convertible Securities: A Toolbox of Flexible Financial Instruments for Corporate Issuers." *Journal of Applied Corporate Finance* 13 (Spring 2000), pp. 22–30.

Henry, David. "An Overdose of Options." *BusinessWeek* (July 15, 2002), pp. 112–14.

Jen, Frank C.; Dosoung Choi; and Seong-Hyro Lee. "Some New Evidence Why Companies Use Convertible Bonds." *Journal of Applied Corporate Finance* 10 (Spring 1997), pp. 44–53.

Lewis, Craig M.; Richard Rogalski; and James K. Seward. "Is Convertible Debt a Substitute for Straight or Common Stock Equity?" *Financial Management* 28 (Autumn 1999), pp. 5–27.

Mayers, David. "Convertible Bonds: Matching Financial and Real Options." *Journal of Applied Corporate Finance* 13 (Spring 2000), pp. 8–21.

Stein, Jeremy C. "Convertible Securities as Backdoor Equity Financing." *Journal of Financial Economics* 32 (August 1992), pp. 3–21.

CHAPTER 20

Becher, David A., and Terry L. Campbell. "Interstate Banking Deregulation and the Changing Nature of Bank Mergers." *Journal of Financial Research* 28 (Spring 2005), pp. 1–20.

Boswell, Stewart. "Buying and Selling Companies in the New Millennium." *Journal of Applied Corporate Finance* 12 (Winter 2000), pp. 70–80.

Doukas, John A., and Ozgur B. Kan. "Excessive Cash Flows and the Diversification Discount." *Financial Management* 33 (Summer 2004), pp. 71–88.

Field, Laura Casares, and Jonathan M. Karpoff. "Takeover Defenses of IPO Firms." *Journal of Finance* (October 2002), pp. 1837–99.

Fuller, Kathleen; Jeffrey Netter; and Mike Stegemoller. "What Do Returns to Acquiring Firms Tell Us? Evidence from Firms That Make Acquisitions." *Journal of Finance* (August 2002), pp. 1763–79.

Kohers, Ninon, and Theodor Kohers. "The Value Creation Potential of High-Tech Mergers." *Financial Analysts Journal* 56 (May–June 2000), pp. 40–50.

Mansi, A. Sattar, and David M. Reed. "Corporate Diversification: What Gets Discounted?" *Journal of Finance* (October 2002), pp. 2167–83.

Song, Moon H., and Ralph A. Walking. "Abnormal Returns to Rivals of Acquisition Targets: A Test of the Acquisition Probability Hypothesis." *Journal of Financial Economics* 55 (February 2000), pp. 143–71.

Stulz, Rene M.; Ralph A. Walking; and Moon H. Song. "The Distribution of Target Ownership and the Division of Gains in Successful Takeovers." *Journal of Finance* 45 (July 1990), pp. 817–33.

Vigh, Anand M. "The Spinoff and Merger Ex-Date Effects." *Journal of Finance* 49 (June 1994), pp. 581–609.

CHAPTER 21

Breger, Ludovic, and Darren Stovel. "Global Integration of Developed Credit Markets." *Journal of Portfolio Management* 31 (Spring 2005), pp. 60–69.

Brennan, Michael J., and H. Henry Cao. "International Portfolio Investment Flows." *Journal of Finance* 52 (December 1997), pp. 1851–80.

Brounen, Dirk; Abe DeJong; and Kees Keodijk. "Corporate Finance in Europe: Confronting Theory with Practice." *Financial Management* 33 (Winter 2004), pp. 71–102.

Chakrabarti, Rajesh. "Just Another Day in the Inter-Bank Foreign Exchange Market." *Journal of Financial Economics* 56 (April 2000), pp. 29–64.

Christoffersen, Peter, and Vihang Errunza. "Toward a Global Financial Architecture: Capital Mobility and Risk Management Issues." *Emerging Markets Review* 1 (Summer 2000), pp. 3–20.

Coffey, Brendan. "Euro Trashed." *Forbes* (April 16, 2002), p. 256.

Ferguson, Bryce. "A Consistent Global Approach to Risk." *Journal of Lending and Credit Risk Management* 82 (February 2000), pp. 20–24.

He, Jia, and Lillian K. Ng. "The Foreign Exchange Exposure of Japanese Multinational Corporations." *Journal of Finance* 53 (April 1998), pp. 733–53.

Murray, Janet Y.; Masaaki Kotabe; and Albert R. Wildt. "Strategic and Financial Performance Implications for Global Sourcing Strategy: A Contingency Analysis." *Journal of International Business Studies* 26 (1st Quarter 1995), pp. 181–201.

Orlowski, Lucjan T. "Monetary Convergence of the EU Accession Countries to the Eurozone: A Theoretical Framework and Policy Implications." *Journal of Banking and Finance* 29 (January 2005), pp. 203–25.

Powell, Bill. "It's All Made in China." *Fortune* (March 4, 2002), pp. 121–28.

Glossary

A

after-acquired property clause A requirement in a bond issue stipulating that any new equipment purchased after the issue be placed under the original mortgage.

aftermarket The market for a new security offering immediately after it is sold to the public.

agency theory This theory examines the relationship between the owners of the firm and the managers of the firm. While management has the responsibility for acting as the agent for the stockholders in pursuing their best interests, the key question considered is: How well does management perform this role?

agent One who sells, or "places," an asset for another party. An agent works on a commission or fee basis. Investment bankers sometimes act as agents for their clients in private placements.

aging of accounts receivable Analyzing accounts by the amount of time they have been on the books.

American Depository Receipts (ADR) These receipts represent the ownership interest in a foreign company's common stock. The shares of the foreign company are put in trust in a major U.S. bank. The bank, in turn, issues its depository receipts to the American stockholders of the foreign firm. Many ADRs are listed on the NYSE and many more are traded in the over-the-counter market.

American Stock Exchange (AMEX) The second largest national physically located security exchange in the United States.

annual percentage rate (APR) A measure of the *effective rate* on a loan. One uses the actuarial method of compound interest when calculating the APR.

annuity A series of consecutive payments or receipts of equal amount.

articles of incorporation A document that establishes a corporation and specifics the rights and limitations of the business entity.

articles of partnership An agreement between the partners in a business that specifies the ownership interest of each, the methods of distributing profits, and the means for withdrawing from the partnership.

asset-backed securities Public offerings backed by receivables as collateral. Essentially, a firm factors (sells) its receivables in the securities markets.

asset depreciation range This represents the expected physical life of an asset. Generally, the midpoint of the ADR is utilized to determine what class an asset falls into for depreciation purposes.

asset utilization ratios A group of ratios that measures the speed at which the firm is turning over or utilizing its assets. They measure inventory turnover, fixed asset turnover, total asset turnover, and the average time it takes to collect accounts receivable.

assignment The liquidation of assets without going through formal court procedures. In order to effect an assignment, creditors must agree on liquidation values and the relative priority of claims.

automated clearinghouse (ACH) An ACH transfers information between one financial institution and another and from account to account via computer tape. There are approximately 30 regional clearinghouses throughout the United States that claim the membership of over 10,000 financial institutions.

average collection period The average amount of time accounts receivable have been on the books. It may be computed by dividing accounts receivable by average daily credit sales.

B

balance of payments The term refers to a system of government accounts that catalogs the flow of economic transactions between countries.

balance sheet A financial statement that indicates what assets the firm owns and how those assets are financed in the form of liabilities or ownership interest.

banker's acceptances Short-term securities that frequently arise from foreign trade. The acceptance is a draft that is drawn on a bank for approval for future payment and is subsequently presented to the payer.

bank holding company A legal entity in which one key bank owns a number of affiliate banks as well as other nonbanking subsidiaries engaged in closely related activities.

bankruptcy The market value of a firm's assets are less than its liabilities, and the firm has a negative net worth. The term is also used to describe in-court procedures associated with the reorganization or liquidation of a firm.

basic earnings per share Earnings per share unadjusted for dilution.

basis point One basis point equals 1/100 of 1 percent.

bear market A falling or lethargic stock market. The opposite of a bull market.

best efforts A distribution in which the investment banker agrees to work for a commission rather than actually underwriting (buying) the issue for resale. It is a procedure that is used by smaller investment bankers with relatively unknown companies. The investment banker is not directly taking the risk for distribution.

beta A measure of the volatility of returns on an individual stock relative to the market. Stocks with a beta of 1.0 are said to have risk equal to that of the market (equal volatility). Stocks with betas greater than 1.0 have more risk than the market, while those with betas of less than 1.0 have less risk than the market.

blanket inventory lien A secured borrowing arrangement in which the lender has a general claim against the inventory of the borrower.

bond ratings Bonds are rated according to risk by Standard & Poor's and Moody's Investor Service. A bond that is rated Aaa by Moody's has the lowest risk, while a bond with a C rating has the highest risk. Coupon rates are greatly influenced by a corporation's bond rating.

book-entry transactions A transaction in which no actual paper or certificate is created. All transactions simply take place on the books via computer entries.

book value (See net worth.)

brokers Members of organized stock exchanges who have the ability to buy and sell securities on the floor of their respective exchanges. Brokers act as agents between buyers and sellers.

bull market A rising stock market. There are many complicated interpretations of this term, usually centering on the length of time that the market should be rising in order to meet the criteria for classification as a bull market. For our purposes, a bull market exists when stock prices are strong and rising and investors are optimistic about future market performance.

business risk The risk related to the inability of the firm to hold its competitive position and maintain stability and growth in earnings.

C

call option An option to buy securities at a set price over a specified period of time.

call premium The premium paid by a corporation to call in a bond issue before the maturity date.

call provision Used for bonds and some preferred stock. A call allows the corporation to retire securities before maturity by forcing the bondholders to sell bonds back to it at a set price. The call provisions are included in the bond indenture.

capital Sources of long-term financing that are available to the business firm.

capital asset pricing model A model that relates the risk-return trade-offs of individual assets to market returns. A security is presumed to receive a risk-free rate of return plus a premium for risk.

capital lease A long-term, noncancelable lease that has many of the characteristics of debt. Under *SFAS No. 13,* the lease obligation must be shown directly on the balance sheet.

capital markets Competitive markets for equity securities or debt securities with maturities of more than one year. The best examples of capital market securities are common stock, bonds, and preferred stock.

capital rationing Occurs when a corporation has more dollars of capital budgeting projects with positive net present values than it has money to invest in them. Therefore, some projects that should be accepted are excluded because financial capital is rationed.

capital structure theory A theory that addresses the relative importance of debt and equity in the overall financing of the firm.

carrying costs The cost to hold an asset, usually inventory. For inventory, carrying costs include such items as interest, warehousing costs, insurance, and material-handling expenses.

cash budget A series of monthly or quarterly budgets that indicate cash receipts, cash payments, and the borrowing requirements for meeting financial requirements. It is constructed from the pro forma income statement and other supportive schedules.

cash discount A reduction in the invoice price if payment is made within a specified time period. An example would be 2/10, net 30.

cash flow A value equal to income after taxes plus noncash expenses. In capital budgeting decisions, the usual noncash expense is depreciation.

cash flow cycle The pattern in which cash moves in and out of the firm. The primary consideration in managing the cash flow cycle is to ensure that inflows and outflows of cash are properly synchronized for transaction purposes.

cash flows from financing activities   Cash flow that is generated (or reduced) from the sale or repurchase of securities or the payment of cash dividends. It is the third section presented in the statement of cash flows.

cash flows from investing activities   Cash flow that is generated (or reduced) from the sale or purchase of long-term securities or plant and equipment. It is the second section presented in the statement of cash flows.

cash flows from operating activities   Cash flow information that is determined by adjusting net income for such items as depreciation expense, changes in current assets and liabilities, and other items. It is the first section presented in the statement of cash flows.

certificates of deposit   A certificate offered by banks, savings and loans, and other financial institutions for the deposit of funds at a given interest rate over a specified time period.

Check Clearing Century Act (Check 21)   A 2004 law that allows banks and others to electronically process checks.

coefficient of correlation   The degree of associated movement between two or more variables. Variables that move in the same direction are said to be positively correlated, while negatively correlated variables move in opposite directions.

coefficient of variation   A measure of risk determination that is computed by dividing the standard deviation for a series of numbers by the expected value. Generally, the larger the coefficient of variation, the greater the risk.

combined leverage   The total or combined impact of operating and financial leverage.

commercial paper   An unsecured promissory note that large corporations issue to investors. The minimum amount is usually $25,000.

common equity   The common stock or ownership capital of the firm. Common equity may be supplied through retained earnings or the sale of new common stock.

common stock   Represents the ownership interest of the firm. Common stockholders have the ultimate right to control the business.

common stock equity   The ownership interest in the firm. It may be represented by new shares or retained earnings. The same as net worth.

common stock equivalent   Warrants, options, and any convertible securities.

compensating balances   A bank requirement that business customers maintain a minimum average balance. The required amount is usually computed as a percentage of customer loans outstanding or as a percentage of the future loans to which the bank has committed itself.

composition   An out-of-court settlement in which creditors agree to accept a fractional settlement on their original claim.

compounded semiannually   A compounding period of every six months. For example, a five-year investment in which interest is compounded semiannually would indicate an n value equal to 10 and an i value at one-half the annual rate.

conglomerate   A corporation that is made up of many diverse, often unrelated divisions. This form of organization is thought to reduce risk, but may create problems of coordination.

consolidation   The combination of two or more firms, generally of equal size and market power, to form an entirely new entity.

contribution margin   The contribution to fixed costs from each unit of sales. The margin may be computed as price minus variable cost per unit.

conversion premium   The market price of a convertible bond or preferred stock minus the security's conversion value.

conversion price   The conversion ratio divided into the par value. The price of the common stock at which the security is convertible. An investor would usually not convert the security into common stock unless the market price were greater than the conversion price.

conversion ratio   The number of shares of common stock an investor will receive if he or she exchanges a convertible bond or convertible preferred stock for common stock.

conversion value   The conversion ratio multiplied by the market price per share of common stock.

convertible Eurobonds   Convertible Eurobonds are dollar-denominated and sold primarily in Western European countries. They have the safety of a bond but the chance to grow with U.S. stock prices since they are convertible into a U.S. firm's stock.

convertible exchangeable preferred   A form of preferred stock that allows the company to force conversion from convertible preferred stock into convertible debt. This can be used to allow the company to take advantage of falling interest rates or to allow the company to change aftertax preferred dividends into tax-deductible interest payments.

convertible security   A security that may be traded into the company for a different form or type of security. Convertible securities are usually bonds or preferred stock that may be exchanged for common stock.

corporate financial markets   Markets in which corporations, in contrast to governmental units, raise funds.

corporate stock repurchase A corporation may repurchase its shares in the market as an alternative to paying a cash dividend. Earnings per share will go up, and, if the price-earnings ratio remains the same, the stockholder will receive the same dollar benefit as through a cash dividend. A corporation may also justify the repurchase of its stock because it is at a very low price or to maintain constant demand for the shares. Reacquired shares may be used for employee options or as part of a tender offer in a merger or acquisition. Firms may also reacquire part of their shares as a protective device against being taken over as a merger candidate.

corporation A form of ownership in which a separate legal entity is created. A corporation may sue or be sued, engage in contracts, and acquire property. It has a continual life and is not dependent on any one stockholder for maintaining its legal existence. A corporation is owned by stockholders who enjoy the privilege of limited liability. There is, however, the potential for double taxation in the corporate form of organization: the first time at the corporate level in the form of profits, and again at the stockholder level in the form of dividends.

cost-benefit analysis A study of the incremental costs and benefits that can be derived from a given course of action.

cost of capital The cost of alternative sources of financing to the firm. (Also see weighted average cost of capital.)

cost of goods sold The cost specifically associated with units sold during the time period under study.

cost of ordering The cost component in the inventory decision model that represents the expenditure for acquiring new inventory.

coupon rate The actual interest rate on the bond, usually payable in semiannual installments. The coupon rate normally stays constant during the life of the bond and indicates what the bondholder's annual dollar income will be.

creditor committee A committee set up to run the business while an out-of-court settlement is reached.

credit terms The repayment provisions that are part of a credit arrangement. An example would be a 2/10, net 30 arrangement in which the customer may deduct 2 percent from the invoice price if payment takes place in the first 10 days. Otherwise, the full amount is due.

cross rates The relationship between two foreign currencies expressed in terms of a third currency (the dollar).

cumulative preferred stock If dividends from one period are not paid to the preferred stockholders, they are said to be in arrears and are then added to the next period's dividends. When dividends on preferred stock are in arrears, no dividends can legally be paid to the common stockholders. The cumulative dividend feature is very beneficial to preferred stockholders since it assures them that they will receive all dividends due before common stockholders can get any.

cumulative voting Allows shareholders more than one vote per share. They are allowed to multiply their total shares by the number of directors being elected to determine their total number of votes. This system enables minority shareholders to elect directors even though they do not have 51 percent of the vote.

currency futures contract A futures contract that may be used for hedging or speculation in foreign exchange.

current cost accounting One of two methods of inflation-adjusted accounting approved by the Financial Accounting Standards Board in 1979. Financial statements are adjusted to the present, using current cost data, rather than an index. This optional information may be shown in the firm's annual report.

current yield The yearly dollar interest or dividend payment divided by the current market price.

D

Data Universal Number System (D-U-N-S) A system in which a unique nine-digit code is assigned by Dun & Bradstreet to each business in its information base.

dealer paper A form of commercial paper that is distributed to lenders through an intermediate dealer network. It is normally sold by industrial companies, utility firms, or financial companies too small to have their own selling network.

dealers Participants in the market who transact security trades over the counter from their own inventory of stocks and bonds. They are often referred to as market makers, since they stand ready to buy and sell their securities at quoted prices.

debenture A long-term unsecured corporate bond. Debentures are usually issued by large firms having excellent credit ratings in the financial community.

debt utilization ratios A group of ratios that indicates to what extent debt is being used and the prudence with which it is being managed. Calculations include debt to total assets, times interest earned, and fixed charge coverage.

decimalization The statement of quotes in decimals rather than fractions.

decision tree A tabular or graphical analysis that lays out the sequence of decisions that are to be made and highlights the differences between choices. The presentation resembles branches on a tree.

deferred annuity An annuity that will not begin until some time period in the future.

deflation   Actual declining prices.

degree of combined leverage (DCL)   A measure of the total combined effect of operating and financial leverage on earnings per share. The percentage change in earnings per share is divided by the percentage change in sales at a given level of operation. Other algebraic statements are also used, such as Formula 5–7 and that in footnote 3 in Chapter 5.

degree of financial leverage (DFL)   A measure of the impact of debt on the earnings capability of the firm. The percentage change in earnings per share is divided by the percentage change in earnings before interest and taxes at a given level of operation. Other algebraic statements are also used, such as Formula 5–5.

degree of operating leverage (DOL)   A measure of the impact of fixed costs on the operating earnings of the firm. The percentage change in operating income is divided by the percentage change in volume at a given level of operation. Other algebraic statements are also used, such as Formula 5–3 and that in footnote 2 in Chapter 5.

depreciation   The allocation of the initial cost of an asset over its useful life. The annual expense of plant and equipment is matched against the revenues that are being produced.

depreciation base   The initial cost of an asset that is multiplied by the appropriate annual depreciation percentage in Table 12–9 to determine the dollar depreciation.

derivative securities   These have a value derived from an underlying security such as common stock or a government bond.

diluted earnings per share   EPS adjusted for all potential dilution from the issuance of any new shares of common stock arising from convertible bonds, convertible preferred stock, warrants, or any other options outstanding.

dilution of earnings   This occurs when additional shares of stock are sold without creating an immediate increase in income. The result is a decline in earnings per share until earnings can be generated from the funds raised.

direct paper   A form of commercial paper that is sold directly by the borrower to the finance company. It is also referred to as finance paper.

discounted loan   A loan in which the calculated interest payment is subtracted, or discounted, in advance. Because this lowers the amount of available funds, the effective interest rate is increased.

discount rate   The rate at which future sums or annuities are discounted back to the present.

disinflation   A leveling off or slowdown of price increases.

dividend payment date   The day on which a stockholder of record will receive his or her dividend.

dividend payout ratio   The percentage of dividends to earnings after taxes. It can be computed by dividing dividends per share by earnings per share.

dividend reinvestment plans   Plans that provide the investor with an opportunity to buy additional shares of stock with the cash dividends paid by the company.

dividend valuation model   A model for determining the value of a share of stock by taking the present value of an expected stream of future dividends.

dividend yield   Dividends per share divided by market price per share. Dividend yield indicates the percentage return that a stockholder will receive on dividends alone.

dual trading   Exists when one security, such as General Motors common stock, is traded on more than one stock exchange. This practice is quite common between NYSE-listed companies and regional exchanges.

Dun & Bradstreet Information Services (DBIS)   A division of Dun & Bradstreet. DBIS is an information company that publishes many different reports that help businesses make credit decisions. Its publications include the reference books *Business Information Report, Financial Stress Report, Payment Analysis Report, Small Business Credit Scoring Report, Commercial Credit Scoring Report, Supplier Evaluation* and various *Industry Credit Score Reports*.

Du Pont system of analysis   An analysis of profitability that breaks down return on assets between the profit margin and asset turnover. The second, or modified, version shows how return on assets is translated into return on equity through the amount of debt that the firm has. Actually return on assets is divided by $(1 - \text{Debt}/\text{Assets})$ to arrive at return on equity.

Dutch auction preferred stock   A preferred stock security that matures every seven weeks and is sold (reauctioned) at a subsequent bidding. The concept of Dutch auction means the stock is issued to the bidder willing to accept the lowest yield and then to the next lowest bidder and so on until all the preferred stock is sold.

E

earnings per share   The earnings available to common stockholders divided by the number of common stock shares outstanding.

economic ordering quantity (EOQ)   The most efficient ordering quantity for the firm. The EOQ will allow the firm to minimize the total ordering and carrying costs associated with inventory.

efficient frontier   A line drawn through the optimum point selections in a risk-return trade-off diagram.

efficient market hypothesis   Hypothesis that suggests markets adjust very quickly to new information and that it is very difficult for investors to select portfolios of securities that outperform the market. The efficient market hypothesis may be stated in many different forms, as indicated in Chapter 14.

elective expensing   Writing off an asset in the year of purchase for tax purposes rather than depreciating it over the life of the asset. The maximum annual deduction is $100,000. This procedure is primarily beneficial to small businesses because its availability is phased out when asset purchases become large.

electronic communications networks (ECNU)   Electronic trading systems that automatically match buy and sell orders at specific prices.

electronic funds transfer   A system in which funds are moved between computer terminals without the use of written checks.

euro   The common currency shared by the 12 members of the European Monetary Union.

Eurobonds   Bonds payable or denominated in the borrower's currency, but sold outside the country of the borrower, usually by an international syndicate.

Eurodollar certificate of deposit   A certificate of deposit based on U.S. dollars held on deposit by foreign banks.

Eurodollar loans   Loans made by foreign banks denominated in U.S. dollars.

Eurodollars   U.S. dollars held on deposit by foreign banks and loaned out by those banks to anyone seeking dollars.

exchange rate   The relationship between the value of two or more currencies. For example, the exchange rate between U.S. dollars and French francs is stated as dollars per francs or francs per dollar.

ex-dividend date   Two business days before the holder-of-record date. On the ex-dividend date the purchase of the stock no longer carries with it the right to receive the dividend previously declared.

exercise price   The price at which a warrant (or other similar security) allows the investor to purchase common stock.

Eximbank (Export-Import Bank)   An agency of the U.S. government that facilitates the financing of U.S. exports through its miscellaneous programs. In its direct loan program, the Eximbank lends money to foreign purchasers of U.S. products, such as aircraft, electrical equipment, heavy machinery, computers, and the like. The Eximbank also purchases eligible medium-term obligations of foreign buyers of U.S. goods at a discount from face value. In this discount program, private banks and other lenders are able to rediscount (sell at a lower price) promissory notes and drafts acquired from foreign customers of U.S. firms.

expectations hypothesis   The hypothesis maintains that the yields on long-term securities are a function of short-term rates. The result of the hypothesis is that, when long-term rates are much higher than short-term rates, the market is saying that it expects short-term rates to rise. Conversely, when long-term rates are lower than short-term rates, the market is expecting short-term rates to fall.

expected value   A representative value from a probability distribution arrived at by multiplying each outcome by the associated probability and summing up the values.

expropriate   The action of a country in taking away or modifying the property rights of a corporation or individual.

ex-rights   The situation in which the purchase of common stock during a rights offering no longer includes rights to purchase additional shares of common stock.

extension   An out-of-court settlement in which creditors agree to allow the firm more time to meet its financial obligations. A new repayment schedule will be developed, subject to the acceptance of creditors.

external corporate funds   Corporate financing raised through sources outside of the firm. Bonds, common stock, and preferred stock fall in this category.

external reorganization   A reorganization under the formal bankruptcy laws, in which a merger partner is found for the distressed firm. Ideally, the distressed firm should be merged with a strong firm in its own industry, although this is not always possible.

F

factoring   Selling accounts receivable to a finance company or a bank.

federal agency securities   Securities issued by agencies such as the Federal Home Loan Banks and the Federal Land Bank.

federal deficit   Government expenditures are greater than government tax revenues, and the government must borrow to balance revenues and expenditures. These deficits act as an economic stimulus.

federally sponsored credit agencies   Federal agencies, such as the Federal Home Loan Banks and the Federal Land Bank, that issue securities.

Federal National Mortgage Association (Fannie Mae)   A former government agency that provides a secondary market in mortgages. It is now private.

Federal Reserve discount rate   The rate of interest that the Fed charges on loans to the banking system. A monetary tool for management of the money supply.

federal surplus   This occurs when government tax receipts are greater than government expenditures. Surpluses may have a dampening effect on the economy.

field warehousing An inventory financing arrangement in which collateralized inventory is stored on the premises of the borrower but is controlled by an independent warehousing company.

FIFO A system of writing off inventory into cost of goods sold, in which the items purchased first are written off first. Referred to as first-in, first-out.

finance paper A form of commercial paper that is sold directly to the lender by the finance company. It is also referred to as direct paper.

Financial Accounting Standards Board A privately supported rule-making body for the accounting profession.

financial capital Common stock, preferred stock, bonds, and retained earnings. Financial capital appears on the corporate balance sheet under long-term liabilities and equity.

financial disclosure Presentation of financial information to the investment community.

financial futures market A market that allows the trading of financial instruments related to a future point in time. A purchase or sale occurs in the present, with a reversal necessitated in the future to close out the position. If a purchase (sale) occurs initially, then a sale (purchase) will be necessary in the future. The market provides for futures contracts in Treasury bonds, Treasury bills, certificates of deposits, GNMA certificates, and many other instruments. Financial futures contracts may be executed on the Chicago Board of Trade, the Chicago Mercantile Exchange, the New York Futures Exchange, and other exchanges.

financial intermediary A financial institution, such as a bank or a life insurance company, that directs other people's money into such investments as government and corporate securities.

financial lease A long-term, noncancelable lease. The financial lease has all the characteristics of long-term debt.

financial leverage A measure of the amount of debt used in the capital structure of the firm.

financial markets The place of interaction for people, corporations, and institutions that either need money or have money to lend or invest.

financial risk The risk related to the inability of the firm to meet its debt obligations as they come due.

financial sweetener Usually refers to equity options, such as warrants or conversion privileges, attached to a debt security. The sweetener lowers the interest cost to the corporation.

fiscal policy The tax policies of the federal government and the spending associated with its tax revenues.

five c's of credit These are used by bankers and others to determine whether a loan will be repaid on time. The five c's are character, capital, capacity, conditions, and collateral.

fixed costs Costs that remain relatively constant regardless of the volume of operations. Examples are rent, depreciation, property taxes, and executive salaries.

float The difference between the corporation's recorded cash balance on its books and the amount credited to the corporation by the bank.

floating rate bond A bond in which the interest payment changes with market conditions.

floating rate preferred stock The quarterly dividend on the preferred stock changes with market rates. The market price is considerably less volatile than it is with regular preferred stock.

floor value Usually equal to the pure bond value. A convertible bond will not sell at less than its floor value even when its conversion value is below the pure bond value.

flotation cost The distribution cost of selling securities to the public. The cost includes the underwriter's spread and any associated fees.

forced conversion Occurs when a company calls a convertible security that has a conversion value greater than the call price. Investors will take the higher of the two values and convert the security to common stock, rather than take a lower cash call price.

Foreign Credit Insurance Association (FCIA) An agency established by a group of 60 U.S. insurance companies. It sells credit export insurance to interested exporters. The FCIA promises to pay for the exported merchandise if the foreign importer defaults on payment.

foreign exchange risk A form of risk that refers to the possibility of experiencing a drop in revenue or an increase in cost in an international transaction due to a change in foreign exchange rates. Importers, exporters, investors, and multinational firms alike are exposed to this risk.

foreign trade deficit A deficit that occurs because Americans buy (import) more foreign goods than American companies sell (export) to foreigners.

forward rate A rate that reflects the future value of a currency based on expectations. Forward rates may be greater than the current spot rate (premium) or less than the current spot rate (discount).

founders' shares Stock owned by the original founders of a company. It often carries special voting rights that allow the founders to maintain voting privileges in excess of their proportionate ownership.

free cash flow Cash flow from operating activities, minus expenditures required to maintain the productive capacity of the firm, minus dividend payouts.

fronting loan A parent company's loan to a foreign subsidiary is channeled through a financial intermediary, usually a large international bank. The bank fronts for the parent in extending the loan to the foreign affiliate.

fully diluted earnings per share Equals adjusted earnings after taxes divided by shares outstanding, plus common stock equivalents, plus all convertible securities.

futures contract A contract to buy or sell a commodity at some specified price in the future.

future value The value that a current amount grows to at a given interest rate over a given time period.

future value of an annuity The sum of the future value of a series of consecutive equal payments.

G

going private The process by which all publicly owned shares of common stock are repurchased or retired, thereby eliminating listing fees, annual reports, and other expenses involved with publicly owned companies.

golden parachute Highly attractive termination payments made to current management in the event of a takeover of the company.

goodwill An intangible asset that reflects value above that generally recognized in the tangible assets of the firm.

H

hedging To engage in a transaction that partially or fully reduces a prior risk exposure by taking a position that is the opposite of your initial position. As an example, you own some copper now but also engage in a contract to sell copper in the future at a set price.

historical cost accounting The traditional method of accounting, in which financial statements are developed based on original cost.

holder-of-record date Stockholders owning the stock on the holder-of-record date are entitled to receive a dividend. In order to be listed as an owner on the corporate books, the investor must have bought the stock before it went ex-dividend.

horizontal integration The acquisition of a competitor.

humped yield curve A yield curve in which intermediate rates are higher than both short- and long-term rates.

hurdle rate The minimum acceptable rate of return in a capital budgeting decision.

I

income statement A financial statement that measures the profitability of the firm over a time period. All expenses are subtracted from sales to arrive at net income.

incremental depreciation The depreciation on a new asset minus the depreciation on an old asset. Incremental depreciation is multiplied times the tax rate to determine its tax shield benefit.

indenture A legal contract between the borrower and the lender that covers every detail regarding a bond issue.

indexing An adjustment for inflation incorporated into the operation of an economy. Indexing may be used to revalue assets on the balance sheet and to automatically adjust wages, tax deductions, interest payments, and a wide variety of other categories to account for inflation.

inflation The phenomenon of prices increasing with the passage of time.

inflation premium A premium to compensate the investor for the eroding effect of inflation on the value of the dollar.

information content of dividends This theory of dividends assumes that dividends provide information about the financial health and economic expectations of the company. If this is true, corporations must actively manage their dividends to provide the market with information.

insider trading This occurs when someone has information that is not available to the public and then uses this information to profit from trading in a company's common stock.

installment loan A borrowing arrangement in which a series of equal payments are used to pay off a loan.

institutional investors Large investors such as pension funds or mutual funds.

interest factor The tabular value to insert into the various present value and future value formulas. It is based on the number of periods (n) and the interest rate (i).

interest rate parity theory A theory based on the interplay between interest rate differentials and exchange rates. If one country has a higher interest rate than another country after adjustments for inflation, interest rates and foreign exchange rates will adjust until the foreign exchange rates and money market rates reach equilibrium (are properly balanced between the two countries).

Intermarket Trading System (ITS) An electronic communications system that links nine markets—NYSE, AMEX, Boston, Chicago, Cincinnati, Pacific, and Philadelphia stock exchanges, the Chicago Board Options Exchange, and the Nasdaq.

internally generated funds Funds generated through the operations of the firm. The principal sources are retained earnings and cash flow added back from depreciation and other noncash deductions.

internal rate of return (IRR) A discounted cash flow method for evaluating capital budgeting projects. The IRR

is a discount rate that makes the present value of the cash inflows equal to the present value of the cash outflows.

internal reorganization   A reorganization under the formal bankruptcy laws. New management may be brought in and a redesign of the capital structure may be implemented.

international diversification   Achieving diversification through many different foreign investments that are influenced by a variety of factors.

international electronic funds transfer   The movement of funds across international boundaries. It is mainly carried out through SWIFT (Society for Worldwide Interbank Financial Telecommunications).

International Finance Corporation (IFC)   An affiliate of the World Bank established with the sole purpose of providing partial seed capital for private ventures around the world. Whenever a multinational company has difficulty raising equity capital due to lack of adequate private risk capital, the firm may explore the possibility of selling equity or debt (totaling up to 25 percent of total capital) to the International Finance Corporation.

intrinsic value   As applied to a warrant, this represents the market value of common stock minus the exercise price. The difference is then multiplied by the number of shares each warrant entitles the holder to purchase.

inventory profits   Profits generated as a result of an inflationary economy, in which old inventory is sold at large profits because of increasing prices. This is particularly prevalent under FIFO accounting.

inverted yield curve   A downward-sloping yield curve. Short-term rates are higher than long-term rates.

investment banker   A financial organization that specializes in selling primary offerings of securities. Investment bankers can also perform other financial functions, such as advising clients, negotiating mergers and takeovers, and selling secondary offerings.

J

just-in-time inventory management (JIT)   A system of inventory management that stresses taking possession of inventory just before the time it is needed for production or sale. It greatly reduces the cost of carrying inventory.

L

lease   A contractual arrangement between the owner of equipment (lessor) and the user of equipment (lessee) that calls for the lessee to pay the lessor an established lease payment. There are two kinds of leases: financial leases and operating leases.

letter of credit   A credit letter normally issued by the importer's bank, in which the bank promises to pay out the money for the merchandise when delivered.

level production   Equal monthly production used to smooth out production schedules and employ manpower and equipment more efficiently and at a lower cost.

leverage   The use of fixed-charge items with the intent of magnifying the potential returns to the firm.

leveraged buyout   Existing management or an outsider makes an offer to "go private" by retiring all the shares of the company. The buying group borrows the necessary money, using the assets of the acquired firm as collateral. The buying group then repurchases all the shares and expects to retire the debt over time with the cash flow from operations or the sale of corporate assets. The firm may ultimately go public again.

LIBOR   (See London Interbank Offered Rate.)

life cycle   A curve illustrating the growth phases of a firm. The dividend policy most likely to be employed during each phase is often illustrated.

LIFO   A system of writing off inventory into cost of goods sold in which the items purchased last are written off first. Referred to as last-in, first-out.

limited partnership   A special form of partnership to limit liability for most of the partners. Under this arrangement, one or more partners are designated as general partners and have unlimited liability for the debts of the firm, while the other partners are designated as limited partners and are only liable for their initial contribution.

liquidation   A procedure that may be carried out under the formal bankruptcy laws when an internal or external reorganization does not appear to be feasible, and it appears that the assets are worth more in liquidation than through a reorganization. Priority of claims becomes extremely important in a liquidation because it is unlikely that all parties will be fully satisfied in their demands.

liquidity   The relative convertibility of short-term assets to cash. Thus, marketable securities are highly liquid assets, while inventory may not be.

liquidity premium theory   This theory indicates that long-term rates should be higher than short-term rates. The premium of long-term rates over short-term rates exists because short-term securities have greater liquidity, and, therefore, higher rates have to be offered to potential long-term bond buyers to entice them to hold these less liquid and more price sensitive securities.

liquidity ratios   A group of ratios that allows one to measure the firm's ability to pay off short-term obligations as they come due. Primary attention is directed to the current ratio and the quick ratio.

listing requirements   Financial standards that corporations must meet before their common stock can be traded on a stock exchange. Listing requirements are not standard, but are set by each exchange. The requirements for the NYSE are the most stringent.

lockbox system   A procedure used to expedite cash inflows to a business. Customers are requested to forward their checks to a post office box in their geographic region, and a local bank picks up the checks and processes them for rapid collection. Funds are then wired to the corporate home office for immediate use.

London Interbank Offered Rate (LIBOR)   An interbank rate applicable for large deposits in the London market. It is a benchmark rate, just like the prime interest rate in the United States. Interest rates on Eurodollar loans are determined by adding premiums to this basic rate. Most often, LIBOR is lower than the U.S. prime rate.

M

majority voting   All directors must be elected by a vote of more than 50 percent. Minority shareholders are unable to achieve any representation on the board of directors.

managing investment banker   An investment banker who is responsible for the pricing, prospectus development, and legal work involved in the sale of a new issue of securities.

marginal corporate tax rate   The rate that applies to each new dollar of taxable income. For a corporation, the maximum rate is 35 percent. The marginal rate is lower for smaller corporations.

marginal cost of capital   The cost of the last dollar of funds raised. It is assumed that each dollar is financed in proportion to the firm's optimum capital structure.

marginal principle of retained earnings   The corporation must be able to earn a higher return on its retained earnings than a stockholder would receive after paying taxes on the distributed dividends.

margin requirement   A rule that specifies the amount of cash or equity that must be deposited with a brokerage firm or bank, with the balance of funds eligible for borrowing. Margin is set by the Board of Governors of the Federal Reserve Board.

market efficiency   Markets are considered to be efficient when (1) prices adjust rapidly to new information; (2) there is a continuous market, in which each successive trade is made at a price close to the previous price (the faster the price responds to new information and the smaller the differences in price changes, the more efficient the market); and (3) the market can absorb large dollar amounts of securities without destabilizing the prices.

market risk premium   A premium over and above the risk-free rate. It is represented by the difference between the market return (K_m) and the risk-free rate (R_f), and it may be multiplied by the beta coefficient to determine the additional risk-adjusted return on a security.

market segmentation theory   A theory that Treasury securities are divided into market segments by various financial institutions investing in the market. The changing needs, desires, and strategies of these investors tend to strongly influence the nature and relationship of short-term and long-term interest rates.

market stabilization   Intervention in the secondary markets by an investment banker to stabilize the price of a new security offering during the offering period. The purpose of market stabilization is to provide an orderly market for the distribution of the new issue.

market value maximization   The concept of maximizing the wealth of shareholders. This calls for a recognition not only of earnings per share but also how they will be valued in the marketplace.

maturity date   The date on which the bond is retired and the principal (par value) is repaid to the lender.

merger   The combination of two or more companies, in which the resulting firm maintains the identity of the acquiring company.

merger premium   The part of a buyout or exchange offer that represents a value over and above the market value of the acquired firm.

modified accelerated cost recovery system (MACRS)   A system that specifies the allowable depreciation recovery period for different types of assets. The normal recovery period is generally shorter than the physical life of the asset.

modified internal rate of return   A method of evaluation combining the reinvestment rate assumption of the net present value method (cost of capital) with the internal rate of return method.

monetary policy   Management by the Federal Reserve Board of the money supply and the resultant interest rates.

money market accounts   Accounts at banks, savings and loans, and credit unions in which the depositor receives competitive money market rates on a typical minimum deposit of $1,000. These accounts may generally have three deposits and three withdrawals per month and are not meant to be transaction accounts, but a place to keep minimum and excess cash balances. These accounts are insured by various appropriate governmental agencies up to $100,000.

money market fund   A fund in which investors may purchase shares for as little as $500 or $1,000. The fund then reinvests the proceeds in high-yielding $100,000 bank CDs, $25,000–$100,000 commercial paper, and other large-denomination, high-yielding securities. Investors receive their pro rata portion of the interest proceeds daily as a credit to their shares.

money markets Competitive markets for securities with maturities of one year or less. The best examples of money market instruments would be Treasury bills, commercial paper, and negotiable certificates of deposit.

mortgage agreement A loan that requires real property (plant and equipment) as collateral.

multinational corporation A firm doing business across its national borders is considered a multinational enterprise. Some definitions require a minimum percentage (often 30 percent or more) of a firm's business activities to be carried on outside its national borders.

municipal securities Securities issued by state and local government units. The income from these securities is exempt from federal income taxes.

mutually exclusive The selection of one choice precludes the selection of any other competitive choice. For example, several machines can do an identical job in capital budgeting. If one machine is selected, the other machines will not be used.

N

National Association of Security Dealers (NASD) An industry association that supervises the over-the-counter market.

National Market List The list of the best-known and most widely traded securities in the over-the-counter market.

net present value (NPV) The NPV equals the present value of the cash inflows minus the present value of the cash outflows with the cost of capital used as a discount rate. This method is used to evaluate capital budgeting projects. If the NPV is positive, a project should be accepted.

net present value profile A graphic presentation of the potential net present values of a project at different discount rates. It is very helpful in comparing the characteristics of two or more investments.

net trade credit A measure of the relationship between the firm's accounts receivable and accounts payable. If accounts receivable exceed accounts payable, the firm is a net provider of trade credit; otherwise, it is a net user.

net worth, or book value Stockholders' equity minus preferred stock ownership. Basically, net worth is the common stockholders' interest as represented by common stock par value, capital paid in excess of par, and retained earnings. If you take all the assets of the firm and subtract its liabilities and preferred stock, you arrive at net worth.

New York Stock Exchange (NYSE) The largest organized security exchange in the United States. It also has the most stringent listing requirements.

nominal GDP GDP (gross domestic product) in current dollars without any adjustments for inflation.

nominal yield A return equal to the coupon rate on a bond.

nonfinancial corporation A firm not in the banking or financial services industry. The term would primarily apply to manufacturing, wholesaling, and retail firms.

nonlinear break-even analysis Break-even analysis based on the assumption that cost and revenue relationships to quantity may vary at different levels of operation. Most of our analyses are based on *linear* break-even analysis.

normal yield curve An upward-sloping yield curve. Long-term interest rates are higher than short-term rates.

O

open-market operations The purchase and sale of government securities in the open market by the Federal Reserve Board for its own account. The most common method for managing the money supply.

operating lease A short-term, nonbinding obligation that is easily cancelable.

operating leverage A reflection of the extent to which fixed assets and fixed costs are utilized in the business firm.

optimum capital structure A capital structure that has the best possible mix of debt, preferred stock, and common equity. The optimum mix should provide the lowest possible cost of capital to the firm.

options These give the owner the right but not the obligation to buy or sell an underlying security at a set price for a given time period.

Overseas Private Investment Corporation (OPIC) A government agency that sells insurance policies to qualified firms. This agency insures against losses due to inconvertibility into dollars of amounts invested in a foreign country. Policies are also available from OPIC to insure against expropriation and against losses due to war or revolution.

P

parallel loan A U.S. firm that wishes to lend funds to a foreign affiliate (such as a Dutch affiliate) locates a foreign parent firm (such as a Dutch parent firm) that wishes to loan money to a U.S. affiliate. Avoiding the foreign exchange markets entirely, the U.S. parent lends dollars to the Dutch affiliate in the United States, while the Dutch parent lends guilders to the American affiliate in the Netherlands. At maturity, the two loans would each be repaid to the original lender. Notice that neither loan carries any foreign exchange risk in this arrangement.

par value Sometimes referred to as the face value or the principal value of the bond. Most bond issues have a par value of $1,000 per bond. Common and preferred stock may also have assigned par values.

participating preferred stock A small number of preferred stock issues are participating with regard to corporate earnings. For such issues, once the common stock dividend equals the preferred stock dividend, the two classes of securities may share equally in additional dividend payments.

partnership A form of ownership in which two or more partners are involved. Like the sole proprietorship, a partnership arrangement carries unlimited liability for the owners. However, there is only single taxation for the partners, an advantage over the corporate form of ownership.

passbook savings account A savings account in which a passbook is used to record transactions. It is normally the lowest yielding investment at a financial institution.

payback A value that indicates the time period required to recoup an initial investment. The payback does not include the time-value-of-money concept.

percent-of-sales method A method of determining future financial needs that is an alternative to the development of pro forma financial statements. We first determine the percentage relationship of various asset and liability accounts to sales, and then we show how that relationship changes as our volume of sales changes.

permanent current assets Current assets that will not be reduced or converted to cash within the normal operating cycle of the firm. Though from a strict accounting standpoint the assets should be removed from the current assets category, they generally are not.

perpetuity An investment without a maturity date.

planning horizon The length of time it takes to conceive, develop, and complete a project and to recover the cost of the project on a discounted cash flow basis.

pledging accounts receivables Using accounts receivable as collateral for a loan. The firm usually may borrow 60 to 80 percent of the value of acceptable collateral.

point-of-sales terminals Computer terminals in retail stores that either allow digital input or use optical scanners. The terminals may be used for inventory control or other purposes.

poison pill A strategy that makes a firm unattractive as a potential takeover candidate. For example, when a potential unwanted buyer accumulates a given percentage of a firm's common stock, such as 25 percent, the other shareholders receive rights to purchase additional shares at very low prices. This makes the firm more difficult to acquire. Poison pills may take many different forms.

pooling of interests A method of financial recording for mergers, in which the financial statements of the firms are combined, subject to minor adjustments, and goodwill is *not* created. The method is being phased out by the Financial Accounting Standards Board (FASB).

portfolio effect The impact of a given investment on the overall risk-return composition of the firm. A firm must consider not only the individual investment characteristics of a project but also how the project relates to the entire portfolio of undertakings.

precautionary balances Cash balances held for emergency purposes. Precautionary cash balances are more likely to be important in seasonal or cyclical industries where cash inflows are more uncertain.

preemptive right The right of current common stockholders to maintain their ownership percentage on new issues of common stock.

preferred stock A hybrid security combining some of the characteristics of common stock and debt. The dividends paid are not tax-deductible expenses of the corporation, as is true of the interest paid on debt.

present value The current or discounted value of a future sum or annuity. The value is discounted back at a given interest rate for a specified time period.

present value of an annuity The sum of the present value of a series of consecutive equal payments.

price-earnings ratio The multiplier applied to earnings per share to determine current value. The P/E ratio is influenced by the earnings and sales growth of the firm, the risk or volatility of its performance, the debt-equity structure, and other factors.

primary market The market for the raising of new funds as opposed to the trading of securities already in existence.

prime rate The rate that a bank charges its most creditworthy customers.

private placement The sale of securities directly to a financial institution by a corporation. This eliminates the middleman and reduces the cost of issue to the corporation.

privatization A process in which investment bankers take companies that were previously owned by the government to the public markets.

profitability ratios A group of ratios that indicates the return on sales, total assets, and invested capital. Specifically, we compute the profit margin (net income to sales), return on assets, and return on equity.

pro forma balance sheet A projection of future asset, liability, and stockholders' equity levels. Notes payable or cash is used as a plug or balancing figure for the statement.

pro forma financial statements A series of projected financial statements. Of major importance are the pro forma income statement, the pro forma balance sheet, and the cash budget.

pro forma income statement A projection of anticipated sales, expenses, and income.

program trading   Computer-based trigger points in the market are established for unusually big orders to buy or sell securities by institutional investors.

prospectus   A document that includes the corporation's important information that has been filed with the Securities and Exchange Commission through the registration statement. It contains the list of officers and directors, financial reports, potential uses of funds, and the like.

proxy   This represents the assignment of the voting right to management or a group of outsiders.

public finance markets   Markets in which national, state, and local governments raise money for highways, education, welfare, and other public activities.

public placement   The sale of securities to the public through the investment banker–underwriter process. Public placements must be registered with the Securities and Exchange Commission.

public warehousing   An inventory financing arrangement in which inventory, used as collateral, is stored with and controlled by an independent warehousing company.

purchase of assets   A method of financial recording for mergers, in which the difference between the purchase price and the adjusted book value is recognized as goodwill. Under new rulings by the FASB, goodwill does not need to be written off under normal circumstances.

purchasing power parity theory   A theory based on the interplay between inflation and exchange rates. A parity between the purchasing powers of two countries establishes the rate of exchange between the two currencies. Currency exchange rates therefore tend to vary inversely with their respective purchasing powers in order to provide the same or similar purchasing power.

pure bond value   The value of the convertible bond if its present value is computed at a discount rate equal to interest rates on straight bonds of equal risk, without conversion privileges.

put option   An option to sell securities at a set price over a specified period of time.

R

real capital   Long-term productive assets (plant and equipment).

real GDP (gross domestic product)   GDP stated in current dollars adjusted for inflation.

real rate of return   The rate of return that an investor demands for giving up the current use of his or her funds on a noninflation-adjusted basis. It is payment for forgoing current consumption. Historically, the real rate of return demanded by investors has been of the magnitude of 2 to 3 percent.

refunding   The process of retiring an old bond issue before maturity and replacing it with a new issue. Refunding will occur when interest rates have fallen and new bonds may be sold at lower interest rates.

regional stock exchanges   Organized exchanges outside of New York that list securities.

reinvestment assumption   An assumption made concerning the rate of return that can be earned on the cash flows generated by capital budgeting projects. The NPV method assumes the rate of reinvestment to be the cost of capital, while the IRR method assumes the rate to be the actual internal rate of return.

repatriation of earnings   Earnings returned to the multinational parent company in the form of dividends.

replacement cost   The cost of replacing the existing asset base at current prices as opposed to original cost.

replacement cost accounting   Financial statements based on the present cost of replacing assets.

replacement decision   The capital budgeting decision on whether to replace an old asset with a new one. An advance in technology is often involved.

required rate of return   That rate of return that investors demand from an investment to compensate them for the amount of risk involved.

reserve requirements   The amount of funds that commercial banks must hold in reserve for each dollar of deposits. Reserve requirements are set by the Federal Reserve Board and are different for savings and checking accounts. Low reserve requirements are stimulating; high reserve requirements are restrictive.

residual claim to income   The basic claim that common stockholders have to income that is not paid out to creditors or preferred stockholders. This is true regardless of whether these residual funds are paid out in dividends or retained in the corporation.

residual theory of dividends   A theory of dividend payout stating that a corporation will retain as much of its earnings as it may profitably invest. If any income is left after investments, the firm will pay dividends. This theory assumes that dividends are a passive decision variable.

restructuring   Process that can take many forms in a corporation, such as changes in the capital structure (liability and equity on the balance sheet). It can also result in the selling of low-profit-margin divisions with the proceeds reinvested in better investment opportunities. Sometimes restructuring results in the removal of the current management team or large reductions in the workforce. Restructuring has also included mergers and acquisitions.

reverse stock split   A firm exchanging with stockholders fewer shares for existing shares with the intent of increasing the stock price.

rights offering   A sale of new common stock through a preemptive rights offering. Usually one right will be issued for every share held. A certain number of rights may be used to buy shares of common stock from the company at a set price that is lower than the market price.

rights-on   The situation in which the purchase of a share of common stock includes a right attached to the stock.

risk   A measure of uncertainty about the outcome from a given event. The greater the variability of possible outcomes, on both the high side and the low side, the greater the risk.

risk-adjusted discount rate   A discount rate used in the capital budgeting process that has been adjusted upward or downward from the basic cost of capital to reflect the risk dimension of a given project.

risk-averse   An aversion or dislike for risk. In order to induce most people to take larger risks, there must be increased potential for return.

risk-free rate of return   Rate of return on an asset that carries no risk. U.S. Treasury bills are often used to represent this measure, although longer-term government securities have also proved appropriate in some studies.

risk premium   A premium associated with the special risks of an investment. Of primary interest are two types of risk, business risk and financial risk. Business risk relates to the inability of the firm to maintain its competitive position and sustain stability and growth in earnings. Financial risk relates to the inability of the firm to meet its debt obligations as they come due. The risk premium will also differ (be greater or less) for different types of investments (bonds, stocks, and the like).

S

safety stock of inventory   Inventory that is held in addition to regular needs to protect against being out of an item.

Sarbanes-Oxley Act of 2002   An act that was intended to restore confidence in the financial markets by demanding accuracy in financial reporting.

Saturday night special   A merger tender offer that is made just before the market closes for the weekend and takes the target company's officers by surprise.

screen-based market   There is no physical location, but trading is based on computers and other communication mediums.

secondary market   The market for securities that have already been issued. It is a market in which investors trade back and forth with each other.

secondary offering   The sale of a large block of stock in a publicly traded company, usually by estates, foundations, or large individual stockholders. Secondary offerings must be registered with the SEC and will usually be distributed by investment bankers.

secondary trading   The buying and selling of publicly owned securities in secondary markets, such as the New York Stock Exchange and the over-the-counter markets.

secured debt   A general category of debt that indicates the loan was obtained by pledging assets as collateral. Secured debt has many forms and usually offers some protective features to a given class of bondholders.

Securities Act of 1933   An act that is sometimes referred to as the truth in securities act, because it requires detailed financial disclosures before securities may be sold to the public.

Securities Acts Amendments of 1975   The major feature of this act was to mandate a national securities market.

Securities and Exchange Commission (SEC)   The primary regulatory body for security offerings in the United States.

Securities Exchange Act of 1934   Legislation that established the Securities and Exchange Commission (SEC) to supervise and regulate the securities markets.

securitization of assets   The issuance of a security that is specifically backed by the pledge of an asset.

security market line   A line or equation that depicts the risk-related return of a security based on a risk-free rate plus a market premium related to the beta coefficient of the security.

self-liquidating assets   Assets that are converted to cash within the normal operating cycle of the firm. An example is the purchase and sale of seasonal inventory.

self-liquidating loan   A loan in which the use of funds will ensure a built-in or automatic repayment scheme.

semivariable costs   Costs that are partially fixed but still change somewhat as volume changes. Examples are utilities and "repairs and maintenance."

serial payment   Bonds with serial payment provisions are paid off in installments over the life of the issue. Each bond has its own predetermined date of maturity and receives interest only to that point.

shareholder wealth maximization   Maximizing the wealth of the firm's shareholders through achieving the highest possible value for the firm in the marketplace. It is the overriding objective of the firm and should influence all decisions.

shelf registration   A process that permits large companies to file one comprehensive registration statement (under

SEC Rule 415) that outlines the firm's financing plans for up to the next two years. Then, when market conditions appear to be appropriate, the firm can issue the securities without further SEC approval.

simulation   A method of dealing with uncertainty, in which future outcomes are anticipated. The model may use random variables for inputs. By programming the computer to randomly select inputs from probability distributions, the outcomes generated by a simulation are distributed about a mean, and, instead of generating one return or net present value, a range of outcomes with standard deviations is provided.

sinking fund   A method for retiring bonds in an orderly process over the life of a bond. Each year or semiannually, a corporation sets aside a sum of money equal to a certain percentage of the total issue. These funds are then used by a trustee to purchase the bonds in the open market and retire them. This method will prevent the corporation from being forced to raise a large amount of capital at maturity to retire the total bond issue.

sole proprietorship   A form of organization that represents single-person ownership and offers the advantages of simplicity of decision making and low organizational and operating costs.

speculative premium   The market price of the warrant minus the warrant's intrinsic value is an example of a speculative premium.

spontaneous sources of funds   Funds arising through the normal course of business, such as accounts payable generated from the purchase of goods for resale.

spot rate   The rate at which the currency is traded for immediate delivery. It is the existing cash price.

standard deviation   A measure of the spread or dispersion of a series of numbers around the expected value. The standard deviation tells us how well the expected value represents a series of values.

statement of cash flows   Formally established by the Financial Accounting Standards Board in 1987, the purpose of the statement of cash flows is to emphasize the critical nature of cash flow to the operations of the firm. The statement translates accrual-based net income into actual cash dollars.

step-up in the conversion price   A feature that is sometimes written into the contract that allows the conversion ratio to decline in steps over time. This feature encourages early conversion when the conversion value is greater than the call price.

stock dividend   A dividend paid in stock, rather than cash. A book transfer equal to the market value of the stock dividend is made from retained earnings to the capital stock and paid-in-capital accounts. The stock dividend

may be symbolic of corporate growth, but it does not increase the total value of the stockholders' wealth.

stock split   A division of shares by a ratio set by the board of directors—two for one, three for one, three for two, and so on. Stock splits usually indicate the company's stock has risen in price to a level that the directors feel limits the trading appeal of the stock. The par value is divided by the ratio set, and the new shares are issued to the current stockholders of record to increase their shares to the stated level. For example, a two-for-one split would increase holdings from one share to two shares.

stockholders' equity   The total ownership position of preferred and common stockholders.

stockholder wealth maximization   The primary goal of financial managers. They maximize the wealth of the firm's shareholders through achieving the highest possible value for the firm.

straight-line depreciation   A method of depreciation that takes the depreciable cost of an asset and divides it by the asset's useful life to determine the annual depreciation expense. Straight-line depreciation creates uniform depreciation expenses for each of the years in which an asset is depreciated.

Subchapter S corporation   A special corporate form of ownership, in which profit is taxed as direct income to the stockholders and thus is only taxed once, as would be true of a partnership. The stockholders still receive all the organizational benefits of a corporation, including limited liability. The Subchapter S designation can apply only to corporations with up to 75 stockholders.

subordinated debenture   An unsecured bond, in which payment to the holder will occur only after designated senior debenture holders are satisfied.

supernormal growth   Superior growth a firm may achieve during its early years, before leveling off to more normal growth. Supernormal growth is often achieved by firms in emerging industries.

sweep account   An account that allows companies to maintain zero balances with all excess cash swept into an interest-earning account.

synergy   The recognition that the whole may be equal to more than the sum of the parts. The "2 + 2 = 5" effect.

T

takeover tender offer   An unfriendly offer that is not initially negotiated with the management of the target firm. The offer is usually made directly to the stockholders of the target firm.

tax loss carryforward   A loss that can be carried forward for a number of years to offset future taxable income and perhaps be utilized by another firm in a merger or an acquisition.

Tax Reform Act of 1986   Tax legislation that eliminated many of the abuses in the tax code and, at the same time, lowered the overall tax rates.

technical insolvency   When a firm is unable to pay its bills as they come due.

temporary current assets   Current assets that will be reduced or converted to cash within the normal operating cycle of the firm.

term loan   An intermediate-length loan, in which credit is generally extended from one to seven years. The loan is usually repaid in monthly or quarterly installments over its life, rather than with one single payment.

terms of exchange   The buyout ratio or terms of trade in a merger or an acquisition.

term structure of interest rates   The term structure shows the relative level of short-term and long-term interest rates at a point in time.

three-sector economy   The economy consists of three sectors—business, government, and households. Typically, households have been major suppliers of funds, while business and government have been users of funds.

tight money   A term to indicate time periods in which financing may be difficult to find and interest rates may be quite high by normal standards.

trade credit   Credit provided by sellers or suppliers in the normal course of business.

traditional approach to cost of capital   Under the traditional approach, the cost of capital initially declines with the increased use of low-cost debt, but it eventually goes up due to the greater risk associated with increasing debt.

transaction exposure   Foreign exchange gains and losses resulting from *actual* international transactions. These may be hedged through the foreign exchange market, the money market, or the currency futures market.

transactions balances   Cash balances held to pay for planned corporate expenditures such as supplies, payrolls, and taxes, as well as the infrequent acquisitions of long-term fixed assets.

translation exposure   The foreign-located assets and liabilities of a multinational corporation, which are denominated in foreign currency units, and are exposed to losses and gains due to changing exchange rates. This is called accounting or translation exposure.

Treasury bills   Short-term obligations of the federal government.

Treasury Inflation Protection Securities (TIPS)   This security pays interest semiannually that equals a real rate of return specified by the U.S. Treasury plus principal at maturity that is adjusted annually to reflect inflation's impact on purchasing power.

Treasury notes   Intermediate-term obligations of the federal government with maturities from 1 to 10 years.

treasury stock   Corporate stock that has been reacquired by the corporation.

trend analysis   An analysis of performance that is made over a number of years in order to ascertain significant patterns.

trust receipt   An instrument acknowledging that the borrower holds the inventory and proceeds for sale in trust for the lender.

two-step buyout   An acquisition plan in which the acquiring company attempts to gain control by offering a very high cash price for 51 percent of the shares of the target company. At the same time, the acquiring company announces a second lower price that will be paid, either in cash, stocks, or bonds, at a subsequent point in time.

U

underpricing   When new or additional shares of stock are to be sold, investment bankers will generally set the price at slightly below the current market value to ensure a receptive market for the securities.

underwriting   The process of selling securities and, at the same time, assuring the seller a specified price. Underwriting is done by investment bankers and represents a form of risk taking.

underwriting spread   The difference between the price that a selling corporation receives for an issue of securities and the price at which the issue is sold to the public. The spread is the fee that investment bankers and others receive for selling securities.

underwriting syndicate   A group of investment bankers that is formed to share the risk of a security offering and also to facilitate the distribution of the securities.

V

variable costs   Costs that move directly with a change in volume. Examples are raw materials, factory labor, and sales commissions.

vertical integration   The acquisition of customers or suppliers by the company.

W

warrant   An option to buy securities at a set price for a given time period. Warrants commonly have a life of one to five years or longer and a few are perpetual.

weighted average cost of capital   The computed cost of capital determined by multiplying the cost of each item in the optimal capital structure by its weighted representation in the overall capital structure and summing up the results.

white knight   A firm that management calls on to help it avoid an unwanted takeover offer. It is an invited suitor.

working capital management   The financing and management of the current assets of the firm. The financial manager determines the mix between temporary and permanent "current assets" and the nature of the financing arrangement.

Y

yield   The interest rate that equates a future value or an annuity to a given present value.

yield curve   A curve that shows interest rates at a specific point in time for all securities having equal risk but different maturity dates. Usually, government securities are used to construct such curves. The yield curve is also referred to as the term structure of interest rates.

yield to maturity   The required rate of return on a bond issue. It is the discount rate used in present-valuing future interest payments and the principal payment at maturity. The term is used interchangeably with market rate of interest.

Z

zero-coupon rate bond   A bond that is initially sold at a deep discount from face value. The return to the investor is the difference between the investor's cost and the face value received at the end of the life of the bond.

Company Index

Page numbers followed by n indicate notes.

Subject Index

Page numbers followed by n indicate notes.